OPEN NETWORKING WITH OSI

Adrian Tang

Computer Science and Telecommunications Program
University of Missouri-Kansas City

Sophia Scoggins

Computer Science and Telecommunications Program
University of Missouri-Kansas City

Prentice Hall, Englewood Cliffs, New Jersey 07632

Editorial/production supervision: *Barbara Marttine*
Cover designer: *Wanda Lubelska*
Prepress buyer: *Mary E. McCartney*
Manufacturing buyer: *Susan Brunke*
Acquisitions editor: *Mary Franz*

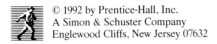
The publisher offers discounts on this book when ordered
in bulk quantities. For more information, write:

> Special Sales/College Marketing
> Prentice-Hall, Inc.
> College Technical and Reference Division
> Englewood Cliffs, New Jersey 07632

Printed in the United States of America

10 9 8 7 6 5 4 3 2 1

ISBN 0-13-351842-6

Prentice-Hall International (UK) Limited, *London*
Prentice-Hall of Australia Pty. Limited, *Sydney*
Prentice-Hall Canada Inc., *Toronto*
Prentice-Hall Hispanoamericana, S.A., *Mexico*
Prentice-Hall of India Private Limited, *New Delhi*
Prentice-Hall of Japan, Inc., *Tokyo*
Simon & Schuster Asia Pte. Ltd., *Singapore*
Editora Prentice-Hall do Brasil, Ltda., *Rio de Janeiro*

CONTENTS

PREFACE

There are two major factors fueling the adoption of OSI communication standards in the 90's. The first one is the integration of the economies of the European Common Market countries. The second one is the Government's mandated use of OSI in a number of countries. These two factors will probably make the 90's the years of OSI. Many open system groups are in the process of migrating to OSI. However, OSI receives very little attention in the US partly because of the popularity of TCP/IP. Many networking professionals realize that OSI is coming, but are thwarted by OSI abstract concepts and acronyms. My goal in writing this book is to explain OSI to these professionals. I try to provide a broad overview of OSI, with emphasis on Layer Seven of the OSI Reference Model.

This book is organized into five parts. The first part (Chapters 1-4) introduces OSI concepts. Chapter 1 gives an overview of open systems environments and basic OSI concepts. In Chapter 2, we explain the abstract OSI architectural concepts. In Chapter 3, we explain the techniques used to describe the service definition and the protocol specification of a protocol standard. Finally in Chapter 4, we explain naming and addressing.

The second part (Chapters 5-9) describes the OSI protocol standards used to support the OSI application protocols. Chapter 5 examines the Network Layer, with emphasis on the interconnection strategies and the routing protocols. Chapter 6 examines the Transport Layer. Chapter 7 examines the Session Layer. Chapter 8 examines ASN.1, the OSI language used to define types in a machine-independent manner. Many believe that the success of OSI is largely due to ASN.1. Chapter 9 covers the Presentation Layer. Note that we do not cover the lower two layers in the OSI Reference Model simply because those two layers are covered in detail in many existing books on data communication.

The third part (Chapters 10-14) examines ASEs (i.e., application service elements) which are the building blocks of Application Layer entities. Chapter 10 examines ACSE, the ASE used for the management of application associations. Chapter 11 examines RTSE, the ASE used to provide a reliable transfer service. Chapter 12 examines CCR, the ASE used to provide the communication support for the two-phase commit protocol in transaction processing. Chapter 13 examines ROSE, the ASE used to transfer remote operations in an interactive environment. Chapter 14 describes two popular tools which are used in the specification of OSI application protocols. They are ASDC (Abstract Service Definition Conventions) and RO-notation.

The fourth part (Chapters 15-24) covers eight OSI application protocols and two interchange formats. Chapter 15 examines the DS (Directory Services) standard, the OSI standard by means of which users can retrieve information of OSI objects. Chapter 16 examines the MHS (Message Handling Systems) standard, the OSI standard for electronic mail. Chapter 17 examines the FTAM (File Transfer, Access, and Management) standard, the OSI standard for file manipulation. Chapter 18 examines the CMIP (Common Management Information Protocol) standard, the OSI standard used to convey systems management information. Chapter 19 examines the VT (Virtual Terminal) standard, the OSI standard by means of which applications can be accessed from a remote terminal, regardless of the make of the terminal. Chapter 20 examines the OSI TP (Transaction Processing) standard, the OSI standard used to support transaction processing. Chapter 21 examines the RDA (Remote Database Access) standard, the OSI standard by means of which a database client can use the same front-end system to various database systems. Chapter 22 examines the MMS (Manufacturing Messaging Specification) standard, the OSI standard used to control factory devices in a manufacturing environment. Chapter 23 examines the use of MHS to carry EDI (i.e., Electronic Document Interchange) documents. Chapter 24 examines the ODA (Office Document Architecture) standard, the OSI standard on the structure and interchange format of office documents.

The fifth part (Chapters 18-25) covers implementation issues and ongoing work in ODP (Open Distributed Processing). Chapter 25 examines a modular design of portable OSI modules. Chapter 26 examines conformance testing. Chapter 27 gives an example of a users' profile, namely, US GOSIP. Finally, Chapter 28 examines the evolving work in ODP which addresses distributed processing in an open systems environment.

This book can be used as a first year two-semester graduate textbook in computer networks. We assume that the students are familar with the lower two layers of the OSI Reference Model. The first three parts of the book can be covered in the first semester. Most of the remaining two parts can be covered in the second semester. We recommend that Chapters 15, 16, 17, 18, and 25 should be covered in all circumstances. Whenever possible, a laboratory should accompany the course in the second semester. Over in this university, we have an OSI laboratory with a LAN of OSI systems from different vendors. Students can perform interoperability testing, design ROSE applications, and design applications using the OSI application program interfaces.

I want to thank all the students in this program to make this book possible. I want to thank Allied Signals and Department of Energy for funding the OSI laboratory in this university which gives me the stimulation to write this book.

I am indebted to Tae Sang Choi who spent many hours doing the drawings and formatting.

Wen-Jung Hsin read through the entire manuscript very carefully and corrected a number of mistakes.

Deokjai Choi, Suzanne Fitzgerald, Tim Hines, Srikanth Kumar, Hung Yu Lin, and Edward Morrow are very helpful in editing various parts of the book.

The following people have made technical contributions to the book: Young Bae Choi, Kanakasabha Kailasam, Sanjay Khurana, Sung Jong Lee, Jeffrey Marx, Vish Narayanan, Anita Reddy, Rajendran Saravanakumar, Xiaojun Shen, Greg Vetter, Wei Wei, and Xiaoyan Wu.

I want to thank my wife Sharon for her patience and understanding while I was writing this book.

I want to dedicate this book to my mother to whose support I am indebted forever.

Adrian Tang

1

Introduction

In recent years, information technology (IT) has become a major part of human civilization. The sheer variety of IT has created a significant problem of interconnecting systems to form networks. Networks make the information available wherever it is most useful, thus increasing the value of information. They also make information distribution possible so that data can be processed on the equipment and in the environment of choice. A typical enterprise-wide network today might contain hundreds and often thousands of small networks. Perhaps the most challenging issue in the past few years has been the interconnection of multi-vendor networks to allow applications in different networks to interwork with each other. Another challenging issue is the applications portability issue which allows an application to run on a wide range of platform.

In an **open systems environment (OSE)**, the computer systems and software of different vendors are interchangeable and can be combined into an integrated operating environment. An OSE encompasses the functionality to provide interoperability, applications portability, and integration of computerized applications across multi-vendor networks. **Interoperability** means that **open systems**, i.e., systems participating in the OSE, can exchange information meaningfully with each other even when they are supplied by different vendors. Interconnection, which is the means to connect computers from possibly different vendors, is an integral part of interoperability. **Applications portability** is the ability to run the same software on a wide variety of platforms.

Scalability, a further constraint on applications portability, means that the same software can run with acceptable performance on different classes of computers, ranging from personal computers to supercomputers. Finally, **integration** means that applications in general provide a consistent and seamless user interface. That is, if a user knows how to operate a few applications, he ought to be able to operate most of the rest.

To an open system user, an OSE means a lot, including:

- the freedom to choose the best solutions among different vendors' products,
- faster access to new technology as it is less costly for vendors to build products on a standardized platform, and
- reduced investments in new computer equipments as systems and applications software are portable among existing computers.

Open system standards, i.e., non-proprietary standards, play the most important role in the realization of an OSE. They provide a standardized operating environment for an OSE. First, architectural standards are needed to build an OSE model. Second, standards are needed to provide the specifications of the different components of the model. These standards include both interoperability and applications portability standards. Finally, functional standards are needed to adapt standards to specific environments.

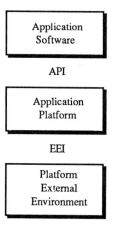

FIGURE 1.1   A Hypothetical OSE Model

The OSE movement evolves through an open consensus-based process for specifying open system standards. In the early stage, the standards defined were primarily aimed at interconnection and interoperability. **Open systems interconnection environment (OSIE)** is a "subset" of OSE in which the open systems use the OSI standards in their communication. OSI standards are fairly well documented today. What open systems users want are standards used to achieve applications portability. Although applications portability does have a large installed base today, it suffers from the lack of applications portability standards.

An open systems model is needed prior to the specifications of open systems standards. Because an unanimous vision of an open system is currently lacking, an OSE Reference Model has not yet been accepted at the international level. A proposed OSE Reference Model is shown in Figure 1.1. In this figure, the application platform is composed of hardware and software components that provide the services used by application programs. Through the use of **Application Program Interfaces (APIs)**, the specific characteristics of the platform are made transparent to the application programs. The API services include information interchange services, communication services, and internal system services. The **Platform External Environment** consists of those system elements external to both the application software and the application platform. Examples of these system elements are human users and external data stores. The **External Environmental Interface (EEI)** is the interface which supports information transfer between the application platform and the platform external environment. For example, it deals with the presentation to human users.

In the first part of this chapter, we examine interoperability and applications portability in detail. Section 1.1 explains the steps leading to interoperability, and Section 1.2 examines applications portability. In the second part (Section 1.3) of this chapter, we study the basics of OSI. We examine the OSI communication services, and we give an overview of the aplication protocols that we are going to cover in this text.

1.1   Interoperability

The path to achieve interoperability requires a series of steps (Figure 1.2). The development of open systems standards is the first step. Standards here include communication standards as well as non-communication standards. The **Open Systems Interconnection (OSI)** standards and the **TCP/IP** standards are examples of open communication standards. Communication standards do not deal with aspects such as data processing and internal functioning of individual systems. Interoperability requires open systems to conform to both the communication standards and the non-communication standards. In this text, we are mainly concerned with the OSI standards.

The International Organization for Standardization (ISO) and the International Electrotechnical Committee (IEC) have jointly formed a committee known as ISO/IEC JTC 1 to develop OSI standards. The other important standard organization for OSI standards is Comité Consultatif Internationale de télégraphique et téléphonique (CCITT) which publishes recommendations. The activities of these two standards organizations will be examined in Section 1.1.1. The most notable OSI standard is ISO/IEC 7498, also known as Recommendation X.200. This architectural standard defines a seven layer framework for the interconnection of heterogeneous systems, known as the **OSI Reference Model**. Within the framework, protocol standards can be specified to detail the functioning of each layer.

The difficulty in implementing the open systems standards is the abstract, often informal, nature of the standards documents as well as the wide variety of options that can be implemented for a protocol. To overcome such difficulties, OSI implementors define **functional profiles** (step 2 in Figure 1.2) in OSI regional workshops. Functional profiles identify specific choices of permitted options and specific values for parameters in the standards for different types of applications. **International Standard Profiles (ISPs)** are functional profiles at the international level. They are designed to achieve harmonization of functional profiles defined in the various OSI regional workshops, so as to provide worldwide interoperability among different implementations. ISPs essentially carry the same status as international standards. Functional profiles and ISPs will be addressed in Section 1.1.2.

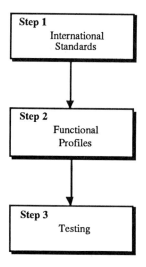

FIGURE 1.2   Steps leading to Interoperability

Step 3 is testing. Testing is an important component in the software engineering cycle. There are two major tests: conformance testing and interoperability testing. **Conformance testing**, performed during the prototype stage of an implementation, is used to verify that an implementation is correct with respect to the relevant standards and profiles. **Interoperability testing** is used to test whether two implementations actually interwork with each other. Interoperability testing is generally considered to be more meaningful when the two implementations have passed conformance testing. Testing will be described in Section 1.1.3.

Thus the path to achieve interoperability is a fairly lengthy process. Given time for the functional profiles to mature, interoperability should not be a problem.

1.1.1   OSI Standard Organizations

Every country has its own standard body which sets standards for products used and sold in that country. In Europe, CEN (Committee European de Normalization) is the official standard body of the European Community while CEN/ELEC is the European electrical standards body.   In US, the two most significant standard bodies involved with communication standards are Accredited Standards Committee X3 (ASC X3) and IEEE Project 802, both operated under the procedures determined by ANSI (American National Standards Institute).   Each of these bodies, accredited by ANSI, present its standards to ANSI for balloting as US National Standards.   X3 is further divided into Technical Committees.   The notable Technical Committees are X3S3, responsible for the OSI lower layers, and X3T5, responsible for OSI architecture and the OSI upper layers.

As far as international standard bodies are concerned, the two most notable ones are ISO and CCITT.   The members of ISO are the various national bodies made up of people from the computer industry, while the members of CCITT are PTT (Post, Telegraph and Telephone) and RPOAs (Recognized Private Operating Agencies) made up of people from the telecommunications industry.

- **ISO/IEC**

ISO/IEC is a voluntary, nontreaty, and specialized agency composed of national standard bodies from 91 countries.   ISO/IEC has intentionally made the processing within end systems separate from the interconnection.   It is divided into Technical Committees (TCs). The most notable TC is ISO/IEC JTC 1 which is responsible to solve the interconnection problem and the information processing problem.   Furthermore, each TC is divided into Subcommittees (SCs) and each SC is subdivided into Working Groups (WGs).

Table 1.1 shows some of the SCs with their associated WGs.   Note that SC 21 has responsibility for architectural issues in the OSI Application Layer in the same way as it has responsibility for the overall OSI Model.   It also has responsibility for standards which are generic to all applications rather than specific to a particular application.   Almost all the OSI architectural standards are produced by SC 21.   The most renowed standard by SC 21 is ISO/IEC 7498 which covers the OSI Reference Model.

As we can see from Table 1.1, ISO/IEC JTC 1 is involved in OSI communications standards (SC 21), information processing standards (SC 18), lower layer information exchange standards (SC 6), security techniques (SC 27), and international functional profiles (SGFS).

The international standards go through a slow and lengthy adoption process that begins when a member organization submits a proposal called a Working Document (WD). This working document is assigned an identification and an SC.   If a consensus can be reached, then the working document is advanced to a Committee Draft (CD).   The TC votes on the CD to be a Draft International Standard (DIS).   Finally the ISO Council approves the DIS to become an International Standard.   It takes an average of five years for a WD to become an International Standard.   This lengthy process ensures that a very wide audience has had an opportunity to agree or disagree with the results.   International Standards can be amended through a similar process involving a Proposed Draft Addendum (PDAD), then a Draft Addendum (DAD), and concluding with an Addendum (AD).

ISO/IEC JTC 1/SC 6:	Telecommunications and information exchange between systems
WG1 WG2 WG3 WG4	Data link layer Network layer Physical layer Transport layer
ISO/IEC JTC 1/SC 18:	Text and office systems
WG1 WG3 WG4 WG5 WG8 WG9	User requirements and SC 18 management support Document architecture Procedures for text interchange Content architectures Text description and processing languages User-systems interfaces and symbols
ISO/IEC JTC 1/SC 21:	Information retrieval, transfer and management for open systems interconnection
WG1 WG3 WG4 WG5 WG6 WG7	OSI architecture Database OSI systems management Specific application services OSI session, presentation and common application services Open distributed processing
ISO/IEC JTC 1/SC 27:	Common security techniques for IT applications
WG1 WG2 WG3	Secret key algorithms and applications Public key crypto-systems and modes of use Use of encipherment techniques in communication architectures
ISO/IEC JTC 1/SGFS:	Special group on functional standards

TABLE 1.1   ISO/IEC Subcommittees and Working Groups

• CCITT

The second most important OSI standard organization is CCITT. CCITT is a subdivision of the International Telecommunications Union (ITU) which operates under the auspices of the United Nations. Its objective is to provide an end-to-end compatibility for international telecommunications. Recommendations are compiled every four years and issued with a colored cover that varies for each four-year period. In 1988, for example, the color was blue; therefore, "Blue Book" refers to the 1988 Recommendations. Study Groups (SGs) and Working Parties (WPs) are the units actually composing CCITT Recommendations. The documents they produce are labelled by a letter, a dot, a number, and a year, e.g., X.25 (1984).

CCITT has been more concerned with issues covered in the lower three layers of the OSI model, and applications using the telecommunications capabilities such as the Message Handling System. There is, though, a great deal of overlap between the work of ISO and the work of CCITT. Indeed, ISO and CCITT publish nearly identical text as both an International Standard and a Recommendation.

The implementation of OSI is a lengthy and costly process. Just on the cost of OSI standards development, one estimate says that it has exceeded four billion dollars. Part of the cost has to do with the length of time for a WD to become an IS. Since a proposal cannot become a standard till everyone involved agrees, the urge to reach compromises greatly increases. Compromises, by trying to please everyone, cause the standards to become large, complex and less workable. Compromised standards do not have the concentration that proprietary standards have. Users may not want to scrap systems that they are familiar with, trust, understand, and have skilled employees dedicated to. In many cases, proprietary products are more efficient because they focus on a smaller set of requirements and functionalities. Furthermore, since OSI implementations often lag behind the development of standards, most users tend to wait until more efficient and stable OSI implementations are available.

Despite the above drawbacks, there are two major factors which facilitate the adoption of OSI standards. Perhaps the biggest factor is the integration of the economies of the European Common Market countries. The governments in different countries also play an important role in promoting OSI. For example, the US Government mandating the use of OSI in procurement of new networks and major upgrades will make the 90's the years of OSI.

1.1.2 Functional Profiles

The existence of OSI standards does not make the design of an OSI system straightforward. While the players in the OSI standard bodies do nothing but develop standards, the implementors are the ones actually building OSI products. The implementation of complete OSI systems comprising the multiple layers of complex protocols is a very challenging task. Some of the problems are listed below:

- The ambiguous nature of the OSI standards makes a correct and efficient implementation of an OSI system a difficult task. Formal specifications would remove the ambiguities.
- OSI standards allow multiple choices in its service elements, service parameters, functional units, and elements of procedures. It is not expected that an OSI product would provide the implementation of every possible feature stated in the standard. A careful selection of such choices is required by any OSI implementation.
- Most of the OSI application standards are object-oriented in their approaches. Different objects are used in different environments. While the standards only give a few tools to define common objects, an implementation must define the objects

necessary to support applications in a given environment. Implementors need to agree on the objects used during the course of communication.

Choosing the protocol features and defining the object classes in a consistent manner require not only a thorough understanding of the standards, but also mutual agreement among the implementors.

The groups involved in defining and applying functional profiles can be divided into three categories: OSI implementor's workshops, industry specific consortia and organizations, and government institutions. These groups are examined next.

* **OSI implementation workshops**

Implementation agreements have been reached mostly in OSI workshops. Each workshop serves as an open public forum for users and suppliers of OSI products to develop functional profiles. The existing three regional workshops are OIW (OSI Implementation Workshop) in the US, EWOS (European Workshop in Open Systems) in Europe and AOW (Asian and Oceanic Workshop) for Japan, Australia and the Pacific Rim countries. OIW, the oldest of all three, is hosted quarterly at NIST (National Institute of Standards and Technology). Once a year, the completed agreements are published as Stable Implementation Agreements.

Each workshop accepts the specifications of the emerging OSI standards as input and produces functional profiles as output.   A functional profile defines, for a particular protocol, a precise combination of options and values to be used in a given environment. A protocol standard can have more than one functional profile. For example, FTAM, the OSI protocol for file manipulation, has a functional profile for file transfer, and another functional profile for file access.

* **industry specific consortia and organizations**

Considering that each OSI layer can have more than one protocol and each protocol can have more than one functional profile, it is not difficult to figure out that there are many functional profiles. Users in a specific environment need only use a subset of such functional profiles. Perhaps they select a few protocols from each layer, and a few functional profiles for each selected protocol. The resulting collection of functional profiles is called a **users' profile**, or just a **profile**. Thus a profile is a consistent selection of functional profiles for a specific environment. The environment can be a manufacturing environment, a testing environment, a government environment, an academic environment, etc.

COS (Corporation for Open Systems), a consortium of computer and communication vendors and users, was founded in 1986 to accelerate the introduction of multivendor interoperable products. One of the most important functions is the development of COS testing profiles and conformance tests of OSI products. Products which have been successfully tested against COS profiles are marked with a COS Mark.

SPAG (Standards Promotion and Application Group), a consortium of leading European IT manufacturers, was founded in 1983 at the request of the European Commission (EC). The objective of EC is to receive guidance from SPAG in the promulgation of an European IT Standards Policy for providing a homogeneous European market for IT products. The plan is that all member countries in Europe will adopt the functional standards published as "European Standards" as of 1992. SPAG also defines its own testing profiles.

General Motors, the giant US car manufacturer, specified MAP (Manufacturing Automation Profile) to link up systems in automated factories. They also designed TOP (Technical Office Profile) and handed the work over to Boeing. Both MAP and TOP are users' profiles.

• **government institutions**

Many government bodies have developed IT policies mandating procurement of OSI computer products. They include US, UK, Canada and Japan.

As of August 15, 1990, the US Government mandated the use of OSI in procurement of new networks and major upgrades to existing networks within the government agencies. The US GOSIP is a Federal Government procurement profile for open systems computer network products in the US. This profile is based on the Stable Implementation Agreements at OIW. NIST issued this profile as Federal Information Processing Standard (FIPS) 146. Version 1.0 of FIPS 146 specified a consistent set of core OSI protocols sufficient to provide electronic mail and file transfer services over LANs and WANs.

Because functional profiles are developed in three different workshops, interoperability among different functional profiles is still a problem. Realizing this serious problem, ISO felt that it had to harmonize these documents and produce a set of international implementation agreements, called ISPs (i.e., International Standardized Profiles), which would carry the same status as the International Standards. A subcommittee of ISO/IEC JTC 1, called Special Group on Functional Standardization (SGFS), was formed in 1987 to define ISPs. It did not take long for the ISO Executive Board and Council to recognize four organizations which have similar interests in converging OSI functional profile development. These four organizations, also known as "feeders" or "OSI User Groups", are SPAG, POSI, COS, and MAP/TOP Users Groups. ISO recognized these four organizations as special S-liaisons to SGFS. As feeders, these organizations informs ISO of the priorities of the needed base standards development. In 1989, the same status was given to the three regional OSI workshops. ISO/IEC JTC1 issued a two-part Technical Report (TR 10000) to cover the framework and taxonomy of ISPs. ISO/IEC TR 10000-1 (Framework) defines the concept of profiles and the way in which ISPs are documented. It gives guidance to organizations making proposals for DISPs (Draft International Standardized Profiles). ISO/IEC TR 10000-2 (Taxonomy) classifies profiles into classes and groups. Since the ISPs will, in general, be evaluated and used by experts in specific areas of standardizations, classification is needed to reflect the main areas of expertise.

Next, we examine how a functional profile turns into an ISP. First a submitting organization which must be authorized proposes a pDISP (Proposed Draft ISP) to SGFS. The pDISP contains an explanatory report such as the purpose of each profile, a statement of the pDISP process, and the extent of international harmonization involved. SGFS then appoints a review team to review the pDISP. The review team prepares and distributes a review report. The pDISP, if approved, advances to the DISP (Draft ISP) level and a ballot takes place. When the majority of members favor the proposal, the DISP will then become an ISP. As soon as the ISP is published, the submitting organization assumes responsibility as the maintenance authority of the ISP. It takes roughly seven months for a pDISP to become an ISP.

One major difference between ISO standards and ISPs should be mentioned. For ISPs, the submitter has the responsibility to prepare the document, ensure global harmonization, and maintain the document after publication. For ISO standards, the ISO committees not only prepare the documents but also maintain them.

TR 10000-2 classifies profiles into classes and groups. Understanding of this classification requires some basic understanding of the OSI layers and protocols. Thus we will postpone our discussion of the classification to Section 1.5.3.

1.1.3   Testing

Testing is crucial to the acceptance of OSI. OSI developers need conformance testing to show the buyers that their products comply to the OSI standards. Buyers need interoperability testing to demonstrate that the products they purchase interoperate with each other.

•   **conformance testing**

Conformance testing examines a product to see if it meets both standards requirements and profile requirements. It is intended to replace protocol verification. Those who have experience with program verification should know that verification is almost an impossible task. Even when it is possible in certain cases, it would be very costly. Although conformance testing is achievable, it may take a long time. But technically speaking, conformance testing is not as thorough as protocol verification. Lack of fault coverage is one of the major problems confronting conformance testing today.

Conformance testing is based on the information in the Protocol Information Conformance Statement (PICS) which is supplied by the vendor. The PICS provides both the static and the dynamic features of an implementation under test (IUT). Conformance testing can be done in-house or by a third party. The IUT is executed by some conformance tester. The tester examines the robustness of the IUT by sending errors to the IUT to see how it handles them.

There are certain limitations of conformance testing. The behavior of the IUT is in general an "infinite" object. This is so because the IUT can execute over infinitely many computation paths. Thus, it is difficult to test an IUT thoroughly. A practical solution is to test the IUT using a finite set of test cases. Testing with a finite set of test cases means that even if an IUT passes all the test cases, we still do not have a thorough proof that the IUT completely conforms to the standard. It only means that no problem is detected by the selected set of test cases. Although increasing the number of test cases may raise the fault coverage, it will increase the development cost significantly. Thus, there is a trade-off between the cost of conformance testing and the fault coverage.

•   **interoperability testing**

While conformance testing gives some degree of confidence to developers, it offers little to users. The point is that two products which have passed conformance testing may not guarantee to interwork with each other. One of the reasons is that the standards allow too many options. If two implementations choose values from the two extreme ends of the range of values for a given option, they may not interwork with each other. Users rely on **interoperability testing** to demonstrate that products from different vendors interoperate with each other. Interoperability testing demonstrates the main objective of OSI: interoperability of heterogeneous systems.

Interoperability testing is performed between two different implementations which have claimed conformance to the same standards and profiles. It is very time-consuming because the tester can only test one pair of implementations at a time. A total of $n*(n-1)/2$ interoperability experiments are needed to demonstrate full interoperability in an environment consisting of n implementations. One way to save time is to test an implementation individually with a "reference" implementation. The idea is that if all the implementations pass this individual test, they will interoperate with each other. Obviously, the last statement is somewhat "grey".

Some differences between interoperability testing and conformance testing should be pointed out. First, interoperability tests are performed by means of commands available at the interfaces provided by the implementations. These commands are fairly high-level. Because interfaces to the OSI "middle" layers may not be as available as interfaces to the Application Layer, interoperability testing is normally performed with application protocols instead of protocols in the "middle" layers. On the other hand, conformance testing can be performed on every protocol. The test commands used for conformance testing are more granular than those used for interoperability testing. Second, conformance testing can be used to test invalid behaviors. For example, a conformance tester can send an invalid protocol data unit to an IUT, expecting it to reject the data unit. There is no way to test invalid behaviors in interoperability testing. Finally, interoperability testing is done in real time in an operational system while conformance testing is seldom done in real time. Indeed, some of the static test cases used in conformance testing can be done manually. Despite the differences mentioned above, conformance testing increases the likeliness of interoperability and should be coupled with interoperability testing.

Even if an implementation passes conformance testing, it does not mean that it can pass interoperability testing. Similarly, even if an implementation passes interoperability testing, it does not mean that it can pass conformance testing. To understand why this is so, one can relate conformance test to taking a written driving test, and interoperability testing to taking a driving test on the road. A student driver can pass a written test and fail in a driving test on the road. It can pass a driving test conducted in a low-traffic area but fails a passing test set by a tough examiner. Another observation is that an implementation may pass a conformance/interoperability testing at one time but fail a conformance/interoperability testing at a later time. This is so because the test cases used each time may be different.

One of the problems with interoperability testing is that whenever an interoperability test case fails, it is hard to determine which system does not follow the standard or profile requirements. We need some tool that can play the role of an arbitrator and monitor the interactions between the two implementations in real time. This tool needs to know the internal implementation details of the two implementations. Since interoperability testing is based on manual procedures which are not specified formally, building such an arbitrator is impossible.

OSINET is an organization established in 1984 to foster the development, the promotion, and the employment of OSI through activities related to interoperability tests. Made up of industry companies, government agencies, and vendors, OSINET is engaged in the testing and registration of OSI products, the demonstration and promotion of the OSI technology, and the research and development of test suites and the conduct of OSI interoperability testing. There are several other extensive networks to provide the interoperability test service to vendors. These include Eurosinet in Europe and OSIcom in Australia. Six of these networks have combined to form a worldwide OSI-interoperability network called OSIOne. A major goal of OSIOne is the establishment of a common platform for regional OSI networks so as to facilitate the promotion of worldwide OSI connectivity and interoperability.

1.2   Applications Portability

Applications portability is as important as interoperability in an OSE. Applications portability means that the purchase and usage of an application software can be separated from the underlying hardware platform so that users can move an application software from one computing environment to another with minor modification.

Applications portability and interoperability are two related but different concepts. Consider OSI application software for example. Applications portability means that a portable OSI software can run in different platforms such as different subnetwork types and different operating systems. On the other hand, interoperability involves at least two different vendors. It means that two vendors of the same type of OSI software can communicate meaningfully with each other. As a matter of fact, applications portability predates interoperability. Even in the old days when computers were stand-alone machines with no communication capability, applications portability was needed for the same application to run in different machines. On the other hand, interoperability has only become a major issue in recent years when applications are designed to be network intrinsic to pave the way for distributed computing.

Like interoperability, application portability is also provided by means of standards. Applications portability standards have a much wider scope than OSI communication standards. Besides addressing communication standards, they also address operating systems standards, data management standards, user interface standards, and programming language standards.

In Section 1.2.1, we examine the major players in applications portability. In Section 1.2.2, we examine a generic applications portability model. In Section 1.2.3, we examine some features of APIs.

1.2.1   Players in Applications Portability

First, let us examine three of the major players in applications portability: IEEE, X/Open, and OSF. These three players play different roles, yet they cooperate to promote applications portability.

•   IEEE

IEEE formed the POSIX Standards Committee in 1985. This POSIX committee first published the Standard P1003.1 on POSIX (Portable Operating System Interface) in 1988 which was accepted as a standard first by ANSI and then by ISO. P1003.1 defines a minimum API to provide operating system services. More specifically, it defines process primitives and environment, files and directories, input and output primitives, device and class-specific functions, language-specific services for C, system databases, and data interchange formats. Other P1003 subcommittees, POSIX.2 through POSIX.12, address the user interface (e.g., shells and tools), transaction processing, supercomputing, validation, real-time extensions, Ada and FORTRAN languages, security, system administration, windowing, and networking. The POSIX specifications represent a milestone in the efforts to standardize an operating environment. The US Government published FIPS 151-1 to ensure POSIX compliance within US government agencies.

•   X/Open

Because the process of IEEE standards is very time-consuming, other organizations also participate in an effort to develop a standard operating environment. X/Open was founded in 1984 by five European computer manufacturers to accelerate the pace of applications portability and to complement the work of POSIX. It is not a standard setting body. It endorses existing International Standards. Where there are no International Standards, X/Open adopts de facto standards, modifying them if necessary. For example, it adopted

X Window System as a user interface and upgraded it by adding a high-level graphical user interface specification.

X/Open developed the Common Applications Environment (CAE) based on de facto and industry standards (Figure 1.3) The foundation of CAE is the POSIX interface definition. However, CAE extends POSIX into a complete operating environment by addressing requirements for data management, data communications, distributed systems, and high-level languages. It comprises all the components of a computer system that need to be specified and standardized to meet the goals of portability and interoperability.

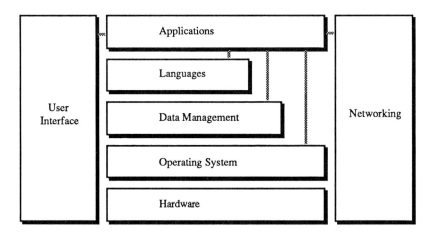

FIGURE 1.3   Common Applications Environment   of X/Open

• **OSF**

While IEEE and X/Open provide standards and specifications, they do not supply implementations. Open Software Foundation (OSF), an industry supported organization formed in 1988, is an integrator and an implementor of existing standards and technologies. Its aim is to provide source code reference implementations. OSF's source code reference implementations are in full compliance with POSIX and X/Open standards. It obtains its source code reference implementations and technology through its Request for Technology (RFT) process, which is an open invitation to the computer industry to submit ideas on a specific topic. In short, source code reference implementations enable vendors to focus their development efforts on creating new technologies and to reduce their cost by building applications on only one interface.

1.2.2   Components of a Generic Applications Portability Model

To accomplish applications portability, it is necessary to shield applications from the underlying operating system and hardware platform by introducing a layer of software in between. This piece of software interfaces with applications on one side and other components on the other side. Figure 1.4 shows the various components of a generic applications portability model. Below we will discuss each of these components.

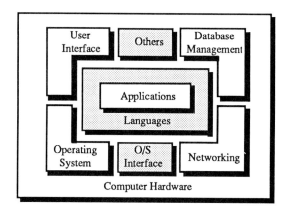

FIGURE 1.4　**Components of a Generic Applications Portability Model**

- **operating systems interface**

This component provides an interface to the operating system services. Currently, the IEEE POSIX standard is the international standard for the operating systems interface.

- **programming languages**

A common language binding interface is being developed to accommodate all language compilers in a reasonable way to promote applications portability. The bindings for the popular high level languages such as C, Ada, and FORTRAN are being developed by the IEEE 1003.1c, IEEE 1003.5, and IEEE 1003.9 working groups respectively.

- **data management**

Many applications require certain data management such as accessing, managing, and interchanging various types of data. Thus a consistent approach to data management is the key to applications portability. Various interfaces and schemes for data management are being developed. For access to a relational database, Structure Query Language (SQL) is the de facto relational database language which has been widely accepted by industries. SQL can be embedded in a general purpose programming language. This feature promotes applications portability since the changes made to the underlying database management system or operating system are transparent to the applications. Not every application requires complex relational database management. Indeed, many applications can function properly with a simple scheme such as Index-Sequential Access Method which provides data access and manipulation by referring to a key field in the data.

Data interchange services establish data formats for interchange of office documents, graphics data, and product description data. Examples of interchange standards are Office Document Language (ODA), Standard Generalized Markup Language (SGML), Computer Graphics Metafile (CGM), and Initial Graphic Exchange Specification (IGES).

• **networking**

Networking is the one of the most important components used to achieve applications portability. It addresses a variety of important issues such as interconnection standards, distributed processing standards, and APIs for communication services.

• **user interface**

The user interface is a major component of the applications portability model since it provides the interface between users and applications. More easy-to-use and object-oriented user interfaces are being developed by vendors. The standardization of the user interface, especially graphical user interface (GUI) with easy-to-use windows, menus, icons, and a mouse appears to be at the heart of the issue.

A generic GUI consists of an API, a windowing system, and an imaging model. The API allows programmers to specify how to manipulate windows, menus, icons, etc. The windowing system is a set of programming tools and commands that allow programmers to build windows, menus, and dialogue boxes. The imaging model defines how fonts and graphics are created on the screen. One good example of a windowing system is the X Window System developed by the MIT Athena project.

1.2.3   Application Programming Interfaces

Portable software can be designed in at least two ways. One way is to design the software using well defined interfaces where the system dependent features are isolated from the system independent features. The other approach is to write the software using a standardized API.

APIs can be either language-dependent or portable. Many APIs today are just libraries of function calls. These are language-dependent APIs. A majority of the language-dependent APIs are based on the language C. In this text, we will cover four language dependent APIs: TLI (Transport Level Interface) in Chapter 6, APLI (Application Level Interface) in Chapter 10, the MAP/TOP FTAM interface in Chapter 17, and CMIP (CMIP Library) in Chapter 18. A portable API is one that is language independent and does not contain any operating system dependencies. Portable APIs are defined in terms of a set of object classes and related operations. Because of their object-oriented nature, they can be easily moved to any platform. We will cover three portable APIs in this text: the XDS API for the OSI Directory Services in Chapter 15 and the two APIs defined for the OSI Message Handling Systems in Chapter 16.

Almost every OSI vendor bundles its OSI products with APIs. In some cases, these APIs are proprietary. Note that although the OSI software has to conform to the standards, APIs are local design matters. In the recent open systems movement, vendors tend to use standardized APIs rather than proprietary APIs. Standardized APIs here refer to APIs that have the blessings of standard bodies (e.g., IEEE), governments (i.e., GOSIP), users' groups (e.g., MAP/TOP), or consortia (e.g., X/Open). A standardized API can be language dependent or portable. For example, TLI is a language dependent API standardized by X/Open.

Some APIs can be very high level. High-level APIs are desirable for average applications programmers. Low-level APIs, on the other hand, allow an application programmer to manipulate some of the parameters used at a lower level of the software. An OSI API can be designed to be both high level and low level at the same time, in view of the fact that an OSI software normally consists of multiple layers. The MAP/TOP FTAM API has this property.

Finally, an API can provide more than one type of service. For example, an integrated API may provide not only communication services but also user interface services (e.g., the MOTIF API), information interchange services (e.g., SGML used for office document interchange), and information services (e.g., the SQL API).

An ideal API for applications portability should be language independent, non-proprietary, both high level and low level, and integrated.

1.3 Basics of OSI

In 1978, ISO proposed to establish a framework for coordinating the development of existing and future standards for the interconnection of heterogeneous systems. The well-known seven-layer OSI Reference Model became an International Standard, ISO/IEC 7498, in the spring of 1983. The original model did not have a detailed description of all possibilities. Since it was published, the following addenda were added to firm up the model:

- ISO/IEC 7498-1 (Connectionless Mode): The original OSI model is connection-oriented, meaning that the communicating parties have to establish a connection before communication can take place. However, there is a demand for connectionless mode communication in LANs, network management, and interactive environments.
- ISO/IEC 7498-2 (Security Architecture): This part of ISO 7498 defines the OSI security architecture as an enhancement to the OSI architecture. It describes security architectural concepts such as security services and security mechanisms. It also suggests how security services can be placed in the OSI Reference Model.
- ISO/IEC 7498-3 (Naming and Addressing): This addendum defines a general mechanism for the use of names and addresses to identify and locate objects in an OSIE.

• ISO/IEC 7498-4 (Management Framework): The OSI management framework defines a framework for management activities pertinent to OSI and management services supported by OSI management protocols. It covers the management concepts, management functional areas, and management structure.

The above addenda provide important support for the OSI Reference Model. The use of OSI in an enterprise network depends much on how well these supporting issues are addressed by OSI. Work is currently underway to combine ISO 7498 and ISO 7498-1 into a single document. Consequently, ISO 7498 will be a four-part document in the future.

1.3.1   OSI Communication Services

In many ways, communication between computers is similar to communication between people using the telephone system, except that the communicating entities are computers rather than people. To facilitate the communication among computer applications in a heterogeneous environment , both the internetworking and the interworking services must be provided. These services are explained next.

The **internetworking service** provides physical connectivity between systems in different networks. Each network, as autonomous as it wants to be, becomes a subnetwork in an internetwork environment. Conceptually, a network is a set of subnetworks, connected by intermediate systems (ISs), and populated by end systems (ESs). ESs are where applications reside. ISs are systems providing the interconnection among ESs. The goal of the internetworking services are twofold: transparency over the topology of the network and transparency over the transmission media used in each subnetwork.

Realization of the transparency goal implies two major functions: addressing and routing. As the network grows in size, some uniform addressing mechanisms are needed to locate the various ESs and ISs in the network. A good network addressing scheme may require addresses to be independent of the network topology and subnetwork transmission media. Once nodes have addresses, the next question is: how is data transferred from the source ES to the target ES? Routing functions determine the next subnetwork and a target IS to use for relaying traffic. There are two levels of routing involved. First, each subnetwork has its own routing strategy. Second, there is the internetwork routing which performs routing over the subnetworks. Ideally, these two routing levels should work independently of each other.

Although the internetworking service can move data from an ES to another ES, reliability is still a problem because the underlying subnetworks may be unreliable. With the help of the transport service and the internetworking service, applications could exchange data reliably with each other as if there were a data pipe connecting them. Applications do not have to worry about communication failures and steps taken to recover from failures.

Even with the provision of a reliable internetworking service, applications may not be able to communicate meaningfully with each other. The reason is that the users of the internetworking services are application processes but not human beings who are smart enough to cope with various problems arising in communication. **Interworking services** contain the communication functionalities for application processes to communicate with each other in a meaningful way. Some of the key interworking services are representation, coordination, and naming. For example, applications need to know how to represent the information in transit. The point is that applications only deal with information structures. These information structures must be represented in some data streams first before the data streams are passed to the lower layers. The transport service only guarantees that the data streams are conveyed reliably from one end to the other end. But if the two communicating applications use different representation strategies, they will not share a common understanding of the information structures exchanged. Thus somewhere in the communication software, the two communicating application processes need to establish a common strategy to represent the information structures. In OSI, the term transfer syntax refers to a set of rules used to encode the values of information structures, and the term abstract syntax means a collection of information structures specified in a representation independent manner. Applications communicate with one another using one or more abstract syntaxes. Each abstract syntax can be represented by one or more transfer syntaxes. Before communication takes place, applications need to establish a common transfer syntax used to represent each abstract syntax.

The interworking service also provides coordination so that applications can carry out their operations accurately in the manner they choose. The transport service only provides a full-duplex data pipe between two communicating applications. But if the applications prefer to operate in a half-duplex mode, then they would rely on some dialogue control facility which controls who can send. This dialogue control facility is provided by the interworking service.

Another useful function provided by the interworking service is naming. Physical connectivity provided by the internetworking service is not sufficient for the open system users to effectively utilize objects (i.e., resources). Uniform mechanisms are needed for identifying and locating objects that are made accessible to the community by their creators or owners. Objects should be given names, which are passed freely around the OSE and shared amongst its users. Once users have a way of referring to objects, services should be provided to bind these objects to their network addresses. Name registration and name resolution are some of the activities provided by the naming service. Without a well-designed naming facility, communication in an enterprise network would be chaotic.

We have identified some of the internetworking and interworking functions. The next step is to provide an infrastructure which lays out these functions.

1.3.2   The OSI Reference Model

The communication software providing the internetworking service and the interworking service is very complex. Using the divide and conquer principle, ISO divides the overall communication functions hierarchically into seven layers (Figure 1.5). Each layer provides services to the layer above by using the services provided by the layers beneath it.

Applications access OSI communication services from the highest layer, i.e., layer seven. For each layer, two types of services (i.e., connectionless and connection oriented) may be provided. For each service type, different protocols are defined. Each protocol is defined to provide a specific set of services, and usually contains a set of mandatory features together with options depending on the system capabilities and the users' requirements.

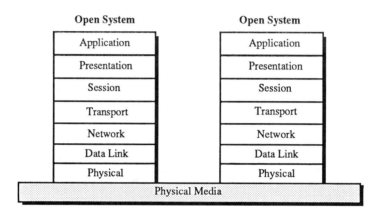

FIGURE 1.5   OSI Reference Model

Layer three, the **Network Layer**, provides the interconnection service. It provides transparency over the topology of the network as well as transparency over the transmission media used in each subnetwork comprising the network. Layer four, the **Transport Layer**, is responsible for moving data reliably from one ES to another ES. While the end-to-end service provided by the Transport Layer deals with data transfer between the ESs, the upper three layers provide an interworking service. These upper layers, starting from the bottom, are the **Session Layer**, the **Presentation Layer**, and the **Application Layer**. The Session Layer is primarily responsible for the coordination function. The Presentation Layer is responsible for the representation function. The Application Layer provides the rest of the communication functions. These functions may be specific or generic to a class of applications. The most important function is the naming function provided by the Directory Services.

Even with the provision of the interworking services, applications still may not be able to interwork with each other. The upper three layers only provide the communication support for interworking. But interworking also requires non-communication support. For example, if the sender and the receiver use different document formats, documents cannot be interchanged meaningfully.

For the rest of this section, we give an overview of each layer.

• **Application Layer**

Layer seven, the **Application Layer**, directly serves applications by providing the required communication support.

First of all, applications do not live in layer seven, although they may have hooks to the communication software in layer seven. Conceptually, we can divide an application into communication components and non-communication components. The communication components are called the application entities (AEs). As an object in Layer seven, an AE derives its services from the Presentation Layer. An application may have one or more AEs. For example, a banking application may have an AE for supporting electronic mail and another AE for supporting file manipulation. The same banking application may have non-communication components such as some word procesing software.

An AE communicates with a peer AE using an **application protocol**. Application protocols vary in complexity. Some involve only two objects, while others involve more than two objects. Some protocols involve a number of systems, and others involve a maximum of two systems. Unlike protocols in the lower six layers, all the application protocols are described using one or more information models. An information model describes how a class of information structures is organized. Information models are practically absent in lower layers, because lower layers deal with data streams which are representations of information structures.

Examples of applications protocols are examined next. **FTAM (File Transfer, Access and Management) protocol** is the protocol used for file handling. The FTAM standard provides three modes of file manipulation. First, file transfer is the movement of an entire file between filestores in two open systems. Second, file access performs reading, writing, or deleting of the selected parts of a remote file. Finally, file management refers to the management of either files or filestores.

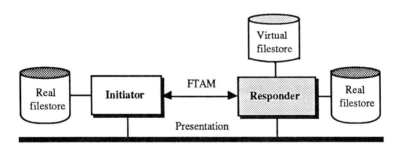

FIGURE 1.6 FTAM Computational Model

The FTAM information model is based on the notions of a virtual file and a virtual filestore. Both notions are defined in terms of attributes and file operations. The virtual filestore contains three types of objects: files, file-directories, and references. In addition to these objects, there are also supporting objects. For example, supporting objects such as document type objects are used to associate a specific type of data with the file contents. Supporting objects are defined by a profile group.

The FTAM computational model is based on the client-server model. There is an initiator (client) initiating and controlling the FTAM association and a responder (server) providing access to its virtual filestore. The initiator reads, writes, accesses, or manages the virtual filestore of the responder's file system. Figure 1.6 shows a model of interaction of an FTAM initiator with an FTAM responder.

Next, we examine the **Common Management Information Protocol (CMIP)** which is the OSI protocol used to support systems management. Network management deals with planning, monitoring, accounting, and controlling the use of network resources. The major problem in network management today is how to eliminate islands of management subsystems in an enterprise network. The OSI management standards define an integrated networking management environment by providing uniformity at three levels: uniformity in the definition of managed objects, uniformity in the definition of systems management functions, and uniformity in the specification of a communication protocol to support the exchange of management information.

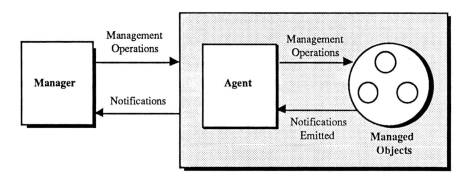

FIGURE 1.7   CMIP Functional Model

Systems management, which is management across multiple layers of the OSI Reference Model, is the primary means of OSI management. ISO/IEC defines CMIP as the communication protocol to support the exchange of systems management information. The CMIP protocol involves two objects: a manager and an agent. The two objects exchange systems management information with each other using management operations and notifications. The manager uses management operations to retrieve or alter a managed object local to the agent. The agent can send notifications to a manager. Figure 1.7 shows a model of interaction between the manager and the agent.

Next, we examine the **Virtual Terminal (VT) protocol.** The VT standard defines a means for VT-users to access applications in remote computing systems through a terminal regardless of the make of the computing systems and the terminal. It introduces the notion of a virtual terminal which is an abstraction of a class of real terminals. Of these classes, the Basic Class Virtual Terminal (BCVT) is character-oriented and provides limited services for manipulating blocks and fields.

The information model of BCVT is defined in an object-oriented manner. All the objects are organized in the shared conceptual communication area (CCA) which contains display objects, device objects as well as control objects. Each object is described in terms of a set of VTE (virtual terminal environment)-parameters. Because there are many choices of VTE-parameters, profile organizations define VTE-profiles. A VTE-profile is a predefined set of VTE-parameters. These VTE-profiles form a basis of negotiation by VT users during the association establishment.

The BCVT service supports both the synchronous mode and the asynchronous mode of operation. The BCVT service also provides delivery control mechanisms by which a VT-user can mark the end of a sequence of updates to objects in the CCA. It also provides a break-in service for VT-users to interrupt each other.

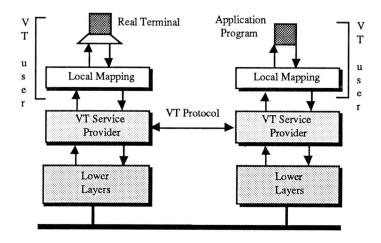

FIGURE 1.8   VT Computational Model

A VT implementation must define a mapping between the virtual terminal and the local terminal characteristics. Figure 1.8 shows the VT computational model.

Next, we examine the **OSI Transaction Processing (TP) protocol**. A transaction is a unit of work consisting of multiple operations that has the four ACID properties: atomicity, consistency, isolation, and durability. For example, the atomicity property means that either all or none of the operations of a transaction are performed. The purpose of the OSI TP standard is to provide an infrastructure through which distributed applications can process transactions reliably across one or more systems.

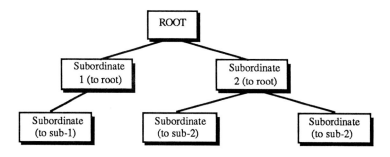

FIGURE 1.9   A TP Transaction Tree Structure

The TP protocol involves two types of objects: a transaction superior and a transaction subordinate. A transaction superior can set up multiple connections with different transaction subordinates and communicate with each of them using TP. A transaction subordinate can also be a transaction superior to another set of subordinates. In this way, a tree of transactions is defined. The transaction tree structure (Figure 1.9) determines the responsibilities of each node in the tree for commitment and recovery. Figure 1.10 shows the use of TP in a travel reservation application. To manage a transaction for a customer, a travel agency may have to set up dialogues with the Airline Reservation System and the Motel Chain. The Airline Reservation System in turn may have to set up dialogues with one or more airlines.

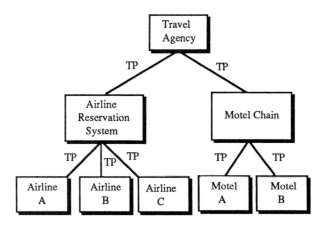

FIGURE 1.10   Use of TP in a Travel Reservation Application

Next, we examine the **Remote Database Access (RDA) protocol**. Today, multi-vendor database interoperability is limited. A database client can only access a limited set of remote database servers. Figure 1.11 gives an example of a database configuration in a manufacturing environment where it is necessary to integrate heterogeneous databases on different floors. RDA enables multi-vendor database interoperability. The RDA standard provides independence such that a RDA user can use the same front end to access different database systems, and a single database may be shared by different workstations.

RDA uses the client-server model. Typically, the client is an application program running in an intelligent workstation, and the server is a remote database server. The current RDA standard is specified in two documents: a generic RDA document and an SQL specialization document. The generic RDA services provide facilities for database management and database access. A specialization standard describes how the generic services can be optimized for a particular class of database systems. For example, the SQL specialization document specifies optimization for SQL access.

Currently, ISO is working closely with **SQL Access Group**, which is an industry consortium group to define specifications to enable multi-vendor interoperability between SQL-based database clients and servers at a faster pace.

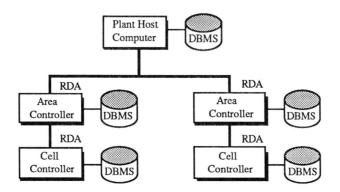

FIGURE 1.11　A Distributed Database Environment

Next we describe the **Manufacturing Message Specification (MMS) protocol**. One of the most well-known requirements for all manufacturing applications is the need for plant floor computers and devices to communicate. MMS is designed to meet this requirement. It allows a central computer, i.e., a host computer, to control any programmable device on a factory floor.

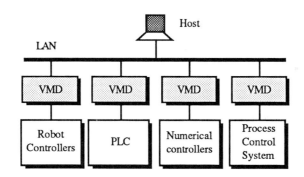

FIGURE 1.12　An MMS Configuration

The MMS standard defines the notion of a virtual manufacturing device (VMD) which is an abstraction of a real device such as a programmable logic controller. Applications communicate with and manipulate the VMD (Figure 1.12). An MMS implementation must define a local mapping between the VMD and the real device. Figure 1.13 shows the MMS model.

MMS is one of the largest and most complex application protocol standards. This is partially due to the wide variety of factory floor devices available. Based on the client-server model, MMS involves only two objects. Typically, the client is a host computer and the server is a factory floor device.

MMS is unique among the OSI application standards due to its companion standards. Companion standards allow MMS to focus on a particular type of factory floor device. Companion standards have been defined for devices such robots, numerical controllers, and programmable logic controllers.

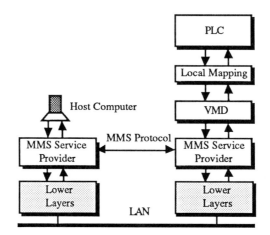

FIGURE 1.13   MMS Computational Model

All the above protocols involve no more than two types of objects. Some applications involve more than two types of objects. For these applications, more than one protocol is needed since a protocol in general specifies interaction rules between a pair of communicating objects. The Message Handling System involves a number of objects and protocols. Although the Directory Services standard involves only two types of objects, it specifies more than one Directory protocol. One protocol specifies the Directory access, while another specifies the interaction among the Directory servers. Below we will briefly examine the Directory services protocols and the Message Handling System protocols .

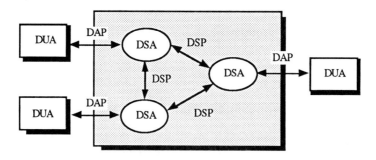

FIGURE 1.14   DS Functional Model

In a distributed computing environment, the **Directory Services (DS)** standard provides a distributed service to manage information that is not likely to change very often. The Directory is the conceptual repository of the such information. Examples of information that can be stored in the Directory are e-mail addresses, network addresses of open systems, and public keys.

Figure 1.14 gives the DS functional model. There are two kinds of objects involved. The client, called the Directory User Agent (DUA), makes a request to the Directory which is made up of one or more Directory Service Agents (DSAs) possibly located at different places. The **Directory Access Protocol (DAP)** specifies how a DUA accesses the DSA. The **Directory System Protocol (DSP)** specifies how the DSAs interact with each other to provide the distributed directory services.

Besides the DS functional model, there are a number of information models described in the DS standard. There is the Directory Information model which describes the structure of the information in the Directory. There is the Directory Administrative Authority Model which describes the Directory from an administrative point of view. And there is the DSA Information Model which describes the information maintained by a DSA. Thus, the Application Layer is bundled with information models which are practically absent in the lower six layers of the OSI model. This in a way explains the object-oriented nature of OSI application protocols.

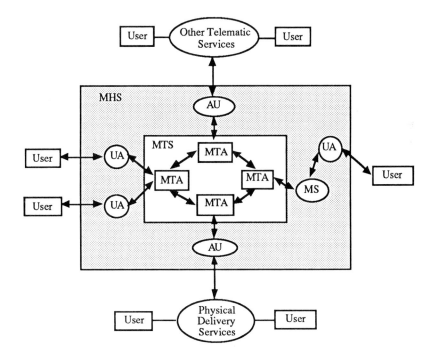

FIGURE 1.15   MHS Functional Model

Message Handling Systems (MHSs) enable users to exchange electronic messages on a store-and-forward basis. The first version of the MHS standard, published in 1984, did not use the presentation services. The latest enhancements to the MHS recommendations, published in 1988, are fully aligned to the OSI model. They include the use of the DS standard, message stores, and distribution lists.

Figure 1.15 shows the MHS functional model. The major components are:

- MHS users which are either people or application processes,
- user agents (UAs) which represent MHS users to do the front end jobs such as submitting and retrieving mail,
- a message transfer system (MTS) which consists of autonomous message transfer agents (MTAs) to transfer the messages,
- the interpersonal messaging service (IPMS) which supports the exchange of messages for human communication,
- message stores (MSs) which provide UAs with mailboxes to store and retrieve messages, and
- access units (AUs) which provide import and export of MHS services to the non-MHS message services.

Thus, four important objects are identified by the MHS standard: UAs, MSs, AUs, and MTAs. The MHS standards define three major protocols: **P1** for the interaction between MTAs, **P3** for a UA to access the MTA service, and **P7** for a UA to access the MS service. Finally, **P2**, which is not a protocol, defines the message content type used in IPMS.

MHS can support a number of applications, such as **Electronic Data Interchange (EDI)** and **Office Document Architecture (ODA)**.

EDIFACT (Electronic Data Interchange for Administration, Commerce, and Transport), published by United Nations Economic Commission of Europe in 1988, has been widely accepted as a de facto EDI standard for the electronic exchange of business documents such as invoices and purchase orders. While the EDI standard defines the structure of an electronic interchange document, it is up to the communication community to develop a standard solution to actually transfer the document. This is where MHS comes into play. CCITT developed an MHS content type for EDI documents.

The ODA standard defines an office document which can be interchanged as a unit between different office systems. Documents here refer to items such as memoranda, letters, forms, journals, books, manuals, catalogues, timetables, directories, and reports. Although the ODA standard defines the Office Document Interchange Format, it is up to the user groups to determine how to transfer a document. Either MHS or FTAM can be used to transfer documents.

- **Presentation Layer**

The Presentation Layer is primarily used to handle the representation of information exchanged between two communicating systems so that the types and values of the information exchanged can be preserved even though each system might choose its own local representation of information.

During connection establishment, the two corresponding presentation entities negotiate to arrive at a set of transfer syntaxes. The term presentation context in OSI refers to a pair of abstract syntax and transfer syntax. Each presentation context determines the transfer syntax of an abstract syntax used during the data transfer phase. Presentation contexts need not be static objects. They can be changed during the data transfer phase. That is, either presentation service user can ask the Presentation Layer to negotiate a transfer syntax for a new abstract syntax that is encountered during the data transfer phase. This type of service is called context management. It is useful when the presentation service users do not know all the abstract syntaxes they will need during connection establishment.

- **Session Layer**

The primary purpose of the session service is to organize and synchronize the dialogue between two communicating session service users and to manage the data exchange.

To organize and synchronize the dialogue, the Session Layer adds structure to the data pipe provided by the Transport Layer. A session connection can be structured into activities. Different activities represent different logical pieces of work. Each activity can be further structured into dialogue units. With the use of this structure, the Session Layer provides facilities for activity management and dialogue control. For example, the dialogue control facility allows a session service user to insert synchronization points. A resynchronization service is also provided to assist orderly reestablishment of communication.

To manage the data exchange, the Session Layer provides four kinds of data transfer facilities: the normal data transfer facility, the expedited data transfer facility, the typed data transfer facility, and the capability data transfer facility. The normal data transfer facility can operate in either a full-duplex or a half-duplex mode. Only the owner of the data token can send data. Note that the use of token requires some token management facility as well. The typed data transfer facility allows both session service users to send data outside the normal data stream independent of the availability and the assignment of the data token. Finally, the capability data transfer facility allows session service users to exchange limited amounts of control information while not within an activity.

The Session Layer provides an orderly release, a service not provided by the Transport Layer. With the use of a release token, an orderly release can be negotiated between the two session service users. A session service user can reply negatively to a release request if it has some more data to send.

- **Transport Layer**

The purpose of the Transport Layer is to provide a reliable end-to-end transport service to its users. Two kinds of transport services are provided: the Connection Oriented Transport Service (COTS) and the Connectionless Transport Service (CLTS). When operating in the connection oriented mode, the Transport Layer provides full-duplex transmission between two transport service users.

The transport functions invoked by the Transport Layer depend on the underlying network type. If the underlying network is unreliable, then some elaborate transport mechanisms are needed to cope with the deficiency. ISO identified five different connection oriented transport protocols to be used for different network types. These five protocols are known as TP 0 through TP 4. Essentially, TP 0 is used for a reliable network, while TP 4 is used for an unreliable network.

Although the Transport Layer provides connectionless service, this service has not yet been used by the existing OSI application protocols which are all connection-oriented. CLTP (Connectionless Transport Protocol), the ISO protocol used to provide CLTS, is very similar in functionality to UDP (User Datagram Protocol) in the Internet.

- **Network Layer**

The Network Layer provides a means for network service users to exchange information without concern about the topology of the network and the transmission media in each constituent subnetwork. It provides two kinds of services: the connection-oriented network service (CONS) and the connectionless network service (CLNS).

The Network Layer is perhaps the most complex of the seven layers of the Reference Model. This is partly due to the fact that many existing diverse subnetwork types do not conform to the OSI network service definition. As a result, ISO defined the IONL model which provides a framework for classifying the network functions into three sublayers. The protocol operating at the lowest sublayer is the protocol associated with the underlying subnetwork. Subnetwork convergence protocols are used in the topmost two layers to augment the services offered by a subnetwork technology into something close to the OSI network service. Using the IONL model, internetworking strategies can be introduced to provide the two modes of network services.

Given a structure by which ESs of different subnetworks are joined together, the Network Layer needs to perform routing and relaying. Routing is hard in a global network because there are many ESs. ISO specified a routing framework, essentially partitioning the network into routing domains where each routing domain can have its own routing protocol. As a result of the partitioning, we need interdomain routing protocols as well as intradomain routing protocols. Intradomain routing protocols include protocols to be used among ISs, and protocols to be used between ISs and ESs. Interdomain routing is more concerned with firewalls, security and policy considerations than with performance.

The Network Layer must also provide a global addressing scheme so that ESs in different subnetworks can be addressed unambiguously.

- **Data Link Layer**

The Data Link Layer is responsible for error free data transmission over a data link. It performs functions such as link establishment, error detection/recovery, and flow control.

The data link service definition of the ISO HDLC (High level Data Link Control) protocol covers both connection mode operation and connectionless mode operation. While HDLC is seen as a superset of data link procedures, many interesting subsets are defined out of it. For example, the HDLC LAP B subset is adopted by CCITT as part of its X.25 packet-switched network standard. HDLC LAP D, a data link standard developed as part of the ISDN standardization, is a subset of LAP B.

The IEEE 802 committee, in an effort to define a means by which devices could communicate over a LAN, came up with a LAN reference model consisting of three layers: the Physical Layer, the Medium Access Control (MAC) Layer, and the Logical Link Control (LLC) Layer. The 802-series of LAN standards fall within the lower two layers of the OSI Reference model, i.e., the Physical Layer and the Data Link Layer. They all share a common transmission medium which is basically a multi-point data link. The LLC layer supports the multi-access nature of a peer multipoint link where there is no primary node. There are three types of LLC services: unacknowledged connectionless service (type 1), connection-oriented service (type 2), and acknowledged connectionless service (type 3).

- **Physical Layer**

The purpose of the Physical Layer is to hide the nature of the physical media from the Data Link Layer in order to maximize the transportability of higher layer protocols. It provides mechanical, electrical, functional, and procedural means to activate, maintain, and de-activate physical connections for serial bit streams between data link entities. The common functions found in the Physical Layer are synchronization and multiplexing.

The Physical Layer standard should be distinguished from the physical interface standards which define the boundary or interface between the Physical Layer and the physical transmission medium. The most common physical interface standards are EIA-232-D, EIA-530, and CCITT X.21.

1.3.3   Taxonomy of ISPs

In this section, we resume our discussion on ISPs which were described in Section 1.1.2. We show here how ISPs are classified. DIS 10000-2 identifies six classes of profiles:

- A (Application profiles using connection mode transport service);
- B (Application profiles using connectionless mode transport service);
- T (Connection mode transport profiles);
- U (Connectionless mode transport profiles);
- R (Relay profiles), for interworking between T- or between U-profiles; and
- F (Interchange format and representation profiles).

A- and B-Profiles are application profiles which define the use of protocols from layers 5 to 7. Each application profile is a complete definition of the use of protocol standards from layers 5 to 7 although it may share one or more common definitions with other application profiles. For example, there is an FTAM ISP specifying the upper layers constraints (i.e., constraints on layer 5, layer 6, and ACSE) that can be shared by the other FTAM ISPs.

Currently, there is no B-Profile simply because all the existing OSI application protocols are connection-oriented. Works on quite a number of A-Profiles are in progress. Examples of such A-Profiles are AFT (for FTAM), AMH (for MHS), AVT (for VT), AOM (for OSI management), and ATP (for TP).

F-Profiles define the structure and content of the information interchanged by A- or B-Profiles. Examples of F-Profiles include FOD (Office document format), FCG (Computer graphics metafile interchange format), and FSG (SGML interchange format).

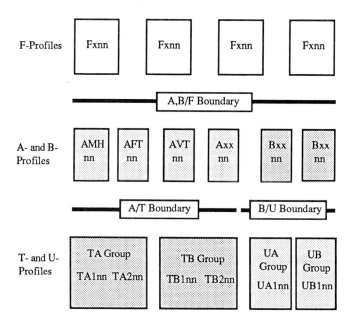

FIGURE 1.16   Relationship between ISP Profiles

The T- and U-Profiles specify the support of the two modes of OSI transport service: COTS and CLTS. T- and U-Profiles are further divided into groups. For example, the T-Profiles can be grouped as follows:

- Group TA: COTS over CLNS,
- Group TB: COTS over CONS with mandatory support of TP0, TP2 and TP4,
- Group TC: COTS over CONS with mandatory support of TP0 and TP2,
- Group TD: COTS over CONS with mandatory support of TP0, and
- Group TE: COTS over CONS with mandatory support of TP2.

The idea behind the grouping is that profiles within a group are compatible, i.e., a system implementing a profile from a group can interwork with any system implementing a different profile from the same group. Through the use of bridges or relays, two profiles from different T-groups may also interwork with each other in some restricted manner. **R-profiles** specify relays needed to enable systems using different T- or U-Profiles to interwork.

Figure 1.16 shows the relationship between profiles from different classes. The combination of A-/B-Profiles with one or more F-Profiles will be selected by a profile organization to meet their users' requirements. A system using an A- or B-Profile must operate in combination with a T- or U-Profile to provide an application protocol over a particular subnetwork type. The location of a set of A-Profiles above a set of T-Profiles, separated by a common A/T boundary, represents the possibility of combining any pair of A- and T-Profiles, with one from each of the two classes. A similar situation exists for B- and U-Profiles.

1.4   Summary

Two of the major user requirements of an open systems environment are interoperability and applications portability. Interoperability is the ability for software from different vendors to communicate meaningfully with each other. Applications portability is the ability to run the same software on a wide variety of platforms.

The path to achieve interoperability requires a series of steps. The development of standards is the first step. Standards include communication standards and non-communication standards. OSI standards and TCP/IP standards are examples of communication standards. Non-communication standards include the evolving ODP standards which address distributed processing in an open systems environment. Step two is the development of functional profiles. Standards allow many choices. A functional profile is a consistent selection of choices from a standard and its supporting standards. There are application profiles, transport profiles, and relay profiles. A users' profile, on the other hand, is a consistent selection of functional profiles based on the needs of the users. Examples of users' profiles are US GOSIP and MAP/TOP. Step three is testing. Conformance testing examines a product to see if it meets the relevant standards requirements and profile requirements. Interoperability testing determines whether products from different vendors interoperate with each other.

To accomplish applications portability, it is necessary to shield applications from its surrounding components by introducing some layer of software, either APIs or user interfaces, in between. This piece of software interfaces with the application on one side and other components such as operating systems, programming languages, database management systems, user interfaces, and networking services on the other side.

The OSI communication services can be grouped into internetworking and interworking services. The internetworking service provides physical connectivity between systems in different subnetworks. The major functions here are routing and relaying. The interworking service provides the communication functionality for applications to communicate meaningfully with each other. The major functions here are representation, coordination, and naming. The lower three layers of the OSI Reference Model provide the internetworking services. Layer four, the Transport Layer, provides an end-to-end reliable transport service to its users. The upper three layers provide the interworking service.

Even with the provision of the interworking services, applications still may not interwork with each other. Interworking may require non-communication support such as an identification of the common objects used during the communication. Such non-communication issues are addressed by functional profiles. Given time for functional profiles to mature, interoperability is achievable.

A layer by layer explanation of the Reference Model was given in this chapter. We also provided an introduction to every application protocol covered in this text.

Related Standards

ISO 7498: Information Processing Systems - Open Systems Interconnection - Basic Reference Model

ISO 7498 AD 1: Information Processing Systems - Open Systems Interconnection - Basic Reference Model - Addendum 1: Connectionless-Mode Transmission

ISO 7498-1 PDAD 2: Information Processing Systems - Open Systems Interconnection Reference Model - Part 1: Basic Reference Model - Proposed Draft Addendum 2 on Multipeer Data Transmission

ISO 7498-2: Information Processing Systems - Open Systems Interconnection - Basic Reference Model - Part 2: Security Architecture

ISO 7498-3: Information Processing Systems - Open System Interconnection - Basic Reference Model - Part 3: Naming and Addressing

ISO 7498-4: Information Processing Systems - Open Systems Interconnection - Basic Reference Model - Part 4: Management Framework

TR 10000-1: Information Technology - Framework and Taxonomy of International Standardized Profiles - Part 1: Framework

TR 10000-2: Information Technology - Framework and Taxonomy of International Standardized Profiles - Part 2: Taxonomy of Profiles

Application Portability Profile. the US Government's Open System Environment Profile, OSE/1 Version 1.0, NIST Publication 500-187

Books on OSI and Open Systems

U. Black, OSI, A Model for Computer Communications Standards, Prentice Hall (1991)

F. Halsall, Data Communications, Computer Networks and OSI, Addison Wesley (1988)

J. Henshall and S. Shaw, OSI Explained, End-to-End Computer Communication Standards, Ellis Horwood (1990)

P. Judge, Open Systems, The Guide to OSI and its Implementation, QED Information Sciences (1988)

J. Pimentel, Communication Networks for Manufacturing, Prentice Hall (1990)

M. Rose, The Open Book, A Practical Perspective on OSI, Prentice Hall (1990)

W. Stallings, Handbook of Computer-Communications Standards, SAMS (1990)

A. Tanenbaum, Computer Networks, Prentice Hall (1990)

2

OSI Architectural Concepts

The OSI Reference Model provides a framework within which protocol standards can be specified for each layer. More fundamental to the framework are the OSI architectural concepts that are formulated independent of the layers and the protocols associated with each layer. The purpose of this chapter is to introduce such basic concepts.

The OSI architectural concepts can be found in ISO/IEC 7498. ISO/IEC 7498 is an example of an **architectural standard** since it only introduces architectural concepts but does not specify any protocol. In contrast, a **protocol standard** specifies one or more protocols. Architectural concepts are studied in Section 2.1.

When ISO/IEC 7498 first appeared, there was no security architecture to support the Reference Model. ISO/IEC 7498-2 was developed to propose an OSI security architecture as an extension of the OSI architecture. Obviously, it would be more cost effective if the network architecture and the security architecture were defined as one architecture in the very beginning. OSI security concepts, as defined in ISO/IEC 7498-2, are explained in Section 2.2.

The Network Layer and the Application Layer are by far the most complicated of all the seven layers, calling for the need for further stepwise refinement of the OSI Reference Model at these two particular layers. ISO/IEC 8648, known as the Internal Organization of Network Layer (IONL), introduces more architectural concepts for the Network Layer and provides further sublayering of the Network Layer based on the network functions. IONL is studied in Section 2.3. ISO/IEC 9545, known as the Application Layer Structure (ALS), attempts to structure an object in the Application Layer into subobjects based on their capabilities. ALS is studied in Section 2.4.

2.1 Basic OSI Architectural Concepts

In this section, we will introduce a number of abstract OSI terms which provide a common vocabulary for the specifications of OSI protocols.

- **open systems**

Since we are going to focus on OSI from this chapter onwards, we will use the term open system in a more restrictive sense. An **open system** will mean a system complying to OSI in its communication. End systems and relay systems are used to qualify the roles played by an open system for its instances of communication. An open system in which there is an application acting either as a source or a destination of data is called an **end system (ES)** for that instance of communication. An open system which is providing a relay function is called a **relay system** for that instance of communication. The same open system may play the role of an end system for an instance of communication and the role of a relay system for a different instance of communication.

- **entities and layers**

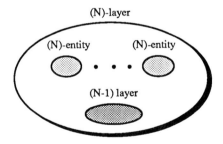

FIGURE 2.1   Decomposition of (N)-layer

The basic structuring technique used by the OSI Reference Model is layering. Layering divides the overall communication functions of an open system into a succession of smaller subsystems. Subsystems of the same rank (N), known as **(N)-subsystems**, collectively form the **(N)-layer** of the OSI Reference Model.

The objects in the (N)-layer are called **(N)-entities**. These (N)-entities use the services provided by the (N-1)-layer. Because the services provided by the (N)-layer is an enhancement of the services provided by the (N-1)-layer, one can suppose that the (N-1)-layer is a subobject of the (N)-layer. In Figure 2.1, the (N)-layer is decomposed into an (N-1)-layer object and a set of (N)-entities.

Each (N)-entity is characterized by a set of communication capabilities. The **(N)-entity-type** describes the capabilities of an (N)-entity. That is, an (N)-entity is an instance of an (N)-entity-type. Entities in the same layer but in different open systems are called **peer entities**. For two peer entities to communicate meaningfully with each other, they must be instances of the same entity type.

A complex (N)-entity can be refined into subobjects based on their communication capabilities. As we will see later on, an application entity in the Application Layer can be decomposed into subobjects called application service objects and application service elements.

The division of OSI objects into layers and entities allows protocol standards to be specified independent of the actual implementation. However, the division is only conceptual and is primarily used for modelling. An OSI implementation is not necessarily structured into layers. For example, an OSI application is often implemented together with the presentation and session capabilities as one module. In this case, the session entity or the presentation entity refers to the same object.

An **(N)-entity-invocation** is a specific utilization of part or all of the capabilities of an (N)-entity. Some of the capabilities associated with the (N)-entity type may be absent in an (N)-entity-invocation. An (N)-entity-invocation is an active object because it has a state which may change dynamically during the communication. An (N)-entity may have one or more (N)-entity-invocations at a given instant. An (N)-entity-invocation is normally implemented by a control block which contains fields such as the current state and the addresses of a set of procedures, where each procedure implements a capability.

Cooperation among the (N)-entities is governed by one or more (N)-protocols. An **(N)-protocol** is a set of rules and formats which govern the exchange of information units between two peer (N)-entity-invocations for an instance of communication. The format specifies the structure and encoding of each information unit exchanged among the (N)-entities. More than one (N)-protocol can be specified for the (N)-layer. Each (N)-protocol is used to exchange information for a certain task. If more than one (N)-protocol exists, then the choice of an (N)-protocol used for the communication is a function of the (N)-layer. The (N+1)-entities are only concerned with the quality of service provided by the (N)-layer. It is entirely up to the (N)-layer to choose an (N)-protocol providing the negotiated quality of service.

Adjacent layers communicate with each other through their common boundary. The service provided by (N)-entities to the layer above it is termed the **(N)-service**. The (N+1)-entities are the **service users** of the (N)-service, while the (N)-entities are the **service providers** of the (N)-service.

- **service access points**

Before an (N+1)-entity can acquire services from the (N)-layer, it must be bound to an **(N)-service access-point ((N)-SAP)**. An (N)-SAP is characterized by the set of service elements or abstract operations that can be invoked by an (N+1)-entity at that point. Service elements and abstract operations will be explained in the next chapter. In the OSI

Reference Model, the (N)-layer is defined so that it has only one type of (N)-SAP at its interface with the (N+1)-layer. Thus, all the (N)-SAPs offer the same set of service elements or abstract operations. As the topmost layer of the OSI Reference Model, the Application Layer does not have any SAPs to provide services to non-OSI entities.

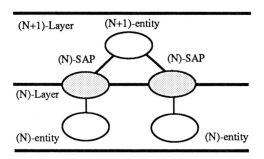

FIGURE 2.2   (N)-SAP

The (N)-service at an (N)-SAP is served by a unique (N)-entity associated with the (N)-SAP. Furthermore at any instant, the service of an (N)-SAP can be used by at most one (N+1)-entity, namely, the (N+1)-entity bound to that (N)-SAP (Figure 2.2).

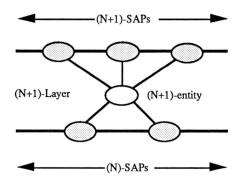

FIGURE 2.3   Relationship between Entities and SAPs

At any instant, an (N)-entity can be bound to more than one (N)-SAP. The relationship among (N+1)-entities, (N+1)-SAPs, and (N)-SAPs is depicted in Figure 2.3.

- **communication modes**

The (N)-layer may offer a connection-oriented service or a connectionless service to the (N+1)-entities. Connection-oriented communication is suitable for applications which involve long-lived and stream-oriented interactions, while connectionless communication is suitable for short-lived applications. For **connection-oriented communication**, an **(N)-association** between the two communicating (N+1)-entities is set by establishing an an **(N)-connection** between two (N)-SAPs, i.e., the (N)-SAPs to which the (N+1)-entities are bound. This (N)-connection must be established prior to the exchange of data.

Example 2.1

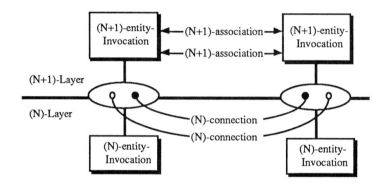

FIGURE 2.4   (N+1)-associations and (N)-connections

Figure 2.4 shows that an (N+1)-entity-invocation is attached to two distinct (N)-SAPs in its local system. It also shows the difference between (N+1)-associations and (N)-connections.

The lifetime of a connection has three distinct phases: connection establishment, data transfer, and connection release. These three phases correspond to dialing a number, conversing with each other, and hanging up respectively in a telephone call. The connection establishment phase normally involves a three-party agreement concerning the parameters (such as quality of service) and options among the two service users and the service provider. Once the connection is established, the service provider at each end provides a **connection endpoint identifier** to its local service user. During the data transfer phase, requests to transfer data may refer to the assigned connection endpoint identifier. The data units transmitted during the data transfer phase are logically related within the context of the connection addressed by the two connection identifiers. Consequently, the data can be numbered, making sequence control, flow control and error control possible.

In the **connectionless mode communication**, there is neither connection establishment phase nor connection release phase. As a result, each data unit transmitted during the data transfer phase must be self-contained, containing all the control information (such as addresses and quality of service) necessary for its transfer. Furthermore, the data units transmitted by the connectionless-oriented service are independent of each other. Consequently, there is no defined context, making flow control, sequence control, and error control more difficult. Data unit independence, however, means that the connectionless-oriented service is more robust than the connection-oriented service.

When the (N+1)-layer wants to provide a given mode of service using the other mode of service from the underlying (N)-layer, some (N+1)-function is required to perform conversion from one communication mode to the other. In order to reduce protocol complexity, ISO/IEC 7498 imposed some restrictions on where conversions can take place (Figure 2.5). They are:

- Conversion at the Session Layer or above is not permitted. For example, this means that the Session Layer must provide its connection-oriented session service using the connection-oriented transport service.
- In a fully open system, the Transport Layer must be able to support a mode using the same mode from the Network Layer. For example, the provision of the connection-oriented transport service must be supported by the connection-oriented network service. This restriction is applied so that systems may communicate without prior agreement on the mode of network service to be used.
- A system which only supports a given mode of transport service by providing conversion in the Transport Layer from a network service of the other mode is not fully open, since such a system cannot communicate with a system which only supports the given mode of transport service over a network service of the same mode. For these two systems to interwork, some kind of interworking unit operating up to the Transport Layer is needed between the two systems. The problem with the use of such an intermediate interworking unit is that the transport service is no longer end-to-end.
- Whenever it is necessary to provide a given mode of network service over a data link or subnetwork service of the other mode, conversion is required at the Network Layer. Support of such conversion is a requirement of OSI.

Thus, the Transport, Network, and Data Link layers may each operate in any mode without considering how the other two are functioning.

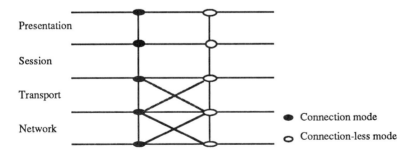

FIGURE 2.5 Conversion Restrictions

There is yet a third kind of communication mode, namely, **store-and-forward communication**. Store-and-forward communication, which is a mixture of connection mode communication and connectionless mode communication, is primarily used for communication in the Application Layer. As Figure 2.6 shows, no end-to-end connection is established, but connections are established with an intermediate system on a hop-by-hop basis. For example, communication between the UAs in MHS uses this kind of mode.

4 2   OSI ARCHITECTURAL CONCEPTS   CHAP. 2

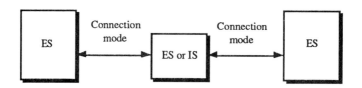

FIGURE 2.6   Store-and-forward Communication

- **data units**

The information units exchanged among the peer (N)-entities are called **(N)-protocol-data-units ((N)-PDUs)**. PDUs for the Network Layer are commonly called **packets**, while PDUs for the Data Link Layer are commonly called **frames**.

Every (N)-PDU has two major components: an (N)-PCI and the user-data. The **user-data** component is what an (N)-entity receives from its user, i.e., some (N+1)-entity. On receiving the user-data, the (N)-entity prefixes the user-data with an **(N)-protocol control information ((N)-PCI)**. This (N)-PCI contains, above all, an indication of the (N)-protocol used, the type of the (N)-PDU, and other parameters such as version number, addressing information, etc.

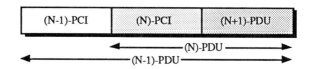

FIGURE 2.7   Encapsulation of PDUs

We can imagine that the (N)-PDUs are conveyed over some logical data circuit connecting the two communicating (N)-entities. What actually happens is that when an (N)-entity in a source system sends an (N)-PDU to a peer (N)-entity, the (N)-PDU will be first moved to the lowest layer in the source system through the use of **encapsulation** (Figure 2.7). Each time when a PDU passes to a lower layer in the source system, the source provider of the lower layer prefixes a PCI to the PDU. By the time the PDU reaches the lowest layer (i.e., the Physical Layer), it has already been encapsulated with layers of PCIs. The encapsulated PDU at the Physical Layer is then ready to be transmitted across one or more transmission media to the lowest layer of the target system. At the target system, the encapsulated PDU is moved upwards towards the receiving (N)-entity. Each time the encapsulated PDU goes up a layer in the target system, one of its PCIs is stripped off. To be precise, a layer in the target system strips off the PCI added earlier by the same layer in the source system. When the receiving (N)-entity receives the PDU, all the PCIs added earlier by the source system have been removed. Consequently, if there is no data loss or data reordering caused by the transmission media, what the receiver receives should be what the sender sends out.

Next, we introduce some OSI terminology to qualify the data units used in the passage of transfer. **(N)-interface-data-units ((N)-IDUs)** are the objects passed between the (N+1)-layer and the (N)-layer of the same open system. For example, if an (N+1)-entity wants to pass an (N+1)-PDU to its peer, it will compose an (N)-IDU which will contain the (N+1)-PDU and other control information. In some cases, the (N)-layer may impose size constraint on an (N)-IDU because of its buffering capabilities. Therefore, the (N+1)-entity may need to compose more than one (N)-IDU in order to pass a single (N+1)-PDU. Since the (N)-IDUs are the objects passed between adjacent layers in the same system, their structures are a local implementation issue. In some cases, an (N)-IDU is used for local management and has nothing to do with (N+1)-PDUs. For example, an (N)-IDU can be used to pass local error information. An (N+1)-entity can use an (N)-IDU to register/deregister itself with the (N)-layer.

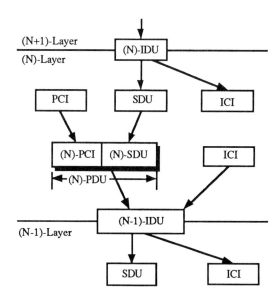

FIGURE 2.8   Building an (N)-PDU

For an (N)-entity, the (N+1)-PDU is treated as an **(N)-service-data-unit ((N)-SDU)**. Upon receipt of the (N)-SDU, the (N)-entity will build an (N)-PDU which is basically made up of the (N)-SDU and an (N)-PCI (Figure 2.8).

• **elements of procedures**

Now that we have explained some of the OSI architectural objects, we can explain the operations that are used to manipulate these objects. In OSI, these operations are called **(N)-functions** or **(N)-operations**. They are also called **elements of procedures** by CCITT.

First, we consider **connection establishment**. The establishment of an (N)-connection requires the availability of an (N-1)-connection. This means that, in the worst case, when none of the layers have an established connection, a connection request from a higher layer would trigger connection establishments from the lowest layers and upwards, one layer at a time. As a result, connection establishment can be very time consuming. There are at least two methods to optimize the cost incurred at connection establishment.

One method is to assign reasonably permanent connections at the layers where the cost is low, regardless of whether a higher layer connection request has been issued.

The other method, **embedding,** attempts to do simultaneous connection establishment. (N+1)/(N) embedding allows an (N+1)-connection request PDU to be carried as user-data inside an (N)-connection service request. In the case when there is no (N-1)-connection, further (N)/(N-1) embedding would allow an (N)-connection request PDU to be carried as user-data inside an (N-1)-connection service request, meaning that the (N-1)-connection request PDU would carry the (N+1)-connection request PDU as well as the (N)-connection request PDU.

It may not be possible to fix the size of connection request PDUs of certain layers for all time, as evolution may require the addition of new parameters to these PDUs. Thus, one can imagine that if embedding at all layers were to be permitted, then the length of the user-data field in a connection request PDU at the Transport Layer may have to be indefinite. The complexity involved in providing arbitrarily long user-data fields may sometimes outweigh the savings that could be accomplished by embedding.

Next, we consider **connection release**. Normally, an (N)-connection will be released by one of the (N+1)-entities associated with it. If some exceptional conditions occur at the (N)-layer, the release of the (N)-connection may be initiated by the (N)-entities. There are three kinds of release: destructive release, orderly release, and negotiated release. In the **orderly release**, there is no loss of data sent earlier by the (N+1)-entity issuing the orderly release service request. A special case of an orderly release is the negotiated release. In the **negotiated release**, an (N+1)-entity can reject a release service request issued by a peer (N+1)-entity. In the **destructive release**, the release of an (N)-connection may disrupt the procedures of some other service requests issued earlier, implying potential loss of data in transit in both directions. The Transport Layer of the OSI Reference Model only provides destructive release while the Session Layer provides all three kinds of release.

Next, we consider **multiplexing** and **splitting**. In the connection-oriented mode, an (N+1)-connection is always mapped to an (N)-connection. The mapping can be one-to-one, many-to-one, or one-to-many. **(N+1)-multiplexing** means that more than one (N+1)-connection is mapped to the same (N)-connection. Obviously, this may result in a more efficient usage of the (N)-service. Care must be taken not to intermix user-data from the various multiplexed (N+1)-connections. This can be achieved by assigning an identifier for each (N+1)-PDU carried in a multiplexed (N+1)-connection. One must also ensure that the total capacity of all the multiplexed (N+1)-connections does not exceed the capacity of the (N)-connection. This can be achieved using flow control. When more than one multiplexed (N+1)-connection wants to send data at the same time, some scheduling mechanism is needed.

When multiplexing is allowed to take place in the (N+1)-layer, it is undesirable to allow embedding. The reason is that embedding can be used only for the first (N+1)-connection request. Consequently, if embedding is allowed for the (N+1)-connections other than the first one, an implementation has to include the non-embedded case for the subsequent (N+1)-connections, producing two different styles of operation and adding complexity without much benefit.

In OSI, there is no reason to preclude the embedding of connection establishment at the upper layers, i.e., layer five and upwards. Transport/Network embedding should be avoided since the Transport Layer supports multiplexing. Embedding is disallowed for the Network Layer and the layers underneath, since multiplexing is frequently used for those layers to provide efficient transportation. Session/Transport embedding is disallowed not because of multiplexing but because of reuse of transport connections. The Session Layer can map a new session connection to an existing transport connection. If reuse and embedding are both allowed, then once again we will have two different styles of session connection establishment.

(N+1)-splitting means that an (N+1)-connection splits into several (N)-connections. This is needed when the bandwidth of an (N)-connection is less than that of an (N+1)-connection. Improving reliability is another benefit of splitting. A function associated with splitting is to resequence the (N+1)-PDUs after they are received from the different (N)-connections.

Flow control is another common function in the lower layers. There are two types of flow control: peer flow control between two open systems and inter-layer flow control between adjacent layers of the same system. **Peer flow control** operates on PDUs. The window mechanism provides the most common peer flow control mechanism. When the two communicating systems are compatible, the static window mechanism using a fixed sized sliding window is applied. When the two systems are not compatible (such as a supercomputer communicating with a personal computer), it would be better to use a variably sized window mechanism where the size of the window can be changed dynamically. This requires each system to send window update control information to the other one. A poor window update mechanism can drastically decrease the throughput. For example, the well known **silly window syndrome** refers to the phenomenon where the receiver system sends several small window allocations rather than waiting for a reasonably sized window to become available. As a result, the sender keeps sending small segments, thus making inefficient use of the network bandwidth. **Inter-layer flow control** operates on IDUs. The implementation of inter-layer flow control is a local issue. Normally, this is achieved by imposing constraints on the size of an IDU, the number of SAPs supported, and the number of connection endpoints supported by an SAP.

Expedited data transfer should be distinguished from **normal data flow**. For example, the expedited data service, provided as an option at the Network Layer, is extremely useful for packet switched networks because of the high potential for blockage of data. It can be also used by an entity to provide some out-of-band signalling mechanism for the management of its own protocol. An **expedited-data-unit** is an SDU which is transferred and/or processed with priority over the normal SDU. The expedited data service guarantees that an expedited-data-unit will not be delivered after any subsequent normal SDU or expedited-data-unit sent on the same connection. Expedited data flow is independent of the states and operations of the normal data flow although the data sent on the two flows may be logically related. Conceptually, a connection that supports expedited flow can be viewed as having two subchannels, one for normal data, and the other for expedited data.

It is important to note that an expedited-data-unit is expedited with respect to a specific connection and has nothing to do with any other connection. Expedited-data-units are intended for use in exceptional cases only. In order not to reserve too many resources, certain restrictions are placed on the usage of expedited-data-units. First, the size of an expedited-data-unit is fairly small. Second, very few expedited-data-units (usually one) may be outstanding at one time.

Assume that an open system provides some queuing mechanism for normal and expedited SDUs, the expedited data service can be provided as follows. Whenever some expedited (N)-SDU is received, it is always placed at the head of the queue unless some expedited (N)-SDU is already in the queue, in which case the new expedited (N)-SDU is placed right after all the existing expedited (N)-SDUs.

Note that it does not make sense to provide expedited data service in the connectionless mode which does not impose any order of delivery.

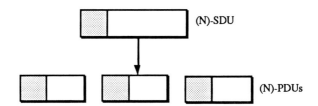

FIGURE 2.9   An (N)-SDU Segmented into (N)-PDUs

Next we consider segmentation and concatenation. **Segmentation**, a one-to-many function, can be performed on SDUs as well as PDUs. Consider the case when an (N)-SDU is too large to be accommodated into the user-data part of an (N)-PDU. The (N)-SDU will be segmented by some (N)-function first and the each segment will be prefixed with an (N)-PCI to form an (N)-PDU. Figure 2.9 shows the case of an (N)-SDU being segmented into three (N)-PDUs. Similarly, segmentation can occur when (N+1)-PDUs are mapped to (N)-IDUs. For example, the size of an (N+1)-PDU may exceed the size of the user-data portion of an (N)-IDU imposed by some implementation of the (N)-layer. In this case, the (N+1)-layer must segment the user-data part of the (N+1)-PDU and prefix each segment with some (N)-ICI to form an (N)-IDU. Whether segmentation is done on an SDU or a PDU, a sequence number identifying the segment must be included in the control information prefixed to each segment. At the target system, reassembly is performed based on the sequence number information.

In OSI, it is common practice for the Network Layer and the Transport Layer to perform segmentation. The Session Layer performs segmentation when the transport software is placed in the kernel code and the session software is written in user space, in which case the operating system would impose constraints on the size of the receiving buffers which holds the incoming IDUs from the Session Layer.

Some (N)-PDUs carry control information only, hence their size is fairly small. **(N)-concatenation,** a many-to-one function, is an (N)-function that concatenates several related small (N)-PDUs into a single (N)-PDU. Not every combination of (N)-PDUs can be concatenated. Figure 2.10 shows that three (N)-PDUs are concatenated into a single (N)-PDU. Concatenation is performed by the lower layers as well as the Application Layer. Examples of application protocols that perform concatenation are FTAM, CCR, and TP.

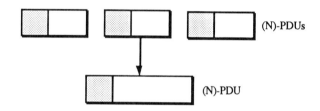

FIGURE 2.10   (N)-PDUs Concatenated into one (N)-PDU

(N+1)-sequencing is used if the (N+1)-layer needs to preserve the order of (N)-SDUs transferred through the (N)-layer. The use of the connection-oriented mode service implies sequencing. Connectionless-oriented mode service does not guarantee sequencing. However, sequencing is still possible over a connectionless-oriented service by assigning identifiers at the sending end and performing reassembly at the receiving end.

Table 2.1 summarizes the functions used in the two different modes of communication.

Functions	**CO**	**CL**
Connection Establishment	Y	
Connection Release	Y	
Multiplexing	Y	Y
Splitting	Y	Y
Normal Data Transfer	Y	Y
Expedited Data Transfer	Y	
Flow Control	Y	Y
Segmenting	Y	Y
Concatenation	Y	Y
Sequencing	Y	Y

TABLE 2.1   Functions used in the two Modes of Communication

2.2   OSI Security Architectural Concepts

Security is important to many IT users. In an OSE, the more information transmitted by IT, the more the information becomes vulnerable. It seems that security might contrast with the concept of open systems. This is not the case. An open system can still participate in an OSE even though access to it is limited to some users. The aim of security in IT is to provide interworking among different vendor systems, yet offer security.

The terms security architectures, security frameworks, security models, and security techniques may be considered as interrelated categories that go from the very general (architectures) to the more specific (techniques). A **security architecture** defines architectural concepts such as security services and security mechanisms. A **security framework** defines generic solutions such as data elements and sequences of operations to provide a security service. A **security model** shows how and when services and framework elements are combined. It provides standard developers with the architectural model for the development of security protocols. Finally, **security techniques** provide the building blocks for an implementation of a secure system. Within each category above, there are a number of components. For example, within the category of architectures, there is the open systems security architecture component which in turn contains the OSI security architecture as a subcomponent.

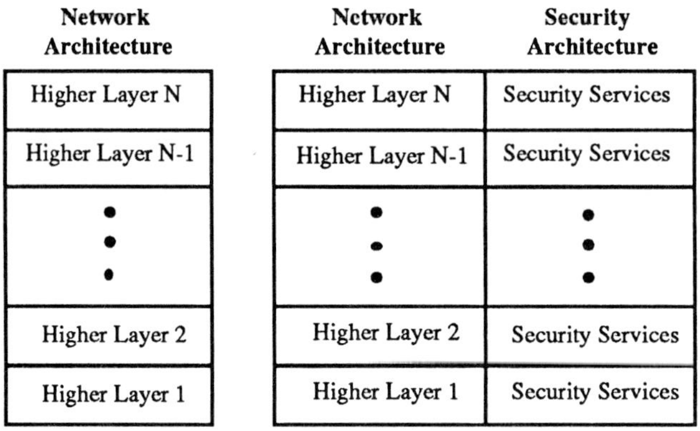

Network Architecture		Network Architecture	Security Architecture
Higher Layer N		Higher Layer N	Security Services
Higher Layer N-1		Higher Layer N-1	Security Services
• • •		• • •	• • •
Higher Layer 2		Higher Layer 2	Security Services
Higher Layer 1		Higher Layer 1	Security Services

FIGURE 2.11   Security Architecture

ISO/IEC 7498-2 describes OSI security architecture as an enhancement of the OSI architecture (Figure 2.11). It describes security architectural concepts such as security services and security mechanisms. It also defines the positions in the OSI Reference Model where the security services and mechanisms may be provided. Although the scope of ISO/IEC 7498-2 is limited to the OSI framework, most of the concepts in ISO/IEC 7498-2 are applicable to an OSE.

Many organizations work separately and sometimes together to develop the required security architectures, frameworks, models, and techniques. Let us briefly describe the players involved in the open systems security standards.

- **ISO/IEC**

Within ISO/IEC JTC 1, the SCs working on security related works include SC 6, SC 14, SC 17, SC 18, SC 21, and the relatively new SC 27. The majority of the security work is done within WG1, WG4, and WG6 of SC 21. WG1 of SC 21 is most renowned for its ISO/IEC 7498-2 standard. Another major ongoing work within WG1 is documentation on various security frameworks. These frameworks are intended to address the provision of security services in an OSE instead of the OSIE.

In the Application Layer, there is ongoing work on the specification of a security protocol used for security exchange.

- **CCITT**

Receiving major inputs from European Computer Manufacturers Association which is responsible for providing standards for use by Europe in 1992, CCITT together with ISO/IEC develops the OSI security architecture, security framework, and the upper layer security model. As far as the Application Layer is concerned, X.509, one part of the DS standard, outlined an authentication framework for use by OSI applications.

- **IEEE**

IEEE, as an ANSI accredited standards organization, is currently preparing a model for use in developing security protocols and services in LANs. The draft standard is 802.10, also known as Standard for Interoperable LAN Security (SILS). SILS sits in between the MAC sublayer and the LLC sublayer of the Data Link Layer.

- **NSA/NCSC**

The Secure Data Networks System (SDNS) is a US Collaborative Program within the National Security Agency (NSA) of the National Computer Security Center (NCSC) to develop OSI security protocols. SDNS addressed both the Internet IP protocol and the ISO/IEC CLNP. The SDNS documentation was published by NIST as three separate reports: security protocols, key management, and access protocol.

The security protocols defined by SDNS are SP3 (Network Layer security), SP4 (Transport Layer security), and MSP (E-mail application security). These protocols are directed at a profile with TP4 over a connectionless network. SP4 resides at the bottom of the Transport layer and can operate over SP3. SP3 and SP4 are both optional in version 2.0 of US GOSIP. MSP was defined because the 1984 MHS standard lacked security features. The 1988 version of the MHS standard took care of this features.

Both the "Orange Book" and the "Red Book" are sponsored by NCSC. The **Orange Book** contained the criteria for evaluating stand-alone computer systems. The **Red Book** attempted to apply the Orange Book evaluation criteria to evaluate networks. The formal evaluation criteria are divided into four hierarchical categories with each category building upon the previous one. Division D is reserved for computer systems that do not achieve a higher evaluation rating while division A, the most sophisticated of the four, requires formal evaluation techniques to verify the security design.

2.2.1   Security Concepts

The security concepts to be studied in this section are fundamental security concepts. We include them here to help the readers understand the OSI security services and security mechanisms presented in Section 2.2.2.

A **threat** is a potential violation of security. Threats can be either accidental or intentional. **Accidental threats** are those that exist with no premeditated intent. Examples of accidental threats are fire, water, heat, cold, system malfunction, software bugs, and carelessness. An **intentional threat** is a plot, by unauthorized means, to read or modify messages/data meant for someone else. Intentional threats may be either passive or active. **Passive threats** do not result in modification to any information. An example is someone monitoring a communication (e.g., a telephone call). They are much more difficult to detect. On the other hand, **active threats** could do something detectable, such as modification of information or changes to the state or operation of the system.

Listed below are the potential threats in an OSE:

- **masquerade:** This is the pretense of a user or entity to be someone or something that is not. Masquerading is often used with other forms of attack such as replay. For example, authentication sequences can be captured and replayed after a valid authentication sequence has taken place.
- **replay:** This is a retransmission of previously transmitted data. For example, a valid message containing authentication information may be replayed by an entity in order to authenticate itself.
- **modification of messages:** This is an unauthorized manipulation of data such as insertion, deletion, or alteration.
- **denial of service**: This is an unauthorized denial of resources to a legitimate user or entity.
- **trapdoor:** When an entity of a system is altered to allow an attacker to produce an unauthorized effect (e.g., skip certain security checks for any user with a given login name), the result is a trapdoor.
- **trojan horse**: A trojan horse is a program that contains unauthorized or unexpected instructions to circumvent existing security policies. For instance, to steal someone's file, one could get a copy of the editor's source code, modify it to steal files, and put it into the victim's directory.
- **insider attacks:** This occurs when legitimate users of a system behave in unintended or unauthorized ways. This is by far the most likely threat.

Next, we explain the notion of a security policy. Before designing a secure system, a system architect should recognize the potential vulnerabilities of the system. A system can be vulnerable in many ways. Only some of them are exploitable because the attacker lacks the opportunity or because the result does not justify the effort and risk of detection. **Threat analysis** is the identification of specific threats against which protection is required.   In general, it involves the following steps: identifying all the possible vulnerabilities of the system, finding out which vulnerabilities are exploitable, assessing the consequences of threats aimed at exploiting the vulnerabilities, estimating the cost of each attack, estimating the cost of potential counter measures, and selecting the security mechanisms that are justified and worthwhile.

Threat analysis is followed up by the definition of a security policy. A **security policy** is a set of rules and definitions of what needs protection during the general operation of a system. These rules govern access rights of any given subject (such as a process or a person) which operates (i.e., read, write, modify, etc.) on any given object (such as a file). This may involve labelling and identification. Labelling of objects is essential in order to enforce access control between subjects and objects. Identification of subjects must be implemented to determine a subject's level of authorization. Policy sets the topmost level of a security specification. It normally does not say how the desired results are to be obtained. A cost effective security policy should provide sufficient security such that the level of effort to circumvent the security mechanisms is too high to make it worthwhile to a potential attacker.

Based upon the nature of the authorization involved, security policies can be divided into rule-based policies and identity-based policies. A **rule-based security policy** is one based on global rules imposed for all users (i.e., independent of user identity). These rules are usually based on sensitivity of the resources (such as security label) being accessed. Users or processes acting on behalf of users may acquire the security label appropriate to their originators. Thus, enforcement is done by a comparison of the sensitivity of the resources being accessed and the possession of the corresponding attributes of users or processes acting on behalf of users. An **identity-based security policy** is one based on the identities and/or attributes of users, a group of users, or entities acting on behalf of the users and the resources being accessed. Depending on whether the information about access rights is held by the accessor or is part of the resources that are accessed, there are two ways to implement an identity-based security policy. The former kind uses **capabilities** while the latter kind uses **access control lists**.

A good security policy should cover all facets. Security facets can be either non-technical or technical. Examples of non-technical facets are physical security (e.g., preventing unauthorized physical access to sensitive areas), personnel security (e.g., careful selection of individuals with access to sensitive data), and procedural security (e.g., assigning security labels to documents). Examples of technical facets are radiation security, communication security, and computer security.

2.2.2   OSI Security Services and Security Mechanisms

The most important security architectural elements given in ISO/IEC 7498-2 are the OSI security services and mechanisms.

- **security services**

Security services are provided to meet the security policies laid by the top level management. ISO/IEC 7498-2 identifies the following security services which can be provided optionally within the OSI framework: authentication services, access control services, confidentiality services, integrity services, and non-repudiation services. Each security service is explained below.

There are two kinds of **authentication services**. The first kind, **data origin authentication**, provides for the corroboration that the source of data received is as claimed. It does not provide protection against the duplication or modification of data units. The second kind, **peer-to-peer entity authentication**, provides for the corroboration that a peer entity in an association is the one claimed. This provides confidence that an entity is not attempting a masquerade or an unauthorized replay of some previous association. It is provided during the connection establishment phase or occasionally during the data transfer phase. In contrast, data origin authentication is normally provided during the data transfer phase.

Access control services protect against unauthorized use of resources accessed via OSI protocols. Examples of access control services are user names/login procedures and file permission rights found in conventional operating systems.

Confidentiality services protect against unauthorized disclosure of information to unauthorized individuals, entities, or processes. ISO/IEC 7498-2 identified four forms of confidentiality services. **Connection confidentiality** provides confidentiality of data in an (N)-connection. **Connectionless confidentiality** provides confidentiality of a single connectionless data unit. **Selective field confidentiality** provides confidentiality of selected fields within the data on a connection or in a single connectionless data unit. Finally, **traffic flow confidentiality** provides protection of information which might be indirectly derived from the observation of traffic flows.

Integrity is the property that data has not been altered or destroyed in an unauthorized manner. **Integrity services** are used to protect against modification, insertion, deletion, or replay. There are five forms of such services. **Connection integrity with recovery** provides integrity of data on an (N)-connection with recovery attempted. **Connection integrity without recovery** provides the detection of data corruption on an (N)-connection. **Selective field connection integrity** provides the integrity of selected fields within data on an (N)-connection. **Connectionless integrity** provides the integrity of a single connectionless data unit. Finally, **selective field connectionless integrity** provides the integrity of selected fields in a single connectionless data unit.

Non-repudiation services are used to protect against denial of originating or receiving data after transfer. There are two forms: non-repudiation with proof of origin and non-repudiation with proof of delivery. In **non-repudiation with proof of origin**, the recipient is provided with proof of origin. This will protect against any attempt by the sender to falsely deny sending the data. In **non-repudiation with proof of**

delivery, the sender is provided with proof of delivery. This will protect against any subsequent attempt by the recipient to falsely deny receiving the data.

- **security mechanisms**

A security policy may be implemented using various security mechanisms, singly or in combination, depending on the policy objectives and the mechanisms used. A security mechanism can be either specific (i.e., addressing particular security concerns), or pervasive. There are a number of security mechanisms including encryption mechanisms, digital signature mechanisms, access control mechanisms, data integrity mechanisms, authentication exchange mechanisms, traffic padding mechanisms, routing control mechanisms, and notarization mechanisms. These mechanisms are explained next.

Encryption or **encipherment**, is used to protect data from modification, unauthorized release, and traffic analysis. Encryption based on the use of keys is performed initially on a cleartext to produce the ciphertext. **Symmetric** (i.e., secret key) **encryption** has the property that knowledge of the encryption key implies knowledge of the decryption key and vice versa. The most well known symmetric encryption algorithm is Data Encryption Standard (DES). DES has been implemented in hardware and runs very efficiently.

Public key encryption or **asymmetric encryption** uses two keys and a trap-door one-way function. The two keys are a public key used to encrypt a message destined for a particular person, and a private key used by that person to decrypt the message. The two keys are mathematically related although one key cannot be feasibly computed from the other. The target person can publicly post his public key so that anyone wishing to send the target person an encrypted message can use it. The private key must be kept secret. A trap-door one-way function, also known as a hash function, is a function which is reasonably easy to compute, but is very difficult to "run backwards". That is, given a value in the range of the function, it is very hard to compute a value in its domain that will yield that value. A message is normally hashed first before encryption is applied. Public key encryption can be used to provide security services such as confidentiality, authentication, and non-repudiation. The prevailing public key encryption algorithm is the RSA algorithm by Rivest, Shamir, and Adleman. It is based on the fact that factorization of large numbers into primes in a reasonable amount of time does not presently exist. The RSA algorithm, although very powerful, is relatively slow when compared with DES.

Digital signature mechanisms can be used to support data origin authentication and non-repudiation of origin. In a digital signature mechanism, the signer (i.e., the sender) uses some private information (e.g., a private key) to produce an encryption of the plain data unit known as the signature. The signature together with the plain data unit are sent to the intended recipient. To verify the data origin, the recipient compares the received plain data unit with that obtained by deciphering the signature using the public key of the signer.

Access control mechanisms are used to enforce a policy of limiting access to a resource to only the authorized users. If an entity attempts to access a resource with an improper type of access, then the mechanism will generate an alarm and/or record it as part of a **security audit trail**. This mechanism can be implemented using access control lists or capabilities. An **access control list** maintains all the entities which are authorized to access a resource. The use of access control lists assumes that peer entity authentication has been assured. A **capability** is a token used as an identifier for a resource such that possession of the token by an entity gives evidence of the right to access the resource. When capabilities are used, they should be unforgeable and should be conveyed in a trusted manneer.

Confidentiality mechanisms which are used to provide the various kinds of confidentiality services rely on encipherment. For example, traffic flow confidentiality can be achieved by inserting a pair of encipherment devices into the physical transmission path. Connection confidentiality can be achieved by the sender encrypting the data with a key private to the intended recipient. Note that the use of encipherment in support of confidentiality implies the use of a key management mechanism. Key management involves generating suitable keys, determining who has access to keys, and making available, and distributing keys in a secure manner.

Data integrity mechanisms are of two kinds: those used to protect the integrity of a single data unit and those used to protect the integrity of a stream of data units against misordering, losing, replaying, inserting, or modifying data. Provision of the first kind, normally accompanying the provision of the second kind, requires the attachment of some integrity check value (ICV) to the data value at the sending site. The ICV is normally obtained as the encipherment of the hashed plain data. Together with the plain data, the ICV are sent to the recipient. The receiving entity generates a corresponding quantity and compares it with the received quantity to determine if the data has been modified in transit. Provision of the second kind against message stream modification requires the use of sequence numbering or time stamping.

There are many choices of **authentication exchange mechanisms**. When communicating entities trust each other and the means of communication, then simple authentication relying on the originator to supply its name/password is sufficient for the peer entity to identify the originator. Passwords, however, do not protect against replay. When each entity trusts its peer entities but does not trust the means of communication, then strong authentication can be provided by a combination of passwords and cryptographic means. Protection against replay attacks may require three-way handshaking protocols or timestamping with trusted clocks. When entities do not trust their peers or the means of communication, non-repudiation services can be used. The non-repudiation service can be achieved using digital signature and/or notarization mechanisms.

An intruder can use traffic analysis to infer information (such as absence, presence, amount, direction, and frequency) from the observation of traffic flows. **Traffic padding mechanisms** can be used to protect against traffic analysis. This involves generating spurious traffic and padding PDUs to a constant length.

Routing control mechanisms enable data transmission through more secure routes using the application of rules during the process of routing.

A notarization mechanism involves the registration of data with a trusted third party notary (trusted by the communicating entities) that allows later assurance of the accuracy of properties about the data such as integrity, origin, time, and destination.

ISO/IEC 7498-2 also indicates the security mechanisms which can be used to provide each security service. The details of how a security mechanism is used to provide a security service can be found in the security frameworks. It is up to the application protocol designers to choose the security mechanism for any security service needed.

Services \ Mechanisms	Encryption	Digital Signature	Access Control	Data Integrity	Authentication Exchange	Traffic Padding	Routing Control	Notarization
Peer entity authentication	Y	Y			Y			
Data origin authentication	Y	Y						
Access control service			Y					
Connection confidentiality	Y						Y	
Connectionless confidentiality	Y						Y	
Selective field confidentiality	Y							
Traffic flow confidentiality	Y					Y	Y	
Connection integrity with recovery	Y			Y				
Connection integrity without recovery	Y			Y				
Connection integrity	Y			Y				
Connectionless integrity	Y	Y		Y				
Connectionless integrity selective field	Y	Y		Y				
Non-repudiation of origin		Y		Y				Y
Non-repudiation of delivery		Y		Y				Y

TABLE 2.2   Security Services vs. Security Mechanisms

2.2.3   Placement of Security Services in the OSI Reference Model

A security service can be provided by more than one layer if its effect on communication security is considered to be different. Table 2.3 shows the placement of security services for connection mode communication, and Table 2.4 shows the placement of security services for connectionless mode communication.

Let us consider the placement of security services for connection oriented communication. First we note that the Application Layer provided all the security services. Three of the services, namely, selected field connection integrity, non-repudiation of origin, and non-repudiation of delivery, are in fact provided by the Application Layer only. Some rationale is given as follows. Since selected field connection integrity provides for the integrity of selected fields which are logical components of machine independent structures, invocation of these services is possible at the Application Layer only. Since non-repudiation services are supported by a notarization mechanism which involves a relay, they are provided by the Application Layer only.

Services	Layer						
	1	2	3	4	5	6	7
Peer entity authentication			Y	Y			Y
Access control			Y	Y			Y
Confidentiality	Y	Y	Y	Y		Y	Y
Selective field confidentiality						Y	Y
Traffic flow confidentiality	Y		Y				Y
Integrity with recovery				Y		Y	Y
Integrity without recovery			Y	Y		Y	Y
Selective field integrity						Y	Y
Non-repudiation of origin							Y
Non-repudiation of delivery							Y

TABLE 2.3   Placement of Security Services for Connection Mode Communication

Services	Layer						
	1	2	3	4	5	6	7
Data origin authentication			Y	Y			Y
Access control			Y	Y			Y
Confidentiality	Y	Y	Y				
Selective field confidentiality						Y	Y
Integrity			Y	Y		Y	Y
Selective field integrity						Y	Y
Non-repudiation of origin							Y
Non-repudiation of delivery							Y

TABLE 2.4   Placement of Security Services for Connectionless Mode Communication

Note that no security services are provided at the Session Layer. Remember that the Session Layer basically provides a structuring of the transport data pipe. It does not modify the data. The moving of data bits which might require security services is a function of the other layers. Thus, security services at the Session Layer would provide no additional benefits over the corresponding security services provided at the lower layers or the upper layers.

Some service is provided at all layers except the Session Layer. This is the case with connection confidentiality, because every layer provides the connection-oriented mode of communication.

Full traffic flow confidentiality is only possible at the Physical Layer since this involves the insertion of a pair of encipherment devices into the physical transmission path.

Note that security services with recovery are not possible at the Network Layer since the Network Layer is not expected to provide error recovery.

2.3   Architectural Concepts for the Network Layer

Taking into account a wide variety of subnetwork types, ISO/IEC 8648 defined more architectural concepts and specified a model of the Network Layer that is similar to the overall OSI model. This model structures the Network Layer into three sublayers which are commonly called the **Internal Organization of the Network Layer (IONL)**. IONL provides a framework which is used in the development and application of protocol standards related to real subnetwork interconnection. We will first describe the architectural concepts in ISO/IEC 8648 before we explain the IONL.

The OSI terminology for the Network Layer must be general enough to address different kinds of existing network types. IONL introduced the following abstract terms: intermediate systems, subnetworks, and relay systems.

A **subnetwork** is basically an abstraction of an isolated network. Public data networks and LANs are examples of real subnetworks. ISO/IEC 8648 defines a subnetwork as any collection of equipments and physical media which forms an autonomy and is used to interconnect real systems for communication purposes. The equipments may be an **interworking units (IWUs)** whose operations provide a network relaying function. An IWU is what we commonly call a gateway or a router. Through interconnection, a set of subnetworks are configured to form a **network**.

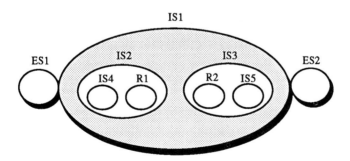

FIGURE 2.12   Decomposition of an IS

While an ES is one where applications reside, an **intermediate system (IS)** is used to forward the data units originated from the ESs. An IS is an abstract concept denoting a collection of real subnetworks or IWUs. Although the functions performed at an IS are typical of functions provided by the lower three layers of the OSI Reference Model, nowadays one often find an IS running all seven layers to support systems management.

An IS may be decomposed into one or more ISs. At a more granular level, an IS can be realized by a single IWU or a single real subnetwork. Figure 2.12 shows a possible decomposition of an IS between two ESs, namely, ES1 and ES2. Here the outermost IS1 is decomposed into IS2 and IS3. IS2 is decomposed into IS4 and a relay object R1, while IS3 is decomposed into IS5 and a relay object R2. IS4 and IS5 model real subnetworks, while R1 and R2 model two "half" gateways.

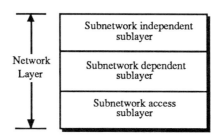

FIGURE 2.13   Sublayers of Network Layer

The IONL model structures the Network Layer into three sublayers (Figure 2.13). The **subnetwork access sublayer** corresponds to some existing network software which may or may not conform to the OSI network requirements. The **subnetwork dependent sublayer** is the layer responsible for augmenting the service offered by a subnetwork technology into something close to the OSI network service. For example, it may map the 1980 version of X.25 (which does not conform to the OSI network standard) to the 1984 version. The **subnetwork independent sublayer** constructs the OSI network service over a well-defined set of underlying capabilities which is intended for use over a wide variety of subnetwork types. It is not necessarily the case that each sublayer of the IONL is fulfilled individually by a discrete protocol. The case where a single network protocol provides the OSI network service may be described as the case where that single protocol fulfills the defined roles for all three sublayers. Presently, such protocol does not exist.

2.4   Architectural Concepts for the Application Layer

The Application Layer needs to provide all kinds of communication capabilities which are not supported by the lower layers. Because of the large number of communication capabilities in the Application Layer, ISO/IEC 9545, known as **Application Layer Structure (ALS)**, provides an object-oriented view of the communication capabilities of an application entity.

The following gives a top-down explanation of some of the ALS concepts, starting from application processes.

- **application processes**

An **application process (AP)** can be a person, an application program, or a physical process. It is an abstract representation of a set of resources that is used to perform a particular information processing activity. An **AP-invocation** represents a particular invocation of an AP. An AP can have zero, one or more AP-invocations at any instant.

- **application entities**

An AP can be conceptually divided into non-communication objects and communication objects. An **application entity (AE)**, i.e., an entity in the Application Layer, is a communication object of an (one and only one) AP. An AP may have multiple AEs. For example, a business application may consist of an AE containing the MHS capabilities, and another AE containing the FTAM capabilities. In this way, any trading document used in any of the non-communication components can be transferred by means of either MHS or FTAM. Note that the actual implementation of an AP may not follow such a division into communication objects and non-communication objects. In many cases, an AP is implemented as a single module with no boundary between the communication objects and the non-communication objects.

Suppose that we have an AP-invocation of an AP. The AP-invocation may trigger an **AE-invocation** (i.e., an invocation of an AE) of one of the AEs contained in the AP. It basically controls the lifetime of this AE-invocation. Even at the end of the AE-invocation, the AP-invocation may still last. That is, we can have an AP-invocation with no AE-invocations at a given instant. All this means is that the AP-invocation does not require any communication support at that instant.

- **application service objects and application service elements**

An AE can be very complex. To understand how an AE communicates with another AE, it is sometimes necessary to refine the AE into one or more component objects, and analyze how these component objects communicate with their peers. This is the divide and conquer approach. Thus, the design of an application protocol between two communicating AEs is reduced to the design of an application protocol between two communicating component objects of less complexity.

An AE can be refined into one or more **application service objects (ASOs)** and **application service elements (ASEs)**. ASO is a composite subobject of an AE, whereas an ASE is a basic subobject of an AE, basic in the sense that it cannot be refined any further. In particular, when an AE contains more than one subobject, the AE itself is an ASO. Considering the structure of an AE in a bottom-up fashion, we can group one or more ASEs into an ASO. This ASO can be combined with one or more ASEs or ASOs into another ASO. Continuing this iteratively, we arrive at the outermost ASO which is equivalent to the AE object. Thus, the internal structure of an AE may contain a number of

ASEs and ASOs. Like an AP or an AE, an ASE/ASO can have zero, one, or more **ASE/ASO-invocations** at any instant.

An ASO, besides containing a number of ASEs and ASOs, also contains a **control function (CF)**. The CF acts as a traffic cop to coordinate the activities of the various ASEs and ASOs within the given ASO. In particular, the CF unifies the services of the various components of an ASO into a single service which can be used by a user of the ASO. This ASO-user may be another ASO or the user of the AE at the highest level of recursion. The CF may add temporal constraints on the use of the combined service in addition to the service constraints on each component. It also maps between the supporting services provided to the ASO and the services required by the components of the ASO.

Example 2.2

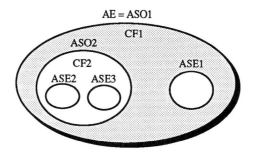

FIGURE 2.14   Decomposition of an AE into ASOs and ASEs

Figure 2.14 gives an example of a decomposition of an AE into ASOs and ASEs. Here, the AE, or the outermost ASO1, is decomposed into ASO2 and ASE1. CF1 serves as a traffic cop for ASO1. ASO2 in turn can be decomposed into ASE2 and ASE3. CF2 serves as a traffic cop for ASO2.

We noted earlier that the Application Layer does not provide any SAP to the outside world. An ASE plays the role of a port (i.e., a SAP) for an AE but not for the Application Layer. Consider Figure 2.15. Here, we have an AE containing three ASEs. Two of the ASEs, ASE1 and ASE2, serve as ports between the two communicating AEs. The third ASE, ASE3, is a port used by the AE to interact with the layer six. In this scenario, ASE1 and ASE2 can be viewed as external ports, while ASE3 is an internal port.

The structuring of an AE into ASOs and ASEs is only a static decomposition. It does not mean that all the ASOs and ASEs in an AE are always involved in an AE-invocation of the AE. For example, we can have an AE containing five ASEs and three ASOs, but for a particular AE-invocation, only three ASEs and two ASOs are utilized.

As mentioned earlier, we want to reduce the design of the application protocol between two communicating AEs to the design of an application protocol between two communicating ASEs/ASOs. Since ASEs are the basic components of an AE, the first thing to standardize are the common ASEs and their protocols. **Common ASEs (CASEs)** refer to those ASEs which provide generic communication capabilities to a number of applications. The use of CASEs ensures that applications can be built in a consistent manner. ACSE and ROSE are examples of CASEs. The **ACSE (Association Control Service Element)** is used to manage the associations between two communicating AEs, such as setting up an association or releasing an association. **ROSE (Remote Operation Service Element)** is used to transport query-like messages from one AE to its peer in an interactive environment. The term **special ASE (SASE)** refers to an ASE which provides specific capabilities to applications. The FTAM ASE defined in the FTAM standard is an example of an SASE.

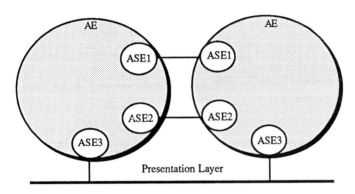

FIGURE 2.15   Viewing ASEs as Ports

• **application associations and application contexts**

Before two AEs can communicate, they must first establish an **application association** with each other. An **application context** is an important attribute of an application association. It defines the rules governing the communication of the two AEs for the entire application association. In particular, it specifies the ASOs and ASEs used for the application association. It defines the abstract syntaxes which may be referenced during the application association. It defines the binding/unbinding information that needs to be exchanged before an application association is established/released. In short, an application context defines the working environment or knowledge that is shared by the AEs for the duration of the application association. The ASEs/ASOs in the application context can be viewed as workers. Each worker communicates with a peer worker (of the same type) using its specialized protocol.

Example 2.3

Consider the P1 protocol in MHS which is used by the MTAs. P1 specifies an optional use of RTSE which is an ASE providing a reliable transfer service. Suppose that an MTA needs to set up application associations with two other MTAs, one over a LAN, and the other over a WAN. For the application context over the LAN, it is not necessary to use RTSE because a LAN is quite reliable. For the application context over the WAN, it is necessary to use RTSE to cope with communication failures. Thus, the P1 protocol can be used in two different application contexts, one with RTSE, and one without RTSE.

Example 2.4

Suppose that an AE, namely, AE1, in one open system wants to communicate with an AE, namely, AE2, in another open system. AE1 may contain ten ASEs in its structure, while AE2 may contain twenty ASEs in its structure. When an application association is established between these two AEs, the application context must specify a set of ASEs common to those of AE1 and AE2. That is, these common ASEs are a subset of the intersection of the ASEs contained in AE1 and AE2. A different application association between the same two AEs may specify an application context given by a different subset.

Suppose that an AE-invocation is involved in more than one application association. We can refine the AE-invocation into component objects, with a component object for each application association. These component objects are called **single association objects (SAOs)**. They are active objects, meaning that they maintain states.

Internally, an SAO consists of a **single application control function (SACF)**, and a set of ASEs and ASOs which are used in the application context of the application association. The SACF is essentially a coordinator of the ASEs and the ASOs in the SAO. If the ASEs and ASOs are viewed as workers, an SACF can be viewed as a manager.

When there are a number of SAOs in an AE-invocation, we may even need a **multiple association control function (MACF)** to coordinate these SAOs. An MACF is similar to an executive manager. In some cases, we need only one MACF to govern all the SAOs in the AE-invocation. In some cases, we may need more than one MACF, with an MACF coordinating a different set of SAOs. And in some other cases, we do not need any SACF at all, because the SAOs do not need to be coordinated. The next example gives a situation when an AE-invocation contains more than one SAO.

Example 2.5

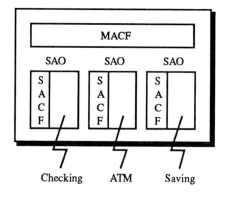

FIGURE 2.16   AE-invocation of the ATM Controller

In this example, we have four systems: an ATM (i.e., automatic teller machine), an ATM controller, a checking account system, and a savings account system. A user can do banking with the ATM. With the help of the ATM controller system, it can manipulate its checking account and savings account. Let us model each system by an AE. Suppose that the ATM sets up an application association with the ATM controller and requests that some fund be moved from the saving account to the checking account. Accordingly, the ATM controller sets up application associations with the checking account system and the savings account system. Figure 2.16 shows an AE-invocation of the ATM controller which can be involved in as many as three application associations at a given instant, one with the ATM, one with the checking account system, and one with the savings account system. Thus, we can refine the AE-invocation of the ATM controller into three SAOs. In the figure, we assume that there is an MACF coordinating the three SAOs.

2.5 Summary

The first part of this chapter introduced OSI architectural concepts. Such concepts include layers, SAPs, communication modes, data units, and elements of procedures.

The security architecture defines an extension of the OSI architecture. It introduces security concepts such as security services and security mechanisms.

Of the seven layers of the OSI Reference Model, the Network Layer and the Application Layer are most complicated, calling the need for further stepwise refinement at these two layers. The IONL standard defines a sublayering of the Network Layer based on the network functions. It provides a basis for interconnection of heterogeneous networks. The ALS standard attempts to structure an object in the Application Layer into objects called ASOs and ASEs based on the communication capabilities.

Related Standards

ISO 7498: Information Processing Systems - Open Systems Interconnection - Basic Reference Model

ISO 7498-2: Information Processing Systems - Open Systems Interconnection - Basic Reference Model - Part 2: Security Architecture

ISO 8648: Information Processing Systems - Open Systems Interconnection - Internal Organization of the Network Layer

ISO 9545: Information Technology - Open Systems Interconnection - Application Layer Structure

ISO 9545 DAM 1: Information Technology - Open Systems Interconnection - Application Layer Structure - Proposed Draft Amendment 1: Extended Application Layer Structure

3

OSI Service Definitions and Protocol Specifications

As computer networks become increasingly important, so does the need for unambiguous and complete specifications of communication protocols. This need is particularly important with respect to protocol standards which are implemented by users and vendors in a heterogeneous environment. The purpose of this chapter is to examine the tools used in OSI service definitions and protocol specifications.

Every OSI protocol standard comprises two sets of documents: the service definition and the protocol specification. A **service definition** is used to describe the boundary between functions of adjacent layers. It can be viewed as a contract between the protocol designers of a layer and the **service users** (i.e., the users of a layer). It defines the functional requirements which the protocol designers must satisfy without implying any specific design or conformance requirements. A **protocol specification** defines requirements for the operation of a protocol in order to provide its service. However, it does not constrain the implementation of the protocol such as the data structures and the software engineering techniques used.

There are currently two sets of conventions to specify the service definition. ISO/IEC TR 8509 describes the **service-primitive-based convention**. This approach is suitable to describe the interface between an OSI layer and a service user of the layer. It is described in terms of service elements and service access points. Section 3.1 gives an account of this approach.

Since the service-primitive-based approach assumes that the interface always involves an OSI layer, it cannot be used to describe the interface between two application entities in the Application Layer. Currently, there are well known object-oriented techniques in software engineering to describe the interface between two interacting objects. In Section 3.2, we give an overview of these object-oriented techniques.

Abstract Service Definition Convention (ASDC), as documented in ISO/IEC 10021-3, is the other set of conventions intended to complement ISO/IEC TR 8509. It is primarily used to describe the static configuration of a distributed application or a distributed system. Objects in the ASDC approach are considered to be peers. Peer-to-peer relationships are described in terms of abstract operations and ports. Abstract operations are invoked from a port. Unlike the service-primitive-based approach where a service user has only one type of interface with the service provider, ASDC allows an object to have more than one interface. The specifications of the major OSI application protocols use ASDC. As a matter of fact, ASDC appears as a part of the MHS standard. ASDC is described in Section 3.3.

In Section 3.4, we study the ingredients of a protocol specification. In particular, we examine a very commonly used tool, finite state machines (FSMs).

Although FSMs are easy to use, they are not formal. It is hard to build automated tools out of FSMs. However, the concepts behind FSMs provide a key building block for **Formal Description Techniques (FDTs)**, which are language-based specification methods using both rigorous and unambiguous rules with respect to the syntax as well as the semantics. The intent of an FDT is to express both the service definition and the protocol specification in a formal way. The application of an FDT can provide benefits such as improving the quality of standards, reducing dependency on the use of natural languages, and reducing engineering development time by using FDT derived tools (such as interpreters, compilers, and syntax-driven editors). In Section 3.5, we give an overview of FDTs and explain some of the features of ESTELLE, one of the FDTs used by ISO.

3.1   Service-primitive-based Conventions

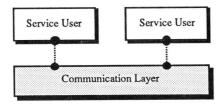

FIGURE 3.1   OSI Service Model

Figure 3.1 depicts a very simple OSI service model where we have two peer service users interacting with each other by means of the services provided by the underlying layer. Let us assume that the two service users are (N+1)-entities and the underlying layer is the (N)-layer. To provide the service, the (N)-entities in the (N)-layer communicate with each other using some (N)-protocol. A service definition of this (N)-protocol is a description of the service which the protocol provides to the (N+1)-entities. It has two major components. The first component defines the service elements and the functional units as seen by a service user. The second component specifies constraints as to how these service elements can be used.

Parameter \ Primitive	S-CONNECT			
	Request	Indication	Response	Confirm
Session connection identifier	U	C(=)	U	C(=)
Calling session address	M	M		
Called session address	M	M		
Responding session address			M	M
Result			M	M(=)
Quality of service	M	M	M	M
Session requirements	M	M(=)	M	M(=)
Initial synchronizatin point serial number	C	C(=)	C	C(=)
Initial assignment of tokens	C	C(=)	C	C(=)
SS-User-Data	U	C(=)	U	C(=)

TABLE 3.1   An Illustration of Service Parameters

First, we describe the notion of a service element. A **service element** consists of **service primitives** which are issued at a SAP. Associated with each service primitive is a set of **service parameters** which are used to provide additional information about the service primitive. The service definition defines the type of each parameter and uses a table to mark the status of each parameter which can be either "M", "C", "M(=)", "C(=)", or "U". Table 3.1 illustrates the specification of the status of the parameters associated with S-CONNECT, a session service element used for session connection establishment. "M" means that the parameter is mandatory. "C" means that the parameter is conditional, depending on some rule in the service definition. "M(=)" means that the parameter is mandatory and its value is the same as the value given in the preceding service primitive. For example, the service primitive preceding an indication primitive is a request primitive. "C(=)" means that the parameter is conditional and its value is the same as the value given in the preceding service primitive. Finally, "U" means that the parameter is optional, at the discretion of the service user.

Next, we consider some classification of the service primitives that can be issued at an (N)-SAP. The S.request primitive is issued by an (N+1)-entity to request a service S from the (N)-layer. The S.indication primitive is issued by the (N)-layer to an (N+1)-entity. It serves two purposes. The (N)-layer can use it to indicate to an (N+1)-entity that the service S has been invoked by some peer (N+1)-entity. It can also use it to report an internal problem. The S.response primitive is issued by an (N+1)-entity in reply to an S.indication primitive. Finally, the S.confirm primitive is issued by the (N)-layer to the originator of the S.request primitive to signal that the service has been completed, either positively or negatively.

There are two types of service elements: user-initiated service elements and provider-initiated service elements. A user-initiated service element is one initiated by a service user. On the other hand, a provider-initiated service element is one that is initiated by the service provider. The service provider, for example, can use a provider-initiated service element to report internal problems to its service users. Typically, a provider initiated service element is made up of just one service primitive, namely, the indication primitive.

A user-initiated service element can be further classified into two kinds: confirmed and unconfirmed. A service element is confirmed if it includes the confirm primitive. Almost all the confirmed service elements also include response primitives. A request from a user leads to an indication to the peer which then issues a response, which then leads to a confirmation to the requesting user. The RT-TRANSFER service element in the service definition of RTSE (Reliable Transfer Service Element), is an exception. Although confirmed, it does not include a response primitive. The lack of a response here has to do with where the responsibility of a reliable transfer ends. In RTSE, the responsibility ends at the RTSE service provider instead of the RTSE service user.

A service element is non-confirmed if it does not include the confirm primitive. A request from the user leads to an indication to the peer with no further primitives following. Thus, a non-confirmed service consists of the request and the indication primitives only. A service is non-confirmed not necessarily because of a lack of reliability but because of a lack of synchronization. For example, an (N+1)-entity, which wants to disconnect an (N)-connection, issues an (N)-DISCONNECT.request primitive but does not care about receiving an (N)-DISCONNECT.confirm primitive.

In most cases, the mode of a service element, i.e., whether it is confirmed or non-confirmed, is specified by the service definition. In some cases, it is up to the user to determine the type. For example, a CMISE user which invokes the M-ACTION service element to have some "minor" action performed on a management object may not want a confirmation of the execution of the requested action.

The service definition of a protocol standard may contain many service elements. For practical reasons, it is not expected that a protocol implementation implements all the service elements. In order for two implementations of the same protocol standard to interwork with each other, it is important that they have a understanding of the common facilities that will be used during the association. The common facilities used for an association may be a subset of the capabilities of an implementation. These common facilities are negotiated during the association or connection establishment. The negotiation may involve all the service users and the service provider. **Functional units** are some of the objects negotiated during the connection establishment phase. A functional unit is some consistent set of facilities. In many cases, a functional unit is specified by a set of service elements. In other cases, a functional unit does not introduce additional service elements but specify some available facilities. For example, the FADU Locking functional unit in FTAM allows the invocation of concurrency control locks on a FADU basis in addition to a file basis, although it does not introduce additional FTAM service elements. Among all the functional units, there is the **Kernel functional unit** which contains a minimal set of facilities. Although this functional unit is expected to be provided by any implementation, the rest of the functional units can be negotiated. A functional profile specifies which functional units are to be supported by an implementation. Note that an implementation can support a functional unit but does not have to use it during an instance of communication.

Example 3.1

The session protocol standard specified twelve optional functional units besides the Kernel functional unit. During a session connection establishment, a session user may propose a set of optional functional units. The local session service provider may not be able to support all the proposed functional units. In that case, it will reduce the number of proposed functional units before conveying the reduced set to the remote session service provider. The remote session service provider may reduce the functional units furthermore before indicating it to its session service user. The remote session service user can respond with a smaller set of functional units.

Service elements must be used properly. The second component of a service definition provides rules that constrain the use and sequencing of the service elements. For example, a service user cannot issue a data transfer request for a connection-oriented operation unless a connection has been established. The sequencing of the service elements can be specified by a finite state diagram. The finite state diagram in Figure 3.2 specifies the sequencing of the service elements used during the connection establishment phase of a simple transport protocol. The set of labelled edges leaving a state denotes the service primitives that can be invoked by a service user at that state.

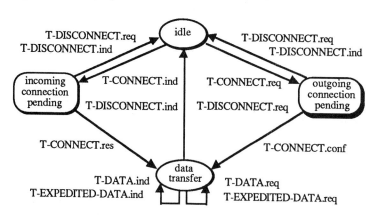

FIGURE 3.2   Sequencing of Service Elements using a Finite State Diagram

The implementation of the service elements should not be constrained by the OSI service definition. It should be left to the implementors to make the decision. In practice, the implementation depends on whether the service user is closely coupled with the service provider. In the case where they are closely coupled with each other, the request and the response primitives can be mapped to procedure calls, where the service user is the caller and the service provider is the callee. The treatment of the indication and confirmation primitive is different. Consider the indication primitive invoked by the service provider. Since a service user has no idea when the service provider will issue an indication primitive, it will handle an indication primitive as an interrupt. Thus, it is necessary for a service user to register the address of some "interrupt handling" procedure with the service provider during the initialization phase. When the service provider issues an indication primitive, it simply invokes the associated interrupt handling procedure.

When the service user and the service provider are loosely coupled with each another, they communicate with each another using the IPC (interprocess communication) facilities offered by the local operating system. In this case, all four primitives will be mapped to IPC messages.

To close our discussion on the service-primitive-based approach, we should note that this approach assumes only one type of (N)-SAP for the interaction between an (N+1)-entity and the (N)-layer, although multiple instances of the same (N)-SAP can be created by the (N)-layer. The ASDC approach, to be discussed in Section 3.3, is more versatile than the service-primitive-based approach because it allows more than one means of interaction between two communicating objects. Each means is modelled by a channel with a pair of bound ports.

3.2   Object-Oriented Modelling Concepts

In object-oriented modelling, an **object** is a discrete distinguishable entity. It may be a physical object such as a printer or a processor. Or it may be a logical object such as an FTAM virtual file. Logical objects can be active or passive. An **active object** is one that has states. An (N)-entity-invocation is an example of an active object. In this section, we give an overview of the object-oriented techniques used to describe the modelling of a system which may be a communication system or a distributed system. To differentiate the static aspects of a system from the dynamic aspects, two kinds of models are used: the **object model** and the **dynamic model**. The object model describes the structure of the objects used in the system, while the dynamic model describes the behavior of the system in terms of the behavior of the objects within the system. The dynamic model is built upon the framework provided by the object model.

- **object model**

The object model describes the static structure of the objects used in a system, and the relationships among the objects.

When a system contains many objects, it is useful to group objects of similar characteristics into classes. For example, similar objects may have common attributes, and common operations. An **object class** is a group of objects with similar characteristics. An object is viewed as an instance of an object class. An **attribute** is a property of an object class. For example, commonName and surname are attributes of the person object class. An attribute can be represented by a pair of the form (attribute type, attribute value). An **instance variable** is an implementation of an attribute. An **operation** is a function that may be applied to or by objects in an object class. For example, the addHobby operation is used to add a hobby to the existing hobbies of a person in the person object class. A **method** is an implementation of an operation. Syntactically, an object class can be viewed as a template of common attributes, operations, instance variables, and methods. Common attributes and operations are stored once per class rather than once per object instance. Furthermore, implementations can be written once for each class so that all the objects in the class can benefit from code reuse.

A very common technique in software engineering is information hiding or encapsulation. **Encapsulation** is a means of separating the external aspects of an object class which are accessible to other objects in its environment from the internal details of the object which are intended to be hidden from the other objects. The **public part** of an object class contains the external aspects while the **private part** contains the internal aspects.

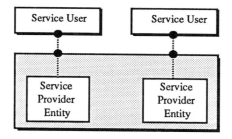

FIGURE 3.3 **Decomposition of the Service Provider into Service Provider Entities**

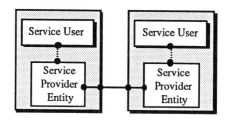

FIGURE 3.4 **A Redrawing of Figure 3.3**

Inheritance allows the construction of new classes from one or more existing classes. An existing class is called a **superclass**. The refined new class is called a **subclass**. Inheriting code enables reusability while inheriting attributes enables structure sharing among object classes. Thus, inheritance avoids redesigning and recording everything from scratch. In OSI, inheritance proves to be a very powerful tool to describe the conceptual information base associated with some application protocols. For example, the DS standard defines many objects for naming purpose. Classes can be used to group objects with common attributes so that subclasses can be defined without redefining the attributes inherited from the superclasses.

An object may be a composite object or a component object. **Composition** is a technique for constructing systems while **decomposition** is a means for designing systems. Through decomposition, a composite object is decomposed into a number of simpler objects. When an object has been decomposed to a level of abstraction where it is obvious that some of the component objects will be distributed, communication objects are introduced to support the distribution of those component objects. In OSI for example, we can compose two objects by introducing another communication object in between. Figure 3.1 illustrates this situation. Here the two peer service users are composed with a communication layer which is viewed as a communication object. Figure 3.3 shows that through decomposition, the communication layer can be decomposed into two service provider entities. Figure 3.4 is a redrawing of Figure 3.3. While Figure 3.3 shows the two service users communicating indirectly via the communication layer, Figure 3.4 shows two system objects communicating directly with each other. Each system object in Figure 3.4 contains a service user object and a service provider object. The ASDC approach is suitable to describe the interaction between the two system objects in Figure 3.4.

• **dynamic model**

The dynamic model describes the control aspects of a system. The major concepts here are activities, events, and states. Objects in the dynamic system are active in the sense that they maintain states. Through activities, their states can change over time.

Objects in a system interact with each other through **activities** at their **interaction points**. An activity may take time to complete. For example, it may be a continuous operation such as displaying a picture on a television screen. It is useful to decompose an activity into a sequence of **atomic events**, atomic in the sense that they will not be subdivided furthermore in a specification. An atomic event is instantaneous in the sense that its duration is relatively insignificant. There are external events as well as internal events. An external event, used to model an external stimulus, can be one sending an operation to another object or one receiving an operation to be performed on an object. An operation associated with an external event must appear in the public part of the object class and can only access public attributes. On the other hand, an internal event of an object class, sometimes called a silent action, is associated with an operation in the private part of an object class. Setting timer values is an example of an internal event in an object class modelling an (N)-entity.

The **state** of an object class is a group of attributes whose attribute values may be affected over time through interaction with other objects in its environment. States and events together can be used to describe the **behavior** of an object class. The behavior of a class can be specified by a finite state diagram. As a directed labelled graph, the finite state diagram contains states as nodes and events as labelled edges. When an event is received at a given state, processing of the event may result in a state transition where the next state is represented by the node at which the labelled edge is pointing. In general, the dynamic model consists of multiple state diagrams, with one state diagram for each object class used in the modelling of the system.

3.3   ASDC

The service-primitive-based approach is limited in the sense that it can only describe the interaction between a service user object and a communication layer. ASDC, which is intended to complement the service-primitive-based approach, is primarily used to describe peer-to-peer interactions in a distributed application or a distributed system. At an abstract level, it does not stipulate the use of a particular communication protocol suite for the communication support of the distributed application/system.

The process of specification in ASDC begins by identifying what the distributed application/system does as a whole. At the highest level, the application/system is composed of a number of objects. An object interacts with another object using a port-pair. A port pair is given by a port on one object and a port on the other. Each port is characterized by a set of abstract operations. When an object wants to request a service from the other object, it invokes the appropriate abstract operation.

ASDC only specifies the object model but does not specify the dynamic model. It provides conventions for abstractly describing a distributed application/system both macroscopically and microscopically. The macroscopic description is called an **abstract model**. It identifies the objects in the application/system. It is based upon the concepts of abstract objects, ports, and refinements. Refinement is used whenever an object needs to be refined to expose its internal component objects. A microscopic description is a specification of the **abstract service**. It describes how the objects in the distributed application/system interact with each other. It is based upon the concepts of abstract operations. In the following, we will describe the abstract model and the abstract service in more detail.

- **abstract model**

Objects in a system are called **abstract objects** in ASDC. There is no difference between abstract objects here and objects described in Section 3.2. Abstract objects interact with each other by means of **abstract ports**. An object may have one or more abstract ports. Ports can be of different types.

Two abstract objects can interact with each other only if they have a pair of bound ports, with a port in one and a port in the other. Two ports can be bound only if they **match**. Any two ports of the same symmetric type match, while two ports of the same asymmetric type match if and only if one is a **consumer** and the other is a **supplier**.

A port is an instance of a port type. An object may have multiple instances of one type, and multiple instances of a different type. A port type is characterized by a set of abstract operations. When an object wants to request a service from another object, it invokes an abstract operation on one of its ports.

A port type can be either symmetric or asymmetric. All instances of a **symmetric** port type are identical, i.e., they offer all the operations associated with the port type. On the other hand, an instance of an **asymmetric** port type is one of two kinds: **supplier** or **consumer**. The object with the consumer port can only invoke an operation associated with the consumer port, while the object with the supplier port can only invoke an operation associated with the supplier port. In general, the operations associated with a supplier port differ from the operations associated with a consumer port. In some cases, the two sets of operations may be completely disjoint from one another.

ASDC provides tools to refine a composite object into component objects. A composite object may have several component objects of the same object class. In this case, the object class is said to be **recurring**. A component object may have **visible ports**, i.e. ports that are visible to the composite object. It may also have ports which are to be **paired** with ports in another component object in the composite object.

In the next three examples, we use ASDC to describe the abstract model of the MHS, the abstract service of the MTA object, and the refinement of the MTS object into one or more MTA objects.

Example 3.2

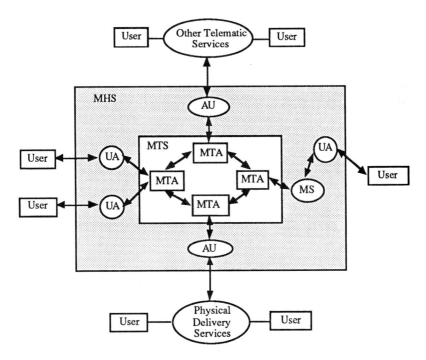

FIGURE 3.5   1984 MHS Functional Model

Figure 3.5 gives an object-oriented view of the 1984 MHS functional model. The MHS, as a composite object, contains the following component objects: an MTS, AUs, and UAs. The MTS is also a composite object. It contains a set of MTAs as component objects. Note that in Figure 3.5, we do not have any MS object which will be present in a 1988 MHS functional model.

Example 3.3

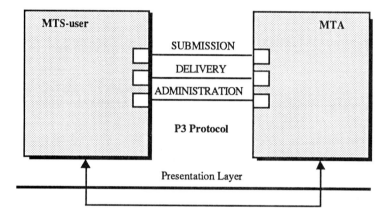

FIGURE 3.6   Interface between an MTS-User and an MTA

Figure 3.6 shows that an MTS-user object interacts with an MTA object using three ports. The MTS-user uses the submission port to submit a message or a probe. An MTA uses the delivery port to deliver a message or a report to an MTS-user. Either an MTS-user or an MTA can use the administration port to change its credentials.

Example 3.4

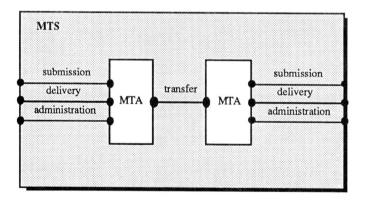

FIGURE 3.7   Refinement of an MTS object

Figure 3.7 shows that the MTS object can be refined to two component MTA objects. An MTA object has three visible ports: the submission port, the delivery port, and the administration port. The transfer port is an invisible internal port pairing up with the two MTAs which want to interact internally for the purpose of relaying messages or MTA-reports. The MTA object is an example of a recurring object.

• **abstract services**

A specification of the abstract services of an application defines how the application is initiated, controlled, and terminated. It is based upon the concepts of abstract bind/unbind operations, abstract operations, and abstract errors.

An **abstract bind operation** is a procedure used to bind one or more pairs of ports. The object which invokes an abstract bind operation is called the **initiator,** and the object which performs the operation is called the **responder.** The abstract bind operation binds a set of ports of the initiator to a matching set of the responder. When the port type of interest is asymmetric, the bind operation must indicate which portside is consumer and which portside is supplier. The initiator may supply binding argument such as authentication information to the responder. The outcome of the bind operation can be conveyed back to the initiator.

An **abstract unbind operation** simply unbinds a set of ports that were bound earlier. It is invoked by the initiator of the abstract bind operation.

An **abstract operation** must be invoked in the context of two bound ports. The object requesting the abstract operation is called the **invoker,** and the object executing the abstract operation is called the **performer.** Note that an invoker/performer can be either an initiator or a responder.

An **abstract error** is an exception condition that may arise during the execution of an operation. When an error is reported, the performer conveys to the invoker the type of the error and possibly other error information.

Overall, an abstract service specification comprises for each port an abstract bind/unbind operation, one or more abstract operations, and zero or more abstract errors reported by each abstract operation.

Example 3.5

Consider the abstract service of the P1 protocol in MHS which defines the interaction between two MTAs. It uses only one port, namely, the transfer port. This port is used to transfer either messages, probes, or reports between two MTAs. The transfer port supports three abstract operations: the message-transfer abstract operation, the probe-transfer abstract operation, and the report-transfer abstract operation.

3.4 Protocol Specification

In this section, we examine the techniques used to specify a protocol. In Section 3.4.1, we describe the various components of a protocol specification. In Section 3.4.2, we demonstrate how an FSM is used to model the behavior of a protocol.

3.4.1   Components of a Protocol Specification

The major components of a protocol specification document include the following:

- the definition of PDUs: this part describes the structure and encoding of each PDU,
- elements of procedures: this component defines the procedures used in the operation of a protocol.
- mapping to underlying services: this component describes how entities exchange PDUs by means of the underlying services.
- the description of a protocol: this component can be described informally by a finite state machine, or it can be described formally using an FDT, and
- the conformance requirements: this component contains conformance requirements to which any implementation claiming conformance to the protocol standard shall comply.

Each component is described next.

One should distinguish between the structure of a PDU from its encoding. The structure of PDUs describes the logical components of a PDU. It can be described using ASN.1, an OSI machine-independent language for defining data types. ASN.1 is covered in Chapter 8. The encoding of PDUs describes how the PDU is transferred between two communicating systems. An application protocol standard does not specify the encoding of its APDUs because their encodings are determined by the communicating presentation entities. In contrast, the encodings of PDUs used for the Presentation Layer and the lower layers are specified in the protocol standards. They cannot be negotiated by the communicating entities.

Example 3.6 shows the structure of an APDU (i.e., application PDU) of ROSE, where no encoding information is specified. In contrast, Example 3.7 shows not only the structure but also the encoding of a transport PDU.

Example 3.6

```
RORJapdu ::= SEQUENCE {
        invokeID    CHOICE {InvokeIDType, NULL},
        problem     CHOICE {
                    [0] IMPLICIT          GeneralProblem,
                    [1] IMPLICIT          InvokeProblem,
                    [2] IMPLICIT          ReturnResultProblem,
                    [3] IMPLICIT          ReturnErrorProblem}}
```

The above illustrates the use of ASN.1 to define the structure of a ROSE PDU. It says that the type of a RORJapdu is SEQUENCE which is similar to the record type in Pascal. It has two fields, invokeID and problem. The type of the problem field may be one of the following: GeneralProblem, InvokeProblem, ReturnResultProblem and ReturnErrorProblem.

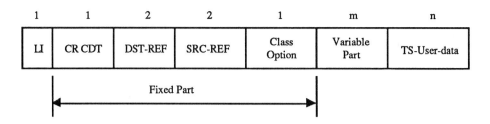

1	1	2	2	1	m	n
LI	CR CDT	DST-REF	SRC-REF	Class Option	Variable Part	TS-User-data

Fixed Part

FIGURE 3.8   A Transport Connection Request PDU

Figure 3.8 gives the structure and encoding of the transport connection request PDU. The structure has seven components. For the encoding, two bytes are used to encode the SRC-REF (source reference) field.

Every protocol specification defines a number of procedures. These procedures, known as **elements of procedures**, are called during the processing of a protocol machine. For example, the transport connection establishment procedure is called when a transport protocol machine receives a transport connection establishment request from a transport service user.

When a protocol machine services an event, it may generate a PDU and then invoke an underlying service primitive to transfer the PDU to its peer. The protocol specification must define how an event is mapped to a PDU and how the PDU is mapped to an underlying service primitive.

The behavior of a protocol describes the operation of the protocol machine. The FSM description is the most common tool to describe the behavior of a protocol. It will be described in more detail in the next section. In short, an FSM description identifies a finite set of states to describe the operation of the protocol machine. It also identifies a set of events which may be incoming or outgoing. States can be changed as a result of the processing of the events.

There are three parts in the conformance requirements component. The first part, the **static conformance** requirement, specifies the minimal capabilities a conforming implementation should include, such as a range of values for certain parameters, functional units, roles of the implementation, or constraints on the capabilities of the supporting lower layers. The second part, the **dynamic conformance** requirement, specifies procedures that determine how an implementation must behave during an instance of communication. The third part, the **PICS (Protocol Implementation Conformance Statement) Proforma**, is a set of tables summarizing the static conformance requirements. A PICS is obtained by completing the PICS Proforma.

Example 3.8

In this example, we consider the conformance requirements of FTAM. A couple of the static requirements are: (1) the system shall act as an initiator, a responder, or both, and (2) it must support at least the kernel group of attributes. A couple of the dynamic requirements are: (1) the system shall follow all procedures group of attributes. A couple of the dynamic requirements are: (1) the system shall follow all procedures relevant to each functional unit that the system claims to perform, and (2) it must support the mapping on the presentation service as specified in the FTAM protocol standard.

We close this section by making a few observations of an application protocol, since most of the protocols described in this text are application protocols.

An application protocol supports the communication of two communicating AEs. It is in fact derived from a number of application protocols. To see this, recall that each AE is made up of a set of ASEs and ASOs. For two AEs to communicate with each other, it is necessary that they have an identical structure of ASEs/ASOs. This structure is described by an application context. An ASE/ASO in one AE communicates with a peer ASE/ASO in its own application protocol. For example, suppose that an FTAM initiator wants to communicate with an FTAM responder in an application context consisting of ACSE and FTAM-ASE. Here, we have the FTAM-ASE in the initiator communicating with the FTAM-ASE in the responder in an application protocol described in the FTAM standard. We also have the ACSE in the initiator communicating with the ACSE in the responder in an application protocol described in the ACSE standard. Thus, the application protocol between the initiator and the responder is actually derived from two application protocols.

The application protocol of some ASE can be very simple. This is the case if an ASE is ROSE user (e.g., CMISE). The standard of a ROSE user normally defines a set of remote operations. When the ROSE user wants to send an operation to its peer, it does not generate any APDU containing a description of the operation. Instead, it issues a ROSE service primitive and passes parameters such as an operation identifier and the arguments of the operation. The point is that all the operations defined by the ROSE user must be registered with the ROSE service provider before any invocation of an operation can be made, hence it is sufficient for a ROSE user to pass an operation identifier and the arguments of the operation to the ROSE service provider. Since a ROSE user does not generate any APDUs, its protocol is relatively simple compared with the protocols of other ASEs which need to generate/process APDUs. Another observation that we can make here is that there are two styles of interaction between two ASEs in an AE. In one style, an ASE interacts with the other ASE by passing operation identifiers and arguments; no APDUs are exchanged. In the other style, an ASE exchanges APDUs with the other ASE. The second style is sometimes called **embedding** in the literature.

Besides containing a service definition and a protocol specification, an application protocol standard may contain a number of information models. An information model describes the structure of a class of information structures which are specific to the application protocol. It is described by a set of object classes. As mentioned in Chapter 1, protocols associated with the lower six layers do not specify any information model because they do not deal with information structures. The objects in an information model are normally defined by a profile group, since they depend on the operating environment. Occassionally, an application protocol standard may provide a few common object classes. It may also provides templates for the definition of object classes. By using these templates, application protocol designers can define object classes in a consistent manner.

Unlike the protocols associated with the lower six layers, an application protocol standard normally defines a number of abstract syntaxes. An abstract syntax, as mentioned in Chapter 1, is a group of related information structures. For example, the FTAM standard has an abstract syntax defining the FTAM constraint sets, and an abstract syntax defining the FTAM document types. Two communicating entities need to have a common understanding of the information structures contained in the abstract syntaxes so that the representation problem can be handled properly by the Presentation Layer. Thus, it is important for an application protocol standard to spell out all the information structures that it has used or defined.

A final observation is that an application protocol standard normally specifies one or more application contexts. Recall that an application context defines a working environment for an application association. In particular, it defines the workers, i.e., the set of ASEs and ASOs used for an application association. The protocol standard of an ASE should state how the ASE can be combined with other ASEs/ASOs to form a working environment. For example, the protocol standard of the RDA-ASE specifies two working environments, one including the TP-ASE, and the other excluding the TP-ASE.

3.4.2   FSM Description

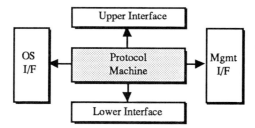

FIGURE 3.9   The Four Interfaces of a Protocol Module

The protocol behavior, which is the most important component of a protocol specification, can be described by a **finite state machine (FSM)**. An FSM is event-driven by a finite set of states. Recall that an event is an atomic action. The type of an event depends on the interfaces to the protocol machine. Some events are communication related and some are not. Every protocol standard identifies the communication related events. The non-communication related events are identified by the implementation.

For the time being, we consider the protocol machine which can be associated with an (N)-entity. It can have the following four possible interfaces: an upper interface with the (N+1)-layer through an (N)-SAP, a lower interface with the (N-1)-layer through an (N-1)-SAP, an operating system interface with a local (N)-entity, and a management interface also with an local (N)-entity (Figure 3.9). The upper and lower interfaces are also called the **external interfaces**, while the operating system and network management interfaces are called the **internal interfaces**. Each interface above can be associated with a set of input and output events.

At the **upper interface**, the machine interacts with the (N+1)-layer via the exchange of (N)-IDUs. Such (N)-IDUs may carry (N+1)-PDUs or some local processing information. For example, receiving a request primitive from an (N+1)-entity is an input event, and issuing an indication primitive to an (N+1)-entity is an output event.

At the **lower interface**, the machine interacts with the (N-1)-layer via the exchange of (N-1)-IDUs. This interface should match with the upper interface of the protocol machine associated with an (N-1)-entity.

From time to time, the protocol machine may interact with the local operating system, in aspects such as buffer management, timer management, and file management. The **operating system interface** serves this purpose. Examples of output events here are requesting for buffers to hold user information received from the (N+1)-layer, setting/cancelling a timer, and writing user information into a file for temporary storage. Notification of time-out is an example of an input event.

When a network management package is in place to provide some kind of layered management, the protocol machine has a **management interface** with a local management entity in the (N)-layer. Through an input event, the machine can perform such functions as resetting or initializing some of its configuration variables. Through an output event, the machine can report the values of its internal variables to the management entity which can perform some performance statistics.

The operation of the protocol machine is extremely simple. At any given state, upon receipt of an input event through one of the above interfaces, the machine may do the following, all in one indivisible action:

- perform some internal action;
- modify the state; and
- output an event to the appropriate interface.

The FSM model calls for the processing of the events one at a time. When there are more than one outstanding input event, the events are queued using the local operating system queuing facilities.

The so called **state explosion problem** refers to the phenomenon in which the state and event spaces become too large to be managed. For example, the use of sequence numbers in a protocol results in a different state for each sequence number. If thirty two bits are used to represent a sequence number, one can imagine that there are many states. Most protocols in the lower layers run into this state explosion problem. In order to mitigate the problem, an **extended state machine description** introduces the notion of state variables and event variables. A **state variable** is used to address a set of related states, while an **event variable** is used to address a set of related events. State variables and event variables are easy to express in an FDT (i.e., Formal Description Techniques) because every FDT has a variable declaration facility. With the use of event and state variables, one can introduce **enabling conditions** which are predicates on (state or event) variables to determine whether an action should be taken upon receipt of an event in some state. It is not hard to see that an extended state machine resembles a computer program which is far more expressive than an FSM. ESTELLE is an FDT based on the use of an extended state machine.

Example 3.9

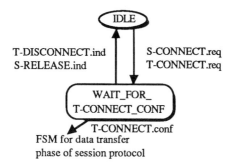

FSM for data transfer
phase of session protocol

FIGURE 3.10   A Finite State Diagram for Connection Establishment

Figure 3.10 gives an FSM modelling the connection establishment phase of the session protocol. There are only two states, the IDLE state and the WAIT_FOR_T-CONNECT_CONF state. On receiving an S-CONNECT.req primitive from a session user in the IDLE state, the session protocol machine will generate a CN PDU, issue a T-CONNECT.request primitive, then move to the WAIT_FOR_T-CONNECT_CONF state. While waiting in the WAIT_FOR_T-CONNECT_CONF state, it may receive two possible events. If it receives a T-CONNECT.confirm primitive, it will move to the initial state of the FSM modelling the data transfer phase of a session protocol. If it receives a T-DISCONNECT.indication primitive, it will issue an S-RELEASE.indication primitive and move to the IDLE state.

Protocol specification using FSMs has one major weakness. It is too simple. A common fact in formal language theory is that FSMs are much weaker than Turing machines. A Turing machine can be specified by any conventional programming language. Thus the question is: why don't we specify a protocol using a programming language? This question is addressed in the next section.

3.5   Formal Description Techniques

The purpose of this section is to give an overview of FDTs and illustrate some of the features of ESTELLE.

3.5.1   An Overview of FDTs

Specifications written in natural languages give the illusion of being easily understood, but often contain ambiguities which implementors need to resolve. Furthermore, most of the tools and methods of protocol validation and testing require that the specifications of the protocol be given in a formal language. It did not take too long for the OSI standard groups to realize the benefit of the use of **Formal Description Techniques** (FDTs). An FDT is a specification language, not a programming language. Three FDTs have been defined: ESTELLE, LOTOS, and SDL.

First, let us give a brief description of each of the three FDTs. **ESTELLE (Extended State Transition Language)** is an FDT developed by ISO for the specification of distributed systems. It can be also used to describe the OSI services and protocols. As the name suggests, it is based on the use of an extended finite state machine. The majority of the ESTELLE features are Pascal like, hence ESTELLE is quite appealing to Pascal programmers. Unlike Pascal, ESTELLE contains concurrency features. A distributed system or a distributed application in ESTELLE is viewed as a set of cooperating subsystems executing asynchronously in parallel with each other. Within each subsystem, synchronous parallelism is permitted. Today, many ESTELLE derived tools such as ESTELLE compilers have been developed.

LOTOS (Language of Temporal Ordering Specifications), another ISO language, is based on Milner's CCS (Calculus of Communicating Systems). CCS is a process algebra providing operators to allow parallel processes to communicate with each other either synchronously or asynchronously. In LOTOS, a system is specified as a hierarchy of process definitions. The behavior of each process is expressed by a behavior expression. The formation rules for these expression are an integral part of LOTOS. In general, the behavior expression can be expressed as a possibly infinite tree-like structure. Communication among processes is handled by applying operators to the processes. The semantics of the process operators is expressed in terms of the behavior expressions.

SDL (System Description Language) was recommended by CCITT as early as 1980. It is related to the programming language CHILL (CCITT High-Level Language) which was designed initially for switching systems.

It is unfortunate that there is presently some competition among the three FDTs, which each having some advantages. ESTELLE has strong backing from the university community where PASCAL is commonly taught. LOTOS has strong backing from the programming language semantics group. The formal semantics of LOTOS can be expressed in LOTOS, although the formal semantics of ESTELLE or SDL has to be expressed in some other meta-language. SDL has strong backing from the telecommunications industry. There is hesitation in the OSI community to adopt any one of the FDTs. Part of the reason is that none of the three languages is truly object oriented.

Before we move on to describe ESTELLE in the next section, we would like to point out that an FDT can accomplish something that the FSM approach fails to accomplish. The FSM approach emphasizes on the state behavior of a protocol and tends to de-emphasize the parameters of the events, states, or actions. ASN.1 notation can be used to give the formal definitions of these parameters. However, FSM combined with ASN.1 still cannot express how the parameter values of the interactions of a protocol machine depend on state variables and/or previously received interaction parameters. The point is that ASN.1 is only a data declaration language, hence it cannot be used to express any control aspects. Such aspects can be expressed by an FDT.

3.5.2   Some Features of ESTELLE

An ESTELLE **specification module** amounts to a program main in Pascal. Within the specification module, there are module definitions. A module definition is similar to an object class definition in an object-oriented programming language. Every module definition is characterized by an external interface and an internal behavior. The external interface can be described by interaction points (analogous to ports), channels (analogous to the binding of two ports), and interactions (analogous to operations). The internal behavior is described by an extended state machine. A **task** is an instance of a module definition. If a module definition is viewed as an object class definition, a task is an object in that object class.

A module definition may include definitions of other modules, thus leading to a hierarchical tree structure of module definitions. The hierarchical structure of modules can be represented in the form of a tree diagram shown in Figure 3.11.

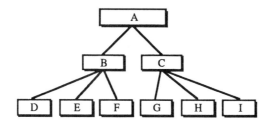

FIGURE 3.11   A Hierarchical Module Structure in ESTELLE

The way tasks behave with respect to each other depends on the way they are nested and "attributed". A module may have one of the following class attributes: systemprocess, systemactivity, process, or activity. All instances of a module have the same attribute as the module. A module, when it is not attributed, provides a framework to define a static structure. Attributed modules are used to describe dynamic structures. Modules attributed with systemprocess or systemactivity are called **system modules**. They serve to identify separate communicating systems within the specification. In particular, the specification module itself may have one of these attributes. In such a case, the specification module describes a single system.

Some rules, known as the attribute principles, are imposed on the nesting of modules within a hierarchical module structure. For example, modules attributed with process or activity shall be nested within a system process. Modules attributed with process or systemprocess may be substructured only into modules attributed with either process or activity. Modules attributed with activity or systemactivity may be substructured only into modules attributed with activity. Modules attributed with activity or process are called **activities** and **processes** respectively.

only into modules attributed with activity. Modules attributed with activity or process are called **activities** and **processes** respectively.

The following example shows a hierarchical module structure and illustrates the attributing principle.

Example 3.10

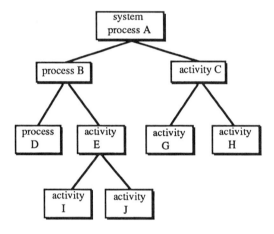

FIGURE 3.12   An Example of a System Process

In Figure 3.12, A is a module attributed with systemprocess. It has two children, B and C, attributed with process and activity respectively. B has a child process D and a child activity E. C has two children activities, G and H. E also has two children activities.

An ESTELLE specification describes a collection of system modules. These system modules run in a parallel asynchronous way with respect to each other. That is, their computation steps are completely independent of each other. Within a system module, one of two possible behaviors among the system's module instances may be specified by means of the attribute assigned to the system module:

- a synchronous parallel execution when the systemprocess attribute is assigned,
- and non-deterministic execution when the systemactivity attribute is assigned.

Let us try to explain what the above means. The behavior of a system module can be explained in terms of computation steps. Each system module executes in a series of computation steps. Each computation step begins by a nondeterministic selection of one (in the case of a "systemactivity" system) or several (in the case of a "systemprocess" system) transitions among those "ready-to-fire" and those "offered" by the system component modules (at most one transition per module may be offered at a given instant). The selected transitions are executed in parallel. A computation step ends when all of them are completed. Note that the relative speed of modules within a "systemprocess" system are synchronized because a selection of new transitions to execute can start only when all of the current selected transitions have completed their executions. In the case of a "systemactivity" system, since only one transition is non-deterministically selected for every computation step, we have purely non-deterministic behavior within such a system.

The following example illustrates the concept of a computation step for a hierarchical module structure.

Example 3.11

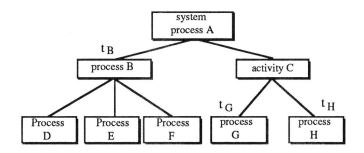

FIGURE 3.13   A Subsystem with a Process and an Activity

A legal set of selected transitions in Figure 3.13 can contain t_B and t_G, or t_B and t_H.

Next, we examine the syntax of ESTELLE. The specification module in ESTELLE is the main program. It may have an attribute which is either systemprocess or systemactivity. It does not have any interaction points, hence it cannot communicate with other external modules. The declaration part of the specification module contains a few channel definitions. The specification module has a body-definition which defines the framework of the system. For example, the body-definition can contain a few module definitions, followed by variables to refer to instances of the module definitions (i.e., tasks). The last part of the specification module describes how the various tasks are configured through links.

Example 3.12

```
specification EXAMPLE;
channel CH(Role1, Role2);
      by Role1:  m1, m2, m3.....
      by Role2:  i1, i2, i3.......

module A systemactivity;
ip a:  CH(Role1);
end;
..........  body AA ..........
```

```
end;

module B systemprocess;
ip b:  CH(Role2);
end;
.........  body BB ........
end;

modvar X:  A, Y:  B;
initialize
     begin
          init X with AA;
          init Y with BB;
          connect X.a to Y.b;
     end;


end.
```

This example gives the skeleton of a specification module which is not attributed. Only one channel (i.e., CH) is declared. To the right of Role1 is a list of messages (i.e., interactions) that can be sent via any interaction point playing the role of Role1 for CH. To the right of Role2 is a list of messages that can be received via any interaction point playing the role of Role2 for CH. The body-definition contains two module definitions: A (attributed with systemactivity) with body AA, and B (attributed with systemprocess) with BB. Within A, the interaction point "a" is declared to be of type CH playing the role of Role1. Within B, the interaction point "b" is declared to be of type CH playing the role of Role2. Two instances (i.e., tasks) are declared: X which is an instance of module A with body AA, and Y which is an instance of module B with body BB. Hence, more than one body may be associated with a module, and this is why the declaration of a task must be attached to a particular body. The last part shows how X and Y are connected with each other, thereby allowing X to send messages to Y.

Next, we consider the structure of a module definition. A module in ESTELLE consists of a header definition and a body definition. The header definition specifies the interaction points, the exported variables, and the same class attribute. The following example illustrates a header definition.

Example 3.13

```
module L process (C:  integer);
ip, p1:  E(Role1) individual queue;
p2, p3:  U(Role2) common queue;
export x, y:  integer; z:  boolean;
end;
```

This example shows that interactions received through p2 or p3 are appended to the same queue.

For each module header definition, there is at least one module body definition. The module body definition begins with the keyword "body", followed by the body name, a reference to the module header name with which the body is associated, and a body definition followed by the keyword "end" or the keyword "external" (i.e., defined externally). The following example illustrates a body definition.

Example 3.14

```
body B1 for L
    "body definition"
end;
body B2 for L; external;
```

Here, two bodies, B1 and B2, are associated with the module L. This in effect defines two distinct modules which can be named by the pairs (L,B1) and (L,B2) respectively. Both modules have the same external visibility in terms of interaction points, exported variables, and class attributes.

A body definition may contain a declaration part, an initialization part, and a transition part that specifies the internal behavior. The declaration part contains Pascal-like declarations and objects such as channels, modules, module variables, states, state sets (i.e., sets of states), and interaction points. The initialization part specifies the initial values of some variables of the module with which every newly created instance of this module begins its execution. Transitions are used to describe the internal behavior.

A transition declaration is composed of two parts: conditions and actions. Conditions are formed by clauses such as "when", "from", "provided", "priority", and "delay". Actions are specified by the clause "to". A transition declaration begins with the keyword "trans". The priority clause introduces a constant which is evaluated during the transition selection to determine which set of transitions is eligible to be selected. The "from" clause ensures that the machine must be in "this" state for the transition to take place. The "this" state is the current state. The "to" clause is the next state after the transition is performed. The "provided" clause introduces a predicate that must evaluate to the boolean true so that the transition is selected and executed. The "when" clause introduces an input interaction. It references the first element in a first-in-first-out queue associated with an interaction point. The action associated with a transition is bracketed by "begin" and "end".

Example 3.15

```
const       RETRtime = 10
type        IDtype = (DATA, ACK)
            SEQtype = 0..3
```

```
state         ESTAB, OPEN, WAIT
stateset      ESOP = (ESTAB, OPEN)
var seq:      SEQtype
function AC(ID: IDtype): boolean;
channel T (USER, PROVIDER)
     by USER: CONNreq;
     by PROVIDER: CONNres;
module M activity (T: integer);
     S1: T (PROVIDER);
     S2: T (USER);
     S3: U (PROVIDER);
end;
modvar        M1, M2, M3: M;

body          MB1 for M; external;
body          MB2 for M; external;
```

The above gives the "body definition" of B1 in Example 3.16. The control states are given by "ESTAB", "OPEN", and "WAIT". A group of control states, referenced by a group name, may be introduced by a stateset declaration. "ESOP" is a stateset, consisting of "ESTAB" and "OPEN". Modvars serve as references to tasks. In the example, M1, M2, and M3 are modvars which are all instances of the module M.

Example 3.16

```
state              state_AA, state_BB;     {state declaration part}
trans                                      {transition declaration}
priority           constant-value
from               state_AA               {current state}
to                 state_BB               {next state}
provided           predicate              {boolean expression}
when               ip1_id.event           {input required}
   begin                                  {transition block}
   output   ip2_id.PDU                    {action}
   end
```

This example illustrates a transition declaration from state_AA to state_BB.

3.6   Summary

Every OSI protocol standard has at least two sets of documents: the service definition and the protocol specification. The service definition describes what services are offered, while the protocol specification describes how the services are offered. Neither one constrains the implementation of a protocol. An application protocol standard may have a third document defining the various information models as needed by the protocol.

There are currently two sets of conventions to give the service definition: the service-primitive-based approach and the ASDC approach. The service-primitive-based approach is intended to describe the interface between an (N+1)-entity and the (N)-layer. It is described using service elements and SAPs. In contrast, the ASDC approach is used to describe peer-to-peer communication in a distributed application/system. At the abstract level, it does not assume that OSI is used to provide the communication support of the distributed application/system. It is described using abstract ports and abstract operations.

A protocol specification consists of a definition of PDUs, a set of elements of procedures, a mapping to underlying services, a definition of PDUs, a protocol behavior description, and a conformance requirements statement. An application protocol specification may also specify the various application contexts in which the protocol can be used.

The protocol behavior is commonly described by an FSM. Four interfaces of an OSI protocol machine can be identified: the upper interface, the lower interface, the operating system interface, and the management interface.

An FSM description is only semi-formal. It is not language-based, making it difficult to build automated tools to assist protocol verification and protocol testing. Recognizing this problem, ISO and CCITT defined FDTs which are language-based specification methods. The three well known FDTs that have been defined are ESTELLE, LOTUS, and SDL.

Related Standards

TR 8509: Information Processing Systems - Open Systems Interconnection - Service Conventions

ISO 8807: Information Processing Systems - Open Systems Interconnection - LOTOS - A Formal Description Technique Based on the Temporal Ordering of Observational Behavior

ISO 9074: Information Processing Systems - Open Systems Interconnection - ESTELLE - A Formal Description Technique Based on an Extended State Transition Model

ISO 9496: Information Processing - Programming Languages - CCITT High Level Language (CHILL)

ISO 10021-3 Title: Information Processing Systems - Text Communication - Message Oriented Text Interchange System - Part 3: Abstract Service Definition Conventions

4

Naming and Addressing in OSIE

Naming services have been provided ever since the beginning of computer networks. There are many kinds of naming conventions around. What is needed in an evolving OSE is a uniform approach to name OSI objects, a set of well defined registration procedures, and perhaps an efficient name resolution mechanism.

ISO/IEC 7498-3 provides guidelines which are to be followed in any OSI standard involving the need for naming and addressing of OSI objects. The general requirement is the following: a real open system, however complicated its internal structure may be, should show a simple naming and addressing structure to other open systems in the OSIE. ISO/IEC 7498-3 does not provide any concrete forms of names and addresses. The concrete forms are to be specified by the profile groups.

In Section 4.1, we discuss naming issues. In Section 4.2, we study OSI names. In Section 4.3, we study OSI addresses as special OSI names. We examine how and in what form OSI addresses appear in OSI service elements and protocols. Finally in Section 4.4, we study OSI network addresses.

4.1 Naming Issues

A **name** is a linguistic construct expressed in some language, i.e., it is a string of symbols taken from some alphabet. It is bound to one or more objects. It lacks a general consensus about what properties distinguish names from other types of identifiers such as addresses and routes. John Schoch made the following distinction:

> "The name of a resource indicates what we seek,
> an address indicates where it is, and
> a route tells us how to get there."

In general, names are chosen by users, and addresses are assigned by system administrators. Historically, the use of names in networking emerged as a convenience to humans who find it difficult to remember strings denoting network addresses. Thus an important property of names is that they are readable by humans. Another desirable property is that an object should be able to migrate to a new location without changing its name, i.e., names should be location independent.

Names can be categorized into primitive names and descriptive names. A **primitive name** is normally assigned by a naming authority. Its internal structure is transparent to the user. Examples of primitive names include social security number, motor license plate number, etc. Primitives names are in general user unfriendly. They are mainly used to build descriptive names. A **descriptive name** is one described by a set of assertions. As such, it may contain a few components. Each component has a primitive name or even a descriptive name. Descriptive names are used in a user friendly naming system.

Aside from the above two categories, **generic names** are used to identify sets of objects. For example, a distributed service can be identified by a generic name since there may be many objects in the distributed system providing the same service. The result of using a generic name ends up selecting exactly one member from the set of objects denoted by the generic name.

Three major issues to be dealt with in any naming system are the form of names, the scope of names, and the procedure of registering names. These issues are addressed next.

Names can appear in different forms. Whenever names have a global significance, their forms should be well understood by the users. For example, users need to know the alphabet defining a name, the maximum size of characters that a name can have, whether a name is case sensitive, etc. In the following, we will examine two name forms: attribute-based name form and object-identifier-based name form.

Attribute-based names are descriptive names used by the OSI DS standard as well as many other naming systems. An attribute-based name consists of a set of **Relative Distinguished Names (RDNs)** where each RDN is a set of attributes. Each attribute is a pair of the form (attribute type, attribute value). For example, a RDN can contain the following the (STATE, Missouri) and (CITY, Kansas City) attributes. Directory names as used by the DS standard have the further constraint that the RDNs must appear in a sequence. The sequence structure is based on a **Directory Information Tree (DIT)**. Figure 4.1 gives an example of a DIT. In this tree, a RDN is assigned to each vertex. A vertex in the DIT is named by the unique path from the root to the vertex. Such a name, called the **Distinguished Name (DN)**, is formed by concatenating the RDNs of all the vertices appearing in that path. For example, Figure 4.1 gives the DN of Edward Morrow. In this example, each RDN contains only one attribute. In general, a RDN can contain more than one attribute.

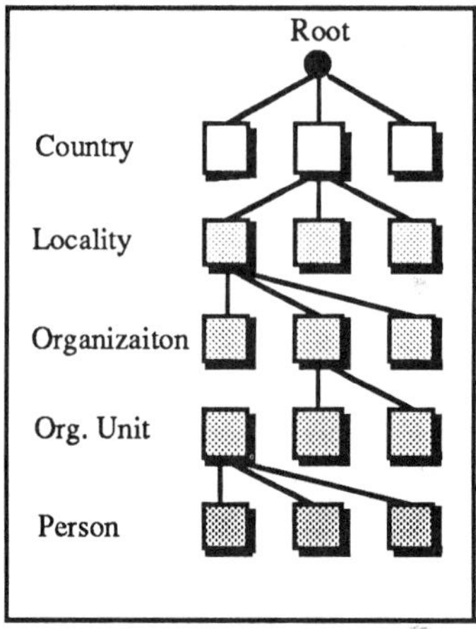

	RDN	Distinguished Name
Country	C = US	{ C = US }
Locality	SP = Missouri	{ C = US, SP = Missouri }
Organizaiton	O = UMKC	{ C = US, SP = Missouri, O = UMKC }
Org. Unit	OU = CSTP	{ C = US, SP = Missouri, O = UMKC, OU = CSTP }
Person	S = Morrow CN = Edward	{ C = US, SP = Missouri, O = UMKC, OU = CSTP, S = Morrow, CN = Edward }

FIGURE 4.1   An Example of a DIT

When registration is put properly in place, DNs provide a means to name objects in an unambiguous manner. While it is difficult to achieve a global DIT, a "profile-dependent" DIT can certainly be defined for a profile group in the least. Consider the usage of DNs by US GOSIP. DNs are used to specify MTAs as well as originators/recipients (O/R) of messages. Below is an example of an O/R name:

Country Name = US
Administration Management Domain Name = attmail
Private Management Domain Name = AlliedSignalKcd
Organization Name = umkccstp
Given Name = Rajendran
Surname = Saravanakumar

Attribute types such as Country Name and Organization Name appearing on the left hand side of the above OR name are defined by a profile group. A profile group also needs to determine whether some of the attribute types are mandatory or optional. Furthermore, it needs to specify the maximum length of some of the attribute values. In the case of US GOSIP, Table 4.1 gives the maximum size of attribute values appearing in O/R names.

Object-identifier-based names are based on the OBJECT IDENTIFIER type, one of the ASN.1 defined types. The possible OBJECT IDENTIFIER values are defined relative to the **Object Identifier Tree (OIT)**, part of which is shown in Figure 4.2. The purpose of the OIT is to provide a means of defining names for registration purposes.

The leaf nodes of the tree denote objects or object classes, and the non-leaf nodes denote administrative authorities. Each administrative authority can delegate responsibility to other administrative authorities to allocate more arcs beneath them. An integer labels each arc of the tree. Each node of the OIT can be named by the ordered sequence of integers that identifies the path from the root to that node. Sometimes, an integer label is accompanied by a mnemonic name describing the meaning of the integer label. The **OBJECT IDENTIFIER** type comprises the names of all of the nodes except the root.

O/R Address Attribute	Maximum Length (Characters)
Country Name	0 3
ADMD Name	1 6
PRMD Name	1 6
Organization Name	6 4
Organizational Unit Name	3 2 (each)
Surname	4 0
Given Name	1 6
Initials	0 5
Generation Qualifier	0 3
Domain Defined Attribute Type	0 8
Domain Defined Attribute Value	1 2 8

TABLE 4.1 Size of O/R Attribute Values for US GOSIP

Let us examine the arcs of the OIT in more detail. The OIT begins with three numbered arcs coming from the root: arc 0 assigned to CCITT, arc 1 assigned to ISO, and arc 2 assigned to joint ISO-CCITT. Below the CCITT arc are arcs leading to recommendations (0), questions (1), administrations (2), and network operators (3). Below the ISO arc are arcs leading to standard (0), registration-authority (1), member-body (2), and identified-organization (3). The arcs below standard shall each have the number of an International Standard. For example, the FTAM standard which is ISO/IEC 8571 is assigned an arc number 8571. Below the arc number 8571 are more arcs specified by the FTAM standard, leading to objects such as FTAM abstract syntaxes and FTAM document types. For example, an FTAM document type may be assigned object identifier {1 0 8571 5 1} which is equivalent to either {iso standard 8571 5 1} or {iso(1) standard(0) 8571 5 1}. Considering the fact that ISO and CCITT publish many standards and recommendations respectively, one can imagine that the subtree below the vertex {iso(1) standard(0)} and the subtree below the vertex {ccitt(0) recommendations(0)} contain many object identifiers.

In common usage, DNs are used to name objects while object-identifier-based names are used to name object classes. Object-identifier-based names are intended to be used in a global environment while DNs are used to name objects in a profile group which defines its own DIT.

Names are always resolved within a scope or context. The same name can be assigned to objects in different scopes. We say that a name is **unambiguous** within a scope if it is resolved to one and only one object. For example, within the scope of an OSIE, network addresses should be unambiguous. This does not mean that the identified object can have only one name. A **synonym** is a name that identifies an object which is also identified by another name(s). Synonyms can be a nuisance because most computer software cannot distinguish among the different synonyms of an object.

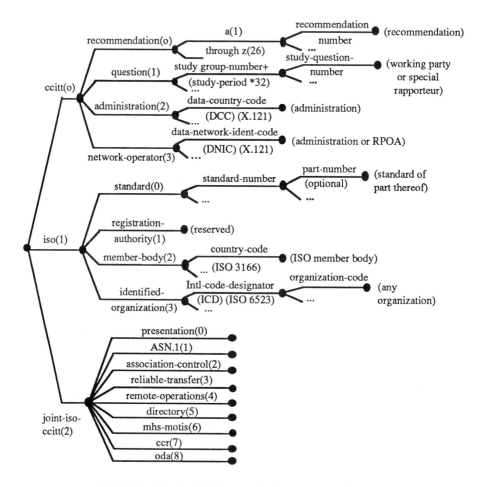

FIGURE 4.2   Initial Part of Object Identifier Tree

Certain objects in the OSIE such as application process titles require an unambiguous identification. This is achieved by registration. The names of such objects are registered with a **naming registration agent** which ensures that every name is unambiguous. A naming registration agent can partition its naming domain and assign the registration responsibility of a partition to a subordinate naming registration agent. This suggests that hierarchically structured names such as object-identifier-based names are useful for registration purpose. To register an object, we still need to know where in the OIT tree to register the object. Obviously this depends on the type of the object.

ISO/IEC 9834-1 describes general procedures for OSI naming registration agents. The registration procedures for specific classes of objects are described in the following documents:

- Document types (ISO/IEC 9834-2),
- Object identifiers (ISO/IEC 9834-3),
- Abstract syntaxes (ISO/IEC 9834-4),
- Transfer syntaxes (ISO/IEC 9834-5),
- Application processes and application titles (ISO/IEC 9834-6),
- Application contexts (ISO/IEC 9834-7),
- System titles (ISO/IEC 9834-8),
- VT profiles (ISO/IEC 9834-9), and
- VT control objects (ISO/IEC 9834-10).

4.2   OSI Names

ISO/IEC 7498-3 identifies three classes of names: titles, identifiers, and addresses. These names are examined next. Titles and identifiers are addressed in this section. Addresses will be examined in more detail in the following section.

A **title**, normally descriptive in nature, is a name assigned to an object in order to distinguish it from other objects. It can be used to identify a system, an application process, an application entity, etc. Let us consider titles for application processes and application entities.

An **application process title (APT)** identifies a particular application process in the OSIE. It must be unambiguous throughout the OSIE and hence it needs to be registered. For example, the following gives an APT for an MTA which is an application process:

Country = US

Administration Management Domain Name = attmail

Private Management Domain Name = AlliedSignalKcd

MTA-name = umkcosil

Address = /31348164751374/30303031//

MTA-id = umkcosi

Number = 1

AEs within an application process are named by **application entity titles (AETs)**. When an OSI software is installed, the system administrator normally has to configure some AET table which is a table consisting of AETs of all the users of this OSI software. An AET is composed of an APT and an application entity qualifier. Since there may be more than one AE in an application process, the application entity qualifier is used to identify a particular AE within an application process. An application entity qualifier needs only be unambiguous within the scope of the APT, hence it does not need to be registered. AETs do not have to be registered because as long as the APT component of an AET is unique, the AET must be unique.

An **identifier** is a name assigned to distinguish among different occurrences of an object. AE-invocation identifiers and (N)-connection-endpoints identifiers are examples of identifiers. Identifiers have only local significance within an open system. Thus different open systems may use different abstract syntaxes for the same type of identifiers. One may use numerals while another may use Roman letters.

Consider an FTAM responder AE. Because multiple FTAM initiators may want to manipulate the filestore associated with the responder, multiple application associations are established. As a result, more than one AE-invocation of the FTAM responder object is created. An **application entity invocation identifier** (AEI) is used to identify an AE-invocation. It is composed of an AET and an invocation qualifier.

Recall from Chapter 2 that when an (N+1)-entity establishes an (N)-connection with another (N+1)-entity, each (N+1)-entity is given an (N)-CEI, i.e., an (N)-connection-endpoint-identifier. The (N+1)-entity can use this CEI to distinguish this new connection from other existing connections which share the same (N)-address at each end. Clearly, this (N)-CEI needs to be unique within the scope of the (N+1)-entity. An (N)-CEI consists of two parts. One part is used to specify the (N)-address of an (N+1)-entity. The other part is used to qualify the (N)-CEI.

4.3   OSI Addresses

An address is a name used to locate an object. For example, an (N+1)-entity can be located by the set of (N)-SAPs to which it is bound. Thus it can be addressed by a name given to that set of (N)-SAPs. Section 4.3.1 describes (N)-addresses, (N)-SAP addresses, and their structures. In Section 4.3.2, we examine how and in what form addressing information appear in OSI service elements and PDUs. Finally in Section 4.3.4, we study NSAP addresses which are the most sought after addresses in an OSIE. In particular, we examine the NSAP address format of version 2.0 of US GOSIP.

4.3.1   (N)-addresses

An (N+1)-entity can be addressed by an **(N)-address** which identifies the set of (N)-SAPs to which the (N+1)-entity is bound. The set membership of an (N)-address is not necessarily known to other open systems. In fact, it may change over time. When an (N)-address contains exactly one (N)-SAP, it is also called an **(N)-SAP address**. If the permanence of attachment between the (N+1)-entity and the (N)-SAP can be ensured, then it is convenient to use an (N)-SAP to address an (N+1)-entity.

Although an (N)-address uniquely locates an (N+1)-entity, the ISO naming standard required that all the (N+1)-entities in a system which have the same (N+1)-entity type to share the same (N)-address. Thus an (N)-address is basically used to name an (N+1)-entity type. This has the advantage of hiding the complexity of differentiating the different (N+1)-entities of the same functionality in a system from the other systems.

Example 4.1

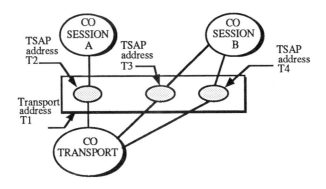

FIGURE 4.3   Transport Address vs Transport SAP Address

Figure 4.3 shows a transport address containing three transport SAP addresses, one used by a connection oriented session entity, and the other two used by a different connection oriented session entity all in one system. The assumption here is that both session entities are of the same type. So to simplify the external view of this system, only one transport address is communicated to the other systems. If this system also supports a connectionless session entity, a different transport address is provided to the other systems.

Example 4.2

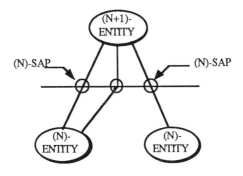

FIGURE 4.4   An (N+1)-entity served by multiple (N)-entities

The (N+1)-entity in Figure 4.4 is attached to three different (N)-SAPs which are served by two different (N)-entities. This example shows that an (N+1)-entity may be concurrently attached to one or more (N)-SAPs served by different (N)-entities.

Next, we examine the structure of an (N)-address. In designing the generic structure of an (N)-address, one is faced with the following question: how much addressing information of the lower layers (i.e., (N-1)-addresses or even (N-2)-addresses)

can an (N)-address convey? We should recognize that when we locate an (N+1)-entity in a remote open system identified by a network address, we need the lower layers addressing information in order to specify a path from the Network Layer all the way up to the target (N+1)-entity. There are two extreme approaches to the solution of the above question. In one approach based on a hierarchical construction, an (N)-address reveals explicitly the (N-1)-address of the supporting (N)-entity, the (N-2)-address of the supporting (N-1)-entity, and so on. That is, an (N)-address implicitly gives the address information of the lower layers. In the other approach based on the use of table lookup, an (N)-address does not imply any lower layers addressing information. It uses some local table lookup facilities to map an (N)-address to an (N-1)-address, an (N-1)-address to an (N-2)-address, and so on. The choice of using either the hierarchical approach or the table lookup approach depends on the following criteria:

- If an (N)-address is always mapped to only one (N-1)-address, then the hierarchical approach is possible.
- If an (N)-address can be mapped to several (N-1)-addresses (as in Example 4.2), then the table lookup approach is the only solution.

Obviously, the hierarchical (N)-address mapping is the more efficient of the two, although some flexibility caused by early binding has to be given up.

When N is greater than three, OSI adopts the hierarchical approach. One obvious reason is efficiency. The other reason has to do with the communication mode constraint studied in Chapter 2 which says, for example, that a connection-oriented presentation entity must be supported by a connection-oriented session entity, which in turn must be supported by a connection-oriented transport entity. This constraint implies that the (N)-address of an (N+1)-entity, in case N is greater than three, is mapped to only one (N-1)-address, thus making the hierarchical approach applicable.

As a result of the use of the hierarchical approach, an (N)-address (for N greater than three) is made up of two components:

- an (N-1)-address of some supporting (N)-entity, and
- an (N)-suffix, known as an **(N)-selector**, which identifies the set of (N)-SAPs to which the (N+1)-entity is bound.

Thus a presentation address is given by a session address and a presentation selector, a session address is given by a transport address and a session selector, and a transport address is given by a network address and a transport selector. In other words, a presentation address can be represented by a quadruple consisting of a presentation selector, a session selector, a transport selector, and a network address.

Since an (N)-selector is used locally to identify a set of (N)-SAPs, its type is determined by the local system. For example, it can be an INTEGER type or a PRINTABLE STRING type. Whatever its type is, a profile group has to determine the maximum size of an encoded value of that type. For example, encoded selector values used for version 2.0 of US GOSIP cannot exceed four octets.

Example 4.3

An FTAM responder in an open system may have the following selector values:

$$P\text{-Selector} = 6$$
$$S\text{-Selector} = 51$$
$$T\text{-Selector} = 41$$

Here, we assume that all the selectors are of INTEGER type. In the same system, we can have three FTAM responders which have identical functionalities. These three FTAM responders will have different P-selectors (such as 61, 62 and 63) internally. However, an external system only knows that there is one P-selector, that of the value 6. In some cases, a system may want another system to know the P-selector value of a particular FTAM responder involved in the application association. It returns the P-selector value, say 62, of that FTAM responder to another system.

4.3.2   Addressing Information

Addressing information can appear in either OSI service elements or PDUs. Sorting out the form of addressing information in either one is the subject of this section.

First, we consider addressing information in OSI service elements. (N)-addresses appearing as parameters of service primitives are of three kinds: calling address, called address, and responding address.

Suppose that an (N+1)-entity wants to establish an (N)-connection or issue a connectionless service request. It must supply the address of the peer (N+1)-entity which is indicated as the "**called (N)-address**" parameter in the connection oriented mode service or the "**destination (N)-address**" parameter in the connectionless mode service. The called (N)-address or destination (N)-address is in general given by a set of (N)-SAPs. When the called system receives the called (N)-address or the destination (N)-address, it needs to use some local means to select an appropriate (N)-SAP out of the set.

The (N)-address of the (N+1)-entity which initiated the connection or issued the connectionless service request is called the **calling (N)-address**. It is normally an (N)-SAP address appearing in an (N)-service indication primitive or an (N)-service request primitive during connection establishment.

The **responding (N)-address** is the (N)-address of a recipient (N+1)-entity. It appears in an (N)-service response primitive or an (N)-service confirm primitive during connection establishment. Some OSI protocols may require that this address be an (N)-SAP address, so that future communication can use this (N)-SAP address rather than the called (N)-address. This (N)-SAP address allows the initiating (N+1)-entity to go back to the specific (N+1)-entity which was selected among all the (N+1)-entities accessible by the called (N)-address at the initial connection establishment. Thus, the responding (N)-

address is not necessarily the same as the called (N)-address provided in the service request primitive. Another situation explaining that the responding address may differ from the called address is as follows. Soon after a called (N+1)-entity receives an indication primitive from the (N)-layer, it fails. As a result of some pre-arrangement, some other (N+1)-entity responds to the initiating (N+1)-entity. In this case, the responding (N)-address would differ from the called (N)-address.

At the protocol level, addressing information is carried between two open systems in the **PAI (protocol address information)** field within the PCI of a PDU. Depending on the layer, it is not necessary for the entire structure of an (N)-address (i.e., an (N)-selector together with an (N-1)-address) to be present in the (N)-PAI.

Full network addresses are carried in the PAI field of a PDU in the Network Layer. This is the case because network addresses, even though they may be bulky, provide an unambiguous identification of network service users in an OSIE.

The addressing information in higher layers (i.e., layers above the Network Layer) is interpreted locally in an open system. To save a few bits in the (N)-PAI, only the (N)-selector instead of the full (N)-address is stored in the (N)-PAI field whenever N is greater than three. For example, only the called and calling session selectors (but not the called and calling transport addresses) are carried in a session connection request PDU. This does not mean that the transport addresses are not passed to the remote system. Eventually the Session Layer will pass the transport addresses as parameters of some transport service primitives. Thus in essence, the remote system does receive the full session addresses. The next example explains how this is done.

Example 4.4

Suppose that an initiator AE1 wants to establish an application association with some application entity AE2 in another system. First of all, it needs to know the presentation address of AE2. With the help of the OSI Directory, this is a simple matter. Let us assume that the returned presentation address of AE2 is (ps2, ss2, ts2, NA2) where ps2 is the presentation selector, ss2 is the session selector, ts2 is the transport selector, and NA2 is the network address of the open system where AE2 is located. Let us also assume that the presentation address of AE1 is (ps1, ss1, ts1, NA1). When the calling presentation address is a set of presentation SAP addresses, normally some local mechanism is used to select a particular presentation SAP address from the set and all the future presentation service primitives will be issued at that SAP.

On receiving a presentation connection request from AE1 through the ACSE, the presentation entity PE1 in the initiating system derives the called session address (ss2, ts2, NA2), the calling session address (ss1, ts1, NA1) as well as some local session SAP address through which future session service primitives can be passed. In addition, PE1 also derives the called presentation selector (i.e., ps2) and the calling presentation selector (i.e., ps1). The selectors ps1 and ps2 will be carried in the PAI field of a CP (Connect Presentation) PDU. On the other hand, the calling session address and the called session address are not packed into the CP PDU, but simply passed as parameters of an S-CONNECT.request primitive.

As mentioned earlier, selectors and their types are chosen locally. They do not have to be registered with any registration authority. The only requirement is that they must be unique within the scope of the system defining the selectors. For example, no two session addresses in the same system can have the same session selectors. Since both the calling and called selectors appear in a connection establishment PDU, it is important that the calling system knows the selector types used in the called system and vice versa. This can be achieved using out-of-band communication. This has an implication. The selector types do not have to be encoded in the PDU, since both communicating systems know the selector types before communication begins.

Besides OSI network addresses, there are also SNPA addresses. A **subnetwork point of attachment (SNPA)** is a point in a subnetwork to which an open system is attached. For example, an open system may be attached to an X.25 network and a LAN. In this case, it has only one OSI network address, but it has two SNPA addresses. In general, the relationship between OSI network addresses and SNPA addresses is one-to-many. All the existing subnetwork protocols only carry SNPA addresses in the PAI field of their PDUs. If these subnetworks are used to provide OSI network service, then the PAI field has to carry not only SNPA addresses but also OSI network addresses. One may wonder whether their PAI field has sufficient space for so much addressing information, especially when OSI network addresses are of varying size. We will address this issue in the next paragraph.

Our discussion in Section 4.3.1 says that a transport address consists of a transport selector and a network address. In general, a transport address may contain more than one network address. Let us explain why. We pointed out in the last paragraph that most subnetwork protocols do not have enough room in the PAI field to carry both the OSI network addresses and the SNPA addresses. One way to solve this problem is to embed an SNPA address as part of a network address. In this case, it is sufficient to carry only the network addresses in the PAI. Note that we lose some flexibility because network addresses defined using SNPA addresses are route dependent. Consider a relay system which is attached to more than one subnetwork. This system has more than one network address. The transport address of this system will therefore contain more than one network address.

4.3.3   NSAP Addresses

A network address locates a network service user. It is made up of one or more NSAP addresses, where an NSAP address is an address of an NSAP (i.e., network service access point). ISO/IEC 8349 AD2 specified a global addressing scheme for NSAP addresses. The objective is that one single global space should be all that is necessary to reach a given destination, irrespective of the number of subnetworks between the source and the destination, the number of subnetworks to which the destination is attached, and the location of the caller.

The set of all the NSAPs in an OSIE forms the **global network addressing domain**. This domain can be partitioned into **network addressing domains** in a hierarchical fashion. Figure 4.5 shows a global tree of the network addressing domain where each node of the tree is a network addressing domain. Each network addressing domain is administered by an address registration authority. An address registration authority may further suballocate its addressing space to another address registration authority. The tree of network addressing domains has seven top level network addressing domains from the root node. They are:

- X.121 (the International plan for public data networks),
- ISO DCC (Data Country Code),
- F.69 (for telex),
- E.163 (for public switched telephone network),
- E.164 (for ISDN),
- ISO 6523-ICD (International Code Designator for identifying organizations), and
- Local.

Each network addressing domain has it own addressing format. For example, the X.121 addresses use up to 14 digits, the ISO DCC addresses use 3 digits, and the ISO 6523-ICD addresses use 4 digits.

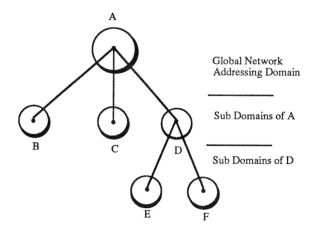

FIGURE 4.5   Global Networking Addressing Domain

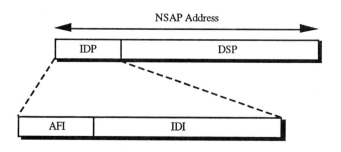

FIGURE 4.6   Structure of an NSAP address

An NSAP address consists of an **Initial Domain Part (IDP)** and a **Domain Specific Part (DSP)** (Figure 4.6) The IDP, in turn, consists of an **Authority and Format Identifier (AFI)** and an **Initial Domain Identifier (IDI)**.

The AFI specifies the format of the IDI (i.e., one of the seven top level addressing domains) and the abstract syntax of the DSP (i.e., binary octets, decimal digits, characters, etc.). It has an integer value between 0 and 99. The proposed allocations are: 36 - 59 to the existing IDI formats, 60 - 69 to the new IDI formats by ISO, and 70 - 79 to the new IDI formats by CCITT.

Figure 4.7 shows how an AFI value determines the IDI format and the DSP syntax. For example, an AFI value of 47 means that the IDI format is ISO 6523-ICD and the DSP abstract syntax is binary.

IDI Format	DSP Syntax			
	Decimal	Binary		
X.121	36	37		
ISO DCC	38	38		
F.69	40	41		
E.163	42	43		
E.164	44	45		
ISO 6523	46	47	Character	National Character
Local	48	49	50	51

FIGURE 4.7   AFI Values

The IDI component contains a value specified by the AFI. Suppose that the AFI value is 47 which implies the ISO 6523-ICD format. The following 4 digit ICD addresses are possible: 0004 for OSINET, 0005 for US GOSIP, 0006 for DOD, and 0014 for OIW.

IDP		DSP							
AFI	IDI								
47	0005	DFI	AAI	Reserved	Routing Domain	Area	End System	NSel
1	2	1	3	2	2	2	6	1

FIGURE 4.8   NSAP Address Format for US GOSIP (version 2.0)

The DSP is the part of an NSAP address assigned by an addressing registration authority specified in the IDI component. Its abstract syntax can be binary octets, decimal digits, characters, etc. As mentioned earlier, it is deduced from the AFI component. For example, if the AFI value is 47, the abstract syntax of the DSP is binary.

The actual length of an encoded NSAP address will vary according to the IDI format, the DSP abstract syntax, and the encoding scheme used by a network protocol. An encoding can be either binary or decimal. Binary encoding provides rules for representing decimal, binary, and character strings in binary strings. Decimal encoding is used for protocols which only permit decimal digits to be transferred. In general, the maximum length is 20 octets (with binary encoding) and 40 digits (with decimal encoding).

Let us consider the NSAP format for version 2.0 of US GOSIP (Figure 4.8). The AFI value is 47 which implies an ISO 6523-ICD format and the binary abstract syntax for the DSP. Under the rules of ISO 6523, NIST has obtained two ICDs for the US Federal Government. One, with the IDI value 0005, is for general Federal Government use and is administered by NIST. The other one, with the IDI value 0006, is for DOD use and is administered by DOD as delegated by NIST. The DSP field is divided into seven subfields:

- the **DSP Format Identifier (DFI)** specifies the version of the DSP structure standard (its present value is '80'H),
- the **Administration Authority Identifier (AAI)**, to be registered with the GSA, identifies an entity in a government agency which is responsible for the organization of its ISs and ESs into Routing Domains and Areas,
- the Reserved field is positioned to be available for encoding higher level routing structures above those of the routing domain or to be used to expand either the Administrative Authority or the Routing Domain fields in the future DSP formats (the value of the reserved field shall be zero unless a separate agreement covering a particular context of use specifies the use of a value other than zero),
- the Routing Domain field identifies a unique Routing Domain within an Administrative Domain,
- the Area field identifies an area within a Routing Domain,
- the End System field identifies a unique end system within an Area, and
- the NSAP SELECTOR subfield identifies a network service user.

The concepts of routing domains and areas will be explained in the next chapter on the Network Layer. Suffices to say at this point that OSI wants to adopt a two-level hierarchical IS-IS routing strategy. The following is an example of an NSAP address used for version 2.0 of US GOSIP:

AFI = 47
IDI = 0005
DFI = 80
AAI = 32 12 00
Reserved = 00 00
Routing Domain = 53 18

Area = 44 27
End System = 22 22 22 22 22 22
N-Selector = 01

The above values except those for the AFI and IDI are expressed in hexadecimal. We mentioned earlier that most network administrators embed an SNPA address in an OSI network address. Note that the End System field, consisting of 6 octets, is an ideal place for an Ethernet SNPA address which is 48 bits long. However, placing an SNPA address within an NSAP address will make the NSAP address subnetwork dependent, hence this method of placement is not recommended.

4.4 Summary

Any object that needs to be referenced deserves a name. The naming service provides the means for users to register/deregister names of objects and to retrieve information about named objects. There are many naming services. They differ from each other principally in the form of names, the scope of names, and the name registration procedures.

Two forms of names are commonly used in an OSIE: attribute-based-names and object-identifier-based names. Attribute-based-names are user friendly. Object-identifier-based names, based on the Object Identifier Tree, are not user friendly. They are mainly used for registration purpose.

An address is a name used to locate an object. Every application entity has a presentation address which is a quadruple made up of a presentation selector, a session selector, a transport selector, and a network address. Whereas presentation addresses are important to network programmers, network addresses are important to network administrators. A network address is an unambiguous name within an OSIE to identify a network service user. It is made up of one or more NSAP addresses. The form of an NSAP address should be general enough to accommodate all the existing non-OSI addresses. The naming standard suggested a hierarchical NSAP address structure which permits delegation of addressing authority.

Related Standards

ISO 7498-3: Information Processing Systems - Open Systems Interconnection - Basic Reference Model - Part 3: Naming and Addressing

DIS 9834-1: Information Technology - Open Systems Interconnection - Procedures for the Operation of OSI Registration Authorities - Part 1: General Procedures

DIS 9834-2: Information Technology - Open Systems Interconnection - Procedures for the Operation of OSI Registration Authorities - Part 2: Registration Procedures for OSI Document Types

DIS 9834-3: Information Technology - Open Systems Interconnection - Procedures for the Operation of OSI Registration Authorities - Part 3: Registration of Object Identifiers Component Values for joint ISO-CCITT Use

DIS 9834-4: Information Technology - Open Systems Interconnection - Procedures for the Operation of OSI Registration Authorities - Part 4: Register of VT Profiles

DIS 9834-5: Information Technology - Open Systems Interconnection - Procedures for the Operation of OSI Registration Authorities - Part 5: Registration of VT Control Object Definitions

DIS 9834-6: Information Technology - Open Systems Interconnection - Procedures for the Operation of OSI Registration Authorities - Part 6: Registration of AP Titles and AE Titles

5

Network Layer

The purpose of the Network Layer is to provide a means for NS-users (i.e., network service users) to communicate without any concern for the topology of the network and the transmission media used in each constituent subnetwork that comprises the network. The Network Layer achieves this by performing functions such as routing and relaying. Due to a variety of networking technologies and complex configurations of subnetworks, the operation of the Network Layer is very complicated, sometimes involving the use of more than one network protocol. There are network protocols for interconnection and network protocols for routing. The network protocols for interconnection are based on the IONL model, introduced in Chapter 2. The routing protocols are based on the OSI Routing Framework which is specified in ISO/IEC TR 9575. ISO/IEC TR 9575 provides a framework to partition the routing functions.

There are two modes of network services: **connection-oriented network service (CONS)** and **connectionless network service (CLNS)**. CONS is studied in Section 5.1. Containing only six service elements, CONS is relatively simple compared with the service of the higher layers. In Section 5.2, we study CLNS, the more common of the two network services. In Section 5.3, we describe how each mode of network service is provided in an internetworking environment. Section 5.4 gives an overview of the OSI routing framework. Routing protocols on IS-IS routing and IS-ES routing are described in Sections 5.5 and 5.6.

5.1　Connection-oriented Network Service

It is worth noting some of the requirements of an internetworking service:

- the details of an internetworking operation and the subnetwork facilities should be transparent to the NS-users,
- the networking service should allow two communicating NS-users to negotiate on QOS (quality of service) and other options during connection establishment; and
- the NS-users should have a uniform and unambiguous way to address each other using some network addressing scheme.

CONS is designed to meet the above requirements.

Peer NS-users such as transport entities use **N-CONNECT**, a confirmed service element, to set up a network connection. During connection establishment, the expedited data selection, the receipt confirmation selection, and the QOS parameters are negotiated. The expedited data selection parameter is used to determine whether expedited data can be sent in the network connection. The receipt confirmation selection parameter is used to determine whether a sender can solicit acknowledgement for some of the data units. This parameter is particularly useful when the underlying subnetworks are unreliable. Both the expedited data and the receipt confirmation are optional features that do not have to be implemented by a network service provider. Within the constraints imposed by the services of the intervening subnetworks, the network service provider tries to provide the requested QOS. Some of the QOS parameters such as throughput and transit delay are subnetwork dependent while others such as protection and priority are not. The ones that are subnetwork dependent can be modified by the network service provider.

Let us examine how the NS-users and the network service provider negotiate over some of the QOS parameters. In an N-CONNECT.request primitive, the calling NS-user can specify the target and lowest acceptable values for each parameter in the QOS parameter set. The target value is the desired value. The lowest quality acceptable value is the lowest acceptable value for the throughput parameter and the highest acceptable value for the transit delay parameter. If the network service provider cannot provide the lowest acceptable value, an N-DISCONNECT.indication is issued to the calling user. Otherwise, it issues an N-CONNECT.indication with both the available value and the lowest acceptable value to the called NS-user. If the called user does not agree with any value between the lowest acceptable and the available, it rejects the connection establishment with an N-DISCONNECT.request. Otherwise, it issues an N-CONNECT.response which includes a selected value for each QOS parameter.

The **N-DATA** service element is used by an NS-user to send normal user data. It contains both the NS-user-data and the confirmation request parameters. The NS-user-data parameter contains the data stream that is dispatched by the sending NS-user. Since the OSI service definition is abstract, it does not specify the maximum size of a data stream which can be sent. If the receipt confirmation service is in use, the confirmation request parameter serves to indicate whether the sending NS-user requires an acknowledgement from the receiving NS-user. The receiving NS-user uses **N-DATA-ACKNOWLEDGE** to acknowledge the receipt when the confirmation request parameter is set. Note that receipt confirmation is done on the basis of every individual NSDU (i.e., network service data unit).

The **N-EXPEDITED** service element is used by an NS-user to send expedited data. This is an optional service. According to the implementation agreements, a maximum of 32 octets of expedited data can be sent.

The **N-RESET** service element is used by an NS-user to synchronize a network connection. For example, the NS-user may be a network administrator. When the reset service completes, the data in the network connection is flushed. Thus it is destructive. However the network connection still exists. Either an NS-user or a network service provider may initiate this service. If an NS-user initiates this service, then N-RESET is a confirmed service. If a network service provider initiates this service, then both NS-users will receive an N-RESET.indication primitive.

The **N-DISCONNECT** service element is used to release a network connection. As mentioned earlier, it can be also used by either an NS-user or a network service provider to reject a network connection establishment. Like N-RESET, it is destructive.

Next we examine how to provide CONS on different types of subnetworks. There is no connection oriented OSI network protocol today, and probably there won't be one in the near future. X.25 falls short of being an OSI network protocol because X.25 is only a network access protocol between a DTE (data terminating equipment) and a DCE (data circuit equipment). The protocol used among the DCEs may be proprietary; for this reason, an X.25 network is sometimes called a "cloud". Thus additional protocols are needed to enhance the functionality of X.25 to that of CONS.

Below we will briefly describe how an X.25 subnetwork provides CONS. An X.25 subnetwork using the 1984 version requires the minimum enhancement. ISO/IEC 8878 described how the 1984 version of X.25 is enhanced to provide CONS. Essentially, it specified how the OSI network primitives are used to create the different types of X.25 packets and how the parameters of the primitives are used to set up the fields within the X.25 packets. The following shows how the OSI network service primitives are mapped to X.25 packets:

- an N-CONNECT.request primitive is mapped to a call request packet (from the calling DTE to the calling DCE) which contains the called address using the called address extension facility,
- an N-CONNECT.indication primitive is mapped to an incoming call packet (from the called DCE to the called DTE),
- an N-CONNECT.response primitive is mapped to a call accepted packet (from the called DTE to the called DCE),
- an N-CONNECT.confirm primitive is mapped to a call connected packet (from the calling DCE to the calling DTE),
- N-DATA.request and N-DATA.indication primitives are mapped to one or more data packets,

•   N-EXPEDITED-DATA.request and N-EXPEDITED-DATA.indication primitives are mapped to an interrupt packet,
•   an N-RESET.request primitive is mapped to a reset request packet,
•   an N-DISCONNECT.request primitive is mapped to a clear request packet, and
•   an N-DISCONNECT.indication primitive is mapped to either a clear indication packet, a restart indication packet, or a clear request packet.

The N-DATA.request and N-DATA.indication primitives correspond to a sequence of one or more X.25 data packets where all except the last have the M-bit set to 1 and the D-bit set to 0. In X.25, the setting of the D-bit to 1 corresponds to the need for an end-to-end acknowledgement. Thus, the setting of the D-bit of the last packet depends on whether the confirmation request parameter of the N-DATA.request primitive is set. If the confirmation request parameter is set, then the D-bit of the last sequence is set to 1.

CONS can also be provided over a LAN. We will briefly describe the provision of CONS over LLC2. In a LAN environment where every DTE is attached directly to the transmission medium, there is no identifiable DCE and thus communication of Layer 2 or above is DTE-to-DTE oriented. ISO/IEC 8881 defined a protocol to enhance the services of LLC2. Essentially this protocol specifies the use of X.25 in the DTE-to-DTE mode in a LAN environment. In the DTE-to-DTE mode, a call request packet and an incoming call are practically the same, and a call accepted packet and a call connected packet are also practically the same. One can imagine that this protocol is quite similar to the X.25 Packet Level Protocol.

5.2   Connectionless Network Service

CLNS, which is mandatory for version 2.0 of US GOSIP, is very simple. There is only one service element, **N-UNIT-DATA**. N-UNIT-DATA is a non-confirmed data transfer service element. The associated parameters are a source address, a destination address, QOS, and user data. If the network service provider cannot provide the requested QOS at certain time, it will still attempt to deliver the data, but indicate to the receiving NS-user the actual QOS provided for that data unit.

CLNP (Connectionless Network Protocol), as specified in ISO/IEC 8473, is the OSI protocol providing CLNS. Because of its similarity to IP (Internet Protocol), CLNP is also known as IP. CLNP is a good example of a subnetwork independent convergence protocol. It assumes minimal services from the underlying subnetwork which may be either connection oriented or connectionless. Thus, CLNP may run on top of LAN or WAN.

ISO/IEC 8473 specifies different types of CLNP functions. All implementations must support Type 1 functions, and may choose to support Type 2 and Type 3 functions at will. If an implementation does not support a Type 2 function selected by a PDU, the PDU is simply discarded and an error report PDU is generated and sent to the originating network entity. If an implementation does not support a Type 3 function selected by a PDU, the PDU is not discarded but is processed as if the function were not selected.

The following gives a short description of each Type 1 function:

- PDU composition: This function constructs the PDU.
- PDU decomposition: This function processes the PCI of a PDU.
- PDU lifetime control: This function enforces a maximum PDU lifetime.
- route PDU: The function determines the next hop to which a PDU should be sent.
- forward PDU: This function issues a subnetwork service primitive supplying the SNPA address of the next hop identified by the route PDU function.
- segment PDU: This function is called when the size of the PDU received from the Transport Layer is too large for the underlying subnetwork to transmit.
- reassembly: This function reassembles the segmented PDUs before they are delivered to the Transport Layer above.
- discard PDU: This function discards a received PDU for reasons such as congestion, expiration of lifetime, an invalid address, and an inconsistent checksum.

Fixed Part	Address Part	Segmentation Part	Options Part	NS-User-Data

FIGURE 5.1   Format of an IP Datagram

Next, we examine the format of an **IP datagram**, i.e., a PDU used by CLNP. Each IP datagram consists of a PCI followed by user data which can contain up to 64K bytes (Figure 5.1). The PCI is made up of a fixed part and a variable part. While the fixed part contains information which every datagram must carry, the variable part contains optional parameters not necessarily present in every datagram. The variable part is made up of an address part, a segmentation part, and an option part. Below we will examine each part.

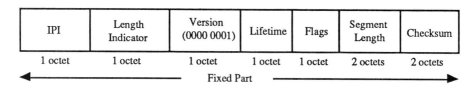

IPI	Length Indicator	Version (0000 0001)	Lifetime	Flags	Segment Length	Checksum
1 octet	1 octet	1 octet	1 octet	1 octet	2 octets	2 octets

Fixed Part

FIGURE 5.2   Fixed Part of an IP Datagram

The fixed part (Figure 5.2) contains the following parameters:

- an **initial protocol identifier (IPI)** which distinguishes CLNP from other network protocols such as those used for routing,
- a length indicator which indicates the total number of octets of the PCI,
- a version number of ISO/IEC 8473 whose current value is '00000001'B,
- the lifetime of an IP datagram,

- flags containing a segmentation permitted flag (indicating whether segmentation can be performed), a more segment flag (indicating whether the data segment of the datagram contains the last octet of the user data in an NSDU), and an error report flag (indicating whether an error report is needed if a PDU is discarded en route),
- a segment length indicator which gives the total length of the header and data in the segment, and
- a checksum which is computed only on the PCI.

Because ISO has defined quite a number of network protocols, ISO requires each network protocol to reserve the first octet as an IPI. For example, the IPI for CLNP is 11000001, and the IPI for the IS-ES routing protocol is 11000011.

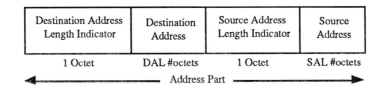

FIGURE 5.3   Address Part of an IP Datagram

The address part (Figure 5.3) contains the source and the destination network addresses. Since OSI addresses are variable in length, the address part contains a source address length (SAL) indicator and a destination address length (DAL) indicator to indicate the length of the respective address fields.

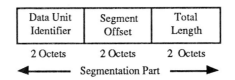

FIGURE 5.4   Segmentation Part of an IP Datagram

Segmentation allows a large datagram to be broken into smaller pieces when it is too large to be transmitted by the underlying subnetwork. CLNP supports the use of a "don't fragment" flag. When this flag is set, segmentation is not allowed. The segmentation part (Figure 5.4), used only if the segmentation permitted flag is set to 1, contains a data unit identifier (identifying a segment), a segment offset from the original TPDU (measured in multiples of 64 bits), and a total length which is equal to the total length of the original TPDU. All the related segments have the same total length value.

The optional part contains optional parameters related to Type 2 and 3 functions (Figure 5.5). Examples of such parameters are:

- source routing which enables the originator of a datagram to dictate the entire route through which a PDU must travel,
- recording of route which allows the originator to indicate that a diagnostic function is to be performed,
- security which assigns a security level to the packet,
- priority which indicates the relative priority of this datagram with respect to other datagrams,
- QOS which specifies reliability and delay values, and
- padding which is used to pad the PDU header to an integral number of octets.

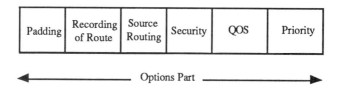

FIGURE 5.5   Options Part of an IP Datagram

The design of connectionless internetworking is reflected in the design of an IP datagram. Some of these issues are mentioned below. First we examine the routing issues. Since there is no connection establishment, the source ES as well as the intervening IWUs (i.e., interworking units) must make some partial routing decision as to where to forward the datagram. Source routing is used when the source ES specifies the entire route through which the datagram must travel. When source routing is not used and an IWU receives a datagram, it must make a routing decision and passes the datagram to the next hop. Thus each IWU maintains a routing table that gives for each destination subnetwork the next IWU to which the datagram should be sent. If an IWU does not recognize the destination address, it will return an error message to the source ES. This error message is different in structure from a datagram carrying data. Because the routing tables maintained by different IWUs may not be well synchronized, it is quite possible that routing loops may occur, causing datagrams to loop indefinitely within the network. A way to tackle this problem is to implement a hop count in each datagram which is initially set to some maximum number of hops. Each time a datagram passes through an IWU, the count is decreased by one. When the count decreases to zero, an IWU simply discards the datagram and returns an error message to the source ES.

Besides performing routing functions, an IWU may also need to perform segmentation of an incoming datagram into smaller pieces before transmitting on to the next subnetwork. Reassembly is normally not performed at an IWU because when dynamic routing is used, there is no guarantee that all the segments of a datagram follow the same route and arrive at the same IWU. Thus, the reassembly function is normally performed at the destination ES.

Protocol combinations to provide CLNS are specified in ISO/IEC 8880-3. For a LAN, connectionless LLC1 is used directly to support the CLNP. For an X.25 subnetwork using the 1984 version, an SNDCP is used in combination with the CLNP.

As X.25 is connection oriented, before an ES wants to send a datagram, an X.25 connection must be established first. Once the data has been sent, the SNDCP then makes local decision to determine whether the connection should be released. If the SNDCP anticipates more data coming, it will keep the connection. The other function of the SNDCP is to embed an IP datagram into the user data field of an X.25 packet.

5.3   Interconnection using IONL

Ideally, it would be desirable to support communication among any combinations of subnetworks which may use different network addressing schemes, different network protocols, and different modes of communication. The current solution is to use IWUs that perform relaying. However, there are practical constraints as the subnetworks may be owned or administered by different organizations. There are also technical constraints as the throughput can decrease and the delay can increase as more subnetworks are involved. Such practical and technical constraints may limit the combinations and configurations of communicating paths in multiple subnetworks. For example, the important consideration for an efficient operation requires that the network protocols on both sides of an IWU be either connection oriented or connectionless and share some common network addressing scheme.

Taking into account of such a wide variance of subnetwork types, ISO/IEC 8648 specified the IONL model which was introduced in Chapter 2. The purpose here is to describe the interconnection strategy using the IONL model.

First, let us examine the protocols found in the sublayers of the IONL model (Figure 5.6).

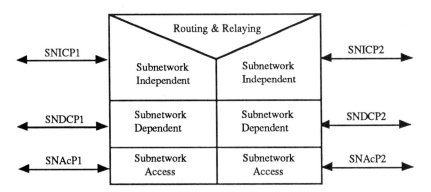

FIGURE 5.6   IONL Model

• subnetwork access sublayer: A **subnetwork access protocol (SNAcP)** operating at this sublayer is a protocol associated with an underlying subnetwork. It may or may not conform to the OSI network service requirements. The X.25 packet level protocol is an example of an SNAcP.

•   subnetwork dependent sublayer: This sublayer is responsible for augmenting the service offered by a subnetwork technology into something close to the OSI network service. A **subnetwork-dependent convergence protocol (SNDCP)** is used for this sublayer. The operation of an SNDCP depends on the network services derived from a particular subnetwork. A common function of an SNDCP is to map between an OSI network address and an SNPA address. The protocol specified in ISO/IEC 8878 is an SNDCP used to augment the 1984 version of X.25 to provide CONS, and the protocol specified in ISO/IEC 8881 is another SNDCP used to augment the services of LLC2 to provide CONS in a LAN.

•   subnetwork independent sublayer: This sublayer provides the OSI network service over a well defined set of underlying capabilities which need not be based on the characteristics of any particular subnetwork. A **subnetwork-independent convergence protocol (SNICP)** is used. It is defined to require a minimal subnetwork service. CLNP is an example of an SNICP.

It is not necessarily the case that each sublayer above is fulfilled individually by a separate protocol. The case where a single network protocol provides the OSI network service may be described as the case where that single protocol fulfills all the defined roles. Currently, no such protocol exists.

In general, there are three basic strategies for the interconnection of subnetworks: interconnection of subnetworks which support all elements of the OSI network service, hop-by-hop enhancement over individual subnetworks, and the use of an internetworking protocol. These strategies are explained below.

In the first strategy, we assume that all the subnetworks involved fully support the OSI network service. Thus, there is no need for an enhancement protocol.

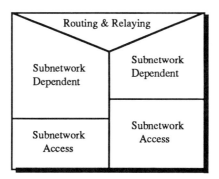

FIGURE 5.7   Hop-by-Hop Enhancement Approach

In the **hop-by-hop enhancement** approach, we assume an environment containing some subnetwork types which do not support the OSI network service. The hop-by-hop enhancement approach takes each of these subnetworks individually and enhances its subnetwork service to the level of the OSI network service. Different

SNDCPs may be required on different subnetworks. Figure 5.7 shows the configuration of an IWU used for such a strategy.

In the **internetworking** approach, again we assume an environment containing some subnetwork types which do not provide the OSI network service. This time we run SNICP on top of every SNAcP in all the ESs and ISs attached to those subnetworks. This SNICP assumes the minimum functionality from each subnetwork. In some cases, it might even duplicate functions already provided in the subnetwork, hence it may be costly. Figure 5.8 shows the configuration of an IWU used for such a strategy. This strategy is most commonly used in the internetworking environment providing CLNS where the SNICP used is CLNP.

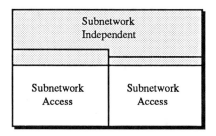

FIGURE 5.8   Internet Approach

We next consider how to apply the above approaches to provide each mode of network service in an interconnection.

First we consider **connection-oriented internetworking (COI)**. CONS is provided in each individual subnetwork using the hop-by-hop approach. An IWU is used to interconnect two or more adjacent subnetworks. ISO/IEC TR 10029 described the operation of an X.25 IWU. A logical connection between two communicating ESs is given by the concatenation of all the intervening logical connections across the subnetworks. Any traffic arriving at an IWU from one connection is retransmitted to the next connection. Thus the operation is very simple. An example to illustrate COI is given below.

Example 5.1

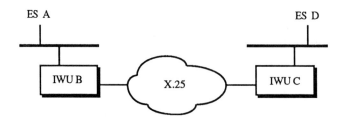

FIGURE 5.9   Connection-oriented Internetworking over Two ESs

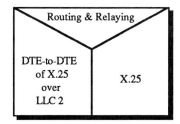

FIGURE 5.10 The Internal Configuration of IWU B

We want to provide COI over a configuration of two communicating ESs (A and D) connected to two separate LANs which are separated by an X.25 network (Figure 5.9). The two IWUs (B and C) are used for the interconnections which behave as DTEs to the X.25 subnetwork. We assume that each ES uses the connection oriented LLC2. Thus the network protocol used between each ES and the local IWU can be the DTE-to-DTE version of X.25 specified in ISO/IEC 8881.

Figure 5.10 depicts the internal configuration of IWU B. It shows the use of an SNDCP on the LAN side. In this scenario, the hop-by-hop enhancement strategy is used for the interconnection. A connection between A and D is obtained as the concatenation of three connections: the first connection between A and B, the second one between B and C, and the third one between C and D.

A point to note here is that when IWU B wants to set up an X.25 connection with IWU C, two addresses are involved: the called DTE address of C, and the called address of D which is an NSAP address. The DTE address of C will be conveyed in the header of a call request packet header while the NSAP address of D is conveyed in the user data field of a call request packet using the optional X.25 user facility.

Next we consider **connectionless internetworking (CLI)**. Every ES or IWU runs CLNP as an SNICP on top of its native SNAcP. For example, if the local system uses X.25, then the user data from the upper layers is first encapsulated in an IP datagram which is then contained in an X.25 packet. An intervening IWU performs routing based on the destination address contained in the header of an IP datagram.

Example 5.2

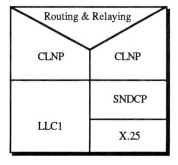

FIGURE 5.11 The Internal Configuration of IWU B using CLI

We want to provide CLI over the configuration in Figure 5.10. This time we assume that connectionless LLC1 is used in ESs A and D. The internal configuration of IWU B is given in Figure 5.11, showing CLNP and the protocol(s) used at each side.

5.4   OSI Routing Framework

Routing deals with the maintenance and the selection of paths through multiple subnetworks to allow PDUs to flow smoothly between ESs. ISO/IEC TR 9575 provides a framework for OSI routing. It has four main sections: routing concepts, environment for OSI routing, goals for OSI routing, and the structure of global OSI routing.

The routing concepts section discussed the major aspects of routing. The four important routing aspects are:

- what routing information is needed?
- how to collect the appropriate routing information?
- how to distribute the routing information to others? and
- how to compute the route based on the collected routing information?

The above considerations lead to the following major routing functions :

- maintaining a routing information base that stores outputs from route calculations, routing updates from other nodes, lists of neighbors, etc.,
- collecting routing information using some routing protocol,
- distributing routing information also using some routing protocol, and
- calculating a route to the next IWU for each destination network.

The environment for OSI routing discussed the various interconnection strategies such as interconnection of LANs, and interconnection of LANs and WANs.

The goals for OSI routing define the general routing principles. The basic principle is that ESs should be kept simple. In general, there are many more ESs than ISs. If possible, one should put the greater complexity in the fewest number of systems. In this way, when the routing protocols change, only a few systems will be affected.

The section on the structure of global OSI routing described an OSI routing architecture. To understand the routing architecture, we need to introduce the notions of a routing domain and an administrative domain. A **routing domain** is a set of ISs and ESs running under the same intra-domain IS-IS routing protocol. An **administrative domain** is a set of ISs and ESs running under a single administration. It may accommodate more than one routing domain with each operating its own IS-IS routing protocol. ISO/IEC TR 9575 divides routing into four functional tiers:

- IS-ES routing, i.e., routing between ESs and ISs,
- intra IS-IS routing, i.e., routing between ISs within a routing domain,
- inter IS-IS routing between ISs in different routing domains, and

- inter IS-IS routing between ISs in different administrative domains.

The first functional tier, IS-ES routing, is the subject of Section 5.6. It provides two kinds of control information to be exchanged among the ESs and ISs. The configuration protocol provides a means for ESs and ISs on a subnetwork to learn of each other's existence. The route redirection provides a means for route redirection information to be sent from an IS to an ES. This allows an IS to inform an ES of a better route towards a given destination. The second functional tier, IS-IS intra-domain routing, is the subject of Section 5.5. It uses a link-state algorithm and a modular approach that divides the routing domain into a 2-level hierarchy. The fourth functional tier, IS-IS inter-domain routing (**policy routing**) is more concerned with firewalls, security, and policy considerations than with performance. Policy routing is still in its infancy. Finally, the third functional tier falls somewhere between tier 2 and tier 4. Presently, there is not much work done for this tier.

5.5   IS-IS Routing

The discussion here is based on ISO/IEC 10589 which specifies an IS-IS intradomain routing protocol used in conjunction with CLNP.

First we review the two well known routing algorithms: vector state algorithm and link state algorithm. In the **vector state algorithm**, an IS periodically sends its routing table to the adjacent neighbors. A routing entry in the routing table is a pair of the form (destination, distance) where the second component gives the distance to the destination in the first component. A receiving IS updates its routing table by simple comparisons and additions. Thus, the processing time is fairly low. However, there are three major drawbacks. First, the routing table sent by an IS can be fairly large because it contains entries for every possible destination. Second, since the routing information propagates from one link to another, routing loops are hard to prevent. Third, it may take considerable time before a remote IS receives the update. In an environment where routes do change quickly, this means that if the route calculation is slow to converge, then an IS may sometimes receive stale information.

The **link state algorithm**, adopted by ISO, requires each IS to maintain a complete topology map. Instead of sending a global routing table to its adjacent neighbors, an IS periodically broadcasts the status of its adjacent links to every IS. The status of a link simply tells whether that link is up or down. On receipt of the link information from other ISs, an IS can build an up-to-date topology map which is modelled as a weighted graph. Using this graph, each IS can apply the **Dijkstra's Shortest Path First (SPF)** algorithm to compute the distance to every destination. The SPF algorithm uses the well known minimum spanning tree algorithm to turn a weighted graph into a tree. Its complexity is of the order of the square of the number of nodes in the graph, assuming a representation of the graph using an adjacency matrix. Since the link state algorithm requires each IS to broadcast its link state status, every IS maintains a consistent view of the entire topology. Thus it precludes two of the major drawbacks such as slow convergence and routing loops associated with the vector state algorithm. Furthermore, since every IS is supposed to have an identical topology map, the faulty ISs are easy to detect. The processing time is considerably higher in the link state algorithm, since an IS may potentially receive link state updates from every IS and the number of link state updates received from an IS can scale as many as the total number of ISs in the entire topology. Thus, the processing time is of the order of the square of the number of ISs.

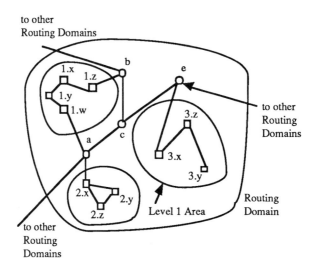

FIGURE 5.12   Two-level Hierarchy of ISs in a Routing Domain

Both link state and vector state algorithms have problems in a very large system. For the link state algorithm, a control burden might result from the distribution of the link status information in a large system. And for the vector state algorithm, a larger system implies slower convergence. A hierarchical construction reduces the amount of routing information maintained at each IS. The idea of reducing complexity using a hierarchical construction is not new. The problem is to determine where and how to define the levels in the hierarchy. A 2-level hierarchy (Figure 5.12) has been chosen. Level 1 ISs form **areas**. Areas are connected by level 2 backbone ISs. The constraint is that level 2 backbone ISs should be fully connected, i.e., any level 2 IS can reach any other level 2 IS by going through only level 2 ISs.

As far as the storage of routing information at each IS is concerned, the 2-level hierarchical design permits a lot of savings. A level 2 IS does not have to store any routing information about level 1 ISs. All it needs to know is the path to its nearest level 1 IS which in turn knows the topology of its own area. As far as level 2 ISs are concerned, each level 1 area is a black box. Similarly, a level 1 IS does not need to store any routing information about level 2 ISs. All it needs to know is a path to its nearest level 2 IS. Thus to relay a message to another level 1 area, a level 1 IS simply forwards the message to its nearest level 2 IS which then computes the shortest path through the level 2 backbone network to the nearest level 2 IS that contains the destination node. This design is modular, as changes at level 2 cause minimal changes to level 1 and vice versa.

When applying the link state algorithm, a level 1 IS in an area only needs to broadcast its link information to level 1 ISs in the same area, while a level 2 IS only needs to broadcast its link information to level 2 ISs. Thus by using hierarchical routing, the scope of broadcast is limited.

As with all other hierarchical routing algorithms, the major penalty paid here is increased path lengths. Routes may not be as good as those found by a "flat" routing scheme. For example, suppose that a message from an ES attached to 1.x is destined to an ES attached to 2.z in Figure 5.12. The path chosen using the hierarchical routing algorithm is 5 hops although the shortest path is only 4 hops.

Flooding is expensive, so the idea is to keep routing updates to the minimum while still keeping track of which neighbors are reachable and which are not. One possible solution, called incremental updates, is to no longer assume that the absence of a neighbor in a routing update indicates that it is unreachable. Instead, anything not listed is assumed to have not changed status. The problem with this partial update is that if a routing update is not received correctly, then the database may be permanently out of synchronization.

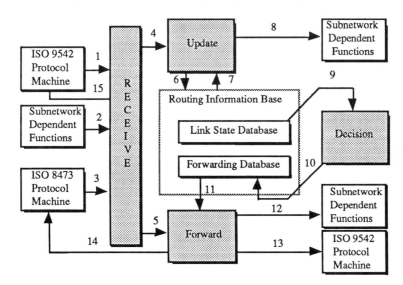

FIGURE 5.13   Design of IS-IS software

Although the link state algorithm and the hierarchical routing are used simultaneously in IS-IS routing, it is important to understand the differences of their roles. The link state algorithm describes the routing entries that an IS should maintain, while hierarchical routing determines the scope of distribution of the routing entries. When used together, a level 1 IS only need to maintain the link information of level 1 ISs in its area.

We have presented the general concept of IS-IS routing over a connectionless subnetwork. Next we explain the design of such software in an IS. Figure 5.13, taken from ISO/IEC 10598, shows that there are four major processes and a routing information database which is made up of a Link State database and a Forwarding database. A routing information database is only a conceptual information model, because, in practice, the routing information is stored in RAM. The four major processes are described below:

- **decision process**

Using the SPF algorithm and the information in the **Link State database**, the decision process calculates routes to each destination in the domain (step 9). It is executed separately within every level for each of the routing metrics supported by the IS. A routing metric can be a delay metric which measures the transit delay, an expense metric which measures the cost, or an error metric which measures the residual error probability. Execution of the decision process results in the determination of adjacency pairs of the form [circuit, neighbor] which are stored in the **Forwarding database** (Step 10).

- **update process**

The update process is responsible for generating and propagating link state information. It performs this by generating **Link State PDUs** as a result of topological changes. Level 1 Link State PDUs are propagated to all the ISs within an area but are not propagated out of an area. Level 2 Link State PDUs are propagated to all Level 2 ISs in the routing domain. Based on Figure 5.13, the update process receives Link State PDUs from the receive process (step 4), places new routing information in the Link State database (step 6), and propagates routing information through Link State PDUs to other ISs (step 8).

- **forwarding process**

The forwarding process supplies and manages the buffers necessary to store datagrams relaying to all destinations. It receives, via the receive process, datagrams to be forwarded (step 5). It performs a lookup in the appropriate Forwarding database (step 11) to determine the possible output adjacencies to use for forwarding to a given destination, chooses one adjacency (step 12), generates error indications to the CLNP protocol machine if necessary (step 14), and signals the ISO/IEC 9542 protocol machine (which performs IS-ES routing) to issue Redirect PDUs (step 13).

- **receive process**

The receive process receives inputs from different sources (steps 1, 2 and 3 in Figure 5.13). It then performs the appropriate actions, which may involve passing the received datagram to the update process (step 4) or the forwarding process (step 5).

5.6 IS-ES Routing

The IS-ES routing exchange protocol provides an automated means for ISs and ESs on a subnetwork to dynamically determine the existence of each other -- **configuration**.

Moreover, it allows an IS to inform an ES of a potentially better route towards a destination -- **route redirection**.

The operation of the IS-ES routing protocol depends on the underlying subnetwork type. ISO/IEC 9542 describes the IS-ES routing protocol used in conjunction with CLNP, while ISO/IEC 10030 describes the IS-ES routing protocol used in conjunction with X.25.

- **IS-ES over the connectionless mode**

There are two types of packets exchanged between ISs and ESs for the purpose of configuration. An **End System Hello (ESH)** packet is periodically generated by an ES and transmitted to every IS on the subnetwork. Similarly, an **Intermediate System Hello (ISH)** packet is generated by an IS and transmitted to every ES on the subnetwork. The primary purpose of a Hello packet is to convey both the SNPA and the network address of a system. The interval between the transmission of Hello packets, known as the **configuration interval**, must be coordinated with the **holding timer** that is transmitted with the Hello packet. The holding timer indicates to the receiving system the number of seconds that the configuration information should be kept. When the holding timer expires, the associated configuration information must be invalidated. Configuration information is normally sent to as many systems as possible in a subnetwork simultaneously. Thus, it is expensive to send configuration information in an X.25 network. When operating over a broadcast network, ESHs and ISHs can be sent to specific multicast addresses, such as "all ISs" or "all ESs".

A **Route Redirection (RD)** PDU, generated by an IS, is used to inform an ES of a potentially better route towards a given destination. The RD PDU may redirect an ES to either the destination ES or a different IS. The lifetime of the information conveyed by the RD PDU is limited by a holding timer. Normally, the redirection information delivered in a RD PDU is specific to a single destination address. However, it is possible for a RD PDU to indicate that the redirection information applies to a larger number of destination addresses. This is accomplished by including an address mask which indicates a larger population of destination addresses.

Example 5.3

Suppose that ES1 wants to send a packet to ES2 located in the same connectionless subnetwork. There are at least three ways to achieve this.

In the first way, ES1 can send it directly to ES2 as long as it knows the SNPA address of ES2. For the remaining ways, we assume that ES1 does not know the SNPA address of ES2. In the second way, ES1 sends a packet to an IS3 located in the same subnetwork. When IS3 receives the data packet from ES1, it decides that ES2 is reachable via the same subnetwork as ES1, and so it forwards the packet to ES2. Note that IS3 knows both ES1 and ES2 because it constantly receives ESH packets from both. In the third way, ES1 does not eavesdrop but instead invokes a function of the IS-ES protocol called query configuration. Essentially, ES1 broadcasts its data packet to all ESs on the subnetwork. When ES2 receives the packet, it knows by the nature of the query configuration packet that ES1 wants to get in touch with it. So ES2 generates an ESH packet and sends it directly to ES1. ES1 can then find out the SNPA address of ES2.

- **IS-ES over the connection-oriented mode**

Based on the use of CONS, ISO/IEC 10030 defines an IS-ES protocol for the exchange of configuration and redirection information between an ES and a **Subnetwork Address Routing Entity (SNARE)**. We will only briefly describe how the configuration information is exchanged.

A SNARE is a network entity which collects configuration information from ESs and distributes configuration and redirection information to them. In order for an ES to exchange configuration information with an SNARE, it must first establish a connection with the SNARE. When the SNARE accepts the call, the ES then transmits its network address to the SNARE. During the connection, the ES may also request information about remote network addresses. When the ES has all the information it requires, it clears the call.

The above procedure assumes that the ES knows at least one SNPA address to access an SNARE. This can be accomplished by an SNARE broadcasting its network address through an **SNARE Hello (SHL) PDU** to the relevant ESs. In case an ES has not received an SHL PDU, it can still discover an SNARE SNPA address by transmitting an **SNARE Request Hello (SRH) PDU** to "all SNAREs" on the subnetwork. An SNARE, on receiving an SRH PDU, then transmits an SHL PDU to that ES.

5.7   Summary

The Network Layer provides a means for network service users to exchange information without concern for the topology of the network and the transmission media in each constituent subnetwork. It is a very complex layer. This is partly due to the fact that many existing subnetwork types do not conform to the OSI network service definition. As a result, ISO defines the IONL model which provides a framework for classifying the network functions into three sublayers. The protocol operating at the lowest sublayer is the protocol associated with an underlying subnetwork. Subnetwork convergence protocols are used in the topmost two layers to augment the service offered by a subnetwork protocol into something close to the OSI network service.

The Network Layer provides both the connection-oriented service and the connectionless service. The network protocol used to provide the connection-oriented service is based on X.25, while the network protocol used to provide the connectionless service is based on IP (Internet Protocol), a protocol used in the TCP/IP communication suite.

Interconnection, which is one of the major functions of the Network Layer, can be described using the IONL model. There are connection-oriented internetworking and connectionless internetworking. In this chapter, we explained three interconnection strategies.

The Network Layer needs to perform routing. Routing is hard in a global network because there are many ESs. ISO/IEC TR 9575 specifies a routing framework, essentially partitioning a network into routing domains where each routing domain can run its own routing protocol. There are interdomain routing protocols as well as intradomain routing protocols. Intradomain routing protocols include protocols to be used among ISs and protocols to be used between ISs and ESs.

The intradomain IS-IS routing protocol essentially partitions the ISs in a routing domain into a 2-level hierarchy. Level 1 ISs forms areas, and areas are connected by level 2 ISs. The constraint is that level 2 ISs should be fully connected.

The intradomain IS-ES routing protocol provides an automated means for ISs and ESs on a subnetwork to dynamically xetermine the existence of each other -- configuration. It alos allows an IS to inform an ES of a potentially better route towards a destination -- route redirection.

Related Standards

ISO 8208: Information Technology - Data Communications - X.25 Packet Layer Protocol for Data Terminal Equipment

ISO 8208 AM 1: Information Technology - Data Communications - X.25 Packet Layer Protocol for Data Terminal Equipment - Amendment 1: Alternative Logical Channel Identifier Assignment

ISO 8208 AM 3: Information Technology - Data Communications - X.25 Packet Layer Protocol for Data Terminal Equipment - Amendment 3: Conformance Requirements

ISO 8348: Information Processing Systems - Data Communications - Network Service Definition

ISO 8348 AD 1: Information Processing Systems - Data Communications - Network Service Definition - Addendum 1: Connectionless Mode Transmission

ISO 8348 AD 2: Information Processing Systems - Data Communications - Network Service Definition - Addendum 2: Network Layer Addressing

ISO 8348 AD 3: Information Processing Systems - Data Communications - Network Service Definition - Addendum 3: Additional Features of the Network Service

ISO 8348 DAM 4: Information Processing Systems - Data Communications - Network Service Definition - Amendment 4: Removal of the Preferred decimal Encoding of the NSAP Address

ISO 8473: Information Processing Systems - Data Communications - Protocol for Providing the Connectionless-Mode Network Service

ISO 8473 PDAD 2: Information Processing Systems - Data Communications - Protocol for Providing the Connectionless-mode Network Service - Addendum 2: Formal Description of ISO 8473

ISO 8473 AD 3: Information Processing Systems - Data Communications - Protocol for Providing the Connectionless-mode Network Service - Addendum 3: Provision of the Underlying Service Assumed by ISO 8473 over Subnetworks which Provide the OSI Data Link Service

ISO 8473 PDAM 4: Information Processing Systems - Data Communications - Protocol for Providing the Connectionless-Mode Network Service - Amendment 4: PICS Proforma and Conformance Clause

ISO 8473 PDAM 5: Information Processing Systems - Data Communications - Protocol for Providing the Connectionless-Mode Network Service - Amendment 5: Provision of the Underlying Service Operation over ISDN Circuit-Switched B-Channel

ISO 8648: Information Processing Systems - Open Systems Interconnection - Internal Organization of the Network Layer

ISO 8878: Information Processing Systems - Data Communications - Use of X.25 to Provide the OSI Connection-mode Network Service

ISO 8878 AD 1: Information Processing Systems - Data Communications - Use of X.25 to Provide the OSI Connection-mode Network Service - Addendum 1: Priority

ISO 8878 AD 2: Information Processing Systems - Data Communications - Use of X.25 to Provide the OSI Connection-mode Network Service - Addendum 2: Use of an X.25 PVC to Provide the OSI CONS

ISO 8878 DAM 3: Information Processing Systems - Data Communications - Use of X.25 to Provide the OSI Connection-mode Network Service - Addendum 3: Conformance

DIS 8880-1: Information Processing Systems - Protocol Combinations to Provide and Support the OSI Network Service - Part 1: General Principles

DIS 8880-2: Information Processing Systems - Protocol Combinations to Provide and Support the OSI Network Service - Part 2: Provision and Support of the Connection-Mode Network Service

DIS 8880-2 DAM 1: Information Technology - Telecommunications and Information Exchange Between Systems - Protocol Combinations to Provide and Support the OSI Network Service - Part 2: Provision and Support of the CONS - Amendment 1: Addition of the ISDN Environment

ISO 8880-2 PDAM 2: Telecommunications and Information Exchange Between Systems - Protocol Combinations to Provide and Support the OSI Network Service - Part 2: Provision & Support of the Connection-Mode Network Service - Amendment 2: Addition of PSTN and CSDN Environments

DIS 8880-3: Information Processing Systems - Protocol Combinations to Provide and Support the OSI Network Service - Part 3: Provision & Support of the Connectionless-Mode Network Service

ISO 8881: Information Processing Systems - Data Communications - Use of the X.25 Packet Level Protocol in Local Area Networks

DIS 8882-1.2: Information Technology - X.25-DTE Conformance Testing - Part 1: General Principles

DIS 8882-2: Information Technology - Telecommunications and Information Exchange Between Systems - X.25-DTE Conformance Testing - Part 2: Data Link Layer Test Suite

ISO 8882-3: Information Technology - Telecommunications and Information Exchange Between Systems - X.25-DTE Conformance Testing - Part 3: Packet Level Conformance Suite

ISO 8882-3 PDAM 1: Information Technology - X.25-DTE Conformance Testing - Part 3: Packet Level Conformance Suite - Amendment 1: Use of Data Link Service Primitives in ISO/IEC 8882-3

ISO 9542: Information Processing Systems - Telecommunications and Information Exchange Between Systems - End system to Intermediate System Routing Exchange Protocol for Use in Conjunction with the Protocol for Providing the Connectionless-mode Network Service

ISO 9574: Information Technology - Telecommunications and Information Exchange Between Systems - Provision of the OSI Connection-mode Network service by Packet Mode Terminal Equipment Connected to an Integrated Services Digital Network

ISO 9574 DAM 1: Information Technology - Telecommunications and Information Exchange Between Systems - Provision of the OSI Connection-mode Network service by

Packet Mode Terminal Equipment Connected to an ISDN - Amendment 1: Operation over an ISDN Circuit-Switched Channel

TR 9575: Information Technology - Telecommunications and Information Exchange Between Systems - OSI Routing Framework

TR 9577: Information Technology - Telecommunications and Information Exchange Between Systems - Protocol Identification in the Network Layer

CD 10028.3: Information Processing Systems - Data Communications - Definition of the Relaying functions of a Network Layer Intermediate System

ISO 10028 PDAM 1: Information Processing Systems - Data Communications - Definition of the Relaying Functions of a Network Layer Intermediate System - Proposed Draft Amendment 1: Connectionless-mode Relaying Functions

DIS 10028-2: Information Technology - Telecommunications and Information Exchange Between Systems - Definition of the Relaying Functions of a Network Layer Intermediate System - Part 2: Connection-mode Network Service

TR 10029: Information Technology - Telecommunications and Information Exchange Between Systems - Operation of an X.25 Interworking Unit

DIS 10030: Information Technology - Telecommunications and Information Exchange Between Systems - End System Routing Information Exchange Protocol for Use in Conjunction with ISO 8878

ISO 10030 PDAM 3: Information Technology - Telecommunications and Information Exchange Between Systems - End System Routing Information Exchange Protocol for Use in Conjunction with ISO 8878 - Amendment 3: Intermediate System Interactions with an SNARE

CD 10030-2: Information Technology - Telecommunications and Information Exchange Between Systems - End System Routing Information Exchange Protocol for Use in Conjunction with ISO 8878 - Part 2: Protocol Implementation Conformance Statement (PICS)

DIS 10039: Information Technology - Local Area Networks - MAC Service Definition

DIS 10177: Information Technology - Data Communications - Intermediate System Support of the OSI Connection-mode Network Service Using ISO/IEC 8208 in Accordance with ISO/IEC 10028

DIS 10733: Information Technology - Telecommunications and Information Exchange between Systems - Elements of Management Information Related to OSI Network Layer Standards

6

Transport Layer

The purpose of the Transport Layer is to provide transparent and reliable data transfer between TS-users (i.e., transport service users).

Like the Network Layer, the service provided by the Transport Layer can be either connection oriented or connectionless. Section 6.1 describes the **connection-oriented transport service (COTS)**. COTS is designed with simplicity in mind so that TS-users can feel that they are given an easy-to-use reliable transport service. On the other hand, the transport protocols that are required to provide the COTS, are quite complex, because they have to cope with an unreliable network. Five connection-oriented transport protocols have been defined by ISO and they are described in Section 6.2. This section also describes the **connectionless transport service (CLTS)**. Section 6.3 describes the X/Open Transport Library Interface which allows network programmers to develop applications on top of the Transport Layer.

6.1 Transport Service

We will first examine COTS. COTS contains only four service elements. A TS-user uses **T-CONNECT** to set up a full duplex transport connection with its peer. During transport connection establishment, the two TS-users and the transport service provider can negotiate the QOS and the expedited data option.

There are two data transfer service elements, T-DATA and T-EXPEDITED-DATA. The **T-DATA** service element is non-confirmed, but still delivers data reliably between TS-users. If any transport failure ever occurs, the transport service provider will notify its TS-users of the failure. The lack of confirmation has to do with a lack of synchronization, not a lack of reliability. If the expedited data option has been selected, then the **T-EXPEDITED-DATA** service element is used to convey expedited data. It has been commonly agreed by implementors that up to 16 octets of expedited data can be carried.

After a connection has been established, either the TS-users or the transport service provider may use the **T-DISCONNECT** service element to release the transport connection. Once this service is invoked, any TSDUs (i.e., transport service data units) or ETSDUs (i.e., expedited transport service data units) in transit may be lost. Thus T-DISCONNECT is destructive. It can be also used for connection rejection by either the transport service provider or the called user.

The service definition of COTS is quite simple. COTS is only an abstract specification. It is not an interface specification. An interface specification contains local processing primitives as well as communication primitives. For example, it may include a primitive by means of which a TS-user can bind to a TSAP, and a primitive for a TS-user to detect the arrival of incoming events from the Network Layer. In Section 6.3, we will examine a transport interface specification by X/Open.

Next we examine CLTS. CLTS provides only one service element, **T-UNIT-DATA**. T-UNIT-DATA has four parameters: source transport address, destination transport address, TS-User-Data, and QOS. Because there is no connection establishment phase, a TS-user cannot negotiate QOS with its service provider. Instead, it is assumed that there is some local means for a TS-user to find out what QOS can be achieved. In this mode of service, there is no guarantee of reliable data transfer. It is left to the upper layers to make the appropriate error recovery.

6.2   Transport Protocols

If the underlying network is fairly reliable, then the transport protocol that is required to accomplish the data transfer does not need to do much work. But if the underlying network is unreliable, then some elaborate transport protocol mechanism is required to cope with the deficiency. ISO has defined five classes of transport protocols, ranging from simple ones to sophisticated ones. During connection establishment, the TEs (i.e., transport entities) negotiate which transport protocol to use based on the QOS parameter requested by the calling TS-user. This allows implementations of more sophisticated transport protocols to provide a superior service to their users whilst retaining interoperation with simpler implementations.

The definitions of the five transport protocol classes depend on the types of network service. ISO identified three types of network services:

- **Type A network service:** Type A network service is essentially perfect. The fraction of packets that are lost, duplicated, or garbled is negligible. N-RESETs are used so rare that they can be ignored. A point-to-point network is an example of a Type A network. Only the simplest possible transport protocol is needed for type A network service.

- **Type B network service:** Type B network service provides network connections with an acceptable residual error rate but an unacceptable signalled failure rate. Residual errors are those that are not corrected, and for which the transport service provider is not notified. On the other hand, a signalled failure is a failure detected by the Network Layer which then signals the TEs for recovery. Examples of signaled failures are internal congestion, hardware problems, or software bugs. It is up to the transport protocol to establish a new network connection and perform resynchronization. Public X.25 networks are of type B.
- **Type C network service:** Type C network service is not reliable enough to be trusted at all, e.g., the residual error rate is unacceptable. These networks do not detect errors if data are lost, duplicated, re-ordered, or corrupted. Transport protocols that must live with class C network service are the most complex of all. A satellite network or an interconnection of LANs and WANs is an example of Type C network.

Based on the three kinds of network services, ISO defines five transport classes:

- TP 0:   Simple class
- TP 1:   Basic error recovery class
- TP 2:   Multiplexing class
- TP 3:   Error recovery and multiplexing class
- TP 4:   Error detection and recovery class

TP 0 and TP 2 are used with Type A networks, TP 1 and TP 3 are used with Type B networks, and TP4 is used with Type C networks. First we give a brief description of these transport classes.

- **TP 0:** TP 0, developed by CCITT for teletex terminals, provides the simplest protocol mechanism to support a Type A network. It does not provide any flow control or connection release service. Its flow control is simply a Network Layer flow control. Its connection release is simply based on the release of the underlying network connection.
- **TP 1:** TP 1, designed to run on top of an X.25 network, provides a connection with minimal service to recover from network signalled failures. This protocol is capable of resynchronization upon receipt of network signalled failures. It is able to reassign a new transport connection in the event of a network failure. Flow control is still provided by the Network Layer.
- **TP 2:** TP 2, basically an enhancement to TP 0, permits multiplexing. To achieve multiplexing, TP 2 provides an explicit flow control because the implicit flow control that is provided by the Network Layer cannot control each individual data flow in the multiplexed transport connections. It is used to support a Type A network.

- **TP 3:** TP 3 is basically a combination of TP 1 and TP 2. It allows an explicit flow control and has the ability to recover from a network failure. It is used to support a Type B network.
- **TP 4:** TP 4 is designed for type C network service. It is the most sophisticated transport protocol. It must be able to handle lost, duplicate, and garbled packets, as well as network failures.

In Section 6.2.1, we examine the structure and encoding of TPDUs which are the objects exchanged by the communicating TEs. In Section 6.2.2, we examine the transport protocol procedures associated with the different transport classes.

6.2.1 Transport PDUs

Length Indicator	Fixed Part	Variable Part	User Data

FIGURE 6.1   Format of a TPDU

The general format of a TPDU is shown in Figure 6.1. A TPDU consists of four parts: a length indicator, a fixed header, a variable header, and a user data field. The latter two fields may not be present. The length indicator specifies the length of a TPDU excluding itself. The fixed part of the header contains parameters that commonly occur. These parameters include the 4-bit TPDU code which indicates the type of the TPDU, the source reference, the destination reference, the sequence number, and the credit allocation. The variable header contains infrequently occurring parameters and variable sized parameters. Most of the parameters in the variable part are used by the CC and CR TPDUs in the connection establishment procedure.

Code	Name
CR	connection request
CC	connection confirm
DR	disconnect request
DC	disconnect confirm
DT	data
ED	expedited data
AK	data acknowledge
EA	expedited acknowledge
RJ	reject
ERR	TPDU error

TABLE 6.1   Transport PDUs

The transport standard defines a total of ten TPDUs (Table 6.1). The examples below illustrate a few of them.

Example 6.1

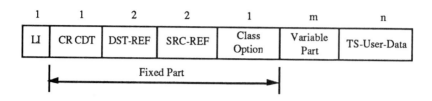

FIGURE 6.2 Encoding and Fields of a CR TPDU

Figure 6.2 gives the encoding and fields of a CR TPDU. The first octet in the fixed part contains the type code of a CR TPDU and a flow control credit indicator (CDT). The source (destination) reference is used by a TE to identify a transport connection in the calling (called) system. These reference parameters are needed because two communicating TS-users can engage in more than one transport connection. The class option indicates one of the five transport classes. Although user data may be conveyed during connection establishment, there is currently no provision for a session entity to pass data prior to the establishment of a transport connection, i.e., no session/transport embedding is allowed. The variable part may contain a checksum (TP4 only), the calling and the called transport selectors, the proposed maximum TPDU size, the version number of transport protocol, the alternate protocol classes (which a TE is willing to negotiate down to), the option selection (which is used to specify use or nonuse of functions such as a checksum in TP4 and acknowledgement in TP1), the QOS parameter, and an acknowledgement timer value. The maximum TPDU size is used to determine a CDT value which is recorded in a CC TPDU and is conveyed to the sending TE. The sending TE uses the acknowledgement timer returned by the receiving TE to compute the retransmission timer value.

Example 6.2

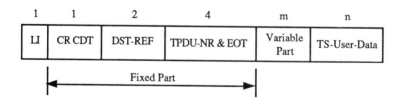

FIGURE 6.3 Encoding and Fields of a DT TPDU

Normal data transfer over a connection is accomplished using DT PDUs. In case a TSDU plus the DT header exceeds the maximum size of a TPDU negotiated during connection establishment, the TE may segment the TSDU and send it out as a sequence of TPDUs. The last TPDU in the sequence has the EOT bit set to 1. A DT TPDU has two formats. They differ in the presence of the destination reference field. The destination reference field is not needed if multiplexing is not allowed. Thus Classes 0 and 1 do not carry the destination reference field because they do not support multiplexing. Figure 6.3 shows the encoding and format of a DT TPDU used for TP 2, TP 3, and TP 4. For the flow control and resequencing purposes, DTs are numbered sequentially in the TPDU-NR field. The variable part contains a checksum field which is unique to TP4.

Example 6.3

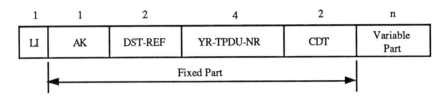

FIGURE 6.4   Encoding and Fields of an AK TPDU

Figure 6.4 gives the encoding and structure of an AK TPDU. Each receiving TE maintains a receive credit window which reflects the number of credits sent by a sending TE for a transport connection. At the same time, each sending TE maintains a send credit window which reflects the number of DT TPDUs that are sent in a transport connection. The YR-TPDU-NR (i.e., your TPDU number) parameter indicates the sequence number of the next DT TPDU that a receiving TE expects from a sending TE. The credit CDT parameter indicates how many more DT TPDUs the receiving TE can let the sending TE send. Note that the acknowledgement of DT TPDUs is decoupled from the credit based flow control mechanism. To illustrate this point, we consider an example. Suppose the last AK TPDU issued by a receiving TE contains the values YR-TPDU-NR and CDT. Even when no additional TPDUs have arrived, the receiving TE can modify its credit by issuing an AK TPDU with the values YR-TPDU-NR and CDT' where CDT' can be either greater than or less than CDT. When a new TPDU arrives and the receiving TE decides not to increase the credit, it can issue an AK TPDU with the values YR-TPDU-NR + 1 and CDT' - 1.

6.2.2   Transport Protocol Procedures

When a TE processes an event, it will call a transport procedure. The transport standard defined a total of twenty three procedures. Each transport class uses only a subset of these procedures. The relationship between these procedures and the five transport classes is summarized in Table 6.2. A procedure marked with "x" in a protocol class means that it is mandatory while the one marked with "o" means that it is optional.

The operation of TP 0 requires the following eight procedures:

• **assignment to a network connection**

This procedure, common to all classes, assigns either an existing or a new network connection to a new transport connection. Whether a transport connection uses an existing or a new network connection, the network connection must meet the QOS requested by the TE.

Elements of Procedure	Variant	Protocol Class 0	1	2	3	4
(1) Assignment to network connection		x	x	x	x	x
(2) TPDU transfer		x	x	x	x	x
(3) DT TPDU length and segmenting		x	x	x	x	x
(4) Concatenation and separation			x	x	x	x
(5) Connection establishment		x	x	x	x	x
(6) Connection refusal		x	x	x	x	x
(7) Normal release	Implicit	x				
	Explicit		x	x	x	x
(8) Error Release		x		x		
(9) DT TPDU numbering	Normal		x	x	x	x
	Extended			o	o	o
(10) Expedited data transfer	Normal		x	x	x	x
	Expedited		o			
(11) Association of TPDUs with TC		x	x	x	x	x
(12) Reassignment after failure			x		x	
(13) Retention until acknowledgement of TPDUs	Confirmation		o			
	Receipt ACK		x		x	x
(14) Resynchronization			x		x	
(15) Multiplexing and demultiplexing				x	x	x
(16) Explicit flow control	With			x	x	x
	Without	x	x	o		
(17) Checksum	Use of					x
	Non-use of	x	x	x	x	o
(18) Frozen references			x		x	x
(19) Retransmission on time-out						x
(20) Resequencing						x
(21) Inactivity control						x
(22) Treatment of protocol errors		x	x	x	x	x
(23) Splitting and recombining						x

TABLE 6.2 Transport Protocol Procedures

- **TPDU transfer**

This procedure, which is common to all transport classes, uses the normal and expedited data services provided by the Network Layer to transfer TPDUs. The sending TE can transmit a number of DT TPDUs up to the specified credit.

- **segmentation**

Because of operating system constraints, a sending TE may need to segment a TSDU into an ordered sequence of DT TPDUs. Reassembly is performed by the receiving TE before an indication primitive is issued to the receiving TS-user.

- **connection establishment**

In all transport classes except TP 4, a two way handshake protocol is used for connection establishment. This involves the sending of a CR TPDU by the initiating TE followed by the sending of a CC TPDU by the responding TE. If a transport connection cannot be accepted, the responding TE shall respond to the CR TPDU with a DR TPDU.

- **implicit normal release**

This procedure applies to TP 0 only. TP 0 assumes a one-to-one correspondence between a network connection and a transport connection. A connection release is achieved by a TE issuing an N-DISCONNECT.request primitive to the Network Layer. When the peer TE receives an N-DISCONNECT.indication primitive, it assumes that the transport connection has been released. Note that no TPDUs are exchanged in this procedure.

- **error release**

When a signalled failure or an N-DISCONNECT.indication primitive is received from the network service provider, the simple transport protocol mechanism used by TP 0 and TP 2 simply releases the transport connection without providing any recovery actions.

- **association of TPDUs with transport connections**

Whenever a TE receives a TPDU from the Network Layer, it will map the TPDU to an appropriate transport connection.

- **treatment of protocol errors**

If the received TPDU cannot be mapped to a transport connection, it is considered to be a protocol error. The detecting TE sends an ER TPDU to its peer, with the received TPDU embedded in the user data part of the ER TPDU.

The purpose of TP 1 is to recover from network resets which can frequently occur in an X.25 network. In addition to the above procedures (except implicit normal release and error release), the following eight procedures are used by TP 1.

- **concatenation and separation**

The purpose of concatenation is to improve efficient use of a network connection. In this procedure, a number of TPDUs can be concatenated into a single NSDU for transmission, and later on separated by the receiving TE. A TE may concatenate TPDUs from the same or different transport connections while maintaining the order of TPDUs for a particular transport connection. The transport protocol standard imposed certain rules on how the

TPDUs can be concatenated. For example, one of the rules says that any TPDU containing user data must be the last TPDU in the concatenated set.

- **explicit normal release**

The explicit normal release procedure is used by a TE to terminate a transport connection. Instead of issuing an N-DISCONNECT.request primitive (as in the case of implicit release), a TE sends a DR TPDU to its peer. Upon receiving the DR TPDU, a TE responds with a DC TPDU unless it has previously sent a DR TPDU. Note that when multiplexing is allowed (as in the case for TP 2, TP 3, and TP 4), explicit normal release is the means to release one of the multiplexed transport connections, whereby the network connection is still maintained.

- **DT TPDU numbering**

To facilitate the use of resynchronization, flow control, and resequencing, it is necessary for each DT TPDU to carry a sequence number. The sequence count field is 7 bits long, but may be extended to 31 bits for TP 2, TP 3, and TP 4.

- **expedited data transfer**

This procedure places expedited user data into the data field of an ED TPDU. All the transport classes but TP 1 use the normal network data transfer service to deliver expedited transport data. Although the expedited transport data service is non-confirmed, the transport protocol requires that each ED TPDU be acknowledged using an EA TPDU. For each direction of data flow, there is at most one outstanding unacknowledged ED TPDU. Hence, hardly any flow control mechanism is used for expedited data.

- **reassignment after failure**

When a TE receives a network signalled failure, it calls this procedure to take care of the problem. The result is that the transport connection is assigned to a different network connection. This network connection may be an existing one owned by the TE or a newly created one. When the reassignment is achieved, the resynchronization procedure is invoked.

- **retention until acknowledgement of TPDUs**

This procedure, applying to TP 1, TP 3, and TP 4, provides a mechanism for the sending TE to retain copies of the TPDUs which were sent until it receives an acknowledgement. Should no acknowledgement be received before a certain period of time has elapsed (TP 4) or should a signalled failure occur (TP 1, TP 3, and TP 4), the unacknowledged TPDUs are retransmitted.

- **resynchronization**

This resynchronization procedure is used by TP 1 and TP 3 to restore a transport connection upon receipt of an N-RESET.indication from the Network Layer. It may involve the retransmission of the unacknowledged TPDUs.

- **frozen references**

This procedure is used to prevent re-use of source/destination references because the TPDUs associated with the old references may still exist somewhere in the network. When a TE determines that a particular connection has been released, it freezes the references which were allocated to the connection. This procedure is invoked when abnormal termination occurs during the data transfer phase.

In addition to the above functions (except DT TPDU numbering, reassignment after failure, resynchronization, and frozen references), TP 2 also performs multiplexing and explicit flow control.

- **multiplexing and demultiplexing**

The multiplexing procedure allows multiple transport connection to share a single network connection. The receiving TE must perform demultiplexing.

- **explicit flow control**

The explicit flow control procedure is used to regulate the flow of DT TPDUs between the TEs. This flow control is independent of the flow control present in the Network Layer. It is optional in TP 2 and mandatory in TP 3 and TP 4. It uses a credit based sliding window scheme (Example 6.3). The receiving TE uses the window to control the flow from its peer. It can modify its credit at any time by sending a window update to the sending TE via an AK TPDU. It uses a RJ TPDU to inform its peer to decrease the size of the window.

The procedures used by TP 3 are a union of the procedures described earlier for TP 1 and TP 2. Minor exceptions from TP 1 are that first, TP 3 uses N-DATA to carry expedited data, and second, TP 3 can use an extended sequence count field of 31 bits.

TP 4 has to provide error detection and recovery. Besides using many of the above procedures (Table 6.2), TP 4 also uses the following procedures.

- **checksum**

This procedure is mandatory for the CR TPDU which is used during the connection establishment phase. Its use is optional during the data transfer phase and is negotiated during connection establishment.

• **retransmission on timeout**

A sending TE uses a local **retransmission timer** T to determine the appropriate time to retransmit a TPDU. A small value of T can detect losses quickly but may inject unnecessary packets into the network. The value may be calculated according to the following formula: $T = kE + AK$, where E is the current estimate of the round trip delay, AK is the value of the acknowledgement parameter received from the remote TE during connection establishment, and k is some weight factor.

• **resequencing**

This procedure is used to sort any misordering of DT TPDUs which may be caused by the underlying network.

• **inactivity control**

This procedure deals with the unsignalled termination of a network connection or the failure of the peer TE (half open connections). It is invoked upon the expiration of an **inactivity timer** which measures the period over which no TPDU is received. It is reset any time when a TPDU is received from a remote TE. To prevent expiration of the remote TE's inactivity timer when no data is being sent, a local TE may send "dummy" AK TPDUs to the remote TE at regular intervals.

• **splitting and recombining**

To achieve a higher throughput or a greater resilience against network failures, this procedure allows a transport connection to be assigned to multiple network connections. Note that the use of splitting may cause the TPDUs to arrive out of sequence.

• **three way handshake connection establishment**

Unlike other transport classes which use a two way handshake for connection establishment, TP 4 uses a three way handshake for connection establishment. The only addition is that after receiving a CC, the initiator must respond. If it has a data request, it responds with a DT or an ED TPDU. Otherwise, it responds with an AK or a RJ TPDU.

Figure 6.5, showing the normal operation of a three way handshake, indicates the use of source and destination reference numbers (i.e., #x and #y). The need for a response from the initiator following the receipt of a CC TPDU stems from the fact that duplicate TPDUs generated as a result of retransmission may hang around in the network after a transport connection has been released. Thus, a TE may receive an old CR or CC TPDU during connection establishment.

In Figure 6.6, B receives an old CR TPDU with a source reference number x, thinking that A wants to establish a connection. B responds with a CC TPDU with its own reference number y. Upon receiving the CC TPDU from B, A responds with a RJ TPDU telling B that the CR TPDU that it received earlier is an old one.

In Figure 6.7, A wants to connect to B by sending a CR TPDU with source reference number x. While waiting for a CC TPDU from B, A receives an old CC TPDU with a source reference number different from x. Therefore, A sends a RJ TPDU to B. When AS finally receives a proper CC TPDU from B, it can then send either a DT or an AK TPDU to B.

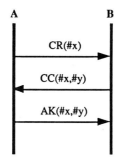

FIGURE 6.5   Normal Operation of the Three Way Handshake

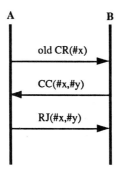

FIGURE 6.6   The Case where an Old CR TPDU is received

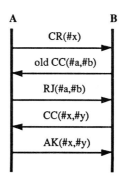

FIGURE 6.7   The Case where an old CC TPDU is received

We have briefly explained the transport protocol procedures. The complexity of TP 4 can be judged from the number of timers that a TE must maintain. We have already seen the use of the retransmission and inactivity timers. Besides these timers, there are also the **persistence timer,** the **window timer,** and some other timers. The persistence timer is used to abort a connection when no TPDUs are acknowledged after a number of retrys. For the window timer, recall that a receiving TE uses an AK TPDU to send its window update to the sending TE. Consider the following situation where a receiving TE wants to close its window by sending a window update with no credit shown. Later on, it sends a different window update with credit. Suppose that the second TPDU is lost. A deadlock occurs because the sending TE which might have data to transmit never receives the window update TPDU, and the receiving TE thinks that it has already informed the sending TE of the window increase. To remedy this situation, a receiving TE maintains a window timer. The value of the **window timer** is set to the maximum time a receiving TE will wait before it transmits a second window update. Thus, whenever an AK is sent, this window timer is reset. Whenever this timer expires, the same AK is retransmitted.

Readers familiar with TCP may find a lot of similarity between the functionalities of TP 4 and TCP. However, there are some differences, some of which are noted below:

- TP 4 uses a destructive disconnect while TCP uses a graceful release. Consequently, TCP uses a three way handshake while TP 4 uses a two way handshake for connection release.
- TP 4 uses a message(i.e., TSDU)-oriented interface while TCP uses a byte-stream oriented interface.
- TP 4 uses a variable sized OSI transport address while TCP uses a fixed size 16 bit address which is also known as a port.
- TP 4 treats the expedited data flow and the normal data flow separately. TCP combines both normal and urgent (i.e., expedited) data in the same data flow.

When the TP 4 checksum is on, the throughput of TP 4 is considerably lower than that of TCP. This is due to the fact that the TP 4 checksum is octet-oriented.

The operation of the **Connectionless Transport Protocol (CLTP)** is very straightforward. On receipt of a valid T-UNIT-DATA.request primitive, the TE generates a UD (UNIT-DATA) TPDU. The UD TPDU contains a calling transport selector, a called transport selector, and a TS-User-Data parameter. It also contains a protocol version number which is provided by the TE. If the length of a TPDU exceeds the maximum NSDU size, then the TE discards the T-UNIT-DATA.request and reports the problem to its TS-user. Otherwise, the TE issues an N-UNIT-DATA.request primitive.

6.3 XTI

Heavily influenced by the OSI transport service definition, AT&T defined the **Transport Level Interface (TLI)** as a programming interface to any transport service provider. It is up to the user of the TLI to specify a transport service provider. TLI is a language dependent API made up of a library of C routines. Because of the significant use of TLI for network programming, X/Open included a minor modification of TLI in its CAE (i.e., Common Applications Environment). The modified version is called **XTI (X/Open Transport Interface)**.

XTI describes a TSAP as a **transport endpoint (TEP)**. The first step in establishing a TEP is to call t_open() with a parameter identifying a particular transport provider. The other parameter associated with t_open is t_info which can be described in C as follows :

```
struct t_info {
    long addr;          /*max size of transport address*/
    long options;       /*max #bytes of protocol-specific options*/
    long tsdu;          /*max size of a TSDU*/
    long etsdu;         /*max size of ETSDU*/
    long connect;       /*max amount of user-data on connection establishment*/
    long discon;        /*max amount of data on disconnection request*/
    long servtype;      /*service type supported*/
};
```

Information regarding the transport service provider is returned to the caller in the above information parameter. t_open() also returns a file descriptor to be used by other XTI functions in the future.

Every TEP has a state which can be modified by events. Because the transport service interface is inherently asynchronous, simultaneous events can occur independent of the actions of a TS-user. The following nine asynchronous events have been identified to cover both the connection oriented mode and the connectionless mode:

- T_LISTEN: This event signals that a connection request from a peer has arrived.
- T_CONNECT: This event signals that a connection confirmation has arrived.
- T_DATA: This event signals that normal data are received.
- T_EXDATA: This event indicates that expedited data are received.
- T_DISCONNECT: This event signals that a disconnection indication has arrived.
- T_ORDREL: This event signals that an orderly release indication has arrived.
- T_UDERR: This event, applied to a connectionless mode only, signals that an error is found in a previously sent datagram.
- T_GODATA: This event signals that flow control on normal data flow has been lifted, enabling normal data to be sent again.
- T_GOEXDATA: This event signals that flow control on expedited data has been lifted, enabling expedited data to be sent again.

All events occurring at a TEP can be retrieved one at a time via t_look(). Every event has a corresponding event clearing function. Unless an event is cleared, it will remain outstanding at a TEP.

Different transport service providers may have different transport address formats. Because XTI wants to accommodate a variety of transport service providers, it does not constrain the format of a transport address. Thus a XTI transport address is simply defined as a sequence of bytes. When t_open() is called, XTI will return with the maximum address length via t_info. A TS-user can call t_alloc() to dynamically allocate memory to a transport address structure based on the returned information from t_open(). Later on, t_free() can be called to release the memory allocated by t_alloc(). Once the address is in a format suitable for the specific transport service provider, a TS-user can use t_bind() to bind a transport address to the TEP. A TS-user can be bound to more than one TEP.

XTI supports two modes for handling events: synchronous (blocking) mode and asynchronous (nonblocking) mode. The mode can be set by using the O_NONBLOCK flag which is passed as a parameter to t_open(). Synchronous mode, the default mode of execution, is useful for applications that need to wait for events to occur, or applications that maintain only a single transport connection. Furthermore, if an application needs to maintain more than one transport connection, the asynchronous mode is better as it would not force the user to wait for the events at a TEP. Suppose that a user wants to receive data via the t_rcv() function in the asynchronous mode. If data is not available, then t_rcv() returns a failure to the caller immediately. At this point, the user has two alternatives. One is to keep on polling for incoming data by repeating the call to t_rcv(). The other is to use t_look() to check for any outstanding events. On the other hand, if the user wants to receive data using the synchronous mode and no data is available, then the call is blocked until either the data, a disconnection indication, or an interrupt signal has arrived.

For the connection-oriented mode, XTI provides functions for the following four phases: initialization/deinitialization, connection establishment, data transfer, and connection release. In this overview, we will only mention the mandatory functions. The following functions are mandatory for the initialization/deinitialization phase:

- **t_open**: This function creates a TEP and returns a file descriptor and protocol specific information associated with the TEP.
- **t_bind**: This function binds a transport address to a TEP, thereby activating it. It also directs the transport service provider to begin accepting connection indications.
- **t_unbind**: This function disables a TEP.
- **t_close**: When the user finishes using a TEP, it calls this function to free the TEP.

Once a TEP has been created and bound to a transport address, a connecting TS-user can use the TEP to connect to a peer, and a listening TS-user can use the TEP as a listening endpoint to receive and enqueue incoming connection indications. The number of outstanding connection requests is limited by the value of the qlen parameter of t_bind(). Overall, the following functions are mandatory for the connection establishment phase:

- **t_connect**: This function requests a connection to a remote TS-user. In the asynchronous mode, this function returns control to the local TS-user before a response arrives.

• **t_rcvconnect**: Used in conjunction with t_connect() in an asynchronous mode, this function allows a TS-user to determine the status of a t_connect() call sent previously.
• **t_listen**: This function allows a listening TS-user to receive connection indications.
• **t_accept**: This function allows a listening TS-user to accept a connection request after it receives an indication.

Once a transport connection has been established, data can be sent or received. XTI supports two modes of data transmission: record-oriented and stream-oriented. In the stream-oriented mode, message boundaries are not preserved, whereas in the record-oriented mode, message boundaries are preserved. Overall, the following XTI functions are mandatory for the data transfer phase are:

• **t_snd**: This function allows a TS-user to send data over a transport connection. There is a parameter in the call to indicate whether the data is expedited or not.
• **t_rcv**: This function allows a TS-user to receive data over a transport connection.

XTI supports both the destructive disconnect and the orderly release. However, its support for the orderly release is optional. The following XTI functions are mandatory for the connection release phase are the following:

• **t_snddis**: A TS-user uses this function to initiate a destructive disconnect or to reject a connection request during the connection establishment phase.
• **t_rcvdis**: This function gives the reason for the destructive disconnect of a transport connection.

The connectionless mode XTI consists of only two phases: initialization/de-initialization and data transfer. The functions that support the initialization/de-initialization phase are the same functions used in the connection mode service. Thus before sending or receiving data units, a TS-user first has to create a TEP and bind to a transport address. The following XTI functions are mandatory for the data transfer phase:

• **t_sndudata**: This function allows a TS-user to send a datagram.
• **t_rcvudata**: This function allows a TS-user to receive datagrams.
• **t_rcvuderr()**: This function allows a TS-user to retrieve error information associated with a previously sent datagram.

Other than the functions mentioned above, there are two other mandatory local management functions which can be issued during any phase. They are:

• **t_look**: This function returns the current event(s) associated with a TEP.

- **t_sync**: Note that a transport service provider treats all users of a TEP as a single user. So if multiple processes use the same endpoint, synchronization is required among the processes so that the state of the TEP remains consistent. This function returns the current state of a TEP to its user, thereby enabling the user to verify the state before taking any further actions.

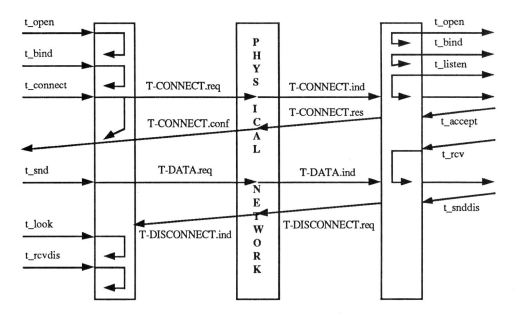

FIGURE 6.8   **Mapping between XTI Functions and Transport Service Primitives**

The next two examples show how the TLI function calls are used in a typical client-server interaction for the two different modes of communication.

Example 6.4

This example illustrates the operation of a server. In the connection-oriented mode, the server first calls t_open(), t_alloc(), t_bind(), and t_listen() in sequence. It then calls t_accept() to accept a connection request. In the connectionless mode, the server first calls t_open(), t_alloc(), and t_bind() in sequence. It then calls t_rcvudata() to indicate that it is ready to receive data.

Example 6.5

This example illustrates the operation of a client. In the connection-oriented mode, the client first calls t_open(), t_alloc(), and t_bind() in sequence. Then it makes a connection request by calling t_connect(). In the connectionless mode, the client first calls t_open(), t_alloc(), and t_bind() in sequence. It then sends data by calling t_sndudata().

It should be apparent from this overview on XTI that there is a clear distinction between the abstract OSI transport service definition and a programmable transport interface. Figure 6.8 shows a partial mapping between the XTI functions and the OSI transport service primitives.

6.4 Summary

The purpose of the Transport Layer is to provide a reliable transport service to its users. Although the transport service definition is quite simple, the transport protocol specification is complicated because it has to cope with the reliability issues. ISO defines five transport protocols to provide the connection-oriented transport service. It also defines a connectionless transport protocol although no existing OSI application protocol uses the connectionless transport service.

At the end of the chapter, we described XTI which is an API on the Transport Layer. This interface is designed to be independent of the underlying transport service provider.

Related Standards

ISO 8072: Information Processing Systems - Open Systems Interconnection - Transport Service Definition

ISO 8072 AD 1: Information Processing Systems - Open Systems Interconnection - Transport Service Definition - Addendum 1: Connectionless-mode Transmission

ISO 8073: Information Processing Systems - Open Systems Interconnection - Connection Oriented Transport Protocol Specification

ISO 8073 AD 1: Information Processing Systems - Open Systems Interconnection - Connection Oriented Transport Protocol Specification - Addendum 1: Network Connection Management Subprotocol

ISO 8073 AD 2: Information Processing Systems - Open Systems Interconnection - Connection Oriented Transport Protocol Specification - Addendum 2: Class Four Operation Over Connectionless Network Service

ISO 8073 AM 3: Information Processing Systems - Open Systems Interconnection - Connection Oriented Transport Protocol Specification - Amendment 3: PICS Proforma

ISO 8073 PDAD 4: Title Information Processing Systems - Open Systems Interconnection - Connection Oriented Transport Protocol Specification - PDAD 4: Protocol Enhancements

ISO 8602: Information Processing Systems - Open Systems Interconnection - Protocol for Providing the Connectionless-Mode Transport Service
DP 10025: Information Processing Systems - Transport Conformance Testing for Connection Oriented Transport Protocol Operating Over the Connection Oriented Network Service - Part 1: General Principles

CD 10025-3: Information Technology - Telecommunications and Information Exchange between Systems - Transport Conformance Testing for Connection Oriented Transport Protocol Operating over the Connection Oriented Network Service - Part 3: Transport Test Mgmt Protocol

TR 10172: Information Technology - Telecommunications and Information Exchange between Systems - Network/Transport Protocol Interworking Specification

CD 10736: Information Technology - Telecommunications and Information Exchange between Systems - Open Systems Interconnection - Transport Layer Security Protocol

CD 10737: Information Processing Systems - Open Systems Interconnection - Transport Layer Management

7

Session Layer

When two application processes communicate with each other, it is desirable to have a third process to organize their dialogues and regulate their data flow so that they can concentrate on the information that they are exchanging. A session entity (SE) is a process for this purpose. With the help of the Session Layer, a session dialogue can be structured into distinct non-overlapping activities. Each activity represents a logical unit of work. In turn, each activity can be structured into dialogue units. Furthermore, SS-users (i.e., session service users) can interact with each other in either a half duplex mode or a full duplex mode.

Unlike the lower layers, the service definition of the Session Layer contains quite a number of service elements. One of the debating questions in OSI is whether we do need all the session functionalites in a real application.

An overview of the session facilities is given in Section 7.1. Here, we describe the major tools used by the Session Layer to structure a session dialogue. The service elements contained in each facility are then explained in Section 7.2. Despite the use of many service elements, the operation of the session protocol is fairly straightforward. Basically, most session requests or responses are mapped one-to-one into corresponding session PDUs (SPDUs). Section 7.3 describes the session protocol.

The connection-oriented session service definition and protocol specification are given in ISO/IEC 8826 and 8827 respectively.

7.1   Session Concepts

The Session Layer has two major functions. The first function is to add structure to the transport data stream. The second function is to regulate the data flow between the two SS-users.

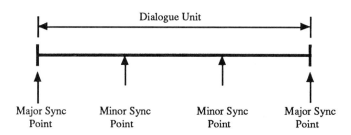

FIGURE 7.1 An Example of a Dialogue Unit

Let us examine the first function which adds structure to the transport data stream. There are two ways to organize a **session dialogue**. One uses the notion of an activity and the other doesn't. In the one not using activity, we insert **major synchronization points** into the data stream to break the stream into **dialogue units**. Thus, a major synchronization point indicates either the end of a dialogue unit, the start of another, or both. Semantically, inserting a major synchronization point means that all the data sent or received prior to that point has been properly processed by both SS-users. In the case that the mode of communication is full duplex, two major synchronization points should be used, with one for each direction. The reason is that a dialogue unit, treated as a unit of a session dialogue, should include data in both directions.

Within each direction of a dialogue unit, checkpoints can be added by using **minor synchronization points** (Figure 7.1). At any given instance, one can only add a minor synchronization point in one direction. This is one of the differences between the use of major and minor synchronization points. Another difference is that although a major synchronization point must be acknowledged immediately, a minor synchronization point does not have to be acknowledged right away. The use of minor synchronization points facilitates the process of recovery. Whenever resynchronization is needed during recovery, an SS-user can resynchronize the dialogue to the previous confirmed minor synchronization point within the current dialogue unit. Application protocols such as CCR or TP relies on the resynchronization facility to perform rollback.

Whether it is major or minor, each synchronization point has a serial number, the **synchronization point serial number (SPSN)**. The session service provider increments the SPSN by one for each synchronization point inserted by an SS-user. While the session service provider maintains and regulates the serial numbers, it makes no association of the serial numbers to any data exchanged between the SS-users. It is the responsibility of the SS-users to properly interpret the SPSNs within the context of their application.

The second way to organize a session dialogue involves the use of **activities**. Conceptually, an activity represents a logical piece of work. A session dialogue can be structured into one or more activities. Activities do not necessarily map to a session connection. A session connection may contain one or more activities (Figure 7.2). It is also possible for a single activity to span over several session connections (Figure 7.3). Internally, an activity can be further structured into one or more dialogue units using major synchronization points. The end of an activity or the beginning of a new activity is indicated by a major synchronization point. Thus overall, a session dialogue is a three level structure. At the topmost level, the dialogue is structured into activities. At the second level, each activity is structured into dialogue units. At the third level, each dialogue unit is structured using minor synchronization points.

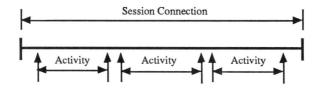

FIGURE 7.2   Activities of a Session Connection

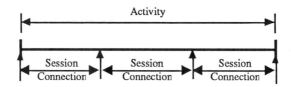

FIGURE 7.3   An Activity Spans over Consecutive Session Connections

The activity management service also allows an SS-user to interrupt an activity or resume an old activity. When an activity is interrupted, the session service provider remembers the last serial number used, but the SS-user has to save any context information that will be needed for the resumption.

The second function of the Session Layer is to regulate the data flow between the two communicating SS-users. The major tool used here is the token management facility. A **token** is an attribute of a session connection. It is dynamically assigned to one of the two communicating SS-users to permit certain services to be invoked. For example, only the owner of the **data token** can send data. In this way, data can be sent in a half-duplex mode even though the underlying transport connection is full-duplex. There are three other tokens used for dialogue control. The **major synchronization/activity token** is used to govern the setting of major synchronization points and to manage the activities. Only the owner of the major synchronization/activity token can insert a major synchronization point to mark the beginning of a dialogue unit, the end of a dialogue unit, the beginning of an activity, or the end of an activity. The **minor synchronization token** is used to govern the setting of minor synchronization points. Only the owner of the minor synchronization token can insert a minor synchronization point within a dialogue unit. The **release token** permits the negotiation of a release. Only the owner of the release token can initiate the negotiated release procedure. The meaning of a negotiated release will be explained later. Any one of the above four tokens is available only if the communicating SS-users agree to use the corresponding functional unit during the session connection establishment. If a token is available, the initial token owner is determined during the connection establishment phase. Thereafter, ownership can change hand. The token management facility provides service elements to allow an SS-user to request a token from its peer.

The Network Layer and the Transport Layer provide only two types of data transfer facilities: normal data transfer and expedited data transfer. With the addition of structure to a transport data stream, some more data transfer facilities are needed. For example, an SS-user not owning the data token may need some means to send control information to its peer. The Session Layer provides four data transfer facilities. The **normal data transfer facility** is used to send normal data in either full duplex or half duplex mode. If the half-duplex mode is chosen, only the owner of the data token can send data. The **expedited data transfer facility** allows an SS-user to send expedited data. In practice, the maximum size of expedited data that can be sent is fourteen octets. The **typed data transfer facility** allows an SS-user to send **typed data** outside the normal data stream and independent of the availability and assignment of the data token. When used properly, this facility gives SS-users a mixed half/full duplex mode which is useful in many applications. The **capability data transfer facility** allows SS-users to exchange limited amount of **capability data** while they are not engaged within an activity. This facility is mainly used to transmit control information without going through the overhead of setting up an activity. No major synchronization point can be inserted within capability data, because major synchronization points are used to structure data but not control information.

The Session Layer provides another useful facility, called the **exception reporting** facility. This exception reporting facility can be used by either an SS-user or a session service provider. Suppose an SS-user detects an abnormal situation that requires an immediate action. Instead of aborting the session connection, it may choose to report an exception to its peer. Upon receiving the exception notification, the SS-user must try to clear the exception by either resynchronizing or aborting the session connection. The session service provider can raise an exception to the SS-users when it detects an internal error.

Recall that the Transport Layer provides a destructive release service. What if an application want an orderly release instead? Thanks to the Session Layer, an SS-user can invoke either an orderly release or a destructive release. The Session Layer provides two kinds of orderly release, **negotiated release** and **non-negotiated release**. The distinction between the two forms of release is based on the availability of a release token. If this token is not available, then release cannot be negotiated, i.e., once a release is requested, the release must be accepted by the peer on receipt of the release indication. If the release token is available, then the release can be negotiated, enabling an SS-user to reply negatively to the release request. For example, an SS-user may choose to reply negatively to a release request if it has some more data to send. Only the owner of the release token can initiate the release procedure. For a destructive release, the Session Layer provides an abortive service which can be either user-initiated or provider-initiated. An SS-user can invoke the user-initiated abort service if it detects a catastrophic error. When a session service provider detects an internal error, it can use the provider-initiated abort service to release a session connection.

Functional Units	Facilities	Token
Kernel	Session connection normal data transfer control release	
Negotiated release Half-duplex Duplex		release data
Expedited data	expediated data transfer	
Typed data	typed data transfer	
Capability data	capability data	
Minor synchronize	minor synchronization point	minor sync/act
Symmetric synchronize	symmetric synchronization	
Major synchronize	major synchronization point	major sync/act
Resynchronize	resynchronize	
Exceptions	exception report	
Activity management	activity management	major sync/act
Token management	token management	

TABLE 7.1   Functional Units and the Associated Facilities

The above session facilities can be grouped into functional units to facilitate negotiation during a connection establishment. At the beginning of a connection establishment, both the calling and the called SS-users specify the functional units which they wish to use. The intersection of the two sets of selections determines which functional units are active during the session connection. There are altogether fourteen functional units (Table 7.1). The Kernel functional unit supports the basic session facilities to establish a session connection, transfer normal data, and release a session connection. Table 7.1 also specifies the type of tokens used in some functional units. When a functional unit implies the requirement of a token, the token management facility must be available in order to request and transfer the token.

Subsets are defined by implementors to group logically related functional units for particular applications. The grouping is not arbitrary. For example, since capability data is sent between two activities, a subset containing the Capability Data functional unit must also contain the Activity Management functional unit. Some of the common subsets are **BCS (Basic Combined Subset), BAS (Basic Activity Subset),** and **BSS (Basic Synchronization Subset).** BCS is used for simple applications, hence it contains only the Kernel, Half Duplex, and Full Duplex functional units. BAS is used primarily for MHS applications. It uses the Activity Management functional unit to provide a reliable message transfer. Finally BSS is used primarily for FTAM applications. For example, it uses the Resynchronize functional unit to do file recovery.

7.2 Session Service

In this section, we examine the service elements associated with each session facility. There are a total of twenty two session service elements.

- **session connection facility**

Parameter \ Primitive	S-CONNECT			
	Request	Indication	Response	Confirm
session connection identifier	U	C(=)	U	C(=)
calling session address	M	M		
called session address	M	M		
responding session address			M	M
result			M	M(=)
quality of service	M	M	M	M
session requirements	M	M(=)	M	M(=)
initial synchronizatin point serial number	C	C(=)	C	C(=)
initial assignment of tokens	C	C(=)	C	C(=)
SS-User-Data	U	C(=)	U	C(=)

TABLE 7.2   Parameters Associated with the S-CONNECT Service Primitives

A SS-user uses **S-CONNECT** to establish a session connection with its peer. Parameters such as functional units, initial SPSNs, and initial token settings are negotiated during the connection establishment. Table 7.2 shows the parameters associated with each S-CONNECT service primitive. The meanings of some of the parameters are explained below:

- session connection identifier: This parameter is used to identify a session connection. The actual structure of the session connection identifier is implementation defined. It may contain a calling session reference, a called session reference, or a common reference.
- QOS: This parameter is used to express session service performance or other session characteristics such as extended control, session connection protection, session connection priority, and optimized dialogue transfer. The **extended control parameter** (a boolean parameter), when enabled, will direct an SE to bypass the normal flow control restrictions when attempting a destructive data action. For example, if an SE decides to discard an activity, it uses the extended control service to send a priority message, known as the **PR (prepare) SPDU**, over the expedited transport data transfer service. The purpose of the PR SPDU is to prompt the peer SE

to start discarding SPDUs received from the network until an SPDU with a special mark is encountered. The **optimized dialogue transfer parameter** (a boolean parameter), when enabled, allows an SS-user to batch several session service primitives together for transmission in a single unit. This in turn allows the session protocol machine (SPM) associated with the SE to perform concatenation of SPDUs. More on concatenation will be discussed at the end of this chapter.

• session requirements: This is a list of the functional units which an SS-user is willing to employ.

• initial synchronization point serial number (ISPSN): If any synchronization functional unit is used for a session connection, then the ISPSN must be negotiated. However, if the Activity Management functional unit is chosen, then there is no need to negotiate the ISPSN because the ISPSN is always set to "1" at the beginning of an activity. Whenever an SS-user inserts a synchronization point, the SPSN is incremented by one. An SPSN does not wrap around, so it is the responsibility of SS-users to keep the serial number within bounds. The **Symmetric Synchronization** addendum was introduced to support the full duplex mode. According to this addendum, if the Symmetric Synchronization functional unit is chosen for the session connection, then two ISPSNs must be negotiated, one for each direction. Furthermore, an SS-user must specify two SPSNs when it wants to add a major synchronization point.

• initial assignment of tokens: The negotiation of the initial assignment of a token deals with the initial ownership of the token. For each token, the value in a request/indication may be one of the following: "calling session service user", "called session service user", or "called session service user decides". The "called SS-user decides" value is used if the calling SS-user invites the called SS-user to determine the initial assignment.

• SS-user-data: This parameter is used to carry user information. For example, a presentation connection request PDU can be embedded in this parameter. The called session service user can also use this parameter to pass information such as acceptance or rejection of a session connection. Version 1 of the session protocol standard restricts the size of the SS-user-data to be a maximum of 512 octets. However, version 2 relaxes this size to a maximum of 10,240 octets. Considering the fact that the SS-user-data may contain application entity titles which are distinguished names, version 1 should be ruled out in any practical application.

Of all the above parameters, only the calling/called session address and the session requirements parameters are mandatory. The called SS-user can respond either positively or negatively to the request. Thus, either an S-CONNECT.confirmation (accept) or an S-CONNECT.confirmation (reject) is passed back to the calling SS-user. The session service provider may also reject a connection establishment request. For example, if the called SS-user is not attached to the called session address, then the session service provider may return to the calling SS-user with the result "reject by SS-provider" and the reason "transient (i.e., the calling SS-user should not try again in a short time)".

- **normal data transfer facility**

Normal data is sent using **S-DATA**. This is a non-confirmed service element. It has a single mandatory parameter, SS-user data. Although the session standard did not impose a bound on the size of normal data, any session implementation would specify a bound.

- **expedited data transfer facility**

Expedited data is sent using **S-EXPEDITED-DATA**. The maximum size of expedited data sent at one time is 14 octets, due to the limitations imposed by the expedited transport data facility.

- **typed data transfer facility**

S-TYPED-DATA, a non-confirmed service element, is used to send typed data outside the normal data stream. For example, this can be used by a presentation entity to negotiate a transfer syntax for an abstract syntax introduced during the data transfer phase. The user of the data transfer facility is not required to own any data token.

- **capability data exchange facility**

S-CAPABILITY-DATA, a confirmed service element, is used to carry capability data in between two activities. For example, at the end of an activity, two SS-users can use capability data to decide which activity to start next. The reason why this service element is made confirmed is that unless a confirmation is received, the sender of S-CAPABILITY-DATA cannot know when to start the next activity.

- **token management facility**

There are three token management services, all of which are non-confirmed. An SS-user uses **S-TOKEN-GIVE** to surrender a token to its peer. It may use **S-CONTROL-GIVE** to surrender the entire set of available tokens. It uses **S-TOKEN-PLEASE** to request its peer to relinquish the ownership of one or more tokens.

- **minor synchronization point facility**

The owner of the minor synchronization token can use **S-SYNC-MINOR** to insert a minor synchronization point in the data flow. This service can only be used for normal or typed data. One of the parameters of S-SYNC-MINOR is the type parameter. The value of the type parameter is either confirmed or non-confirmed. In most cases, the value of the type parameter is set to non-confirmed. If the requesting SS-user needs a confirmation of a minor synchronization point, it sets the type parameter value to confirmed. An explicit confirmation of a minor synchronization service is similar to a confirmed normal data service, but has the advantage of identifying checkpoints in the data flow if resynchronization becomes necessary.

If every minor synchronization point is confirmed, then network traffic is increased. An efficient approach to reduce the network burden is to use a sliding window technique. Applications negotiate the window size as part of the initialization procedure so that the receiver is aware that it must confirm minor synchronization points within the defined window size. Before the window reaches its maximum size, a confirmation should be sent to confirm all the previously non-confirmed minor synchronization points.

• **major synchronization point facility**

The owner of a major synchronization/activity token (and the data and minor synchronization tokens if available) can use **S-SYNC-MAJOR** to insert a major synchronization point in the data flow. A major synchronization point signals either the end of a dialogue unit or the beginning of a new dialogue unit. Unlike the minor synchronization service, this service may be used with expedited data. S-SYNC-MAJOR has only two parameters: the SPSN parameter which gives the next serial number for the session connection, and the SS-user-data parameter .

The session standard imposes some constraints on the use of S-SYNC-MAJOR. For example, it said that after a requesting SS-user issues an S-SYNC-MAJOR.request primitive, it must wait for an S-SYNC-MAJOR.confirm primitive. The only primitive that it is allowed to issue while it is waiting is an S-TOKEN-GIVE.request or a destructive primitive such as an S-ACTIVITY-INTERRUPT.request primitive, an S-U-ABORT.request primitive, or an S-RESYNCHRONIZE.request primitive.

• **symmetric synchronize facility**

This facility allows SS-users to establish major synchronization points in both directions. This is necessary when SS-users want to communicate in a full duplex mode. Thus major synchronization primitives used with this facility carry two serial numbers, one for each direction of the data flow.

• **activity management facility**

If the Activity Management functional unit is active, then five activity management service elements are available. They are S-ACTIVITY-START, S-ACTIVITY-END, S-ACTIVITY-INTERRUPT, S-ACTIVITY-RESUME, and S-ACTIVITY-DISCARD. All except S-ACTIVITY-START and S-ACTIVITY-RESUME are confirmed. An SS-user issuing an activity request primitive must own the major synchronization/activity token, and the data and the minor synchronization tokens if they are available.

Referring to Figure 7.4, an SS-user can initiate a new activity using **S-ACTIVITY-START**. When an activity is started, a major synchronization point is implicitly issued (this is why a single major synchronization/activity token is used instead of two separate tokens) and the value of the next SPSN is set to one. S-ACTIVITY-START has only two parameters: an activity identifier parameter to identify the activity, and an SS-user-data parameter.

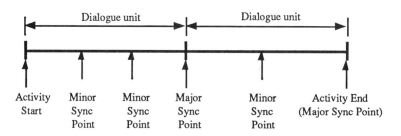

FIGURE 7.4   Structuring an Activity into Dialogue Units

An SS-user invokes **S-ACTIVITY-END** to complete an activity. When the activity is ended, a major synchronization point is implicitly issued.

An SS-user can interrupt the current activity using **S-ACTIVITY-INTERRUPT,** possibly resuming it later on. S-ACTIVITY-INTERRUPT is confirmed. Its use may cause loss of data in transit. Upon completing S-ACTIVITY-INTERRUPT, all available tokens must be transferred to the requesting SS-user. Confirmation is needed here so that the requesting SS-user has all the available tokens before it can initiate another activity.

An SS-user uses **S-ACTIVITY-RESUME** to resume a previously interrupted activity. It may provide a new activity identifier, an old activity identifier identifying the activity to be resumed, and an SPSN. If the resumed activity was originally started on some previous session connection, the session connection identifier of that session connection must be also provided. The SPSN indicates the point at which the activity should be resumed. A new activity identifier should be used whenever the old activity identifier has some conflict with an activity identifier in the current session connection. If the Symmetric Synchronization functional unit is active, then two SPSNs are provided, one for each direction. When the accepting SS-user receives an S-ACTIVITY-RESUME.indication, it should retrieve all the information associated with the previously interrupted activity from its stable storage. Although S-ACTIVITY-RESUME is non-confirmed, an implicit major synchronization point is added to the data flow.

A SS-user can terminate an activity abruptly by using **S-ACTIVITY-DISCARD.** On completion of this service, all the available tokens are transferred to the requesting SS-user. Confirmation is needed here so that the requesting SS-user has all the available tokens before it initiates another activity.

• **exception reporting facility**

When an SS-user does not own the data token, it may use **S-U-EXCEPTION-REPORT,** a non-confirmed service element, to report an exception to its peer. If the session service provider detects some internal error, it can use **S-P-EXCEPTION-REPORT** to indicate the malfunction to both SS-users. Both S-P-EXCEPTION-REPORT and S-U-EXCEPTION-REPORT are destructive. An SS-user can try to clear an exception by giving up the data token, resynchronizing the dialogue, issuing an activity interrupt or discard, or aborting the session connection.

- **resynchronization facility**

An SS-user can reset the session dialogue to a known state using **S-RESYNCHRONIZE** which is a confirmed service element. There are three types of resynchronization. The **abandon** type simply discards the current dialogue and the session service provider then assigns the next unused serial number to the connection. The **restart** type is used to return to an agreed point no earlier than the last confirmed major synchronization point. Finally the **set** type is used to synchronize to any valid synchronization point specified by the SS-users. Theoretically, a requesting SS-user can set to a future point. It may also set to a previous non-confirmed minor synchronization point if it guesses that its peer has secured all the data before the non-confirmed point. Besides carrying the type parameter, S-RESYNCHRONIZE also carries the assignment of token parameter. The requesting SS-user uses the assignment of tokens parameter to indicate who should own the available tokens after resynchronization. There are three possible choices: "requesting SS-user", "accepting SS-user", and "accepting SS-user chooses".

It is possible for both SS-users to issue a S-RESYNCHRONIZE.request primitive simultaneously. To resolve those colliding requests which are destructive in nature, the session standard defined a set of rules. The following destructive service primitives are given from highest to lowest precedence: S-U-ABORT.request, S-ACTIVITY-DISCARD.request, S-ACTIVITY-INTERRUPT.request, S-RESYNCHRONIZE.request (abandon > set > restart), and S-U-EXCEPTION-REPORT.request. The requesting SS-user who issues a session service primitive with a higher precedence wins the collision. If both SS-users request the same type of resynchronization, then the request with the lower SPSN takes precedence. Implicit in the collision rules is that the SS-user requesting S-U-ABORT.request is always the winner.

- **session connection release facility**

A session connection can be released in either an orderly or destructive manner. **S-RELEASE**, a confirmed service element, releases a session connection in an orderly manner. When the Negotiated Release functional unit is active, the result parameter of an S-RELEASE.response primitive is used to indicate whether or not the session connection release should be granted. **S-U-ABORT**, a non-confirmed service element, releases a session connection in a destructive manner. A session service provider uses **S-P-ABORT** to indicate to its SS-user the release of the session connection because of some internal malfunction. Like S-U-ABORT, S-P-ABORT is destructive.

We have completed our discussion on the connection-oriented session service. The session standard also defined a connectionless session service. Considering the fact that the purpose of the Session Layer is to add structure to a transport data stream, one can immediately conclude that in the absence of a session connection, the connectionless session service does not provide any extra service other than what is provided by the connectionless transport service. OSI defines the connectionless session service and protocol because the layering principle requires a connectionless presentation service to access a connectionless session service first before it can access a connectionless transport service. An implementation would obviously want to violate this layering principle to avoid any inefficiency.

The connectionless session service is defined in ISO/IEC 8326 DAD 3. There is one confirmed service element, **S-UNIT-DATA**, which carries parameters such as calling and called session addresses, QOS, and SS-user-data.

7.3   Session Protocol

In Section 7.3.1, we examine the structure of an SPDU (i.e., session PDU). In Section 7.3.2, we examine some of the session protocol procedures.

7.3.1   Structure of an SPDU

The session protocol uses a total of thirty six types of SPDUs (Table 7.3). It is not surprising due to the large number of session service elements. The session protocol maps most of the session service primitives to the corresponding SPDUs in a one-to-one manner.

Like any PDUs in other layers, an SPDU consists of a header and user data. Let us examine the structure of a header. The first octet of a header is an SPDU identifier (SI) which specifies the type of the SPDU. The second octet (LI) indicates the length of the header. The rest of the header contains parameters whose sizes are variable. As some SPDUs such as CN and AC may contain quite a number of parameters, it makes sense to combine the related parameters into a parameter group. For example, it may combine all the mandatory parameters in one group, and all the optional parameters in another group. Thus within the header of an SPDU, one may find either a single parameter (Example 7.1), a set of parameters, a single parameter group, or several parameter groups.

Next, we examine the structure of a parameter and a parameter group. Every individual parameter is structured into three fields: a PI field identifying the parameter, an LI field indicating the length, and a PV field containing the parameter value. Likewise, every parameter group is structured into three fields: a PGI field identifying the group, an LI field indicating the length of the parameter group, and a value field made up of the various parameters constituting the group. Figure 7.5 gives an example of a parameter group containing two parameters. Note that the first LI indicates the length of the parameter group, while the second and the third LIs indicate the lengths of the two parameters.

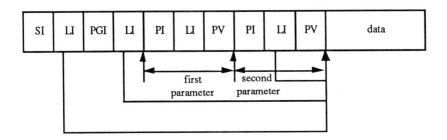

FIGURE 7.5 An Example of a Parameter Group

Code	Name	Code	Name
CN	connect	MIP	minor sync point
AC	accept	MIA	minor ack
RF	refuse		
FN	finish	MAP	major sync point
DN	disconnect	MAA	major ack
AB	abort	PR	prepare
AA	abort accept		
DT	data transfer	RS	resync
		RA	resync ack
PT	please token		
GT	give token	EX	expedited data
GTA	give tokens ack		
GTC	give tokens confirm	AS	act start
		AR	act resume
ER	exception report	AI	act interrupt
ED	exception data	AIA	act interrupt ack
		AD	act discard
TD	typed data	ADA	act discard ack
		AE	act end
NF	not finished	AEA	act end ack
CDO	connect data overflow	CD	capability data
OA	overflow acknowledge	CDA	capability data ack

TABLE 7.3 Session PDUs

Example 7.1

The GT SPDU does not contain any parameter group. Instead, it contains only the token parameter which indicates which tokens are surrendered by the requesting SS-user.

Example 7.2

The CN SPDU contains two parameter groups. The first parameter group contains information about the session connection identifier such as the calling SS-user reference, the common reference, and the additional reference. None of the information in this group is mandatory. The second parameter group contains parameters such as protocol options, the version number, the TSDU maximum size, the ISPSN, the token setting item, session user requirements, the calling session selector, and the called session selector, all but the first two are not mandatory.

7.3.2 Session Protocol Procedures

The SPM maps session service primitives to SPDUs. In many cases, one can guess how the SPDUs are exchanged from the use of the session service primitives. Although not always true, a confirmed session service element would result in the exchange of two SPDUs: a request SPDU and a response SPDU. Table 7.4 shows the possible request and response SPDUs being used for each session service element. The generation of some of the SPDUs, however, depends on whether the extended control QOS parameter is enabled during connection establishment. In the following, we will rely on examples to illustrate some of the session procedures.

Session Element	Request SPDU	Response SPDU
S-CONNECT	CN	AC
S-SYNC-MAJOR	MAP	MAA
S-SYNC-MINOR	MIP	MIA
S-RESYNCHRONIZE	RS	RA
S-ACTIVITY-END	AE	AEA
S-ACTIVITY-INTERRUPT	AI	AIA
S-ACTIVITY-RESUME	AR	
S-ACTIVITY-DISCARD	AD	ADA
S-TOKEN-GIVE	GT	GTA
S-CAPABILITY-DATA	CD	CDA
S-RELEASE	FN	DN or NF
S-U-ABORT	AB	AA

TABLE 7.4   Mapping Session Service Elements to SPDUs

Example 7.3

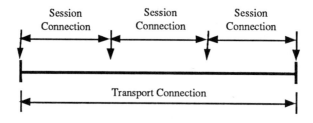

FIGURE 7.6   A Transport Connection over Several Session Connections

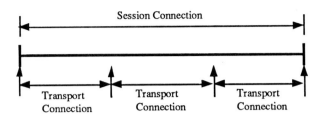

FIGURE 7.7 A Session Connection over Consecutive Transport Connections

At any given instant, there is a one-to-one relationship between a session connection and a transport connection. The Session Layer does not perform any multiplexing although a transport connection can support consecutive but non-overlapping session connections (Figure 7.6). A session connection can span over several consecutive transport connections (Figure 7.7).

Only the SE which is the initiator of a transport connection is permitted to issue a CN SPDU. This takes care of the problem of the collision problem during the session connection establishment. A connection request may be responded positively with an AC SPDU or negatively with an AB SPDU. The responding SS-user may accept the connection request but proposes session parameters which are unacceptable to the initiating SS-user. In this case, the initiating SS-user can abort the session connection by issuing an S-U-ABORT.request primitive. This will trigger an AB SPDU sent by the initiating SE. The responding SE will respond with an AA SPDU.

Example 7.4

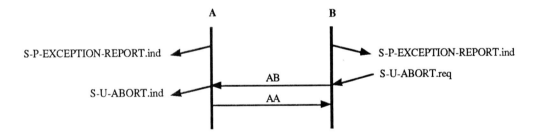

FIGURE 7.8   Session Service Provider Raising an Exception

In Figure 7.8, an S-P-EXCEPTION-REPORT.indication is indicated to both SS-users. On receiving the indication primitive, an SS-user may resynchronize the state to some previously defined state or abort the connection. A decision to abort will trigger the requesting SE to send an AB SPDU. If the extended control QOS parameter is set, the AB SPDU is sent using the expedited transport data flow. The accepting SE will respond with an AA SPDU.

One may wonder why the AA SPDU is needed at all. Consider the case that the SS-user who aborted earlier wants to establish another session connection using an existing transport connection. The receipt of the AA SPDU informs the requesting SE that its peer is ready for a new session connection, hence it can start sending data to the reused transport connection.

Example 7.5

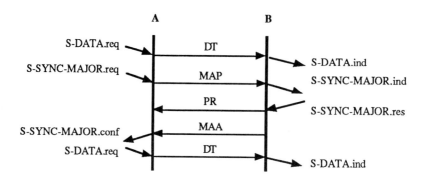

FIGURE 7.9   SPDUs Exchanged using Major Synchronization

Figure 7.9 shows the exchange of SPDUs using major synchronization when the extended control QOS parameter is enabled. An S-SYNC-MAJOR.request triggers an MAP SPDU to be sent to the other side. Upon receipt of a response from the SS-user, the accepting SE will send a PR SPDU on the expedited transport flow (assuming that the extended control QOS parameter is set) and an MAA SPDU on the normal transport flow. The PR SPDU alerts the requesting SE that an MAA is arriving on the normal transport flow. Recall that after issuing an S-SYNC-MAJOR.request primitive, the requesting SS-user is limited to the invocation of very few session primitives until it receives a confirmation. Thus, the receipt of a PR SPDU allows the requesting SE to prepare for receiving more primitives from its SS-user. A PR SPDU can be also used in conjunction with the RS, RA, AI, AIA, AD, ADA, and AEA SPDUs.

Example 7.6

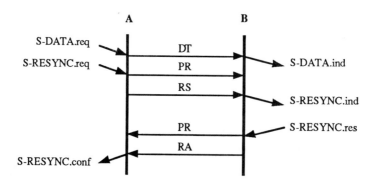

Figure 7.10   Use of PR SPDUs with RS and RA SPDUs

Figure 7.10 shows further use of PR SPDUs in conjunction with RS and RA SPDUs. This time, a PR SPDU is sent in either direction. The use of a PR SPDU can purge incoming SPDUs on the transport normal data flow unintentionally.

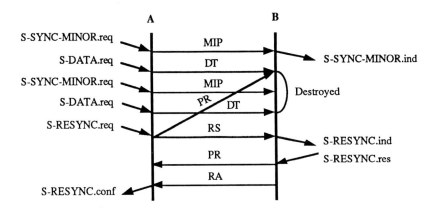

FIGURE 7.11   **Destruction of Minor Synchronization Points by the PR SPDU**

Figure 7.11 shows that a PR SPDU destroys one or more minor synchronization points. The accepting SE receives a PR SPDU prior to the arrival of DT and MIP SPDUs. Thus, it discards the incoming SPDUs until it spots the RS SPDU. Since the accepting SE discards an MIP SPDU unintentionally, upon receipt of the RS SPDU, it acknowledges the requesting SE with PR and RA SPDUs indicating a serial number less than the one proposed by the requesting SE. The CCR and TP protocols experience such an undesirable situation when they attempt to use the resynchronization service.

Example 7.7

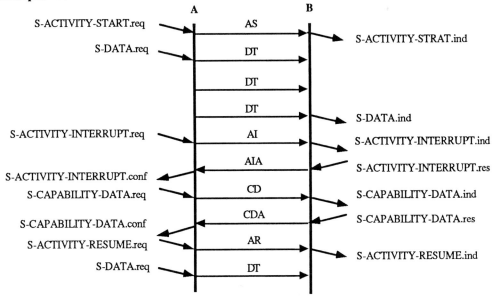

FIGURE 7.12   **The Use of Activity Management SPDUs**

Figure 7.12 illustrates the use of activity management SPDUs.

Example 7.8

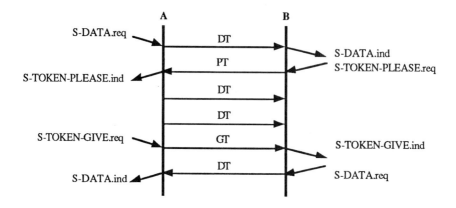

FIGURE 7.13   Use of Token Management

Figure 7.13 illustrates token management. Note that on receiving the S-TOKEN-PLEASE.indication primitive, A is under no duress to surrender the token. Instead, it sends some more data before it issues an S-TOKEN-GIVE.request primitive.

Example 7.9

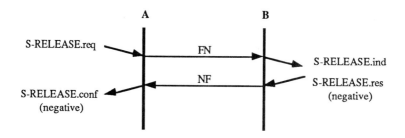

FIGURE 7.14   Negotiated Release

While a non-negotiated release results in the exchange of FN and DN SPDUs, a negotiated release allows an SS-user to reply negatively to the release request by sending an NF SPDU (Figure 7.14).

Internally, an SPM may perform segmentation and concatenation which are invisible to its SS-users. We have seen that segmentation is performed by both the Network Layer and the Transport Layer. If the transport software is implemented in the kernel of the operating system and the session software is implemented as user code, then operating system buffer constraints may require an SPM to perform segmentation.

As a way to minimize the number of interactions at the session/transport interface, an SPM can concatenate a number of SPDUs into a single TSDU. There are two kinds of concatenation. **Basic concatenation** permits concatenation of two SPDUs while

extended concatenation permits concatenation of up to four SPDUs. Extended concatenation is possible only if the optimized dialogue transfer QOS parameter is enabled. Not every arbitrary set of SPDUs can be concatenated. The session standard divided SPDUs into three categories. Category 0 SPDUs may be mapped one-to-one onto a TSDU or can be concatenated with up to three category 2 SPDUs. Examples of category 0 SPDUs are GT and PT. Category 1 SPDUs are always mapped one-to-one onto a TSDU. Examples of category 1 SPDUs include EX, PR, TD, and those used for connection establishment, connection release, and connection abort. Category 2 SPDUs are never mapped one-to-one onto a TSDU. Examples of category 2 SPDUs include DT, synchronization related SPDUs, activity management SPDUs, exception reporting SPDUs, and capability SPDUs. The category 2 SPDUs are processed in a certain order before they are concatenated with a category 0 SPDU. For example, an activity start SPDU or an activity resume SPDU must be processed before a data transfer SPDU which in turn must be processed before a synchronization related SPDU or an activity end SPDU. Here are some examples of legal concatenations:

- a data transfer SPDU (category 2) followed by a token give SPDU (category 0), and
- an activity start SPDU (category 2) followed by a data transfer SPDU (category 2) followed by a token give SPDU (category 0).

7.4 Summary

The primary purpose of the session service is to organize a session dialogue, and to manage the data exchange between two communicating SS-users.

To organize a session dialogue, the Session Layer adds structure to a transport pipe. A session connection can be structured into activities. Different activities represent different logical pieces of work. An activity can be structured further into dialogue units. With the use of this structure, the Session Layer provides service elements for activity management and dialogue control. The dialogue control facilities allow an SS-user to insert either major synchronization points or minor synchronization points. Major synchronization points are used to separate dialogue units whereas minor synchronization points can appear anywhere within a dialogue unit. A resynchronization service is also provided to assist orderly re-establishment of communication.

To manage the data exchange, the session services provides four kinds of data transfer facilities: the normal data transfer facility, the expedited data transfer facility, the typed data transfer facility, and the capability data transfer facility. The normal data transfer facility can operate in either full duplex or half duplex mode. Only the owner of the data token can send data. The typed data transfer facility allows an SS-user to send data outside the normal data stream independent of the availability and the assignment of the data token. Finally, the capability data transfer facility allows SS-users to exchange limited amounts of user data while not within an activity.

The Session Layer provides orderly release, a service not provided by the Transport Layer. With the use of a release token, an orderly release can be negotiated between two SS-users. An SS-user can reply negatively to a release request if it has some more data to send.

Despite the large number of session service elements, the session protocol machine does not have to worry about the reliability problem of the underlying network. Indeed, the session protocol machine operates in a very straightforward manner. The only interesting aspect is the use of the prepare PDU by a session entity to alert the remote session entity of what it might receive. The prepare PDU is sent over an expedited transport flow. On receipt of a prepare PDU, a session entity might purge incoming session PDUs. This might create problems for some application protocols such as TP and CCR.

Related Standards

ISO 8326: Information Processing Systems - Open Systems Interconnection - Basic Connection Oriented Session Service Definition

ISO 8326 DAD 1: Information Processing Systems - Open Systems Interconnection - Basic Connection Oriented Session Service Definition - Addendum 1: Session Symmetric Synchronization for the Session service

ISO 8326 DAD 2: Information Processing Systems - Open Systems Interconnection - Basic Connection Oriented Session Service Definition - Addendum 2: Incorporation of Unlimited User Data

ISO 8326 DAD 3: Information Processing Systems - Open Systems Interconnection - Basic Connection Oriented Session Service Definition - Addendum 3: Connection-mode Session Service

ISO 8326 DAM 4: Information Processing Systems - Open Systems Interconnection - Basic Connection Oriented Session Service Definition - Proposed Draft Amendment 4 to Incorporate additional synchronization Functionality

ISO 8327: Information Processing Systems - Open Systems Interconnection - Basic Connection Oriented Session Protocol Specification

ISO 8327 DAD 1: Information Processing Systems - Open Systems Interconnection - Basic Connection Oriented Session Protocol Specification - Addendum 1: Session Symmetric synchronization for the Session Protocol

ISO 8327 DAD 2: Information Processing Systems - Open Systems Interconnection - Basic Connection Oriented Session Protocol Specification - Addendum 2: Incorporation of Unlimited User Data

ISO 8327 DAM 3: Information Processing Systems - Open Systems Interconnection - Basic Connection Oriented Session Protocol Specification - Proposed Draft Amendment 3 to Incorporate additional synchronization Functionality

CD 8327-2.2: Information Processing Systems - Open Systems Interconnection - Basic Connection Oriented Session Protocol Specification - Part 2: Protocol Implementation Conformance Statement (PICS) Proforma

DIS 9548: Information Processing Systems - Open Systems Interconnection - Connectionless Session Protocol to Provide the Connectionless-Mode Session Service

CD 9548-2: Information Processing Systems - Open Systems Interconnection - Connectionless Session Protocol Implementation Conformance Statement (PICS) Proforma

TR 9571: Information Processing Systems - Open Systems Interconnection - LOTOS Description of the Session Service

TR 9572: Information Processing Systems - Open Systems Interconnection - LOTOS Description of the Session Protocol

DIS 10168-1: Information Processing Systems - Open Systems Interconnection - Conformance Test Suite for the Session Protocol - Part 1: Test Suite Structure and Test Purposes

8

ASN.1

At the Application Layer, AEs exchange information in the form of APDUs (i.e., application PDUs). An APDU in transit can be represented in many ways. Agreeing on a common representation is important for interoperability. The goal of the Presentation Layer is to free the AEs of the representation problem. AEs only need to know the structure and content of the APDUs, but not the representation of the APDUs. **ASN.1 (Abstract Syntax Notation One)** is a language used to describe the structure and content of a structured object. It is described in ISO 8824.

ASN.1 is similar to the data declaration part of a high level programming language. It provides language constructs to define types and values. Types correspond to structures and values correspond to content. But unlike any programming language, ASN.1 types need not be implemented by any machine. For example, the ASN.1 INTEGER type allows all integers as values; obviously, such a type cannot be represented in any real machine.

It is common practice to group related abstract types into a module which can be referenced externally by an object identifier. For example, an application protocol designer may want to group all the APDUs of an application protocol into a module. **An abstract syntax** is such a named group of abstract types, and an **ASN.1 module** is the ASN.1 notation to define an abstract syntax. ASN.1 types and modules are studied in Section 8.1.

An ASN.1 value may be represented in different ways. A **print value** is a representation of an ASN.1 value in a printable form. It is strictly for presentation to the human beings, hence it does not have to depend on any machine architecture. A **local value** is a value used by a programming language or a system to represent an ASN.1 value. A **transfer value** is a representation of an ASN.1 value in transit. It is a bit stream obtained from applying a set of rules, known as a **transfer syntax**, to an ASN.1 value. BER (Basic Encoding Rules), a transfer syntax specified by the ASN.1 standard, is covered in Section 8.2. It is important to note that the same ASN.1 value can be mapped to many possible print values, local values, or transfer values.

The ASN.1 standard also defines a macro notation to extend its type/value notation. ASN.1 macros are covered in Section 8.3.

8.1 ASN.1 Types

An abstract syntax is a named group of types. It can be an abstract syntax of an application protocol defined by the standard groups, an abstract syntax of a profile defined by the implementation profile groups, or an abstract syntax of a class of objects defined by the user groups. An ASN.1 module is the ASN.1 notation to define an abstract syntax. The general form of an ASN.1 module is as follows:

```
<moduleIdentifier> DEFINITIONS TagDefault ::=
    BEGIN
        EXPORTS
        IMPORTS
        AssignmentList
    END
```

The **moduleIdentifier** is a module name followed optionally by an object identifier to identify the module. The first letter of the module name must be in upper case. The **TagDefault** construct has to do with tags which will be explained later. The **EXPORTS** construct specifies the definitions in the module that can be imported by other modules. The **IMPORTS** construct is used to import types or values defined in other modules. Neither IMPORTS nor EXPORTS may be used unless the moduleIdentifier includes an object identifier value. The AssignmentList of the module contains type assignments, value assignments, and macro definitions. A **type assignment** is of the following form:

```
<typeReference> ::= <typeDescription>
```

where the typeReference is an identifier whose first letter must be in upper case and the typeDescription describes a type. Similarly, a **value assignment** assigns a value to a valueReference name whose first letter must be in lower case.

Example 8.1

```
ModuleExample1 DEFINITIONS ::=
```

```
BEGIN
    TypeA ::= INTEGER
    TypeB ::= BOOLEAN
    valueA TypeA ::= 10
    valueB TypeB ::= TRUE
END
```

This module contains two type assignments (i.e., TypeA and TypeB) and two value assignments.

Example 8.2

```
ModuleExample2 {1 4 12 32} DEFINITIONS IMPLICIT TAGS ::=
BEGIN
    IMPORTS ...
    EXPORTS...
    TypeA ::= ImportedType
    TypeB ::= BIT STRING
END
```

Unlike moduleExample1 in the previous example, this module uses the TagDefault, IMPORTS, and EXPORTS construct. The name of this module is followed by an object identifier, i.e., {1 4 12 32}.

An ASN.1 type can be either simple or structured. Simple ASN.1 types include INTEGER, REAL, BOOLEAN, CHARACTER STRING, BIT STRING, OCTET STRING, NULL, and OBJECT IDENTIFIER. Structured types are built from simple types. Simple types and structured types are covered in Sections 8.1.1 and 8.1.2 respectively. The ASN.1 standard provides its own print values for the ASN.1 types. As we introduce the types, we will also introduce these print values.

8.1.1   Simple Types

- **BOOLEAN Type**

There are only two values: TRUE and FALSE.

- **INTEGER**

ASN.1 deals with integers of "unbounded" precision. Thus the ASN.1 INTEGER type is quite different from the integer type in conventional programming languages.

Example 8.3

```
ExInt ::= INTEGER
```

```
intA ExInt  ::= 2              -- IntA is of type ExInt and has a value 2
intB ExInt  ::= -10
intC ExInt  ::= 99             -- same as '63'H
```

Comments begin with a double hyphen (--) and end with another double hyphen or the end of the line.

Example 8.4

```
IntColor ::= INTEGER {red(0), blue(1), green(2), white(3), black(4)}
intD IntColor ::= green     -- OR
intD IntColor ::= 2
```

In this example, red, blue, green, white, and black are identifiers. The integers next to the identifiers need not be a contiguous range of integers. The type, IntColor, includes all other integer values.

• BIT STRING

The values of this type are ordered as a sequence of zero, one, or more bits. A BIT STRING value can be denoted by a binary string (BString) item or hexadecimal string (HString) item. Like INTEGER, the BIT STRING type may contain a named number list.

Example 8.5

```
ExBitString1 ::= BIT STRING
bitA ExBitString1 ::= '10001'B              -- 5 bits
bitB ExBitString1 ::= '1A2B3'H              -- 20 bits
```

Example 8.6

```
ExBitString2 ::= BIT STRING {attribute1(0), attribute2(1), attribute3(2)}
bitC ExBitString2 ::= {attribute1, attribute3}     -- or '101'B
```

The named numbers in the BIT STRING type show the bit positions. The numbers that are present/absent in the list are assigned "1"/"0" bits with respect to their bit positions.

• OCTET STRING

The values of this type are ordered as a sequence of zero, one, or more octets. An OCTET STRING value may be denoted by a BString item or an HString item.

Example 8.7

```
ExOctetString ::= OCTET STRING
```

```
octetA ExOctetString ::= '00010001 10001000 11001100 'B    -- 3 octets
octetB ExOctetString ::= '1A2B'H                           -- 2 octets
```

- **NULL**

This is a simple type which consists of a single value, NULL. It is mainly used as a place holder.   If the value of a type is not known precisely at a particular time, it is wiser to send a value of the NULL type to indicate that the value is unknown.

- **OBJECT IDENTIFIER**

Object identifiers and the Object Identifier Tree were introduced in Chapter 4.

Example 8.8

```
ExObjectID ::= OBJECT IDENTIFIER
ftam ExObjectID  ::= {iso standard 8571}
-- the following values are equivalent
valObjectID1  ExObjectID       ::= {ftam abstract-syntax(2) pci(1)}
valObjectID2  ExObjectID       ::= {iso standard 8571 abstract syntax(2) pci(1)}
valObjectID3  ExObjectID       ::= {1 0 8571 2 1}
```

This example illustrates a number of equivalent print values of the OBJECT IDENTIFIER type.

- **ObjectDescriptor**

As can be seen from the above example, an OBJECT IDENTIFIER value consists of a list of integers. Thus, it is not very user friendly. An ObjectDescriptor value is meant to provide a human readable reference for a particular OBJECT IDENTIFIER value. An ObjectDescriptor value is not necessarily unique, hence it cannot be used for identification.

Example 8.9

```
ExName ::= ObjectDescriptor
name ExName  ::= "An example of Object Descriptor"
```

- **REAL**

This type contains all the real numbers as values. Since every real number can be expressed as $M \times B^E$ where M is the mantissa, B is the base and E is the exponent, a print value of the REAL type is represented by a triple {M, B, E}. Furthermore, ASN.1 uses special print notation to include the values 0, + infinity, and - infinity. These special print notations are 0, PLUS-INFINITY, and MINUS-INFINITY respectively.

Example 8.10

    pi REAL ::= {31415928, 10, -8}

• **ENUMERATED**

This type is useful when the scope of the value is limited.

Example 8.11

    MonthsOfTheYear ::= ENUMERATED
    {jan(1), feb(2), mar(3), apr(4), may(5), jun(6), jul(7), aug(8), sep(9), oct(10), nov(11), dec(12)}
    coldestMonth MonthsOfTheYear ::= dec -- OR
    coldestMonth MonthsOfTheYear ::= 12

• **CHARACTER STRING types**

ASN.1 defines several CHARACTER STRING types. The values of each character string type are strings of characters taken from a character set. A character set contains a G (graphics) set and a C (control) set. For example, the G set in the ASCII character set consists of the characters with ASCII numbers 33 through 126 while the C set consists of characters with ASCII numbers 0 through 31. The characters SPACE (number 32) and DELETE (number 127) are in both sets. Examples of CHARACTER STRING types are briefly described below:

    • **NumericString**: This character set consists of digits 0 through 9 and space. There is no C set.
    • **PrintableString**: This character set consists of all uppercase and lowercase letters, digits, punctuation marks, and space. There is no C set.
    • **IA5String**: This character set consists of characters taken from IA5 (International Alphabet number 5) which is almost identical to ASCII.
    • **VisibleString**: This character set consists the graphic characters taken from IA5. There is no C set.
    • **GeneralString**: This character set is the union of all the standardized character sets.

Example 8.12

    -- IA5String
    ExCharString1 ::= IA5String
    charStr1 ExCharString1 ::= "Example of IA5String"

    -- NumericString

ExCharString2 ::= NumericString
charStr2 ExCharString2 ::= "1234568890"

-- PrintableString
ExCharString3 ::= PrintableString
charStr4 ExCharString3 ::= "A..Za..z0..9'()+,-./:=? "

-- VisibleString
ExCharString4 ::= VisibleString
charStr5 ExCharString4 ::= "A..Za..z0..9~`!@#$%^&*()_+=-[]{};':",.<>?/\ "

•   **GeneralizedTime type**

ASN.1 defines two useful types for the applications to reference the time of a day. One is GeneralizedTime, and the other is UTCTime.

Let us describe the GeneralizedTime type. The values of this type take one of three possible forms. The first form is intended for local time, the second form is intended for **UTC (Coordinated Universal Time)** which is equivalent to Greenwich mean time, and the third form is basically a union of the first two forms -- it shows the local time plus the differential from UTC time. In the first form, the date is expressed as a four-digit year, two-digit month, and a two-digit day while the time is expressed in hours, minutes, seconds, and fractional sections of arbitrary decimal precision. The second form is the same as the first form except that it ends with an indicator "Z". The third form is the same as the first form except that it ends with an indication of the differential from UTC time. The following example illustrates the three forms.

Example 8.13

   -- Two useful types
   -- GeneralizedTime format is YYYYMMDDHHMMSS.S and an optional indicator
   -- to show the local time

   ExTime ::= GeneralizedTime
   time1 ExTime ::= "19900811131510.5"
   -- time1 is of the first form indicating that local time is 15 minutes 10.5 secs past 1 pm on
   -- Aug 11, 1990

   time2 ExTime ::= "19900811121510.5Z"
   -- time2 is of the second form

   time3 ExTime ::= "19900811131510.5+400"
   -- time3 is of the third form and +400 means that the local time is 4 hours ahead of UTC time

8.1.2   Structured Types

• **SEQUENCE**

A SEQUENCE value is an ordered list of zero or more component elements. Each component element is of some ASN.1 type. Often a textual name in the form of an identifier (which begins with a lower case letter) is associated with the component element for readability purpose. The identifier is followed by a type description describing the type of the component element. The type description of each component element may be followed by the OPTIONAL or DEFAULT keyword. The OPTIONAL keyword implies that the component element need not be present in a SEQUENCE value. The DEFAULT keyword indicates the same but prescribes a value that will be assigned if a value for that component is absent. The COMPONENTS OF keyword is used within the SEQUENCE type to indicate the inclusion of all the components of some given sequence.

Example 8.14

```
F-SELECT-response ::= SEQUENCE {
      stateResult              StateResult DEFAULT success,
      actionResult             ActionResult DEFAULT success,
      attributes               SelectAttributes,
      sharedASEinform          SharedASEinform OPTIONAL,
      diagnostic               Diagnostic OPTIONAL }
```

This example gives the definition of one of the FTAM PDUs using the SEQUENCE construct. It shows the use of the DEFAULT and OPTIONAL constructs.

Example 8.15

```
Address ::= SEQUENCE {
            local    COMPONENTS OF LocalAddress,
            organizationname Name OPTIONAL  }

LocalAddress ::= SEQUENCE {...}
```

This example shows that all the component elements of the LocalAddress type are included as component elements of the Address type. Thus if LocalAddress has n component elements, then Address contains n+1 component elements.

Example 8.16

```
ValidSeq ::= SEQUENCE {
            a    INTEGER OPTIONAL,
```

```
                    s    BOOLEAN,
                    n    INTEGER  }
       val ValidSeq ::= {    a  5,
                             s  TRUE,
                             n  20   }
```

This example illustrates the print values of the SEQUENCE type.

Example 8.17

```
       Fadu ::= SEQUENCE {
           node         NodeDescriptor,
           data         DU OPTIONAL,
           children     SEQUENCE OF Fadu}
```

This example, taken from the FTAM standard, shows that ASN.1 allows the definition of recursive types.

• SEQUENCE OF

The SEQUENCE OF type is a special kind of the SEQUENCE type where all the component elements must be of same ASN.1 type.

Example 8.18

```
       Words ::= SEQUENCE OF VisibleString
       buildWords Words ::= {"applications","elements","protocols"}
```

• SET

A SET type contains an unordered list of zero or more components. The component elements involved must be distinct. As the ordering is not important, it is essential that identifiers be included to ensure an unambiguous value notation.

Example 8.19

```
       TypeSet ::= SET {
                       a    BOOLEAN,
                       s    INTEGER,
                       n    BIT STRING  }
       valSet TypeSet ::= {
                       a    TRUE,
                       n    '10001'B,
                       s    520   }
```

Each value of TypeSet must contain one value of component a, one value of component s, and one value of component n. The order in which they appear is not important.

Example 8.20

```
Address ::= SET {
                name            [0]  VisibleString OPTIONAL,
                organization    [1]  VisibleString OPTIONAL,
                countryName     [2]  VisibleString OPTIONAL }
add Address::= {  name              "John Doe",
                organization      "CSTP"   }
```

The countryName component is absent in the value of add.

Example 8.21

```
Typeset ::= SET {    a   BOOLEAN,
                     s   INTEGER,
                     n   REAL OPTIONAL  }
TypeCompOfSet ::= SET {     o              BIT STRING,
                           t              NULL,
                           i              PrintableString,
                           COMPONENTS OF TypeSet  }
```

The TypeCompOfSet has components o, t, i, a, s, and n.

• SET OF

A SET OF type contains an unordered list of zero or more elements, all of which must be of same ASN.1 type.

Example 8.22

```
Words ::= SET OF VisibleString
buildOSIWords Words ::=  {"entities", "protocols", "pdu"}
```

• CHOICE

A CHOICE type contains a list of alternatives of known types. Each value of the new type is a value of one of the component types. This type is useful especially when the values to be described can be of different types under different circumstances, and where all possibilities are known in advance. Although not shown in the examples below, it is customary to tag the components of a choice type.

Example 8.23

```
CurrentTime ::= CHOICE {
                current-time-available        UTCTime,
                current-time-not-available    NULL   }
timeofrun CurrentTime ::= {current-time-available    "900811132012Z"}
timeofrun-unknown CurrentTime ::= {current-time-not-available NULL}
```

This example shows the print values of the CHOICE type.

Example 8.24

```
ROSEapdus ::= CHOICE {
                roiv-apdu ROIVapdu,
                rors-apdu RORSapdu,
                roer-apdu ROERapdu,
                rorj-apdu RORJapdu}
```

This example shows the four APDUs used by the ROSE protocol.

• ANY

When a data type is not known at specification time, ANY is used. At a later time, the ANY type can be replaced by an ASN.1 type.

Example 8.25

```
Allowed ::= SEQUENCE {
                a    INTEGER    OPTIONAL
                s    BOOLEAN    OPTIONAL
                n    ANY        OPTIONAL  }
```

Let us assume that for some value of Allowed, the BOOLEAN component is absent and that the ANY component is filled by an INTEGER type. It is not clear whether the INTEGER component is "a" or "n". To remove the ambiguity, the Allowed type should be tagged. The use of tags will be explained shortly.

The ANY DEFINED BY construct provides the source of the type which fills the ANY type.

Example 8.26

```
ROIVapdu ::= SEQUENCE {
                invokeID            InvokeIDType,
```

linked-ID	InvokeIDType OPTIONAL,
operation-value	OPERATION,
argument	ANY DEFINED BY operation-value OPTIONAL }
	-- ANY is filled by the single ASN.1 type following the
	-- keyword ARGUMENT in the type definition of a particular
	-- operation.

ROIVapdu is a ROSE APDU. Here the type of argument will be filled by the argument type of a remote operation defined by the user of ROSE, where the remote operation is defined as an instance of the OPERATION macro.

- **EXTERNAL**

This is a type whose values need not be described using ASN.1, although ASN.1 may be used. The EXTERNAL type permits the inclusion of any data value from an identified set of data values. It is assumed that some mechanism is provided to encode/decode the values in the set.

- **Tagged Types**

Type	Tag	Type	Tag
BOOLEAN	1	SET OF	17
INTEGER	2	NumericString	18
BIT STRING	3	PrintableString	19
OCTET STRING	4	TeletexString	20
NULL	5	VideotexString	21
OBJECT IDENTIFIER	6	IA5String	22
ObjectDescriptor	7	UTCTime	23
EXTERNAL	8	GeneralizedTime	24
REAL	9	GraphicString	25
ENUMERATED	10	VisibleString	26
SEQUENCE	16	GeneralString	27
SEQUENCE OF	16	ANY	none
SET	17	CHOICE	none

TABLE 8.1   Predefined Tags

A **tag** consists of a tag class and a non-negative tag number. There are four different tag classes. They are listed as follows:

- **Universal**: Universal tags are defined only by the ASN.1 standard, its addenda, or CCITT Recommendations. They are globally unique. Except for Choice and Any types, all simple and structured types are assigned universal tags. Table 8.1 shows the ASN.1 types and their associated universal tags.

• **Application**: Application tags are defined for abstract syntaxes of application protocol standards. They must be unique within an ASN.1 module.
• **Private**: Private tags are available to any enterprise. They must be unique within an enterprise.
• **Context-specific**: Context-specific tags are used to remove ambiguities. They must be unique in a structured type. The same context specific tag number can be used many times within a module. These tags do not have any meaning outside of the ASN.1 type where they are defined.

Example 8.27

```
Exuniv ::= [UNIVERSAL 2] INTEGER
valA Exuniv ::= 9

Exappl ::= [APPLICATION 0] INTEGER
valB Exappl ::= 10

Expriv ::= [PRIVATE 1] INTEGER
valC Expriv ::= 11

Excont ::= SET {
            type1 [0]      INTEGER OPTIONAL
            type2 [1]      INTEGER OPTIONAL }
```

Since both components of the Excont type are of the same type (i.e., INTEGER) and optional, a print value of Excont type containing only one component value needs to indicate which component element the component value comes from. Thus, context specific tags (i.e., [0] and [1]) are used to remove ambiguities.

A tagged type essentially creates a new type. For example,

Expriv ::= [PRIVATE 1] INTEGER

is different from

Expriv ::= INTEGER

Whenever a value of a tagged type is transmitted on the network, additional information must be encoded. In order to avoid unnecessary encoding, a tag may be followed by the keyword IMPLICIT to indicate that the new tag overrides, instead of prefixing, an existing tag. Thus, we can define:

Expriv ::= [PRIVATE 10] IMPLICIT INTEGER

When IMPLICIT is used, only the [PRIVATE 10] tag but not the predefined [UNIVERSAL 2] tag associated with INTEGER is transmitted on the network. When large data structures are transmitted, the use of IMPLICIT can save considerable amount of encoding octets. Note that although the tag is not transmitted, the receiving end can deduce the tag information from the DCS (i.e., defined context set).

      The ANY and CHOICE types cannot be tagged as IMPLICIT. If it were used with ANY, it would not be possible to tell which ASN.1 type is present. If it were used with CHOICE type, it would not be possible to tell which element of the choice is present.

- **SUBTYPE**

A **subtype** is a "subset" of some parent type. For example, the set of positive integers can be defined as a subtype of the INTEGER type using some subtype specification. Depending on the parent type, subtype specifications may impose restrictions on the alphabet of character strings, the size of strings, the value range of numeric types, etc. The parent type in turn may be a subtype of some other parent type.

Example 8.28

```
Months ::= ENUMERATED
           {   january          (1),
               february         (2),
               ......
               december         (12) }
First-quarter ::= Months
           {january | february | march}
```

First-quarter is a subtype of the Months type. The "|" is interpreted as a sort of choice.

Example 8.29

```
Name      ::= StringType (SIZE (1..20))
Address   ::= SEQUENCE (SIZE (1..5)) OF ...
```

SIZE is used to indicate the smallest and largest length (in the case of Name), or the maximum number of components of a sequence (in the case of Address).

8.2   Basic Encoding Rules

While ASN.1 provides a notation to describe the structure and content of an abstract syntax, **Basic Encoding Rules (BER)** describes how the content can be represented in the transfer. Thus BER is a transfer syntax. The ASN.1 standard group is in the process of defining some other transfer syntaxes. They are Distinguishing Encoding Rules, Packed

Encoding Rules, and Light Weight Encoding Rules. In this section, we will only describe BER.

Every BER encoded value has three fields: a tag (identifier) field that conveys information on the tag and the encoding form, a length field that defines the size of the value in octets, and a content field that conveys the actual value. Hence a BER encoded value is called a **TLV triple**. Each field has octet aligned and self delimiting properties. **Octet aligned** means that the entire encoded value is made up of an integral number of octets. **Self delimiting** means that the end of the encoded value can be deduced.

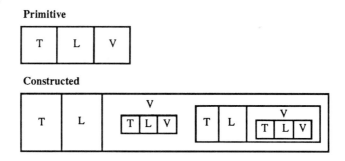

FIGURE 8.1   Encoding Forms

The encoding can be either primitive or constructed (Figure 8.1). It is **primitive** if it denotes a complete and explicit value of some simple type, and **constructed** if it denotes a value with a nested structure. Thus all simple types allow primitive encoding, and all structured types allow only constructed encoding. Some simple types such as OCTET STRING and BIT STRING also allow constructed encoding which is used when the length of the string is unknown when encoding begins. Note that if all the simple types use primitive encoding and all the structured types use constructed encoding, then we do not need to indicate the encoding form in the tag field.

All the encodings in this section are given in hex, unless stated otherwise.

8.2.1   Tag Field

In the tag field, we encode the tag class, the tag number, and the encoding form. Since there are only four tag classes, 2 bits are sufficient to encode the tag class: "00" for UNIVERSAL, "01" for APPLICATION, "10" for CONTEXT SPECIFIC, and "11" for PRIVATE. One bit is used to indicate the encoding form, "0" for primitive and "1" for constructed. If a tag number is in the range from 0 to 30, then the tag number can be encoded using 5 bits. Thus as long as the tag number is less than 31, we need only one octet for the tag field: bits 8 and 7 for the tag class, bit 6 for the encoding form, and the remaining five bits for the tag number. If the tag number is 31 or more, then more than one octet is needed for the tag field. In this case, the low order 5 bits of the leading octet are set to 1. The high order bit is set to 1 in all the subsequent octets except the last one. The concatenation of the rightmost seven bits of the subsequent octets gives the tag number.

Table 8.2 shows the encoded tags of some ASN.1 types, all of which are expressed in hex. In the cases where both primitive and constructed encodings are allowed.

Type	Encoded Tag
BOOLEAN	0 1
INTEGER	0 2
BIT STRING	0 3 or 2 3
OCTET STRING	0 4 or 2 4
NULL	0 5
OBJECT IDENTIFIER	0 6
ENUMERATED	0A
SEQUENCE	3 0
SEQUENCE OF	3 0
SET	3 1
SET OF	3 1

TABLE 8.2 Encoded Tags

Example 8.30

Consider the tag [APPLICATION 23]. The encoded tag field consists of one octet "01110111"B. The leftmost two bits (i.e., 01) indicates the application tag class, the next bit (i.e, 1) indicates that the encoding form is constructed, and the subsequent bits (i.e., 10111) represents the tag number 23. Now consider the tag [PRIVATE 42]. The binary representation of 42 (i.e., 101010) takes up more than five bits, hence two octets are needed to encode this tag. The encoded tag is 11111111 00101010 in binary. The leftmost octet indicates the private tag class and the constructed encoding form. The rightmost octet has the highest bit set to 0 showing that it is the last octet in the tag encoding. The rightmost seven bits (i.e., 0101010) gives the encoding of 42.

When a type is tagged, both the predefined tag and the user defined tag have to be encoded. Thus the presence of a tag increases the size of the encoding. In order to save bits in the encoding, the TagDefault construct is used in the ASN.1 module definition. If the TagDefault is set to IMPLICIT, then only the user defined tag (but not the predefined tag) of the type is encoded, unless there is an EXPLICIT keyword after the user defined tag, in which case both the user defined tag and the predefined tag have to be encoded. If the TagDefault construct is not used in a module definition, then both the predefined tag and the user defined tag type have to be encoded, unless there is an IMPLICIT keyword after the user defined tag, in which case only the user defined tag of the type is encoded .

8.2.2 Length Field

The length field of the TLV triple indicates the length of the content field. It can be encoded in three forms: short, long, and indefinite forms. It is up to the encoder to decide which one to use. Either the short form or the long form is called a **definite form**. Definite here means that the exact length of the content field is known. The **indefinite form** is used when the length of the content field is unknown at the time when encoding begins. If the number of octets of the content field is less than 128, then the **short form** is used. The short form uses a single octet where the highest order bit of the octet is set to 0 and the length is encoded in the remaining seven bits. For example, the length of 6 is encoded in short form as '00000110'B.

If the length is longer than 128, the **long form** is used. The long form length encoding starts with an octet which indicates the number of octets required to encode the length of the content field. The leading octet is followed by octets encoding the length of the content field. The highest order bit of the first octet is 1 to indicate that the long form is used. The remaining 7 bits of the leading octet are used to specify the number of the subsequent octets of the length field. For example, if the length of the content is 960, then two octets are needed to encode the length of the content. Thus three octets are needed in the length field in the long form encoding. The value of the length field is '82 03 C0'H.

The long form can be used even if the length of the content is less than 128. For example, suppose that the length of the content is 6. Although the short form can be used, one can also give a long form encoding as '10000010 00000000 000000110'B where the middle octet contains all 0's.

The indefinite form of length encoding is used when the length of the content is not known when encoding begins. It uses a pair of delimiters to mark the start and finish of the encoded value. The start delimiter is given by '10000000'B, and the finish delimiter is given by a pair of octets consisting of 0's. In between the start and the finish delimiters is the content which consists of a number of TLV triples.

8.2.3   Content Field

• **BOOLEAN**

The encoding of BOOLEAN values is primitive. FALSE is encoded by '00'H while TRUE can be encoded by any other octet, depending on the choice of the encoder.

Example 8.31

The TLV encoding of FALSE is '01 01 00'H (01 for tag, 01 for length, and 00 for value). If we encode TRUE by using an octet which consists of all 1's, then the TLV encoding of TRUE is '01 01 FF'H.

• **INTEGER**

The encoding of INTEGER values is primitive. An integer value is encoded as a twos complement binary number. One should use a minimum number of octets to encode an INTEGER value.

Example 8.32

> smallestNum INTEGER ::= -2

The TLV encoding of smallestNum is 02 01 FE, where the number -2 in twos complement form is FE.

• BIT STRING

The encoding of BIT STRING values can be either primitive or constructed. The content octets for the primitive encoding contain an initial octet followed by zero, one or more subsequent octets. The subsequent octets encode the bitstring. The initial octet indicates the number of unused bits in the last octet of the encoding of the content since a BIT STRING value may not be octet-aligned. This number must be in the range zero to seven. For example, if the BIT STRING value is '101'B, then the number of unused bits is 5 and the encoded content is '05A0'H. If the length of the BIT STRING value is unknown when encoding begins, the constructed encoding with indefinite length form is used.

Example 8.33

> first BIT STRING ::= '0011 1010 1010 1010 1010'B -- 20 bits long

The TLV encoding of first is '03 04 043AAAA0'H, where 03 is the encoded tag, 04 is the encoded length, 04 is the number of unused bits, and 3AAAA0 is the encoded value.

• OCTET STRING

The encoding of OCTET STRING values is either primitive or constructed.

Example 8.34

This example illustrates the constructed encoding of an OCTET STRING value. Suppose the OCTET STRING is '0123456789ABCDEF'H. We can segment this string into two parts: '01234567'H and '89ABCDEF'H. The first part is encoded in a primitive form as '04 04 01234567'H, and the second part is encoded in a primitive form as '04 04 89ABCDEF'H. Using the indefinite form, we enclose these two parts by a pair of start and finish delimiters. The TLV encoding of the OCTET string is:

```
24 80
    04 04 01234567
    04 04 89ABCDEF
00 00
```

The leading octet 24 shows that the constructed encoding is used (Table 8.2), and 80 (the same as '10000000'B) is the start delimiter.

Example 8.35

second OCTET STRING ::= '0AB2B0'H

The TLV encoding of second in a primitive form is '04 03 0AB2B0'H, where 04 is the encoded tag, 03 is the encoded length, and 0AB2B0 is the encoded value.

- **NULL**

The encoding of NULL is primitive.

Example 8.36

The NULL value is encoded as '05 00'H, where 05 is the encoded tag and 00 is the encoded length.

- **OBJECT IDENTIFIER**

Each subidentifier is encoded into a series of octets. The high order bit of each octet except the last one is set to 1. The value of the subidentifier is encoded into the rightmost seven bits of the octets.

   According to the Object Identifier Tree, the first subidentifier value is either 0, 1, or 2, while the second subidentifier value must be less than 40 if the first subidentifier value is 0 or 1. Because of the spareness of the range of the first subidentifier, the first and the second subidentifiers are combined to form a subidentifier with a value of $(X * 40) + Y$, where X is the value of the first subidentifier, Y is the value of second subidentifier, and 40 is in decimal.

Example 8.37

ftam1 OBJECT IDENTIFIER ::= {1 0 8571 2 1}

The TLV encoding of ftam1 is 06 05 28 C2 7B 02 01, where the first two subidentifiers are combined to form an integer of value (1x40)+0=40 which is 28 in hex.

- **Tagged type**

The encoding of a tagged value is derived from the encoding of the corresponding data value. If the IMPLICIT keyword is not used, then the encoding is constructed. If the IMPLICIT keyword is used, the encoding is constructed provided that the encoding of the data value is constructed, otherwise it is primitive.

Example 8.38

Question1 ::= [17] BOOLEAN
result1 Question1 ::= TRUE

The TLV encoding of result1 is B1 03 01 01 FF where B1 is the (constructed) encoded tag for [17], 03 is the encoded length, and 01 01 FF is the encoded content. The constructed encoding form is used because IMPLICIT is not used.

Question2 ::= [17] IMPLICIT BOOLEAN
result2 Question2 ::= TRUE

The TLV encoding of result2 is 91 01 FF, where 91 is the (primitive) encoded tag for [17]. Note that the T and L encodings of TRUE are left out.

• SEQUENCE

SEQUENCE values are the most frequently used values in the Application Layer. A SEQUENCE value is an ordered list of TLV encodings of the components of the sequence.

Example 8.39

```
Constructed ::= SEQUENCE
                    {    name          OCTET STRING
                         place         INTEGER { room1(0), room2(1) room3(2)}
                         persons       INTEGER OPTIONAL   }
meeting Constructed ::=
                    {    name          '1AA2FFGH',
                         place         room3}
```

The TLV encoding of meeting is: 30 09
                                                04 04 1A A2 FF GH
                                                02 01 02

where 30 is the encoded tag, 09 is the encoded length, and the rest gives the TLV encodings of the two components.

• SEQUENCE OF

The encoding of SEQUENCE OF values is always constructed. Unlike a SEQUENCE value, a SEQUENCE OF value may contain arbitrarily many components, so long as they are all of the same type.

Example 8.40

> Data ::= SEQUENCE OF INTEGER {-120.. 120}
> actual Data ::= { 15, -2, -4}

The TLV encoding of actual is:

> 30 0C
>   02 01 0F
>   02 01 FE
>   02 01 FC

where 30 is the encoded tag, 0C is the encoded length, and the rest gives the TLV encodings of the components.

- **SET**

The encoding of SET is basically the same as the encoding of SEQUENCE values except that the TLV encodings of the components may appear in any order.

Example 8.41

> Constructed ::= SET
>   {   name   OCTET STRING
>   place   INTEGER { room1(0), room2(1) room3(2)}
>   persons   INTEGER }
> meeting Constructed ::=
>   {   name   '1AA2FFFH',
>   persons   12
>   place   room3   }

The TLV encoding of meeting is:

> 31 0C
>   04 04 1AA2FFFH
>   02 01 0C
>   02 01 02

- **CHOICE**

The encoding of CHOICE values is same as the encoding of the values of the chosen components. For example, if the chosen component is of an INTEGER type, then the CHOICE value is encoded as if it were an INTEGER value.

• ENUMERATED

The encoding of ENUMERATED values is always primitive. The only difference in encoding an ENUMERATED value and an INTEGER value is the associated tag.

Example 8.42

Rate ::= ENUMERATED {bad(-1), ok(0), good(1)}

The TLV encoding of good is 0A 01 01, where 0A is the encoded tag, the first 01 is the encoded length, and the second 01 is the encoded value for good.

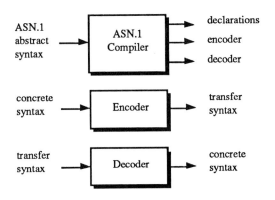

FIGURE 8.2   ASN.1 Compiler

We have completed our discussion on BER. BER has some deficiencies. The use of type and length fields introduce unnecessary overhead, since in many cases the receiver knows the type of data being sent to it. The encoding/decoding process is highly CPU consuming because BER is based on byte-based, variable sized representation. Another problem is that an array length is not known until the end of the array is received, which may create storage problems at the receiver's end. To overcome these problems, the **lightweight transfer syntax (LWTS)** has been proposed. The two major principles used by LWTS are the following: avoid unnecessary information in the encoding, and use fixed representations whenever possible. LWTS does not use TLV encodings. Experiments show that the encoding/decoding time of LWTS is up to six times faster than that of BER.

We close this section by examining some of the ASN.1 tools. There are many ASN.1 tools around. These tools include tools to create ASN.1 modules, perform ASN.1 syntax checking, compile ASN.1 types to programming language types, and create encoding/decoding routines for a programming language. Let us examine the last two.

An **ASN.1 compiler** (Figure 8.2) takes an ASN.1 abstract syntax as input and generates three outputs, all pertaining to a common target programming language. The first output is a set of declarations of data structures expressed in the target language. There should be at least one data structure associated with each ASN.1 type appearing in the input abstract syntax. For example, if one of the ASN.1 types is a SEQUENCE type and the target language is PASCAL, then one of the corresponding outputs would be some PASCAL record structure. The second output is an encoder. This encoder receives a local value of the target language as input, and applies BER to convert it to a transfer value. The third output is a decoder. The decoder takes a transfer value as input and converts it to a local value of the target language.

8.3   ASN.1 Macros

The macro facilities of ASN.1 allow an application protocol designer to use non-standard notations to define types and values. Types defined by macros are basically ASN.1 types supplemented with narrative constraints and semantic footnotes. As the constraints and footnotes are only narrative in nature, they do not have any impact on encoding. Thus, as far as encoding is concerned, ASN.1 macros can be always reduced to ASN.1 types.

A macro can be viewed as a template which is used to derive a set of related types and values. For example, a macro definition for remote operations may specify a template consisting of a field for argument types, a field for result types, and a field for error types. Since the macro does not specify any argument, result, or error types, it is not a type. However, an application protocol designer can use this macro to define a remote operation type by simply plugging in the argument, result, and error types.

Most of the syntax appearing in a macro definition, known as syntax items or literals, are intended primarily for presentation to the user. For example, one can use a macro to write a fancy type, or a fancy value. Once again, these fancy notations are not used in the encoding. They are strictly syntactic sugar.

Although the ASN.1 macro facility is attractive in terms of its expressive capabilities, it does have significant drawbacks. One of the major drawbacks is that it is difficult to fully specify a macro compiler. A macro compiler would need to know the grammatical rules of all the macros defined and used in an ASN.1 module before it can compile the ASN.1 module. The other drawback is that the ASN.1 standard is quite difficult to read. As a result, many macro features defined in the ASN.1 standard are not used in practice. One of the reasons why macros are still in use is the macro facilities offered by RO-notation and ASDC. As we will see in Chapter 14, RO-notation and ASDC provide a useful set of macros to application protocol designers.

A macro can be defined as follows. First a name is assigned to the macro. Types and values within the macro are specified using Backus Naur Form (BNF). The form of a macro is as follows:

```
<name> MACRO ::= BEGIN
TYPE NOTATION ::= <new type notation>
VALUE NOTATION ::= <new value notation>
<supporting syntax>
END
```

where
- the name, written in all uppercases, is the name of the macro,
- the new type notation contains a set of BNF rules to describe the new type,
- the new value notation contains a set of BNF rules to describe the values of the new type, and
- the supporting syntax expands the nonterminals and types referenced within the macro definition.

The MACRO keyword serves to indicate a macro definition. The "TYPE NOTATION" keyword is used to introduce a set of production rules for the new types. The "VALUE NOTATION" keyword is used to introduce the values of the new types.

Within the production rules, there are alternatives, terminal symbols, and nonterminal symbols. Commonly occurring terminal symbols are empty, identifier, number, string, value, and type. The type symbol stands for any ASN.1 type description. The identifier symbol stands for any name starting with a lowercase letter. The VALUE symbol specifies how instances of the macro should be encoded. A commonly used nonterminal symbol is NamedType, defined as follows:

NamedType ::= identifier type I type

The presence of alternatives in a macro definition allows different types to be derived from a macro definition. As mentioned earlier, a macro is used as a type definition facility.

Within the production rules, one finds quoted strings such as "example" and "andChapterEndsSoon" as in Example 8.44. Think of these quoted strings as semantic footnotes. These strings will appear in type derived from the macro. This is how we can derive fancy types. Within the production rules, one also finds the value symbol followed by a type description, e.g. value (Printable String) and value(VALUE INTEGER) in Example 8.43. Although quite a few occurrences of the value symbol can appear within a macro, at most one of them is of the form value (VALUE <type>), e.g., value(VALUE OBJECT IDENTIFIER). The idea is that the type appearing immediately after VALUE is the macro's returned type, i.e., any value of an object in a type derived from the macro is encoded as a value of that type. Before we proceed furthermore, let us give a few examples on macro definitions.

Example 8.43

```
ANOTHER-EXAMPLE MACRO ::=
BEGIN
TYPE NOTATION  ::=
                "example" "number"
                value(Printable String)
VALUE NOTATION ::=
                value(VALUE INTEGER)
```

END

This macro allows fancy types to be written. There is hardly any production rule in the value notation. The new type notation contains the "example" string, which is followed by the "number" string, which is followed by a printable string. Note that value(printable String) has nothing to do with encoding. The new value notation says that the macro should be encoded as INTEGER.

Example 8.44

```
YET-ANOTHER-EXAMPLE MACRO ::=
BEGIN
TYPE NOTATION ::=
            "aStreamOfExamples"
VALUE NOTATION ::=
            "example" value(VALUE INTEGER) "andChapterEndsSoon"
END
```

This macro allows a fancy value to be written. The new value notation contains the "example" string, which is followed by an INTEGER value, which is followed by the "andChapterEndsSoon" string.

Example 8.45

```
OBJECT MACRO ::=
BEGIN
TYPE NOTATION    ::= "PORTS" "{" PortList "}" I empty
VALUE NOTATION ::= value(VALUE OBJECT IDENTIFIER)
PortList            ::= Port "," PortList I Port
Port                ::= value (Port) PortType
PortType            ::= Symmetric I Asymmetric
Symmetric           ::= empty
Asymmetric          ::= Consumer I Supplier
Consumer            ::= "[C]"
Supplier            ::= "[S]"
END
```

This macro, taken from ASDC, allows fancy types to be defined. It contains a number of production rules.

Example 8.46

```
ExampleType ::= ANOTHER-EXAMPLE
                example number "an example on macro usage"
exType ExampleType ::= 46
```

This example shows how a fancy type, ExampleType, is derived from the macro definition given in Example 8.43. Note that all the quoted strings appearing in the ANOTHER-EXAMPLE macro also appear in ExampleType.

Example 8.47

```
OneMoreType ::= YET-ANOTHER-EXAMPLE
            aStreamOfExamples


exValue OneMoreType ::= example 47 andChapterEndsSoon
```

This example shows how a fancy value, exValue, is derived from the macro definition in Example 8.44.

Example 8.48

```
directory OBJECT
      PORTS {    readPort [S],
                 searchPort [S],
                 modifyPort [S] }
   ::= id-ot-directory
```

This example shows that the Directory object in the DS standard is defined using the OBJECT macro.

Example 8.49

```
LADY MACRO ::=
BEGIN
TYPE NOTATION ::= "Wimbledon statistics"
VALUE NOTATION ::= "wins" "Wimbledon" value(VALUE INTEGER) "times"
END


navratilova LADY ::= wins Wimbledon 9 times
```

This example shows that one can define a fancy value without defining a fancy type first.

As mentioned earlier, the upthrust of the ASN.1 macro facility is to introduce a notation to define remote operations. The ROSE protocol standard defines a set of macros which allows ROSE users to define remote operations for their application needs. Two of the macros, BIND and OPERATION, are examined next to illustrate some other features of the macro facility, namely, local variables and embedded definitions.

No remote operations may be invoked until a binding has been established between two AE-invocations. The BIND macro provides a facility for an application protocol designer to specify information accompanying a bind request and its corresponding result. The definition of the BIND macro is shown below:

```
BIND MACRO ::=
BEGIN
TYPE NOTATION      ::=    Argument Result Error
VALUE NOTATION     ::=    Argument-value | Result-value | Error-value
Argument           ::=    empty | "ARGUMENT" Namedtype (Argument-type)
Result             ::=    empty | "RESULT" NamedType (Result-type)
Error              ::=    empty | "BIND-ERROR" NamedType (Error-type)
Namedtype          ::=    type | identifier type
Argument-value     ::=    empty | "ARGUMENT" value(Argument-value Argument-type)
                          <VALUE Argument-type ::= Argument-value>
Result-value       ::=    empty | "RESULT" value(Result-value Result-type)
                          <VALUE Result-type ::= Result-value>
ERROR-value        ::=    empty | "ERROR" value(Error-value Error-type)
                          <VALUE Error-type ::= Error-value>
END
```

In the above definition, one finds Argument-type, Result-type, and Error-type. They are local variables known as **localtypereference** . Each one of them is assigned a particular type. One also finds Argument-value, Result-value, and Error-value. They are local variables known as **localvaluereference**. Each one of them is assigned a particular value of some type. For example, the Argument-value localvaluereference is assigned the Argument-type type. This is indicated by the embedded definition <VALUE Argument-type ::= Argument-value>. Note that the alternatives present in the value notation allows any object derived from the BIND macro to be encoded in three possible ways.

Example 8.50

```
Bind1 ::= BIND
        ARGUMENT    BindArgumentType1
        RESULT      BindResultType1
```

The Bind1 type is derived from the BIND macro. Here, the ERROR nonterminal in the macro definition is chosen to be empty.

Once a binding has been established, operations may be invoked. The OPERATION macro provides a template for an application protocol designer to define remote operations. The definition of the OPERATION macro is shown below:

```
OPERATION MACRO   ::=
BEGIN
```

TYPE NOTATION	::=	Argument Result Errors LinkedOps
VALUE NOTATION	::=	value(VALUE CHOICE{
		localValue INTEGER,
		globalValue OBJECT IDENTIFIER})
Argument	::=	"ARGUMENT" NamedType l empty
Result	::=	"RESULT" ResultType l empty
ResultType	::=	NamedType l empty
Errors	::=	"ERRORS" "{"ErrorNames"}" l empty
LinkedOps	::=	"LINKED" "{LinkedOpNames"}" l empty
ErrorNames	::=	ErrorList l empty
ErrorList	::=	Error l ErrorList","Error
Error	::=	value (ERROR) l type
LinkedOpNames	::=	OperationList l empty
OperationList	::=	Operation l OperationList","Operation
Operation	::=	value(OPERATION) l type
NamedType	::=	type l identifier type
END		

The value notation shows that an operation can be encoded as either INTEGER or OBJECT IDENTIFIER. The next two examples show how to define instances and types using the OPERATION macro.

Example 8.51

```
OperationType ::= OPERATION
        ARGUMENT    ArgumentType
        RESULT      ResultType
```

Here, the OPERATION macro is used to define a type called OperationType.

Example 8.52

```
operation OPERATION
        ARGUMENT    ArgumentType3
        RESULT      ResultType3
        ERROR       {error1, error5}
        LINKED      {operation1, operation2}
        ::= 30
```

We assume that error1, error5, operation1, and operation2 identifiers are defined elsewhere.

As mentioned in the beginning of the chapter, the ASN.1 standard is hard to read. Although the purpose of the macro facilities is to extend the ASN.1 types and values, it has seldom been used that way. In almost all the applications, the macro facility is used to define an object class. The ASN.1 standard group is currently in the process of replacing (not extending) the macro facility. They add some constructs to the ASN.1 standard by means of which an application protocol designer can define object classes, objects, and object sets directly without using macros. We close this section by giving an overview of these new constructs.

To begin, an **object class** is not an ASN.1 type. Like a macro, it is a template used to specify the various fields of an object class. For example, OPERATION may be defined as an object class which contains fields for the arguments, the results, and the errors. Every object of the Operation class must have these fields. Another example of an object class is ATTRIBUTE. This class contains fields for the attribute syntax, the attribute name, and an indication of whether the attribute values are single- or multiple-valued.

An **object** of an object class must provide a more concrete specification of the types associated with the fields in the object class. For example, one can specify a remote operation as an object by specifying the types used for the argument, the result, and the error fields.

An **object set** is a set of objects of the same class. For example, we can collect a set of remote operations (e.g., those associated with a port) into an object set. This object set may be referenced by any module. This object set construct can be used to replace the ANY or the ANY DEFINED BY ASN.1 constructs.

A good way to relate the above constructs is a table. An information class can be viewed as the layout of a table. An object is a row in a particular table. Finally, an object set is a set of rows that make up a particular table.

8.4   Summary

The structure and content of an object should be independent of the representation of the object. The ASN.1 notation provides a tool to specify the structure and content of an object in a representation-independent manner.

Similar to the declaration part of a high level programming language, ASN.1 provides language constructs, called ASN.1 modules, to define types and values. An ASN.1 module contains a group of related ASN.1 types used for an application.

For every abstract type in ASN.1, the ASN.1 standard provides a transfer syntax to represent values of that type. This transfer syntax is called Basic Encoding Rules (BER).

The macro facility of the ASN.1 standard allows an application protocol designer to extend the types and value notations of ASN.1. For example, an application protocol designer can use ASN.1 macros to define object classes and remote operations. Because of the broad use of remote operations in OSI application protocols and the increasing use of object-oriented concepts in modelling information, ASN.1 macros are used in many OSI application protocol standards.

Related Standards

DIS 8824: Information Technology - Open Systems Interconnection - Specification of Abstract Syntax Notation One (ASN.1)

DIS 8824 PDAM 2: Information Technology - Abstract Syntax Notation One (ASN.1) - Amendments to ISO 8824 - Part 1: Basic ASN.1

CD 8824-2: Information Technology - Open Systems Interconnection - Abstract Syntax Notation One (ASN.1) - Part 2: Information Object Specification

CD 8824-3: Information Technology - Open Systems Interconnection - Abstract Syntax Notation One (ASN.1) - Part 3: Constraint Specification

CD 8824-4: Information Technology - Open Systems Interconnection - Abstract Syntax Notation One (ASN.1) - Part 4: Parameterization of ASN.1 Specification

DIS 8825: Information Technology - Open Systems Interconnection - Specification of Basic Encoding Rules for Abstract Syntax Notation ONE (ASN.1)

ISO 8825 PDAM 2: Information Technology - Specification of ASN.1 Encoding Rules - Amendments to ISO 8825 to Give ISO 8825 Part 1: Basic Encoding Rules

CD 8825-2: Information Technology - Open Systems Interconnection - Specification of ASN.1 Encoding Rules - Part 2: Packed Encoding Rules

CD 8825-3: Information Technology - Open Systems Interconnection - Specification of ASN.1 Encoding Rules - Part 3: Distinguished Encoding Rules

9

Presentation Layer

The Presentation Layer provides two types of service. The first type is to handle the representation of information exchanged between two communicating AEs (i.e., application entities) so that the types and values of the information exchanged will be preserved. These two AEs are also called presentation service users (PS-users). The second type is session related. The only reason why such session related service is provided at the Presentation Layer is because OSI layering principle requires session related requests be passed through the Presentation Layer first. Since the OSI standard does not impose conformance to the layering principle, an OSI implementation may choose to violate the layering principle and pass session related requests directly to the session module.

In Section 9.1, we explain some presentation concepts. In Section 9.2, we examine the presentation service. In Section 9.3, we study the presentation protocol.

The connection-oriented presentation service definition and the protocol specification are specified in ISO/IEC 8822 and 8823 respectively.

9.1   Presentation Concepts

A common representation of information exchanged between two communicating AEs ensures that the sending AE and the receiving AE understand the same data types and data values. During a presentation connection establishment, the AEs and the presentation service provider negotiate on the use of a transfer syntax for every abstract syntax involved in the communication. In general, an abstract syntax can be represented by more than one transfer syntax. At the end of the negotiation, exactly one transfer syntax is selected for every abstract syntax. Each negotiated abstract/transfer syntax pair is called a **presentation context**. A presentation context is named by a **presentation context identifier (PCI)**. The set of all the presentation contexts available at any given time on a presentation connection is called the **defined context set (DCS)**. In particular, the DCS obtained at the end of the connection establishment phase is called the **initial DCS**.

During the connection establishment phase, the AEs may assume the availability of a mutually understood **default context**, and skip the process of negotiation of presentation contexts. Since the default context amounts to a single presentation context, some facility may be needed for the AEs to add presentation contexts to the DCS during the data transfer phase. The **presentation context management** facility permits an AE to request the presentation service provider to negotiate a transfer syntax for any abstract syntax introduced during the data transfer phase. For example, an FTAM initiator may not know the abstract syntax of a file that it wants to open when the FTAM dialogue is established. The presentation context management facility also allows presentation contexts to be deleted from the DCS during the data transfer phase.

Let us briefly explain how encoding is done by the sending AE. During the data transfer phase, the sending AE passes PSDUs (i.e., presentation service data unit) to an underlying presentation entity (PE). In general, a PSDU is a sequence of one or more **presentation data values (PDVs)**. For example, an FTAM protocol machine may concatenate a sequence of F-WRITE PDUs first before it invokes the presentation service; in this case, the file data from each F-DATA is mapped to a PDV. Besides containing some locally encoded value, each PDV also contains a PCI to inform the remote system of the presentation context associated with the value. On receiving a PSDU, the PE transforms each PDV in the PSDU into a bit stream using the transfer syntax specified in the PCI. It then uses some mechanism defined by the presentation protocol standard to concatenate all the bit streams into a single bit stream. The concatenated bit stream is then passed as SS-user-data to the underlying Session Layer.

9.2 Presentation Service

The presentation standard defines the following connection-oriented presentation facilities (Table 9.1):

- connection establishment facility which is used to select presentation functional units, establish session connection characteristics, and define an initial DCS or a default context,
- context management facility which is used to add or delete presentation contexts within the lifetime of a presentation connection,
- data transfer facilities, dialogue control facilities, and connection termination facilities which are all inherited from the Session Layer.

The first two facilities are examined next.

Facility	Service Elements	Type
Connection Establishment	P-CONNECT	Confirmed
Context Management	P-ALTER-CONTEXT	Confirmed
Normal Data	P-DATA	Non-Confirmed
Typed Data	P-TYPED-DATA	Non-Confirmed
Expedited Data	P-EXPEDITED-DATA	Non-Confirmed
Capability Data	P-CAPABILITY-DATA	Confirmed
Dialogue Control	See Table 9.3	
Connection Release	P-RELEASE P-U-ABORT P-P-ABORT	Confirmed Non-Confirmed Provider-Initiated

TABLE 9.1   **Presentation Service Elements Provided by each Facility**

• **connection establishment facility**

Parameter Name	Request	Indication	Response	Confirm
Calling-presentation-address	M	M		
Called-presentation-address	M	M		
Responding-presentation-address			M	M
Presentation context definition list	U	C(=)		
Presentation context definition result list		C	C	C(=)
Default context name	U	C(=)		
Default context result			C	C(=)
Quality of service	S	S	S	S
Presentation requirements	U	C	U	C(=)
Mode	M	M(=)		
Session requirements	S	S	S	S
ISPSN	S		S	S
Initial assignment of tokens	S	S	S	S
Session connection identifier	U	S	S	S
PS-user data		S	U	C(=)
Result		C(=)	M	U(=)

TABLE 9.2   **Parameters of P-CONNECT**

A PS-user uses **P-CONNECT** to establish a presentation connection with its peer. Table 9.2 shows the parameters associated with each of the P-CONNECT service primitives. Many of them are session related, thus they are mapped onto equivalent parameters of the corresponding S-CONNECT service primitive. Let us explain some of the presentation related parameters.

- presentation context definition list: The initiating PS-user uses this list to propose a set of presentation contexts. Each item in the list contains two components: a PCI and an abstract syntax name.
- presentation context definition result list: This parameter indicates the acceptance or rejection of each item in the presentation context definition list.
- default context name: This parameter identifies a default presentation context.
- default context result: This parameter is used to indicate the acceptance or rejection of the proposed default context.
- presentation requirements: This is a list of functional units that the PS-users are willing to employ.
- mode: This parameter indicates the mode of the operation of the Presentation Layer. Its value can be either X.410-1984 or normal. The X.410-1984 mode exists primarily for compatibility with the 1984 version of MHS which does not use the presentation service. Use of this mode for applications other than MHS is discouraged. On the other hand, the normal mode supports all the presentation service, therefore it is the preferred mode for supporting all new application protocols.
- PS-user-data: This parameter is made up of one or more PDVs.

Note that the session connection identifier instead of the presentation connection identifier appears as a parameter of P-CONNECT (Table 9.2). The reason is that there is a one-to-one correspondence between a presentation connection and a session connection.

Let us describe how to derive the initial DCS during connection establishment. First, the calling PS-user issues a P-CONNECT.request primitive. Among the various parameters associated with this primitive is the presentation context definition list. On receiving the P-CONNECT.request, the local PE determines which transfer syntax(es) to use. It then sends a presentation context definition result list to the peer PE. The remote PE examines each presentation context in the result list and decides if it can support any of the proposed transfer syntaxes. It then issues a P-CONNECT.indication with a possibly modified presentation context definition result list to the called PS-user. The called PS-user may respond with a different presentation context definition result list which is eventually passed back to the initiating PS-user. At this stage, the initial DCS is established.

- **context management facility**

Using **P-ALTER**, a PS-user can modify the DCS. P-ALTER-CONTEXT, a confirmed service element, is used as follows. The requesting PS-user provides a presentation context addition list or/and a presentation context deletion list to the local PE. The PE passes these lists to the remote system together with an indication of which proposed contexts it can support. The remote PS-user and the remote PE may make further changes to the lists. The final presentation context addition result list and presentation context deletion list are conveyed back to the requesting PS-user.

- **data transfer facilities**

The data transfer facilities are those offered by the Session Layer. They comprise of **P-TYPED-DATA**, **P-DATA**, **P-CAPABILITY-DATA**, and **P-EXPEDITED-DATA**. The user data parameter in the first three service elements is encoded using the current DCS or the default context. Expedited data is encoded using the default context. This choice is made because it is possible for an expedited data request to overtake a P-ALTER request, hence the DCS may not be the one agreed by both sides when the expedited data arrive.

- **dialogue control facility**

Service Elements	Type
P-U-EXCEPTION-REPORT	Non-Confirmed
P-P-EXCEPTION-REPORT	Provider Initiated
P-TOKEN-GIVE	Non-Confirmed
P-TOKEN-PLEASE	Non-Confirmed
P-CONTROL-GIVE	Non-Confirmed
P-SYNC-MINOR	Optionally Confirmed
P-SYNC-MAJOR	Confirmed
P-RESYNCHRONIZE	Confirmed
P-ACTIVITY-START	Non-Confirmed
P-ACTIVITY-RESUME	Non-Confirmed
P-ACTIVITY-END	Confirmed
P-ACTIVITY-INTERRUPT	Confirmed
P-ACTIVITY-DISCARD	Confirmed

TABLE 9.3   Service Elements Provided by the Dialogue Control Facility

The service elements here (Table 9.3) are similar to the session service elements.

- **connection release facility**

The presentation service provides three different ways to release a connection: orderly release (**P-RELEASE**), user abort (**P-U-ABORT**), and provider abort (**P-P-ABORT**).

Next, we describe the presentation functional units. The presentation functional units fall into two categories. The first category contains the Kernel, Context Management, and Context Restoration functional units. The second category contains all the functional units in the Session Layer. Let us examine the functional units in the first category.

The Kernel functional unit supports the basic presentation service elements such as P-CONNECT, P-DATA, P-RELEASE, P-U-ABORT, and P-P-ABORT. If only the Kernel functional unit is selected, then either the presentation contexts in the initial DCS or the default context would be used during the lifetime of a presentation connection.

The Context Management functional unit supports the modification of the DCS during the lifetime of the presentation connection.

The Context Restoration functional unit is used for the interaction between context management and session resynchronization. It may be selected only if the Context Management functional unit is chosen for use. It works as follows. If the DCS can be altered and a resynchronization occurs, it is necessary to determine the DCS that is previously in effect. Resynchronization using restart or set to a point known to the presentation service provider is not a problem. If the point is lower than those known to the presentation service provider, the DCS will be restored to the initial DCS. If the point specified is higher than those known to the presentation service provider or if the abandon resynchronization type is requested, the DCS is left unchanged.

The presentation standard also specifies a connectionless presentation service. There is only one service element, **P-UNIT-DATA**. Its parameters are PS-user-data and QOS. In the absence of the connection establishment phase, the sending PS-user must specify the presentation context(s) when it invokes P-UNIT-DATA.

9.3   Presentation Protocol

Code	Name
CP	Connect Presentation
CPA	Connect Presentation accept
CPR	Connect Presentation Reject
ARP	Abnormal Release Provider
ARU	Abnormal Release User
NR	Normal Release
NRA	Normal Release Acknowledge
CD	Capability Data
CDA	Capability Data Acknowledge
PD	Presentation Data
ED	Expedited Data
PTD	Presentation Typed Data
RS	Resynchronize
RSA	Resynchronize Acknowledge
AC	Alter Context
ACA	Alter Context Acknowledge

TABLE 9.4   Presentation PDUs

The operation of the presentation protocol machine (PPM) is very straightforward. The Presentation Layer does not generate any PPDU for the pass-through service elements. Since most of the presentation service elements are session related, there are not as many PPDUs as SPDUs. Table 9.4 displays the PPDUs used by the presentation protocol. It is interesting to note that the data transfer and resynchronize facilities are not considered to be pass-through facilities. Consider the resynchronize facility. When a PPM receives a P-RESYNCHRONIZE.request primitive, it has to adjust the DCS and send that information in a PPDU to its peer. Since control information needs to be exchanged, the resynchronize facility is not pass-through.

The next three examples illustrate how the PPDUs are used by the presentation protocol.

Example 9.1

This example shows the protocol exchanges during a presentation connection establishment. When the initiating PPM receives a P-CONNECT.request service primitive, it prepares and sends a CP PPDU to its peer, the responding PPM. An interesting question here is how the initiating PPM represents the PS-user-data field of a CP PPDU in the absence of an initial DCS during this early part of the connection establishment phase. What the initiating PPM may do is to represent each PDV in the PS-user-data field using a number of transfer syntaxes, and hope that the responding PPM may support at least one of them. In the worst case, if the responding PPM does not support any of the transfer syntaxes, it can refuse the presentation connection by sending a CPR PPDU with a provider reason value of "user data not readable". Otherwise, it issues a P-CONNECT.indication service primitive to its PS-user and then waits for a response. If it receives a P-CONNECT.response with a result parameter value of "acceptance", it sends a CPA PPDU to the initiating PPM. And if it receives a P-CONNECT.response with a result parameter value of "user-rejection", it sends a CPR PPDU.

Example 9.2

This example illustrates the protocol exchanges during context management. When the requesting PPM receives a P-ALTER-CONTEXT.request primitive, it sends an AC PPDU to the accepting PPM. When the accepting PPM receives the AC PPDU, it may refuse some of the proposed presentation context additions/deletions. It issues a P-ALTER-CONTEXT.indication primitive in which it marks the refused proposals with a value of "provider-rejection". When it receives a P-ALTER-CONTEXT.response from its PS-user, it modifies its own DCS and then sends an ACA PPDU to the requesting PPM. This ACA PPDU indicates the acceptance or rejection of each presentation context addition/deletion. When the requesting PPM receives the ACA PPDU, it makes changes to its own DCS accordingly and issues a P-ALTER-CONTEXT.confirm primitive to its PS-user.

The interesting presentation protocol procedures have been examined. Next we examine the structure of a generic PPDU. One of the design issues in the structure of a PPDU is how much information should be put inside a PPDU. As pointed out earlier, some of the parameters associated with a presentation service primitive are session related.

To save a few bits in the encoding of a PPDU, it seems better to put only the presentation related parameters inside a PPDU and pass the session related parameters to the Session Layer when a session service primitive is issued. To illustrate what we meant, let us consider the presentation address parameter of P-CONNECT. Remember that a presentation address is made up of a presentation selector and a session address. The presentation selector is presentation related whereas the session address is session related. Thus the presentation selector is put inside the CP PDU while the session address is passed as a parameter to the S-CONNECT service element.

Next, we examine the encoding of a PPDU. BER is used to encode each PPDU. The only interesting part is how to encode the User-data field of a PPDU if it is present. The following definition says that there are two ways to encode the User-data field: simple encoding and full encoding.

```
User-data ::= CHOICE {
                    [APPLICATION 0] IMPLICIT     Simply-encoded-data
                    [APPLICATION 1] IMPLICIT     Fully-encoded-data }


Simply-encoded-data ::= OCTET STRING


Fully-encoded-data ::= SEQUENCE OF PDV-list


PDV-list ::= SEQUENCE {
                    transfer-syntax-name             Transfer-syntax-name OPTIONAL,
                    presentation-context-identifier  Presentation-context-identifier,
                    presentation-data-values
                        CHOICE{
                            single-ASN1-type     [0]     ANY,
                            octet-aligned        [1]     IMPLICIT OCTET STRING,
                            arbitrary            [2]     IMPLICIT BIT STRING}
                        }
```

These two encodings are explained next.

Simple encoding is used when only one presentation context is involved. This is the case if either the default context is used, or the initial DCS contains only one context and the Context Management functional unit is not active. The encoding of User-data is obtained by the concatenation of the encodings of all the PDVs contained within the User-data. No delimiter is inserted between the encodings of two adjacent PDVs. This means that the transfer syntax used (there is only one transfer syntax since we assume that there is one presentation context) must be self-delimiting. There is an exception to the above rule. The exception applies to those cases where the User-data of the PPDU maps directly to a parameter of a session element. For example, the User-data of the PD PPDU maps directly to a parameter of the S-DATA service element. In those cases, the tag and the length octets are left out in order to save a couple of octets in the encoding. The reason is that the tag and length information will be supplied by the SI and LI fields within an SPDU (see Section 7.3.1).

Full encoding is used when the default context is not used and furthermore, either the DCS contains more than one presentation context or the Context Management functional unit has been selected. The basic idea behind full encoding is whenever adjacent PDVs happen to belong to the same presentation context, we can group them into a PDV-list -- this can save a few bits because we do not have to encode the same PCI more than once. In case the transfer syntax for the presentation context of the group produces octet-aligned encoding, then each PDV in the group is serialized and the resulting encodings are concatenated to form an OCTET STRING. Otherwise, the "arbitrary" alternative is used where each PDV in the group is serialized and the resulting encodings are concatenated to form a BIT STRING. The "single-ASN1-type" alternative is used whenever the group contains only one PDV. In this case, encoding is done according to the corresponding transfer syntax specified in the PCI.

When a presentation service primitive is pass-through, the PPM will not generate any PPDU. However, it still needs to encode the PS-user-data parameter of the service primitive (if present) before it issues a corresponding session service primitive. For example, P-ACTIVITY-START.request is pass-through and does contain the PS-user-data parameter. Encoding of PS-user-data in such a case is given by simple encoding with the BER tag and length octets left out.

9.4 Summary

The primary service of the Presentation Layer is to handle the representation of information structures exchanged between two communicating AEs so that the types and values of the information structures can be preserved.

During connection establishment, the two corresponding presentation entities negotiate to arrive at an initial Defined Context Set (DCS). This DCS is a set of presentation contexts, with one for each abstract syntax specified in the application context. Each presentation context determines the transfer syntax used for the associated abstract syntax. Presentation context management allows presentation contexts to be added to or deleted from the DCS.

The operation of the presentation protocol is quite straightforward. Because most of its service elements are pass-through service elements from the Session Layer, it does not use too many presentation PDUs.

Related Standards

ISO 8822: Information Processing Systems - Open Systems Interconnection - Connection Oriented Presentation Service Definition
ISO 8822 DAD 1: Information Processing Systems - Open Systems Interconnection - Presentation Service Definition - Draft Addendum 1 Covering the Connectionless-Mode Presentation

ISO 8822 PDAD 2: Information Processing Systems - Open Systems Interconnection - Connection Oriented Presentation Service Definition - Addendum 2: Support of Session Symmetric Synchronization Service

ISO 8822: PDAM 2 Information Processing Systems - Open Systems Interconnection - Connection-oriented Presentation Service Definition - Proposed Draft Amendment 2: Unlimited User Data

ISO 8822: PDAM 3 Information Processing Systems - Open Systems Interconnection - Connection-oriented Presentation Service Definition - Proposed Draft Amendment 3 to Specify registration of Abstract Syntaxes

ISO 8822 DAM 5: Information Processing Systems - Open Systems Interconnection - Connection Oriented Presentation Service Definition - Proposed Draft Amendment 5 to Deliver Additional Session Synchronization Functionality to the Presentation Service User

ISO 8823: Information Processing Systems - Open Systems Interconnection - Connection Oriented Presentation Protocol Specification

ISO 8823 PDAD 2: Information Processing Systems - Open Systems Interconnection - Connection Oriented Presentation Protocol Specification - Addendum 2: Support of Session Symmetric Synchronization Service

ISO 8823: PDAM 2 Information Processing Systems - Open Systems Interconnection - Connection Oriented Presentation Protocol Specification - Proposed Draft Amendment 2: Unlimited User Data

ISO 8823: PDAM 3 Information Processing Systems - Open Systems Interconnection - Connection Oriented Presentation Protocol Specification - Proposed Draft Amendment 3 to Specify Registration of Transfer Syntaxes

ISO 8823 DAM 5: Information Processing Systems - Open Systems Interconnection - Connection Oriented Presentation Protocol Specification - Proposed Draft Amendment 5 to Deliver Additional session Synchronization Functionality to the Presentation Service User

ISO 8823-2: Information Processing Systems - Open Systems Interconnection - Connection-oriented Presentation Protocol Specification - Part 2: Protocol Implementation Conformance Statement (PICS) Proforma

DIS 8824: Information Processing Systems - Open Systems Interconnection - Specification of Abstract Syntax Notation One (ASN.1)

DIS 8825: Information Processing Systems - Open Systems Interconnection - Specification of Basic Encoding Rules for Abstract Syntax Notation One (ASN.1)

DIS 9576: Information Processing Systems - Open Systems Interconnection - Connectionless Presentation Protocol Specification

DIS 9576-2: Information Processing Systems - Open Systems Interconnection - Connectionless Presentation Protocol to Provide the Connectionless-Mode Presentation Service - Part 2: Protocol Implementation Conformance Statement (PICS) Proforma

10

Association Control Service Element

Association Control Service Element (ACSE) is defined for the purpose of management of application associations. It provides facilities for the establishment and release of application associations. An application association is a presentation connection with additional application layer semantics such as application context negotiation and peer-to-peer authentication. At present, there is a one-to-one mapping between application associations and presentation connections. However, future versions of the ACSE standard might permit a presentation connection to be reused for a new association or multiple associations to be interleaved onto a single presentation connection.

Because the sole purpose of ACSE is to manage application associations, ACSE does not provide any data transfer service elements. Thus, in any application context containing ACSE, there is one or more user-ASEs which will provide some data transfer service elements.

Sections 10.1 and 10.2 describe the ACSE service definition and the ACSE protocol respectively. Section 10.3 describes the ACSE/Presentation (A/P) library which provides a programming interface on top of ACSE and the Presentation Layer. Later in Chapter 18 on OSI Management, we will see how a CMISE API can be integrated with the A/P library.

The service definition and the protocol specification of ACSE are given in ISO 8649 and 8650 respectively.

10.1 ACSE Service

Parameter Name	Req	Ind	Rsp	Cnf
Mode	U	M(=)		
Application Context Name	M	M(=)	M	M
Calling AP Title	U	C(=)		
Calling AE Qualifier	U	C(=)		
Calling AP Invocation-identifier	U	C(=)		
Calling AE Invocation-identifier	U	C(=)		
Called AP Title	U	C(=)		
Called AE Qualifier	U	C(=)		
Called AP Invocation-identifier	U	C(=)		
Called AE Invocation-identifier	U	C(=)		
Responding AP Title			U	C(=)
Responding AE Qualifier			U	C(=)
Responding AP Invocation-identifier			U	C(=)
Responding AE Invocation-identifier			U	C(=)
User Information	U	C(=)	U	C(=)
Result			M	M(=)
Result Source				M
Diagnostic			U	C(=)
Calling Presentation Address	P	P		
Called Presentation Address	P	P		
Responding Presentation Address			P	P
Presentation Context Definition List	P	P		
Presentation Context Definition Result List			P	P
Default Presentation Context Name	P	P		
Default Presentation Context Result			P	P
Quality of Service	P	P	P	P
Presentation Requirements	P	P	P	P
Session Requirements	P	P	P	P
Initial Synchronization Point Serial Number	P	P	P	P
Initial Assignment of Tokens	P	P	P	P
Session-connection Identifier	P	P	P	P

TABLE 10.1   Parameters of A-ASSOCIATE

There are only four ACSE service elements. An AE uses **A-ASSOCIATE** to establish an application association with its peer. This service element uses over thirty parameters (Table 10.1). More may be added in the future to provide additional semantics of an application association. Let us describe some of the parameters.

 •   application context name: This parameter, perhaps the most important of all, identifies the application context used for the application association. The initiating AE (initiator) first proposes an application context. The accepting AE (acceptor) returns either the same or a different one. If the initiator cannot operate in the acceptor's application context, it issues an A-ABORT.request primitive.

- mode: This parameter specifies the mode in which the ACSE service will operate for the association. Its value can be either normal or X.410-1984.
- AP Titles/qualifiers: An application entity is identified by an AET (i.e., application entity title) which consists of an APT (i.e, application process title) and an AE qualifier.
- presentation context definition list: This list contains at least one PCI (i.e., presentation context identifier) for every ASE contained in the application context. In particular, it includes a PCI for ACSE.
- result and result source: The result parameter is provided by either the acceptor, the ACSE service-provider, or the presentation service provider. Its value can be either "accepted", "rejected (permanent)" or "rejected (transient)". The result source parameter identifies the creating source of the result parameter and the diagnostic parameter if present. Its value can be either "ACSE service user", "ACSE service provider", or "presentation service provider".
- diagnostic: This parameter is used only if the result parameter has the value "rejected". For example, an ACSE service user may reject an association because it does not support the application context, and an ACSE service provider may reject an association because there is no common ACSE version.
- user information: Either the initiating AE or the responding AE may include the user information. Its meaning depends on the application context that accompanies the request. For example, in a FTAM application context, the F-INITIALIZE-request PDU generated by the FTAM ASE is passed as user information to the A-ASSOCIATE.request primitive.

An application association can be released in an orderly manner by means of **A-RELEASE**. If the Negotiated Release functional unit in the Session Layer is active, the accepting AE may refuse the release. If an AE detects an unrecoverable error, it uses **A-ABORT** to abort an application association with possible loss of data that are in transit. The ACSE service provider can also abort an application association using **A-P-ABORT** if it has detected some internal problem. A-P-ABORT is a pass through service element from the Presentation Layer, i.e., A-P-ABORT is semantically identical to P-P-ABORT.

ACSE has a total of two functional units. The functions described above form the Kernel functional unit. ISO/IEC 8649/AM 1 defined the Authentication functional unit which, if active, can provide peer entity authentication. The addendum called for the addition of three new parameters to the A-ASSOCIATE service element: authentication value, ACSE requirements, and authentication mechanism. The ACSE requirements parameter is used to indicate the ACSE functional units requested by an ACSE service user, while the authentication mechanism parameter is used to specify the authentication mechanism used to process the authentication values.

10.2   ACSE Protocol

The ACSE Protocol Machine (ACPM) operates in either the normal mode or the X.410-1984 mode. When operating in the latter mode, the ACPM does not exchange any ACSE

APDUs with its peer. For example, if the ACPM receives an A-ASSOCIATE.request primitive with the mode equal to X.410-1984, it does not generate any APDU and immediately issues a P-CONNECT.request primitive with the same mode. The following discussion assumes that the ACPM operates in the normal mode.

Code	Name
AARQ	A-ASSOCIATE.request PDU
AARE	A-ASSOCIATE.reponse PDU
RLRQ	A-RELEASE.request PDU
RLRE	A-RELEASE.reponse PDU
ABRT	A-ABORT.request PDU

TABLE 10.2   ACSE APDUs

The ACPM is driven by the receipt of input events from its ACSE service user or the presentation service provider. It uses five APDUs (Table 10.2) and three procedures. These procedures are association establishment, normal release, and abnormal release procedures.

The AARQ APDU is used in the association establishment procedure. Upon receiving an A-ASSOCIATE.request primitive from its ACSE service user, the requesting ACPM forms an AARQ APDU. The AARQ APDU is then sent as the user data parameter of a P-CONNECT.request primitive. The ASN.1 definition of the AARQ APDU is shown below:

```
AARQ-apdu :: = [APPLICATION 0]    IMPLICIT SEQUENCE {
    protocol-version              [0]    IMPLICIT BIT STRING DEFAULT {version 1}
    application-context-name      [1]    Application-context-name OPTIONAL,
    called-AP-title               [2]    AP-title OPTIONAL,
    called-AE-qualifier           [3]    AE-qualifier OPTIONAL,
    called-AP-invocation-id       [4]    AP-invocation-id OPTIONAL,
    called-AE-invocation-id       [5]    AE-invocation-id OPTIONAL,
    calling-AP-title              [6]    AP-title OPTIONAL,
    calling-AE-qualifier          [7]    AE-qualifier OPTIONAL,
    calling-AP-invocation-id      [8]    AP-invocation-id OPTIONAL,
    calling-AE-invocation-id      [9]    AE-invocation-id OPTIONAL,
    implementation-inf            [29]   IMPLICIT Implementation-data OPTIONAL,
    user-information              [30]   IMPLICIT Association-information OPTIONAL}
```

Note that the protocol-version and implementation-inf fields are filled in by the ACPM.

When the accepting ACPM receives an AARQ APDU, it checks if the AARQ APDU is acceptable syntactically. If not, the association establishment procedure is disrupted and no A-ASSOCIATE.indication is issued. If the accepting ACPM does not support the protocol version requested by the initiating ACPM, it will respond with an AARE APDU and indicate the result value of "rejected (permanent)".

When the accepting ACPM receives an A-ASSOCIATE.response primitive, the result parameter should specify whether its user has accepted or rejected the association. The accepting ACPM forms an AARE APDU and sends it to the requesting ACPM using a P-CONNECT.response primitive. If its user accepted the association request, the accepting ACPM sets the result parameter of P-CONNECT.response to "acceptance", otherwise "user-rejection" is set to indicate that its user has rejected the association.

The RLRQ and RLRE APDUs are used in the normal release of an association. When an ACPM receives an A-RELEASE.request primitive, it forms a RLRQ APDU and sends it as the user data of a P-RELEASE.request primitive. When the accepting ACPM receives an A-RELEASE.response primitive, it forms a RLRE APDU and sends it as the user data of a P-RELEASE.response primitive. Thus, the purpose of RLRE is to acknowledge the received RLRQ.

The ABRT APDU is used in the abnormal release procedure. There are only two fields in an ABRT APDU: abort source (mandatory) and user information (optional). When an ACPM receives A-ABORT.request, it forms an ABRT APDU with the abort source field set to "ACSE service user". It then sends the ABRT APDU as user data of a P-U-ABORT.request primitive to release the association. When an ACPM detects a protocol error, it issues an A-ABORT.indication primitive to its service user, forms an ABRT APDU with the abort source field set to "ACSE service provider", and sends it as the user data of a P-U-ABORT.request primitive.

The choice of the version of the session protocol does affect the abnormal release procedure. The procedure described above is used for version 2 which essentially relaxes the size of the SS-user-data to "infinite". If an ACPM receives an A-ABORT.request primitive while version 1 is used for an association, it does not generate the ABRT APDU. It simply issues a P-U-ABORT.request primitive. This is understandable because an ABRT APDU, if generated, will increase the size of the SS-user-data.

ACSE Primitive	APDU	Presentation Primitive
A-ASSOCIATE.request/indication	AARQ	P-CONNECT.request/indication
A-ASSOCIATE.response/confirm	AARE	P-CONNECT.response/confirm
A-RELEASE.request/indication	RLRQ	P-RELEASE.request/indication
A-RELEASE.response/confirm	RLRE	P-RELEASE.response/confirm
A-ABORT.request/indication	ABRT	P-U-ABORT.request/indication
A-P-ABORT.indication	–	P-P-ABORT.indication

TABLE 10.3   Mapping of ACSE Primitives to Presentation Primitives

If the Authentication functional unit is supported, then the AARQ and AARE APDUs should also include fields such as authentication value, authentication mechanism name, and ACSE requirements.

Table 10.3 summarizes the mapping of ACSE primitives to presentation primitives.

10.3   ACSE/Presentation Library Interface

Functions	Parameters
ap_open	(pathname, oflags)
ap_init_env	(fd, env_file, flags)
ap_get_env	(fd, attr, val)
ap_set_env	(fd, attr, val)
ap_save	(fd, savefd)
ap_restore	(fd, savefd)
ap_snd	(fd, sptype, cdata, ubuf, flags)
ap_rcv	(fd, sptype, cdata, ubuf, flags)
ap_error	()
ap_free	(kind, val)
ap_close	(fd)

TABLE 10.4   APLI Functions

The **ACSE/Presentation (A/P) library**, by UNIX Systems Laboratory, is a library of C functions that provides the users an API to the ACSE and presentation services. It comprises a small set of functions and an environment. The A/P library environment simplifies the programmer's task by maintaining information that is needed to set up and maintain the application association. For example, some environment default values can be established before an association is made. The A/P library functions (Table 10.4) can be used to establish/release a communication endpoint, manage the A/P library environment, send/receive A/P library service primitives, and share an instance of the A/P library. The use of these functions is explained below.

•   **establishing and releasing a communication endpoint**

In order to use the A/P library, the user must first obtain a supporting communication endpoint. This can be accomplished by calling the **ap_open()** function. This function takes two arguments. The first argument specifies the name of a communication provider. The second argument, oflags, is used to request the asynchronous mode of operation. When the ap_open() function is successfully executed, it returns an integer that is used to identify a communication endpoint in subsequent interactions with the A/P library. The **ap_close()** function is used to indicate that the supporting communication endpoint is no longer needed.

•   **managing the A/P library environment**

The A/P library environment is the repository of the information necessary to establish and maintain an association. Information in the environment is stored as attributes. Below is a description of some of the environment attributes:

- AP_ACSE_SEL: This indicates which version of the ACSE protocol standard has been selected for use within the current association.
- AP_BIND_PADDR: This indicates the presentation address to which the communication endpoint should be bound.
- AP_CLD_AEID: This is the called AE-invocation identifier.
- AP_CNTX_NAME: This indicates the application context of the association.
- AP_DCS: This is the defined context set.
- AP_DPCN: This is the default context name.
- AP_INIT_SYNC_PT: This is the initial synchronization point serial number.
- AP_MODE_SEL: This indicates the mode in which the A/P-Library is to be used.
- AP_PCDL: This is used to specify the proposed presentation context definition list.
- AP_ROLE_ALLOWED: This indicates the roles (i.e., initiator or responder) which the library user may play.
- AP_SESS_SEL: This indicates the version number of the session protocol selected for the current association.
- AP_SFU_AVAIL: This indicates which session functional units are available.

Note that some of the above attributes are static, while some are dynamic.

Four functions are provided to perform operations on the A/P library environment. First, **ap_init_env**() function creates an instance of the A/P library environment specified by some communication endpoint. An instance of the A/P library can be viewed as a collection of information kept in the user's data space. After the library instance is created, some of the attributes may be set. This is achieved by calling **ap_set_env**() which will set an attribute to a specified value. The **ap_get_env**() function is used to retrieve the value of a particular attribute. After the value is retrieved and the examination is over, the **ap_free**() function can be called to free the memory allocated to the retrieved value.

- **sending and receiving A/P library service primitives**

Assuming the user has initialized the AP environment, in particular the presentation addresses and the presentation contexts, it can issue or receive service primitives using the **ap_snd**() and **ap_rcv**() functions. Each ACSE or presentation service primitive can be viewed as an event which is passed as a parameter to the ap_snd() or ap_rcv() function. The A/P library designates an event for every possible ACSE or presentation primitive. For example, if the sender wants to send some data, it calls ap_snd() with "P_DATA_REQ" as a parameter. And if it wants to receive data, it calls ap_rcv() with "P_DATA_IND" as a parameter. Note that the invocation of either ap_snd() or ap_rcv() may produce side effects on the environment attributes.

- **sharing an A/P library instance**

A user can share its A/P library instance with some other user. The **ap_save**() and **ap_restore**() functions are provided to facilitate sharing an instance of the A/P library among cooperating processes. The ap_save() function saves the current workspace into an opened file. The ap_restore() function recreates the saved workspace in the calling process's data space. Note that the calling process may not be identical to the process which calls ap_save(). Thus, if some process A calling ap_save() wants to do something else, another process B can continue the work of A by calling ap_restore(). Of course, B needs to know the communication endpoint which identifies the library instance saved by A.

• **error reporting**

Error reporting is accomplished using the global variable, ap_error. Through ap_error, the library reports internal error conditions caused, for example, by an invalid argument or a primitive issued in an invalid state. The **ap_error**() function is provided in the A/P library to return a pointer to a message that describes the latest error encountered by the library.

The following examples illustrate some of the functions in C format.

Example 10.1

```
int ap_init_env (fd, env_file);
int fd;
char *env_file;
```

This function establishes an instance of the A/P library and initializes the A/P environment. The fd argument is the communication endpoint returned by ap_open(). If no environment exists when ap_init_env() is called, memory will be allocated for the environment attributes in the calling process's data space and the attributes will be set to their default values. If an environment already exists when ap_init_env() is called, attributes will be assigned values from an initialization file, env_file. In this case, attributes will not be automatically set to their default values.

Example 10.2

```
int ap_snd (fd, sptype, cdata, ubuf, flags);
int fd;
unsigned long sptype = A_ASSOC_REQ;
ap_cdata_t *cdata;
struct osi_buf *ubuf;
int flags;
```

This function is used to issue an A-ASSOCIATE.request primitive. The cdata argument is used to contain control information such as the initial token assignment and the length of user-information field of an APDU. The ubuf argument points to a buffer containing user-information. The flags argument is used to indicate whether there are some more user data coming.

Example 10.3

```
int ap_restore (fd, savef);
int fd;
FILE *savef;
```

Used in conjunction with ap_save(), this function restores an instance of the A/P library. Essentially, it recreates the A/P library instance that was saved in the file associated with savef in the calling process's data space. The restored A/P library instance will be supported by the communication endpoint identified by fd. This must be the same communication endpoint that supported the instance of the A/P library when it was saved.

We close this section by summarizing the steps which an application program might use to manage an association. First, the application program obtains a communication endpoint by calling ap_open(). Afterwards, it may initialize some of the environment attributes by calling ap_init_env(). For example, if the application program is the initiator, it can specify the called presentation address and the presentation defined context set by setting the AP_BIND_PADDR attribute and the AP_PCDL attribute respectively. Once all the appropriate environment attributes have been set, the application program playing the initiator role may attempt to establish an association by calling ap_snd() with "A_ASSOC_REQ" as a parameter. After the association is established, data can be exchanged using ap_snd() and ap_rcv(). When the application program wants to release the association, it calls ap_snd() with "A_RELEASE_REQ" as a parameter.

10.4 Summary

ACSE provides facilities for the management of application associations. Since all the existing OSI application protocols are connection oriented, ACSE is contained in every application context.

ACSE provides only four service elements. It is interesting to note that the A-ASSOCIATE service element uses more than thirty parameters, most of which are inherited from the lower layers. It is anticipated that more parameters will be added to A-ASSOCIATE in the future. Thus for now, ACSE serves as a place holder to allow future addition of more complex application semantics.

A useful API, known as the A/P library, is provided by UNIX Systems Laboratory. It provides a simple interface to ACSE and presentation service. When future operating systems include the OSI upper layers in their kernels, this A/P library may replace TLI for network programming.

Related Standards

ISO 8649: Information Processing Systems - Open Systems Interconnection - Service Definition for the Association Control Service Element

ISO 8649 AM 1: Information Processing Systems - Open Systems Interconnection - Service Definition for the Association Control Service Element - Amendment 1: Authentication During Association Establishment

ISO 8649 DAD 2: Information Processing Systems - Open Systems Interconnection - Service Definition for the Association Control Service Element - Draft Addendum 2 Covering Connectionless-mode ACSE Service

ISO 8650: Information Processing Systems - Open Systems Interconnection - Protocol Specification for the Association Control Service Element

ISO 8650 AM 1: Information Processing Systems - Open Systems Interconnection - Protocol Specification for the Association Control Service Element - Amendment 1: Authentication During association Establishment

DIS 8650-2: Information Processing Systems - Open Systems Interconnection - Protocol Specification for the Association Control Service Element - Part 2: Protocol Implementation Conformance Statement (PICS) Proforma

DIS 10035: Information Processing Systems - Open Systems Interconnection - Connectionless ACSE Protocol to Provide the Connectionless-Mode ACSE Service

ISO 10169-1: Information Technology - Open Systems Interconnection - Conformance Test Suite for the ACSE Protocol - Part 1: Test Suite Structure and Test Purposes

11

Reliable Transfer Service Element

If a network failure occurs while a bulky APDU such as a large file or a long message is transferred over a wide area network, then the entire APDU may have to be retransmitted. **RTSE (Reliable Transfer Service Element)** ensures that the APDU, whatever its size, is transferred exactly once or that the sender is warned of an exception. RTSE provides such service through the use of the session service. To the RTSE users, RTSE provides a simple reliable transfer facility by hiding the complexity of the session service.

The RTSE standard, as specified in ISO/IEC 9066, is primarily used by MHS. Formerly called **RTS (Reliable Transfer Server)**, RTSE is used to regulate and control mail transfer between local and remote MTAs. In particular, it is used by the P1 protocol over a wide area network. When sending mail over a reliable LAN, the overhead incurred by RTSE cannot not be justified, hence RTSE is not used.

Let us describe how RTS works in conjunction with a 1984 MHS product. Figure 11.1 shows how an MTA process interacts with a RTS process and a UA process. The MTA process maintains two queues with the UA: a submission queue and a delivery queue. It also maintains two queues with the RTS process: an input queue and an output queue. When the MTA receives a message through the submission queue, it will insert the message into its output queue which also serves as the input queue to the RTS process. The RTS process encodes the message using BER, chops up the encoded string into segments, and uses the underlying communication mechanism to dispatch the segments to a remote RTS process. If there is any network failure, the RTS process only has to retransmit the segments sent since the last confirmed checkpoint. The entire mail does not have to be retransmitted. In its use of the session service, the MTA process creates an activity for every message it processes. Checkpoints within the message correspond to minor synchronization points within an activity. Note that no major synchronization points are used within an activity, hence the operation of RTS does not require the Major Synchronize functional unit to be active.

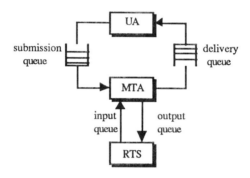

FIGURE 11.1   RTS used with 1984 MHS

Section 11.1 describes the RTSE service. Section 11.2 describes the RTSE protocol.

11.1 RTSE Service

Service	Type
RT-OPEN	Confirmed
RT-CLOSE	Confirmed
RT-TRANSFER	Confirmed
RT-TURN-PLEASE	Non-confirmed
RT-TURN-GIVE	Non-confirmed
RT-P-ABORT	Provider-initiated
RT-U-ABORT	Non-confirmed

TABLE 11.1   RTSE Service Elements

Table 11.1 lists the RTSE service elements. An initiating RTSE user invokes **RT-OPEN** to establish an application association with its peer which is the responding RTSE user. One of the mandatory parameters of this service element is dialogue-mode, whose value is either monologue-mode (meaning that only the AE which has the turn can request transfer) or two-way alternate (meaning that either AE can request transfer). Another mandatory parameter, initial-turn, specifies which RTSE user initially owns the turn. The mode parameter, an optional parameter, specifies the mode in which the RTSE service will operate for the association. It has two values: normal mode and X.410-1980 mode. The normal mode provides the full use of RTSE services while the X.410-1980 mode is based on RTS, the older version of RTSE. The X.410-1980 mode is primarily used to allow interworking with the older 1984 MHS implementations.

A RTSE user must own the turn before it can send an APDU using RTSE. Suppose it does and there is no outstanding RT-TRANSFER confirm primitive, it uses **RT-TRANSFER** to request the reliable transfer of the APDU. The request primitive contains a mandatory transfer-time parameter which defines the time period within which the requesting RTSE user would want to have the APDU transferred to its peer. Unlike many other OSI confirmed service elements, this service element does not have a response primitive. Thus, a confirm primitive received by the requesting RTSE user does not mean that its peer has secured the APDU. It only means that the peer RTSE protocol machine (RTPM) has received the APDU.

A RTSE user uses **RT-TURN-PLEASE** to request the turn from its peer, and **RT-TURN-GIVE** to relinquish the turn to its peer.

Provided that a RTSE user possesses the turn, it can use **RT-CLOSE** to request an orderly release of an established application association.

11.2   RTSE Protocol

RTSE APDU	RTSE Service Elements
RTORQ	RT-OPEN-REQUEST
RTOAC	RT-OPEN-ACCEPT
RTORJ	RT-OPEN-REJECT
RTTR	RT-TRANSFER
RTTP	RT-TOKEN-PLEASE
RTAB	RT-ABORT and RT-U-ABORT

TABLE 11.2   RTSE APDUs and corresponding Service Elements

First, we examine the use of each RTSE APDU (Table 11.2). The RTORQ APDU is used by an initiating RTPM to establish an application association. It is also used in the association recovery procedure to be explained later. Some of the fields, namely, checkpoint-size and window size, are options of the RTPM. The checkpoint-size field allows negotiation of the maximum amount of data (in units of 1024 octets) that can be sent between two minor synchronization points. The window-size field allows negotiation of the maximum number of outstanding minor synchronization points before data transfer shall be suspended. The default value is three. When a RTSE user registers with the RTSE service, it can specify its preferred values for the checkpoint-size and window-size fields.

The accepting RTPM uses RTOAC in a positive response to an association establishment request. It fills in the checkpoint-size and window-size fields, the values of which must be less than or equal to the corresponding values in the RTORQ APDU. The RTORJ APDU is used in a negative response to the association establishment request.

The RTTR APDU is used in the transfer and error recovery procedures.

The RTTP APDU is used during the servicing of the RT-TURN-PLEASE service element. No APDUs are exchanged during the servicing of the RT-TURN-GIVE service element.

The RTAB APDU is used during the servicing of the RT-U-ABORT and RT-P-ABORT service elements

No APDUs are exchanged for the orderly release of an association.

The RTPM maps association management service elements such as RT-OPEN, RT-CLOSE, RT-U-ABORT, and RT-P-ABORT to ACSE service elements in a natural way. Service elements used during the data transfer phase are mapped to the underlying presentation service elements. We should point out that if an application context uses RTSE, then RTSE is the sole user of ACSE in that application context, i.e., any other ASE in the application context has to go through RTSE to access association management facilities.

Next, we discuss the procedures used in the RTSE protocol. The RTSE standard defined nine procedures to cope with reliable transfer, error handling, and error recovery.

• **transfer procedure**

The transfer procedure is used to transfer an APDU. The RTPM accomplishes this by means of a single session activity. To explain this procedure, let us assume that a RTSE user wants to send an APDU to the local RTPM which is the requesting RTPM. Upon receipt of the APDU, the requesting RTPM issues a P-ACTIVITY-START.request primitive to create a new activity for the APDU. It encodes the APDU using an appropriate transfer syntax. Assuming that checkpointing is used, the RTPM chops the encoded value into segments with the length of each segment limited to the maximum checkpoint-size negotiated during association establishment. Each segment is next embedded in the user-data-part of a RTTR APDU. Each RTTR APDU is then presented as a PDV (i.e., presentation data value) to the Presentation Layer via P-DATA. If a RTTR APDU is not the last in a series of RTTR APDUs used to transfer the encoded string, the requesting RTPM inserts a checkpoint by issuing a P-SYNC-MINOR.request primitive. It may issue further P-DATA.request primitives until the agreed window-size has been reached. If the RTTR APDU is the last in the series of RTTR APDUs, the requesting RTPM issues a P-ACTIVITY-END.request primitive to signal the end of the transfer of the encoded string.

Next, we consider the accepting RTPM. A P-ACTIVITY-END.indication primitive issued to the accepting RTPM indicates that the entire encoded APDU has been received. The accepting RTPM decodes the value, issues a RT-TRANSFER.indication primitive to the accepting RTSE-user, and then issues a P-ACTIVITY-END.response primitive to the Presentation Layer.

Note that the requesting RTPM instead of the PPM (i.e., presentation protocol machine) encodes the APDU received from the requesting RTSE user. The reason is simple. The RTSE-user APDU is only an abstract structure. Without converting the abstract structure into a bit string, checkpointing cannot be performed. Since the requesting RTPM has all the checkpointing information, it can perform the segmentation. One may ask why the RTPM does not pass the checkpointing information to the PPM and let the PPM take care of the encoding and checkpointing. If the PPM does perform checkpointing, it may as well take care of the error handling and recovery procedures associated with checkpointing. There is then not much left for the RTPM to do.

• **error handling procedures**

There are four error handling procedures. They are the transfer-interrupt, transfer-discard, association-abort, and association-provider-abort procedures. The use of these procedures depends on how severe the error situation is.

The transfer-interrupt procedure is used by a RTPM to handle a less severe local error situation during the transfer procedure. Less severe here means that at least one checkpoint is confirmed during the transfer procedure. No RTSE APDUs are used in this procedure. The requesting RTPM uses P-ACTIVITY-INTERRUPT to interrupt the transfer. The responding RTPM, when notified, initiates some local recovery.

The transfer-discard procedure is used by the sending RTPM to escape from a more severe local error situation when no checkpoint is confirmed during the transfer procedure. No RTSE APDUs are used in this procedure. P-ACTIVITY-DISCARD is used to abort the activity associated with the APDU. Eventually, all knowledge of the APDU is deleted by the receiving RTPM.

The association-abort procedure is used by a RTPM to handle the most severe error situation. This is performed between a RT-TRANSFER.request primitive and its corresponding RT-TRANSFER.confirm primitive. The procedure uses the RTAB APDU. A-ABORT is used to abort the association. The initiating RTPM calls the association recovery procedure. After a successful association recovery, it calls the transfer-resumption procedure to resume the transfer. Both the association recovery procedure and the transfer-resumption procedure will be discussed shortly.

The association-provider-abort procedure is used to handle a presentation service-provider abort. No APDUs are used. As soon as an A-P-ABORT.indication primitive is received, the initiating RTPM calls the association-recovery procedure. If the association-recovery procedure is successfully completed, it calls the transfer-resumption procedure, otherwise it informs the requesting RTSE user that the APDU cannot be transferred.

• **error recovery procedures**

There are three error recovery procedures. They are the transfer-resumption, transfer-retry, and association-recovery procedures.

The transfer-resumption procedure resumes a transfer by using P-ACTIVITY-RESUME. If at least one checkpoint is confirmed in the interrupted transfer procedure, the sending RTPM sends a RTTR APDU for the segment following the last confirmed checkpoint. If no checkpoint was confirmed in the interrupted transfer procedure, then the original transfer is discarded and another transfer is retried from start.

The transfer-retry procedure is used to retry a transfer. P-ACTIVITY-START is used with a new activity identifier value.

During the association-recovery procedure, the initiating RTPM forms a RTORQ APDU and attempts to send it using a new application association. The requested application association may not be accepted by the ACSE service provider. If it is accepted and the responding RTPM finds everything acceptable, a RTOAC APDU will be returned by the responding RTPM. But if the responding RTPM finds something unacceptable, it will respond with a RTORQ APDU. If the rejection is transient, the responding RTPM may call the association-recovery procedure again after some period of time.

The operation of RTSE requires the following presentation functional units to be active: Half Duplex, Exceptions, Minor Synchronize, and Activity Management. The mapping of RTSE service elements to presentation service elements is quite straightforward.

11.3   Summary

RTSE is used primarily by an MHS application to send a bulky message over an unreliable network. The purpose of RTSE is to ensure that an APDU is transferred at most once. RTSE relies on the session checkpointing facilities.

Before any RTSE-user APDU can be transferred, both RTPMs have to agree on the size of a checkpoint. After the requesting RTPM receives an RTSE-user APDU, it first encodes it using BER, then chops up the encoded string into segments. Thus, a RTPM performs the encoding/decoding function which is normally performed by the Presentation Layer. Each segment is wrapped inside a RTSE APDU, and all the segments are sent to the remote RTPM using a single session activity. Minor synchronization points can be inserted in between the segments. When all the segments have been secured by the requesting RTPM, the transfer is considered to be complete.

Related Standards

ISO 9066-1: Information Processing Systems - Text Communication - Reliable Transfer - Part 1: Model and Service Definition

ISO 9066-2: Information Processing Systems - Text Communication - Reliable Transfer - Part 2: Protocol Specification

12

Commitment, Concurrency, and Recovery

The **Commit, Concurrency, and Recovery (CCR)** standard, as specified in ISO/IEC 9804 and 9805, provides the communication mechanism for the two-phase commit protocol on a single application association between two CCR service users. It provides the CCR service users with service primitives to commit, rollback, and recover from failures. It does not provide any data transfer facilities. Therefore, the CCR-ASE must be used with one or more user-ASEs which can supply the data needed for an atomic action.

Section 12.1 presents the CCR concepts. Section 12.2 describes the CCR service. Finally, Section 12.3 describes the CCR protocol.

12.1 CCR Concepts

An **atomic action** is a well-defined set of operations which has the following **ACID** properties:

- **Atomicity** means that to an outside observer, either all the operations pertaining to the atomic action are completed or none of them is executed.

- **Consistency** means that the outcomes of the operations are consistent with the application semantics.
- **Isolation** means that a user cannot have access to any partial results of the operations of an atomic action before the completion of the entire action.
- **Durability** means that the operations must endure any communication or application failure.

Preserving the ACID properties requires that the state be remembered prior to any work, so that an earlier consistent state can be recreated if the work is damaged. The notion of recreating an earlier state is called **rollback**. The primary method to preserve the ACID properties is to use the **two-phase commit protocol** taken from database theory. First, let us describe how the two-phase commit protocol works (Figure 12.1).

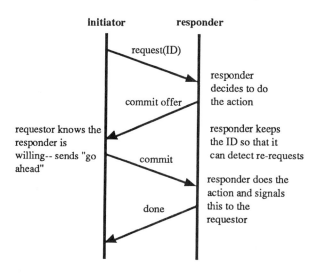

FIGURE 12.1   Two-party Two-phase Commit

- **phase 1**

Imagine a situation where a superior A asks a subordinate B if it can perform an atomic action. When B receives the request, it can either agree or refuse to perform the action. B informs A of its choice. If it agrees to perform the action, it sends an "offer to commit" message to A. If it refuses to perform the action, it sends a refusal message to A. In any case, B needs not perform the atomic action during this phase, although it may put a lock on the **bound data**, i.e., data which may be affected by the atomic action.

- **phase 2**

A receives the refusal or the "offer to commit" message from B. If B sent an "offer to commit" message, then A can decide whether it wants to follow through. In the meantime,

B is in a doubt period because it does not know whether A wants to follow through with the commit. If A decides to follow through, then it sends a commit signal to B. B then performs the atomic action and sends a done signal to A when it is finished. If A decides not follow through, it sends a rollback signal to B. When B receives the rollback signal, it drops the task. Had it put a lock on its bound data earlier, it should remove the lock.

Recovery is different from rollback. Rollback prevents an atomic action from being inappropriately performed. **Recovery** is the process whereby the status of an atomic action is determined after a crash and the correct steps to recover are undertaken by an application. A crash could leave one communicating party with one value and the other communicating party with a different value. Recovery may perform rollback but it may also complete an atomic action. The recovery choice is determined by the application using CCR. For example, if the CCR-ASE is used together with the TP-ASE, the recovery choice can be made by the TP-ASE.

The two-phase commit protocol described earlier only covers two parties. Figures 12.2 and 12.3 illustrate a multi-party arrangement ("?" indicates a request) which is a typical environment where CCR is used to support distributed transaction processing. A tree structure, called the **atomic action tree**, is imposed on the communicating parties. There is a CCR service user at each node of the tree. Each branch of the tree, known as an **atomic action branch,** represents the relationship between two adjacent CCR service users. The tree is built dynamically and only exists for the duration of the atomic action. With respect to the atomic action tree, a CCR service user can be a master, an intermediate, or a leaf. The master, which creates the tree, has the superior role. The intermediate has both the subordinate and superior roles, being subordinate to the master (or a more superior intermediate) and superior to a subordinate. Finally, the leaf, which is superior to no other node in the tree, is only a subordinate.

Requests trickle downwards through the tree. Subordinates send their commit signals upwards. This seems to suggest that "higher" nodes are more important than "lower" nodes. Actually, a single subordinate can halt the process even when all the others agree to go ahead. Commitment occurs only after all CCR service users that are subordinate to the master agree to commit, and the master decides to follow through. When a subordinate finishes execution, it releases its portion of the bound data. The operations of an atomic action may modify the bound data, changing them from an initial state to a final state. Commitment releases bound data in their final state. A rollback forces a subordinate to return its portion of the bound data to the initial state.

The coordination of all the nodes in an atomic action tree is quite complicated. CCR is only concerned with a single branch of the atomic action tree. It is not concerned with the overall coordination although the CCR standard does provide some guidelines about the usage of CCR by an application. The TP protocol is an application of CCR. It provides a command and control environment whereby some automated decision at different nodes of an atomic action tree may be made by the TP service provider. Since it is an application of CCR, it imposes some constraints on the usage of CCR service elements. For example, although CCR requires rollback to propagate down the tree, TP requires rollback to propagate throughout the tree.

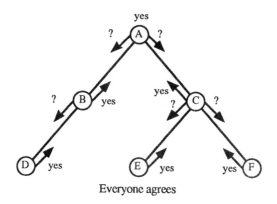

Everyone agrees

FIGURE 12.2   Multi-party Two-phase Commit: everyone agrees

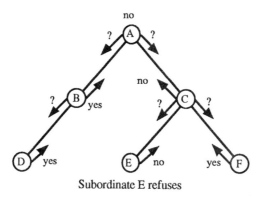

Subordinate E refuses

FIGURE 12.3   Multi-party Two-phase Commit: someone refuses

We close this section by examining the concepts of presumed rollback and heuristic commit. A recovery mechanism determines when a CCR service user acquires recovery responsibility for an atomic action branch. **Atomic action data,** which is made up of control information such as the state of an atomic action, is used for recovery. CCR adopts the **presumed rollback recovery mechanism.** In this mechanism, a subordinate acquires the responsibility when it decides to offer commitment, and a superior acquires the responsibility when it decides to order commitment. Both keep recovery responsibility until the atomic action is completed. A CCR service user uses atomic action data to determine if it has recovery responsibility. A CCR service user, which assumes the responsibility, must maintain atomic action data, be able to set its bound data to either the initial state or the final state, and be able to initiate recovery whenever needed.

After a subordinate offers commitment, not only does it acquire recovery responsibility, but also is in a doubt period, not knowing whether its superior wants to commit or rollback. In the meantime, it must retain the capability to commit or rollback until it gets a message from its superior. The bound data affected must be locked using some concurrency control mechanism. However, this arrangement is not practical as it does not set a time limit on how long the locking should continue. This is an important problem as the bound data may be needed by other applications and their indefinite lockup can halt or delay work. **Heuristic commitment or rollback** is an attempt to deal with this problem. With heuristic commitment or rollback, a subordinate makes a guess as to whether it should commit or rollback if it has not received an indication from its superior for some time. A subordinate must also consider whether a wrong guess will do more harm than good. If the guess is wrong, then the CCR mechanism is thwarted. There is no longer an atomic action and the bound data may be left in an inconsistent state. To improve the decision process, CCR allows a superior to determine how long its subordinate should wait before making a guess. CCR also allows a superior to indicate a preference for the heuristic action, which is either commit, rollback, or "let the subordinate choose". Unlike normal commitment and rollback, heuristic commitment/rollback requires a subordinate to keep a record of the selected heuristic choice. It must keep this record until its superior is informed of its heuristic choice and has acknowledged that it is informed.

12.2 CCR Service

There are a total of six CCR service elements (Table 12.1). Some service elements are invoked by a superior only, while some are invoked by a subordinate only. To be more precise, a superior may invoke C-BEGIN, C-PREPARE, C-COMMIT, C-ROLLBACK, or C-RECOVER, while a subordinate may invoke C-READY, C-ROLLBACK, or C-RECOVER. In short, C-BEGIN creates a branch, and the completion of a branch is achieved either by commit using C-PREPARE, C-READY, C-COMMIT, and C-RECOVER, or by rollback using C-ROLLBACK and C-RECOVER. These CCR service elements are explained next.

Service	Type	Requestor
C-BEGIN	Optionally confirmed	Superior
C-PREPARE	Non-confirmed	Superior
C-READY	Non-confirmed	Subordinate
C-COMMIT	Confirmed	Superior
C-ROLLBACK	Confirmed	Superior or subordinate
C-RECOVER	Confirmed or Optionally confirmed	Superior Subordinate

TABLE 12.1   CCR Service Elements

A superior invokes **C-BEGIN** to start a branch with its subordinate. C-BEGIN has three parameters: atomic action identifier, branch identifier, and user data. The **atomic action identifier** is used to identify the atomic action associated with the branch. This identifier is created by the master of the atomic action when the first branch of the atomic action begins. The superiors of later branches use the same value. If a failure occurs, the identifier is used in recovery. The **branch identifier** is used to identify a branch of an atomic action inside the scope of the atomic action identifier's value.

Following the creation of a branch by C-BEGIN, an exchange of bound data can occur to define the requested atomic action. The exchange is accomplished by the use of service elements of some user-ASE in the application context. At the end of the exchange, the superior may invoke **C-PREPARE** to request its subordinate to offer commitment. It can no longer send bound data to its subordinate. The use of C-PREPARE is optional. If the end of the exchange is implicit, then the use of C-PREPARE is not needed.

C-READY, a non-confirmed service element, is invoked by the subordinate to signal its superior that it is ready to commit. A subordinate must safeguard its bound data before issuing a C-READY.request primitive. Afterwards, it can no longer send bound data to its superior.

A superior orders commitment by invoking **C-COMMIT** which is a confirmed service element. This occurs only when it has its bound data in the final state, and its subordinate has offered to commit. On receiving a C-COMMIT.indication primitive, a subordinate releases its bound data in the final state. When a superior receives a C-COMMIT.confirm primitive, it does not have to attempt recovery even if a failure occurs -- the atomic action is complete.

C-ROLLBACK, a confirmed service element, is used to force completion of a branch. This, however, can result in loss of data still in transit. The superior invokes this service element to command its subordinate to rollback. It can do this only if it has not yet invoked C-COMMIT. The subordinate uses this service to let its superior know it is not ready to commit. It can only do this if it has not yet invoked C-READY. If it invokes C-ROLLBACK, it should release its bound data in the initial state.

C-RECOVER can be invoked by either a superior or a subordinate to initiate recovery. Both CCR service users are permitted to invoke it because, as described earlier in the presumed rollback recovery mechanism, either user at various times may be required to initiate recovery following a failure. When the superior invokes C-RECOVER, the service is confirmed. When the subordinate invokes C-RECOVER, the service can be either confirmed or non-confirmed. One of the parameters of C-RECOVER is the recovery state parameter. The requestor of C-RECOVER uses this parameter to disclose what it thinks is the state of the branch. The acceptor uses this parameter to indicate its reply. This parameter has five possible values.

- The value "ready" is used when the subordinate wants to tell its superior that it has offered commitment. The subordinate has recovery responsibility for that branch.
- The value "commit" is used when the superior wants to tell its subordinate that it ordered commitment earlier. The superior has recovery responsibility.

• The value "unknown" is used when the superior wants to tell its subordinate that it does not have any atomic action data for the branch.

• The value "retry-later" is used by the acceptor, which can be either a superior or a subordinate, to inform the requestor that it is not prepared to proceed with recovery (e.g, because of its inability to establish an application association with one or more of its subordinates) and the requestor should retry in the future.

• The value "done" is used by the subordinate to inform its superior that the commitment is finished.

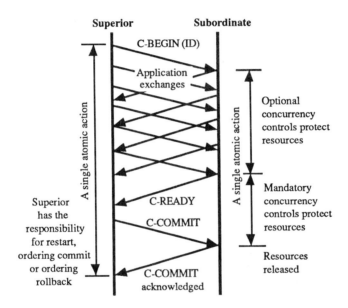

FIGURE 12.4   Typical Exchange of CCR service primitives

The following sequence of steps shows a typical scenario of how the CCR service primitives are used in a two-party exchange (Figure 12.4):

1. The superior issues a C-BEGIN primitive to begin an atomic action.

2. Data exchange is made.

3. The superior wants to know if its subordinate will commit. This is explicitly done with C-PREPARE or implicitly done through the semantics of the data exchange.

4. The subordinate offers commitment with a C-READY.request primitive or refusal with a C-ROLLBACK.request primitive.

5. The superior uses a C-COMMIT.request primitive to order commitment, or uses a C-ROLLBACK.request primitive to order rollback.

6. Commitment or rollback is acknowledged by the subordinate. The subordinate no longer needs to maintain atomic action data about the atomic action. When the superior receives the acknowledgement, it can also throw out its atomic action data.

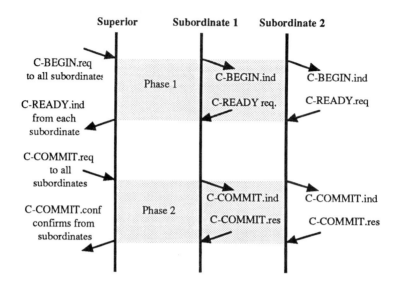

FIGURE 12.5   The Superior and the two Subordinates agree to Commit

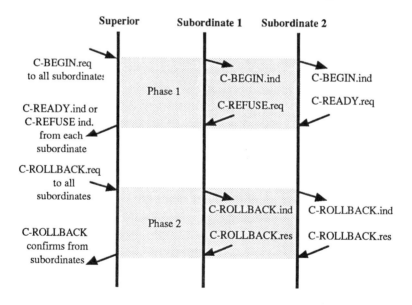

FIGURE 12.6   Commitment by one Subordinate and Refusal by the Other

An example depicting an exchange between a superior and two subordinates is illustrated in Figures 12.5 and 12.6. In Figure 12.5, both the subordinates and the superior agree to commit. In Figure 12.6, one of the subordinates refuses to commit.

Unless the CCR service elements are used properly, the ACID properties of an atomic action may not be preserved. For this reason, the CCR standard defines four sets of CCR service user rules. Some of these rules are described below.

The "CCR service primitive usage" rules define constraints on the use of the CCR service primitives. Consider the use of the C-COMMIT.request primitive. The "multi-branch sequence" rule says that an intermediate can issue this primitive only if it has received a C-COMMIT.indication or C-RECOVER (commit).indication primitive from its superior. The "single branch recovery" rule says that a superior can issue this primitive only if it has recorded all the atomic action data. The "association use" rule says that a CCR service user can issue this primitive only if it owns the major sync/activity token.

The "atomic action data manipulation" rules specify when to record/forget atomic action data for an atomic action branch. There are rules to record/forget atomic action data indicating an offer of commitment, and rules to record/forget atomic action data indicating an order of commitment. For example, one of the rules says that a subordinate can forget its atomic action data indicating an offer of commitment, if a C-ROLLBACK.indication primitive or a C-RECOVER.confirm (unknown) primitive is received from its superior. Another rule says that a superior can forget its atomic action data indicating an order of commitment, if a C-COMMIT.confirm or C-RECOVER.confirm (done) primitive is received from each of its subordinates.

The "bound data manipulation" rules impose constraints on the manipulation of bound data. For example, one of the rules says that an intermediate can release its bound data in the initial state as part of rollback if atomic action data indicating an order of commitment has not been recorded, or if an offer of commitment is recorded and a C-ROLLBACK.indication/C-RECOVER.confirm (unknown) primitive has been received from the superior.

Finally, the "CCR service user data transfer" rules impose constraints on the use of the presentation primitives to transfer bound data. For example, one of the rules says that a superior can issue a P-DATA.request primitive to manipulate bound data if it has not received a C-READY.indication/C-ROLLBACK.indication primitive, or if it has not issued a C-PREPARE.request/C-READY.request/C-ROLLBACK.request primitive.

12.3 CCR Protocol

CCR APDUs	
C-BEGIN-RI	C-ROLLBACK-RC
C-BEGIN-RC	C-COMMIT-RI
C-PREPARE-RI	C-COMMIT-RC
C-READY-RI	C-RECOVER-RI
C-ROLLBACK-RI	C-RECOVER-RC

TABLE 12.2 APDUs Used by CCR

This section describes the CCR protocol in terms of the APDUs, the procedures, and the use of the presentation services.

CCR uses a total of ten APDUs (Table 12.2). A CCR APDU ending with RI (such as C-BEGIN-RI) means that the APDU is moving from the request CCR service user to the indication CCR service user. A CCR APDU ending with RC (such as C-BEGIN-RC) means that the APDU is moving from the response CCR service user to the confirm CCR service user. All the CCR APDUs, except C-BEGIN-RI APDU, contain only one field, the user-data field. The C-BEGIN-RI APDU also contains an atomic action identifier field.

For optimization purpose, the CCR standard permits certain concatenations of CCR APDUs with other CCR APDUs or APDUs from other user-ASEs. Some examples of concatenation sequences (read from left to right) are shown below:

- (User-ASE-APDUs, C-BEGIN-RI, User-ASE-APDUs, C-PREPARE-RI),
- (C-COMMIT-RI, C-BEGIN-RI), and
- (C-ROLLBACK-RI, C-BEGIN-RI).

where the User-ASE-APDUs above represent a sequence of APDUs defined by the user-ASE standard.

CCR Procedures	CCR Service Elements
Begin branch	C-BEGIN
Prepare subordinate	C-PREPARE
Offer commitment	C-READY
Order commitment	C-COMMIT
Rollback	C-ROLLBACK
Branch recovery	C-RECOVER
Order commitment & begin new branch	C-COMMIT, C-BEGIN
Rollback & begin new branch	C-ROLLBACK, C-BEGIN

TABLE 12.3   CCR Service Element Protocol Procedures

The CCR protocol procedures are described next. The CCR standard defines a total of eight procedures (Table 12.3). In general, the procedures are very straightforward. We will illustrate the operation of the CCR protocol machine (CCRPM) by describing the rollback procedure and the "rollback and begin new branch" procedure next.

The rollback procedure is used to force completion of an atomic action branch. Suppose that a CCRPM receives a C-ROLLBACK.request primitive. It will form a C-ROLLBACK-RI APDU and issue a P-RESYNCHRONIZE.request (restart) primitive with the APDU as the PS-user-data. Since P-RESYNCRONIZE is destructive, this means that CCR APDUs other than the C-ROLLBACK-RI APDU from the association initiator may be discarded by the presentation service provider. Hence, the rollback procedure takes precedence over all other allowed CCR protocol procedures. It could happen that two C-ROLLBACK-RI APDUs may collide because both the association initiator and the responder issue a C-ROLLBACK.request primitive simultaneously. In this case, the CCR standard says that the association initiator is the winner, hence the C-ROLLBACK-RI APDU generated by the association responder is discarded by the presentation service provider.

CCR primitive	CCR APDU	Presentation primitive
C-BEGIN.req/ind	C-BEGIN-RI	P-SYNC-MINOR.req/ind
C-BEGIN.rsp/cnf	C-BEGIN-RC	P-SYNC-MINOR.rsp/cnf
C-BEGIN.rsp/cnf where C-BEGIN.req was given with C-ROLLBACK.req or C-COMMIT.req	C-BEGIN-RC	P-TYPED-DATA.req/ind
C-PREPARE.req/ind	C-PREPARE-RI	P-TYPED-DATA.req/ind
C-READY.req/ind	C-READY-RI	P-TYPED-DATA.req/ind
C-ROLLBACK.req/ind	C-ROLLBACK-RI	P-RESYNC(restart).req/ind
C-ROLLBACK.rsp/cnf	C-ROLLBACK-RC	P-RESYNC(restart).rsp/cnf
C-ROLLBACK.req/ind + C-BEGIN.req/ind	C-ROLLBACK-RI followed by C-BEGIN-RI	P-RESYNC(restart).req/ind
C-ROLLBACK.rsp/cnf + C-BEGIN.rsp/cnf	C-ROLLBACK-RC followed by C-BEGIN-RC	P-RESYNC(restart).rsp/cnf
	C-ROLLBACK-RC followed by C-BEGIN-RI	P-RESYNC(restart).rsp/cnf
C-COMMIT.req/ind	C-COMMIT-RI	P-SYNC-MAJOR.req/ind
C-COMMIT.rsp/cnf	C-COMMIT-RC	P-SYNC-MAJOR.rsp/cnf
C-COMMIT.req/ind + C-BEGIN.req/ind	C-COMMIT-RI followed by C-BEGIN-RI	P-SYNC-MAJOR.req/ind
C-COMMIT.rsp/cnf + C-BEGIN.rsp/cnf	C-COMMIT-RC followed by C-BEGIN-RC	P-SYNC-MAJOR.rsp/cnf
C-RECOVER.req/ind	C-RECOVER-RI	P-TYPED-DATA.req/ind
C-RECOVER.rsp/cnf	C-RECOVER-RC	P-TYPED-DATA.req/ind

TABLE 12.4   Mapping of CCR Service Primitives to Presentation Primitives

The "rollback and begin branch" procedure is used by a superior to request its subordinate to rollback on an atomic action branch while trying to begin a new atomic action branch with the same subordinate. Suppose that a CCRPM receives a C-ROLLBACK.request primitive and a C-BEGIN.request primitive. It will form a C-ROLLBACK-RI APDU and a C-BEGIN-RI APDU, concatenate them, then issue a P-RESYNCHRONIZE.request (restart) primitive with the concatenated APDU as the PS-user-data. Collisions with CCR APDUs other than the C-ROLLBACK-RI APDU are resolved in favor of the C-ROLLBACK-RI APDU + C-BEGIN-RI APDU (i.e., the concatenation of the two APDUs). Resolution of the collision of the C-ROLLBACK-RI APDU + C-BEGIN-RI APDU with the C-ROLLBACK-RI APDU depends on which side is the association initiator. The CCR standard says that the association initiator is always the winner. Therefore, if the association initiator issues the C-ROLLBACK-RI APDU, then the C-ROLLBACK-RI + C-BEGIN-RI APDU will be discarded.

The CCR protocol relies heavily on the session-related presentation service. The following presentation service elements are used by CCR: P-DATA, P-TYPED-DATA, P-SYNC-MAJOR, P-SYNC-MINOR, and P-RESYNCHRONIZE. Hence, an application association supporting the use of CCR must arrange for the following presentation functional units to be selected: Kernel, Typed Data, Major Synchronize, Minor Synchronize, and Resynchronize.

The use of the expedited transport service by the Session Layer brings up an interesting point. Recall that the rollback procedure uses the session resynchronization service. If the extended control QOS parameter is enabled, the session protocol machine receiving an S-RESYNCHRONIZE.request primitive would send a PR SPDU using the expedited transport data transfer service to inform its peer to discard some of the SPDUs. As a result, C-BEGIN-RI and possibly some other User-ASE-APDUs preceding the C-ROLLBACK-RI could be purged unintentionally. Because of this, the CCR standard requires a CCR service user, after issuing a C-BEGIN.request primitive, not to issue a C-ROLLBACK.request primitive until receiving a C-BEGIN.confirmation primitive.

Table 12.4 shows the mapping of CCR primitives to presentation primitives. Note that although C-BEGIN.request/indication is mapped to P-SYNC-MINOR.req/ind, if it is issued immediately after C-ROLLBACK.req/ind, then both service primitives will be mapped to P-RESYNC (start) req/ind.

12.4 Summary

The CCR-ASE provides a set of service elements to coordinate two AEs involved in an atomic action. An atomic action, as a sequence of operations, is characterized by four properties collectively known as the ACID properties. The atomicity property means that to an outside observer, either all of the operations are completed or none of them are executed. The consistency property means that the operations are performed correctly with respect to the application semantics. The isolation property means that any partial results of the operations composing the atomic action are not accessible before the completion of the atomic action. Finally, the durability property means that the action must endure a communication or an application failure.

To preserve the ACID properties, the two-phase protocol taken from database theory is used. CCR supports the communication aspects of the two-phase protocol. For example, a CCR service user can use CCR service elements to request its peer to offer commitment, to signal to its peer that it is ready to commit, and to command a peer to rollback or to initiate recovery.

Bound data refers to the data whose state may be affected by an atomic action. The two-phase protocol makes sure that the modification of the bound data is done indivisibly.

Commitment releases bound data in the final state while rollback releases bound data in the initial state.

Atomic action data consists of state information about an atomic action. When a communication or an application failure occurs, a CCR service user relies upon the atomic action data to perform recovery. CCR uses the presumed rollback recovery mechanism. For this mechanism, the subordinate acquires the recovery responsibility when it decides to offer commitment, while the superior acquires the recovery responsibility when it decides to order commitment.

The CCR-ASE is not a stand-alone ASE. It is used in conjunction with a referencing application which models a CCR service user. In order to preserve the ACID properties of an atomic action, the CCR service definition provides rules to CCR service users.

The CCR protocol relies heavily on the session service. An application association supporting the use of CCR must arrange for the following session functional units to be selected: Kernel, Typed Data, Major Synchronize, Minor Synchronize, and Resynchronize.

Related Standards

ISO 9804: Information Technology - Open Systems Interconnection - Service Definition for the Commitment, Concurrency and Recovery Service Element

ISO 9804 DAM 2: Information Technology - Open Systems Interconnection - Service Definition for the Commitment, Concurrency and Recovery Service Element - Amendment 2: Session Mapping Changes

ISO 9805: Information Technology - Open Systems Interconnection - Protocol Specification for the Commitment, Concurrency and Recovery Service Element

ISO 9805 DAM 2: Information Technology - Open Systems Interconnection - Protocol Specification for the Commitment, Concurrency and Recovery Service Element - Amendment 2: Session Mapping Changes

CD 9805-2.2: Information Technology - Open Systems Interconnection - Commitment, Concurrency and Recovery Protocol Specification - Part 2: Protocol Implementation Conformance Statement Proforma

13

Remote Operation Service Element

In a typical interactive environment, an AE requests a remote AE to perform some operation. The remote AE executes the operation and returns either an outcome or an error. Since many distributed applications are written in this kind of interactive environment, it is useful to provide an ASE to support the communications aspects of such applications. **Remote Operation Service Element (ROSE)** is such an ASE. That is, ROSE conveys the invocations or the replies from an AE to a remote AE.

In an application context, ROSE must be used with one or more user-ASEs which supply the remote operations. A user-ASE defines a set of remote operations based on the application needs. It can be a proprietary ASE or an ASE defined by the standard groups. ROSE does not define remote operations. It only acts as a courier for remote operations. The ROSE standard, however, does provide a set of templates for the definition of remote operations. These macros, collectively called the RO-notation, will be examined in the next chapter. Using RO-notation, application protocol designers of ROSE-user-ASEs (i.e., user-ASEs which are users of ROSE) can define remote operations in a consistent manner.

In Section 13.1, a simple model of remote operations is presented. Section 13.2 and Section 13.3 describe the ROSE service and protocol respectively.

The ROSE service definition and protocol specification are given in ISO/IEC 9072-1 and 9072-2 respectively.

13.1 A Model for Remote Operations

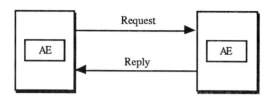

FIGURE 13.1   Invoker/Performer Interaction Model

Interactions among the AEs in an OSI application can be modelled as **Remote Operations** or simply **operations**. An operation is requested by an invoking AE (**invoker**). The performing AE (**performer**) attempts to perform the operation and then reports the outcome which may be normal or an exception. Figure 13.1 illustrates such an interaction.

Operations may be classified according to whether the performer reports the outcome. Alternatively, they may be classified according to the mode which is either asynchronous or synchronous. As a result, five different operation classes are defined:

- **Operation Class 1:**   synchronous, reporting success or failure
- **Operation Class 2:**   asynchronous, reporting success or failure
- **Operation Class 3:**   asynchronous, reporting failure only
- **Operation Class 4:**   asynchronous, reporting success only
- **Operation Class 5:**   asynchronous, nothing reported

A ROSE implementation may support some or all of the above operation classes.

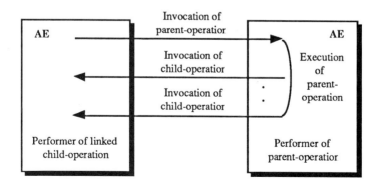

FIGURE 13.2   Use of Linked Operations

Every operation is identified by an operation number. An invocation of an operation is identified by an **invocation identifier**. Invocation identifiers can differentiate invocations of the same operation. Finally, an operation may have a **linked invocation identifier**, indicating that the operation is part of a group of **linked-operations** formed by one **parent-operation** and one or more **child-operations**. The performer of the parent-operation may invoke zero, one or more child-operations to be performed by the invoker of the parent-operation although a child-operation may be a parent-operation of another group of linked-operations in a recursive manner (Figure 13.2).

Note that the initiator of an application association may not be the invoker, and the acceptor of an association may not be the performer. Some rules are needed in an application context to determine which AE may invoke operations. An association class is an attribute of an application context. Three association classes have been identified:

- **Association Class 1**: only the initiator can invoke operations
- **Association Class 2**: only the acceptor can invoke operations
- **Association Class 3**: both the initiator and the acceptor can invoke operations

although they may invoke different kinds of operations

Association Class 1 is used in a client-server interaction. Of the three classes, Association Class 3 is perhaps the most frequently used because it supports peer-to-peer interaction. For example, the application context of CMIP uses Association Class 3.

13.2 ROSE Service

Service	Type
RO-INVOKE	Non-confirmed
RO-RESULT	Non-confirmed
RO-ERROR	Non-confirmed
RO-REJECT-U	Non-confirmed
RO-REJECT-P	Provider-initiated

TABLE 13.1   ROSE Service Elements

Table 13.1 displays the ROSE service elements. An invoker uses **RO-INVOKE** to request an operation to be performed by a performer. There are six parameters: operationValue, operationClass, argument, invokeId, linkedId, and priority. The operationValue and the argument parameters identify the remote operation and its arguments. The priority parameter is a hint to the ROSE service provider as to the priority assigned to the transfer of the corresponding APDU with respect to the other APDUs to be exchanged. It is used strictly by the ROSE service-provider, hence is not conveyed to the performing AE.

A performer returns a positive result using **RO-RESULT**. The invokeId parameter of RO-RESULT has the same value as the invokeId parameter of RO-INVOKE. A performer returns a negative reply using **RO-ERROR**. Information about the error may be placed in the errorParameter parameter. When a ROSE user detects a problem with the invocation, it can use **RO-REJECT-U** to reject the request or the reply. Sometimes, the ROSE service provider may not convey the operation because it detects a bad problem such as a badly structured APDU. In this case, it uses **RO-REJECT-P** to inform the ROSE users of the problem. The following examples illustrate how ROSE is used.

Example 13.1

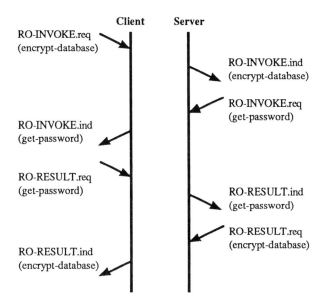

FIGURE 13.3   Use of Linked Operations

This example illustrates the use of a linked operation in a remote database application. We assume an application has defined the following operations: "open-database", "read-record", "encrypt-database", "get-password", and "close-database". To begin an interaction, the client establishes an application association with the database server. It then sends an "open-database" operation to the server using RO-INVOKE. If the database can be opened, the server would reply positively using RO-RESULT. If the client wants to read a record next, it sends a "read-record" operation using RO-INVOKE. Using RO-RESULT, the server sends the record back to the client.

On the other hand, suppose that the client wants to encrypt the remote database (see Figure 13.3). The invocation of the "encrypt-database" might require the client to present a password first. For security, the client's password is not sent immediately by the client. Instead, it sends a parent "encrypt-database" operation with no password to the server. The server responds by sending a linked child "get-password" operation to the client. This request by the linked child process has its own invokeId. When the client receives the linked child operation request, it replies with the password and an invokeId the same as the invokeId of the child operation. After the server receives the password, it encrypts the database and then generates a response to the original "encrypt-database" request by the client. The invocation id in this response is set to the one that was sent earlier by the client in the parent "encrypt-database" operation.

Example 13.2

This example illustrates a very simple file transfer using ROSE. We assume that two file operations, "open-file" and "transfer-file", are defined by some application. Using RO-INVOKE, the initiator sends the "open-file" operation to the responder. Assuming that the file is found, the responder replies with the same invokeId. Next, the initiator sends the "transfer-file" operation to the responder with a different invokeId. The responder then responds with the requested file content. Note that this simple file transfer facility can only be used to transfer small files which can be encapsulated within a ROSE APDU. It does not provide the file access and file recovery capabilities as provided by FTAM.

13.3   ROSE Protocol

The ROSE protocol is very simple. It uses four ROSE APDUs, the ASN.1 definitions of which are given below:

```
ROIVapdu ::= SEQUENCE {    invokeID    InvokeIDType,
                           linked-ID   [0] IMPLICIT InvokeIDType OPTIONAL,
                           op-value    OPERATION,
                           argument    ANY DEFINED BY op-value OPTIONAL }

RORSapdu ::= SEQUENCE {    invokeID    InvokeIDType,
                           SEQUENCE {
                           op-value    OPERATION,
                           result      ANY DEFINED BY op-value OPTIONAL }
                                       OPTIONAL }

ROERapdu ::= SEQUENCE {    invokeID    InvokeIDType,
                           err-value   ERROR,
                           param       ANY DEFINED by err-value OPTIONAL }

RORJapdu ::= SEQUENCE {    invokeID    CHOICE { InvokeIDType, NULL},
                           problem     CHOICE {
                                       [0] IMPLICIT   GeneralProblem,
                                       [1] IMPLICIT   InvokeProblem,
                                       [2] IMPLICIT   ReturnResultProblem,
                                       [3] IMPLICIT   ReturnErrorProblem }
```

Note that all the fields in the ROSE APDUs can be derived directly from the parameters of the corresponding service primitive.

      The ROSE Protocol Machine (ROPM) maps a ROSE service primitive to a ROSE APDU which is then mapped to either a RTSE or a presentation service primitive. Whenever the ROPM issues a RT-TRANSFER.request primitive, it must possess the turn. If it does not, it must issue a RT-TURN-PLEASE.request primitive.

Occasionally, the ROPM is also responsible for managing the turn. For example, if the operationClass parameter of a RO-INVOKE.request primitive indicates that the performer should return the outcome and the Half Duplex functional unit is active, then the ROSE-service provider has to make sure that the performer side receives the data token in time to return the outcome.

The ROSE standard defines five procedures: invocation, return-result, return-error, user-reject, and provider-reject. These procedures are described next.

The invocation procedure is used when the invoker requests an operation to be performed by the performer. The requesting ROPM forms a ROIV APDU which is transferred as user data to an underlying transfer service. The underlying transfer service can be provided by either RTSE or the Presentation Layer.

The return-result procedure is used when the performer returns a positive result to the invoker. The performing ROPM forms a RORS APDU which is transferred as user data to an underlying transfer service.

The return-error procedure is used when the performer returns error information to the invoker. The performing ROPM forms a ROER APDU which is transferred as user data to an underlying transfer service.

The user-reject procedure is used when an AE rejects a request or a reply of the remote AE. The requesting ROPM forms a RORJ APDU which is transferred as user data to an underlying transfer service.

The provider-reject procedure is used by a ROPM to inform its ROSE user and the peer ROPM of some internal problem such as the reception of a badly structured APDU. The requesting ROPM forms a RORJ APDU. It can happen that the badly structured APDU is a RORJ APDU. In this case, no new RORJ APDU is formed, and the ROPM might choose to abort the application association.

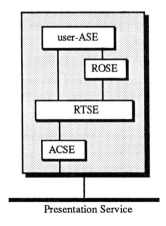

FIGURE 13.4 A ROSE Application Context with RTSE

There are two application contexts to use ROSE, one with RTSE, and one without RTSE. Whenever RTSE is present (Figure 13.4), RTSE manages the association and

ROSE transfers the operations using RTSE. Whenever RTSE is absent (Figure 13.5), ACSE manages the association and ROSE can access the presentation service directly. Either application context contains one or more user-ASEs to supply the remote operations.

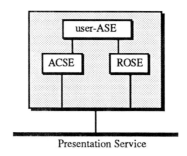

FIGURE 13.5   A ROSE Application Context without RTSE

ROSE Service	APDU	RTSE Service
RO-INVOKE request/indication	ROIV	RT-TRANSFER request/indication/confirm
RO-RESULT request/indication	RORS	RT-TRANSFER request/indication/confirm
RO-ERROR request/indication	ROER	RT-TRANSFER request/indication/confirm
RO-REJECT-U request/indication	RORJ	RT-TRANSFER request/indication/confirm
RO-REJECT-P indication	RORJ	RT-TRANSFER request/indication/confirm

TABLE 13.2   Mapping of ROSE Primitives to RTSE Primitives

ROSE Service	APDU	Presentation Service
RO-INVOKE request/indication	ROIV	P-DATA request/indication
RO-RESULT request/indication	RORS	P-DATA request/indication
RO-ERROR request/indication	ROER	P-DATA request/indication
RO-REJECT-U request/indication	RORJ	P-DATA request/indication
RO-REJECT-P indication	RORJ	P-DATA request/indication

TABLE 13.3   Mapping of ROSE Primitives to Presentation Primitives

Before a ROSE user can invoke any operation, it must first register a set of remote operations with the ROSE service provider even before an application association is made with a peer. At the time of application association establishment, it must specify whether the application context should contain RTSE or not.

Tables 13.2 and 13.3 show how a ROSE service primitive is mapped to a ROSE APDU which is then mapped to either a RTSE service primitive or a presentation primitive, depending on the application context.

13.4 Summary

ROSE provides the communication support for a typical request-reply interaction. In an application context containing ROSE, there is one or more user-ASEs which supply the requests or replies in the form of remote operations to ROSE. On receiving a remote operation, the ROSE protocol constructs a ROSE APDU and sends it using either RTSE or the presentation service.

The ROSE service definition provides service elements to invoke an operation, to return a result/reply, or to reject the execution of an operation. It also supports the use of linked operations. For example, using the linked operations feature, a management agent can link multiple replies to a single request from a manager.

Related Standards

ISO 9072-1: Information Processing Systems - Text Communication - Remote Operations - Part 1: Model, Notation, and Service Definition

ISO 9072-2: Information Processing Systems - Text Communication - Remote Operations - Part 2: Protocol Specification

14

Application Design Tools using ASDC and RO-notation

The purpose of this chapter is to examine two popular tools in the specification of application protocols, namely, RO-notation (Remote Operations Notation) and ASDC (Abstract Service Definition Convention). RO-notation provides a set of templates for the specification of a distributed application/system both macroscopically and microscopically. Both notations rely on the use of ASN.1 macros. RO-notation can only be used within the OSI framework. A macroscopic description of ASDC identifies the objects and ports used in a distributed application/system. It does not require the use of OSI in its communication support. In contrast, a microscopic description of ASDC, which gives the computational flow of the communicating objects in a distributed application/system, heavily relies on RO-notation. When ASDC is realized in an OSI environment, it provides a very powerful tool for the specification of an interface between two communicating AEs. RO-notation and ASDC notation are examined in Section 14.1 and Section 14.2 respectively.

14.1 RO-notation

RO-notation (i.e., **remote operations notation**) is concerned with the specification of an application context. An application context defines the knowledge shared by two communicating AEs during an application association. It has the data part and the control part. RO-notation relies on ASN.1 macros to specify the data part of an application context. The data part includes the ASEs used in the application context, the binding/unbinding information exchanged between the communicating AEs, and the abstract syntaxes used during the application association. There are certain "control" features of an application context (such as the interleaving rules of the ASEs) which can only be specified using a state machine. Since RO-notation relies on ASN.1 which is a data declaration language, it cannot completely describe an application context.

RO-notation provides macros for the specification of the different components of the data part of an application context. It defines six ASN.1 macros. These macros are briefly described as follows:

- the **BIND/UNBIND** macro is used to specify the information exchanged between two AE-invocations during the binding/unbinding process,
- the **OPERATION** macro is used to specify a remote operation,
- the **ERROR** macro is used to specify an error which occurs during the execution of an operation,
- the **APPLICATION-SERVICE-ELEMENT** macro is used to specify an ASE, and
- the **APPLICATION-CONTEXT** macro is used to specify an application context.

In the following, we will explain the above macros in detail and illustrate how they are used.

- **BIND macro**

No remote operation can be invoked until an application association has been established between two AE-invocations. An application association establishes an application context. A bind type is used to specify the the type of information which an initiator of the association may supply, the type of information which an acceptor may return, and the type of error which may occur during the binding process. It is an integral part of an application context. The BIND macro is used to define a bind type.

The definition of the BIND macro is given as follows:

```
BIND MACRO ::=
BEGIN
TYPE NOTATION       ::=     Argument Result Error
VALUE NOTATION      ::=     Argument-value | Result-value | Error-value
Argument            ::=     empty | "ARGUMENT" NamedType (Argument-type)
Result              ::=     empty | "RESULT" NamedType (Result-type)
Error               ::=     empty | "BIND-ERROR" NamedType (Error-type)
NamedType           ::=     type | identifier type
```

```
Argument-value          ::=      empty !"ARGUMENT" value(Argument-value Argument-type)
Result-value            ::=      empty I "RESULT" value(Result-value Result-type)
Error-value             ::=      empty I "ERROR" value(Error-value Error-type)
END
```

The type/value notation of the BIND macro is used to specify the data types/values to be exchanged during the binding process. A typical way to use this macro is to define a bind type and use this bind type in the definition of an application context. Note that there is no value(..) clause in the macro definition. This means that we do not transfer an instance of a bind type, which is sometimes called a bind-operation. The following example illustrates how to define bind types.

Example 14.1

```
Bind1 ::= BIND
        ARGUMENT        BindArgumentType1
        RESULT          BindResultType1
        BINDERROR       BindErrorType1


Bind2 ::= BIND
```

Bind1 and Bind2 are both bind types. In Bind2, no information is specified.

In an application, two communicating AE-invocations may need to communicate with each other in more than one channel. A **port pair**, which is similar to a channel, is a pair of bound ports. Thus, two communicating AE-invocations may be bound to each other via multiple port pairs. The BIND macro is used to specify the bind type for a port pair. In general, the same bind type can be used for a set of port pairs. This can also be specified using the ABSTRACT-BIND macro in ASDC.

• UNBIND macro

When two communicating AE-invocations are through with their communication, they need to unbind from each other. As a result, all the port pairs between the two communicating AE-invocations are released. An unbind type is used to specify the information exchanged between two AE-invocations during the unbinding process. It is an integral part of an application context. The UNBIND macro is used to define an unbind type.

The definition of the UNBIND macro is given as follows:

```
UNBIND MACRO ::=
BEGIN
TYPE NOTATION       ::=      Argument Result Error
VALUE NOTATION      ::=      Argument-value I Result-value I Error-value
```

Argument	::=	empty | "ARGUMENT" NamedType (Argument-type)
Result	::=	empty | "RESULT" NamedType (Result-type)
Error	::=	empty | "UNBIND-ERROR" NamedType (Error-type)
NamedType	::=	type | identifier type
Argument-value	::=	empty | "ARGUMENT" value(Argument-value Argument-type)
Result-value	::=	empty | "RESULT" value(Result-value Result-type)
Error-value	::=	empty | "ERROR" value(Error-value Error-type)
END		

A typical use of this macro is to define an unbind type and use this unbind type in the definition of an application context. Note that there is no value(..) clause in the macro definition. This means that we do not transfer an instance of an unbind type, which is sometimes called an unbind-operation.

Example 14.2

```
Unbind ::= UNBIND
        ARGUMENT    UnbindArgumentType
        RESULT      UnbindResultType
```

Unbind is an unbind type with no specification of error information.

• OPERATION macro

Once an application association has been established, operations may be invoked. The OPERATION macro is used to specify an operation. Unlike a bind/unbind-operation, an operation can be transferred. Every operation has a transfer value which may be an INTEGER value or an OBJECT IDENTIFIER value. An operation may be the parent-operation of a group of linked operations. As a result, the OPERATION macro contains the LinkedOperations component which is used to specify the child-operations. The OPERATION macro may call the ERROR macro to specify errors encountered during the execution of the operation.

The definition of the OPERATION macro is given as follows:

OPERATION MACRO	::=	
BEGIN		
TYPE NOTATION	::=	Argument Result Errors LinkedOperations
VALUE NOTATION	::=	value(VALUE CHOICE {
		localValue INTEGER,
		globalValue OBJECT IDENTIFIER})
Argument	::=	"ARGUMENT" NamedType | empty
Result	::=	"RESULT" ResultType | empty
ResultType	::=	NamedType | empty

Errors	::=	"ERRORS" "{"ErrorNames"}" I empty
LinkedOperations	::=	"LINKED" "{"LinkedOpNames"}" I empty
ErrorNames	::=	ErrorList I empty
ErrorList	::=	Error I ErrorList","Error
Error	::=	value(ERROR) I type
LinkedOpNames	::=	OperationList I empty
OperationList	::=	Operation I OperationList","Operation
Operation	::=	value (OPERATION) I type
NamedType	::=	type I identifier type
END		

A typical way to use this macro is to define operations instead of operation types, and use these operations in the definition of an ASE.

Example 14.3

```
operation1 OPERATION
        ARGUMENT     ArgumentType1
        RESULT       ResultType1
        ERRORS       {error1}
        ::= 27


operation2 OPERATION
        ARGUMENT     ArgumentType2
        RESULT       ResultType2
        ::= 32


operation3 OPERATION
        ARGUMENT     ArgumentType3
        RESULT       ResultType3
        ERRORS       {error1,error5}
        LINKED       {operation1,operation2}
        ::= 36
```

Note that operation3 is the parent of operation1 and operation2.

• ERROR macro

The ERROR macro is used to define an error which may be encountered during the execution of an operation. The definition of the ERROR macro is given as follows:

```
ERROR MACRO ::=
BEGIN
```

```
TYPE NOTATION          ::=    Parameter
VALUE NOTATION         ::=    value(VALUE CHOICE{
                                  localValue    INTEGER,
                                  globalValue  OBJECT IDENTIFIER})
Parameter              ::=    "PARAMETER" NamedType I empty
NamedType              ::=    type I identifier type
END
```

Since an error can be passed between two communicting AE-invocations during the transfer, it needs to have a transfer value. The macro above says that an error value can be transferred as an INTEGER value or an OBJECT IDENTIFIER value.

Example 14.4

```
error1 ERROR
PARAMETER    ParameterType1
::= 6
```

ParameterType1 is used to specify the error information in error1.

• APPLICATION SERVICE ELEMENT macro

Recall that an ASE specifies a set of related capabilities of an AE, where the capabilities can be given in terms of operations. In the context of a pair of communicating AEs, some of the capabilities are contained in both AEs, while others are contained in one but not the other.

The APPLICATION-SERVICE-ELEMENT macro is used to specify an ASE. Its definition is given as follows:

```
APPLICATION-SERVICE-ELEMENT MACRO ::=
BEGIN
TYPE NOTATION      ::= SymmAse I ConsInvokes I SuppInvokes I empty
VALUE NOTATION     ::= value(VALUE OBJECT IDENTIFIER)
SymmAse            ::= "OPERATIONS" "{"OpList"}"
ConsInvokes        ::= "CONSUMERINVOKES" "{"OpList"}" I empty
SuppInvokes        ::= "SUPPLIERINVOKES" "{"OpList"}" I empty
OpList             ::= Operation I OpList","Operation
Operation          ::= value(OPERATION)
END
```

An ASE is characterized by the operations which a user of the ASE can invoke. It is either symmetric or asymmetric. When two **asymmetric ASEs** communicate with each other, one is the **consumer ASE** and the other one is the **supplier ASE**. The operations which may be invoked by a user of the consumer ASE are in general different from the operations which may be invoked by a user of the supplier ASE. In the macro definition above, the operations which a user of the consumer ASE may invoke are listed after the keyword "CONSUMERINVOKES", while the operations which a user of the supplier ASE may invoke are listed after the keyword "SUPPLIERINVOKES". When two **symmetric ASEs** communicate with each other, the users of either one can invoke the same operations which are listed in the OpList after the keyword "OPERATIONS". Parent-operations may be listed in the OpList. When a parent-operation is in the ConsumerInvokes list, its child-operations are implicitly listed in the SupplierInvokes OpList. If one of these child-operations also appears explicitly in the SupplierInvokes OpList, then a user of the supplier ASE may invoke that child operation either as a child-operation or as a non-child operation (i.e., outside the set of linked-operations).

ASEs are like workers in an application context. They need to be referenced. The macro above says that an ASE value is transferred as an OBJECT IDENTIFIER value. The reason is that application contexts are meant to be globally unambiguous within an OSIE. A typical way to use the ASE macro is to define one or more ASEs, and use them in the definition of an application context.

Example 14.5

```
ase1 APPLICATION-SERVICE-ELEMENT
CONSUMERINVOKES {operation3}
::= objectidentifier6

ase2 APPLICATION-SERVICE-ELEMENT
CONSUMERINVOKES {operation3}
SUPPLIERINVOKES {operation2}
::= objectidentifier7
```

Both ase1 and ase2 are asymmetric. Note that the user of supplier ase1 can invoke either operation1 or operation2 (Example 14.3) as a child operation, and the user of supplier ase2 can invoke operation2 as a child-operation or a non-child operation.

• **APPLICATION CONTEXT macro**

An application context is used to specify the knowledge shared between two communicating AE-invocations during an application association. While it is not possible to express some of the common knowledge (such as rules) in ASN.1, it is possible to use the APPLICATION CONTEXT macro to specify the data part of an application context.

The definition of the APPLICATION-CONTEXT macro is given as follows:

```
APPLICATION-CONTEXT MACRO ::=
BEGIN
```

TYPE NOTATION	::=	NonROelements Binding ROelements ASs
VALUE NOTATION	::=	value(VALUE OBJECT IDENTIFIER)
NonROelements	::=	"APPLICATION SERVICE ELEMENTS" "{"AseList"}"
Binding	::=	"BIND" type
		"UNBIND" type
ROelements	::=	"REMOTE OPERATIONS" "{"AseID"}"
		SymmetricAses AsymmetricAses I empty
SymmetricAses	::=	"OPERATIONS OF" "{"AseList"}" I empty
AsymmetricAses	::=	InitConsOf RespConsOf
InitConsOf	::=	"INITIATOR CONSUMER OF" "{"AseList"}" I empty
RespConsOf	::=	"RESPONDER CONSUMER OF" "{"AseList"}" I empty
ASs	::=	"ABSTRACT SYNTAXES" "{"AseList"}"
AseList	::=	AseId I AseList","AseID
AseId	::=	value (APPLICATION-SERVICE-ELEMENT)
ASList	::=	ASs I ASList","AbstractSyntax
AbstractSyntax	::=	value(OBJECT IDENTIFIER)
END		

The binding component specifies a bind type and an unbind type. As pointed out earlier, the bind/unbind type may be an abstract-bind/abstract-unbind type obtained by using the ABSTRACT-BIND/ABSTRACT-UNBIND macro in ASDC. The ASList component specifies the abstract syntaxes which may be referenced during the application association. The macro makes a distinction as to whether an ASE in the application context is a user of ROSE. The user-ASEs which are not users of ROSE (e.g., ACSE) are listed after the keyword "APPLICATION SERVICE ELEMENTS", while the user-ASEs which are users of ROSE are listed after the keyword "REMOTE OPERATIONS". Finally, the macro attempts to qualify the role of an ASE of the initiator/acceptor of an application association. The consumer ASEs which are in the initiator object are listed after the keyword "INITIATOR CONSUMER OF", while the consumer ASEs which are in the responder object are listed after the keyword "RESPONDER CONSUMER OF". The following example illustrates a very simple application context which uses ase1 and ase2 as defined in Example 14.5.

Example 14.6

```
context1 APPLICATION-CONTEXT
        APPLICATION SERVICE ELEMENTS        {acse}
        BIND                                Bind1
        UNBIND                              Unbind1
        REMOTE OPERATIONS                   {rose}
        INITIATOR CONSUMER OF               {ase1}
        RESPONDER CONSUMER OF               {ase2}
        ......
```

The above gives the definition of context1 which contains acse, rose, ase1, and ase2 as ASEs. Since the initiator contains consumer ase1, it can invoke operation3. Since the responder contains consumer ase2, it can invoke operation3. Finally, since operation3 is a parent operation, both the initiator and the responder can invoke the child operations which are operation1 and operation2. Thus, the initiator and the responder in this application context can invoke the same set of operations.

The next two examples illustrate how to use the APPLICATION-SERVICE-ELEMENT and the APPLICATION-CONTEXT macros in the abstract service specification of the P3 protocol in MHS. The P3 protocol specifies how a UA can access the MTS service. Access to the MTS service is supported by three asymmetric ASEs: the message submission service element (mSSE), the message delivery service element (mDSE), and the message administration service element (mASE). All three ASEs use ROSE. The next example gives the definition of mSSE.

Example 14.7

```
mSSE APPLICATION-SERVICE-ELEMENT
CONSUMERINVOKES {
        msg-submission,
        probe-submission,
        cancel-deferred-delivery}
SUPPLIERINVOKES {submission-control}
::= id-ase-msse
```

Since mSSE is asymmetric, there is a consumer mSSE and a supplier mSSE. An application context of P3 will determine whether the initiator contains the consumer mSSE or not.

The next example shows the use of the APPLICATION-CONTEXT macro to define "mts-forced-reliable-access", which is one of the four application contexts in which P3 can be used.

Example 14.8

```
mts-forced-reliable-access APPLICATION-CONTEXT
APPLICATION SERVICE ELEMENTS {aCSE, rTSE}
BIND MTSBind
UNBIND MTSUnbind
REMOTE OPERATIONS {rOSE}
RESPONDER CONSUMER OF {mSSE, mDSE, mASE}
ABSTRACT SYNTAXES {
        id-ase-acse,      - of ACSE
        id-ase-msse,      - of MSSE
        id-ase-mdse,      - of MDSE
```

id-ase-mase,   - of MASE
id-ase-mts-rtse   -of MTSBind, MTSUnbind and RTSE}
::= id-ac-mts-forced-reliable-access

Note that mts-forced-reliable-access contains both rTSE and aCSE as non-users of ROSE. The MTSBind/MTSUnbind type is defined using the ABSTRACT-BIND/ABSTRACT-UNBIND macro.

14.2 ASDC

ASDC, which was studied earlier in Chapter 3, is a set of conventions for describing a distributed application/system both macroscopically and microscopically. The macroscopic description is called the abstract model. It is concerned with the specification of the structure of a distributed application/system. It identifies the objects involved in the computation, although it is not concerned with computational details such as the information exchanged among the objects. In contrast, the microscopic description, which is called the abstract service, is concerned with the computation flow. It defines how the distributed application/system is initiated, controlled, and terminated. ASDC provides tools in the form of macros for each description. The ASDC macros used for the microscopic description turn out to be very tightly coupled with the macros in RO-notation. For example, the ABSTRACT-BIND macro in ASDC is always used together with the BIND macro, and the ABSTRACT-OPERATION macro in ASDC is in fact identical to the OPERATION macro.

While RO-notation assumes that the communicating objects are AE-invocations, ASDC does not assume that the communicating objects are OSI objects. For example, one can use ASDC to describe an application where the communicating tasks are all residing in the same system. In this case, the tasks can communicate with each other using local interprocess communication (instead of OSI communication) facilities.

- **macros used in the abstract model**

Three macros are available in the abstract model. They are the OBJECT, the PORT, and the REFINE macros.

Every communicating object belongs to some object class. The **OBJECT macro** is used to specify an object class. Its definition is given as follows:

```
OBJECT MACRO ::=
BEGIN
TYPE NOTATION       ::=     "PORTS" "{"PortList"}" | empty
VALUE NOTATION      ::=     value(VALUE OBJECT IDENTIFIER)
PortList            ::=     Port","PortList | Port
Port                ::=     value (PORT) PortType
PortType            ::=     Symmetric | Asymmetric
Symmetric           ::=     empty
```

Asymmetric	::=	Consumer | Supplier
Consumer	::=	"[C]"
Supplier	::=	"[S]"
END		

Thus an object class is characterized by the ports at its external interface. More than one port pair can exist between two communicating objects. Every port has a port type which is either symmetric or asymmetric. All instances of a symmetric port type offer identical operations. An asymmetric port type is one of two kinds: supplier or consumer. The object with the consumer port can invoke only an operation associated with the consumer port, while the object with the supplier can invoke only an operation associated with the supplier port.

The **PORT macro** is used to define a port type. Its definition is given as follows:

PORT MACRO ::=		
BEGIN		
TYPE NOTATION	::=	Operations | empty
VALUE NOTATION	::=	value(VALUE OBJECT IDENTIFIER)
Operations	::=	Symmetrical | Asymmetrical
Symmetrical	::=	"ABSTRACT OPERATIONS" "{"OpList"}"
Asymmetrical	::=	OneSided | TwoSided
OneSided	::=	Consumer | Supplier
TwoSided	::=	Consumer Supplier | Supplier Consumer
Consumer	::=	"CONSUMER INVOKES" "{"OpList"}"
Supplier	::=	"SUPPLIER INVOKES" "{"OpList"}"
OpList	::=	Operation","OpList | Operation
Operation	::=	value(ABSTRACT-OPERATION) | type
END		

It is necessary that two ports are of the same port type before they can be bound to each other. Any two ports of the same symmetric type match. If the two ports are of the same asymmetric port type, one is the consumer and the one is the supplier. A port operation is either symmetric or asymmetric. A symmetric port operation may be invoked by any object with the port. In contrast, an asymmetric port operation may be invoked by either the object with the consumer port or the object with the supplier port. A port operation can be specified by using the ABSTRACT-OPERATIONS macro. The following example shows how the OBJECT and the PORT macros are used in the macroscopic description of a part of the MHS standard.

Example 14.9

mTS OBJECT
    PORTS {submission[S], delivery[S], administration[S]}

```
                    ::=  id-ot-mts

mTSUser OBJECT
PORTS {submission[C], delivery[C], administration[C]}
::= id-ot-mts-user

submission PORT
CONSUMER INVOKES {MsgSubmission, PrbSubmission, CancelDeferredDelivery}
SUPPLIER INVOKES {SubmissionControl}
::= id-pt-submision

delivery PORT
CONSUMER INVOKES {DeliveryControl}
SUPPLIER INVOKES {MsgDelivery, RepDelivery}
::= id-pt-delivery

administration PORT
CONSUMER INVOKES {ChangeCredentials, Register}
SUPPLIER INVOKES {ChangeCredentials}
::= id-pt-administration
```

This example gives the definition of the mTS and the mTSUser object classes. All the port types are asymmetric. The ports at the mTS object class are supplier ports, while the ports at the mTSUser object class are consumer ports. All the port operations in this example are asymmetric.

When an object class is composite, it may be necessary to refine the object class to one or more component object classes. The **REFINE macro** is used for this purpose. Its definition is given as follows:

```
REFINE MACRO ::=
BEGIN
TYPE NOTATION          ::=      Object "AS" ComponentList
VALUE NOTATION         ::=      value(VALUE OBJECT IDENTIFIER)
ComponentList          ::=      Component ComponentList | Component
Component              ::=      ObjectSpec Ports
ObjectSpec             ::=      Object | Object "RECURRING"
Ports                  ::=      PortSpecList | empty
PortSpecList           ::=      PortSpec PortSpecList | PortSpec
PortSpec               ::=      value (PORT) PortSide PortStatus
PortSide               ::=      Consumer | Supplier | empty
Consumer               ::=      "[C]"
Supplier               ::=      "[S]"
PortStatus             ::=      "VISIBLE" | "PAIRED""WITH" ObjectList
```

ObjectList	::=	Object","ObjectList I Object
Object	::=	value(OBJECT)
END		

The refinement of an object class requires the specification of the component object classes and their ports. A component object class may be paired with another component object class. It can communicate with the composite object class using a "visible" port. If a composite object class contains more than one instance of a component object class, we say that the component object class is recurring.

Example 14.10

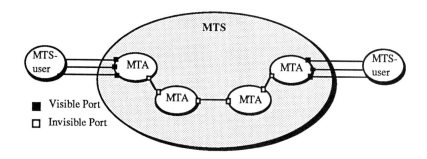

FIGURE 14.1   Refinement of the MTS Object

```
MTSRefinement ::= REFINE mTS AS
mTA RECURRING
          submission      [S]      VISIBLE
          delivery        [S]      VISIBLE
          administration  [S]      VISIBLE
          transfer             PAIRED WITH mTA
mTA OBJECT
PORTS {submission[S], delivery[S], administration[S], transfer}
::= id-ot-mta

transfer PORT
ABSTRACT OPERATIONS {MsgTransfer, PrbTransfer, RepTransfer}
::= id-pt-transfer
```

The mTS object class in Example 14.9 is refined to a set of recurring mTA component object classes (Figure 14.1). The mTA object class has visible ports such as submission-ports, delivery-ports, and administration ports. It can be also paired with another mTA object class using the transfer port. A transfer-port here is used to transfer messages, probes, and reports from one mTA to another mTA.

- **macros used in the abstract service**

From macros used for the abstract model specification, we move to macros used for the abstract service specification. ASDC defines four macros for the specification of abstract bind operations, abstract operations, abstract errors, and abstract unbind operations. These macros are examined below.

The **ABSTRACT-BIND macro** is used to specify a set of port pairs between two communicating objects. The bind type used for these port pairs is specified using the BIND macro. The definition of the ABSTRACT-BIND macro is given as follows:

```
ABSTRACT-BIND MACRO ::=
BEGIN
TYPE NOTATION          ::=      Ports Bind
VALUE NOTATION         ::=      value(VALUE BindType)
Ports                  ::=      "TO""{"PortList"}" I empty
PortList               ::=      Port","PortList" I empty
Port                   ::=      value(PORT) PortSide
PortSide               ::=      Consumer I Supplier I empty
Consumer               ::=      "[C]"
Supplier               ::=      "[S]"
Bind                   ::=      type (BindType) I empty
                                <BindType ::= BIND>
END
```

Note that when the port type is asymmetric, one port in a port pair is the consumer port and the other port is the supplier port. A typical way to use this macro is to define an abstract-type, and use it in the definition of an application context.

Example 14.11

```
MTSBind ::= ABSTRACT-BIND
TO {submission, delivery, administration}
BIND
        ARGUMENT SET {
            initiator-name        ObjectName,
            messages-waiting      [1] EXPLICIT MessageWaiting OPTIONAL,
            initiator-credentials [2] InitiatorCredentials,
            security-context      [3] SecurityContext OPTIONAL}
        RESULT SET {
            responder-name        ObjectName,
            messages-waiting      [1] EXPLICIT MessageWaiting OPTIONAL,
            responder-credentials [2] ResponderCredentials}
        BIND-ERROR INTEGER {
```

```
busy (0)
authentication-error (2),
unacceptable-dialogue-mode (3),
unacceptable-security-context (4)}
```

The MTSBind type is used for three port pairs.

The **ABSTRACT-UNBIND macro** is used to specify an abstract unbind-type for a set of port pairs. Its definition is given as follows:

```
ABSTRACT-UNBIND MACRO ::=
BEGIN
TYPE NOTATION        ::=      Ports Unbind
VALUE NOTATION       ::=      value(VALUE UnbindType)
Ports                ::=      "FROM" "{"PortList"}"
PortList             ::=      Port","PortList I empty
Port                 ::=      value(PORT) PortSide
PortSide             ::=      Consumer I Supplier I empty
Consumer             ::=      "[C]"
Supplier             ::=      "[S]"
Unbind               ::=      type (UnbindType) I empty
                             <UnbindType ::= UNBIND>
END
```

A typical way to use this macro is to define an abstract-unbind type, and use it in the definition of an application context.

Example 14.12

```
MTSUnbind ::= ABSTRACT-UNBIND
FROM {submission, delivery, administration}
```

The MTSUnbind type is used for three port pairs. Note that no unbind type information is exchanged.

The ABSTRACT-OPERATION/ABSTRACT-ERROR macro is syntactically identical to the OPERATION/ERROR macro, i.e.,

```
ABSTRACT-OPERATION MACRO   ::= OPERATION
ABSTRACT-ERROR MACRO       :: = ERROR
```

It is important to note that an abstract operation defined using the ABSTRACT-OPERATION macro is not semantically identical to an operation defined using the OPERATION macro. An operation is always supported by ROSE, whereas an abstract operation is not necessarily supported by ROSE. For example, one can use abstract operations to describe the abstract services of a distributed application at the level of the Network Layer; in this case, it does not make sense to support abstract operations using ROSE. The next example shows how to define an abstract-operation type.

Example 14.13

```
MsgDelivery ::= ABSTRACT-OPERATION
ARGUMENT SEQUENCE {
        COMPONENTS OF MessageDeliveryEnvelope,
        content Content}
RESULT SET {
        recipient-certificate [0] RecipientCertificate OPTIONAL,
        proof-of-delivery [1] ProofOfDelivery OPTIONAL} DEFAULT {}
ERRORS {
        DeliveryControlViolated,
        SecurityError,
        UnsupportedCriticalFunction}
```

The MsgDelivery operation is used in the delivery port of an mTA object class.

We close this section by examining a realization of the abstract service in an OSI application context. Assuming that ROSE is used in the application context, the realization can be accomplished as follows:

- each object in the abstract model is mapped to an application process,
- each port is mapped to an ASE which is a user of ROSE, and
- each abstract-operation is mapped to a remote operation.

From an implementation point of view, an ASE is implemented as a function library, and an operation is implemented as a function in the library. An important point to observe is that port operations are mapped to ASEs which are users of ROSE. When an ASE is a user of ROSE, it does not need a protocol engine. A remote operation must be registered with the ROSE software before it can be invoked. Thus, there is no point for a ROSE user to pass an APDU containing a description of the operation. It is sufficient for the ROSE user to pass an operation identifier and the arguments for the invocation as parameters of the RO-INVOKE.request primitive.

14.3 Summary

In this chapter, we examined two popular tools used in the specification of OSI application protocols: RO-notation and ASDC macros.

RO-notation provides a set of macros to specify the various pieces of an OSI application context.   ASDC provides a set of macros to describe a distributed application/system both macroscopically and microscopically.   In the macroscopic description, it provides macros to define the structure of a communication framework in terms of object classes and ports.   In the microscopic description, it provides macros to describe the computational flow in terms of abstract operations.   When ASDC is used together with RO-notation, it provides a very powerful tool for the specification of the interface between two communicating AEs.

Related Standards

ISO 9072-1: Information Processing Systems - Text Communication - Remote Operations - Part 1: Model, Notation and Service Definition

ISO 9072-2: Information Processing Systems - Text Communication - Remote Operations - Part 2: Protocol Specification

DIS 10021-3: Information Processing Systems - Text Communication - Message Oriented Text Interchange System - Part 3: Abstract Service Definition Conventions

15

Directory Services

An OSI network is filled with a large multitude of objects of different types. It is constantly changing as objects are added and subtracted at ease. While things change in general, certain information may not change often and will be looked up far more often than it is changed. Primary examples of such information are presentation addresses of application entities, network addresses of open systems, and people's e-mail addresses. The OSI **Directory Services (DS)** standard, as defined in ISO/IEC 9594, provides a means of looking up such kind of information.

The DS functional model (Figure 15.1) was described in Chapter 1. Its key component is the **Directory.** The Directory is composed of **Directory Service Agents (DSAs).** The DSAs cooperate through the **Directory Service Protocol (DSP)** to provide the Directory services to the Directory users. A Directory user is either a human being or an application program. It requests the Directory services through a **Directory User Agent (DUA). Directory Access Protocol (DAP)** is the protocol used by a DUA to request services from a DSA.

In Section 15.1, we examine the Directory Information Base model. In Section 15.2, we study the DAP and give its service specification in ASDC. In Section 15.3, we study the DSP and examine the distributed operation of the Directory. In Section 15.4, we examine the authentication framework proposed in the DS standard. In Section 15.5, we examine some of the proposed 1992 additions to the 1988 DS standard. They include access control, replication, and a few more models. In Section 15.6, we describe XDS, a Directory API endorsed by X/Open.

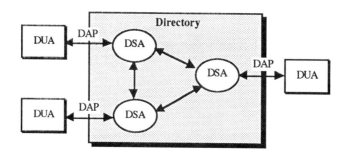

FIGURE 15.1   The DS Functional Model

15.1   The Directory Information Base

The **Directory Information Base (DIB)** model is a conceptual information model storing information about OSI objects. It is structured hierarchically using a tree structure known as the **Directory Information Tree (DIT).** The DS standard provides Directory schema which can be used by a profile group to define its DIT.

In Section 15.1.1, we examine Directory names and the structure of a DIT. In Section 15.1.2, we examine Directory schema and illustrate how they are used. In Section 15.1.3, we examine various means of implementing the DIB.

15.1.1   Directory Information Tree

The DIB is composed of **Directory entries** (or just **entries**). An entry can be either an **object entry** or an **alias entry**. An object entry is an entry which is the primary collection of information in the DIB about an object in the real world. On the other hand, an alias entry points to another object entry. It is primarily used to provide a user-friendly name to the referenced object entry. An object in the real world can be represented by more than one alias entry although it can be represented by at most one object entry in the DIB.

An entry is described by a set of attributes. Table 15.1 shows some of the attribute types defined by the DS standard. Attribute types can be also defined by profile groups. Among the attributes of an entry, there are the **distinguished attributes** which are used to name the entry. The type used in a distinguished attribute is called a **distinguished attribute type**, while some of the attribute values (normally at most one) of a distinguished attribute type are called **distinguished values**.

Entries of similar characteristics are grouped into object classes. Examples of object classes are Country, Organization, Person, Alias, Application Entity, DSA, and Device. A specification of an object class describes (mandatory) attributes which must belong to the class and (optional) attributes which may appear in the class. For example, we can specify the Person object class by requiring the commonName and surname attributes to be mandatory, and the telephoneNumber and userPassword attributes to be optional. A subclass inherits the mandatory and optional attribute lists from its superclass. Figure 15.2 shows an inheritance hierarchy constructed by using the subclass relationship.

X.500 Attribute Types			
System	Object Class Aliased Object Name Knowledge Information	Labelling	Common Name Surname Serial Number
Geographical	Country Name Locality StateOrProvince Street Address	Organizational	Organization Organization Unit Title
Explanatory	Description Search Guide Business Category	Postal	Postal Address Postal Code Post Office Box Physical Delivery Office
Telecommunications	Telephone Number Telex Number Telex Terminal ID Fax Telephone Number X.121 Address International ISDN Number Registered Address Destination Indicator	Preferences	Preferred Delivery Method
		OSI Application	Presentation Address Supp. Application Context
Relational	Member Owner Role Occupant	Security	User Password User Certificate CA Certificate Authority Revocation List Certificate Revocation List Cross Certificate Pair

TABLE 15.1   Directory Attribute Types

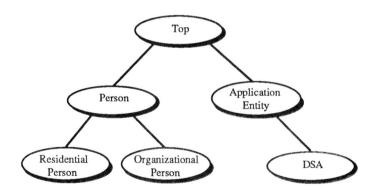

FIGURE 15.2   An Example of the Inheritance Hierarchy for the Directory

Entries in the DIB are placed as nodes of a hierarchical structure called the **Directory Information Tree (DIT)**. Each node of the DIT, except the root, corresponds to a set of entries. It is characterized by one or more attributes, e.g. C = US. These attributes together with the attributes associated with the nodes preceding the given node describe a set of entries. For example, the node with the attribute OU = CS in Figure 15.3 describes the set of entries which possess the following attributes: OU = CS, O = UMKC, and C = US. Alias entries must appear as leaves of the DIT.

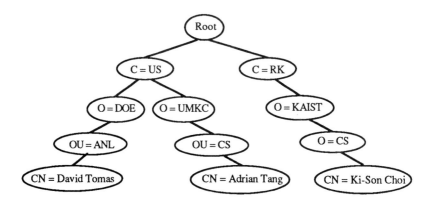

FIGURE 15.3 An Example of a DIT

The DIT structure is chosen for two reasons. First, because every node in a tree structure has a unique path to the root, the path can serve as an unambiguous name to the entry associated with the node. Second, whenever the number of entries grows, it is possible to delegate the management of the names in a subtree to other name servers.

Every level of the DIT is assigned an attribute type. Referring to the DIT in Figure 15.3, the first level is assigned the countryName attribute type, the second level is assigned the organizationName attribute type, the third level is assigned the organizationunitName attribute type, and the fourth level is assigned the commonName attribute level. Each attribute type belongs to a Directory object class. For example, the countryName attribute type is an attribute type in the Country object class, and the commonName attribute type is an attribute type of the Organization Person object class. Thus in the design of a level of a DIT, a Directory administrator has to first determine a Directory object class, then an attribute type of that object class. In a more general case, a Directory administrator can even choose a set of attribute types, all from the same Directory object class, for the same level of the DIT. The attribute types in the set, called distinguished attribute types, are studied in the following section.

Next, we examine how the Directory entries are named. Two kinds of names are provided by the Directory: distinguished names and aliases. Relative distinguished names (RDNs) and distinguished names (DNs) have been examined briefly in Chapter 4.

Each entry in the DIB is assigned a RDN when it is created. A RDN is a subset of attributes taken from the attributes of an entry. It describes some properties of the entry. Not all the attributes of an entry may be in the RDN of the entry. Those attributes which are not in the RDN can be considered as "secondary" properties of the entry. Thus, we need to distinguish between those attributes of an entry which are in the RDN and those attributes which are not. An attribute in the RDN is called a **distinguished attribute**. The type of a distinguished attribute is called a **distinguished attribute type**, while the value of a distinguished value is called a **distinguished attribute value**. Consider a person entry. A Directory administrator can require the commonName attribute to be a distinguished attribute, although it may not require the telephoneNumber attribute to be a distinguished attribute. The decision as to which attributes or attribute values should be distinguished is up to a Directory administrator, although the DS standard does provide some guidelines on the selection of distinguished attributes from a Directory object class.

A DN is formed by appending the entry's RDN to the DN of its immediate superior. In other words, the DN is an ordered sequence of RDNs from the root of the DIT to the entry, where the DN of the root is defined to be the empty set.

A leaf of the DIT modelling an alias entry points to some other node of the DIT. As a result, an entry may have one or more **alias names**. The following example illustrates how alias names are constructed.

Example 15.1

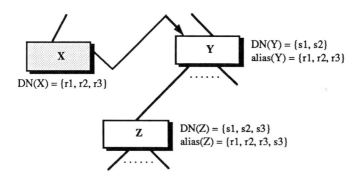

FIGURE 15.4   Illustration of Alias Names

In Figure 15.4, X is an alias entry pointing to Y. Assume that X and Y have DNs given by {r1, r2, r3} and {s1, s2} respectively. Y acquires an alias name given by {r1, r2, r3}. Z, a subordinate of Y, also acquires an alias name given by {r1, r2, r3, s3}, where s3 is the RDN of Z.

15.1.2 Directory Schema

The structure of the DIB is described by the **Directory schema**. The Directory schema consists of a set of structural rules on the DIT. It provides templates for the definition of object classes, attribute types, and abstract syntaxes. Figure 15.5 shows the relationships between the schema definitions on one side, and the DIT, directory entries, attributes, and attribute values on the other. Note that the DIT, object classes, attribute types, and attribute syntaxes are defined by a profile group or a Directory administrator. The Directory schema, in providing templates for these definitions, can improve consistency in the definitions. For instance, it prevents the creation of an inappropriate containment relation in the DIT, the use of an inappropriate attribute type in an object class definition, and the addition of an inappropriate value of a syntax not matching the syntax defined for the attribute type. In the following, we will describe the structural rules in the Directory schema.

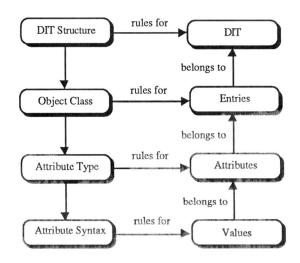

FIGURE 15.5   Directory Schema

- **DIT structure definition**

The DS standard suggests a DIT structure which is used to derive DITs. The **DIT structure**, as depicted in Figure 15.6, has Directory object classes as nodes. It also specifies one or more attribute types for each Directory object class. Using these Directory object classes and attribute types, we can derive a DIT since each level of a DIT is characterized by a Directory object class and one or more of its attribute types. For example, Figure 15.6 says that the country object class should be used as the first level of a DIT, and that the countryName attribute type (not shown in Figure 15.6), which is one of the attribute types of the Country object class, should be used as a distinguished attribute type.

Two observations can be made about this hierarchy. First, Locality is a repeating object class. It may appear above or beneath the Organization object class. Second, OrganizationalUnit is repeating and can be interleaved with Locality.

A DIT can be derived by duplicating the repeating objects in the DIT structure to make it a tree structure. Every implementation should determine the maximum number of times an object class in the DIT structure can repeat in the DIT. For example, it should specify the maximum number of times an organization unit can appear within an organization unit, assuming that the organization unit object class can be used for more than one level in the DIT.

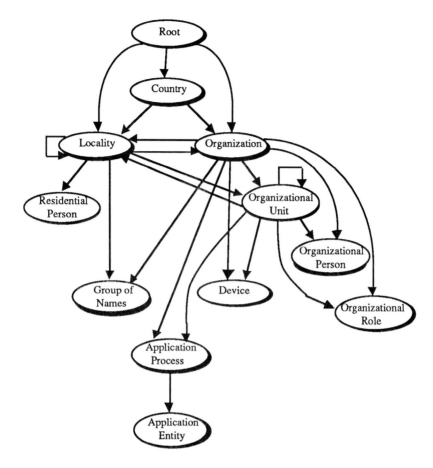

FIGURE 15.6   A DIT Structure suggested by the DS standard

- **object class definition**

List of X.500 Object Classes	
TOP	alias
country	residential Person
locality	application Process
organization	application Entity
organization Unit	DSA
person	device
organizational Person	strong Authentication User
organizational Role	certification Authority
group of Names	

TABLE 15.2   Directory Object Classes

The DS standard defines an OBJECT-CLASS macro which is used by DS application
designers to define their object classes. Rather than giving the definition of this macro, we
will describe the basic ingredients of the macro and use examples to illustrate the use of this
macro.

In a nutshell, the OBJECT-CLASS macro specifies a list of superclasses, a list of
subclasses, a list of mandatory attribute types, and a list of optional attribute types. The DS
standard defined a number of object classes, some of which are shown in Table 15.2.

The following examples illustrate the use of the OBJECT-CLASS macro.

Example 15.2

```
top OBJECT-CLASS
        MUST CONTAIN {objectClass}
        ::= {objectClass 0}
```

Every object class is a subclass of top. Since the top object class must contain the objectClass attribute,
every object class inherits this attribute. The objectClass attribute is used to identify the object class to
which an entry belongs.

Example 15.3

```
person OBJECT-CLASS
        SUBCLASS of top
        MUST CONTAIN { commonName, surName}
        MAY CONTAIN {description, seeAlso, telephoneNumber, userPassword}
        ::= {objectClass 1}

residentialPerson OBJECT-CLASS
        SUBCLASS OF person
        MUST CONTAIN {localityName}
        MAY CONTAIN {localAttributeSet, postalAttributeSet, preferredDeliveryMethod,
        telecommunicationAttributeSet, businessCategory}
        :: = {objectClass 2}

organizationalPerson OBJECT-CLASS
        SUBCLASS OF person
        MAY CONTAIN {localAttributeSet, postalAttributeSet, organizationalUnitName, title,
        telecommunicationAttributeSet}
        ::= {objectClass 3}
```

The person object class is defined to be a subclass of top. It contains residentialPerson and
organizationPerson as subclasses.

Example 15.4

```
applicationEntity OBJECT-CLASS
        SUBCLASS OF top
        MUST CONTAIN {commonName, presentationAddress}
        MAY CONTAIN {description, localityName, organizationName, organizationalUnitName,
        seeAlso, supportApplicationContext}
        ::= {objectClass 4}

dSA OBJECT-CLASS
        SUBCLASS OF applicationEntity
        MUST CONTAIN {knowledgeInformation}
        ::= {objectClass 5}
```

This example shows that applicationEntity is a subclass of top, and that dSA is a subclass of applicationEntity.

- **attribute syntax definition**

The ATTRIBUTE-SYNTAX macro is used to define an abstract syntax. It specifies the basic data type of the attribute value(s), the permitted size range for each attribute value, and the matching rules (such as equality, substrings, and ordering) for matching a presented value with a target attribute value held in the DIB. An example follows.

Example 15.5

```
caseIgnoreStringSyntax ATTRIBUTE-SYNTAX
        CHOICE {T61 String, PrintableString}
        MATCHES FOR EQUALITY SUBSTRINGS
        ::= {attributeSyntax 1}
```

- **attribute type definition**

The ATTRIBUTE macro is quite similar to the ATTRIBUTE-SYNTAX macro. It specifies the abstract syntax of an attribute type which may either point to a separately defined attribute syntax or explicitly define an attribute syntax by using the ATTRIBUTE-SYNTAX macro. It also indicates whether the attribute is single-valued or multi-valued. The next example illustrates the use of this macro.

Example 15.6

```
countryName ATTRIBUTE
        WITH ATTRIBUTE-SYNTAX
```

PrintableString (SIZE(2))
MATCHES FOR EQUALITY
SINGLE VALUE
::= {attributeType 1}

15.1.3 DIB Implementation

The DIB is only a conceptual information model. It can be implemented by storing the DIB information in the main memory or in a database system. For example, the QUIPU Directory, a public domain DS implementation, operates with all the Directory information in the main memory. This facilitates implementation, flexibility, and performance to a large extent. A database is invoked every time the system is booted, and any modification made to the information must be stored in a disk once the system is shut down.

Consider a database implementation of the DIB. Although the DIT has a hierarchical structure, the database model chosen does not have to be hierarchical. Any database system that can capture the characteristics of the DIT can be used to implement the DIB. In the following, we examine different database models for the DIB implementation.

The hierarchical database model follows the DIT structure very closely. However, it searches and retrieves single records instead of sets of records which may be required by the browsing feature of the Directory services.

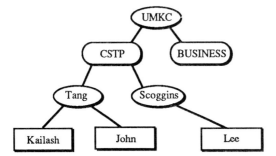

ENTRY_ID	SUBORDINATE_ID
UMKC	CSTP
UMKC	BUSINESS
CSTP	Tang
CSTP	Scoggins
Tang	Kailash
Tang	John
Scoggins	Lee

FIGURE 15.7 Structure Table for the DIT

The relational database model frees users from the frustration of having to deal with the clutter of storage representation details which may be required by the hierarchical database model. The simple tabular form of relations together with the simple non-procedural query language facilities provide a consistent user interface. In relational queries, the user describes what it wants and not how to get to it. The relational model is flexible and easier to use than any other traditional database models because inter-record relationships need not be pre-defined. The join operator allows a user to relate records based on attribute values. When using a relational database model, we need to map a DIT into tables or relations, and create a naming context table, a knowledge reference table, and a structure table. Figure 15.7 illustrates a structure table which captures the tree structure of a DIT.

The basic types provided to users in the relational database model are limited to simple data types. Modelling complex data types and storing multiple instances of the same relation are not possible. There is no facility for a user to define its own data types. When a relational database system is used, complex objects have to be transformed and treated as tables. The tables are related by means of common attributes, thereby resulting in redundancy. At runtime, entries from the tables need to be put back to retrieve the original objects. This is done by selecting the required data from different tables and then joining them. The overhead involved with the join operation is very high, resulting in degraded performance.

Object-oriented database models support complex data structures that match real world objects closely, and allow objects to be stored and manipulated directly as there is no need to transform objects into tables. Data types can be user-defined. Since the object-oriented database model can model objects directly, run time performance is better than that of relational database models. Experiments have shown the object-oriented database models to be 10 to 100 times faster than the relational database models.

In general, all DIB implementations should avoid large flat DITs as the performance improves with a deeper and a less wide tree. Furthermore, management is easier for such "non-flat" trees.

15.2   Directory Access Service

Section 15.2.1 gives an informal description of the Directory services. Section 15.2.2 gives an ASDC description of the Directory access service.

15.2.1   An Overview of the Directory Access Service

A DUA requests the Directory services on behalf of its Directory user. Before requesting any service, the DUA must first bind to the Directory. Once bound, the DUA can request a Directory service through the invocation of a remote operation. Each invocation is accompanied by arguments specific to the operation. The outcome of each request is a result, a referral, or an error. A result is returned when the request has been carried out successfully. A referral is returned if the service is unobtainable at a DSA or more easily "reached" through another DSA. An error is returned if the request cannot be carried out. When no further requests are anticipated, the DUA can unbind from the Directory.

The DS standard defines the arguments, the results, and the errors of each Directory operation. Using the principle of commonality, it defines a commonArguments parameter and a commonResult parameter. The commonArguments parameter groups all the attributes which appear in almost every operation request. Similarly, the commonResults parameter groups all the attributes which appear in every result. The use of commonArguments and commonResults will simplify the definition of a Directory operation.

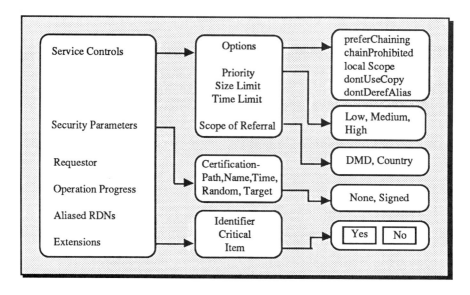

FIGURE 15.8   A User Interface to the Common Arguments

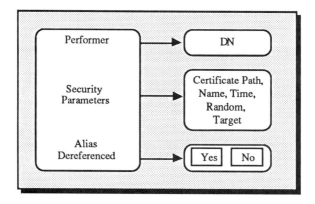

FIGURE 15.9   A User Interface to the Common Results

The **commonArguments** parameter is used to qualify a Directory request. It contains the following subparameters: serviceControls, securityParameters, DN, operationProgress information, and extensions. The DN subparameter identifies the originator of the request. The operationProgress subparameter defines the role that the DSA should play in the distributed evaluation of the request. The extension subparameter provides a mechanism to allow extensions to the argument of a Directory operation. The serviceControl and securityParameters subparameters are explained in the next two paragraphs. The **commonResults** parameter is used to qualify the result of a request. It contains the following subparameters: securityParameters, DN, and aliasDereferenced. The DN subparameter identifies the performer (i.e., some DSA) of the Directory operation. The aliasDereferenced subparameter is set to TRUE when the purported name of the target of the operation included an alias which was dereferenced. Figures 15.8 and 15.9 provide an example of a user interface for commonArguments and the commonResults.

To make service requests practical, every invocation of a Directory operation is qualified by service controls. Service controls impose limits on the use of the Directory resources. The ASN.1 definition of service controls is given below.

```
ServiceControls ::= SET {
    options             [0]  BIT STRING {  preferChaining (0),
                                           chainingProhibited (1),
                                           localScope (2),
                                           dontUseCopy (3),
                                           dontDereferenceAliases (4) } DEFAULT {},
    priority            [1]  INTEGER {low(0), medium(1), high(2)} DEFAULT medium,
    timeLimit           [2]  INTEGER OPTIONAL,
    sizeLimit           [3]  INTEGER OPTIONAL,
    scopeOfRef          [4]  INTEGER {dmd(0), country(1)} OPTIONAL
```

The timeLimit field designates a cutoff point for requests that take too long to answer. The sizeLimit field imposes an upper bound on the size of the response to a request. The scopeOfRef field defines the scope of the request which can be a DSA, a country, or a collection of DSAs administered under the same authority. The priority limit field indicates a priority on the request. The options field has to do with the distributed operation of the Directory. A Directory operation operates in two modes: chaining and referrals. These modes will be explained in Section 15.3. The chainingProhibited option indicates that referrals instead of chaining should be used. The dontUseCopy option indicates that information should not be returned from a copy of the target entry. The dontDereferenceAliases option, if omitted, indicates that aliases are always dereferenced.

The SecurityParameters subparameter of the commonArguments parameter is used to qualify the invocation of each operation as well as the result of each retrieval operation. Its ASN.1 definition is given below.

```
SecurityParameters ::= SET {
    certificationPath        [0]  CertificationPath OPTIONAL,
    name                     [1]  DistinguishedName OPTIONAL,
    time                     [2]  UTCTime OPTIONAL,
    random                   [3]  BIT STRING OPTIONAL,
    target                   [4]  ProtectionRequest OPTIONAL}
```

The certificationPath field is used to carry the sender's certificate for authentication purpose. The name field identifies the intended recipient. The time field indicates the expiration time for the validity of the signature. The random number field is used in conjunction with the time field to enable the detection of replay attacks when the argument or the result has been signed.

A DUA requests a service from the Directory via three ports: read, search, and modify. Future versions of the DS standard may introduce more port types. Each port supports a number of Directory operations. Each Directory operation contains an argument, a result, and a set of possible errors. Possible errors include nameError (e.g., no such object), serviceError (e.g., the Directory is busy at present or unavailable), securityError (e.g., insufficient access rights), attributeError (e.g. no such attribute for a read operation), abandoned, updateError, and referral. Referral is not really an error, but rather suggests that the DUA should try another DSA to obtain the requested information. The Abandoned error is returned if an Abandon request is received during processing.

The **read port** allows a DUA to read information from a target entry. It supports three operations: read, compare, and abandon. It is assumed that the DUA has foreknowledge of the DN of the target entry. The three operations are explained below:

- **Read**: The Read operation allows a DUA to retrieve information of an object entry in the Directory. The Read argument contains the DN of the object entry to be retrieved and a selection field indicating what information of the object entry is requested. The argument is qualified by the commonArguments parameter. Note that the DN of the object entry may contain one or more aliases which should be dereferenced unless deferencing is prohibited in the service control specification. The Read result contains the requested information of the object entry, should the request succeed. It is qualified by the commonResults parameter. The Read errors include attributeErrors, nameErrors, serviceErrors, referral, abandoned, and securityError.

- **Compare**: The Compare operation compares the value of a particular object entry to one or more values submitted in the Compare query. An example of the use of this operation is the comparison of a password to a list of passwords to gain admission to some service. The Compare argument specifies the DN of the object entry concerned and the purported attribute value assertion to be applied to the object entry. The Compare result holds the result of the comparison, and may specify whether the information is compared against the object entry or a copy. The Compare errors include attributeError, nameError, serviceError, referral, abandoned, and securityError.

- **Abandon**: A DUA uses the Abandon operation to inform the Directory that it wants to terminate some outstanding interrogation launched earlier. The Abandon argument contains an invoke identifier of the operation to be abandoned. The Abandon result is null. If the abandon request fails, an abandonFailed error is reported. The abandonFailed error values are "no such operation", "too late", and "cannot abandon". The Abandon operation is only applicable to interrogation operations such as Read, Compare, List, and Search.

The **search port** enables browsing of the DIB. It supports two operations: List and Search.

- **List**: The List operation is used to return the immediate subordinates of an object entry. The List argument contains the DN of the object entry whose immediate subordinates are to be listed. The List request succeeds if the object entry is located, regardless of whether there is any subordinate information to return. The List result may include subordinate information (such as indicating whether the subordinate is an alias entry or not), a partialOutcomeQualifier indicating whether the time limit or the size limit has been exceeded, or whether some portion of the DIT has not been explored. If indeed a portion of the DIT has not been explored, then some "continuation" references may be supplied to indicate where the search should continue. The List errors include nameError, serviceError, referral, abandoned, and securityError.

• **Search**: Unlike the List operation which retrieves only the information about the first level subordinates of a base object entry, the Search operation allows an entire subtree (headed by the base object entry) to be searched. The Search argument includes the DN of the base object entry, the subset parameter, the filter parameter, and the selection parameter. A filter is a set of conditions that essentially narrow down the volume of results returned. The selection parameter indicates what information from the entries is requested. The subset parameter is used to limit the search to explore the base object, the base object and the first level subordinates, or the entire subtree headed by the base object entry. The search request succeeds if the base object entry is located, regardless of whether there are any subordinates to return.

The **modify port** allows the DIB to be modified in a restricted manner. It supports four operations: AddEntry, RemoveEntry, ModifyEntry, and ModifyRDN.

• **AddEntry**: The AddEntry operation adds a new leaf entry to the DIT. The leaf entry can be an object entry or an alias entry. It may be extended in the future to allow a subtree to be added to the DIT. The AddEntry argument contains the DN of the superior object entry under which the new object entry is to be added and the set of entry information to comprise the new entry. In processing this operation, the Directory ensures that the new entry conforms to the Directory schema. One of the errors associated with the addEntry operation is updateError. For example, placing an entry as a subordinate of an alias entry is an updateError.

• **RemoveEntry**: The RemoveEntry operation is used to remove a leaf entry . It may be extended in the future to allow the deleting of a subtree from the DIT.

• **ModifyEntry**: The ModifyEntry operation is used to perform a series of one or more of the following modifications to an entry: add a new attribute, remove an attribute, add attribute values, remove attribute values, replace attribute values, or modify an alias. It is atomic, meaning that either all the changes take place or none of the changes are made. Atomicity ensures consistency of the DIB with its schema.

• **ModifyRDN**: This operation is used to change the RDN of a leaf entry. The ModifyRDN argument contains the new RDN and the DN of the entry whose RDN is to be modified. The new RDN may replace or overlay some of the old RDN values, depending on the setting of the deleteOldRDN flag. If the deleteOldRDN flag is set, all the attribute values in the old RDN which are not in the new RDN are deleted. If the flag is not set, the old values will remain in the entry. This operation returns "null" as an indication of success. The ModifyRDN errors include nameError, serviceError, referral, securityError, and updateError.

15.2.2 Abstract Service of DAP

The purpose of this section is to apply ASDC to specify the abstract service of DAP. First we consider the macroscopic description.

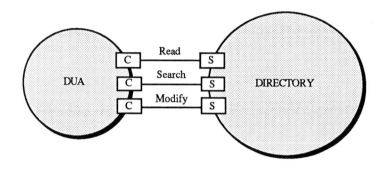

FIGURE 15.10   DAP Ports

The two objects involved in the communication of DAP are the Directory object and the DUA object. Figure 15.10 shows that they interact with each other via three ports: the read port, the search port, and the modify port. All three ports are asymmetrical with the ports in the DUA playing the consumer role. The following shows the specification of the Directory, the DUA, and the readPort using the OBJECT macro:

```
directory OBJECT
    PORTS {readPort[S], searchPort[S], modifyPort[S]}
    ::= id-ot-directory

dua OBJECT
    PORTS {readPort[C], searchPort[C], modifyPort[C]}
    ::= id-ot-dua

readPort PORT
    CONSUMER INVOKES {Read, Compare, Abandon}
    ::= id-pt-read
```

The microscopic description describes how the Directory services can be initiated, controlled, and terminated. In the next three examples, we select an operation from each port and gives its specification using the ABSTRACT-OPERATION macro. The selected operations are Read, Search, and AddEntry .

Example 15.7

```
Read ::= ABSTRACT-OPERATION
    ARGUMENT     ReadArgument
    RESULT       ReadResult
    ERRORS       {attributeError, nameError, serviceError, referral, abandoned, securityError}

ReadArgument ::= OPTIONALLY-SIGNED SET {
    object          [0]  Name,
    selection       [1]  EntryInformationSelection DEFAULT {},
    COMPONENTS OF CommonArguments}
ReadResult ::= OPTIONALLY-SIGNED SET {
    entry           [0]  EntryInformation,
    COMPONENTS OF CommonResults}
```

The selection field of ReadArgument specifies the attributes to be read.

Example 15.8

```
Search ::= ABSTRACT-OPERATION
    ARGUMENT     SearchArgument
    RESULT       SearchResult
    ERRORS       {attributeError, nameError, serviceError, referral, abandoned, SecurityError}

SearchArgument ::= OPTIONALLY-SIGNED SET {
    baseObject      [0]  Name,
    subset          [1]  INTEGER {
                            baseObject (0),
                            oneLevel (1),
                            wholeSubtree (2)} DEFAULT baseObject,
    filter          [2]  Filter DEFAULT and {},
    searchAlias     [3]  BOOLEAN DEFAULT TRUE,
    COMPONENTS OF CommonArguments}
SearchResult ::= OPTIONALLY-SIGNED
    CHOICE {
        searchinfo SET {
                    distinguishedName        DistinguishedName OPTIONAL,
                    entries                  [0]  SET OF EntryInformation,
                    partialOutcomeQualifier  [2]  PartialOutcomeQualifier OPTIONAL,
                    COMPONENTS OF CommonResults}
        uncorrelatedSearchInfo     [0]  SET OF SearchResult}
PartialOutcomeQualifier ::= SET {
    limitProblem                 [0]  LimitProblem OPTIONAL,
```

```
        unexplored                  [1]  SET OF ContinuationReference OPTIONAL,
        unavailableCriticalExt      [2]  BOOLEAN DEFAULT FALSE}
LimitProblem ::= INTEGER {
                         timeLimitExceeded (0),
                         sizeLimitExceeded (1),
                         administrativeLimitExceeded (2)}
```

The subset field of SearchArgument indicates the scope of the search. The filter field specifies a test to be applied to the scope of the search. If an entry passes the test, its information is returned. In some cases, the partialOutcomeQualifier is used to qualify the outcome. For example, it may indicate that either the time or the size limit is exceeded. It may also indicate a set of continuation references to be pursued by the requestor.

Example 15.9

```
AddEntry ::= ABSTRACT-OPERATION
        ARGUMENT    AddEntryArgument
        RESULT      AddEntryResult
        ERRORS      {attributeError, nameError, serviceError, referral, securityError, updateError}


AddEntryArgument ::= OPTIONALLY-SIGNED SET {
        object          [0]  DistinguishedName,
        entry           [1]  SET OF Attribute,
        COMPONENTS OF CommonArguments}
AddEntryResult ::= NULL
```

Note that the argument of AddEntry may be signed by the requestor.

In the realization of the abstract service, abstract objects are mapped to AEs, and ports are mapped to ASEs. The three ports of DAP are mapped to the following ASEs: readASE, modifyASE, and searchASE (Figure 15.11). These ASEs can be specified using the APPLICATION-SERVICE-ELEMENT macro. For example, the readASE can be specified as follows:

```
readASE APPLICATION-SERVICE-ELEMENT
                CONSUMER INVOKES {read, compare, abandon}
 ::= id-ase-readASE
```

The DUA object is mapped to an AE containing readASE, modifyASE, searchASE, ROSE, and ACSE. The DSA communicating with the DUA, is mapped to the same AE structure. The DS standard specifies only one DAP application context, directoryAccessAC. DirectoryAC can be specified using the APPLICATION-CONTEXT macro as follows:

directoryAccessAC APPLICATION-CONTEXT
                 APPLICATION SERVICE ELEMENTS {aCSE}
                 BIND DirectoryBIND
                 UNBIND DirectoryUnbind
                 REMOTE OPERATIONS {rOSE}
                 INITIATOR CONSUMER OF {
                     readASE,
                     searchASE,
                     modifyASE}
                 ABSTRACT SYNTAXES {id-as-acse, id-as-directoryAccessAS}
::= id-ac-directoryAccessAC

Since the DUA is normally the initiator, the DUA is the consumer in the directoryAccesAC application context. Thus, the DUA and the Directory interact with each other using the client-server paradigm, where the DUA is the client.

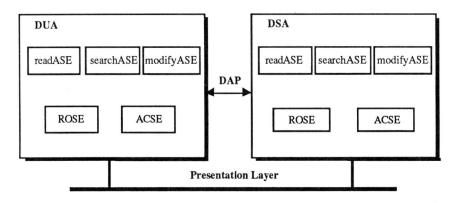

FIGURE 15.11   DirectoryAccessAC

15.3   The Distributed Directory

In a large network environment, the Directory services may be distributed among multiple DSAs. Despite the distributed nature, the basic philosophy of the Directory services is transparent distribution, i.e., a DUA views the Directory as a single object. This means that the object entry information retrieved by a DUA from a particular DSA should be the same, had the object entry information been retrieved from a different DSA. To preserve the DUA's view of a single Directory object, mechanisms must be defined to allow partitioning of the DIB.

     In Section 15.3.1, we study the Distributed Directory model and show how the DIT is partitioned among the DSAs. Furthermore, we examine the knowledge information which a DSA must hold about other DSAs so that it can intelligently navigate in the DIT.

In Section 15.3.2, we examine the abstract service specification of DSP in ASDC. In Section 15.3.3, we examine an internal organization of a DSA.

15.3.1 Distributed Directory Model

One of the design goals of the Directory services is that requests addressed to any DSA must produce results which are the same regardless of the DSA contacted. To satisfy this goal, a DSA must have some knowledge of the place where the requested information is located in the DIT. In the extreme case, the entire DIB is contained within a single DSA, in which case the goal is trivially satisfied. In fact, a centralized DSA was very common during the early DSA implementations. In general, information in the DIB is distributed among the DSAs. Each DSA maintains one or more substructures of the DIT. Consequently, the DSAs may need to communicate with each other to resolve requests from a DUA.

First, we examine the different modes in which the DSAs interact with each other. Then we introduce the concept of naming contexts which is used to partition a DIT. Finally, we introduce the DSA knowledge information model.

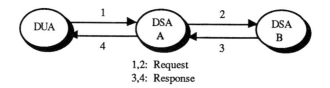

1,2: Request
3,4: Response

FIGURE 15.12   Chaining

The DSAs interact with each other in three different modes: chaining, referral, and multicasting. Figure 15.12 illustrates **chaining**. Here a DSA passes a request to another DSA until a DSA that can provide the information requested is found. In the figure, B has the requested information and passes it to A which then returns the result to the DUA.

Figure 15.13 illustrates **multicasting**. This mode is used by a DSA to chain an identical request in parallel or sequentially to one or more DSAs. In the figure, A first chains the request to B and then to C in a sequential manner. Multicasting can be viewed as a particular form of chaining.

Figure 15.14 illustrates **referrals**. The DUA first makes a request to A. A does not have the requested information but refers B to the DUA. The DUA then contacts B. Referral is used here because A and B do not have chained ports with each other.

Figure 15.15 illustrates another usage of referral when the DSAs have chained ports with one another. Here A chains the request to B which sends back a referral of C to A. A then chains the request to C. C has the information and returns the information to A.

A DUA can prohibit chaining through the service control parameter of a Directory operation. In this case, the contacted DSA will return a referral if does not have the entry information. The DSA can also choose not to chain, in which case it returns a referral.

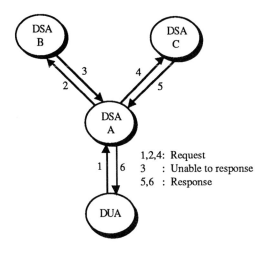

FIGURE 15.13   Multicasting

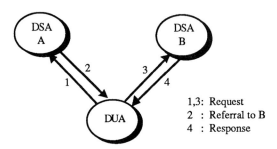

FIGURE 15.14   Referral

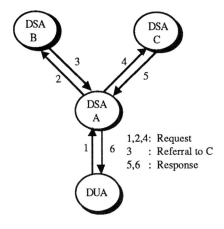

FIGURE 15.15   Another Referral

As the DIB grows, a DSA may delegate authority to other DSAs. Delegation of authority begins with the root of the DIT and proceeds downwards to the leaf entries. For example, Figure 15.16 shows that A delegates authority for entry 4 to B and entry 7 to C. As a result, each DSA holds one or more partial subtrees of the DIT. A **naming context** is a partial subtree of the DIT defined as starting at a vertex (known as the root vertex of the naming context) and extending downwards to leaf and/or non-leaf entries. For example, the DIT in Figure 15.17 is partitioned into 5 naming contexts. Note that the naming context C is not a subtree because it does not extend to all the leaf entries. Hence a name context is a partial subtree in general. Also note that context E is "subordinate" to context C, because the root of context E is a child of the root of context C. Similarly, context D is subordinate to context B.

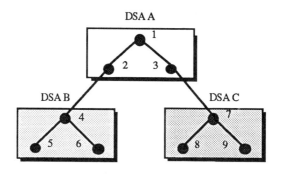

FIGURE 15.16   Delegation of Authorities

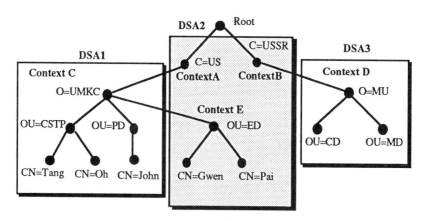

FIGURE 15.17   Partitioning a DIT into Naming Contexts

Naming contexts have an important property. The immediate superior of any entry in a naming context (except the root of the naming context) is also in the naming context, i.e., a naming context does not have any "hole". Using this property, we can define a **naming context tree** where the nodes are given by the naming contexts. The child/parent relationship in this tree is given by the subordinate/superior relationship among the naming contexts. Figure 15.18 shows the naming context tree derived from the DIT in Figure 15.17.

In an extreme case, a naming context contains only a single entry or the entire DIT. The naming context containing only the root of the DIT is known as the **root context**. A DSA holding the root context is called a **root DSA**. A DSA holding naming contexts that are immediately subordinate to the root context is called a **First Level DSA**. DSA 2 in Figure 15.17 is a First Level DSA.

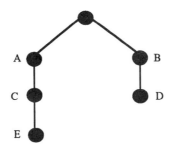

FIGURE 15.18   A Naming Context Tree

Every naming context is named by a context prefix. A **context prefix** of a naming context is defined to be the DN of the root vertex of the naming context. For example, the context prefix of the naming context E in Figure 15.17 is {C=US, O=UMKC, OU=ED}.

Directory administrators need to decide how to assign naming contexts to the various DSAs. Assignment of naming contexts must be done to optimize **name resolution** which is the process of locating the **administrative DSA** of an entry, i.e., the primary DSA holding the entry in one of its naming contexts (primary means that there may be a secondary DSA holding replicated copies of the entry). There is no standardized assignment procedure, but the following guidelines can be applied:

- In a small network, the root context is normally replicated in all the DSAs. In this way, a DSA can immediately navigate to the root of the DIT during name resolution.
- In a large network, the root context contains a bunch of information about the DIB. In this case, some DSAs should be set aside to hold only the root context. Cross references to these DSAs should be contained in every other DSA.

Next, we describe the knowledge that may be held by a DSA so that it can navigate intelligently in the DIT. While a DSA must hold Directory information for the entries contained in its own naming contexts, it must also hold references to Directory information held by other DSAs. This internal knowledge together with references to external knowledge constitute the **knowledge information** of a DSA. When a DSA is not an administrative authority of an entry, it relies on its knowledge information to locate the administrative authority of the root of a naming context containing the entry.

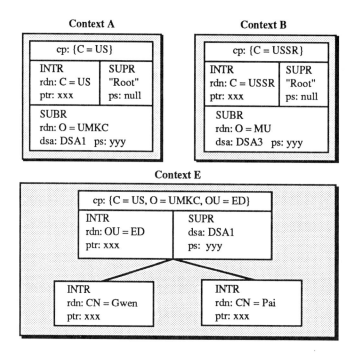

FIGURE   15.19   Knowledge Information of DSA 2 in Figure 15.17

Knowledge information can be expressed in terms of five kinds of references. These references are described below:

• **internal references**: A DSA needs to maintain an internal reference for every entry of which it is the administrative authority. An internal reference consists of the RDN of the entry and an address to the location where the entry is stored. For example, DSA 1 in Figure 15.17 must hold an internal reference to each of the six entries contained in context C.

• **subordinate references**: A DSA needs to maintain a subordinate reference to an immediate subordinate entry (i.e., one that is a subordinate to an entry in a naming context maintained by the DSA) and an access point of the Administrative Authority of that subordinate entry. For example, DSA 2 in Figure 15.17 holds a subordinate reference for context A and a subordinate reference for context D.

• **superior references**: Every non-first level DSA must maintain a superior reference pointing to a DSA which holds a naming context "closer" to the root than any naming context held by the non-first level DSA. For example, DSA 3 (a non-first level DSA) in Figure 15.17 holds a superior reference pointing to DSA 2, an administrative authority of naming context B which is in turn the superior of context D.

• **cross references**: A cross reference consists of a context prefix of a naming context and the access point of a DSA which is the administrative authority of that naming context.   Referring to Figure 15.17, DSA 3 may contain a cross reference pointing to context C. This type of reference is optional for a DSA. It serves to speed up the name resolution process. A DSA may acquire cross references from other DSAs at the end of a Directory operation.

• **non-specific subordinate references**: A non-specific subordinate reference consists of an access point of a DSA which holds one or more immediate subordinate naming contexts. Unlike a specific subordinate reference, a non-specific subordinate reference does not contain a context prefix of a naming context. A non-specific subordinate reference is held by a DSA when the context prefix of a subordinate of one of its naming contexts is unknown to the DSA. For example, DSA 1 in Figure 15.17 may hold a non-specific subordinate reference pointing to DSA 2 because DSA 2 holds context E which is a subordinate to context C held by DSA 1.

Figure 15.19 shows the knowledge held by DSA 2 in Figure 15.17. Note that internal references, specific subordinate references, and non-specific subordinate references are defined relative to a naming context, while superior references and cross references are defined relative to a DSA.

15.3.2 Abstract Service of DSP

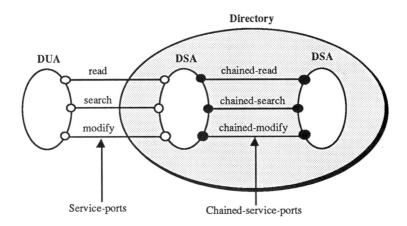

FIGURE 15.20   DSP Chained Ports

In this section, we examine an ASDC abstract service specification of DSP, the protocol used among the DSAs to provide the Directory services. Figure 15.20 shows that two DSAs communicate with each other in DSP using three chained-service-ports: chained-readPort, chained-searchPort, and chained-modifyPort. These three ports are invisible to a DUA. Externally, a DSA interacts with a DUA using the three service-ports described in the previous section. Thus the ports associated with a DSA are of two types: service-ports for interaction with a DUA, and chained-service-ports for interaction with a DSA.

When a Directory operation is chained from one DSA to another, a DSA needs to maintain the status of the chaining operation, suggest continuation references to the other

DSAs, detects possible chaining loops, etc. These additional arguments and results, known as **chained arguments** and **chained results**, are encompassed around the arguments and results of the chained operations used among the DSAs. These chained operations are quite similar to the DAP operations except that there are additional arguments and results for each chained operation.

A macroscopic description of the abstract service of DSP is obtained by first refining the Directory object into DSA objects and then specifying the ports of each DSA object as follows :

```
DirectoryRefinement ::= REFINE directory AS
    dsa                 RECURRING
    readPort        [S]     VISIBLE
    searchPort      [S]     VISIBLE
    modifyPort      [S]     VISIBLE
    chainedReadPort     PAIRED WITH dsa
    chainedSearchPort   PAIRED WITH dsa
    chainedModifyPort   PAIRED WITH dsa


dsa OBJECT
    PORTS {     readPort            [S]
                searchPort          [S],
                modifyPort          [S],
                chainedReadPort,
                chainedSearchPort,
                chainedModifyPort }
::= id-ot-dsa


chainedReadPort PORT
ABSTRACT OPERATIONS {ChainedRead, ChainedCompare, ChainedAbandon}
::= id-pt-chained-read


chainedSearchPort PORT
ABSTRACT OPERATIONS {ChainedList, ChainedSearch}
::= id-ot-chained-search


chainedModifyPort PORT
ABSTRACT OPERATIONS {ChainedAddEntry, ChainedRemoveEntry, ChainedModfiyEntry,
    ChainedModifyRDN}
::= id-pt-chained-modify
```

A chained operation is obtained by adding the ChainingArguments and the ChainingResults to the non-chained operation. For example, ChainedRead is specified as follows:

```
ChainedRead ::= ABSTRACT-OPERATION
    ARGUMENT    OPTIONALLY-SIGNED SET {
                    ChainingArguments,
                    [0] ReadArguments}
    RESULT      OPTIONALLY-SIGNED SET {
                    ChainingResults,
                    [0] ReadResult}
    ERRORS      {..., DSAReferral, ...} -- this includes all the errors of Read
```

where ReadArguments and ReadResults are the arguments and the results of the Read operation respectively defined in Section 15.2.2.

ChainingArguments is used to indicate to a performing DSA the information needed to successfully perform its part of the overall distributed Directory operation. Its ASN.1 definition is given as follows:

```
ChainingArguments ::= SET {
    originator          [0]  DistinguishedName OPTIONAL,
    targetObject        [1]  DistinguishedName OPTIONAL,
    operationProgress   [2]  OperationProgress OPTIONAL DEFAULT {notStarted},
    traceInformation    [3]  TraceInformation,
    aliasDereferenced   [4]  BOOLEAN DEFAULT FALSE,
    aliasedRDNs         [5]  INTEGER OPTIONAL,
    returnedCrossRefs   [6]  BOOLEAN DEFAULT FALSE,
    info                [7]  DomainInfo OPTIONAL,
    timeLimit           [9]  UTCTime OPTIONAL,
    securityParameters  [10] SecurityParameters DEFAULT {}}
```

The meanings of some of the fields of ChainingArguments are explained next. The originator field identifies the very first originator of the request. The targetObject field identifies the object currently being sought after. This object may be the object whose entry is to be operated upon or some base object identifying the scope of a set of objects to be acted upon. If the value of AliasedDereferenced is "true", then the targetObject may be different from the object originally specified by the DUA.

The operationProgress field is used to inform the performing DSA of the progress of the operation. Its ASN.1 definition is given as follows:

```
OperationProgress ::= SET {
    nameResolutionPhase     [0]  ENUMERATED {
                                     notStarted (1),
                                     proceeding (2),
                                     completed (3)},
    nextRDNToBeResolved     [1]  INTEGER OPTIONAL}
```

The nameResolutionPhase field is used to indicate one of the three phases in the name resolution process to be described in Section 15.3.3. When the nameResolutionPhase is "notStarted", it means that a DSA has not yet been reached with a naming context whose context prefix matches with some initial part of the name. When the nameResolutionPhase is "proceeding", it means that the initial part of the name has been recognized although the administrative DSA of the target object may not have been reached yet. The nextRDNToBeResolved subcomponent qualifies the "proceeding" phase by indicating to the performing DSA which RDNs in the targetObject name should be resolved next. When the nameResolutionPhase is "completed", it means that the administrative DSA of the target object has been reached.

The TraceInformation field is used to prevent looping. Prior to chaining an operation to another DSA, a DSA adds its own name and the targetObject value to TraceInformation. Before performing any operation, a DSA should check the TraceInformation value to see if it has been associated with an earlier execution of this operation. If so, looping is detected.

The returnCrossedRefs field indicates whether or not knowledge references used during the course of performing a distributed operation should be passed back to the initial DSA as cross references. A DSA can add these cross references to its knowledge information to speed up name resolution in the future.

The referenceType field indicates to the performing DSA what type of knowledge (i.e., superior, subordinate, cross, or non-specific subordinate) was used to route the request to it. Based on this knowledge, the performing DSA may be able to detect inconsistency in the knowledge held by the invoking DSA.

Finally, the timeLimit field indicates the time by which the distributed operation should be completed. Its value is extrapolated from the original time limit set by the requesting DUA.

ChainingResults is used by a performing DSA to provide feedback to the invoking DSA. Its ASN.1 definition is given as follows:

```
ChainingResults ::= SET {
    info              [0]  DomainInfo OPTIONAL,
    crossReferences   [1]  SEQUENCE OF CrossReferences OPTIONAL,
                      [2]  SecurityParameters DEFAULT {}}
```

If the returnedCrossRefs argument of a request has been set to TRUE by the invoking DSA, the crossReferences field is used to return cross references.

Figure 15.21 shows two DSAs communicating with each other in "directorySystemAC", the only DSP application context defined by the DS standard. The ports are mapped to the following three ASEs: chainedReadASE, chainedSearchASE, and chainedModifyASE. For example, the chainedReadASE and the directorySystemAC are specified as follows:

chainedReadASE APPLICATION-SERVICE-ELEMENT

OPERATIONS {chainedRead, chainedCompare, chainedAbandon}
::= id-ase-chainedReadASE

directorySystemAC APPLICATION-CONTEXT
APPLICATION SERVICE ELEMENTS {aCSE}
BIND DSABind
UNBIND DSAUnbind
REMOTE OPERATIONS {rOSE}
OPERATIONS OF {chainedReadASE, chainedSearchASE, chainedModifyASE}
ABSTRACT SYNTAXES {id-as-acse, id-as-directorySystemAS}
::= id-ac-directorySystemAC

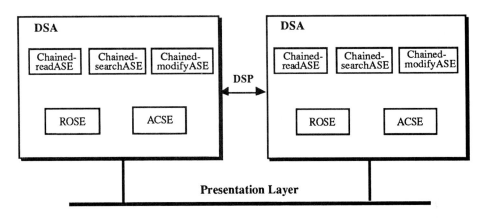

FIGURE 15.21   DirectorySystemAC

15.3.3 Internal Organization of a DSA

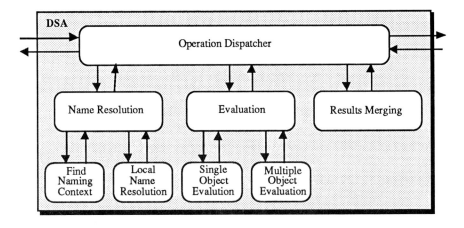

FIGURE 15.22   Internal Organization of a DSA

In this section, we examine an internal organization of a DSA. Each DSA in the Directory is equipped with procedures capable of executing the Directory operations. Figure 15.22, which is taken from the DS standard, shows an internal organization of a DSA. The **Operation Dispatcher** is the nucleus controlling the different procedures. Upon receiving an operation, it first validates the operation, checking for any chaining loop or authentication error. If none are found, it proceeds to execute the following three phases: Name Resolution, Evaluation, and Results Merging. These phases are described below.

- **name resolution phase**

In this phase, the purported name of an entry for which an operation is to be performed is used to locate the administrative DSA of the entry. The Operation Dispatcher calls the Name Resolution procedure which returns either a found indication, a reference, or an error indication. References are handled by either a referral or a chain action. Found indications are handled by calling the Evaluation procedure. The Name resolution procedure may call the Find Naming Context and the Local Naming Resolution procedures internally.

- Find Naming Context: This procedure attempts to match the purported name against context prefixes held by the DSA. If there are no matches, then it attempts to identify a cross reference or a superior reference. If a context prefix is matched, it returns either an indication that a suitable local naming context was found, or a cross reference relating downwards in the DIT. On the return of a local context, the Name Resolution procedure calls the Local Name Resolution procedure. Otherwise, it returns a cross reference to the Operation Dispatcher and terminates.
- Local Name Resolution: This procedure attempts to match the RDNs in the purported name internally until it can return a found indication. If it is unable to match all the RDNs internally, it attempts to identify subordinate references and return these to the Name Resolution procedure.

- **evaluation phase**

This phase is entered only if the Local Name Resolution procedure returns a found indication to the Name Resolution procedure. The principle procedure used during this phase is the Evaluation procedure. The Evaluation procedure may call the Single Object Evaluation and the Multiple Object Evaluation procedures internally.

- Single Object Evaluation: If the Directory operation is a single-object operation (i.e., one which affects only a single entry), the Evaluation procedure calls the Single Object Evaluation procedure. In this case, the entire Directory operation can be performed within the DSA. Examples of single-object operations are read, compare, addEntry, modifyEntry, modifyRDN, and removeEntry.
- Multiple Object Evaluation: If the Directory operation is a multiple-object operation such as Search or List, the Evaluation procedure calls the Multiple Object Evaluation

procedure. Multiple-object operations may affect entries which may or may not be co-located in the same DSA, hence this procedure requires some cooperative effort by several DSAs to locate and operate on the affected entries.

- **results merging phase**

This phase is entered once some of the results of the evaluation phases are available. The Results Merging procedure is invoked to merge the results obtained from different DSAs. The permissible responses returned to the requestor can be a complete result, a partial result which is not complete because some parts of the DIT have not yet been explored, or a chaining result if the requestor is a DSA.

The Name Resolution procedure is illustrated in the following examples. The next three examples refer to the DIT in Figure 15.17 and assume a chaining mode.

Example 15.10

Suppose that DSA 1 receives a request with the DN {C=US, O=UMKC, OU=CSTP, CN=Tang}. After routine authentication and loop tests, the Operation Dispatcher at DSA 1 calls its Name Resolution procedure which then calls the Find Naming Context procedure. The Find Naming Context procedure finds out that the given DN does match with the context prefix of context C. Hence, it returns the context prefix of context C to the Name Resolution procedure which then calls the Local Name Resolution procedure. The Local Name Resolution procedure proceeds downwards in context C, successfully matching each one of the remaining RDN until CN=Tang is located. It returns a found indication to the Name Resolution procedure which then proceeds to the evaluation phase.

Example 15.11

Say DSA 1 receives a request with the DN {C=US, O=KU}. The Operation Dispatcher at DSA 1 calls the Find Naming Context procedure. Since it cannot find any matching prefix, it returns the superior reference of naming context C which points to context A held by DSA 2. On receiving the superior reference, the Operation Dispatcher forwards the request to DSA 2. The Find Naming Context procedure at DSA 2 finds that the request matches with the prefix {C=USA} of context A and so it returns context A to the Name Resolution procedure at DSA 2. The Naming Resolution procedure calls the Local Name Resolution procedure which proceeds downwards in context A. However, it does not find a subordinate of C=US to match the RDN O=KU. Hence, the request fails and the name is determined to be invalid.

Example 15.12

In this example, DSA 1 receives a request with the DN {C=USSR, O=MU, OU=MD}. Since this name does not match the context prefix of any context held by DSA 1, DSA 1 will forward the request to DSA 2 because the superior reference of context C held by DSA 1 points at DSA 2. At DSA 2, the request is found to match the context prefix {C=USSR} of context B held locally. Hence, the Local Name Resolution procedure at DSA 2 is called with the context B. As the Local Name Resolution procedure attempts to match O=MU, it finds a subordinate reference indicating that {C=USSR, O=MU} is the start of a context held by DSA 3, thus it returns the subordinate reference to the Local Name Resolution procedure at DSA 2. Name resolution then migrates to DSA 3, where the Find Naming Context procedure locates the object identified by {C=USSR, O=MU, OU=MD}. However, the object turns out to be an alias entry which points to an entry whose DN is {C=USA, O=UMKC, OU=CSTP, CN=Scoggins}. Hence, the Find Naming Context procedure at DSA 3 returns an alias found indication to the Operation Dispatcher. DSA 3 resumes the processing of the request using the target name obtained by dereferencing.

Example 15.13

Suppose that a DSA maintains three contexts A, B and C which have the names {a, b}, {a, b, g}, and {a, b, c, d} respectively. It receives a request with the DN {a, b, c, d, e, f}. The Find Naming Context procedure returns context C since C seems to have the best match with the given DN. There is a problem. It is possible that the requested name is in context A but not in context C. A way to solve this is not to allow a DSA to maintain two contexts where the name of one is a prefix of the name of the other.

15.4 An Authentication Framework for OSI Applications

Part 8 of ISO/IEC 9594 defines an authentication framework for use by other OSI application protocols. In particular, it:

- specifies the form of authentication information held by the Directory,
- describes how authentication information may be obtained from the Directory, and
- defines ways in which applications may use the authentication information.

Two levels of authentication are defined. **Simple authentication** relies on the originator supplying its name/password which are then checked by the recipient. Obviously, it offers very limited protection against unauthorized access. **Strong authentication** relies on the use of cryptographic techniques to protect the exchange of validating information. It is based upon the use of certificates which may be held in the Directory.

15.4.1 Simple Authentication

There are three types of simple authentication. They are explained below.

- **Type A**

First, the originating user, say A, sends its DN and its password to its peer, say B. B then sends A's name and password to the Directory for verification. It is then notified of the success/failure of the authentication from the Directory. It may convey the result to B.

- **Type B**

First, A sends its protected identification information, Authenticator, to B. Authenticator1 is defined as follows:

    Protected1 = f1(timestamp1, randomnum1, nameA, passwordA)
    Authenticator1 = (timestamp1, randomnum1, nameA, Protected1)

where f1 is a 1-way hash function, and timestamp1 is a time-stamp, and randomnum1 is a random number. The time-stamp and the random number are used to minimize replay. B verifies the protected identification information by generating a local protected copy of A's password, ProtectedB, which is defined as follows:

    ProtectedB = f1(timestamp1, randomnnum1, nameA, passwordatB)

where passwordatB is a copy of A's password kept locally by B. B checks to see if ProtectedB is equal to Protected1. Note that A and B must use the same hash function.

- **Type C**

Type C is similar to Type B except that Protected1 is hashed with a 1-way hash function f2 to yield Protected2 which is equal to f2(timestamp2, randomnum2, Protected1). Instead of sending Authenticator1 to B, A will send Authenticator2 which is a 5-tuple consisting of timestamp1, timestamp2, randomnum1, randomnum2, and Protected2. On receiving Authenticator2 from A, B generates its local version of Protected2 and compares it for equality with what it received from A.

15.4.2 Strong Authentication

Strong authentication is based on public key cryptosystems, where the pair of keys involved must have the mutual encipherment property:

$$Xp*Xs = Xs*Xp$$

where Xp/Xs are the encipherment/decipherment function using the public/secret keys of user X. Both keys can be used for encipherment. For instance, if the secret (public) key is used for encipherment, then the public (secret) key is used for decipherment.

    The principle behind strong authentication is very simple. Each user is identified by the possession of its secret key. For a user to determine that its communicating partner possesses a secret key, it must have its communicating partner's public key. Thus, user's public keys need to be distributed and readily available. The public keys can be stored in the Directory.

First, we introduce the notion of certificates and describe how a user can obtain the public key of its communicating partner from the Directory. Then we describe three kinds of strong authentication.

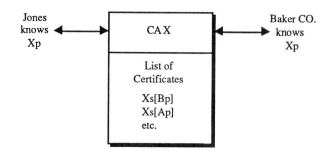

FIGURE 15.23   A Certification Authority Example

An incorrect public key is useless, hence certification of a key is required. There must be a chain of trusted points in the Directory from the user which seeks certification of a public key to the **certification authority (CA)** which will produce a public key **certificate**. Figure 15.23 illustrates a very simple arrangement for the Jones-to-Baker Co. example. In the figure, X is the trusted CA for both parties. The certificate has the verified public key of a user and other information. They also have a lifetime associated with them. Regenerating a certificate must then be possible. This is a responsibility of the CA. The certificate is encrypted using the CA's private key. This makes the certificates unalterable and unforgeable. They are thereby safe to "display", or make publicly available, to users who have the right to use the CA. Only the CA is allowed to modify certificates. There may be several CAs, each with their own, perhaps unique, store of certificates. The CA itself has its own public key. Any user with the key of a CA can obtain a certificate held by that CA.

Some notation may be helpful. Assume that X_p is the public key of X, X_s is the private key of X, and CA(X) is the certification authority for X. A nested chain of certification authorities is possible, wherein one CA is CA for another. $CA^n(X)$ is the notation for the situation where there are n steps in the chain of CAs. A certificate is represented by $X_1<<X_2>>$, where X_1 is the CA and X_2 is the certified user, i.e., the user associated with the certificate. For example, A<<C>> is the certificate for C, and CA(C) is A. If a user has A_p (i.e., the public key of the CA A), then it can get the certified public key of C, C_p.

More formally, a certificate is produced by a CA signing a collection of information, including the user's DN, the user's public key, the user's algorithm identifier, the validity period of the certificate, the CA's DN, and the CA's algorithm identifier.

The Directory entry of a CA usually contains more than one certificate. These certificates are of two kinds: **forward certificates** and **reverse certificates**. For a CA X, the forward certificates of X are generated by other CAs. The reverse certificates of X are generated by X and are the certified public keys of other CAs. Both of these certificates are used to construct certification paths. A **certification path** is an arbitrarily long list of certificates necessary for a user to get the public key of another user. Each list item is a certificate of the CA of the next list item. A chain of certificates is represented by notation of the form: $X_1<<X_2>>X_2<<X_3>>$. For example, $A<<B>>B<<C>>$ yields the same certificate as $A<<C>>$. In $A<<B>>B<<C>>$, A is the CA for B. If a user has A_p, then it can get B_p. B is the CA for C. With B_p, we can get C_p. This can be represented by the notation $A_p \cdot A<<B>>B<<C>>$, which denotes the operation of using A_p to "unwrap" a chain of certificates to extract the public key of the rightmost item, here C_p. A --> B denotes the certification path from A to B, formed by a chain of certificates, starting with the CA for A and finally yielding B_p.

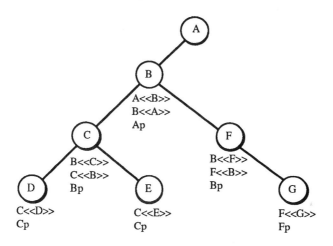

FIGURE 15.24   A Hierarchy of Certification Authorities

A certification path can be viewed logically as a chain formed by trusted points in the DIT between two users seeking to authenticate each other. There are more than one way to put together this chain. A hierarchy of CAs could be formed. Figure 15.24 illustrates an example of a hierarchy of CAs. In the figure, the nodes represent users. The nodes contain certain information about the tree structure that allows them to determine who is their superior CA. We also assume that each node knows its own public and private keys and the public key of its CA. To establish a path from D to G, D acquires certificates from the Directory to build a certification path to G. These certificates are:

$$C<<B>>, B<<F>>, F<<G>>$$

After G gets these certificates, it can unwrap the path to get G_p and C_p.

$$G_p = C_p \cdot C<<B>> B<<F>> F<<G>>$$

Node G needs to know the return path to D. For this, it gets the following certificates from the Directory:

$$F<<B>>, B<<C>>, C<<D>>$$

Unwrapping this yields:

$$D_p = F_p \bullet F<<B>> \; B<<C>> \; C<<D>>$$

In the general case, the Directory supplies both paths, but the amount of information required from the Directory can be reduced in a number of ways.

- When two users, such as D and E, share the same CA (here C), they need not go to the Directory. They can unwrap the certificates directly. For example, $E_p = C_p \bullet$ C<<E>>.
- In a hierarchical arrangement of CAs, we could record at each CA the public keys and reverse certificates of all the nodes higher in the tree. Then, the user would be halfway to his target and would only need to trace a path downwards from the first node that was superior to both the starting user and the target user.
- If a user communicates frequently with a certain CA, then it could store the path to that CA and the return path from that CA.
- CAs can cross-certify each other. This knowledge would speed the process.
- Finally, if two users have communicated, then they have established the two paths. Storing the paths would avoid the cost of rediscovering them if they are needed in the future.

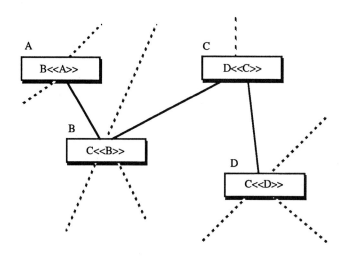

FIGURE 15.25   A finding a Certification Path to D

It is more often the case that the CAs do not form a hierarchical structure. In that case, it may be possible to force a hierarchical form on them, but we could view the certificates as arcs between the nodes which represent users and CAs. Finding a path would then be the same as finding a path in a directed graph and an appropriate algorithm for that purpose. Figure 15.25 gives a small example. If user A must build a certification path to D, then A must do a search for a path from B to D. This yields:

$$B<<C>>, C<<D>>$$

When this path has been discovered, the reverse path is simply a matter of backtracking. Such an approach, however, is subject to the major problem associated with graph algorithms. It may be slow. Precautions against looping are needed, and paths may be longer than necessary.

Next, we examine the authentication procedures. The authentication framework in the DS described three different authentication procedures with each carrying different kinds of authentication information. The bottom line is the corroboration of identity by demonstrating possession of the secret key. In all cases, let us assume that A wants to send to B.

In **1-way authentication**, A first generates a random number to detect replay attacks. A then sends to B its name and signature of a token containing the random number, the generation time (optional), the expiry date, and the DN of B. On receiving the information, B gets the certificate of A from the Directory and verifies that A's certificate has not expired. Then, it checks the signature. Finally, it checks that the timestamp is current and the random number has not been replayed. Thus, 1-way authentication involves a single transfer of information from A to B, and establishes the following:

- the identity of A, and that the token was actually generated by A,
- the identity of B, and that the token was intended to be sent to B, and
- the integrity of the token.

2-way authentication involves a reply from B to A. A generates the security token as described for 1-way authentication. B checks the security token as described for 1-way authentication. Furthermore, B generates a new security token using a random number and a timestamp generated by B and including the random number previously generated by A. On receiving the token from B, A checks the reply token in the same way as B checks A's token. The reply from B to A establishes the following:

- the token generated in the reply was generated by B and was intended to be sent to A, and
- the integrity of the token sent in the reply.

Thus, 2-way authentication is more suitable for mutual authentication.

The **3-way authentication** provides the same properties as 2-way authentication without using timestamp. This procedure is the subject of a defective report in progress, since the absence of timestamps is considered to be insecure.

15.5   More New Developments

The above sections were based on the 1988 DS standard. The management of the distributed Directory has been the main theme of the 1989 - 1992 period. Managers are concerned with issues such as access control and replication. The following sections present some of the management issues.

15.5.1   Some Directory Management Models

The 1992 DS standard presents a number of Directory models. We have covered the Directory functional model, the Distributed Directory model, and the DIB model in the previous sections. The 1992 DS standard adds a few more models, such as the Directory Administrative Authority Model, the Model of Directory Administrative and Operational Information, and the DSA Knowledge Model. The Directory Administrative Authority Model describes the structure of a DIT from the perspective of a DSA. The Model of Directory Administrative and Operational Information describes the structure of administrative information. The DSA Information Model describes the knowledge to be held by a DSA for its distributed operation. These models are examined in this section.

• **Directory Administrative Authority Model**

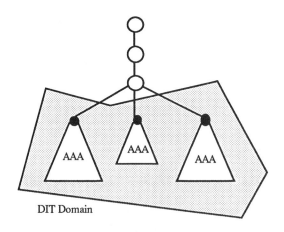

DIT Domain

FIGURE 15.26   A DIT Domain

The Directory Administrative Authority Model describes the structure of a DIT from the viewpoint of a Directory administrator. In the following, we will describe some management terminology and show how the DIT is structured for administration purpose.

A **Directory Management Domain (DMD)** is a set of DSAs and DUAs managed by a single organization, called the **Domain Management Organization (DMO)**. The portion of a DIT held by the DSAs in a DMD is called a **DIT domain**. A DIT domain may be partitioned into one or more non-overlapping Autonomous Administrative Areas (Figure 15.26). The structure of an Autonomous Administrative Area is described next.

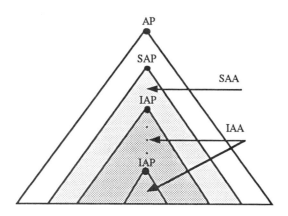

FIGURE 15.27   IAAs nested within a SAA

An **Autonomous Administrative Area (AAA)** is some "convex" substructure of the DIT. It begins at a single **administrative point (AP)** and continues downwards through the DIT till it runs into another administrative point associated with a subordinate AA (Figure 15.26). Since an AAA may not continue downwards to the leaves of the DIT, it is in general not a subtree of the DIT, although it has the convex property of a tree structure, i.e., the parent of any non-root node in the AAA is also in the AA.

For each specific concern, an AAA may be independently partitioned into similar convex substructures called **specific administrative areas (SAAs)**, with each SAA starting at a **specific administrative point (SAP)**. For example, the **Access Control Specific Area (ACSA)** is used for access control. The **Subschema Specific Area (SSA)** is used for schema management, i.e., it defines DIT structural rules for the AAA. The SAP of each SAA is represented in the DIT by an administrative entry. This entry contains an administrativeRole attribute which describes the role of the SAA. For example, the value of this attribute is "access-control-specific-area" if the SAA is an ACSA.

To facilitate delegation of administration, an SAA can be further subdivided into convex substructures called **inner administrative areas (IAAs)**, with each starting at an **inner administrative point (IAP)**. IAAs can be nested within each other (Figure 15.27), so that overlaying of administration attributes is possible. For example, a Security Administrative Authority which is in charge of an ACSA may partition its ACSA into one or more **Access Control Inner Areas (ACIAs)**. Each ACIA has an associated access control list which is applicable to a subset of the ACIA. The access control of an entry in the ACSA is then governed by the totality of the access control lists of those ACIAs which include the entry in their subsets. In contrast, an SSA does not allow nesting of IAAs within.

- **Model of Directory Administrative and Operational Information**

There are a variety of attributes in the DIB. First, there are the user attributes of interest to users. Then, there are attributes (e.g., access control information and schema information) required for the regulation of user information. Finally, there are attributes required by the DSAs for their support of the distributed Directory operation. The last two kinds of attributes are called **operational attributes**. Operational attributes are normally visible to Directory administrators but not Directory users. Access to these attributes is defined by the policy of an administrative authority.

Operational attributes can be categorized into three types: Directory operational attributes, DSA-shared operational attributes, and DSA-specific operational attributes. **Directory operational attributes** are found in the DIB and are used to represent control information (e.g., access control information and schema information) or other information such as indicating whether an entry is a leaf or non-leaf entry. **DSA-shared operational attributes** and **DSA-specific operational attributes**, which are described in the DSA Information Model, are used to support the distributed operation of a DSA. A knowledge reference is an example of a DSA-shared operational attribute, while DSE type (to be explained in the DSA Knowledge Model) is an example of a DSA-specific operational attribute.

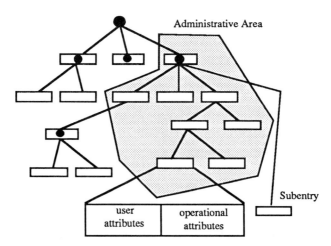

FIGURE 15.28　Subentry

Operational attributes are applicable to either an entry or a set of entries. When they are applicable to a single entry, they are stored with the entry. For example, an access control list is stored with an entry if its scope only applies to the entry. In some cases, operational attributes are applicable to a set of entries. This is the case if the scope of an access control list is a subarea of an ACSA. A **subentry**, positioned as a child of an administrative point, stores operational attributes about an area or a subtree refinement. A **subtree refinement** is a subset of a convex structure specified by a filter. The elements of a subtree refinement consist of those entries which pass the filter test. For example, a subtree refinement can be a subset to which an access control list is applicable. It can be a subset to which a schema is applicable. Or it can be a subset to which a collection of attributes is applicable. An operational attribute within a subentry is used to indicate the type of the subentry. The three types which we have mentioned are "access control", "subschema", and "collective attributes".

Figure 15.28 illustrates the relative position of a subentry. In general, an administrative point may have more than one subentry as children. In some cases, more than one subentry are required to serve a specific purpose. For example, access control information may be placed in more than one subentry. Figure 15.28 also shows that both user attributes and operational attributes can be stored with an entry in the DIB.

• DSA Information Model

A DSA defined in the 1988 DS standard is like a black box in terms of management. The DSA Information Model, as defined in the 1992 DS standard, is concerned with knowledge held by the DSAs to perform name resolution, how Directory information is mapped onto the DSAs, and how copies of Directory information may be held by the DSAs. It is made up of a set of DSEs, and structured into a DSA Information Tree similar to how the DIB is structured into a DIT. In the following, we will describe some of the aspects of the Directory Information Model.

Knowledge, as described in Section 15.5.3, is some kind of operational information held by a DSA to represent a partial description of entry and entry-copy information held by other DSAs. There are two categories of knowledge: **master knowledge** and **shadow knowledge**. Both categories are related to shadowing which is studied in Section 15.5.2. Master knowledge is knowledge of the access point of the "master DSA", i.e., the administrative authority of a naming context. Shadow knowledge is knowledge of the "shadow" DSAs, i.e., the DSAs holding replicated copies. A DSA may hold both master and shadow knowledge references. The latter sometimes involves multiple shadow DSAs regarding a particular naming context.

For each category of knowledge, a knowledge reference can be a superior reference, an immediate superior reference, a subordinate reference, a non-specific subordinate reference, or a cross reference. In addition to these references, there are also references used for replication purpose.

In the DSA Information Model, the information repositories holding the information associated with a particular entry are called **DSA-specific Entries (DSEs)**. The **DSA information tree** is the set of all the DSEs held by a DSA. Within a DSE, one may find a Directory entry/subentry, DSA-shared operational attributes, and DSA-specific operational attributes (Figure 15.29). The information contained within a DSE depends on the purpose of the DSE. For example, if the DSE is used to hold a subordinate reference, it does not contain a Directory entry/ subentry although it will have a DSA-shared attribute to indicate the master access point and a DSA-specific attribute to indicate that the DSE is a subordinate reference. If the DSE is associated with a subentry, it will definitely contain a Directory subentry and a DSA-specific attribute to indicate that it is holding a subentry.

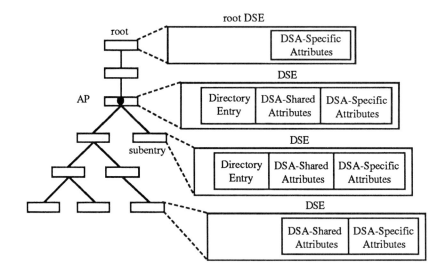

FIGURE 15.29   Information Stored in a DSE

The purpose of a DSA-specific attribute is to indicate the purpose or the type of a DSE. The DS standard defined fifteen DSE types, some of which are mentioned below:

- root: The root DSE contains DSA-specific attributes that characterize the DSA as a whole.
- cp: The DSE represents the context prefix of a naming context.
- glue: A glue DSE represents knowledge of a name only. Glue DSEs arise in the DSA Information Model to represent names that are known by a DSA as a result of holding information associated with other names. For example, a DSA holding a context prefix DSE may hold a glue DSE to represent the name of the superior of the context prefix if no operational information is associated with the name. A glue DSE does not contain any entry.
- entry: The DSE holds an object entry.
- alias: The DSE holds an alias entry.
- subr: The DSE holds a subordinate reference.
- nssr: The DSE holds a superior reference.
- xfr: The DSE holds a cross reference.
- admPoint: The DSE is associated with an administrative point.
- subentry: The DSE holds a subentry.

- shadow: The DSE holds a shadow copy received from a shadow supplier.
- immSupr: The DSE holds an immediate superior reference.

Note that a DSE can be of more than one DSE type.

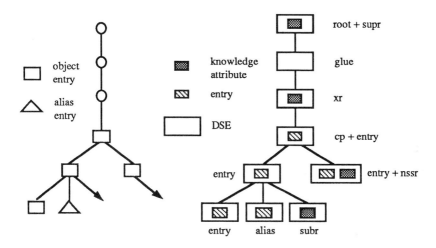

FIGURE 15.30   Mapping of DIT's Naming Context to a DSA

The DIB information needs to be mapped to the DSA information. Figure 15.30 illustrates the mapping for a DIT subtree corresponding to a naming context. In addition to the naming context information, the DSA's root DSE contains its superior reference, a glue DSE, and a DSE representing a reference to an immediately superior naming context are also shown in the figure.

15.5.2   DSA Replication

To improve the performance of the Directory, replication is used to "spread around" information. There are two approaches to replication: caching and shadowing. Caching involves a DSA obtaining and using copies of information in ways specified by local policies. Thus caching is outside the scope of the DS standard. Shadowing involves a DSA obtaining and using copies of information in ways specified by the DS standard. Shadowing is the subject of this section.

There are three possible parties involved in shadowing: a master DSA, a shadow supplier, and a shadow consumer. A **master DSA** is the DSA holding the original information. A **shadow supplier** is a DSA that provides shadow copies. A **shadow consumer** is a DSA which receives shadow copies from a shadow supplier. There are two arrangements of shadowing: primary and secondary shadowing. **Primary shadowing** is the arrangement where a shadow supplier DSA must be the master DSA. **Secondary shadowing** is the arrangement where a shadow supplier DSA is not the master DSA. Thus, a shadow supplier in secondary shadowing could obtain its shadow copies from the master DSA and supplies the copies to a shadow consumer.

Before shadowing takes place between two DSAs, a bilateral shadow agreement is established between the administrative authorities of the two DSAs. Among the ingredients of a shadow agreement are:

- the subject of shadow which specifies the subtree, entries, and attributes to be replicated,
- the update mode which specifies when updates of a shadowed area are scheduled to occur, and
- policy conditions for the treatment of the shadowed data upon termination of the agreement.

The shadowing agreement may be activated by means of the **Directory Operational Binding Management Protocol (DOP)**. The DOP allows DSAs to establish, modify, and terminate operational bindings. An **operational binding** is the mutual understanding between two DSAs which, express their agreement to engage in some sort of interaction. The attributes of a shadowing agreement can be viewed as operational bindings.

Once a shadowing agreement has been activated, shadowing may take place by means of the **Directory Information Shadowing Protocol (DISP)**. Three abstract operations are available for the Directory information shadow service. The service can be initiated by the shadow supplier or the shadow consumer.

If the shadow supplier initiates the Directory Information shadowing service, then it first invokes the **CoordinateShadowUpdate** operation which identifies a shadowing strategy and a shadowing agreement for which it intends to send an update. The strategy may be either incremental or total, where incremental means that only changes which have occurred since the last update are sent by the shadow supplier. Upon receipt of a positive acknowledgement from the shadow consumer, the shadow supplier sends the update by using the **UpdateShadow** operation.

If the shadow consumer initiates the Directory information shadowing service, it first invokes the **RequestShadowUpdate** operation which identifies a shadowing strategy and a shadowing agreement for which it wishes to receive an update. If the shadow supplier finds the arguments of the RequestShadowUpdate operation acceptable, it then sends the update using the UpdateShadow operation.

It should be obvious that DISP relies on ROSE. In case the replication information is huge, RTSE may be used.

We close this section by describing the notion of a unit of replication. A **unit of replication** is an indivisible subset of the DIT to be shadowed. A unit of replication is described as follows (Figure 15.31):

- area: This defines the replicated area. Because shadowing is only defined between pairs of DSAs, there is a constraint that the shadowed information must be contained completely within a DSA. Thus, although the unit of replication may extend beyond a naming context, the replicated area is limited to a naming context which is a unit of DIT information held by a DSA. The area specification contains the context prefix of the naming context for the replicated area and the subtree specification relative to that context prefix. The subtree specification can be found in a subentry associated with the root of the naming context.

• attributes: This defines the set of attributes to be replicated within the area. In general, not all the attributes of an entry information in an area need to be replicated.

• knowledge: This specifies a set of master/shadow knowledge references. If a DSA is a shadow supplier, it holds a **consumer reference** for each of its shadow consumers. The consumer reference keeps track of the access point of the shadow consumer, and the shadowing agreement that the supplier has established with the consumer. If a DSA is a shadow consumer, it holds a **supplier reference** for each shadow supplier from which it receives its shadow copies. The supplier reference keeps track of the following: the access point of the shadow supplier, the shadow agreement that the consumer has established with the supplier, and an indication if the shadow supplier is the master of the replicated area or not. The knowledge component also indicates whether the knowledge requested is extended knowledge or not. If extended knowledge is specified, then all the subordinate and the non-specific subordinate references of a naming context which is subordinate to the area prefix are included in the unit of replication.

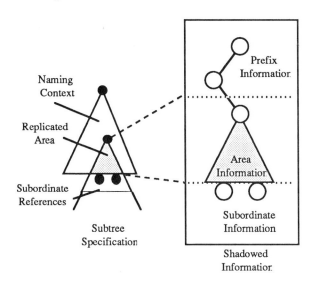

FIGURE 15.31   Shadow Copy Subset of Shadow Supplier's Copy

The shadowed information is built out of shadowed DSEs. A **shadowed DSE (SDSE)** is the information to be replicated from a DSE. It is analogous to a DSE and consists of a SDSE type (such as cp, entry, alias, subr, nssr, etc.), user attributes, operational attributes, and an attribute-completeness flag. The attribute-completeness flag is true if and only if all the user attributes of the entry are present in the SDSE. Only SDSEs containing entry information use the attribute-completeness flag. In general, a SDSE inherits the SDSE type from the corresponding DSE type.

15.5.3 Access Control

In this section, we describe the **Basic Access Control Scheme** which controls access to the user/operational information related to the DIT. The Basic Access Control Scheme defines the protected items, the user classes, the permission categories required to perform each Directory operation, and the Access Control Decision Function used to decide whether a particular requestor has a particular permission.

The **protected items**, i.e., the items to be protected, consist of entries, attributes, and attribute values. Hence, access to protected items is either entry access, attribute access, or attribute value access. To perform a Directory operation on an entire entry (such as entry deletion), it is not necessary for permission to be granted for attribute access or attribute value access to that entry. However, to perform a Directory operation on attributes or attribute values, it is necessary to have entry access permission to the entry.

Access is controlled by either granting or denying permissions. There are a number of **permission categories**. There are permission categories for entry access, attribute access, and attribute value access. These permission categories are described next.

The permission categories used to control entry access are Read, Browse, Add, Remove, Modify, Rename, DiscloseOnError, Export, Import, and ReturnDN. For example, the Read permission, if granted, permits a user to invoke the Read operation. The DiscloseOnError permission, if granted, permits the name of an entry to be disclosed in an error result. The Export permission, if granted, permits an entry and its subordinates to be exported, i.e., removed from the current location and placed in a new location subject to the granting of suitable permissions at the destination.

The permission categories used to control attribute/attribute value access are Compare, Read, FilterMatch, Add, Remove, and DiscloseOnError. For example, the Compare permission, if granted, permits attributes and values to be compared. The FilterMatch permission, if granted, permits evaluation of a filter within a search criterion. The Remove permission, if granted for an attribute, permits removing of an attribute completely. If granted for an attribute value, it permits removing of an attribute value from an attribute.

The user requesting the operation is identified by a **user class** type. Possible values of the userClass type include "allUsers", "name", and "userGroup", where "name" identifies a specific user by a distinguished name, and "userGroup" identifies some group of users.

Using the access control information, the **Access Control Decision Function (ACDF)** decides whether a requestor has a particular permission to a protected item. A denial specified in the access control information always overrides a grant, all other factors being equal. Access is allowed only when there is an explicitly provided grant present in the access control information. In the absence of explicit access control information that grants access, the only default access decision is to deny access.

Recall that an ACSA in the Directory Administrative Authority Model is an SAA defined for the purpose of access control. The root of an ACSA is called the **Access Control Specific Point (ACSP)**. The ACSP is represented in the DIT by an entry whose administrativeRole operational attribute value is "access-control-specific-area". The ACSP can have one or more subentries which contain access control information. Each subentry has a subentry-class operational attribute whose value is "basic-access-control". The scope of a subentry that contains access control information, as defined by a subtree specification, is called a **DACD (i.e., Directory Access Control Domain)**. A Security Administrative Authority can divide an ACSA into ACIAs (i.e., Access Control Inner Areas). Subentries can be associated with the administrative point of each ACIA. The purpose of the use of ACIAs is to permit delegation of access control authority within an ACSA.

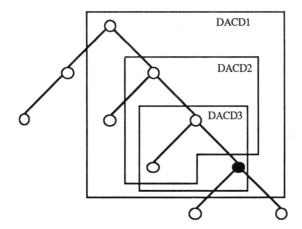

FIGURE 15.32   DACDs

Access control information that may affect access to an entry can be stored in two different ways in the DIT. It can be stored with the entry in the **EntryACI attribute**. Or it can be stored in one or more subentries in the the **PrescriptiveACI attribute**. Both the EntryACI attribute and the PrescriptiveACI attributes are multi-valued operational attributes. Either attribute value is a set of ACIItems. Each ACIItem grants or denies permissions with regard to certain specified users and protected items. Access to an entry is governed by the ACIItems in the EntryACI attribute value for that entry (if present) and the ACIItems contained in those subentries whose scopes, i.e., DACDs, include the entry. In other words, access to an entry is controlled by the "totality" of superior ACSPs (both inner and specific) up to and including the first non-inner access control administrative point or autonomous administrative point encountered moving up the DIT from the entry towards the root. Referring to Figure 15.32, access control information that may affect access to the shaded entry is stored in the EntryACI attribute of the entry as well as the subentries whose scopes are DACD1 and DACD3.

The **Access Control Decision Function (ACDF)** for the Basic Access Control Scheme determines whether to grant or deny a specified permission to a requestor based on the access control information in the DIT. It works in a very simple manner. First, it collects all the ACIItems that are relevant to the protected item. For simplicity sake, we assume that each ACIItem is a 4-tuple consisting of the userClass, the protectedItem, the grantsAndDenial, and the precedence. The ACIItems that apply to the protected item are grouped as a set of 4-tuples. The ACDF then proceeds to discard the irrelevant 4-tuples. For example, it discards those 4-tuples that do not include the requestor in the userClass, or do not have set permission bits for one of the requested permissions. It orders the remaining rows from highest to lowest precedence, and discard all but those of the highest precedence. Permission is granted if and only if the resulting rows all grant access.

15.6   X/Open Directory API

The **X/Open Directory Services (XDS)** is an API to the Directory Services. Unlike TLI and A/P Library, it is not language-dependent. Instead, it is abstract in the sense that it is specified in terms of a set of objects and operations. The abstract nature of XDS is designed so that it can be implemented by one or more vendors working independently. The X.400 APIs are also defined in a similar manner.

Both XDS and X.400 APIs depend on the Object Management API. The Object Management API is designed to support multiple application specific APIs. It provides tools to create, examine, modify, and destroy objects which are specific to an API.

In Section 15.6.1, we examine the OSI Object Management API. In Section 15.6.2, we examine XDS.

15.6.1   OSI Object Management API

The purpose of the **Object Management (OM) API** is to provide an information architecture for structuring complex information objects, and functions for manipulating such objects. One of the design goals of the OM API is to avoid imposing constraints on the representation of objects that the service (i.e., the software that implements the OM API) maintains internally. The internal representation of such objects is chosen by the service. A client (i.e., a user of the OM API) can access these objects using the OM functions. The second design goal of the OM API is to allow the co-existence of multiple application specific APIs in an environment, with each application specific API providing its own implementation of the OM API. In such an environment, we can have the same object class appearing in more than one application specific API although the objects in that object class may be represented differently by different APIs. To facilitate the cooperation of the various APIs, the OM API provides the notion of a workspace to store "private" objects of an application specific API, and functions to move objects from one workspace to another.

First, we examine the information architecture. The architecture, consisting of objects, classes, packages, and workspaces, is composed hierarchically, .

There are two kinds of objects: public and private. A **public object** is represented by a data structure whose format is part of a service's specification. Its structure is made explicit to the clients. A client can manipulate a public object directly. Thus it can use programming language constructs to create a public object and then modify it afterwards. On the other hand, a **private object** is meant to be hidden from the clients. Its structure is implementation dependent and varies from one service to another. A client can only access a private object indirectly, by means of the API functions. To illustrate the use of public and private objects, we consider an application program written to read the social security number of a particular person. The Read operation takes in a number of arguments. Some of the arguments are public objects and some are private objects. Arguments such as social security numbers and object entry are declared to be public objects. However, arguments such as session and context which define the working environment are declared to be private objects in the interest of efficiency.

Public objects can be divided into two kinds: client- and service-generated objects. A **client-generated public object** is created by clients while a **service-generated public object** is created by the service. The storage occupied by a public object is directly accessible to a client. The storage occupied by a private object is not accessible to a client although a client can destroy a service-generated public object by using OM_delete.

There are two types of object classes: **concrete** and **abstract**. A client may create objects of concrete classes, but not objects of abstract classes. The purpose of an abstract class is to collect a set of logically related attributes which can be inherited by its subclasses. In XDS for example, Object, Address, and Presentation-Address are three distinct object classes. Address is a subclass of Object, while Presentation-Address is a subclass of Address. Since a client can define instances of Presentation-Address, Presentation-Address is a concrete class. However, a client neither defines instances of Object nor Address, because these two classes are used primarily for an inheritance purpose. Thus, both Object and Address are abstract classes.

A group of logically related object classes is called a **package**. For example, we can group all the classes related to the basic Directory Services into a package.

As said earlier, the OM API is designed to be implemented by one or more vendors working independently, e.g., one developing the MHS system, and the other developing the DS system. Each vendor effectively provides the programmer with the ability to manipulate objects of a particular kind. Interworking between different service implementations is accomplished by means of **workspaces**. A workspace is a repository of private objects. A client must obtain a workspace that supports an object class before it can create any object of that class. For example, to obtain a workspace that supports all the object classes in the Directory Services package, a DUA invokes DS-Initialize(), a function of XDS. Besides supporting all the OM API functions, a workspace may support one or more packages. For example, it can support both the Directory Services package and the

Interpersonal Message package. Interworking between two workspaces is possible. For example, the OM API includes functions for effectively copying and moving objects of an object class from one workspace to another, provided that the object classes are associated with both.

The OM API does not define any object class hierarchy. An object class hierarchy is to be defined by an application specific API. However, the OM API does provide functions which will allow a client to create, examine, modify, and destroy objects of any object class associated with an application specific API. Examined next are some of the OM API functions:

- Copy: This function creates a new private object that is an exact but independent copy of an existing private object.
- Create: This function creates a private object of a particular concrete object class.
- Decode: This function creates a private object that is an exact but independent copy of the object that an existing private object encodes.
- Delete: This function deletes a private or service-generated public object. If applied to a service-generated public object, it deletes the object and releases any resources associated with the object. If applied to a private object, it makes the object inaccessible.
- Encode: This function creates a private object that encodes an existing private object. Both the Encode function and the Delete function enable copying from one workspace to another when the two workspaces come from different vendors.
- Get: This function creates a public copy of all or particular parts of a private object.
- Instance: This function determines whether a service-generated public or private object is an instance of a particular object class.
- Put: This function places or replaces in a private object copies of an attribute value of another object. The source values may be inserted before any existing destination values, before the value at a specified position in a destination attribute, or after any existing destination values. Note that the representation of the object may have to be changed during the copying.
- Read: This function reads a segment of an attribute value in a private object.
- Remove: This function removes and discards particular values of an attribute of a private object.
- Write: This function writes a segment of an attribute value in a private object. The value must be a string. This function enables a client to write an arbitrarily long value without having to place a copy of the entire value in memory.

We will provide the C format of two of the above functions in the following examples.

Example 15.14

```
OM_return_code
om_create (
```

```
OM_object_identifier      class,
OM_boolean                initialize,
OM_workspace              workspace,
OM_private_object         •object
     );
```

The above gives a macro of the create function in the C interface. There are three arguments of this function. The class argument is an object identifier identifying the class of the object to be created. The initialize argument indicates whether the created object is to be initialized as specified in the definition of its class. The workspace argument specifies a workspace in which the object is to be created. The specified class shall be in a package associated with the workspace. On return, this function indicates success or failure of the object creation.

Example 15.15

```
OM_return_code
om_write (
     OM_private_object      subject,
     OM_type                type,
     OM_value_position      value_position,
     OM_syntax              syntax,
     OM_element_position    *element_position,
     OM_string              elements
          );
```

The above provides the C macro for the write function in the C interface. There are six arguments. The subject argument specifies the subject which is to be accessed. The type argument specifies an attribute, one of whose values is to be written. The value_position argument specifies the position within the above attribute of the value to be written. The syntax argument specifies the syntax of the value if the value written does not exist in the subject. The element_position argument specifies the position of the first element to be written. Finally the elements_argument specifies the string. On return, the function will indicate success or failure as well as the position within the value of the element following the last element written.

15.6.2 XDS

XDS provides an API to the Directory Services. Figure 15.33 shows where XDS is used with the DS functional model. In the figure, XDS is provided on top of a DUA instead of a DSA.

   XDS defines its own object classes and packages. Most of the objects are used as arguments or results of the Directory operations. It relies partially on the OM functions to manipulate its objects. XDS models Directory interactions as service requests made through a number of interface functions. These interface functions resemble the Directory operations.

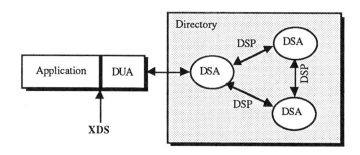

FIGURE 15.33   Use of XDS with the DS Functional Model

To begin, a Directory user invokes DS-Initialize() which will return a workspace to hold the DS package. From this point onward, all interactions between the user and the Directory belong to a session. A **session** identifies to which DUA and to which suite of DSAs a particular Directory operation will be sent. It is an object of a DS object class, namely, Session. It is created by the om_create() function. A Directory session is then started with the Bind() function and is later terminated with Unbind() function. In each Directory service request, the user needs to pass the session as the first argument. It is possible for a Directory user to hold more than one session concurrently.

Function	Description
Abandon	abandon the result of a pending, asynchronous operation.
Add-Entry	add a leaf entry to the DIT.
Bind	open a session with a DUA.
Compare	compare a purported attribute value with the attribute value stored in the directory for a particular entry.
Initialize	initialize the XDS.
List	enumerate the immediate subordinates of a Directory entry.
Modify-Entry	perform an atomic modification of a Directory entry.
Modify-RDN	change the RDN of a leaf entry.
Read	query information on a Directory entry by name.
Receive-Result	retrieve the result of an asynchronously executed function.
Remove-Entry	find entries of interest in a portion of the DIT.
Search	remove a leaf entry from the DIT.
Shutdown	discard a workspace.
Unbind	unbind from a Directory session.
Version	negotiate features of the XDS and service.

TABLE 15.3   XDS Service Functions

Another important object is context. A **context** defines the characteristics of the Directory interaction that are specific to a particular Directory operation, but often are unchanged for many operations. It generally includes the ComonArguments and the Service Controls as described earlier in the chapter. Since these parameters are relatively static, they are grouped into a DS object (of the Context object class) which is supplied as the second argument of each Directory service request.

XDS provides a number of interface functions (Table 15.3). An abstract Directory operation essentially maps to an interface function. Thus, DirectoryBind maps to Bind(), DirectoryUnbind maps to Unbind(), Read maps to Read(), Compare maps to Compare(), RemoveEntry maps to RemoveEntry(), etc. Arguments and results of the interface functions can be either public or private objects. Some of the arguments are public and some are service specific. The first two arguments, session and context, are common to many interface functions. Service specific arguments include objects of the Attribute, the AVA (i.e., Attribute Value Assertion), the Entry Information Selection, and the Name object classes. The above object classes will be explained in a short while.

The interface functions return three types of results: Status, Invoke-ID, and Result. Status is a result returned by all the functions. Its value is either "success" or "error". Invoke-ID is an integer identifying a particular invocation of an operation. Result is the result returned by a Directory interrogation operation.

The following XDS functions have no corresponding abstract Directory operation: Receive-Result(), DS-Initialize(), Shutdown(), and Version(). The Receive-Result() function retrieves the result of an asynchronously executed function. The DS-Initialize() function initializes the XDS software which returns the DS package and may be more packages, depending on the vendor of the XDS software. The Version() function returns the object identifiers that identify additional packages. Finally the Shutdown() function is used to free the XDS resources including the workspace and its associated private objects.

In the following examples, we provide the C format of two XDS functions.

Example 15.16

```
DS_status ds_compare (
        OM_private_object       session,
        OM_private_object       context,
        OM_object               name,
        OM_object               ava,
        OM_private_object       * result_return,
        OM_sint                 * invoke_id_return
        );
```

The above provides the C macro for the compare function in the C interface. There are four arguments. The session argument indicates the session against which this operation is performed. The context argument indicates the context to be used for this operation. The name argument specifies the name of the target object entry. The ava argument specifies the attribute value assertion. The function has three results.

Status indicates whether the comparison was completed or not, if used synchronously, or whether the operation was initiated, if used asynchronously. Result_return contains the flags indicating whether the values matched and whether the comparison was made against the original entry. It also contains the DN of the target object if an alias was dereferenced. Finally, invoke_id_return gives the Invoke-ID of an asynchronous Directory operation.

Example 15.17

```
DS_status ds_list (
        OM_private_object      session,
        OM_private_object      context,
        OM_object              name,
        OM_private_object      * result_return,
        OM_sint                * invoke_id_return
        );
```

The above provides the C macro for the list function in the C interface. There are three arguments. The name argument specifies the name of the target object entry whose immediate subordinates are to be listed. There are three kinds of results. Status indicates whether the named object was located or not, if used synchronously, or whether the operation was initiated, if used asynchronously. Result_return contains some information about the target object's immediate subordinates. It also contains the DN of the target object if an alias was dereferenced. Aliases in the subordinate names are not dereferenced. There may be a partial outcome qualifier, which indicates that the result is incomplete. Finally, invoke_id_return gives the Invoke-ID of an asynchronous Directory operation.

We close this section by examining the object classes in the **Directory Service (DS) package** to get a more concrete idea of the objects passed as arguments to the XDS interface functions. The classes in the package are organized hierarchically. Each class inherits additional attributes from its superclasses. Subclassification is indicated by indentation, and names of abstract classes are given in italics form. Examples of object classes are given below, and brief explanations are given to some of them.

Object
- Access-Point -- identifies a particular point at which access to a DSA can occur.
- *Address* -- represents the address of a particular entity or service.
  - Presentation-Address
- Attribute
  - AVA -- a proposition concerning the values of a Directory entry.
  - Entry-Modification -- describes a single modification to a specified attribute of a Directory entry.
  - Filter-Item -- an assertion about the existence of values of a single attribute type in a Directory entry.
- Attribute-List -- a list of Directory attributes.

- Entry-Information -- contains selected information from a single Directory entry.
- *Common-Results* -- results that are returned by, and thus common to, the Directory interrogation operations.
  - Compare-Result
  - List-Info
  - Read-Result
  - Search-Info
- Context -- comprises of operation arguments that are accepted by most of the interface functions.
- Continuation-Reference
- Entry-Information-Selection -- identifies the information to be extracted from a directory entry.
- Entry-Modification-List -- comprises of a sequence of changes to be made to a Directory entry.
- *Error* -- comprises of the parameters common to all errors.
  - Abandon-Failed
  - Attribute-Problem
  - Communication-Error
  - Name-Error
  - Security-Error
- Extension
- Filter
- List-Info-Item -- comprises details of a single subordinate object returned by List() function.
- List-Result -- comprises the results of a successful call to the List() function.
- *Name*
  - DS-DN -- represents a name of a Directory object.
- Operation-Progress
- Partial Outcome Qualifier
- *Relative-Name*
  - DS-RDN -- represents a RDN.
- Search-Result -- comprises the result of a successful call to the Search() function.
- Session

15.7   Summary

The primary purpose of the Directory Services (DS) standard is to provide a means for a user to find out information about those OSI objects which do not change very often. The DS standard defines a conceptual information model called the Directory Information Base (DIB). Directory entries in the DIB are placed in a hierarchical structure, called the Directory Information Tree (DIT). This hierarchical structure not only allows a convenient way of assigning user friendly names to Directory entries but also permits delegation of naming authority in a large network.

The DS functional model is made up of DUAs and DSAs. A DUA models an application program/user which needs to access the Directory services. The DAP is the Directory access protocol by means of which a DUA interacts with the Directory. The DSP is the protocol used among the DSAs to provide the Directory services. Both protocols are interactive in nature, hence require the use of ROSE.

The distributed operation of the Directory requires more than the specification of the DAP and the DSP. It needs to provide a DSA Knowledge Model so that a DSA would know who has what. This knowledge is crucial when a DSA needs to resolve a name.

The 1988 version of the DS standard provides the basic services. The 1992 version adds a few more models such as the Directory Administrative Authority Model, the Model of Directory Administrative and Operational Information, and the Basic Access Control Model. It also supports DSA replication.

The XDS is an API to the Directory Services. By enabling the Directory to be accessed from applications in a standardized manner, it promotes applications portability.

Related Standards

ISO 9594-1: Information Technology - Open Systems Interconnection - The Directory - Part 1: Overview of Concepts, Models and Services

ISO 9594-1 PDAM 1.2: Information Technology - Open Systems Interconnection - The Directory - Part 1: Overview - Proposed Draft Amendment 1: Replication, Schema and Access Control

ISO 9594-2: Information Technology - Open Systems Interconnection - The Directory - Part 2: Models
ISO 9594-2 PDAM 1.3: Information Technology - Open Systems Interconnection - The Directory - Part 2: Information Framework - Proposed Draft Amendment 1: Access Control

ISO 9594-2 PDAM 2.2: Information Technology - Open Systems Interconnection - The Directory - Part 2: The Models - Proposed Draft Amendment 2.2: Schema Extensions

ISO 9594-2 PDAM 3.2: Information Technology - Open Systems Interconnection - The Directory - Part 2: Models - Proposed Draft Amendment 3: Replication

ISO 9594-3: Information Technology - Open Systems Interconnection - The Directory - Part 3 Abstract Service Definition

ISO 9594-3 PDAM 1.3: Information Technology - Open Systems Interconnection - The Directory - Part 3: Abstract Service Definition - Proposed Draft Amendment 1: Access Control

ISO 9594-3 PDAM 2.2: Information Technology - Open Systems Interconnection - The Directory - Part 3 Abstract Service Definition - Proposed Draft Amendment 2: Replication, Schema and Enhanced search

ISO 9594-4: Information Technology - Open Systems Interconnection - The Directory - Part 4: Procedures for Distributed Operations

ISO 9594-4 PDAM 1.3: Information Technology - Open Systems Interconnection - The Directory - Part 4: Procedures for Distributed Operations - Proposed Draft Amendment 1: Access Control

ISO 9594-4 PDAM 2.2: Information Technology - Open Systems Interconnection - The Directory - Part 4: Procedures for Distributed Operations - Proposed Draft Amendment 2.2: Replication, Schema and Enhanced Search

ISO 9594-5: Information Technology - Open Systems Interconnection - The Directory - Part 5: Protocol Specifications

ISO 9594-5 PDAM 1.2: Information Technology - Open Systems Interconnection - The Directory - Part 5: Protocol Specifications - Proposed Draft Amendment 1.2: Replication

ISO 9594-6: Information Technology - Open Systems Interconnection - The Directory - Part 6: Selected Attribute Types

ISO 9594-6 PDAM 1.2: Information Technology - Open Systems Interconnection - The Directory - Part 6: Selected Attribute Types - Proposed Draft Amendment 1 for Schema Extensions

ISO 9594-7: Information Technology - Open Systems Interconnection - The Directory - Part 7: Selected Object Classes

ISO 9594-7 PDAM 1.2: Information Technology - Open Systems Interconnection - The Directory - Part 7: Selected Object Classes - Proposed Draft Amendment 1 for Schema Extensions

ISO 9594-8: Information Technology - Open Systems Interconnection - The Directory - Part 8: Authentication Framework

ISO 9594-8 PDAM 1.2: Information Technology - Open Systems Interconnection - The Directory - Part 8: Authentication Framework - Proposed Draft Amendment 1 for Access Control

CD 9594-9.2: Information Technology - Open Systems Interconnection - The Directory - Part 9: Replication

16

Message Handling Systems

The current trends towards electronic office automation and the growth of workstations have created a demand for universal message communication. Most of all, advances in network technology have made universal message communication possible.

The **Message Handling Systems (MHS)** standard facilitates the exchange of all kinds of information among MHS users through the OSI communication system. Although MHS users mainly exchange interpersonal messages, the MHS service may be also used to exchange business documents and others. One of the principle features of MHS is its operation in a store-and-forward manner so that the originator's system does not have to be attached to the recipient's system. Instead, the message may be routed via one or more intermediate systems.

CCITT first published the well known X.400 standard in 1984. Since then, CCITT and ISO/IEC have worked together to harmonize their activities and produced parallel standards with almost identical text. They are the CCITT's X.400 (1988) and the ISO/IEC 10021 or MOTIS (i.e., Message Oriented Text Interchange System). The differences between the X.400 standard and the MOTIS standard are minor. Throughout this chapter, the 1988 MHS standard refers to one of these standards.

The 1988 MHS standard contains many improvements over the 1984 MHS standards. These improvements include the use of user friendly Directory names instead of user unfriendly O/R addresses to identify MHS users, the use of distribution lists to name groups of recipients, the provision of security services which were practically absent in the 1984 MHS standard, and the use of the full OSI stack for compatibility with other OSI system software.

Section 16.1 examines the MHS functional model. Section 16.2 studies the Interpersonal Message Handling System which is a specialization of MHS to handle interpersonal communication. Section 16.3 studies the service specifications of three MHS protocols: two MHS access protocols and the message transfer protocol. Section 16.4 explains the operation of the P1 protocol. Section 16.5 shows how security services are provided by the MHS. Section 16.5 examines two MHS APIs.

16.1 MHS Model

Section 16.1.1 describes the MHS functional model. Section 16.1.2 considers the different configurations of MHS functional objects. Section 16.1.3 studies the naming and addressing issues. Finally, Section 16.1.4 describes how MHS uses the Directory services.

16.1.1 MHS Functional Model

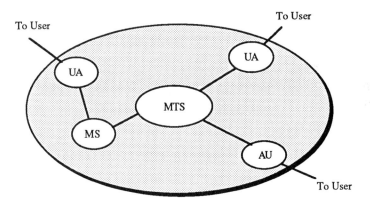

FIGURE 16.1 MHS 1988 Functional Model

Figure 16.1 shows the MHS functional model. The major functional objects in this model are the User Agents (UAs), the Message Stores (MSs), the Access Units (AUs), and the Message Transfer System (MTS).

An **MHS user**, sitting outside the MHS object, can be either a person or an application process that originates and receives messages. An **MHS message** consists of an envelope and its contents. The **envelope** identifies the message's originator and recipient(s), characterizes its contents (e.g., indicates whether it is for interpersonal communication or business communication), and contains administrative information needed to convey the message from the originator to the recipient(s).

There are three types of messages. A **user message**, which is the most common of the three, is the basic message type used to send information from one MHS user to another. A **delivery report message**, which is generated by the MTS, informs the message originator of the outcome of the delivery of a user message or a probe message. A **probe message** enables an MHS user to determine whether a particular user message is deliverable. Unlike the other two message types, a probe message does not contain any content.

Next, the MHS functional objects are examined in more detail. A UA provides access to the MTS or an MS on behalf of its user. It submits and delivers messages for its user. It may provide text processing facilities for the composition of messages. Some UAs are specialized to handle person-to-person communication, some are specialized to handle business documents, and others are for some specialized content type. In general, a UA can only process a certain content type. Currently, only two content types have been standardized: the IPM content type and the Pedi (edi standing for electronic data exchange) content type. An IPM content type is used for person-to-person communication, while a Pedi content type is used for business trading. Thus, there are IPM-UAs and Pedi-UAs.

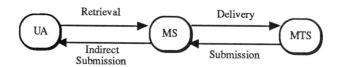

FIGURE 16.2   MS Services

An MS provides a secure, continuously available storage mechanism on behalf of a UA. Consider the case when a UA is implemented on a PC. The PC may be powered-down causing queued messages for the UA to be declared undeliverable by the MTS. The MS, serving as an intermediary entity between a UA and the MTS (Figure 16.2), can store the incoming messages from the MTS until the UA is brought up and is ready to process the messages. The MS can also provide a summary of the stored messages and perform auto-forwarding to another UA when the UA is not active. An MS is always associated with a UA although not every UA is associated with an MS. If a UA is supported by an MS, all the messages destined for the UA are delivered to its MS.

The value of the MHS can be increased if the MHS can be connected to other non-MHS communication systems such as the traditional postal systems. An AU is a functional object that links a non-MHS communication system to the MHS. There are a number of AU types. For example, a **physical delivery access unit (PDAU)** can convert an electronic message to a physical form before passing it to a physical delivery system for further relaying and physical delivery. A **telematic agent (TLMA)** allows teletex users to subscribe to the IPM service. A **telex access unit (TLXAU)** allows telex users to access the IPM service. There are also AUs for facsimile and videotex.

The MTS provides the distributed store-and-forward message transfer service. Serving as the backbone communications system of the MHS, it conveys messages regardless of their content types. It does not examine or modify the content of messages unless content conversion is explicitly requested by the originator. It relies primarily on the information in the envelope to transfer a message.

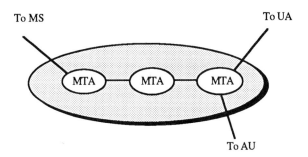

FIGURE 16.3   MTS Objects

Because of the distributed nature of the MTS service, the MTS object can be refined to **message transfer agent (MTA)** objects (Figure 16.3). The MTAs collectively provide the MTS service. An MTA can interact with a UA or an MTA.

Consider the case when a UA submits a user message to an MTA which is called the originator MTA. First, the originator MTA validates the submission envelope and records appropriate administrative information on the envelope. Next, the MTA tries to deliver the message to its recipient(s). If the recipient is a client of the originator MTA, then the delivery is straightforward because it will not involve another MTA. In the case where the recipient is not a client of the originator MTA, the originator MTA needs to relay the message to some other MTA(s). When there is more than one recipient, the originator MTA needs to perform message replication. A distinct copy of the message must be created for each distinct MTA which the message is relayed to. An MTA, on receiving the relayed message from the originating MTA, may be held responsible for progressive delivery of the message to the intended recipient(s). There is a boolean responsibility flag on the envelope indicating to the MTA its responsibility. An MTA, if held responsible, can discharge its responsibility by either delivering the message, if the recipient is local to the MTA or transferring the message to another MTA closer to the recipient. If delivery is unsuccessful, then its responsibility ends with the generation of a non-delivery report.

Another service provided by an MTA is the conversion of the **encoded information types (EITs)** of the body parts. In general, the content of a message may have one or more body parts, where each body part has an EIT. For example, an EIT can be IA5 text, facsimile, voice, or telex. The purpose of conversion is to improve the communication possibilities among MHS users who use terminals of different capabilities. Some conversions such as IA5 to Telex may result in a loss of information. A message originator may explicitly request a particular conversion to be performed on the message by the originator MTA before it is delivered. This is used when the message originator knows in advance that the recipient UA is unable to handle a particular EIT. A message originator may also specify conversion only if loss of information would not occur.

16.1.2 Physical and Organizational Configurations

The purpose of this section is to identify some of the common configurations of the MHS functional model. These configurations include the physical configurations as well as the organizational configurations.

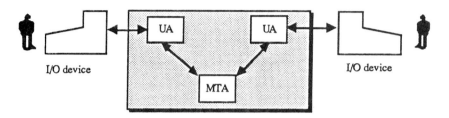

FIGURE 16.4   Co-resident UA and MTA Messaging System

A **messaging system** is a physical configuration or a realization of the MHS model as a set of interconnected computer systems. Some of the functional objects in the MHS functional model can be co-located in the same messaging system. For example, Figure 16.4 shows that an MTA is co-located with two UAs.

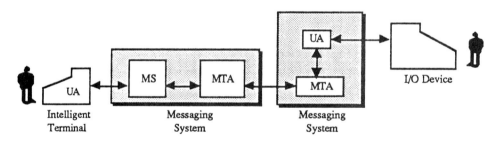

FIGURE 16.5   Co-resident MS and MTA Messaging System

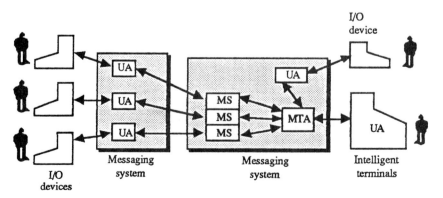

FIGURE 16.6   Co-resident MS, UA and MTA Messaging System

Communication between two messaging systems can be achieved via standardized MHS protocols or proprietary means. Consider the communication between a UA and a remote MTA. If the UA software is implemented in a workstation powerful enough to run the full OSI stack, then communication between the UA and the MTA is possible via the P3 protocol which is a standardized MHS access protocol. If the UA is run on a diskless workstation, communication between the UA and MTA is still possible via some proprietary filesystem software where the MTA plays the role of a fileserver. When a UA composes a message on behalf of its user, it automatically creates a file in the filesystem of the MTA. When the message is ready to be submitted by the UA, the MTA will remove the message from its filesystem and insert it into an outgoing queue.

With the addition of the MS object to the MHS model in 1988, some additional messaging systems are possible. Figure 16.5 shows a messaging system with a co-resident MTA and MS communicating with another messaging system with a co-resident MTA and UA. Figure 16.6 shows another feasible messaging system.

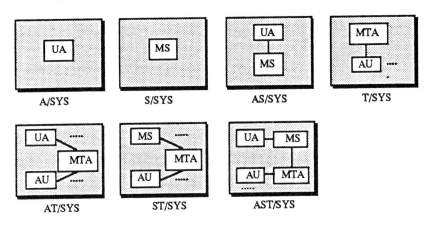

FIGURE 16.7   Messaging Types

The MHS standard identifies seven common messaging system types to reflect the commonly occurred messaging systems (Figure 16.7). An AST/SYS type, for example, is an access, storage, and transfer system containing one or more UAs, one or more MSs, one MTA, and optionally one or more AUs. Note that an AU is typically co-located with an MTA because there is no standardized protocol to govern their interaction.

An organizational configuration is a realization of the MHS as a set of interconnected management domains. A **Management Domain (MD)** is a set of messaging systems owned by either an administration or an organization. An administration can be a central PTT authority or a RPOA (i.e., recognized private operating agency). An organization may be a company or a non-commercial organization. An MD managed by an administration is called an **Administration Management Domain (ADMD)**, while an MD managed by an organization other than an administration is called a **Private Management Domain (PRMD)**. For example, "ATTMAIL" is an ADMD in the US, and "ALLIEDSIGNALS-KCD" is a PRMD in Kansas City.

In the CCITT's view of MDs, inter-PRMD communication is not allowed. To communicate with another PRMD, a PRMD has to go through one or more ADMDs. Furthermore, international message transfer must be done on an ADMD-to-ADMD basis. Thus, a PRMD in one country cannot access an ADMD in another country directly. In this sense, the PRMDs play a peripheral role in the MHS, while the ADMDs essentially provide a backbone connecting all the PRMDs. The MOTIS's view of MDs is different from the CCITT's view. MOTIS allows the PRMDs to communicate directly with each other. A PRMD, in the MOTIS's view, can span over a few countries.

16.1.3 Naming and Addressing

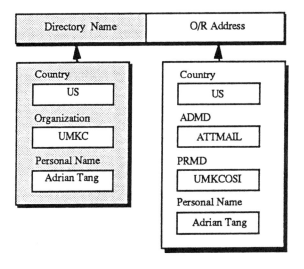

FIGURE 16.8   An Example of O/R Name

An **O/R (i.e., originator/recipient) name** is a two-slot data structure used to identify an originator or a recipient. It contains two components: a Directory name and an O/R address. The Directory name component is a distinguished name identifying an MHS user. It uses attribute types such as country, organization, commonName, and personalName. It may also use **domain defined attributes** to supply domain-specific information. For example, the information on the Internet address or the social security number of an MHS user can be supplied using domain defined attributes. The **O/R address component** gives the location of a user in terms of attribute types such as ADMD and PRMD. It locates the MD to which a user belongs. Figure 16.8 shows an example of an O/R name.

There are three kinds of O/R addresses. A **mnemonic O/R address** is one that mnemonically identifies a user. The example in Figure 16.8 is a mnemonic O/R address. A **numeric O/R address** is one which identifies a user numerically. The number is normally assigned by an ADMD. Finally, a **postal O/R address** identifies a user by means of a postal address.

Although O/R names are primarily used to identify MHS users, they can be also used to name **distribution lists (DLs)**. Using DLs, a user can send a message to a group of recipients by naming the entire group instead of having to name each of the recipients in the group. Each member of a DL is an MHS user or possibly another DL. By allowing DLs in a DL, the DL can be used to name a group of groups. In general, one cannot determine whether an O/R name refers to an MHS user or a DL.

A DL is owned by a **DL owner**. This owner specifies who are allowed to use the DL to send a message to the DL's members. At certain points in the delivery route, a DL is expanded to its DL members. Such points are known as **DL expansion points**. Only the MTA at a DL expansion point can tell if an O/R name refers to a DL or an MHS user.

Example 16.1

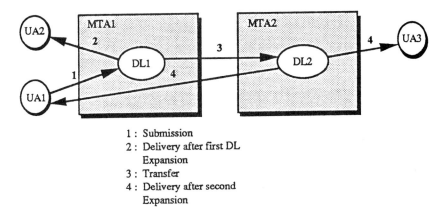

1 : Submission
2 : Delivery after first DL
    Expansion
3 : Transfer
4 : Delivery after second
    Expansion

FIGURE 16.9   DL Expansion Example

Figure 16.9 illustrates the concept of DL expansion. In Step 1, UA1 sends a message to DL1. Assume that the members of DL1 are DL2 and UA2. Also assume that the DL1 expansion point is at MTA1. In Step 2, the DL1 expansion at MTA1 results in the message being delivered to UA2 and the DL2 expansion point at MTA2. When MTA2 receives the message, it expands DL2. Assume that the members of DL2 are UA3 and UA1. In step 4, the message is delivered to UA3 and UA1.

16.1.4   MHS Use of the OSI Directory Services

MHS can make use of the OSI Directory Services in a number of ways, including:

- user-friendly naming: An MHS user can be identified by a Directory Name instead of a less user unfriendly O/R address. At any time, a UA or an MTA can send to a DSA (i.e., Directory Services Agent) the Directory Name of a communicating partner to obtain its partner's O/R Address.

- user capabilities: The capabilities of a UA can be stored in a Directory entry. Such capabilities include the EITs which a UA can interpret or the content types it can process.
- DLs: A DL owner can store the Directory names of the DL members in the Directory.
- security authentication: An MHS functional object can establish the identity of a communicating partner by retrieving its partner's certificate from the Directory. Certificates, which were studied in Chapter 15, provide a tool for authentication.

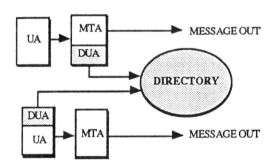

FIGURE 16.10   Possible Placements of a DUA in MHS

At submission, a UA may include one or both components of each O/R name that it supplies. If only the Directory Name is present, the UA or the originator MTA will use the Directory name to look up the O/R Address in the Directory. If only the O/R Address is present, the originator MTA will use the O/R address to route the message to its destination. If both components are present, the originator MTA first uses the O/R Address to route the message. If the O/R Address fails, then the Directory name will be used to look up the correct O/R address in the Directory. In a messaging system, it is customary to co-locate a UA or an MTA with a DUA. Figure 16.10 illustrates.

16.2   Interpersonal Messaging System

UAs are grouped according to their capabilities of processing the content type of a message. A set of UAs and MTAs which can process the IPM content type forms an **Interpersonal Messaging System (IPMS)**. The UAs in an IPMS are called **IPM-UAs**.

An **interpersonal message (IPM)** consists of an envelope and a content of IPM type. The IPM content consists of a header and a body (Figure 16.11). The fields or attribute types associated with a header and a body are examined next. Some of the header fields are described below:

- this-IPM: This field identifies an IPM.
- originator: This field identifies the identity of a message originator.

• authorizing-users: This field enables an originator to tell the recipient the user(s) who are authorized to send this message.

• primary-recipients: This field identifies the recipients of a message.

• copy-recipients: This field identifies the carbon copy recipients.

• blind-copy-recipients: This field identifies the blind copy recipients.

• replied-to-IPM: This field identifies an IPM to which this-IPM replies.

• obsoleted-IPMs: This field identifies the previously sent IPMs which would be made obsolete by this-IPM.

• related-IPMs: This field identifies other IPMs related to this-IPM.

• subject: This field identifies the subject of this-IPM.

• expiry-time: This field indicates the time and date after which an originator considers this-IPM to be no longer valid.

• reply-time: This field indicates the time and date after which a reply to this-IPM is no longer useful.

• reply-to-users: This field identifies the users to whom a reply should be sent.

• importance: This field indicates the level of importance of this-IPM.

• sensitivity: This field identifies the level of confidentiality attached to this-IPM.

• auto-forwarded: This field indicates whether or not this-IPM should be auto-forwarded.

Table 16.1 shows the IPM header fields defined by the MHS standard.

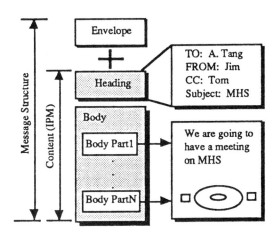

FIGURE 16.11   Basic Structure of a Message

The body is a sequence of **body parts**. Each body part is of some EIT. For example, an IA5 text body part contains a character string made up of characters from the IA5 character set, a voice body part contains a bit string for representing digitized voice, and an IPM body part consists of a complete IPM which is intended to be forwarded by the originator IPM-UA.

IPM Header Fields		
this-IPM originator authorizing-users primary-recipients copy-recipients blind-copy-recipients	replied-to-IPM obsoleted-IPMs related-IPMs subject expiry-time reply-time	reply-recipients importance sensitivity auto-forwarded extensions

TABLE 16.1   IPM Header Fields

Besides exchanging IPMs, IPM-UAs also exchange **IPNs (interpersonal notifications)**. IPNs provide a mechanism for a recipient IPM-UA to acknowledge receipt of an IPM or report a non-receipt. For example, if the originator IPM-UA requests a receipt notification, then a **receipt notification (RN)** is sent by the recipient IPM-UA to the originator IPM-UA. If the originator IPM-UA requests a non-receipt notification, then a **non-receipt notification (NRN)** is sent by the recipient IPM-UA. For example, the expiration date has been passed or the recipient IPM user no longer subscribes to the IPMS service. The originator IPM-UA can also request for the IPM content type to be returned in the case of non-receipt.

RNs should be distinguished from delivery notifications. A RN is generated by either an IPM-UA or an MS. On the other hand, a delivery notification is generated by an MTA. The receipt of a delivery notification by the originator IPM-UA does not imply that the intended recipient IPM user has received the message from its IPM-UA.

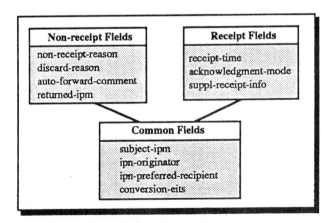

TABLE 16.2   Content of an IPN

Like an IPM, every IPN has an envelope and a content. The IPN content is described using fields (Table 16.2). Some of the fields are common to both RN and NRN. For example, the subject-IPM field identifies the original IPM, which is the subject of the notification. The ipn-originator field identifies an originator of the IPN. The ipn-preferred-recipient field indicates the intended recipient in case the IPM is received by an alternate recipient because of message redirection. Finally, the conversion-eits field identifies the final EIT of the subject-IPM in case conversion has taken place.

In addition to the common fields, a RN also contains a receipt-time field and an acknowledge-mode field. The former field indicates the time the IP message is received. The latter field indicates whether the sending of the RN results from the automatic activity of the UA or the MS.

An NRN also contains a non-receipt-reason field indicates why the subject IPM is not received, a discard-reason field which indicates why the IPM is discarded, an auto-forward-comment field which indicates whether auto-forwarding has been enabled by the recipient, and an IPM-return field which is the subject IPM if the originator requests to have it returned.

16.3   MHS Protocols

This section describes the service specifications of three MHS protocols. The two MHS access protocols are: P3 which is used to access the MTS, and P7 which is used to access an MS. The message transfer protocol is P1. All the service specifications are described using ASDC.

Both P3 and P7 may optionally use RTSE. RTSE ensures that messages, reports, or probes are transferred reliably between two systems intact without duplication. If the underlying network is reliable, it is not necessary to use RTSE. However, RTSE is mandatory for P1 because the MTS may transfer a message over a variety of subnetwork types, some of which are unreliable. Both P3 and P7 use ROSE because of their interactive nature. P1 is not interactive. An MTA, after relaying a message to another MTA using P1, does not need a reply.

16.3.1   MTS Access Protocol

P3, as defined in ISO/IEC 10021-6, is the MHS protocol used to access an MTA from an MTS-user. There are two objects involved in the P3 protocol: the MTS object and the MTS-user object which may be a UA or an MS. Figure 16.12 shows that the two objects interact with each other using three ports. The MTS-user uses the submission port to submit a message or to probe the ability of the MTS to deliver a message. The MTS uses the delivery port to deliver either a message or an MTA-report to an MTS-user. The administration port enables either the MTS or an MTS-user to change its credentials.

Before an MTS-user can invoke any service from the MTS, it must first invoke the MTS-bind operation to establish an association with the MTS. The MTS-bind operation establishes the credentials of both the MTS-user and the MTS, an application context, and perhaps a security context (which is defined by a set of security labels) of the association.

Next, the operations supported by each P3 port are examined. Figure 16.13 shows the ports together with their associated operations. The **submission port** supports four asymmetric operations: message-submission (MTS-user), probe-submission (MTS-user), cancel-deferred-delivery (MTS-user), and submission-control (MTS), where an operation can only be invoked by the object shown on the right-hand side of the operation. An MTS-user invokes the message-submission operation to submit a message, the probe-submission operation to submit a probe, and the cancel-deferred-delivery operation to request cancellation of a previously submitted message. The MTS invokes the submission-control operation to constrain the use of the submission port by an MTS-user. For example, it may want to constrain the size of messages submitted by an MTS-user.

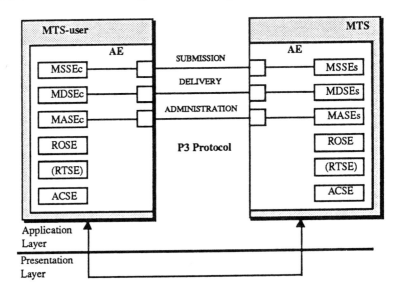

FIGURE 16.12   P3 Computational Model

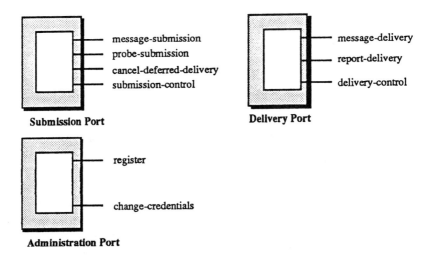

FIGURE 16.13   P3 Ports and Operations

Originator arguments	Originator-name (M)
Recipient arguments	Recipient-name (M) Alternate-recipient-allowed DL-expansion-prohibited Disclosure-as-recipients Recipient-reassignment-prohibited Originator-requested-alternate-recipient
Priority argument	Priority
Conversion arguments	Implicit-conversion-prohibited Explicit-conversion Conversion-with-loss-prohibited
Delivery time arguments	Deferred-delivery-time Latest-time
Delivery method arguments	Requested-delivery-method
Physical delivery arguments	Registered-mail-type Physical-delivery-modes Recipient-number-for-advice Physical-rendition-attributes Originator-return-address Physical-forwarding-prohibited Physical-forwarding-address-request
Report request arguments	Originator-report-request (M) Content-returned-request Physical-delivery-report-request
Security arguments	Originator-certificate Message-token Content-integrity-check Message-origin-authentication-check Message-security-label Proof-of-submission-request Proof-of-delivery-request Content-confidentiality-algorithm-identifier
Content arguments	Original-encoded-information-types Content-type (M) Content-identifier Content-correlator Content (M)

TABLE 16.3   Arguments of P3 Submission Operation

The **delivery port** supports three asymmetric operations: message-delivery, report-delivery, and delivery-control. The MTS invokes the message-delivery operation to deliver a message to an MTS-user. It invokes the report-delivery operation to acknowledge to an MTS-user the outcome of an outstanding message-submission operation or probe-submission operation. An MTS-user uses the delivery-control operation to constrain the use of the delivery port by the MTS. For example, it may not want certain content types to be delivered.

The **administration port** supports the register operation and the change-credentials operation. An MTS-user invokes the asymmetric register operation to register or change long term parameters such as O/R names. Either an MTS-user or the MTS can invoke the change-credential operation to change credentials such as security related information.

Consider a simple scenario to illustrate how the P3 operations are used. An MTS-user first invokes the register operation to specify some content type of messages that it wishes the MTS to deliver. Then, it submits a message with a request for a delivery report. If the message is indeed delivered, the MTS will invoke the report-delivery operation to send a delivery report to the MTS-user. At a later time, the MTS might invoke the delivery operation to deliver a message to the MTS-user.

Each P3 operation involves quite a number of arguments. Table 16.3 displays the arguments used by the P3 submission operation. There are thirty-seven arguments listed, only five of which (those marked with "M") are mandatory.

In a realization of the MTS abstract service, each port is mapped to an ASE. The three ASEs are **message submission service element (MSSE)**, **message delivery service element (MDSE)**, and **message administration service element (MASE)**. These ASEs are supported by ROSE, RTSE (optional), and ACSE.

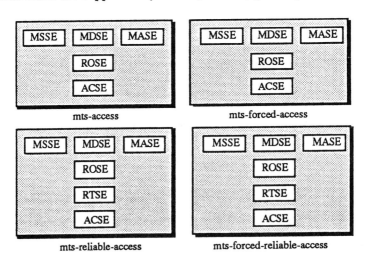

FIGURE 16.14 P3 Application Contexts

The MHS standard specifies four P3 application contexts. Theese application contexts are "mts-access", "mts-forced-access", "mts-reliable-access", and "mts-forced-reliable-access" (Figure 16.14). All four application contexts include MSSE, MDSE, and MASE as users of ROSE and ACSE. RTSE is included in the "mts-reliable-access" and the "mts-forced-reliable-access" application contexts. If the MTS-user is the consumer of the ASEs, the application context is "not forced", otherwise it is "forced".

16.3.2   MS Access Protocol

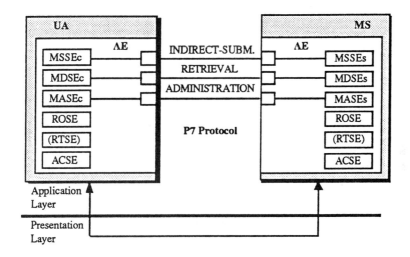

FIGURE 16.15   P7 Computational Model

P7, as defined in ISO/IEC 10021-5, is the MHS protocol used for accessing an MS from a UA. There are two objects involved in the P7 protocol: the UA and the MS. Figure 16.15 shows that the two objects interact with each other via three ports.

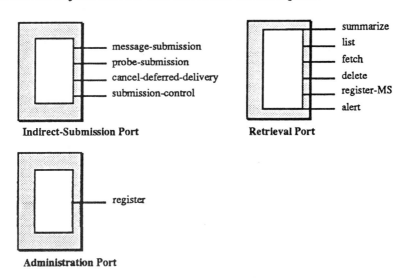

FIGURE 16.16   P7 Ports and Operations

Before we examine the operations supported at each port, it is necessary to associate an MS with an information base. An information base is a conceptual database of entries, where each entry is an object manipulated by the message store operations. For example, the **Stored-Message Information Base (SMIB)** is used to store messages for the IPMS. Thus an entry in the SMIB can be an IPM or an IPN. The MS assigns a sequence number to each entry it creates. It also maintains the entry-status of each entry which describes whether the entry is new, listed, or processed. An entry is considered to be processed if the UA associated with the MS has previously read the entry or the MS has performed some auto-action on the entry.

Figure 16.16 lists the operations supported by each P7 port. The P7 indirect-submission port and the P7 administration port will not be described here since they are similar to the P3 submission port and the P3 administration port respectively. We will only describe the retrieval port.

The **retrieval port** supports six asymmetric operations: summarize (UA), list (UA), fetch (UA), delete (UA), register-MS (UA), and alert (MS). A brief description of these operations follows:

- summarize: A UA invokes the summarize operation to obtain a summary of selected entries in an information base.
- list: A UA invokes the list operation to search for entries of interest.
- fetch: A UA invokes fetch to get selected information of a specific entry in an information base.
- delete: A UA invokes the delete operation to delete selected entries from an information base.
- register-MS: A UA invokes the register-MS operation to register or deregister information with the MS. The information can be auto-actions, new credentials, or a default list of attribute types.
- alert: An MS invokes the alert operation to inform the UA of a new entry having been entered into the MS, whose attributes match the selection criteria of one of those previously supplied by a UA using the register-MS operation.

Consider a simple scenario to illustrate how the P7 operations are used. A UA invokes the list operation to retrieve a list of selected information from the MS. The MS associated with the UA returns this list together with the sequence number of the next entry beyond those that have already been selected. If one of the returned entries is of interest, the UA invokes the fetch operation to retrieve the message. While the fetched message is being examined, the UA could get an alert indication from the MS. The alert indication may inform the UA that a new message has arrived. After the UA completes the examination of the message, it could invoke the register-MS operation to enter auto-forwarding actions.

For a second scenario, suppose that a UA invokes the summarize operation. The MS associated with the UA first identifies the information base which is addressed by the summarize operation. It accumulates counts in accordance with the supplied argument attributes and then returns the results to the UA. Figure 16.17 shows the information which the MS may return to the UA.

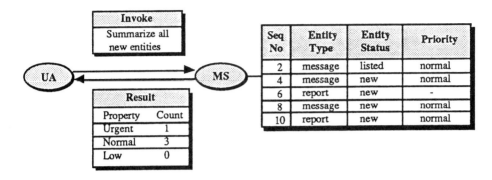

FIGURE 16.17   Summarize Operation

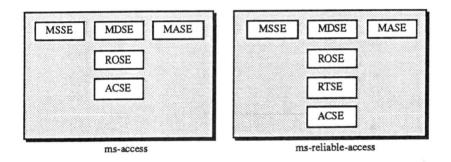

FIGURE 16.18   MS Access Application Contexts

Each P7 port is mapped to an ASE. Hence there are three ASEs, which are the **message submission service element (MSSE)**, the **message delivery service element (MDSE)**, and the **message administration service element (MASE)**. The MHS standard specifies two P7 application contexts: ms-access and ms-reliable-access (Figure 16.18). Both application contexts include MSSE, MDSE, and MASE as users of ROSE and ACSE. RTSE is included in the ms-reliable-access application context. The UA is always the initiator of the application association. Note that it does not make sense to specify an application context where the MS is the initiator.

16.3.3   Message Transfer Protocol

P1, as defined in ISO/IEC 10021-5, is the MHS protocol used by the MTAs to transfer a message, a probe, or a report. Figure 16.19 shows that P1 involves two MTA objects interacting with each other via the transfer port. The transfer port supports three symmetric operations: message-transfer operation, probe-transfer operation, and report-transfer operation.

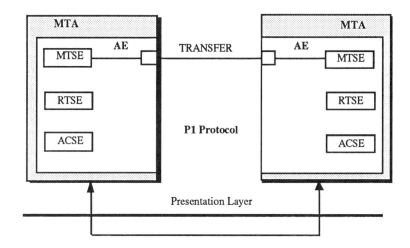

FIGURE 16.19 P1 Computational Model

An MTA must first invoke MTA-bind to establish an association with another MTA. After this, an MTA can use the message-transfer operation to transfer a message, the report-transfer operation to transfer a report, or the probe-transfer operation to transfer a probe to another MTA.

The arguments of the message-transfer operation are examined next. The MHS standard defines forty-six arguments, only ten of which are mandatory. These arguments can be grouped as follows:

• relaying arguments: These arguments are used to route the message through the MTS. Examples of such arguments are message-identifier, trace information, recipient-names, and responsibility.

• redirection arguments: These arguments are used to redirect a message to some other UA. Examples of these arguments are alternate-recipient-allowed, recipient-redirection-allowed, and redirection reason.

• conversion arguments: These arguments allow a message originator to specify whether EIT conversion should be performed by the MTS. Examples of these arguments are originally-encoded-information-types, conversion-prohibited, explicit-conversion, and conversion-with-loss-prohibited.

• delivery time arguments: These arguments allow a message originator to specify either a delay in the delivery of a message or a date and time after which the message should not be delivered. Examples of these arguments are deferred-delivery-time and latest-delivery-time.

• delivery report request arguments: These arguments control the generation of the delivery and the non-delivery reports. Examples of these arguments are originator-delivery-report-request, MTA-delivery-report-request, and content-return-request.

• security arguments: These arguments are used to provide MHS security services. Examples of these arguments are originator-certificate, message-token, content-

confidentiality-algorithm-identifier, content-integrity-check, and message-origin-authentication-check. These arguments will be studied in detail in Section 16.5.
• content arguments: These arguments specify the content type in addition to the actual content.

A brief description of the mandatory arguments follows:

• message-identifier: This argument distinguishes the message from all other messages in the MTS. This identifier should have the same value as the message-submission-identifier submitted to the MTS by an originator MTS-user.
• trace information: This argument documents the actions taken on the message by each managing domain through which the message passes. This information is used by the MTS to detect looping.
• originator-name: This is the O/R name of an originator MTS-user.
• recipient-name: This argument contains the O/R name of each recipient.
• originally-specified-recipient-number: This argument contains a distinct integer value for each recipient. This argument together with the message-identifier argument unambiguously identify the copy of the message delivered to each recipient.
• responsibility: This argument indicates whether the receiving MTA should have the responsibility to deliver the message to a recipient or transfer it to another MTA for subsequent delivery to the recipient. For example, the receiving MTA may be asked to deliver the message only if the recipient is local to the MTA. A different value of this argument may be specified for each recipient of the message.
• originator-report-request: This argument, as generated by the originator MTS-user, may have one of the following values: no-report, non-delivery-report, and report. A different value of this argument may be specified for each recipient of the message.
• originating-MTA-report-request: This argument indicates the kind of report requested by the originating MTA. The value must be at least equal to the level of report requested by the originator MTS-user. A reporting level is either no-report, basic, confirmed, or audit-and-confirmed. The audit-and-confirmed level means that the delivery report must contain all the trace information.
• content-type: This argument describes the content type of the message.
• content: This argument contains the content of the message. Except when conversion is allowed, the content cannot be modified by the MTS. However, it can be encrypted to provide confidentiality.

The **message type**, as an object type, is characterized by the above attributes and some more. Conceptually, it can be divided into an envelope and a content. The fields in an envelope can be split into the per-message-transfer fields (Figure 16.20) which apply to an envelope as a whole, and the per-recipient fields (Figure 16.21) which apply to each recipient listed on an envelope.

In a realization of the abstract service of P1, the transfer port is mapped to the **message transfer service element (MTSE)**. This MTSE is supported by ACSE and optionally RTSE. Three P1 application contexts are defined in the MHS standard. Only one of them, mts-transfer, works over a pure 1988 stack containing MTSE and the 1988 versions of RTSE and ACSE. It uses RTSE but does not use ROSE. MTSE uses three APDUs: Message, Probe, and Report. The Message APDU is of the message type mentioned in the last paragraph.

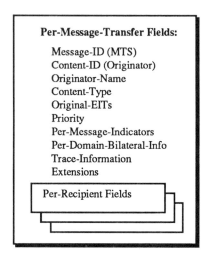

FIGURE 16.20   Per-Message-Transfer Fields

```
Per-Recipient Fields:

   Recipient-Name
   Originally-Specified-Recipient-Number
   Per-Recipient-Indicators
   Explicit-Conversion
   Extensions:
       Originator-Requested-Alternate
       Requested-Delivery-Method
       Physical-Delivery-Controls
       Message-Token (Security)
       Content-Integrity-Check
       Proof-of-Delivery-Request
```

FIGURE 16.21   Per-Recipient Fields

Considering the use of RTSE by MTSE, MTA-bind and MTA-unbind are mapped to RT-OPEN and RT-CLOSE respectively. If MTSE wants to transfer a message and it possesses the turn, it will issue the RT-TRANSFER.request primitive. If MTSE does not possess the turn, it may issue the RT-TURN-PLEASE.request primitive.

16.4   Distributed Operations of the MTS

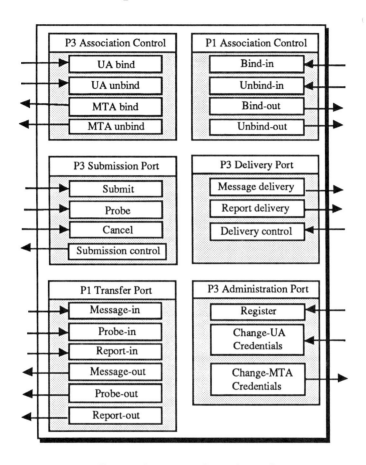

FIGURE 16.22   Design of a DSA

The MTAs collectively provide a distributed service to the MTS-users. In this section, we examine an internal design of an MTA which is taken from the MHS standard.

The design of an MTA can be described by a set of modules. Every external port of an MTA object (i.e., the submission port, the delivery port, the administration port, and the transfer port) is mapped to an external module. External modules interact with external MHS objects which are either MTS-user objects or MTA objects. Each external module contains a number of procedures (Figure 16.22). For example, the external module associated with the transfer port contains six procedures: message-in, message-out, probe-in, probe-out, report-in, and report-out (note that there are two procedures for each operation supported by the transfer port, namely, one for input and the other for output).

Besides external modules, there are also internal modules which are used for internal processing. The MHS standard describes three internal modules: the deferred delivery module, the main module, and the report module. The deferred delivery module provides the deferred delivery service. Recall that one of the arguments of the P3 submission-operation is the deferred-delivery-time argument. This argument specifies the time before which a message should not be delivered to the recipient(s). When an MTA receives a submitted or transferred message from another MTA, its deferred delivery module will check if the deferred-delivery-time field is present, and if so, whether the deferred-delivery-time has expired.

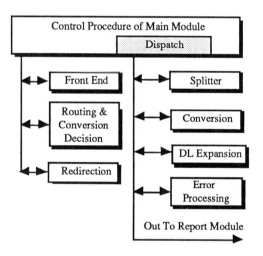

FIGURE 16.23   Organization of the Main Module

The main module, which is the most important of the three internal modules, is responsible for performing the processing on the incoming messages and probes. Figure 16.23 shows the organization of the main module. There is a control procedure controlling seven other procedures. Its flowchart is shown in Figure 16.24. Below is a brief description of the seven procedures:

- front-end procedure: This procedure performs the front-end processing on incoming messages and probes. The front-end processing tasks include trace initialization, detection of message expiration, initial security check, and loop detection.
- routing and conversion decision: For each recipient for which the MTA is responsible, this procedure determines the routing and conversion actions to be taken, if any are present. These actions are subsequently carried out by other procedures internal to the routing and conversion decision procedure.
- redirection: This procedure redirects a message to an alternate recipient.
- conversion: This procedure performs message conversions. For a probe, it indicates conversions that would have been performed.
- distribution list expansion: This procedure expands a DL. For a probe, it verifies whether DL-expansion would occur.
- error processing: This procedure is called whenever errors occur. When invoked, this procedure determines if delivery can be achieved by some other means.

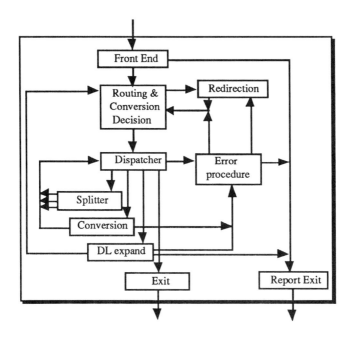

FIGURE 16.24   Flow Chart of Control Procedure

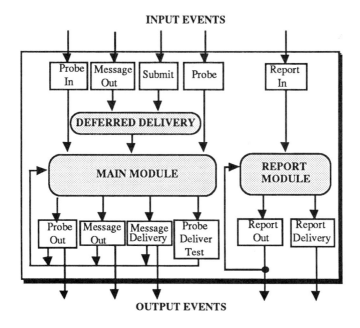

FIGURE 16.25   Relationship of the Internal Modules with the External Modules

- splitter: This procedure replicates messages and probes to indicate the distribution of responsibility for the various recipients. For example, when more than one relaying path outwards from the MTA is needed, a separate copy of the message is created for each path and responsibility is also assigned to the recipients along each path.

    The third internal module is the report module. It can be invoked by the main module or the external module associated with the transfer port. If it is invoked by the main module, it will generate a report and then determine a route for the generated report. If it is invoked by the external module associated with the transfer port with an incoming report, it simply determines a route to relay the report.
    Figure 16.25 shows the relationship among the internal modules and the procedures associated within the external modules. Not all the procedures associated with the external procedures interact with the internal modules. For example, the procedures associated with the P3 association control module, the P1 association control module, or the administration port module do not interact with any of the internal modules.

16.5   MHS Security

The highly distributed nature of the MHS mandates the need to protect against various security threats. The following sections describe the potential MHS threats and various services and mechanisms to counter them.

16.5.1 MHS Security Threats

- **masquerade**

The most likely form of such threats is impersonation of an MTS-user/MTA. An unauthorized MTS-user may impersonate another MTS-user to gain unauthorized access to MTS capabilities, to discard the messages of a valid MTS-user, to falsely claim to originate a message, to falsely acknowledge receipt by a valid recipient, etc. An unauthorized MTA may impersonate an MTA to an MTS-user to falsely claim that a user message has been delivered. The secure access service must be provided.

- **message sequencing**

This threat takes the form of reordering, timeshifting, or repeating parts or all of a message. The message sequence integrity service must be provided.

- **modification of information**

Messages for an intended recipient and management information may be intentionally modified by an unauthorized object. The connection integrity and the content integrity services must be provided.

*   **repudiation**

Repudiation threats occur when MHS participants deny their involvement such as submitting a message, receiving a message, or originating a message. This is a serious threat if, for example, financial transactions are being communicated via the MHS. The non-repudiation of origin, the non-repudiation of submission, and the non-repudiation of delivery services must be provided.

*   **leakage of information**

This threat takes the form of listening to messages, illegal access to information stored in an MHS object, or analysis of traffic to gain information about the message exchange. The message content confidentiality and the message flow confidentiality services must be provided.

*   **other threats**

Other threats include unauthorized routing of messages through unreliable domains, setting up or accepting an association with a security context for which the communicating entities do not have clearance, etc. The secure access management and the message security labelling services must be provided.

16.5.2 MHS Security Services

Every MHS management domain has its own security policy. MHS security services must be able to support a wide range of security policies for the needs of the management domains. The following gives a brief description of the MHS security services.

*   **origin authentication security services**

These security services provide for the identifications of the communicating peer entities and the source of data. They are: the **message/probe/report origin authentication security service** which enables the corroboration of the source of a message/probe/report, the **proof of submission security service** which enables the originator of a message to obtain corroboration that the message has been received by the MTS for delivery to the intended recipient(s), and the **proof of delivery security service** which enables the originator of a message to obtain corroboration that the message has been delivered by the MTS to its intended recipient(s).

*   **secure access management security services**

These security services provide protection of resources against their unauthorized use. Two services are provided: the **peer entity authentication security service** which provides confidence that an unauthorized entity is not attempting a masquerade or replaying a previous connection, and the **security context security service** which is used to limit the scope of messages passed between MHS objects by reference to security labels associated with the messages.

- **data confidentiality security services**

These security services provide protection of data against unauthorized disclosure. Two services are provided: the **content confidentiality security service** which provides assurance that the content of a message is only known to the sender and the intended recipients, and the **message flow confidentiality security service** which provides the protection of information which might be derived from observation of the flow of the messages.

- **data integrity security services**

These services provide the protection of message content and message sequence against modification during transmission. Two services are provided: the **content integrity security service** which provides integrity for the content of a message, and the **message sequence integrity security service** which protects the originator and recipient(s) of a sequence of messages against re-ordering of the sequence.

- **non-repudiation security services**

These services provide irrevocable proof to a third party that the message has been originated, submitted, or delivered. Three services are provided: the **non-repudiation of origin security service** which provides the recipient(s) of a message with irrevocable proof of the origin of the message, its content, and associated message security label, the **non-repudiation of submission security service** which provides the originator of the message with irrevocable proof that the message was submitted to the MTS for delivery to the intended recipient(s), and the **non-repudiation of delivery security service** which provides the originator of the message with irrevocable proof that the message was delivered to the specified recipient(s).

- **message security labelling security service**

This service allows security labels to be associated with the MHS objects. With the help of the security context service, it can be used to specify a security policiy.

- **security management security services**

MHS requires a number of security management services. They include the **change credentials security service** which enables an MHS object to change its credentials which are held by another MHS object, and the **register security service** which enables permissible security labels to be registered at an MTA for a specific MTS-user or MS-user.

Service	UA/ UA	UA/ MS	MS/ MTA	UA/ MTA	MTA/ MS	MTA/ MTA	MTA/ UA	MS/ UA
Origin Authentication								
Message origin authentication	X	X	-	X	-	-	-	-
Probe origin authentication	-	-	X	X	-	-	-	-
Report origin authentication	-	-	-	-	X	X	X	-
Proof of submission	-	-	-	-	-	-	X	-
Proof of delivery	X	-	-	-	-	-	-	-
Secure Access Management								
Peer entity authentication	-	X	X	X	X	X	X	X
Security context	-	X	X	X	X	X	X	X
Data Confidentiality								
Connection confidentiality	-	X	X	X	X	X	X	X
Content confidentiality	X	-	-	-	-	-	-	-
Message flow confidentiality	X	-	-	-	-	-	-	-
Data Integrity								
Connection integrity	-	X	X	X	X	X	X	X
Content integrity	X	-	-	-	-	-	-	-
Message sequence integrity	X	-	-	-	-	-	-	-
Non-repudiation								
Non-repudiation of origin	X	-	-	X	-	-	-	-
Non-repudiation of submission	-	-	-	-	-	-	X	-
Non-repudiation of delivery	X	-	-	-	-	-	-	-
Message Security Labelling								
Message security labelling	X	X	X	X	X	X	X	X
Security Management								
Change credentials	-	X	-	X	X	X	X	-
Register	-	X	-	X	-	-	-	-

TABLE 16.4 MHS Security Services

The above MHS security services can be provided at eight possible interfaces: UA/UA, UA/MS, MS/MTA, UA/MTA, MTA/MS, MTA/MTA, MTA/UA and MS/UA. For each interface, the object on the left provides the service to the object on the right. Table 16.4 indicates the services provided at each interface. For example, end-to-end security services can occur only at the UA/UA interface. On the other hand, message security labelling service is possible at every interface. Both peer entity authentication and security context services can be provided wherever an application association can exist. Hence, this occurs at every interface except the UA/UA interface. Also note that the services provided at the UA/MTA interface and the MTA/UA interface differ from each other. For example, since a probe originates from a UA but not an MTA, the probe origin authentication service is provided at the UA/MTA interface but not the MTA/UA interface.

16.5.3 MHS Security Arguments

In this section, we examine the MHS security mechanisms used to provide the MHS security services. MHS security mechanisms are based on the Authentication Framework defined in ISO/IEC 9594-8. The authentication principle outlined in ISO/IEC 9594-8 is very straightforward. Each MHS user is identified by the possession of a secret key. Suppose that the UA A wants to provide message origin authentication service to another UA B (Figure 16.26). When A sends a message to B, it first computes a signature which is obtained by hashing and encryption. First, a 1-way hash function is applied to the message, ensuring that false information cannot be substituted. Then the hashed message is encrypted using the secret key of A. The encrypted string is the signature. A sends the signature and the message to B. Upon receipt of the signature and the message, B applies the same hash function to the received message. It then decrypts the signature using A's public key. Note that B can retrieve A's public key from the Directory or may receive it directly from A. Finally, B compares the hashed result with the decrypted signature. If they are equal, B has proof that the message must have come from A since only A possesses the secret key.

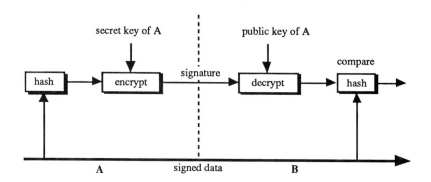

FIGURE 16.26   Authentication Procedure

MHS security services are provided by means of the security arguments and the security results of the port operations. In P3 for example, security arguments and security results appear in operations such as message-submission, probe-submission, message-delivery, probe-delivery, register, change-credentials, MTS-bind, and MTS-unbind. Table 16.5 shows the security arguments of the message-submission operation, some of which are relevant to the entire message while some are relevant to a particular recipient.

Below is a description of how the MHS security services are provided.

Security Arguments	Pre-message Field	Pre-recipient Field
Originator-certificate	X	
Message-token		X
Content-confidentiality-algorithm-identifier	X	
Content-integrity-check		X
Message-origin-authentication-check	X	
Message-security-label	X	
Proof-of-submission-request	X	
Proof-of-delivery-request		X

TABLE 16.5   Security Arguments of Message Submission operation

- **provision of message origin authentication security service**

The message origin authentication security service is provided by a message originator to enable corroboration of the source of the message. This service is provided at the UA/MS, the UA/MTA, and the UA/UA interfaces.

At the UA/MTA interface, assume that the originator UA is A and the originator MTA is B. The message origin authentication service is provided using the **message-origin-authentication-check argument** in the message-submission operation (Table 16.5). This argument actually contains two components. The first component contains a message-origin-authentication-algorithm-identifier. The second component is obtained by encrypting (using A's secret key) a hashed version of the message-origin-algorithm-identifier, the message content, the content-identifier, and the message-security-label. When B receives the message-origin-authentication-check argument, it uses A's public key to validate the information in message-origin-authentication-check. In this way, the message-origin-authentication-check provides both message origin authentication and non-repudiation of origin of the message content.

Because the message-origin-authentication-algorithm is applied to the unencrypted version of the message content, the message content will be disclosed to B. In order not to disclose the content to B, A could have applied the message-origin-authentication-check algorithm to an encrypted version of the message content. The message-origin-authentication-check obtained in this way would still provide for message-origin authentication but not for non-repudiation of the origin of the message content.

- **provision of message content confidentiality security service**

The message content confidentiality service is an end-to-end service between an originator UA and a recipient UA. Assume that the originator UA is A and the recipient UA is B. The message content confidentiality security service is provided as follows. First, A encrypts the message content using B's public key. A then sends the encrypted message together with the content-confidentiality-algorithm-identifier to B. Upon receipt of the encrypted message content, B uses its secret key to decrypt the encrypted message. Since B is the only holder of its secret key, the message content can be known to A and B only.

- **provision of content integrity security service**

The content integrity security service, which is an end-to-end service, is provided using the **content-integrity-check argument** in the message-submission operation. Assume that the originator UA is A and one of the recipient UAs is B. Upon submission, A supplies the content-integrity-check argument which contains two components. The first component is the content-integrity-algorithm-identifier, and the second component is obtained by encrypting (using A's secret key) a hashed version of the content-integrity-algorithm-identifier and the message content. When B receives the content-integrity-check argument, it uses A's public key to validate the content-integrity-check argument.

- **provision of proof of submission security service**

The proof of submission security service is provided by using the **proof-of-submission result** parameter of the message-submission operation. Assume that the originator UA A requests proof of submission by setting the proof-of-submission-request result of the message-submission operation to true. Upon correct submission, the originator MTA B returns the originator-MTA-certificate and the proof-of-submission result to A. The proof-of-submission result contains two components. The first component is a proof-of-submission-algorithm identifier. The second component is obtained by encrypting (using B's secret key) a hashed version of the proof-of-submission-algorithm-identifier, the arguments of the submitted message, the message-submission-identifier, and the message-submission-time. Upon receipt of the proof-of-submission result from B, A first derives B's public key, then it uses this key to validate the proof-of-submission argument.

- **provision of proof of delivery security service**

The proof of delivery security service is an end-to-end service between an originating UA and a recipient UA. It uses the **proof-of-delivery result** in the message-delivery operation. Assume that the originator UA is A and one of the recipient UAs is B. Upon submission, A requests the proof of delivery service by setting the proof-of-delivery-request result to true. Upon successful delivery, B returns its certificate and the proof-of-delivery result to A. The proof-of-delivery result contains two components. The first component is a proof-of-delivery-algorithm-identifier, and the second component is obtained by encrypting (using B's secret key) a hashed version of the proof-of-delivery-algorithm-identifier, the delivery-time, the this-recipient-name, the originally-intended-recipient-name, the message content, the content-identifier, and the message-security-label of the delivered message arguments. Upon receipt of the proof-of-delivery result from B, A will first derive B's public key from B's certificate, then it uses this key to validate the proof-of-delivery result with the public key.

- **provision of security access services using message security label**

Security labels are used to associate security relevant information with MHS objects. A message originator can associate a security label with a message, a probe, or a report in line with some rule-based security policy in force. The security label of a report should be identical to the security label of the message or probe which is the subject of the report. During an application association establishment, the two communicating MHS objects negotiate a security context which defines a set of security labels common to both objects.

A security label can be described attributes such as the security-policy attribute and the security-classification attribute. The security-policy attribute identifies the security policy in force to which the security label relates. The security-classification attribute indicates the sensitivity level (such as "unclassified" and "confidential") of the object.

- **message-token**

The message-token argument is the primary method of distributing and conveying security related information in MHS. While security arguments are used to provide security services, some means are needed to protect the security arguments/results from modification and disclosure. A message-token is a collection of security arguments/results, some of which are signed/encrypted.

Consider the signed data part of a message-token containing public security relevant information. This will be signed by an originator UA using some signature algorithm. The signed data may contain security arguments such as the content-confidentiality-algorithm-identifier, the content-integrity-check, the message-security-label, the proof-of-delivery request argument, and the message-sequence-number arguments. An MHS object can check the signed data as long as it has access to the public key of the signed data. For example, a recipient UA can use the signed data to provide non-repudiation-of-origin of a message to a third party if the signed data includes the content-integrity-check.

The encrypted data part of a message-token contains secret security relevant information. This part is encrypted by an originating UA using the public key of the intended recipient of the token. Note that the encryption algorithm used here may be different from the signature algorithm. The encrypted data may contain security arguments such as the content-integrity-check, the message-security-label, and the message-sequence-number arguments. Note that the encrypted data can be decrypted by the intended recipient only. The effect of this end-to-end service is that the originator UA can transfer a security label end-to-end.

16.6 MHS APIs

In the transition from isolated proprietary messaging systems to a global messaging system using gateways, a group of leading computer and communications vendors formed the **X.400 Application Program Interface Association (XAPIA)** in late 1988. In the first phase of its work, the XAPIA established the **MHS Gateway API specification**.

The objective of this interface is to divide the work of developing an MHS gateway between the supplier of a proprietary messaging system and the supplier of the MHS software. In the second phase of its work, the XAPIA produced the **MHS Application API specification**. The objective of this interface is to standardize the services offered by the MHS to applications. The specification of Gateway API and Application API is covered in Section 16.6.1. These interfaces achieve their functionalities by accessing three packages: IM package, MH package, and SM package. Section 16.6.2 briefly explains these three packages. Both the Gateway and the Application APIs utilize the OM API which was described in Chapter 15.

16.6.1 Specifications of MHS APIs

• **MHS Gateway API**

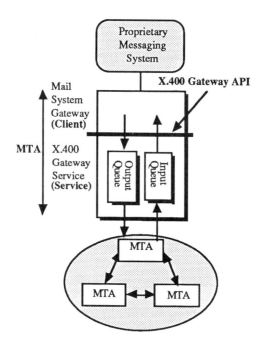

FIGURE 16.27   Conceptual Model of Gateway API

Figure 16.27 illustrates the conceptual model of the MHS Gateway API. The two major objects are the X.400 gateway service (i.e., the software implementing the MHS Gateway API) and the Mail System Gateway (which is the client). The service maintains two queues: an input and an output queues. The output queue is filled by the client and emptied by the gateway service. It contains objects which the gateway service will convey, by means of MHS, to the intended recipients. An object here is a message, a probe, or a report. The input queue is filled by the gateway service and emptied by the client. It contains objects for the client to convey to its users by local means. An object here is either a message, a probe, or a report. The client can access an object in the input queue without first removing it from that queue on the condition that no other client can access that object simultaneously.

One of the client's principle tasks is to transfer out objects that functionally approximate objects in its local environment. To do this, the client establishes a session with the gateway service using open(), creates a new object using create(), places the local information in the object using put() and write(), transfers out the object using transfer_out(), and terminates the session using close() .

Another important task of the client is to inject into the local environment objects that functionally approximate objects transferred in. To do this, the client establishes a session with the gateway service using open(), awaits the next inbound object using wait(), obtains access to it using start_transfer_in(), gets information from it using om_get(), injects information into the local environment using om_read(), accepts responsibility for the object using finish_transfer_in(), and terminates the session using close().

Function	Description
Close	Terminate an MT session
Finish Transfer In	conclude one of the "transfers in" in progress in a session
Open	establish an MT session
Size	Determine the size of the input queue
Start Transfer In	Begin the "transfer in" of a communique or a report
Transfer Out	Add a communique or report to the output queue
Wait	Return when an object is available for transfer in

TABLE 16.6   Gateway API Service Functions

Table 16.6 gives a brief description for each function. The next example describes the C format of the mt_transfer_out function.

Example 16.2

```
OM_return_code
mt_transfer_out (
        OM_private_object     session,
        OM_object             object,
        );
```

The purpose of the transfer out function is to add a communique or a report to the output queue. The session argument is an established MT session between the client and the service. The object argument is the object to be added to the output queue. The object can be a communique or a report.

- **MHS Application API**

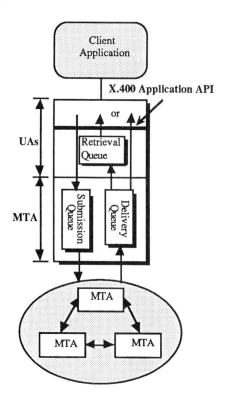

FIGURE 16.28　　Conceptual Model of Application API

Figure 16.28 shows the conceptual model of the MHS Application API. The service (i.e., the software that implements the MHS Application API) maintains a submission queue and either a delivery queue or a retrieval queue for each local user, except that a single delivery queue may be shared by a group of local users. The choice between a delivery or retrieval queue is an option of an application. The submission queue is filled by the client and emptied by the service. It contains objects which the service will convey to their intended recipients. An object here is either a message or a probe. The delivery or retrieval queue is filled by the service and emptied by the client. It contains objects for the client or its human user. An object here is either a message or a report.

One of the client's principle tasks is to submit objects that functionally approximate objects in its local environment. To do this, the client establishes a session with the service using open(), creates a new object using om_create(), places the local information in the object using om_put() or om_write(), transfers out the object using transfer_out(), and terminates the session using close(). Another important task of the client is to inject into its local environment information drawn from the delivered objects. To do this, the client establishes a session with the service using open(), awaits the next inbound object using wait(), obtains access to the object using start delivery() or start retrieval(), gets information from the object using om_get(), injects information into its local environment using om_read(), accepts responsibility for the object using finish_delivery() or finish_retrieval(), and terminates the session using close().

Function	Description
Cancel Submission	cancel the deferred delivery of a submitted message
Close	terminate an MA session
Finish Delivery	conclude the delivery in progress in a session
Finish Retrieval	conclude the retrieval in progress in a session
Open	establish an MA session
Size	determine the size of the delivery or retrieval queue
Start Delivery	begin the delivery of a message or a report
Start Retrival	begin the retrieval of a message or a report
Submit	submit a communique
Wait	retrun when an object is available for delivery or retrieval

TABLE 16.7   Application API Service Functions

Table 16.7 gives a brief description of each function. The next example describes the C format of the mt_transfer_out() function.

Example 16.3

```
OM_return_code
mt_transfer_out (
            OM_private_object           session,
            OM_object                   communique,
            OM_private_object           * submission_results
    );
```

The purpose of the submit function is to submit a communique by adding it to the submission queue to which a session provides access. The session argument is an established MA session between the client and the service. The communique argument is the object to be submitted. On return, the function indicates whether it succeeds or not. An instance of the submission results class is returned as a submission result.

16.6.2. MHS API Packages

This section explains three packages which can be accessed by both MHS APIs. They are the **Interpersonal Messaging (IM) Package**, the **Message Handling (MH) Package**, and the **Secure Messaging (SM) Package** Examples of object classes in these packages are given below, and brief explanations are given to some of them.

- **IM Packages**

  - *Body Part*
    - Bilaterally Defined Body Part -- comprises of arbitrary binary data. The client is presumed to know the syntax or the semantics of the data.
    - Externally Defined Body Part -- comprises of an information object whose syntax and semantics are not defined.
    - IA5 Text Body Part -- comprises IA5 text
    - Message Body Part -- represents an IPM and, optionally, its delivery envelope.
    - Mixed-mode Body Part -- comprises of a final-form document of the kind that mixed-mode Teletex and G4 Classes 2 and 3 facsimile terminals can process.
  - *Content*
    - Interpersonal Message -- is a primary information object conveyed between IPMS users.
    - *Interpersonal Notification*
      - Non-receipt Notification
      - Receipt Notification -- reports its originator's receipt, or the expected and arranged future receipt, of an IPM.
  - IPM Identifier -- uniquely identifies an IPM.
  - OR Descriptor -- identifies a user.

- **MH Package**

  - Algorithm -- identifies a mathematical (typically cryptographic) algorithm.
  - Asymmetric Token
  - *Content* -- is the information that a message is intended to convey to its recipients.
    - General Content -- is the information that a message is intended to convey to its recipients and is made available as binary data.
  - Delivered Message
  - Delivery Confirmation
    - Local Delivery Confirmation -- comprises confirmations of the delivery of a message (but not a report) to zero or more local recipients.
  - EITs
  - Expansion Record -- documents the expansion of a DL.
    - *Communique* -- is a primary information object conveyed by users via the MTS.
      - Message
      - Probe
    - *Delivered Per-recipient Report* -- gives information about the successful or unsuccessful delivery, or the deliverability or undeliverability, of the subject message to a particular recipient.
      - Delivered Per-recipient DR
      - Delivered Per-recipient NDR

- *Delivery Report* -- is a secondary information object delivered by the MTS to its users. It reports the successful or unsuccessful delivery, or the deliverability or undeliverability of the subject message to some or all of its recipients.
    - Delivered Report -- gives to the originator of a submitted communique, information about the successful or unsuccessful delivery of the message to a particular recipient.
- Delivery Envelope
- *Per-recipient Report* -- gives information about the successful or unsuccessful delivery, or the deliverability or undeliverability, of the subject message to a particular recipient.
    - Per-recipient DR -- gives information about the successful delivery, or the deliverability of the subject message to a particular recipient.
    - Per-recipient NDR -- gives information about the unsuccessful delivery, or the undeliverability, of the subject message to a particular recipient.
- *RD* -- identifies an intended recipient of a communique and records certain information about that recipient.
    - Submitted Probe RD -- identifies an intended recipient of a submitted probe (or message) and records certain information about that recipient.
        - Probe RD -- identifies an intended recipient of a probe (or message) and records certain information about that recipient.
    - Submitted Message RD
        - Message RD -- identifies an intended recipient of a message and records certain information about that recipient.
- Submission Results -- is an acknowledgement of the successful submission to the MTS of a submitted communique. The MTS provides the acknowledgement.
- *Submitted Communique* -- is a primary information object submitted by users to the MTS.
    - Submitted Message
    - Submitted Probe
- External Trace Entity -- describes one or more actions that a management domain takes with respect to a communique or report.
- Internal Trace Entry -- describes one or more actions that an MTA takes with respect to a communique or report.
- Local Delivery Confirmation
- Local Non-delivery Report
- Local Per-recipient Non-delivery Report
- MTS Identifier -- distinguishes a communique or report from other communiques and reports in the MTS.
- OR Address
    - OR Name
- Redirection Record -- documents a communique's redirection.
- Security Label

- Session -- is an MA or MT session between the client and the service. Among other things, a session comprises of information about an MTA's environment, especially information about the subject domain, and the management domain that contains the MTA.

- **SM Package**

  - Integrity Check Basis -- provides the basis for enabling any recipient of a message to verify that its content is unchanged.
  - Origin Check Basis -- provides the basis for enabling a third party to verify the origin of portions of a communique or a report.
  - Per-recipient Check Basis -- provides the basis for enabling a third party to verify the origin of a portion of a per-recipient report.
    - Per-recipient Delivery Check Basis -- provides the basis for enabling a third party to verify the origin of a portion of a per-recipient DR.
    - Per-recipient Non-delivery Check Basis -- provides the basis for enabling a third party to verify the origin of a portion of a per-recipient NDR.
  - Proof of Delivery Basis -- provides the basis for enabling the originator of a message to prove that it has been delivered to a particular recipient.
  - Proof of Submission Basis -- provides the basis for enabling the originator of a message to prove that it has submitted the message.
  - Public Information Basis -- provides the basis on which a token protects public security-related information.
  - Secret Information Basis -- provides the basis on which a token protects secret security-related information.

16.7 Summary

The MHS service provides the electronic messaging service in a global network. Improving the 1984 version, the 1988 MHS version provides more security services through the use of the evolving Directory Services. A secured electronic messaging system is what some applications such as EDI and ODA have been waiting for.

The MHS functional model is made up of a number of objects, among which are the UAs, the MSs, and the MTAs. Interactions between these objects are specified using the MHS protocols.

The P1 protocol specifies the protocol between the MTAs for the transfer of messages, probes, and reports. In an unreliable environment, it relies on the use of RTSE. Unlike the other MHS protocols, it is non-interactive, hence it does not use ROSE.

The P3 protocol is an interactive protocol used between a UA and an MTA. With P3, a remote UA can submit messages and probes. In practice, the UA and MTA can interact with each other through some other proprietary means. Many existing MHS products do not provide a P3 implementation.

The P7 protocol is an interactive protocol used between a UA and an MS which is the message store. This protocol is useful if the UA runs on a PC (personal computer) which does not operate twenty-four hours a day. When the PC is on, the UA uses the P7 protocol to retrieve messages received when the PC was off. Although the message store is a 1988 feature, most 1984 implementations provide some partial P3 features.

The MHS standard also specifies P2. P2 is not a communication protocol. It defines the interpersonal messaging content type which is used for person-to-person communication. It defines the structure of an interpersonal notification which is used by a recipient to acknowledge receipt of an interpersonal message.

The distributed nature of the MHS is exposed to security threats such as message access threats, message relay threats, and message store threats. The MHS security mechanisms used to provide the MHS security services are based on the Authentication Framework defined in ISO/IEC 9594-8.

In this chapter, we examined two MHS APIs. Both APIs make use of the OM API introduced in the last chapter. Both are object-oriented and language-independent in the sense that they are defined using object classes and functions. The MHS Gateway API divides the work of developing an MHS gateway between the supplier of a proprietary messaging system and the supplier of the necessary MHS software. The MHS Application API standardizes the functionality of the MHS based messaging system to promote applications portability.

Related Standards

ISO 10021-1: Information Processing - Text Communication - Message Oriented Text Interchange System - Part 1: System and Service Overview

ISO 10021-2: Information Processing Systems - Text Communication - Message Oriented Text Interchange System - Part 2: Overall Architecture

ISO 10021-2 PDAM 1: Information Processing Systems - Text Communication - Message Oriented Text Interchange System - Part 2: Overall Architecture - Amendment 1: Representation of O/R Addresses for Human Exchange

ISO 10021-2 PDAM 2: Information Processing Systems - Text Communication - Message Oriented Text Interchange System - Part 2: Overall Architecture - Amendment 2: Minor Enhancements

ISO 10021-3: Information Processing Systems - Text Communication - Message Oriented Text Interchange System - Part 3: Abstract Service Definition Conventions

ISO 10021-4: Information Processing Systems - Text Communication - Message Oriented Text Interchange System - Part 4: Message Transfer System: Abstract Service Definition and Procedures

ISO 10021-4 PDAM 1: Information Processing Systems - Text Communication - Message Oriented Text Interchange System - Part 4: Message Transfer System: Abstract Service Definition and Procedures - Amendment 1: Minor Enhancements

ISO 10021-5: Information Processing Systems - Text Communication - Message Oriented Text Interchange System - Part 5: Message Store: Abstract Service Definition

ISO 10021-6: Information Processing Systems - Text Communication - Message Oriented Text Interchange System - Part 6: Protocol Specifications

ISO 10021-7: Information Processing Systems - Text Communication - Message Oriented Text Interchange System - Part 7: Interpersonal Messaging System

CD 10021-11: Information Technology - Text Communication - Message Oriented Text Interchange System - Part 11: MTS Routing

17

FTAM

File handling is one of the principal services in a networking environment. Many existing file protocols are concerned primarily with moving complete files. The **File Transfer Access Management (FTAM)** standard, which is specified in ISO/IEC 8571, has broadened the scope of these protocols by offering three modes of file manipulation: file transfer, file access, and file/filestore management. **File transfer** is the movement of a complete file between two filestores in different open systems. **File access** performs reading, writing, or deleting of selected parts of a remote file. **File/filestore management** refers to the management of a remote file/filestore.

Files are viewed differently on different systems. On a system like UNIX (trademark of UNIX Systems Laboratory), a file is as simple as a sequence of bytes. But on a system like IBM's MVS, a file is a series of records. In general, the organization of a file is operating system specific. In order to accommodate heterogeneous file systems, the FTAM standard introduces the concepts of a virtual file and a virtual filestore. Virtual files and virtual filestores are the OSI abstractions of real files and real filestores. The use of virtual files and virtual filestores permits applications to perform file operations over a variety of file types without detailed knowledge of the characteristics of the remote file systems. Since virtual filestores and virtual files are only abstractions, an FTAM implementation needs to provide translation between virtual files and system-specific files.

FTAM is an asymmetric protocol involving two objects: an initiator and a responder (Figure 17.1). An initiator initiates an application association with a responder for its subsequent file activities, while a responder maintains a virtual filestore containing virtual files which are the subjects of file activities by different initiators. The initiator is normally invoked by a local user's request and supplied with information about a local file and a remote virtual file. The responder is informed of the file operations through the PDUs exchanged with the initiator.

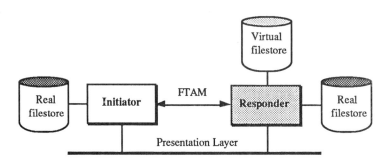

FIGURE 17.1   The FTAM Configuration

The term **FTAM dialogue** is used to qualify the application association between an initiator and a responder. It is possible that the same responder maintains more than one FTAM dialogue, or the same initiator maintains more than one FTAM dialogue. An initiator or a responder identifies a role of an application entity for an FTAM dialogue. The same entity can simultaneously play different roles for different FTAM dialogues.

Section 17.1 introduces virtual files. Section 17.2 describes the FTAM service. Section 17.3 illustrates the operation of the FTAM protocol. Finally, Section 17.4 introduces virtual filestores and filestore management .

17.1   Virtual Files

Virtual files and virtual filestores are the OSI abstractions of real files and real filestores respectively. We will study virtual files in this section. Virtual filestores will be studied in Section 17.4.

Like any object, a virtual file is characterized by its structure and its content. The FTAM standard describes the structure of a file as a **hierarchical access structure** which is a tree (Figure 17.2). Each node may contain structural information such as its name and level, and content information called a **data unit** (DU). Every DU has an associated abstract syntax which might vary for each DU. A **file access data unit** (FADU) is a subtree of the hierarchical access structure. It identifies the location of a substructure of the file access structure. For file access, an initiator first specifies the location of a file structure using a FADU, then directs subsequent file operations to this FADU.

FADU R

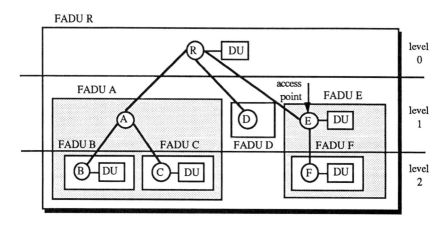

FIGURE 17.2 Hierarchical File Access Structure

When a FADU is moved from one FTAM system to another FTAM system, both the structural and the content information may have to be transferred as a sequence of FTAM data elements. An **FTAM data element**, which is defined as a unit of information to be transferred between two FTAM systems, can be one of the following types:

- node-descriptor: This gives the name of a node (if present), the level of the node in the file access structure, and the "data-exists" indicator which is a boolean value indicating if a DU is attached to the node.
- file-contents: This is a DU associated with a node.
- enter-subtree: This is used to indicate that a subtree is entered.
- exit-subtree: This is used to indicate that an exit from a subtree is made.

In general, only certain data elements of specific types are transferred, depending on what the initiator wants to read. For example, the initiator may only care about the content information but not the structural information. Hence, the notion of a file access context is introduced. A **file access context** is an initiator's view of a FADU. It defines a sequence of data elements of interest to the initiator. For example, if the initiator does not care about the structure, it can use the UA (Unstructured Access) access context in which only data elements of the file-contents type are transferred. On the other hand, if it wants all the information, it will use the HA (Hierarchical Access) access context in which all data elements relevant to the FADU are transferred. Figure 17.3 shows the three possible file access contexts associated with a flat file access structure. Only the data elements that are marked with an "X" are transferred. The transferring order depends on the traversal sequence used.

Next, we consider file actions on file structures. A file action is either a complete file action or a file access action. A complete file action operates on the entire file structure. Examples of complete file actions are "create", "select", and "change attribute". For example, an initiator invokes the "select" action to select a file, and the "change attribute" action to change the existing attributes of a file. A file access action operates on a specified part of a file structure. Examples of file access actions are "read", "insert", "replace", "extend", "erase", and "locate". All these file access actions take a FADU as an input parameter. Consider the write action. There are three kinds of write actions. The "extend" action adds data to the end of the DU associated with the root node of an addressed FADU. The "replace" action replaces either a FADU or the DU of the root of an addressed FADU. A FADU is replaced only if the structural information of the FADU is available. The "insert" action inserts a FADU as either a sibling or a child of an addressed FADU.

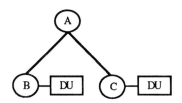

Traversal Sequence	Access Context		
	HA	FA	UA
Node (A)	x		
Enter Subtree	x		
Node (B)	x	x	
Data Unit (B)	x	x	x
Node (C)	x	x	
Data Unit (C)	x	x	x
Exit Subtree	x		

FIGURE   17.3   File Access Contexts of a Flat File Access Structure

In general, the meaning of a file action depends on the file structure. Furthermore, not every file action is applicable to a file structure. For example, the only file actions that are meaningful to the flat file structure are "locate", "read", "insert", and "erase". There are certain constraints on the use of "insert" and "erase". The "insert" action is allowed only at the end of the file, and the new node is inserted following all existing nodes in the file. The "erase" action is only allowed at the root node to empty the file.

FADUs may not have names. Since a FADU is the target of subsequent file activities, it needs to be identified. As a substructure of a tree structure, it can be identified by its position in a well-defined tree traversal sequence of the FADUs of the tree. A tree traversal on the subtrees of a tree is similar to a tree traversal of the tree nodes. The three popular tree traversal algorithms in literature are the pre-order, the in-order, and the random-order traversal algorithms. The random-order traversal algorithm works only if the nodes in the tree have names. Assuming that the pre-order traversal sequence is used, we can use the following terms to identify a FADU:

- "first" returns the first FADU that has a DU in the sequence,
- "last" returns the last FADU in the sequence,
- "next" returns the FADU following the currently identified FADU in the sequence,
- "previous" returns the FADU preceding the currently identified FADU in the sequence,
- "begin", whose meaning depends on the file structure, has the effect that "next" immediately after "begin" gives the first FADU, and
- "end" establishes a state of the file where there is no current location, but the use of "previous" will identify the last FADU.

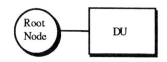

FIGURE 17.4   **Unstructured File**

The hierarchical access structure is the most general structure. In practice, only degenerate substructures of the hierarchical access structure are found in existing file systems. Among the common degenerate substructures are the unstructured file structures and the flat file structures. An **unstructured file structure,** which is a one-level structure, consists of only one node, namely, the root node (Figure 17.4). The root node does not have a name because it does not need one. As a DU is atomic for file operations, an unstructured file structure must be transferred or accessed as a whole. All UNIX files have this structure. A **flat file structure,** such as the structure in Figure 17.3, is a two-level structure, consisting of a level 1 root node and a series of level 2 nodes (i.e., leaves). There are three kinds of useful flat file structures. They are:

- **sequential flat structure**: This is a flat file structure in which the nodes are not named. The root node does not have any DU. The only file access contexts of interest are FA and UA.
- **ordered flat structure**: This is a flat file structure in which the leaf nodes are named. The root neither has a name nor a DU.
- **ordered flat structure with unique names**: This is a special case of an ordered flat structure with uniquely named leaf nodes.

A degenerate file structure is specified using a **constraint set**. A constraint set is a set of restrictions and refinements of the hierarchical file access structure, specifying a less general model tailored to the needs of a particular class of applications. The items it specifies include:

- file access actions: This defines a subset of file actions that are applicable to the constraint set. For example, the file actions which are applicable to the unstructured constraint set are "read", "replace", "extend", and "erase".

• file access contexts: This is a list of the file access contexts that are meaningful to the constraint set. The FTAM standard has defined seven file access contexts. For example, only the UA access context is meaningful to the unstructured constraint set.
• creation state: This describes the state of the file structure immediately after creation. For example, an unstructured file structure has an empty DU immediately after creation.
• beginning/end of file: This describes the beginning/end FADU of the file structure. For example, the beginning of the sequential file structure is the root node.
• location after open: This indicates the location of the FADU immediately after successful completion of the "open" action. For example, it may be "first", "beginning of file", etc. For the sequential flat structure, the location after open is the root node. In general, the location after open does not have to be identical to the beginning of the file.
• read/write whole file: This describes the file access context and the FADU identity when the whole file is read/written. For the sequential flat structure, the access context is either FA or UA, and the FADU identity is "begin".

Every constraint set has a constraint set identifier which can be referenced by either an OSI standard or a functional profile. Table 17.1 gives the specification of the unstructured constraint set. The format of Table 17.1 is based on a template defined by the FTAM standard.

Constraint set descriptor	Unstructured
Constraint set identifier	{iso standard 8571 constraint-set (4) unstructured (1)}
Node names	None
File access actions	"Read", "Replace", "Extend", "Erase"
Qualified actions	None
Available access contexts	UA
Creation state	Root node with an empty data unit
Location after open	First
Beginning of file	Not applicable
End of file	Not applicable
Read whole file	Read in access context UA with FADU Identity of "first"
Write whole file	Transfer a single DU (without a node descriptor) with FADU Identity of "first" and file access action of "replace"

TABLE 17.1   Unstructured Constraint Set

Note that a constraint set does not specify the abstract syntaxes associated with the DUs of a file. A further step towards facilitating applications is the concept of a **document type**. A document type specifies not only the structure of a file, but also its file contents. For example, the FTAM-1 document type describes a virtual file whose structure is defined by the unstructured constraint set, and whose contents can contain characters from any defined character set in the ASN.1 standard. Table 17.2 gives the specification of the FTAM-1 document type, using a template defined by the FTAM standard. Other FTAM document types are:

- FTAM-2: This is a sequential flat file of text data.
- FTAM-3: This is an unstructured file of binary data.
- FTAM-4: This is a sequential flat file of binary data.
- NBS-6: This is a sequential flat file. The types of DUs associated with the level 1 nodes include INTEGER, REAL, BOOLEAN, BIT STRING, and CHARACTER STRING.
- NBS-7: This is an NBS-6 file where the level 1 nodes are ordered, thus permitting random access.

document type name	{iso standard 8571 document-type (5) unstructured-text (1)} "ISO FTAM unstructured text"
abstract syntax names a) name of asname1	{iso standard 8571 document-type (5) unstructured-text (1)} "FTAM unstructured text abstract syntax"
transfer syntax names	{joint-iso-ccitt asn1(1) basic-encoding (1)} "Basic encoding of a single ASN.1 type"

Parameter syntax
    PARAMETERS ::= SEQUENCE
        { universal-class number [0] IMPLICIT INTEGER OPTIONAL,
        maximum-string length [1] IMPLICIT INTEGER OPTIONAL,
        string-significance [2] IMPLICIT INTEGER
        {variable (0), fixed (1), not-significant (2)} OPTIONAL}	

file model	{iso standard 8571 file-model (3) hierarchical (1)} "FTAM hierarchical file model"
constraint set	{iso standard 8571 constraint-set (4) unstructured (1)} "FTAM unstructured constraint set"

File contents
    Datatype1 ::= CHOICE
 	
        { PrintableString, TeletexString, VideotexString, IA5String,
        GraphicString, VisibleString, GeneralString }	

TABLE 17.2 FTAM-1 Document Type

With the above background on a virtual file, we are ready to describe a virtual file in terms of attributes. A virtual file can be described by two classes of attributes: file attributes and activity attributes. The values of a **file attribute** remain constant throughout the lifetime of a file unless specifically modified. For example, the name of a file is a file attribute. The date and time of creation of a file is another one. An **activity attribute** describes a file relative to a particular FTAM dialogue in progress. It is dynamic in nature and has no meaning outside the dialogue. For example, the current location of a file is a dynamic attribute. The current access request is another. Unlike a file attribute, an activity attribute (such as the current identity) may not have a file associated with it

filename
permitted actions
contents type
storage account
date and time of creation
date and time of last modification
date and time of lastread access
date and time of last attribute modification
identity of creator
identity of last modifier
identity of last reader
identity of last attribute modifier
file availability
filesize
future filesize
access control
legal qualifications
private use

TABLE 17.3   File Attributes

current access request
current initiator identity
current location
current processing mode
current calling AET
current responding AET
current account
current concurrency control
current locking style
current access passwords

TABLE 17.4   Activity Attributes and their Types

Table 17.3 lists a few file attributes. Some of them are explained below:

• permitted actions: This is a boolean vector attribute indicating the set of file operations that can be performed on a file.
• contents type: This is a scalar attribute indicating the document type of a file.
• storage account: This is a scalar attribute identifying the authority responsible for the charges of the accumulated file storage.
• file availability: This is a scalar attribute indicating if a delay is to be expected before the file is opened. The value can be either "immediate availability" or "deferred availability."
• access control: This is a set attribute defining conditions under which access to the file is valid.

• legal qualifications: This is a scalar attribute conveying information about the legal status and usage of the file. For example, its value can be "copyright protected - not to be reproduced without permission."

Table 17.4 lists a few activity attributes. Some of them are explained below:

• active contents type: This is a scalar attribute identifying the document type used for the FTAM dialogue. It is derived from the contents type attribute.
• current location: This is a scalar attribute indicating the current position within the file.
• current access request: This is a vector attribute indicating the requested file actions.
• current concurrency control: The initiator of the FTAM dialogue uses this attribute to specify a concurrency control mode for each requested access action in the current access request attribute. The value of this attribute is one of the following: "not required", "shared", "exclusive", and "no access".
• current initiator identity: This is a scalar attribute that indicates the authentication information established by the file service provider about the initiator when the FTAM dialogue is established. Note that this attribute is not specific to a file.
• current access passwords: This is a vector attribute in which each component gives a value associated with each action of the current access request attribute.

Because there are many file attributes and activity attributes, related attributes can be grouped into an **attribute group**. The **kernel group** contains the important attributes that should be supported by any FTAM implementation. The **security group** contains security-related attributes such as access control, legal qualifications, and current access passwords. The **storage group** consists of storage-related attributes such as storage account and filesize. Finally, the **private group** consists of user-defined attributes for a specific application. These attribute groups are negotiated during the FTAM dialogue establishment.

17.2 FTAM Service

Because there are many FTAM service elements, they are grouped by means of functional units. The FTAM functional units are:

• Kernel: This supports the basic functions for establishing and releasing an FTAM association, and selecting and deselecting of a file for further processing.
• Read: This supports data transfer from a responder to an initiator.
• Write: This supports data transfer from an initiator to a responder.
• File Access: This is used to locate a specific FADU for subsequent file operations.
• Limited File Management: This supports file management operations such as creating and deleting files, and interrogating the attributes of files.

Functional Unit	Service Elements	Functional Unit	Service Elements
Kernel	F-INITIALIZE F-TERMINATE F-ABORT F-SELECT F-DESELECT	File access Limited file management	F-LOCATE F-ERASE F-CREATE F-DELETE F-READ-ATTRIB
Read	F-READ F-DATA F-DATA-END F-TRANSFER-END F-CANCEL F-OPEN F-CLOSE	Enhanced file management Grouping Recovery	F-CHANGE-ATTRIB F-BEGIN-GROUP F-END-GROUP F-RECOVERY
Write	F-WRITE F-DATA F-DATA-END F-TRANSFER-END F-CANCEL F-OPEN F-CLOSE	Restart FADU Locking	F-CHECK F-CANCEL F-RESTART F-CHECK F-CANCEL

TABLE 17.5   Functional Units and their Service Elements

• Enhanced File Management: This is used to change the attributes of files.
• Grouping: This allows several regimes (to be explained shortly) to be established in one exchange.
• FADU Locking: Two types of concurrency control are provided by the FTAM standard. They are File concurrency and FADU locking. File concurrency is individually applied to each of the possible permitted actions on a virtual file. It is first applied when the file is selected and later applied when the file is opened. FADU locking provides concurrency control on a FADU basis. The FADU Locking functional unit allows both types of concurrency control.
• Recovery: This allows an initiator to perform recovery actions when a failure occurs after a file is opened.
• Restart: This allows a data transfer to be interrupted and restarted at some checkpoint.

Table 17.5 shows the service elements contained in each functional unit. These service elements allow peer FTAM processes to build a working environment. For example, the initiator and the responder establish their identities and determine the functional units to be used over the FTAM dialogue at the first stage. At the next stage, the initiator identifies the file which is the subject of the file operation. At later stages, the peer FTAM processes perform file operations. These stages are known as **regimes**. Thus an FTAM dialogue is structured into regimes (Figure 17.5) which are completely nested within each other. These regimes are the FTAM regime, the file selection regime, the file open regime, and the data transfer regime. During each regime, only certain service elements can be invoked. Thus, regimes are used to constrain the use of service elements.

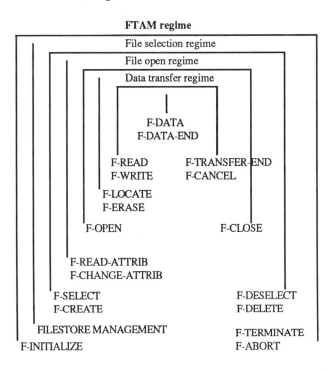

FIGURE 17.5   FTAM Regimes

state result	functional units
action result	attribute groups
called AET	shared ASE information
calling AET	FTAM QOS
responding AET	communication QOS
called presentation address	contents type list
calling presentation address	initiator identity
responding presentation address	account
presentation context management	filestore password
application context name	diagnostic
service class	checkpoint window

TABLE 17.6   Parameters of F-INITIALIZE

The outermost regime, the **FTAM regime**, is established between peer FTAM processes by use of **F-INITIALIZE**. Table 17.6 gives the parameters associated with F-INITIALIZE. Some of these are explained below:

- state result: This parameter indicates whether the FTAM regime has been established. The value is either "success" or "failure."
- presentation context management: This indicates whether the Presentation Context Management functional unit is to be used or not.
- attribute groups: This parameter negotiates the set of attribute groups to be used over the application association.
- FTAM QOS: The initiator uses this parameter to specify the class of error recovery capability. There are four classes. Class 0 means that no error recovery is to be provided. Class 1 means that recovery is needed to correct any damage in the data transfer regime. Class 2 means that recovery is needed to fix any damage within the file open regime. Class 3 means that recovery is needed to fix any damage within any regime. Obviously, recovery mechanisms needed for Class 3 are more complex than recovery mechanisms needed for the other classes.
- diagnostic: This parameter, as used in almost all the FTAM service elements, conveys detailed information on the failure of a requested action. The information indicates the diagnostic type, the error-identifier, who observed the error, and who caused the error.
- checkpoint window: This parameter indicates, for each direction of transmission, the maximum number of checkpoints which may remain unacknowledged.

For normal termination, an FTAM dialogue can leave the FTAM regime only if it has left all the inner regimes. **F-U-ABORT**, on the other hand, is available for a user to abnormally terminate all the regimes. The service provider can also use **F-P-ABORT** to inform its users that it cannot continue to provide the service and all regimes are lost. The F-P-ABORT service element generally results from an A-P-ABORT passed up by ACSE. The initiator can also terminate a regime by using **F-TERMINATE**. While either F-U-ABORT or F-P-ABORT does a disorderly closing, F-TERMINATE does an orderly closing.

The **file selection regime**, the first of the inner regimes, identifies a specific file (either old or new) which is the subject of the subsequent file operations. This regime is entered either by selecting a file using **F-SELECT** or by creating a new one using **F-CREATE**. File contents are not accessible in this regime. Either F-SELECT or F-CREATE can specify activity attributes such as current requested access, current access password, and current concurrency control. Once the file selection regime has been established, all the subsequent file activities are directed at the specified file until the regime is closed. Certain file management activities can be undertaken within the file selection regime when no further inner regime is in force. These activities are achieved by the use of **F-READ-ATTRIBUTE** and **F-CHANGE-ATTRIBUTE** which allows the initiator to read and change the attributes of the selected file respectively. The file selection regime is closed by the use of either **F-DESELECT** or **F-DELETE**, the latter causing the file to be destroyed.

The **file open regime** makes the file contents available for reading/writing. It is entered by **F-OPEN** which includes the processing mode, the contents type, and the activity identifier parameters. The processing mode parameter has the effect of reducing the actions which were earlier established by the requested access parameter of F-SELECT/F-CREATE. The contents type parameter is used to make sure that the structure of the file is understood by both the initiator and the responder. For example, if the initiator wants to read from a file, it needs to know the structure of that file. The contents type parameter is used to pass this structural information. The activity identifier is used to identify a record for error recovery purpose. The initiator must secure the record in its docket before it invokes F-OPEN. A **docket** here is a set of information (e.g., an activity identifier) about a regime which must be preserved for the purpose of error recovery. When the responder receives the activity identifier via the F-OPEN.indication primitive, it should secure the activity identifier which may be used for recovery in the future. To exit the file open regime, the initiator invokes **F-CLOSE**. After exiting, the initiator can use F-OPEN again to enter a different file open regime.

Within the file open regime, there are two service elements providing file management services to an initiator: **F-LOCATE** and **F-ERASE**. F-LOCATE allows the initiator to locate a specific FADU in the opened file, so subsequent file activities will be directed to this FADU. F-ERASE, on the other hand, erases a FADU from the file.

Any number of consecutive data transfer regimes can be established within the file open regime. Each data transfer regime is associated with a FADU. A **data transfer regime** supports the transfer of data for reading or writing a FADU. It is established by means of either **F-READ** or **F-WRITE**. These service elements determine the data flow of the DUs. F-READ implies data flows from the responder to the initiator, while F-WRITE implies data flows from the initiator to the responder. They both contain a FADU identity parameter which is the subject of transfer. F-READ contains a file access context parameter which specifies the data elements of the subject FADU that the initiator would like to read. F-WRITE contains a parameter to distinguish the various write actions, i.e., "extend", "insert" or "replace".

Once the data transfer regime has been established by either F-READ or F-WRITE, the non-confirmed **F-DATA** service element can be invoked. Each invocation of F-DATA causes the transfer of a single data element associated with the FADU. The order of transfer of these data elements depend on the file access context. In general, the sender would need to issue a sequence of F-DATA.request primitives before it can finish the data transfer of a FADU. When it is done, it invokes **F-DATA-END**. On a bulky data transfer, the initiator indicates the completion of a transfer by invoking **F-TRANSFER-END**. Receipt of an F-TRANSFER-END.indication or F-TRANSFER-END.confirm (as appropriate) primitive informs the sender of the F-DATA.request primitive that no further error recovery actions are required. Within a data transfer regime, **F-CANCEL** is used to cancel a data transfer regime. This confirmed service element can be invoked by either the initiator or the responder.

So far, we have discussed regimes and most of the service elements. The remaining service elements are those found in the Grouping, the Recovery, and the Restart functional units. The Grouping functional unit, if available, serves to reduce the number of interactions between the initiator and the responder. It contains two service elements, F-

BEGIN-GROUP and **F-END-GROUP**. The initiator invokes F-BEGIN-GROUP to indicate to the responder that it is about to invoke a set of "grouped" service primitives which may have the effect of establishing or closing more than a single regime. For example, the initiator can group an F-CREATE.request primitive and an F-OPEN.request primitive together. F-GROUP-END conveys the end of such a grouping.

The **F-CHECK** service element, which is present in both the Recovery and the Restart functional units, provides a facility for the sender to insert checkpoints in the data flow. This is a confirmed service. However, the issuer of an F-CHECK.request primitive may keep on sending data without waiting for an F-CHECK.confirm primitive until the number of outstanding checkpoint requests reaches a certain window size. The window size, which is a parameter of F-INITIALIZE, is negotiated during the establishment of the FTAM dialogue. The **F-RESTART** service element in the Restart functional unit is used primarily to recover from Class 1 errors. Either the initiator or the responder can invoke F-RESTART to negotiate a secured checkpoint where the data transfer can be restarted. Hence, F-RESTART should be used in conjunction with F-CHECK.

The **F-RECOVER** service element in the Recovery functional unit is used to recover from Class 2 or Class 3 errors. If an FTAM entity detects a Class 2 error, it should first invoke F-CANCEL. After this, the two FTAM entities should close the file to prepare for the F-RECOVERY exchange. If an FTAM entity detects a Class 3 error (e.g., it receives a F-P-ABORT.request primitive), it should first locate its docket possibly by means of an F-INITIALIZE exchange. It fetches the activity identifier from its docket before it initiates the F-RECOVERY exchange. The recovery procedures to be applied are negotiated at the time of the FTAM regime establishment. In general, F-RECOVER is followed by F-RESTART, or F-READ/ F-WRITE.

Because of the large number of functional units, the FTAM standard defined five service classes where each service class is characterized by a set of functional units addressed to a specific range of applications. These service classes are: **Access (A)**, **Transfer and Management (TM)**, **Transfer (T)**, **Management (M)**, and **Unconstrained (U)**. Table 17.7 shows the mandatory and optional functional units in each service class. In negotiating an FTAM regime, the initiator proposes a combination of service classes. The responder modifies this combination by removing the classes that it cannot support and returning the remaining combination to the initiator. The initiator then compares the combination proposed on the F-INITIALIZE.request primitive with the value returned. It then selects the highest service class, with the service classes ranked from highest to lowest in the following order: A, TM, T, M, and U. For example, if the initiator proposes TM, T, and M which can all be supported by the responder, then the service class selected will be TM because TM has a highest priority of the three. Each service class is briefly described below.

- **Access class**: This class, which is the richest class in terms of the variety of functional units required, permits an initiator to read or modify certain substructures of a file. There is no constraint on any sequence of events.

• **Transfer class**: This class permits transfer of files between peer FTAM entities. By requiring the Grouping functional unit, it emphasizes simplicity in file transfer. For example, the F-SELECT.request and the F-OPEN.request primitives are concatenated to establish a file open regime.

• **Management class**: This allows the initiator to interrogate or change the attributes of an existing file. It emphasizes simplicity in file management by including the Grouping functional unit. For example, the F-SELECT.request, the F-READ-ATTRIBUTE.request, and the F-DESELECT.request primitives can be concatenated to provide a more efficient way to interrogate an attribute of a file. Similarly, the FSELECT.request, the F-CHANGE-ATTRIBUTE.request, and the F-DESELECT.request primitives can be concatenated. Note that the Enhanced File Management functional unit is only optional for this class.

• **Transfer and Management class**: This is essentially the union of the transfer class and the management class.

• **Unconstrained class**: Only the Kernel functional unit is mandatory. There is no constraint imposed on the use of the service elements. Therefore, this class leaves the selection of functional units entirely open to negotiation. This class is suitable for future requirements that have not yet been well defined.

Functional Unit	Service Classes				
	T	A	M	TM	U
Kernel	M	M	M	M	M
Read	#	M	-	#	O
Write	#	M	-	#	O
File access	-	M	-	-	O
Limited file management	O	O	M	O	O
Enhanced file management	O	O	O	O	O
Grouping	M	O	M	M	O
Recovery	O	O	-	O	O
Restart data transfer	O	O	-	O	O

M: mandatory   O: optional   -: not available
#: at least one of read or write must be included

TABLE 17.7 FTAM Service Classes

17.3   FTAM Protocol

The FTAM protocol is quite straightforward. First we examine a couple of FTAM APDUs. Then we illustrate the operation of the FTAM protocol using a few examples.

An FTAM PDU has the same name as the corresponding service primitive. For example, the PDU sent as a result of an F-INITIALIZE.request primitive is called an F-INITIALIZE-request FPDU. Two examples on FTAM FPDUs are given next.

Example 17.1

```
F-INITIALIZE-request ::= SEQUENCE {
    protocol-version              Protocol-Version DEFAULT {version-1},
    implem-inform                 Implementation-Information OPTIONAL,
    present-context-inform        IMPLICIT BOOLEAN DEFAULT FALSE,
    service-class                 Service-Class DEFAULT {transfer-class},
    functional-units              Functional-Units,
    attribute-groups              Attribute-Groups DEFAULT {},
    shared-ASE-inform             Shared-ASE-Information OPTIONAL,
    ftam-qos                      FTAM-QOS,
    contents-type-list            Contents-Type-List OPTIONAL,
    initiator-identity            User-Identity OPTIONAL,
    account                       Account OPTIONAL,
    filestore-password            Password OPTIONAL,
    checkpoint-window             IMPLICIT INTEGER DEFAULT 1}
```

It is useful to compare the fields here with the parameters of an F-INITIALIZE.request primitive.

Example 17.2

```
F-OPEN-response ::= SEQUENCE {
    state-result                  State-Result DEFAULT success,
    action-result                 Action-Result DEFAULT success,
    contents-type                 Contents-Type-Attribute,
    concurrency-control           Concurrency-Control OPTIONAL,
    shared-ASE-information        Shared-ASE-Information OPTIONAL,
    diagnostic                    Diagnostic OPTIONAL,
    recovery-mode                 IMPLICIT INTEGER
                                  {none(0), at-start-of-file(1), at-any-active-checkpoint(2)}
                                  DEFAULT none,
    presentation-action           IMPLICIT BOOLEAN DEFAULT FALSE}
```

The above gives the structure of an F-OPEN-response FPDU. The presentation-action flag is set if the responder follows the response by a P-ALTER-CONTEXT exchange.

Note that the F-DATA and the F-CHECK service elements are not associated with any FPDUs since they are pass through service elements.

The FTAM protocol uses services from ACSE and the Presentation Layer. The use of the Context Management functional unit is optional. If an initiator needs to define abstract syntaxes during the file open regime establishment, then the Context Management functional unit must be available. Both the Restart and the Recovery functional units require the availability of the Minor Synchronize functional unit.

FTAM FPDUs are sent as data values, either on a presentation primitive or in the user information of an ACSE primitive. The following FTAM FPDUs are carried by the ACSE primitives: F-INITIALIZE-request, F-INITIALIZE-response, F-TERMINATE-request, F-TERMINATE-response, F-P-ABORT-request, and F-U-ABORT-request. The following FTAM FPDUs are carried by the P-RESYNCHRONIZE primitives: F-CANCEL-request, F-CANCEL-response, F-RESTART-request, and F-RESTART-response. The F-CHECK-request and the F-CHECK-response FPDUs are carried by the P-SYNC-MINOR primitives. The rest of the FTAM FPDUs are carried by the P-DATA primitives. Since the FTAM protocol machine can perform concatenation of FPDUs, the PSDU carried in a P-DATA primitive is in general a sequence of PDVs.

Next, we illustrate the operation of the FTAM protocol using a few examples.

Example 17.3

This example explains how the initiator sets up an FTAM regime. Upon receipt of an F-INITIALIZE.request primitive from the initiator, the initiating protocol machine constructs an F-INITIALIZE-request FPDU. This PDU is passed as user-data to ACSE using an A-ASSOCIATE.request primitive. The presentation requirements and session requirements parameters of the A-ASSOCIATE.request must be set to at least the corresponding functional units derived from the parameters of the F-INITIALIZE.request primitive. The initiating protocol machine then waits for the receipt of an A-ASSOCIATE.confirm primitive which will contain an F-INITIALIZE-response FPDU as user information. If the result parameter of the A-ASSOCIATE.confirm primitive indicates success, then an F-INITIALIZE.confirm primitive will be issued by the initiating protocol machine.

The next three examples illustrate pieces of the operation to transfer a big file. FPDUs generated by this protocol are carried by P-DATA or P-RESYNCHRONIZE whose type is either "abandon" or "restart".

To illustrate the operation, we introduce a few data structures: read/write indicator, discard indicator, checkpoint identifier expected, next synchronization point number, synchronization offset, and outstanding checkpoint counter. The read/write indicator records the direction of the data transfer; its value is either "reading", "writing", or "unset". The discard indicator is used to signal that data received during cancellation or before recovery are invalid and should be thrown away; its value is either "unset" or "set". The checkpoint identifier expected identifies the next checkpoint in the current sequence of checkpoints associated with the data. The next SPSN gives the serial number of the next session synchronization point. The synchronization offset is a constant established when a read or write bulk data transfer is initiated or recovered, giving the difference between the checkpoint identifier expected and the next SPSN. Finally, the outstanding checkpoint counter records the number of checkpoints which have not been acknowledged.

Example 17.4

Here is how an initiator reads bulky data. Upon receipt of an F-READ.request primitive from the initiator, the initiating protocol machine sends an F-READ-request FPDU using P-DATA. If the Minor Synchronize functional unit is active, it will issue a P-TOKEN-GIVE.request for the minor synchronize token, set the appropriate checkpoint identifier and outstanding checkpoint counter, calculate the synchronization offset, and set the read/write indicator to "reading".

Example 17.5

This example explains the write actions during a bulk data transfer. Upon receipt of an F-DATA.request primitive from the initiator, the initiating protocol machine will add the data element given by an F-DATA.request primitive to the current PSDU. Note that the data elements given by a sequence of F-DATA.request primitives can be concatenated into a single PSDU, provided that no checkpoints need to be inserted in the sequence. Upon receipt of an F-CHECK.request primitive from the initiator, the initiating protocol machine should terminate the current PSDU, increase the outstanding checkpoint counter, verify that the checkpoint window has not been exceeded, issue a P-SYNC-MINOR.request primitive, and finally increase the expected checkpoint identifier and the next SPSN.

Example 17.6

This example explains some of the actions taken by an FTAM entity to cancel a data transfer. Assume that the Resynchronize functional unit is active. Upon receipt of an F-CANCEL.request primitive from an FTAM entity, the FTAM protocol machine will issue a P-RESYNCHRONIZE.request primitive of the "abandon" type. It then sets the discard indicator. If the issuer of F-CANCEL is an FTAM responder, the responder must return the synchronization minor token to the initiator, and set the outstanding checkpoint counter to zero. Upon receipt of an F-CANCEL-request FPDU, the initiator will discard any undelivered user data, issue an F-CANCEL.indication primitive, and set the outstanding checkpoint counter to zero.

17.4 FTAM Filestore Management Services

Note from Figure 17.6 that filestore management can be performed as soon as the FTAM dialogue is established. To accommodate filestore management, the concept of a virtual filestore is broadened to include not only files, but also file-directories and references. This generalization calls for the addition of a few more functional units, and a redefinition of the regimes studied in Section 17.2.

There are three types of objects in a filestore: files, file-directories, and references. A **file-directory** is an object maintaining a parenthood relation with zero or more subordinate objects. A **reference** object maintains a link to another object which is either a file-directory or a file. The objects in the filestore can be structured as a tree using the parenthood relation. The root of this tree is either a file or a file-directory. It cannot be a reference. When the root is a file, that file is the only object within the filestore.

The tree structure of a filestore permits naming of objects in the filestore using path names. The sequence of parenthood relations starting from the root to an object in the tree is the **primary path** to the object. The sequence of object names in the primary path to an object is the **primary pathname** of the object.

Just as a file is described by file and activity attributes, a file-directory object or a reference object can be also described by object and activity attributes. An **object attribute** is an attribute used to describe an object in a virtual filestore. Thus, it can be used to describe a file, a file-directory, or a reference. Some object attributes, called the **generic object attributes,** are so general that they can be used to describe all three kinds of objects in a virtual filestore. Examples of generic object attributes are:

- object name: Its value is a scalar attribute of type GraphicString.
- object type: Its value is either "file", "file-directory", or "reference".
- others are storage account, date and time of creation, identity of creator, legal qualifications, date and time of last attribute modification, identity of last attribute modifier, access control, permitted actions, object size, future object size, and unique permanent identifier.

Examples of object attributes specific to file-directory objects are:

- identity of last reader: This indicates the identity of the last initiating user that listed the file-directory.
- date and time of last access: This indicates when the parenthood relation maintained by a file-directory was last listed.
- date and time of last modification: This indicates when the parenthood relation maintained by a file-directory was last modified.

Examples of object attributes specific to reference objects are:

- linked object: This identifies the object to which a reference links.
- linked object type: This indicates the type of the linked object to which a reference links. The possible values are either "file" or "file-directory".

In addition to object attributes, there are activity attributes which are used to describe a file regime. Examples of activity attributes are:

- current name prefix: This attribute value gives part of the complete pathname which prefixes incomplete pathnames.
- generalized selection group: This attribute value is a group of pathnames, identifying one or more files in the filestore. Note that this attribute describes a

property of the generalized selection regime. It does not address any object in the filestore.

• current pathname: This attribute value gives the complete pathname of a selected object in the filestore.

Functional Unit	Service Elements
Limited Filestore Management	F-CHANGE-PREFIX F-LIST
Enhanced Filestore Management	F-CREATE-DIRECTORY F-LINK F-UNLINK F-READ-LINK-ATTRIBUTE
Object Manipulation	F-MOVE F-COPY
Group Manipulation	F-GROUP-SELECT F-GROUP-DESELECT F-GROUP-MOVE F-GROUP-COPY F-GROUP-LIST F-SELECT-ANOTHER

TABLE 17.8   Functional Units in Filestore Management

With the inclusion of file-directories and references in a filestore, more service elements (Table 17.8) have to be introduced for the purpose of filestore management. These service elements are briefly explained below.

• **F-CHANGE-PREFIX:** This is used to update the value of the current name prefix attribute.
• **F-LIST:** This is used to list all the objects subordinate to a file-directory.
• **F-GROUP-SELECT:** This is used to identify a group of pathnames of file objects with attributes matching a given attribute value assertion list.
• **F-GROUP-DESELECT:** This is used to disassociate a group of pathnames identified earlier by F-GROUP-SELECT.
• **F-GROUP-MOVE:** This is used to place a selected group of objects in a specified file-directory.
• **F-GROUP-COPY:** This is used to duplicate the objects in a selected group and place the duplicates in a specified file-directory.
• **F-GROUP-LIST:** This is used to list the pathnames and selected attributes of the objects in a selected group.
• **F-SELECT-ANOTHER:** This is used to select the next object which has not yet been selected. It must be used in conjunction with a selected group.

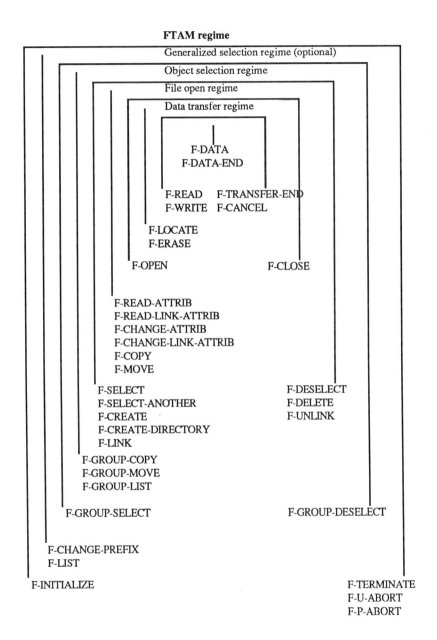

FIGURE 17.6   FTAM Regimes with the addition of Filestore Management

- **F-SELECT**: This is used to select a specific object by a pathname.
- **F-CREATE-DIRECTORY**: This is used to create a file-directory.
- **F-LINK**: This is used to create a reference.
- **F-UNLINK**: This is used to delete an existing reference, leaving the object to which it was linked intact in the filestore.

- **F-READ-LINK-ATTRIBUTE**: This is used to interrogate the object attributes of a reference.
- **F-CHANGE-LINK-ATTRIBUTE**: This is used to modify the object attributes of a reference.

To accommodate file-directories and references in a virtual filestore, the semantics of some of the service elements in Table 17.5 have to be generalized. For example, the F-SELECT service element can be used to select not only files but also file-directories or references. The regimes given in Figure 17.6 have to be modified as well. Figure 17.7 gives the new FTAM regime diagram. Note the addition of the generalized selection regime and the replacement of the file selection regime by the object selection regime. The FTAM regime is the same as before, except some filestore management services such as F-LIST and F-CHANGE-PREFIX can be performed. The generalized selection regime and the object selection regime are briefly explained below.

An FTAM user enters the **generalized selection regime** by invoking the F-GROUP-SELECT service element. Access passwords may be needed to enter this regime. F-GROUP-SELECT is used to identify a group of file objects and reference objects. Note that no file-directory objects are allowed in the group. This service is extremely useful when there is a need to apply the same operation to each file in a group of files.

When there is no need to access a group of file objects, the initiator can bypass the generalized selection regime and move directly to the **object selection regime**. Thus, the use of the generalized selection regime is optional. The filestore management service elements allowed during the generalized selection regime are F-GROUP-COPY, F-GROUP-MOVE, and F-GROUP-LIST. F-GROUP-DESELECT is used to exit from this regime.

The object selection regime allows the initiator to select/create a file, a directory, or a reference. Figure 17.6 shows the five service elements which are used to enter the object selection regime and the three service elements which are used to exit the regime. In addition, there are six service elements available within the regime to perform object management such as reading or modifying object attributes.

The file open regime and the data transfer regime are basically the same as before. Note that in the file open regime, F-COPY is similar to F-MOVE, except that it leaves the original object in place.

17.5   MAP 3.0 FTAM API

Currently, we are facing an FTAM API "muddle". Almost every major FTAM vendor has its own proprietary FTAM API, but no FTAM API has yet been endorsed by multiple vendors. The MAP 3.0 FTAM API which we are going to describe in this section is the only existing non-proprietary FTAM API. It is part of the MAP 3.0 specification which was published in 1988. Presently, X/Open and IEEE are developing their non-proprietary FTAM APIs, known as XFTAM and IEEE 1238 respectively.

The MAP FTAM API consists of two levels of services: Context Free services and Context Sensitive services. **Context Free Services** provide a high-level service. Users do not need any knowledge of the FTAM protocol. For example, a user can move a file from one filestore to another without any interaction with the FTAM protocol machine. Instead, between the FTAM API and the FTAM protocol machine, there is a special High Level Service Provider. This provider will ensure that the protocol exchange between the FTAM entities is carried out in a proper order to complete a context free request. On the other hand, **Context Sensitive Services** are more primitive in nature and require knowledge of the FTAM protocol. A context sensitive request is sensitive to the previous requests. For example, it is improper to issue an F-SELECT.request primitive before issuing an F-INITIALIZE.request primitive.

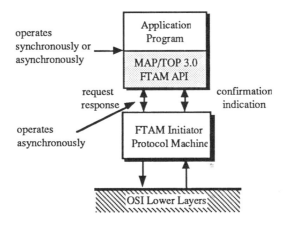

FIGURE 17.7   Conceptual Model of MAP/TOP FTAM API

Figure 17.7 shows that an application program can call an MAP FTAM API function either synchronously or asynchronously. The API then issues a request to the FTAM initiator, and finally the FTAM initiator sends a request to the remote system.

Next, we describe the functions available in the MAP FTAM API. The first group of functions are used for connection management. In essense, it provides an API to ACSE. The second group specifies the functions for the context free services. The third group defines the functions for the context sensitive services. There are also functions for the memory management and event management services which we will not discuss in this text. Event management services are used to retrieve the events arriving from the FTAM protocol machine when the asynchronous mode is selected by the application program.

- **Connection Management functions**

The functions here provide an interface to ACSE. Not only can they be used with the FTAM API, but they can be also used with the MMS API which is also specified as part of the MAP 3.0 specification. A brief description of each function follows:

- **ft_aeactivation:** This function activates an FTAM AE. This function must precede connection establishment and any file operations.
- **ft_aedeactivation:** This function deactivates an FTAM AE.
- **ft_abort:** This function brings the FTAM association regime to an abrupt halt at any time after an ft_connect request has been issued.
- **ft_aereset:** This function aborts all open and pending connections.
- **ft_connect:** This function establishes a connection with a peer FTAM AE.
- **ft_ireceive:** This function allows all abort indications to be passed to the user.
- **ft_rrequest:** This function releases an association between two FTAM AEs.

- **Context Free functions**

Below is a short description of each context free function.

- **ft_fcopy:** This function allows a file to be copied between any two filestores.
- **ft_fmove:** This function allows a file to be moved between any two filestores.
- **ft_fdelete:** This function deletes a file from a filestore.
- **ft_frattributes:** This function allows a user to read the values of a file attribute.
- **ft_fcattributes:** This function allows a user to modify a file attribute.

Example 17.7

```
Return_code
ft_fcopy (source_aet, source_filename, destination_aet, destination_filename,
        return_event_name, input_dcb, output_dcb).


Applic_entity_title            source_aet;
Filename                       source_filename;
Appli_entity_title             destination_aet;
Filename                       destination_filename;
Return_event_name              return_event_name;
struct ft_fcopy_in_dcb {
    Initiator_identity         source_init_id;
    Account                    source_account;
    File_store_password        source_filestore_pw;
    struct File_password       source_file_passwords;
    Initiator_identity         dest_init_id;
    Account                    dest_account;
    File_store_password        dest_filestore_pw;
    struct File_password       dest_file_passwords;
}
struct ft_fcopy_out_dcb {
    unit16                     size;
```

    struct Attributes   attributes;
    enum Action_result   action_result;
    Return_code   return_code;
    struct Diagnostic   *diagnostic;
}

The above gives the declaration of the ft_fcopy function in C format. Some of the parameters are explained next. The source_aet and the destination_aet are the AE titles of the FTAM filestore associated with the source system and the destination system respectively. The source_filename contains the name of the file of which a copy is made. The dest_filename contains the name of the file to which a file is copied on the destination system. The return_event_name contains the name of the return event. The input_dcb is a pointer to an input data block where the optional parameters of the ft_fcopy function are stored. The output_dcb is a pointer to an output data block which stores the results of the ft_fcopy function.

- **Context Sensitive functions**

Context sensitive functions can be either high-level or low-level. A high-level function is "grouped" in the sense that it is equivalent to a sequence of low-level functions. However, it still requires knowledge of the FTAM protocol. A brief description of the grouped high-level functions follows.

- **ft_fopen:** This function allows a user to open a file and access the contents of a file in the filestore.
- **ft_fclose:** This function allows a user to close a file. The file closed is the file which was most recently opened on the specified connection.
- **ft_freset:** This function allows a user to rewind the file to the beginning of the file.
- **ft_fseek:** This function allows a user to locate a specified FADU within the file.
- **ft_fextend:** This function allows a user to position at the end of the file.

The low-level functions are described below:

- **ft_select:** This function is used to make a file available for access.
- **ft_deselect:** This function is used to end the access to a file previously selected.
- **ft_open:** This function is used to make a previously selected file available for access to its contents. Note that this function is similar in functionality to ft_fopen.
- **ft_close:** This function is used to make a previously opened file unavailable for access to its content.
- **ft_create:** This function creates a file.
- **ft_delete:** This function deletes a file.
- **ft_rattributes:** This function is used to read the values of the attributes of a selected file.
- **ft_cattributes:** This function is used to modify the values of the attributes of a selected file.

- **ft_read:** This function is used to transfer part, or all, of the contents of a previously opened file in the filestore.
- **ft_write:** This function is used to transfer data which is to be placed into a previously opened file in the filestore.
- **ft_erase:** This function is used to remove part, or all of contents of a previously opened file.
- **ft_locate:** This function is used to move to a specified position of a previously opened file.
- **ft_sdata:** This function is used to transfer a block of data to a previously opened file.
- **ft_rdata:** This function is used to receive a block of data from a previously opened file.
- **ft_edata:** This function is used to indicate the end of a sequence of ft_sdata invocations and mark the end of the data being transferred to a previously opened file.
- **ft_etransfer:** This function is used to indicate the end of the data transfer phase for a previously opened file.
- **ft_bgroup:** This function allows a user to designate the beginning of a series of primitive requests to be treated by the FTAM protocol machine as one PSDU.
- **ft_egroup:** This function allows a user to designate the end of a series of primitive requests to be treated by the FTAM protocol machine as one PSDU.
- **ft_cancel:** This function allows a user to end the data transfer in progress to/from the filestore.
- **ft_rcancel:** This function allows a user to acknowledge the end of the data transfer in progress to/from a filestore.

We have described the functions of the MAP FTAM API. As mentioned earlier, IEEE is currently working on an FTAM API known as the IEEE 1238 API. Hopefully, the IEEE 1238 API will be compatible with the MAP FTAM API.

17.6 Summary

The FTAM standard provides three modes of file manipulation. File transfer is the movement of an entire file between filestores in two open systems. File access performs reading, writing, or deleting of selected parts of a remote file. File management refers to the management of remote files/filestores.

The FTAM information model is based on the notions of a virtual file and a virtual filestore. Both notions are defined in terms of attributes and operations. The virtual filestore contains three types of objects: files, file-directories, and references.

A virtual file has a hierarchical access structure in general. Constraints can be applied to this hierarchical structure to obtain specific structures. A document type is used to associate data types with the file contents of a specific access structure.

The FTAM computational model is based on a client-server model. The initiator (client) initiates and controls the FTAM association, while the responder (server) provides access to its virtual filestore. An FTAM association can be structured into regimes. At any time, an FTAM user is limited to a set of service elements available within the active regimes. The FTAM protocol is quite straightforward. When a bulky file is to be transferred, the protocol relies on the use of the session synchronization services.

Filestore management extends the scope of a virtual filestore to include file-directory and reference objects. This requires the addition of a few more service elements. For example, it provides the facility to move a group of files from one location to another.

Related Standards

ISO 8571-1: Information Processing Systems - Open Systems Interconnection - File Transfer, Access and Management - Part 1: General Introduction

ISO 8571-1 DAM 1: Information Processing Systems - Open Systems Interconnection - File Transfer, Access and Management - Part 1: General Introduction - Amendment 1: Filestore Management

ISO 8571-1 DAM 2: Information Processing Systems - Open Systems Interconnection - File Transfer, Access and Management - Part 1: General Introduction - Amendment 2: Overlapped Access

ISO 8571-1 PDAM 3: Information Processing Systems - Open Systems Interconnection - File Transfer, Access and Management - Part 1: General Introduction - Proposed Draft Amendment 3: Service Enhancement

ISO 8571-2: Information Processing Systems - Open Systems Interconnection - File Transfer, Access and Management - Part 2: Virtual Filestore Definition

ISO 8571-2 DAM 1: Information Processing Systems - Open Systems Interconnection - File Transfer, Access and Management - Part 2: Virtual Filestore Definition - Amendment 1: Filestore Management

ISO 8571-2 DAM 2: Information Processing Systems - Open Systems Interconnection - File Transfer, Access and Management - Part 2: Virtual Filestore Definition - Amendment 2: Overlapped Access

ISO 8571-3: Information Processing Systems - Open Systems Interconnection - File Transfer, Access and Management - Part 3: File Service Definition

ISO 8571-3 DAM 1: Information Processing Systems - Open Systems Interconnection - File Transfer, Access and Management - Part 3: File Service Definition - Amendment 1: Filestore Management

ISO 8571-3 DAM 2: Information Processing Systems - Open Systems Interconnection - File Transfer, Access and Management - Part 3: File Service Definition - Amendment 2: Overlapped Access

ISO 8571-3 PDAM 3: Information Processing Systems - Open Systems Interconnection - File Transfer, Access and Management - Part 3: File Service Definition - Proposed Draft Amendment 3: Service Enhancement

ISO 8571-4: Information Processing Systems - Open Systems Interconnection - File Transfer, Access and Management - Part 4: File Protocol Specification

ISO 8571-4 DAM 1: Information Processing Systems - Open Systems Interconnection - File Transfer, Access and Management - Part 4: File Protocol Specification - Amendment 1: Filestore Management

ISO 8571-4 DAM 2: Information Processing Systems - Open Systems Interconnection - File Transfer, Access and Management - Part 4: File Protocol Specification - Amendment 2: Overlapped Access

ISO 8571-4 PDAM 3: Information Processing Systems - Open Systems Interconnection - File Transfer, Access and Management - Part 4: File Protocol Specification - Proposed Draft Amendment 3: Service Enhancement

DIS 8571-5: Information Processing Systems - Open Systems Interconnection - File Transfer, Access and Management - Part 5: Protocol Implementation Conformance Statement (PICS) Proforma

DIS 10170-1: Information Technology - Open Systems Interconnection - Conformance Test Suite for the File Transfer, Access and Management (FTAM) Protocol - Part 1: Test Suite Structure and Test Purposes

ISP 10607-1: Information Technology - International Standardized Profile AFTnn - File Transfer, Access and Management - Part 1: Specification of ACSE, Presentation and Session Protocols for the Use by FTAM

ISP 10607-2: Information Technology - International Standardized Profile AFTnn - File Transfer, Access and Management - Part 2: Definition of Document Types, Constraint Sets and Syntaxes

DISP 10607-2 DAD 1: Information Technology - International Standardized Profile AFTnn - File Transfer, Access and Management - Part 2: Definition of Document Types, Constraint Sets and Syntaxes Addendum 1: Additional Definitions

ISP 10607-3: Information Technology - International Standardized Profile AFTnn - File Transfer, Access and Management - Part 3: AFT11 - Simple File Transfer Service (Unstructured)

DISP 10607-4: Information Technology - International Standardized Profile AFTnn - File Transfer, Access and Management - Part 4: AFT12 - Positional File Transfer Service (Flat)

DISP 10607-5: Information Technology - International Standardized Profile AFTnn - File Transfer, Access and Management - Part 5: AFT22 - Positional File Access Service (Flat)

DISP 10607-6: Information Technology - International Standardized Profile AFTnn - File Transfer, Access and Management - Part 6: AFT3- File Management service

18

CMIP and OSI Systems Management

Network management is concerned with planning, monitoring, accounting, and controlling the use of network resources and their activities. The complexity of network management lies in the size and diversity of network resources. Today's network management only provides solutions to management over specific classes of resources, resulting in islands of management subsystems. The primary goal of network management is to bring all the management subsystems together to provide a single point of control by the manager. The goal of the OSI management standards is to define an integrated networking management system by providing uniformity at the following three levels:

- uniformity in the definition of managed objects,
- uniformity in the definition of systems management functions, and
- uniformity in the specification of a communication protocol to support the exchange of management information.

As of today, we do not have uniformity in the definition of managed objects. To achieve interoperability, it is important to have a single dictionary of managed objects.

Although OSI management is only concerned with the management of OSIE resources, the basic principles of OSI management can be applied to areas outside the scope of OSI management. For example, it can be applied to manage stand-alone computer systems and non-OSI resources.

The OSI Management framework is studied in Section 18.1. Section 18.2 gives an overview of systems management. Sections 18.3 describes the management information model. Section 18.4 gives a brief description of the OSI systems management functions. Section 18.5 covers CMIP, the OSI communication protocol used to exchange systems management information. Section 18.6 describes a CMISE API by AT&T. Finally in Section 18.7, we examine two OSI management profiles.

18.1   OSI Management Framework

ISO/IEC 7498-4 describes a framework of OSI management. It covers the fundamental management concepts, the management functional areas, and the management structure.

- **OSI Management Concepts**

OSI Management consists of facilities to control, coordinate, and monitor the OSI resources. A **managed object** is a management view of a resource, i.e., it logically characterizes the actual resource for the purpose of managing it. It models the permissible management operations on the managed object, the permissible notifications that the object may wish to send, and the attributes associated with the object. Managed objects specific to a layer are called **(N)-layer managed objects**, while managed objects relevant to more than one layer are called **systems managed objects**.

Within the OSI Management environment, a **manager** is responsible for any management activities needed to support the users' management needs. An **agent** manages the managed objects within its local environment, performs management operations on managed objects as a result of management operations requested by a manager, and forwards notifications emitted by locally managed objects to a manager.

- **Management Functional Areas**

The users' requirements of OSI Management can be grouped into five **Management Functional Areas (MFAs)**. The concept of MFAs provides a frame of reference within which management functions may be identified. Each requirement is satisfied by one or more functions, while each function may satisfy one or more requirements. A brief description of each MFA follows.

- **Fault Management:** Fault Management is the management and monitoring of abnormal operations. It provides the functions to maintain error logs, respond to error notifications, locate and isolate faults, carry out diagnostic tests to identify types of faults, and finally correct faults.
- **Accounting Management:** Accounting Management handles costs and charges for the use of specific resources. It provides the functions to inform users of costs

incurred or resources used, enable accounting threshold points to be set, and combine costs with others when more than one resource is used.

- **Configuration Management:** Configuration Management exercises control over, collects configuration data from, and provides configuration data to other open systems. It provides the functions to initialize and delete managed objects, set parameters where appropriate to control the routine operation, and collect information about the status.

- **Performance Management:** Performance Management enables the evaluation of the behavior of resources. It provides the functions to gather and disseminate statistical data, maintain historical logs of system performance, and simulate various systems modes of operations.

- **Security Management:** Security Management addresses functions to protect access to an open system. It provides the functions to support security services, maintain security logs, and distribute security relevant information to other open systems.

- **OSI Management Structure**

The OSI management standards identified three forms of management: systems management, (N)-layer management, and (N)-layer operation.

Systems management, which is the normal and preferred form of management information exchange, is the management of OSI resources across all layers of the OSI model. **(N)-layer management** is used to carry management information specific to the operation of the (N)-layer. Occasionally, limited **management (N)-operations** are embedded within an (N)-protocol. Management information carried by an (N)-protocol exists for the purpose of controlling and monitoring a single instance of communication. The Reset operation in the X.25 protocol is an example of a management operation. Despite the three different approaches, all of them can occur simultaneously in the management of a network system. For example, the (N)-layer can be managed through the simultaneous use of systems management and (N)-layer management.

18.2 Systems Management Overview

The early work by ISO on management has focused on systems management. The work accomplished is represented by a number of standards on systems management. ISO/IEC 10040 describes a model for systems management. The remaining standards can be categorized into three groups: standards relating to the specification of managed objects, standards specifying systems management functions, and standards for communicating management information. Figure 18.1 illustrates the relationship among the three groups.

At the top level, systems management is a distributed application made up of agents and managers. Figure 18.2 shows a model of systems management. In particular, it shows that an agent performs operations on managed objects as a result of management operations requested by a manager, and forwards notifications to a manager. Not shown in the figure is the interface between an agent and the network resources or a database system. Such an interface is system specific, hence it is outside the scope of OSI. The remainder of this section will briefly describe three refinements of the systems management model: information aspects, functional aspects, and communication aspects.

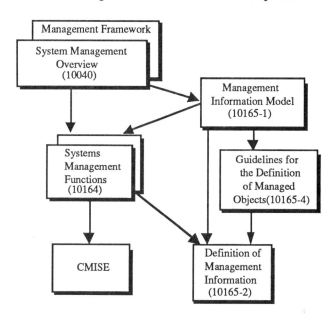

FIGURE 18.1   Relationship Between Systems Management Standards

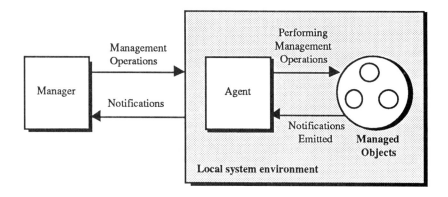

FIGURE 18.2   A Model of Systems Management

The set of systems managed objects in a system constitutes a system's **Management Information Base (MIB)**. The MIB should be viewed as a conceptual schema for management. It can be implemented by a database, but it does not have to be.

ISO/IEC 10165 gave a very detailed description of the MIB. Some of the key concepts of ISO/IEC 10165 will be given in Section 18.3.

System Management Functions	ISO/IEC	CCITT
Object Management Function	IS 10164-1	X.730
State Management Function	IS 10164-2	X.731
Attributes for Representing Relationships	IS 10164-3	X.732
Alarm Reporting Function	IS 10164-4	X.733
Event Report Management Function	IS 10164-5	X.734
Log Control Function	IS 10164-6	X.735
Security Alarm Reporting Function	IS 10164-7	X.736
Security Audit Trail Function	IS 10164-8	X.740
Objects and Attributes for Access Control	DIS 10164-9	X.741
Accounting Meter Function	IS 10164-10	X.742
Workload Monitoring Function	IS 10164-11	X.739
Test Management Function	IS 10164-12	X.745
Measurement Summarization Function	IS 10164-13	X.738

TABLE 18.1   Systems Management Functions

As noted earlier in Section 18.1, ISO has identified five MFAs. Each MFA is supported by one or more management functions. Table 18.1 lists some of the systems management functions. The more frequently used functions are the Object Management function, the Event Reporting function, and the Alarm Control function. Systems management functions are studied in Section 18.4.

At the Application Layer, there is a **systems management application entity (SMAE)** which contains an ASE known as the **Systems Management Application Service Element (SMASE)**. Depending on the role of an open system for a particular instance of communication, there is an agent SMASE and a master SMASE. The agent SMASE and the manager SMASE exchange APDUs with each other using a communication protocol. The communication service may be provided by CMISE, FTAM ASE, or TP ASE. The TP ASE is used to provide coordination and concurrency control of distributed management transactions if the managers choose to synchronize changes across distributed resources. A typical SMAE using CMISE contains the following ASEs in its application context: SMASE, CMISE, ROSE, and ACSE (Figure 18.3). In this application context, SMASE contains a set of systems management capabilities, CMISE defines the management operations which carries the systems management information, and ROSE conveys the management operations from one system to another. The capabilities of an SMASE is chosen from the systems management functions to be studied in Section 18.4.

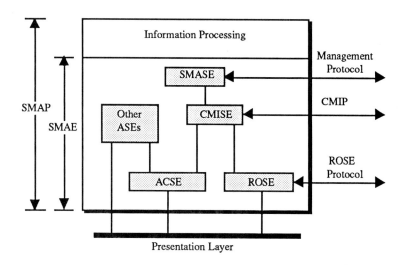

FIGURE 18.3   Application Context of an SMAE

18.3 Structure of Management Information

ISO/IEC 10165 is a five-part document defining the **structure of the OSI management information service (SMI)**. We will only cover Parts 1, 2, and 4 in this chapter. Part 1, known as the **Management Information Model**, defines the logical structure of systems management information. This part is studied in Section 18.3.1. Part 2, known as the **Definition of Management Information (DMI)**, provides templates for the definition of managed object classes in accordance with the guidelines in Part 4, known as the **Guidelines for the Definition of Managed Objects (GDMO)**. Section 18.3.2 covers Parts 2 and 4 of SMI.

18.3.1 Management Information Model

The purpose of the Management Information Model is to give structure to the management information conveyed externally by the systems management protocols, and thereby provide a consistent means for viewing objects from the management point of view.

A **managed object class** is a set of managed objects with similar characteristics. It can be described in terms of a set of attributes, management operations, and notifications.

A managed object is an instance of a managed object class. Some of the commonly used managed object classes are briefly described below.

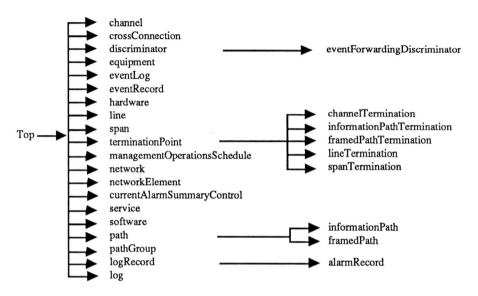

FIGURE 18.4   Inheritance Hierarchy of OSI/NMF

• **top**: Every object class is a subclass of this object class. Top is characterized by the following attributes: objectClass, packages, nameBindings, allomorphs, and name. Hence these attributes are inherited by all other object classes.

• **log**: Defined as a subclass of top, this object class is used to define the criteria for controlling the logging of managed information. Some of the attributes in this object class are discriminatorConstruct and maxLogSize.

• **log record**: Defined as a subclass of top, this object class is used to define the records contained in a log managed object. A log is typically maintained at a managed agent to store internal notifications from the managed objects. Two of the attributes in this object class are logRecordId and loggingTime. This object class contains a number of subclasses depending on the specialization of the record. Examples of subclasses are event log records (as a result of receiving events), attribute value change records (as a result of receiving attribute value change notification), object creation/deletion records (as a result of receiving object creation/deletion notification), relationship change records (as a result of receiving relationship change reports), object name change records (as a result of receiving object name change notification), state change records (as a result of receiving state change reports), and security alarm report records (as a result of receiving security alarm reports).

• **discriminator**: Defined as a subclass of top, this object class is used to specify conditions that must be satisfied before a notification is issued.

Refinement is a process of extending a managed object class in a number of ways such as addition of more attributes, extension or restriction of the range of an existing attribute, addition of new actions and notifications, addition of arguments to actions and notifications, and extension or restriction of the ranges of arguments to actions and notifications. Through refinement, an inheritance hierarchy of managed object classes can be obtained. Figure 18.4 shows the inheritance hierarchy used by OSI/NMF.

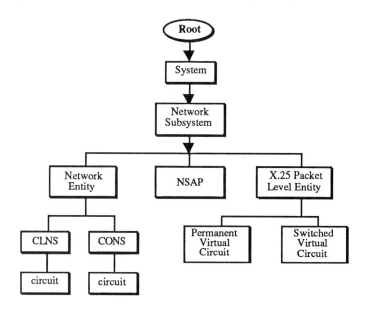

FIGURE 18.5   Example of a MIT structure

Naming of managed objects can be accomplished by first defining a **Managed Information Tree (MIT) structure** which is quite similar to the DIT structure studied in Chapter 15. The only difference is that the MIT structure deals with managed object classes while the DIT structure deals with Directory object classes. Managed objects are structured into a **Managed Information Tree (MIT)** just like the way Directory objects are structured into a DIT. Similarly, a MIT is derived from a MIT structure just like the way a DIT is derived from a DIT structure. Figure 18.5 shows a very simple MIT structure. It defines a managed object class and a set of distinguished attribute at each level. It also defines a containment relation for each tree edge. For example, the NSAP object class is "contained" in the Network Subsystem managed object class. Using these distinguished attributes, we can assign DNs to managed objects. For example, the following DN can be assigned to a switched virtual circuit managed object:

system-title = UMKC
subsystem = UNIX3
X.25PLE = CO
switched virtual call = 10

A managed object is encapsulated. Encapsulation preserves the integrity of an object by distinguishing the external view from the internal view. The external view, which is used by the managers and the agents to communicate management information, is discussed next.

Attributes of a managed object are either group attributes or set-valued attributes. A **group attribute** refers to a collection of logically related attributes. A managed object class can have more than one group attribute. The value of a **Set-valued attribute** is a set of elements. The set is of variable size. In particular, it can be empty.

Managed objects emit **notifications** when an internal event occurs. Whether a notification is sent to a manager or logged depends on the criteria established through the event reporting management function and the log control management function. Any one of the following can cause the emission of a notification: attribute value change, communication alarm, equipment alarm, object creation/deletion, object name change, relationship change, security service/mechanism violation, and state change.

There are two types of management operations: attribute-oriented operations and object-oriented operations. **Attribute-oriented operations** are applied to the attributes of a managed object. Examples of attribute-oriented operations are "get", "replace", "add", and "remove". **Object-oriented operations** are operations applied to a managed object as a whole. Examples of object-oriented operations are "create", "delete", and "action". A short description of these operations follows:

- **get**: This operation reads the values of the requested attributes, or reads all the attribute values if no attribute is supplied.
- **replace**: This operation replaces the values of specified attributes with supplied values.
- **replace-with-default**: This operation directs the managed object to replace the values of attributes to default values which are specified in the managed object class definition.
- **add**: This operation adds a new member to a set-valued attribute value
- **remove**: This operation removes a member from a set-valued attribute value.
- **create**: This operation requests the creation and initialization of a managed object.
- **delete**: This operation requests the deletion of a managed object.
- **action**: This operation requests the managed object to perform an action and to indicate the result of the action. The set of possible actions are a part of the definition of a managed object class.

A managed system can be requested to perform an operation on one or more managed objects. This is accomplished through the use of filters. A **filter** applies a test to a managed object. For example, a filter can be used to check whether an attribute value is equal to, greater than, or less than some specified value. Some objects may pass the filter and some may not. When a filter is evaluated to "true" on a managed object, the requested operation will be performed on that object. Synchronization can be specified on the collection of managed objects selected. Two types of synchronization can be requested:

"atomic" and "best effort". **Atomic synchronization**, if selected by a manager, requires the operation be successfully applied to all objects of interest or no operation be performed at all. **Best effort synchronization** attempts to perform the operation on all the managed objects selected, whether or not the operation can be performed.

Related attributes, notifications, and operations within a managed object class can be grouped into **packages**. Within a managed object class, some packages are mandatory and some are optional. A **conditional package** is a collection of optional attributes, notifications and operations which are either all present or all absent in a managed object. It reflects optional functionality of the resource. Packages are instantiated at the same time as the managed object. Every managed object has at most one instance of every possible conditional package. For example, we can use a conditional package to indicate how frequently we want to update a manager with the information in an agent's log. We can have a conditional package for daily scheduling, a conditional package for weekly scheduling, and a conditional package for monthly scheduling.

Allomorphism is another useful concept supported in the definition of a managed object class. Allomorphism is very similar to polymorphism used in an object-oriented design. **Polymorphism** provides the capability to implement the same operation in different object classes, while **allomorphism** refers to the capability of an object class to imitate or emulate the behavior of another object class known as the **allomorphic superclass**. Through allomorphism, a manager can manage an object in the same way as an older object, i.e., the emulated object. In order to support allomorphism, a managed object class definition includes a set-valued attribute identifying its class and all its allomorphic superclasses, i.e., all the classes which it can imitate. When allomorphism is not required, this attribute has only one member, namely, itself. It is necessary to place restrictions on the way an allomorphic subclass is specialized from its allomorphic superclasses. These restrictions may apply to attributes, operations and notifications. Consider a restriction on attributes. For an allomorphic subclass, the range of values of an inherited attribute must be the same as or a subset of the range in the superclass. It cannot be an extension of the range in the superclass. In this way, any value which is acceptable in the subclass must be also acceptable in the superclass.

So far, we have examined managed information from an abstract view. Let us briefly examine how the management information is stored in practice. MIB information is distributed in nature. Not all the managed information has to be stored in a database. Some of the static object attributes may be stored in a PROM (i.e., Programmable Read-only Memory) contained within a resource, and some of the dynamically changing attributes may be stored in the RAM (i.e., Random-Access Memory). For example, a resource may contain within its PROM configuration information about resources in its neighborhood, hence this configuration information does not have to be stored in a database. In general, if a resource can store non-volatile management information and is capable of being queried for that information, that information does not have to be stored in a database.

Certain management information such as graphical information may be retrieved more efficiently if they are stored in a manager's system. The point is that most managed agents run in cheap devices which lack fancy graphics or database facilities. Security sensitive information should be also stored in a manager's system.

18.3.2 Use of Management Templates

To provide uniformity in the definition of managed objects, the OSI management standards defined GDMO which is a set of management tools or templates in the form of ASN.1 macros. Systems managers can use these templates to define managed objects. The use of a common set of templates encourages consistency among managed object definitions and reduces duplication of effort among object definers. In the following, we introduce some of the templates and illustrate how they are used.

• **managed object class specification template**

The managed object class template forms the basis of the definition of a managed object class. It identifies the inheritance relationships existing between the class and other managed object classes, the packages of behavior, attributes, notifications, and operations pertinent to the managed object class definition. The major elements of the definition are:

• Object-class-name	MANAGED OBJECT CLASS
• Inheritance	DERIVED FROM
• Allomorphs	ALLOMORPHIC SET
• Mandatory Packages	CHARACTERIZED BY
• Conditional Packages	CONDITIONAL PACKAGES
• Class Naming	REGISTERED AS

where the keywords used in the template are shown on the right.

Example 18.1

```
top MANAGED OBJECT CLASS
CHARACTERIZED BY
topPackage PACKAGE
    BEHAVIOR DEFINITIONS
    topBehavior;
    ATTRIBUTES
    objectClass GET,
    packages GET,
    nameBindings GET,
    allomorphs GET,
    name GET;;;
REGISTERED AS objectClass-example-one
```

The top object class is the class of which every other object class is a subclass. There is a mandatory package (i.e., topPackage) in top. The attributes within topPackage are inherited by every managed object class. Note that the operations that are applicable to each attribute are shown on the right.

Example 18.2

```
discriminator MANAGED OBJECT CLASS
    DERIVED FROM  top;
    CHARACTERIZED BY
discriminatorPackages PACKAGE
    ATTRIBUTES
    discriminatorID  GET,
    discriminatorConstruct  GET-REPLACE,
    administrativeState  GET-REPLACE,
    operationalState  GET,
    usageState  GET,
    availabilityStatus  PERMITTED VALUES  Attribute-ASN1Module.DiscriminatorAvailability
    GET;
    NOTIFICATIONS
    stateChange,
    attributeValueChange;;;
CONDITIONAL PACKAGES
    dailyScheduling PRESENT IF
    both the weekly scheduling package and external scheduler packages are not present in an instance,
    weeklyScheduling
    PRESENT IF
    both the daily scheduling package and external scheduler packages are not present in an instance,
    externalScheduler
    PRESENT IF
    both the daily scheduling package and weekly scheduling packages are not present in an instance;
    REGISTERED AS  object-class-example-two
```

The discriminator object class is used to define the criteria for controlling management services. Note that there is one mandatory package and three conditional packages.

Example 18.3

```
eventForwardingDiscriminator MANAGED OBJECT CLASS
DERIVED FROM  discriminator;
CHARACTERIZED BY
efd PACKAGE
    ATTRIBUTES
    destinationAddress  GET-REPLACE,
```

```
    backUpAddressList GET-REPLACE,
    activeAddress GET-REPLACE,
    allomorphicList GET ADD-REMOVE;;;
REGISTERED AS  object-class-example-three
```

This object class, defined as a subclass of the discriminator object class, is used to define the conditions that shall be satisfied by potential event reports before an event report is forwarded to a particular destination system. The only mandatory package here is efd.

Example 18.4

```
log  MANAGED OBJECT CLASS
    DERIVED FROM  top;
    CHARACTERIZED BY
    logPackage  PACKAGE
        ATTRIBUTES
        logID GET,
        discriminatorConstruct GET-REPLACE,
        administrativeState GET-REPLACE,
        operationalState GET-REPLACE,
        usageState GET,
        availabilityStatus PERMITTED VALUES Attribute-ASN1Module.LogAvailability GET,
        maxLogSize GET,
        capacityAlarmThreshold GET-REPLACE ADD-REMOVE,
        logFullAction GET-REPLACE;
        NOTIFICATIONS
        attributeChange,
        stateChange,
        processingErrorAlarm;;;
    CONDITIONAL PACKAGES
        dailyScheduling  PRESENT IF  both the weekly scheduling and external scheduler packages
        are not present,
        weeklyScheduling  PRESENT IF  both the daily scheduling and external scheduler packages
        are not present,
        externalSchedular  PRESENT IF  both the daily scheduling and weekly scheduling packages
        are not present;
REGISTERED AS objectClass-example-three
```

Let us explain some of the attributes in the logPackage. The discriminatorConstruct attribute specifies tests on the information to be logged. The administrativeState, operationalState, availabilityStatus, and usageStatus attributes are used to specify the state. The capacityAlarmThreshold attribute specifies the points at which an event generates a log full or log wrap condition. The logFullAction attribute specifies the actions to be taken when the maximum log size is reached. Possible actions are wrap (i.e., deleting the earlier records to make room for new records) and halt (i.e., disallowing further logging). Finally, the packages attribute identifies the conditional packages instantiated for that log instance. The conditional packages here are the scheduling packages which provide the logs with the ability to automatically switch between logging-in and logging-off.

- **package specification template**

This template provides the means to define a package consisting of of behavior, attributes, attribute groups, actions, and notifications. The major elements of the definition are:

• Object-class-name	PACKAGE
• Behavior	BEHAVIOR DEFINITIONS
• Contained attributes	ATTRIBUTES, ATTRIBUTES GROUPS
• Operations	ACTIONS
• Notifications	NOTIFICATIONS
• Class Naming	REGISTERED AS

The following example gives the definition of the dailyScheduling package which was referenced in Examples 18.2 and 18.4.

Example 18.5

```
dailyScheduling  PACKAGE
     ATTRIBUTES
     intervalsOfDay    GET ADD-REMOVE;
REGISTERED AS package-example-one
```

This package provides the capability of scheduling reports on a daily basis.

- **attribute specification template**

This template provides the means to define an attribute. It is quite similar to the ATTRIBUTE SYNTAX macro defined by the DS standard. The definition of an attribute type includes the definitions of the attribute syntax that is used to convey values of the attribute. The definition of an attribute syntax indicates whether the attribute value is a single- or set-valued attribute type. The definition may include the valid ways in which the value of an instance of the type may be tested. The major elements of the definition are:

• Attribute name	ATTRIBUTE
• Inheritance	DERIVED FROM
• Attribute Syntax	WITH ATTRIBUTE SYNTAX
• Value test	MATCHES FOR
• Value Constraint	PERMITTED VALUES

- Behavior   BEHAVIOR
- Type naming   REGISTERED AS

Example 18.6

objectName ATTRIBUTE
    WITH ATTRIBUTE SYNTAX AttributeModule.ObjectName;
    MATCHES FOR Equality;
    REGISTERED AS attribute-example-one

Note that this attribute is referenced in the top managed object class.

Example 18.7

capacityAlarmThreshold ATTRIBUTE
    WITH ATTRIBUTE SYNTAX
    AttributeASN1ModuleCapacityAlarmThreshold;
    MATCHES FOR Set Comparison, Set Intersection;
    REGISTERED AS attribute-example-two

A threshold is the general mechanism for generating a notification from changes in numeric attributes values. This example shows the definition of the capacityAlarmThreshold attribute which is referenced in the log managed object class. Other threshold attributes can be defined for counters and gauges used in performance management.

- **attribute group specification template**

This template is used to define an attribute group, i.e., a group of related attributes. The major elements of the definition are:

- Attribute group name   ATTRIBUTE GROUP
- Contained attribute   GROUP ELEMENTS
- Semantic description   DESCRIPTION
- Class naming   REGISTERED AS

Example 18.8

qOS-Group   ATTRIBUTE GROUP
    GROUP ELEMENTS qOS-Error-Cause, qOS-Error-Counter;
    DESCRIPTION Group attribute that includes all QOS-related attributes in a managed object class;
    REGISTERED AS attributeGroup-example-one

Here we group two attributes together.

Example 18.9

>   relationships ATTRIBUTE GROUP
>   GROUP ELEMENTS
>   userObject, providerObject, peer, primary, secondary, backUpObject, backedUpObject, member,
>   owner;
>   DESCRIPTION This is a group of all relationship attributes defined in ISO/IEC 10165-3;
>   REGISTERED AS attributeGroup-example-two

This attribute group is used for the Relationship Management function specified in ISO/IEC 10165-3.

- **notification specification template**

This template is used to define a notification type. Notification types defined by means of this template may be carried in event reports. The definition of a notification type shall specify the circumstances under which a notification of the type is generated. It should indicate whether the action may be confirmed, non-confirmed, or both. It should also specify any syntax that is used to convey the event information and the event reply parameters. The major elements of the definition are:

• Notification-label	NOTIFICATION
• Behavior	BEHAVIOR
• Confirmation Mode	MODE
• Data syntax	WITH DATA SYNTAX
• Result syntax	WITH RESULT SYNTAX
• Notification naming	REGISTERED AS

Example 18.10

>   stateChange
>   NOTIFICATION
>   BEHAVIOR stateChangeBehavior;
>   MODE CONFIRMED AND NON-CONFIRMED;
>   WITH INFORMATION SYNTAX Notification-ASN1Module.StateChangeInformation
>   AND ATTRIBUTE IDS
>   oldOperationalState   oldOperationalState,
>   newOperationalState   newOperationalState,
>   oldUsageState   oldUsageState,
>   newUsageState   newUsageState,
>   oldAdministrativeState   oldAdministrativeState,
>   oldRepairState   oldRepairState,
>   newRepairState   newRepairState,
>   oldInstallationStatus   oldInstallationStatus,

```
        newInstallationStatus        newInstallationStatus,
        oldAvailabilityStatus        oldAvailabilityStatus,
        newAvailabilityStatus        newAvailabilityStatus,
        oldControlStatus             oldControlStatus,
        newControlStatus             newControlStatus,
        additionalStateChangeInfo    additionalStateChangeInfo;
        WITH REPLY SYNTAX;
    REGISTERED AS  notification-example-one
```

Note that this notification type is referenced in the definition of the discriminator object class (Example 18.2). Also note that both confirmation modes are allowed.

Example 18.11

```
    objectNameChange
        NOTIFICATION
        BEHAVIOR objectNameChangeBehavior;
        MODE CONFIRMED AND NON-CONFIRMED;
        WITH INFORMATION SYNTAX Notification-ASN1Module.ObjectNameChangeInfo
        AND ATTRIBUTE IDS
        newName                      newName,
        additionalNameChangeinfo     additionalNameChangeInfo,
        sourceIndicator              sourceIndicator;
        WITH REPLY SYNTAX;
    REGISTERED AS  notification-example-two
```

This notification type is used to report the name change of a managed object to other systems.

• behavior specification template

This template is used to define the behavioral aspects of managed object classes, attribute operation, and notification types. The current description technique used in the body of a behavior template is informal.

Example 18.12

```
    topBehavior BEHAVIOR
        DEFINED AS
        This is the top level of managed object class hierarchy and every other managed object class is a
        refinement of either this generic class (top) or a refinement of subclass of Top;
```

Note that topBehavior is referenced in the definition of the top managed object class in Example 18.1. Note that the body is described in a natural language.

Example 18.13

```
stateChangeBehavior  BEHAVIOR
    DEFINED AS
    This notification type is used to report the change in the value of one or more state attributes of a
    managed object.
```

Note that stateChangeBehavior is referenced in the definition of the stateChange notification type in Example 18.10. Also note that the description is very informal.

• **name binding template**

The name binding template is used to assign distinguished attribute types of a managed object class in the context of a superior class. The major elements of the template are:

• Name-binding-label	NAME BINDING
• Subclass name	SUBORDINATE OBJECT CLASS
• Superclass name	NAMED BY SUPERIOR OBJECT CLASS
• Naming attribute	WITH ATTRIBUTE
• Class naming	REGISTERED AS

Example 18.14

```
log-system   NAME BINDING
    SUBORDINATE OBJECT CLASS  log;
    NAMED BY
    SUPERIOR OBJECT CLASS  system;
    WITH ATTRIBUTE  logID;
    CREATE
    with-reference-object,
    with-automatic-instance-naming;
    DELETE
    only-if-no-contained-objects;
REGISTERED AS  nameBinding-example-one
```

The above says that the log-system object class is contained in the system object class, and contains the log object class as a component. It also says that logID, one of the attribute types of the log-system object class, is used as a distinguished attribute type to name log-system objects.

18.4 Systems Management Functions

ISO/IEC identified a number of systems management functions to satisfy the users' requirements (Table 18.1). The set of of systems management functions contained in an application depends on the needs of the users of the application. The SMASE in the application context of a management entity provides the systems management functions required for an application.

Suppose that the users of an application require some configuration management capabilities. Some of the requirements are to initialize/ delete managed objects, alter configurations, and set parameters to control the operation of a system. These requirements can be met by the Object Management function. One requirement is to collect information about the current status of a system. This requirement can be met by the State Management function. Finally, the requirement to obtain notification of events in a system can be met by the Event Reporting function. Thus, to satisfy the needs of the users of this particular application, we can build an SMASE containing the Object Management function, the State Management function, and the Event Reporting function.

A systems management function is used as follows. First, a management user issues a service request at the interface provided by a systems management function. Associated with the service request may be parameters supplying appropriate management information. The systems management function maps the service request to a CMISE service request. It can mapped either directly or indirectly. When the mapping is indirect, the service request is first mapped to a service element of the Object Management function which is then mapped to a CMISE service element. When the mapping is direct, the systems management function operates by parameterizing some CMISE service request with the management information it receives from the user. Whether the mapping is direct or indirect, the systems management function does not generate any APDUs.

Systems management functions are described next. We will indicate the mapping of the corresponding service elements, i.e., whether it is direct or indirect.

- **Object Management Function**

The **Object Management function** provides the systems management services for the reporting of creation and deletion of managed objects, the reporting of name changes of managed objects, and the reporting of changes in the attribute values of managed objects. Of the ten service elements of the Object Management function, six of them are pass-through. Pass-through service elements are prefixed with the "PT". An invocation of a pass-through service element would trigger an invocation of an underlying communications service element without the addition of any new parameters.

PT-CREATE, a confirmed service element, is used to create a managed object together with its identification and the values of its associated management information. This service element is mapped to the M-CREATE service element of CMISE.

PT-DELETE, a confirmed service element, is used to delete a managed object and to deregister its identification. This service element is mapped to the M-DELETE service element of CMISE.

The **PT-ACTION** service element is used to perform an action on one or more managed objects. This service element is mapped to the M-ACTION service element of CMISE.

The **PT-SET** service element is used to modify the attribute values of a managed object. This service element is mapped to the M-SET service element of CMISE.

The **PT-GET** service element is a confirmed service used to retrieve attribute values. This service element is mapped to the M-GET service element of CMISE.

The **PT-EVENT REPORT** service element is used to report an event. This service element is mapped to the M-EVENT-REPORT service element of CMISE.

The **Object Creating Reporting** service element allows a system to keep other systems aware of the creation of new managed objects. This service element is mapped to the M-EVENT-REPORT service element of CMISE.

The **Object Deleting Reporting** service element is used to notify a system about the deletion of existing managed objects. This service element is mapped to the M-EVENT-REPORT service element of CMISE.

The **Object Name Change Reporting** service element is used to notify a system about name changes of existing managed objects. This service element is mapped to the M-EVENT-REPORT service element of CMISE.

The **Attribute Change Reporting** service element is used to inform a system about changes in the attributes of managed objects. This service element is mapped to the M-EVENT-REPORT service element of CMISE.

All the above service elements except PT-CREATE, PT-DELETE, and PT-GET can be either confirmed or non-confirmed.

- **State Management Function**

The **State management function** provides generic definitions for inquiring about and changing the management state of a managed object, and for reporting changes in the management state of a managed object.

The following attributes can be used to describe a management state:

- **operational state attribute:** The operability of a resource is described by this attribute having one of two possible values: "disabled" and "enabled". A resource is "disabled" if it is totally inoperable. It is "enabled" if it is partially or fully operable and available for use.
- **usage state attribute:** The usage of a resource is described by this attribute having one of four possible values: "idle", "active", "busy", and "unknown". A resource is "idle" if it is currently not in use. It is "active" if it is currently in use and has sufficient spare operating capacity for additional simultaneous users. Managed objects whose associated resource supports only one user do not exhibit the active usage state. A resource is "busy" if it is in use but has no spare operating capacity for additional users. Finally, managed objects having no knowledge of their usage are in the "unknown" usage state.
- **administrative state attribute:** The attribute has one of the three possible values: "locked", "unlocked", and "shutting down". A resource is "locked" if it is administratively prohibited from performing services for its users. It is "unlocked" if it

is administratively permitted to perform services. A resource is "shutting down" if use of the resource is administratively permitted only on existing instances.

•   **management state attribute:**   This attribute is a 3-tuple made up of the operational state, the usage state, and the administrative state. For example, if an administrator prohibits the use of a resource, then the management state of the resource is either (disabled, idle, locked) or (enabled, idle, locked). Note that some 3-tuples such as (disabled, active, locked) and (disabled, active, shutting down) cannot be realized.

The **State Change Reporting** service element is used to convey changes in the values of the management state attributes. It can be used as either a confirmed or a non-confirmed service. It is mapped to the M-EVENT-REPORT service element of CMISE.

•   **Relation Management Function**

The **Relation Management function** is used by a management user to examine and change the relationships between the various parts of a system.

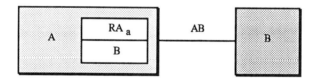

FIGURE 18.6   A Reciprocal Relationship

The standard defines a number of relationships. We will only describe the reciprocal relationship. A **reciprocal relationship** is a binding between two managed objects represented as a set of attributes. Figure 18.6 illustrates a reciprocal relationship between objects A and B where RA is the attribute value of some **relationship attribute type**. The standard identified a number of relationship attribute types. For example, both the service provider and the service user attribute types are used to describe a service relationship between two managed objects, where the managed object with the service provider attribute type plays the role of a service provider and the managed object with the service user attribute type plays the role of a service user.

The **Relationship Change Reporting** service element is used to report any change in any one of the relationship attributes of a managed object. It is mapped to the M-EVENT-REPORT service element of CMISE.

•   **Alarm Reporting Function**

The **Alarm Reporting function** provides a means to report alarms detected in a resource. Alarm reporting may not indicate an error. It is used to understand the cause of a potential abnormal situation.

The **Alarm Reporting** service element allows a management user to notify another user of an alarm detected in a resource. It can be used as either confirmed or non-confirmed service. It is mapped to the M-EVENT-REPORT service element of CMISE.

Alarms can be categorized into communications alarms, QOS alarms, processing alarms, equipment alarms, and environment alarms. The alarm-type parameter of the Alarm Reporting service element indicates the type of the alarm. Alarm Reporting also has a severity level parameter indicating how the capability of a managed object may have been affected. For example, the "minor severity" level indicates existence of an error condition which is not currently degrading the capability of a managed object.

- **Event Reporting Management Function**

Event reports are generated as a result of notifications issued by managed objects. The **event reporting management (ERM) function** allows a manager to establish and control discrimination tests which determine when an event report should be forwarded to another system.

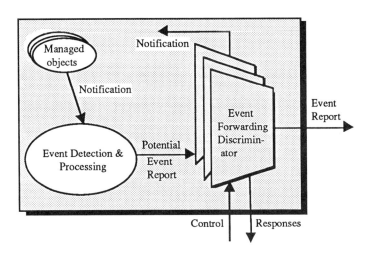

FIGURE 18.7   Event Reporting Management Function

First we explain how the Event Reporting Management Function works (Figure 18.7). Local managed objects emit notifications to an Event Detection and Processing module. If the conditions of the Event Detection and Processing are met, a Potential Event Report will be formed and sent to all the Event Forward Discriminators in the local system. The **Event Forwarding Discriminator** is used to determine which event reports are forwarded to a particular destination system during specified time periods. The discriminator consists of a scheduling capability which determines intervals during which event reports are selected for forwarding, and a discriminator construct which specifies the conditions for a potential event report to satisfy. If the discriminator construct of the Event Forwarding Discriminator evaluates to true and the period falls within the scheduling capability, then an event report is sent to its destination(s) as soon as possible. An Event Forwarding Discriminator may also send a notification to the initiating managed object.

There are four **event report forwarding (ERF)** service elements. The **ERF-CREATE** service element allows a system to request another system to create an event forwarding discriminator, thereby requesting that new or additional event forwarding controls be imposed. It is mapped to PT-CREATE.

The **ERF-DELETE** service element allows a system to request another open system to delete one or more event forwarding discriminators, thereby requesting that some event forwarding controls be terminated. It is mapped to PT-DELETE.

The **ERF-SUSPEND/RESUME** service element allows a system to request another system to change the administrative state of the event forwarding discriminator. It is mapped to PT-SET.

Finally, the **ERF-SET** service element allows a system to request another system to change some of the attribute values of the event forwarding discriminators. It is mapped to PT-SET.

The Event Forwarding Discriminator is a supporting managed object. As a managed object, it generates a notification whenever it is created, terminated, suspended or modified. Whether this notification results in the transmission of an event report depends on the management state and the discriminator construct of the discriminator which processes the potential event report.

• **Log Control Function**

For management purposes, it is useful to maintain a supporting managed object to preserve information about events that have occurred or operations that have been performed on managed objects. A log is such an object composed of log records, with each log record containing information derived from some received event report. The **Log Control function (LCF) function** provides functionality needed by a manager to allow selection of particular event reports for automatic logging. Logging can be initiated, terminated, suspended, and resumed.

There are four LCF service elements. The **LCF-CREATE** service element allows a system to request another system to create a log. It is mapped to PT-CREATE.

The **LCF-DELETE** service element allows a system to request another system to delete one or more logs. It is mapped to PT-DELETE.

The **LCF-SUSPEND/RESUME** service element allows a system to request another system to change the administrative state of a log. It is mapped to PT-SET.

The **LCF-SET** service element allows a system to request another system to change the non-state attributes of a log. It is mapped to PT-SET.

• **Other Systems Management Functions**

There are a number of systems management functions other than the ones mentioned above. Some of them are as follows:

• **Security Alarm Reporting Function:** This function provides a means for a management user to receive notifications of security related events.

• **Security Auditing Function:** The function is used to maintain a security audit log. The types of security auditing events include connections/disconnections, security mechanism utilization, management operations, and usage accounting.

• **Objects and Attributes for Access Control function:** The standard for this function models access control for management communication associations. It specifies managed objects and attributes to be used to grant or to deny access according to some access control policy.

• **Accounting Meter function:** The standard for this function provides a model for accounting meters and logs. It indicates which usage data to be collected and under what conditions they are to be reported.

• **Workload Monitoring function:** The standard for this function models gauges to be used for monitoring resource utilization. It specifies the gauge managed object, the mean monitor metric object for deriving the instantaneous mean value of an associated gauge object, the notifications that can be emitted, and the operations for initiating, terminating, suspending, and resuming the monitoring process.

• **Test Management function:** This function supports remote control tests in open systems. It also provides the specification of tests which exercise resources in open systems.

• **Measurement Summarization function:** The standard for this function provides a model for sampling, aggregating, and reporting summaries of management attributes of specified managed objects. It specifies services for reporting such summaries and for initiating and terminating summarization activities.

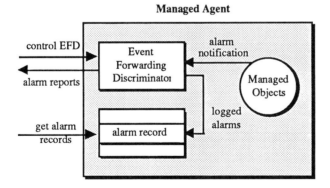

FIGURE 18.8   An Implementation of Alarm Surveillance Capabilities

We close this section by giving an example to illustrate how the systems management functions are applied. Consider a management application where the users require some alarm surveillance capabilities to monitor and control managed objects at one or more managed agents (Figure 18.8). First, we identify the required capabilities. The manager must be able to establish and control discrimination tests and forward alarm reports from an agent. An agent must be able to notify the manager of any alarm detected in a resource that it manages. Finally, the manager must be able to retrieve alarm records from the log located at an agent. Next, we identify the systems management functions needed to support the above capabilities. The first capability can be supported by the Event Reporting Management function. EFR-CREATE is used to initiate alarm reporting by creating an ERF object, and ERF-SET is used to modify the discriminatorConstruct attribute of the ERF object. The second capability is supported by the Alarm Reporting function. The third capability is supported by the PT-GET service element of the Object Management function. Thus, three systems management functions are needed to support this particular application. We can build an SMASE containing these three functions as part of the capabilities of the management application.

18.5 CMISE

CMISE is an ASE defined to convey management information from one system to another in an interactive environment. CMISE is not the only ASE that can convey management information. The FTAM ASE can be also used to provide bulk transfer of software configuration loads or transmission of huge management reports. The TP ASE can be used to provide coordination and concurrency control of distributed management transactions if the managers choose to synchronize changes across distributed resources.

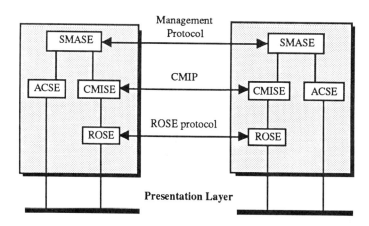

FIGURE 18.9   Interaction Between SMAEs

Figure 18.9 shows a model of interaction between two SMAEs. The SMASE within an SMAE conveys systems management information to its peer by invoking a CMISE service element at the SMASE/CMISE interface. CMIP, the protocol engine of CMISE, then invokes a ROSE service element at the CMISE/ROSE interface. Thus, there are two levels of parameterization. The first one occurs at the SMASE/CMISE interface and the second one occurs at the CMISE/ROSE interface (Figure 18.10). Neither CMISE nor SMASE generates any APDU.

Section 18.5.1 describes CMISE and Section 18.5.2 describes CMIP.

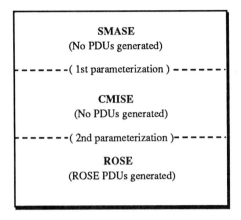

FIGURE 18.10   Tightly Coupled CMISE Software

18.5.1 CMISE Service

CMISE Parameters	
access control	invoke identifier
action information	linked identifier
action reply	managed object class
action type	managed object instance
attribute identifier list	mode
base object class	reference object instance
base object instance	scope
filter	superior object instance
get invoked identifier	synchronization

TABLE 18.2   CMISE Service Parameters

CMISE provides two types of management information transfer services: a management notification service and a management operation service. The **management notification service**, consisting of the M-EVENT-REPORT service element, allows a CMISE service user (i.e., an SMASE) to report an event about a managed object to its peer. The **management operation service** provides a set of operations which allows an invoking CMISE service user to request its peer to manipulate its managed objects. There are altogether six management operation service elements. They are M-GET, M-SET, M-ACTION, M-CREATE, M-DELETE, and M-CANCEL-GET.

CMISE service elements use quite a number of parameters although only a few parameters are mandatory (Table 18.2). Some of the parameters are used for the purpose of selection. CMISE allows a service user to select more than one managed object. Managed object selection involves two phases: scoping and filtering. Scoping involves the identification of a set of managed objects to which a filter is applied. Four specifications for the level of scoping are possible, indicating to what part of the MIT the filter can be applied:

- the base object alone,
- the (n)-level subordinates of the base object,
- the base object and all of its subordinates down to and including the (n)-level, and
- the base object and all of its subordinates (whole subtree).

Figure 18.11 displays all of the four possible cases for selecting objects from the the MIT. Filtering applies a test to each managed object in a scope. If a managed object passes the filter test, then it will be selected for the performance of some management operation.

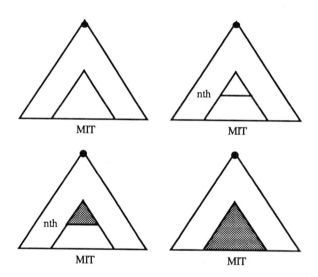

FIGURE 18.11   Four Different Styles of Selecting Objects from the MIT

Considering the parameters of the CMISE service elements (Table 18.2), the following observations can be made:

- All the service elements contain the invocation identifier parameter. This is because each CMISE service element is mapped to a ROSE service element which always uses the invocation identifier parameter.
- Whenever a service element can be used as either confirmed or non-confirmed service, the mode parameter is used by a requesting CMISE service user to indicate the choice.

• The only CMISE service elements to which scoping and filtering can be applied are M-GET, M-SET, M-ACTION, and M-DELETE. Whenever scoping and filtering are applicable to a CMISE service element, the service element may contain the following parameters: linked identifier, base object class, base object instance, scope, filter, access control, and synchronization. The linked identifier parameter is needed whenever multiple replies are needed. All the replies will have a value of the linked identifier parameter equal to the value of the invocation identifier parameter in the indication primitive. The last reply is indicated by a response primitive without the linked identifier. Both the base object class and the base object instance parameters are used to indicate the starting point of the selection of the managed objects to which the filter is applied. The access control parameter is used to pass access control information to some access control function. Finally, the value of the synchronization parameter can be either "atomic" or "best effort".

Table 18.3 displays the CMISE service elements. The description of each service element and its parameters follows.

Service	Type
M-CANCEL-GET	confirmed
M-EVENT-REPORT	confirmed/non-confirmed
M-GET	confirmed
M-SET	confirmed/non-confirmed
M-ACTION	confirmed/non-confirmed
M-CREATE	confirmed
M-DELETE	confirmed

TABLE 18.3   Types of CMISE Service Elements

The **M-EVENT-REPORT** service element is used by a CMISE service user to report an event about a managed object to its peer. The mandatory parameters are invocation identifier, mode, managed object class, managed object instance, and event type. The event type parameter is used to carry the type of an event. For example, the Alarm Reporting service element of the Alarm Reporting function is mapped to the M-EVENT-REPORT service element with the alarm type parameter mapped to the event type parameter.

The **M-GET** service element is used by a CMISE service user to request the retrieval of attribute values of one or more managed objects from its peer. A reply is expected. This service may be cancelled by means of M-CANCEL-GET. The mandatory parameters are invocation identifier, base object class, and base object instance. There is an optional attribute identifier list parameter. This parameter specifies a set of attribute identifiers for which the attribute values are to be returned by the performing CMISE service user. If this parameter is omitted, then all the attribute identifiers are assumed.

The **M-SET** service element is used by a CMISE service user to request its peer to modify the attribute values of one or more managed objects. The mandatory parameters are invocation identifier, mode, base object class, base object instance, and modification list. The modification list parameter is a set of 3-tuples where each 3-tuple contains an attribute identifier, an attribute value, and a modify operator. The value of the modify operator can be either "replace", "add values", "remove values", or "set to default".

The **M-ACTION** service element is used by a CMISE service user to request its peer to perform an action on one or more managed objects. The mandatory parameters are invocation identifier, mode, base object class, base object instance, and action type. The action type parameter specifies a particular action to be performed. The action which is performed on a managed object is a part of the definition of a managed object class.

The **M-CREATE** service element is used by a CMISE service user to create and register a new managed object. The only mandatory parameters are invocation identifier and managed object class. It is optional for a user to supply a managed object instance parameter and an attribute list parameter. If a managed object instance parameter is not supplied, then the performing CMISE service user will assign a name to the new managed object. The attribute list parameter is used by the performing CMISE service user to assign attribute values to the new managed object. The requesting CMISE service user can also supply a superior object instance and a reference object instance. The superior object instance is the superior of the new managed object, while the reference object instance is an existing managed object of the same class as the managed object to be created. Attribute values associated with the reference object instance become the default values for those attributes not specified by the attribute list parameter.

The **M-DELETE** service element is used by a CMISE service user to request a peer service user to delete and de-register one or more managed objects.

The **M-CANCEL-GET** service element is used by a CMISE service user to request the cancellation of a previously requested and currently outstanding invocation of the M-GET service element. The only mandatory parameters are invocation identifier and get invocation identifier. The get invocation identifier specifies the identifier assigned to a previously requested and currently outstanding M-GET service element.

The CMISE service elements carry many parameters. Functional units are primarily used in CMISE to determine when some of the parameters can be used. All of the CMISE service elements except M-CANCEL-GET are included in the Kernel functional unit. The Multiple Object Selection functional unit makes available the use of the scope and synchronization parameters in the service elements of the Kernel functional unit. If the Multiple Object Selection functional unit is proposed, then the Multiple Reply functional unit should also be proposed. The Filter functional unit makes available the use of the filter parameter in the service elements of the Kernel functional unit. The Multiple Reply functional unit makes available the use of the linked identification parameter in the service elements of the Kernel functional unit. The Extended Service functional unit makes available other presentation service elements in addition to the P-DATA service element. The Cancel Get functional unit makes available the use of the M-CANCEL-GET service element. The negotiation of the functional units is done during application association establishment. Note that CMISE does not provide any association management service element, hence a CMISE service user has to rely on ACSE for association management. By using the user information parameter of A-ASSOCIATE, a CMISE service user can pass information such as CMISE functional units and security information.

18.5.2 CMIP

CMIP is a ROS-based protocol. It maps every CMISE service primitive to a remote operation. An invocation of a CMISE service primitive would trigger the invocation of a ROSE service primitive. In this section, we will show by way of examples how a CMISE service primitive in a given mode is mapped to a remote operation.

CMISE Primitive	Mode	Linked-ID	CMIP Operation
M-CANCEL-GET.req/ind	C	NA	m-Cancel-Get-Confirmed
M-CANCEL-GET.rsp/conf	NA	NA	m-Cancel-Get-Confirmed
M-EVENT-REPORT.req/ind	NC	NA	m-EventReport
M-EVENT-REPORT.req/ind	C	NA	m-EventReport-Confirmed
M-EVENT-REPORT.rsp/conf	NA	NA	m-EventReport-Confirmed
M-GET.req/ind	C	NA	m-Get
M-GET.rsp/conf	NA	absent	m-Get
M-GET.rsp/conf	NA	present	m-Linked-Reply
M-SET.req/ind	NC	NA	m-Set
M-SET.req/ind	C	NA	m-Set-Confirmed
M-SET.rsp/conf	NA	absent	m-Set-Confirmed
M-SET.rsp/conf	NA	present	m-Linked-Reply
M-ACTION.req/ind	NC	NA	m-Action
M-ACTION.req/ind	C	NA	m-Action-Confirmed
M-ACTION.rsp/conf	NA	absent	m-Action-Confirmed
M-ACTION.rsp/conf	NA	present	m-Linked-Reply
M-CREATE.req/ind	C	NA	m-Create
M-CREATE.rsp/conf	NA	NA	m-Create
M-DELETE.req/ind	C	NA	m-Delete
M-DELETE.rsp/conf	NA	absent	m-Delete
M-DELETE.rsp/conf	NA	present	m-Linked-Reply

C - confirmed, NC - non-confirmed, NA - not

TABLE 18.4 Mapping CMISE Service Primitives to Remote Operations

Table 18.4 shows the correspondence between CMISE service primitives and CMIP operations. For example, suppose a CMISE service user issues an M-GET.request service primitive. This primitive is mapped to the m-Get operation. The underlying CMIP machine will convey the m-GET operation to the other side using a RO-INVOKE.request primitive. Upon receiving this operation, the remote CMIP machine will issue an M-GET.indication primitive to its user. Since M-GET is a confirmed service, the remote CMIP machine will wait for one or more response primitives from its user. If there is more than one response, all except the last will contain a linked identifier. Any M-GET.response primitive received containing a linked identifier is mapped to an m-Linked-Reply operation which is sent using a RO-INVOKE.request primitive to the invoking CMIP machine. The M-GET.response primitive not containing a linked identifier (i.e., the last response) is mapped to an m-Get operation which is sent using a RO-RESULT.request primitive to the invoking CMIP machine. The next three examples show how some of the CMIP operations are defined using RO-notation.

Example 18.15

```
m-Action OPERATION
     ARGUMENT ActionArgument
     ::= local-value-action

ActionArgument ::= SEQUENCE{
                        COMPONENTS OF  BaseManagedObjectId,
                        accessControl     [5] AccessControl OPTIONAL,
                        sync              [6] IMPLICIT CMISSync DEFAULT bestEffort,
                        scope             [7] Scope DEFAULT baseObject,
                        filter            CMISFilter DEFAULT and { },
                        actionInfo        [12] IMPLICIT ActionInfo }
BaseManagedObjectId ::= SEQUENCE{
                        baseManagedObjectClass        ObjectClass,
                        baseManagedObjectInstance   ObjectInstance}
```

The above gives the definition of the m-Action operation in the non-confirmed mode.

Example 18.16

```
m-Action-Confirmed OPERATION
     ARGUMENT      ActionArgument
     RESULT        ActionResult
     ERRORS        {accessDenied, classInstanceConflict, invalidScope, etc.}
     LINKED        {m-Linked-Reply}
     ::= local-value-action-c

ActionResult ::= SEQUENCE {
                        managedObjectClass       ObjectClass OPTIONAL,
                        managedObjectInstance    ObjectInstance OPTIONAL,
                        currentTime              [5] IMPLICIT GeneralizedTime OPTIONAL,
                        actionReply              [6] ActionReply OPTIONAL }
```

The above gives the definition of the m-Action-Confirmed operation in the confirmed mode.

Example 18.17

```
m-Create OPERATION
    ARGUMENT      CreateArgument
    RESULT        CreateResult
    ERRORS        {invalidAttributeValue, noSuchReferenceObject etc.}
    ::= local-value-create


CreateArgument ::= SEQUENCE {
    managedObjectClass  ObjectClass
                        CHOICE  {managedObjectInstance  ObjectInstance,
                                 superiorObjectInstance [8] ObjectInstance} OPTIONAL,
    accessControl       AccessControl OPTIONAL,
    referenceObjectInst ObjectInstance OPTIONAL,
    attributeList       IMPLICIT SET OF Attribute OPTIONAL }
```

The above gives the definition of m-Create, and illustrates the parameters to create a managed object.

Earlier it was described how two levels of parameterization are used. We close this section by showing how parameterization occurs at the SMASE/CMISE interface. We will illustrate this with the Alarm Reporting function.

Example 18.18

Alarm Reporting	M-EVENT-REPORT
invocation identifier	invocation identifier
mode	mode
managed object class	managed object class
managed object instance	managed object instance
alarm type	event type
event time	event time
alarm information	event information

The Alarm Reporting service element is mapped to the M-EVENT-REPORT service element. The mapping between the Alarm Reporting parameters and the M-EVENT-REPORT parameters is shown above. Note that the alarm type parameter is mapped to the event type parameter.

18.6   CMIP Library

The **CMIP (CM) library**, developed by UNIX Systems Laboratory, provides an API to CMISE and ACSE. Network management applications can be built by using the CM library. The designs of the CM library and the A/P library are consistent with each other.

Like the A/P library, the CM library uses the concept of a library environment. Indeed, some of the CM library environment attributes are A/P library environment attributes, thus the CM library environment provides transparent access to the A/P library environment attributes. The CM library provides functions to maintain an association, maintain the CM library environment, exchange CMISE service primitives, and pass error reports during the processing of a CMISE service request. These functions are examined next.

Initially, a management application calls cl_open() to obtain a communication endpoint. This function will return a file descriptor which identifies a CM library instance. Like ap_open(), cl_open() contains an oflags argument. If the application wants the mode to be synchronous, it should set oflags to NULL (or 0), otherwise it should set oflags to O_NDELAY. To terminate a CM library instance, the cl_close() function is called. A CM library instance also terminates automatically when the application terminates.

The next step that an application should do is to create a CM library instance. There are two ways to do this. The first way is to use the cl_init_env() function which behaves quite similarly to the ap_init_env() function in the A/P library. One of the arguments of cl_init_env() is the name of an environment initialization file. The environment initialization file contains a number of default attribute settings. The cl_init_env() function essentially copies the attribute settings from the environment initialization file into a CM library instance. The second way to create a CM library instance is to call the cl_restore() function which essentially recreates an environment set earlier by some other application.

Certain CM library environment attributes are not part of the environment initialization file. Such attributes have to be explicitly placed in the CM library instance by means of the cl_set_env() function. For example, if the application is the initiator, it must set the AP_BIND_PADDR attribute to bind its presentation address, the AP_CNTX_NAME attribute to propose an application context to the remote application entity, and the AP_REM_PADDR attribute to specify the presentation address of a remote application entity. Note that all the above three attributes are A/P library environment attributes. This shows that the A/P library environment attributes can be accessed transparently by the CM library.

Explained below are some of the CM library environment attributes:

- CL_CREQ_LAST_INV: This indicates the last outstanding confirmed request.
- CL_CREQ_FIRST_INVK: This indicates the first outstanding confirmed request.
- CL_MAX_CREQ_INVK: This gives the maximum number of outstanding confirmed service requests that are allowed.
- CL_NUM_CREQ_INVK: This gives the current number of outstanding confirmed requests.
- CL_FU_AVAIL: This shows the functional units supported by CMIP.
- CL_FU_SEL: This gives the CMIP functional units for a particular library instance.

Note that the first four attributes above have to do with confirmed requests. Outstanding confirmed requests exist if the asynchronous mode is selected for cl_open(). Similarly,

CM library environment attributes exist for outstanding confirmed indications which are meaningful to an application playing the responder role.

After the CM library instance has been created, the CM library environment attributes can be read by calling cl_get_env(). When the cl_get_env() is called, a pointer is supplied by the caller to point to a storage area where the retrieved value is stored. Later on, this storage area can be freed by calling the cl_free() function. The CM library environment can be saved or restored by means of the cl_save() function or the cl_restore() function. The cl_save() and cl_restore() functions work similar to the ap_save() and ap_restore() functions in the A/P library.

Next, the initiator application can establish an association by calling the cl_snd() function. To indicate that an association is requested, the "M_INIT_REQ" event is passed as an argument of cl_snd(). If the acceptor application wants to accept an indication, it calls the cl_rcv() function with the "M_INIT_IND" event as an argument. The initiator application can terminate an association by calling cl_snd() with the "M_TERM_REQ" event as an argument. Note that by providing these events to manage an association, the CM library effectively provides an interface to ACSE.

Once the association has been set up, CMISE service primitives can be passed. The CM library designates an event for every CMISE service primitive. Every CMISE event is passed as an argument of the cl_snd() or the cl_rcv() function. For example, if a manager application wants to crate a managed object, it calls cl_snd() with the "M_CRT_REQ" event as a parameter. If it wants to receive an event report, it calls cl_rcv() with the "M_EVT_RPT_IND" event as a parameter. The letter "M" here stands for management.

The CM library also provides a set of CMIP error primitives to report failure during the processing of a CMISE service request. Some examples of errors are given below:

- classInstanceConflict: This indicates that the specified managed object instance is not a member of the specified object class.
- invalArgVal: This indicates that the argument value is invalid.
- noSuchArgument: This indicates that the argument specified is invalid.
- noSuchEvtType: This indicates that the event type specified is invalid.
- noSuchInvokeID: This indicates that the invocation identifier specified is invalid.
- noSuchObjClass: This indicates that the object class specified is invalid.

Depending on which CMISE service primitive is used, different CMISE errors may occur. The CMISE errors occurred depend on the CMISE service primitive processed. For example, the following CMISE errors can arise during the servicing of the M-EVENT-REPORT service element: invalArgVal, noSuchArgument, noSuchEvtType, noSuchObjClass, and noSuchObjInst.

18.7 OSI Management Profiles

For two OSI management applications to interwork with each other, they must use the same OSI management functional profile. An OSI management profile is more than a

CMIP profile. Besides specifying constraints on CMIP, an OSI management profile must also specify the systems management functions and managed objects supported by the profile. Thus we can have two OSI management applications, both conforming to CMIP, which fails to interwork with each other because they use incompatible managed object class definitions. Although the OSI management standards provide tools for the definitions of managed object classes, the managed objects are defined by a profile group.

Many groups are involved in defining managed objects. Examples are:

- OIW NMSIG extending the managed objects that have been defined in the standards,
- T1M1.5 defining telecommunication objects,
- OSI/NMF defining telecommunication objects, protocol layer objects, computer related objects as well as interconnection objects,
- IEEE 802 defining LAN objects,
- ISO SC 21/WG 4 defining management support objects, and
- ISO/IEC SC 6 defining OSI lower layer objects.

Currently there are efforts to define an **International Managed Information Library (IMIL)**. The goal of IMIL is to reconcile the differences in the definitions of managed objects from different groups and put them in a common place for reference. The IMIL will eventually become a widely and readily accessible repository that lists or points to all the object definitions in the standard GDMO syntax. It would give a widespread public disclosure to managed objects of all sorts. It would also promote reuse and refinement of the existing management information definitions. A manager can use IMIL to manage not only the standard objects but also the proprietary objects of other vendors to some extent. Government agencies can also use IMIL as a dictionary for the procurement purpose.

There are two very popular existing OSI management profiles. They are the NMF profile and the T1M1 profile. A brief overview of these profiles is given next.

The **OSI/Network Management Forum (OSI/NMF)** was created in 1988 with a mission to accelerate the development and use of OSI standards for network management. Fundamental to the mission is the objective of achieving interoperability between disparate network management systems. The idea is to define a single implementation of emerging network management standards which can be used as the definition of a common network management interface to allow their products to interoperate. This single implementation, known as the **OSI/NMF profile**, consists of sifting through the many allowed options, and selecting those that best suit a network management application. This work is nontrivial considering the fact that the network management standards are not yet fully defined. So in many cases, the Forum works from draft standards if available, and makes informed judgements where they are not. The Forum does not create standards. Rather it encourages standard bodies to move quickly and adopt a common approach. As part of the efforts to promote interoperability in a broader spectrum of users, OSI/NMF includes many non-OSI objects in its managed object library.

The first specification of OSI/NMF profile was released in 1990. This release emphasized fault management and configuration management. It defined thirty five managed object classes covering a wide range of resources. Release 2 work is currently underway. It addresses diagnostic and testing management messages, and the use of FTAM to enable the bulk transfer of logs between systems for analysis. The OSI/NMF operating environment consists of a group of systems called **Conformant Management Entities (CMEs)**. These entities communicate with each other using the OSI/NMF Protocol Stack (**"P" Stack**) and exchange OSI/NMF defined messages (**"M" messages**) for the purpose of network management. Figure 18.12 illustrates the "P" Stack.

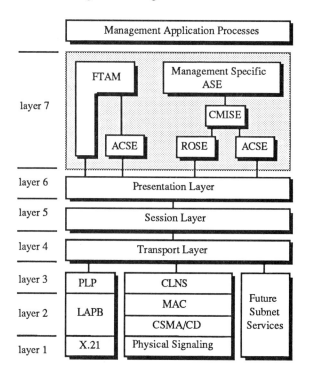

FIGURE 18.12   "P" Stack

Next, we describe the T1M1 profile. Formed before OSI/NMF, T1M1.5 is a subgroup of the Exchange Carriers Standards Association which has the mandate to define interface standards for **Operations Administration, Maintenance, and Provisioning (OAM&P)**. The T1M1 activities are focused on network management in a telecommunications environment. Thus they employ primarily telecommunications objects.

Management in T1M1 is provided by a distributed **Telecommunications Management Network (TMN)** which is essentially an integrating management system. A TMN is made up of a number of **operations systems (OSs)** and **mediation devices (MDs)**. An OS corresponds to a manager, and an MD corresponds to an agent.

The resources managed by an MD are known as **network elements (NEs)**. Early work by T1M1.5 has focused on the interface between an OS and an NE. This interface is known as the **"Q3" interface**. Current emphasis is on the definition of the OS/OS interface. Figure 18.13 illustrates the T1M1 stack. To facilitate interworking, T1M1 and NMF have established a formal liaison whose objective is to converge their object definitions and systems management functions.

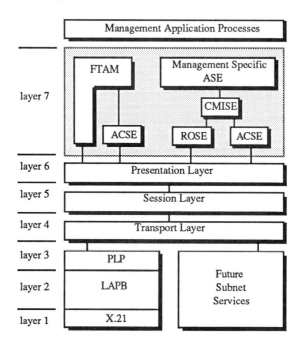

FIGURE 18.13   T1M1 stack

18.8   Summary

Network management is concerned with planning, monitoring, accounting, and controlling the use of network resources. The major problem in network management today is how to eliminate islands of management subsystems in a corporate or enterprise network. The OSI standards attempt to define an integrated networking management system by providing uniformity at three levels: uniformity in the definition of managed objects, uniformity in the definition of systems management functions, and uniformity in the specification of a standard communication protocol to support the exchange of management information.

A managed object is the management view of a network resource. It is defined in terms of attributes it possesses, operations it may perform, notifications it may issue, and relationships with other objects. The Management Information Base is the repository of managed objects. To provide uniformity in the definition of managed objects, the GDMO document defined a set of management templates. These templates allow object definers to define managed objects in a consistent manner. Without GDMO, the same network resource may have more than one definition.

Users' requirements on systems management can be divided into five different Management Functional Areas (MFAs). They are Configuration Management, Fault Management, Accounting Management, Security Management, and Performance Management. To support these MFAs in a uniform manner, ISO/IEC defines a number of systems management functions. These functions include the Object Management function, the State Management function, the Relation Management function, the Alarm Reporting function, the Event Report Management function, and the Log Control function. The Object Management function, for example, provides the users with the ability to create, delete, examine, and modify managed objects. Uniformity in the definition of systems management functions means that the same function can be used to meet the requirements of more than one MFA.

To provide a uniform communication standard for conveying management information, ISO defines CMISE. CMISE defines a number of management operations which allow a manager to retrieve or alter information associated with a managed object. Through scoping and filtering, management operations can be performed on multiple objects.

A typical application context contains SMASE, CMISE, ROSE and ACSE as ASEs. An SMASE provides the systems management functions to support the management requirements of an application. SMASE is very closely coupled with CMISE and ROSE. SMASE essentially parameterizes the CMISE management operations with management information, while CMISE parameterizes the ROSE interface with operations and invocation identifiers.

While the OSI management standards are aimed at uniformity at all three levels, they do not define the managed objects that a profile may need. However, tools and some common objects are provided by the standards. It is up to a profile group to define their managed objects using the tools. There are many profile groups involved in the definitions of managed objects. Both OSI/NMF and T1M1.5 are briefly examined in this chapter. There is an ongoing effort to define an International Management Information Library (IMIL). The goal of IMIL is to reconcile the differences in the definitions of managed objects from different groups and put them in one common place for reference. The IMIL is to be a widely and readily accessible repository that lists or points to all object definitions. It would provide the users with a single complete dictionary of OSI objects as well as non-OSI objects.

Related Standards

CMISE

ISO 9595: Information Technology - Open Systems Interconnection - Common Management Information Service Definition

ISO 9595 DAM4: Information Technology - Open Systems Interconnection - Common Management Information Service Definition - Amendment 4: Access Control

ISO 9595 PDAM X: Information Technology - Open Systems Interconnection - Common Management Information Service Definition - Amendment X: Allomorphism

ISO 9596-1: Information Technology - Open Systems Interconnection - Common Management Information Protocol Specification - Part 1: Specification

CD 9596-2 Title: Information Technology - Open Systems Interconnection - Common Management Information Protocol Specification - Part 2: Protocol Implementation Conformance Statement (PICS) Proforma

ISO 9596 PDAM X: Information Technology - Open Systems Interconnection - Common Management Information Protocol Specification - Amendment X: Allomorphism

Structure of Management Information (SMI)

DIS 10165-1: Information Technology - Open Systems Interconnection -Management Information Services - Structure of Management Information - Part 1: Management Information Model

ISO 10165-2: Information Technology - Open Systems Interconnection -Management Information Services - Structure of Management Information - Part 2: Definition of Management Information

ISO 10165-4: Information Technology - Open Systems Interconnection -Management Information Services - Structure of Management Information - Part 4: Guidelines for the Definition of Managed Objects

CD 10165-5: Information Technology - Open Systems Interconnection -Management Information Services - Structure of Management Information - Part 5: Generic Management Information

CD 10165-6: Information Technology - Open Systems Interconnection - Requirements and Guidelines for Implementation Conformance Statement Proformas Associated with Management Information

Elements of Management Information

DIS 10733: Information Technology - Telecommunications and Information Exchange between Systems - Elements of Management Information Related to OSI Network Layer Standards

Systems Management (SM)

ISO 7498-4: Information Processing Systems - Open Systems Interconnection - Basic Reference Model - Part 4: Management Framework

ISO 10040: Information Technology - Open Systems Interconnection - Systems Management Overview

DIS 10164-1: Information Technology - Open Systems Interconnection - Systems Management - Part 1: Object Management Function

DIS 10164-2: Information Technology - Open Systems Interconnection - Systems Management - Part 2: State Management Function

DIS 10164-3: Information Technology - Open Systems Interconnection - Systems Management - Part 3: Attributes for Representing Relationships

DIS 10164-4: Information Technology - Open Systems Interconnection - Systems Management - Part 4: Alarm Reporting Function

DIS 10164-5: Information Technology - Open Systems Interconnection - Systems Management - Part 5: Event Report Management Function

DIS 10164-6: Information Technology - Open Systems Interconnection - Systems Management - Part 6: Log Control Function

DIS 10164-7: Information Technology - Open Systems Interconnection - Systems Management - Part 7: Security Alarm Reporting Function

DIS 10164-8: Information Technology - Open Systems Interconnection - Systems Management - Part 8: Security Audit Trail Function

CD 10164-9.2: Information Technology - Open Systems Interconnection - Systems Management - Part 9: Objects and Attributes for Access Control

CD 10164-10.2: Information Technology - Open Systems Interconnection - Systems Management - Part 10: Accounting Meter Function

CD 10164-11.2: Information Technology - Open Systems Interconnection - Systems Management - Part 11: Workload monitoring Function

CD 10164-12: Information Technology - Open Systems Interconnection - Systems Management - Part 12: Test Management function

CD 10164-13: Information Technology - Open Systems Interconnection - Systems Management - Part 13: Summarization Function

SC 21 N 6021: Information Technology - Open Systems Interconnection - Systems Management - Part s: Scheduling Function

SC 21 N 6040: OSI Software Management - Working Draft

SC 21 N 6041: General Relationship - Working Draft

SC 21 N 6047: First Working Draft on Management Domains

SC 21 N 6048: Working Document on Management Knowledge Management

SC 21 N 6049: Working Document on Synchronization

SC 21 N 6307: Information Technology - Open Systems Interconnection - Systems Management - Confidence and Diagnostic Test Classes

Performance Management

SC 21 N 6306: Information Technology - Open Systems Interconnection - Systems Management - Performance Management Working document - Seventh Draft

Accounting Management

SC 21 N 4971: Information Technology - Open Systems Interconnection - Accounting Management Working Document - Fourth Version

19

Virtual Terminal

In an OSE, it is desirable to access applications in a remote computer system through a terminal regardless of the make of the computer system and the terminal. In practice, this is not feasible as most application programs are built to interact with a limited range of terminals. The **Virtual Terminal (VT)** standard provides a solution to this problem by describing how a virtual terminal simulates a real terminal. A VT is an abstraction of a class of related terminals. A terminal user and an application program can interact with each other via a VT class which is established during the application association establishment. In the model shown in Figure 19.1, both the terminal driver and the application program are VT-users. They communicate with the VT software by means of a local mapping. The local mapping performs the translation between the VT software and the terminal/application program.

Classes of VT services have been defined to meet the needs of a specific range of applications and terminal functions. ISO/IEC 9040 describes the **Virtual Terminal Basic Class (BCVT)**. Being character-oriented, BCVT supports a wide range of applications. It also provides a limited set of services for manipulating blocks and forms. The Forms facilities, for example, can handle operations associated with forms mode terminals. Other classes of VT services include the graphics class and the image class. Only BCVT will be examined in this chapter.

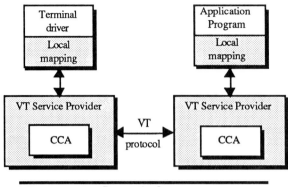

FIGURE 19.1 Terminal User and Application Program Interaction.

In Section 19.1 we provide an overview of BCVT and its model. In Section 19.2, we examine the attributes associated with the various components of the model. Section 19.3 describes the block and field structuring facilities and their associated objects. Section 19.4 describes the VT service definition. Finally, Section 19.5 describes the VT protocol.

19.1 BCVT Concepts

BCVT supports character oriented terminals. In this section, we cover the BCVT concepts.

- **VTE**

There are many classes of character oriented terminals. It is infeasible to standardize a single VT environment providing the services of all the character-oriented terminals. Realizing this, the VT standard introduced the concept of a **Virtual Terminal Environment (VTE)**. A VTE is a set of logically related parameters, known as **VTE-parameters**, defining the data structuring and operational characteristics for a particular VT-association. A VTE can be built upon a **VTE-profile** which is a predefined set of VTE-parameters. VT-users can start from a default VTE-profile and negotiate VTE-parameter values to arrive at a VTE. The VTE may be subsequently replaced or modified depending upon the type of negotiation facilities available.

OIW has defined the following VTE-profiles:

- The **TELNET Profile** is intended for terminal transactions characterized by simple line-at-a-time or character-at-a-time dialogues. It is based on the TELNET protocol of the Internet. TELNET is built on the concept of a **Network Virtual Terminal (NVT)** which is a bi-directional character-oriented device with a display and a keyboard. The display shows data from the application program and the keyboard sends user data to the application program. NVT is a scroll mode device with

an unlimited line length and unlimited number of lines. TELNET commands are sent as control signals which occur as byte strings embedded in the normal data stream.
• The **Transparent Profile** supports a simultaneous two way exchange of uninterpreted sequences of characters. Using this profile, a VT-user can control terminals directly through the use of embedded control characters and escape sequences.
• The **Forms Profile** supports forms-based applications with local entry and validation of data by the terminal system. For example, an application in a mainframe can download a form to a terminal with some of the fields being read-only and other fields to be filled in by the terminal user.
• The **Scroll Profile** supports line-at-a-time interactions between a terminal and a computer system. Scrolling is bi-directional, i.e., it can be either forward or backward. This profile supports what is often referred to as "type-ahead". This allows input from the terminal user to be available to the host application as soon as the application is ready for input.
• The **S-mode Page Profile** supports the interaction in which the data is displayed on a full screen (page) basis. Thus, a terminal user can fill all the fields on a screen and then send the entire screen to the host.
• The **X3 Profile** supports functionality similar to the CCITT Packet Assembler/Disassembler (PAD) recommendations (X.3/X.29).

• **display objects**

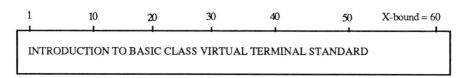

FIGURE 19.2   Single Line or One Dimensional Screen Display.

A **display object** is a one, two, or three dimensional array of character array elements together with a display pointer. A one dimensional array corresponds to a single line display (Figure 19.2), a two dimensional array corresponds to a multi-line screen display, and a three dimensional array corresponds to a multi-page display. The Transparent and X.3 profiles use a one dimensional array, the TELNET and Scroll profiles use a two dimensional array, and the Forms profile uses a three dimensional array. Each array dimension has a lower bound of 1 and an upper bound which may be defined or declared as unbounded. The dimensions are named X, Y and Z, where X is the lowest order dimension. A set of array elements identified by a contiguous set of x-coordinate values is known as an **X-array**. A **Y-array** is a set of X-arrays identified by a set of contiguous y-coordinate values. A **Z-array** is a set of Y-arrays identified by a set of contiguous z-coordinate values. A **primitive display pointer** is used to identify an array element in the display object. When blocks are in use, an **extended display pointer** is also used to identify an array element within a block.

At any given time, an array element may contain a **primary attribute value** selected from a character repertoire available within the current VTE. In addition, each array element may contain **secondary attribute values** which specify the character repertoire in use and the render attributes for that array element. Examples of render attributes are emphasis, font, foreground color, and background color.

Operations on a display object can be either addressing operations or updating operations. Addressing operations enable the moving of the display pointer or the cursor. They can move a pointer to an absolute position by some relative amount, or to the home position which corresponds to the upper left hand corner of the first page. A few updating operations are explained next. The TEXT operation enters a specified primary attribute value into the array element identified by the display pointer. It then increments the x-coordinate value of the primitive display pointer by one. The ATTRIBUTE operation sets the secondary attribute of some or all the array elements. The ERASE operation cancels the character content of an array element .

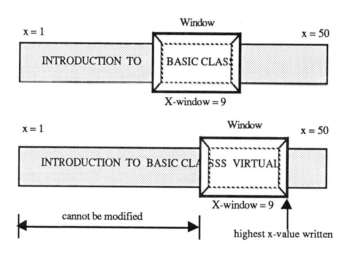

FIGURE 19.3   Update Window

Each dimension of the display object can have an **update window** determining the region where editing is allowed. The purpose of the use of an update window is to limit the amount of display object content which an implementation must store. The update window places lower limits on locations which may be modified by the update operations. If the display pointer is moved to an address below the lower limit of the update window, the TEXT operation will not be invalid. However, the update window does not constrain the upper limit of the TEXT operation which can cause the update window to be moved to include a set of higher coordinate values, i.e., the update window will be moved or scrolled forward with the window size unchanged (Figure 19.3). At any time, the upper limit is at the highest coordinate value that is last updated by the TEXT operation. The **d-window**

VTE-parameter (d for dimension) describes the number of positions in the window minus one. For example, the d-dimension in Figure 19.3 is 9. Using this d-window parameter, one can describe various terminal capabilities starting with the simplest terminals with no editing capabilities (by setting the update window size to zero) to the more sophisticated page-mode terminals with full screen editing capabilities.

• **modes of operations**

The BCVT service supports two modes of operation: the S-mode (synchronous mode) and the A-mode (asynchronous mode). These two modes have their origins from two of the common terminals types, namely, the IBM 3270 (S-mode) and the DEC VT 100 (A-mode). The **S-mode** allows at most one VT-user to transmit at any time. If a VT-user is entering data from a keyboard in the S-mode, data from the remote computer cannot appear on the terminal display screen. This mode is supported by the Forms and Paged profiles. The **A-mode** permits both VT-users to transmit data at the same time. This mode, as found in most personal computers, is useful for real time applications where the terminal must be updated with status changes at the same time data entry is occurring at the terminal keyboard. The Transparent and Scroll profiles support the A-mode. The TELNET profile supports either mode.

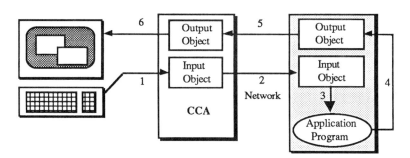

FIGURE 19.4 A-mode Operation

The mode of operation can be modelled by one or two display objects. For the A-mode, each end of the VT-association maintains two display objects, one for input and one for output. Modifying the output (input) display object at one end will only affect the output (input) display object at the other end, so basically the output (input) objects at both ends are identical to each other. Figure 19.4 illustrates the A-mode. Note that the display object for input is independent of the display object for output. For example, one can include certain control characters in the display object for input but exclude them from the display object for output. For the S-mode, the two ends share the same display object, hence each end maintains only one display object. Consistency of the two objects at either end is provided through the exchange of VT APDUs and tokens which prevent both sides from modifying the display object simultaneously. Figure 19.5 illustrates the S-mode.

The mode of operation must be specified during the VT-association establishment. The BCVT standard defines two default VTE-profiles: the **S-mode VTE-profile** and the **A-mode VTE-profile**. If the initiating VT-user does not specify a VTE-profile during the VT-association establishment, either the S-mode VTE-profile or the A-mode VTE-profile may be chosen by the VT service provider to be used as a basis for further negotiation.

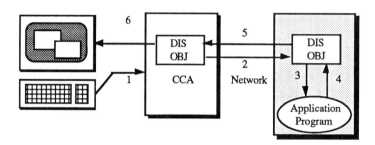

FIGURE 19.5   S-mode Operation

*   **device objects**

A **device object** is an abstraction of a real device object. There is at least one device object for each real device attached to the terminal (Figure 19.6). In TELNET for example, there is a device object associated with the keyboard and a device object associated with the display.

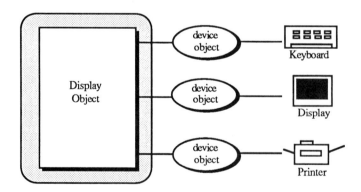

FIGURE 19.6   Device Objects

*   **access rules**

When the S-mode is used, access rules must be used to determine whether and when each VT-user is permitted to update the single display object. The BCVT standard defined seven different access rules. In the S-mode, the single display object always has the **WAVAR**

(write access variable) access rule whose ownership can be passed between the two VT-users. In the A-mode, the **WACI (write access connection initiator)** is owned at all times by the initiating VT-user, while the **WACA (write access connection acceptor)** is owned at all times by the accepting VT-user.

Consider the TELNET profile which supports both modes. For the A-mode, the TELNET Profile maintains two display objects, one for the display output and the other for the keyboard input. The access rule of the display object for displaying output is WACA, which is owned by the accepting application VT-user. The access rule of the display object for the keyboard input is WACI which is owned by the initiating terminal VT-user.

- **control objects**

Control objects are used to handle control information related to VT functions and real devices. Examples of control objects are given below:

- Data received at a terminal from an application program may cause audible/visual warnings or enable/disable the use of the keypad and the keyboard. A control object of category "symbolic" is used to convey symbolic signals to the terminal from the application. OIW has defined two control objects for this purpose: SA (sequenced application) and UA (unsequenced application). These two objects will be described in Section 19.2.2.
- A default control object is implicitly defined when a device object is defined. It holds a boolean value which signals on/off . This allows a remote switch to turn on/off the device.
- The **Echo Control Object (ECO)** is used by an application VT-user in the A-mode to notify a terminal VT-user whether echoing should be on or off. If no echo control object exists, it is the local VT-user's decision whether input updates are echoed locally or not.
- When controlled data entry is to be done, an application VT-user may update the **FDCO (Field Definition Control Object)**, the **FEICO (Field Entry Instruction Control Object)**, and the **FEPCO (Field Entry Pilot Control Object)** with field information defining the entry rules and reactions, and then updates the **CCO (Context Control Object)** to indicate whether data entry can be started by the terminal VT-user. These control objects will be explained in Section 19.3.2.
- A **Termination Control Object (TCO)**, other than the default control object, can be also linked to a device object. Consider the situation when a device object models some update object device such as a keyboard. A terminal VT-user can use the TCO to notify the application VT-user of certain events. This is achieved by writing a termination event-id to the TCO. By selecting the CO-trigger field of the TCO, a VT-user can have events automatically signal its peer.

A control object is either simple or structured. A **simple control object** has a single data element which can be either a character string, a boolean string, a symbolic value, or a bitstring. **Parametric control objects** can contain several data elements, all of which need not be the same type. Changes to these data elements can be made by negotiation. More complex control objects are the **non-parametric control objects**. Although changes to individual elements of a non-parameteric control are possible, they cannot be negotiated as in the case of parametric control objects. Examples of these complex control objects are FDCO, FEICO, and FEPCO which are used to control the process of data entry.

Like a display object, a control object also has access rules to determine which VT-user may update it and when it may be updated. Accordingly, the BCVT standard defines a few access rules in addition to the ones applicable to a display object. These extra rules are: no-access, WACI, WACA, WAVAR & WACI, WAVAR & WACA, and NSAC.

- The **no-access** rule means that neither VT-user may update the control object.
- The **WACI** access rule means that the control object may be updated by the VT-initiator only.
- The **WACA** access rule means that the control object may be updated by the VT-acceptor only.
- The composite value **WAVAR & WACI** means that the acceptor does not have access and the initiator has access only if it owns WAVAR.
- The composite value **WAVAR & WACA** means that the initiator does not have access and the acceptor has access only if it owns WAVAR.
- The **NSAC** access rule means that the control object may be updated by either VT-user at any time.

For example, the access rules that can be applied to ECO (i.e., Echo Control Object) are "WACA", "WACI" or "NSAC". The WAVAR mode which is used for S-mode does not apply to ECO which is used only for the A-mode.

- **conceptual communication area**

The display objects, device objects, and control objects make up the so called **shared conceptual communication area (CCA)**. Information exchanged between two VT-users is modelled by one VT-user updating the contents of the CCA using the VT service elements.

Internally, the CCA can be organized into four areas: a **conceptual data store (CDS)** containing one or two display objects, a **control, signalling, and status store (CSS)** containing zero or more control objects used for device control, signaling and status information, an **access control store (ACS)** maintaining the current WAVAR access rights, and a **data structure definition (DSD)** containing the definitions for the various objects. Figure 19.7 illustrates the internal organization of the CCA when the mode of operation is A-mode.

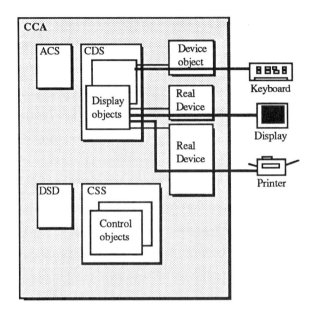

FIGURE 19.7 Internal Organization of the CCA in A-mode.

* **delivery control**

The BCVT service provides delivery control mechanisms by means of which a VT-user may mark the end of a sequence of updates to either display objects or control objects. This marking initiates delivery of data accumulated in buffers from one VT-user to its peer. The BCVT standard defined three kinds of delivery control: "no delivery control", "simple delivery control", and "quarantine delivery control".

No delivery control simply means that a VT-user cannot mark the end of a sequence of updates. It only means that a VT-user can deliver updates by issuing a data transfer request primitive which updates the value of some control object whose CO-trigger capability is selected. The BCVT standard did not constrain how an implementation of the VT service provider delivers the updates.

With simple delivery control, a VT-user can explicitly mark the end of a sequence of updates, causing delivery of the stored sequence of updates and thereby indicating to its peer that the data is more or less complete. The VT-user initiating the delivery can also request acknowledge of delivery from its peer. The VT service provider here can also deliver updates even if the VT-user does not initiate the delivery function.

Quarantine delivery control is simple delivery control with a constraint that the VT-service provider is not permitted to deliver updates before the delivery function is initiated by a VT-user. However, the VT service provider is permitted to concatenate or "net-effect" the accumulated updates between two deliveries. If applied, net-effecting may remove changes to the character stored in a particular array element which has been obviated by changes later in the sequence of updates to the same character. Net-effecting is not permitted in the first two kinds of delivery control.

Some VT service elements may cause implicit delivery. For example, if a VT-user wants to release a VT-association by issuing a VT-RELEASE.request primitive, updates are delivered to its peer before the peer receives the VT-RELEASE.indication primitive. If the peer VT-user responds positively to the release, then updates accumulated at the peer VT-user should be delivered to the initiating VT-user before the initiating VT-user receives the VT-RELEASE.confirmation primitive. However, if the peer VT-user refuses the release, then updates need not be delivered to the initiating VT-user.

An **update priority** is assigned to a control object to reflect the urgency with which the VT service provider will attempt to notify an update requested by a VT-user to its peer. Its value can be either "normal", "high", or "urgent". A control object with a **normal update priority**, which is subject to delivery control, is ordered (i.e., in a first in first out manner) with respect to the display object updates. A control object with either high or urgent update priority is not subject to delivery control. **High priority updates** can be delivered when normal updates are held by the quarantine delivery control. If the Urgent Data functional unit is selected, then updates to control objects with an **urgent update priority** will be delivered before normal updates.

- **break-in**

The BCVT service provides a break-in service for VT-users to interrupt each other during the data transfer phase. There are two kinds of interrupts: destructive interrupt and non-destructive interrupt.

Destructive interrupt is used in a situation when a terminal user wants to stop some current activity. In this situation, the terminal user needs to advise the application program to stop whatever information exchange is currently in progress and requests the VT service provider to purge all the outstanding updates which have not been delivered. As a result, the objects at either end may be unsynchronized. The use of this service requires the initiating VT-user to provide resynchronization information to its peer, and optionally specify which VT-user should have the reassignable access-right at the conclusion of the service.

Non-destructive interrupt is used in a situation when a VT-user needs to send out-of-band information to its peer. For example, an application program may want to send a signal to a terminal user by displaying an attention message on the bottom line of the display screen, without interrupting the current dialogue flow. Deferred actions may be taken by the VT-user receiving the attention message. This kind of non-destructive interrupt is supported implicitly by sending updates to "high" or "urgent" priority control objects using the underlying expedited data transfer service. The use of the underlying expedited data service means that only a small amount of information can be carried in an "urgent" priority update. In contrast, "high" priority updates can carry a large amount of information.

19.2 VTE-parameters

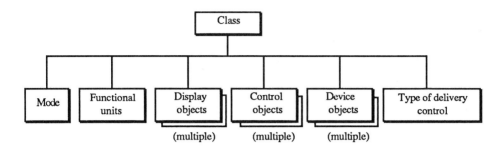

FIGURE 19.8   Top Level of the VTE-parameter Graph

Every BCVT object is described in terms of a set of VTE-parameters. The VTE-parameters can be arranged into a directed graph. Figure 19.8 shows the top part of the graph. Note that mode, class, and functional units are not VTE-parameters. They are service parameters supplied during a VT-association establishment. Display objects, control objects, and device objects in the graph can have multiple occurrences, where each occurrence has its own set of VTE-parameters. In the following sections, the VTE-parameters of different objects will be described.

19.2.1 Display Object VTE-parameters

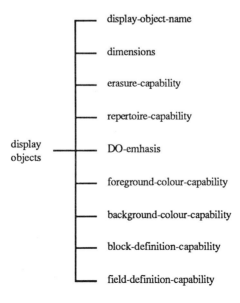

FIGURE 19.9   Primary VTE-parameters of a Display Object.

The VTE-parameters of a display object can be primary, secondary, or tertiary. Figure 19.9 shows the primary VTE-parameters of a display object. Some of these VTE-parameters are explained below:

- display-object-name: This name identifies a display object.
- DO-access: This has three possible values: "WAVAR", "WACI", or "WACA".
- dimensions: This is either "one", "two", or "three". The default is "two". Each dimension is specified by a set of secondary VTE-parameters such as d-bound, d-addressing, d-absolute, and d-window. The d-bound parameter is used to define the upper bound of the d dimension, the d-addressing parameter indicates whether the value of the display object pointer can be altered by an explicit addressing operation, the d-absolute parameter indicates whether the value of the display object pointer for the d dimension can be set to a new value by a pointer-absolute addressing operation, and the d-window parameter defines the update-window-size for the d-dimension.
- erasure-capability: This parameter is used to indicate the availability of the erase operation.
- block-definition-capability: This parameter is present only if the Block functional unit is selected.
- field-definition-capability: This parameter is present only if the Field functional unit is selected. It is further qualified by three secondary parameters: max-fields, max-field-elements, and access-outside-fields. These parameters will be explained later in Section 19.3.
- repertoire-capability: This parameter specifies the maximum number of repertoires. For each repertoire, there are two secondary VTE-parameters: font-capability and repertoire-assignment. The font-capability parameter indicates the number of fonts available for each repertoire appearing in the list associated with the repertoire-assignment parameter. The repertoire-assignment parameter defines an ordered list of repertoires. Each display object position stores, in addition to a character value, an identification of the repertoire to which the character value belongs. If the repertoire assignment parameter is absent, then the default repertoire assignment method is the one specified in ISO/IEC 2022. Control characters as used in ISO/IEC 2022 are not supported by BCVT, meaning that the occurrence of a control character in the TEXT operation only indicates that a value should be written to a display object position and no control function should occur.
- foreground-color-capability and background-color-capability: These parameters are used to specify the maximum number of foreground-color values and background-color-values. They are further qualified by two secondary VTE-parameters: foreground-color-assignment and background-color-assignment. Each assignment is described by a color-assignment-type and a color-assignment-value.
- DO-emphasis: This secondary parameter defines an ordered list of registered emphasis sets. Examples of emphasis values are NORMAL, BOLD, ITALIC, UNDERLINED (single), UNDERLINED (double), and SHADOW.

Examples of VTE-parameters for some display objects are given below:

Example 19.1

```
Display-objects *(single occurrence)* =
{
    display-object-name = D,
    do-access = "WAVAR",
    dimension = 2,
    x-dimension =
    {
        x-bound = 80,
        x-window = 0
        *(x-addressing and x-absolute assume default values)*
    },
    y-dimension =
    {
        *(y-bound, y-addressing, y-absolute and y-window all assume default values)*
    }
},
```

The above is a display object for the default VTE-profile in the S-mode.

Example 19.2

```
-- A-mode
Display-objects = *(double occurrence)*
{
{
display-object-name = D, *(DISPLAY)*
do-access = "WACA",
dimensions = "two",
    x-dimension =
    {
        x-bound = "unbounded,"
        x-addressing = "no constraint,"
        x-absolute = "no,"
        x-window = profile-argument-r1
    }
    y-dimension =
    {
        y-bound = "unbounded,"
        y-addressing = "higher only,"
```

```
                y-absolute = "no",
                y-window = 1
        },
        erasure-capability = "yes",
        repertoire-capability = 2,
        repertoire-assignment = profile-argument-r2,
        repertoire-assignment = <ESC>2/5 2/15 4/2
        },
        {
        display-object-name = K, *(KEYBOARD)*
        do-access = "WACI,"
        dimensions = "two",
                x-dimension =
                {
                        x-bound = "unbounded,"
                        x-addressing = "no constraint,"
                        x-absolute = "no,"
                        x-window = profile-argument-r1
                }
                y-dimension =
                {
                        y-bound = "unbounded,"
                        y-addressing = "higher only,"
                        y-absolute = "no,"
                        y-window = 1
                },
        erasure-capability = "yes,"
        repertoire-capability = 2,
        repertoire-assignment = profile-argument-r2,
        repertoire-assignment = <ESC> 2/5 2/15 4/2
        }
},

-- S-mode
Display-objects *(single occurrence)* =
        {
        display-object-name = A,
        do-access = "WAVAR,"
        dimensions = "three,"
                x-dimension =
                        {
                        x-bound = profile-argument-r1,
                        x-addressing = "no constraint,"
```

```
            x-absolute = "yes,"
            },
        y-dimension =
            {
            y-bound = profile-argument-r2,
            y-addressing = "no constraint,"
            y-absolute = "yes,"
            y-window = y-bound
            },
        z-dimension =
            {
            z-bound = "unbounded,"
            z-addressing = "no constraint,"
            z-absolute = "no,"
            z-window = profile-argument-r3
            },
    erasure-capability = "yes,"
    repertoire-capability *(implicitly defined by r4)*,
    repertoire-assignment = profile-argument-r4,
    font-capability *(implicitly defined by r5)*,
    font-assignment = profile-argument-r5,
    do-emphasis = profile-argument-r6,
    foreground-color-capability = profile-argument-r7,
    foreground-color-assignment = profile-argument-r8,
    background-color-capability = profile-argument-r7,
    background-color-assignment = profile-argument-r9
    block-definition-capability = "no,"
    field-definition-capability = "yes,"
    max-fields = "unbounded,"
    max-field-elements = profile-argument-r10,
    access-outside-fields = profile-argument-r11
    },
```

The two display objects used by the TELNET profile are shown above. The A-mode uses two two-dimensional display objects, one modelling the display for displaying data from the application program, and the other modelling the keyboard for receiving user data from the keyboard operator. Some of the VTE-parameters, called profile-arguments (e.g., r1 and r2), are negotiated during the association establishment.

19.2.2 Control Object VTE-parameters

The following VTE-parameters (Figure 19.10) are used to describe a control object:

• CO-name: This identifies a control object.

• CO-type-identifier: This parameter specifies the source of semantics definition for the control object.

• CO-structure: This parameter is used only if the Structured Control Objects functional unit is selected. When present, its value can be either "non-parametric" or an integer value indicating the number of data elements in the information structure associated with a parametric control object. Each data element is in turn described by a set of VTE-parameters such as CO-element-id (used only if the number of data elements exceeds one), CO-category, CO-repertoire-assignment, and CO-size. The CO-category can be either "character", "boolean", "symbolic", "integer, or "transparent" -- the default is "boolean". The CO-size parameter gives the data storage for that data element. Its value depends on the value of CO-category. For the "character" category, the default maximum number of characters is 16. For the "integer" category, the default maximum value of an integer is 65535. For the "boolean" category, a maximum of 16 booleans may be stored. For the "symbolic" category, the default maximum number of distinct values is 255.

• CO-access: This parameter specifies the access rule for the control object.

• CO-priority: The value of this parameter is either "normal", "high" or "urgent".

• CO-trigger: The value of this parameter is either "selected" or "non-selected". It may only be selected if the CO-priority is "normal". If "selected", any updates to the control object must be delivered immediately.

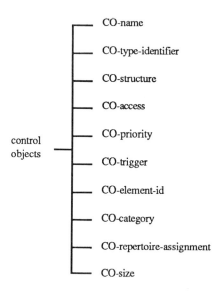

control
objects

— CO-name

— CO-type-identifier

— CO-structure

— CO-access

— CO-priority

— CO-trigger

— CO-element-id

— CO-category

— CO-repertoire-assignment

— CO-size

FIGURE 19.10   VTE-parameters for a Control Object

Example 19.3

CO-name: E
CO-type-identifier: vt-b-sco-echo

CO-access: "WACA", "WACI" or "NSAC"
CO-priority: "normal"
CO-trigger: "selected" or "not-selected" (default is "selected")
CO-category: "boolean"
CO-size: 1 boolean

The above gives the definition of the Echo Control Object.

Example 19.4

CO-name: any value unique to the VTE
CO-type-identifier: vt-b-sco-tco
CO-access: any valid value except "NSAC"
CO-priority: "normal"
CO-trigger: any valid value
CO-category: "integer" used to specify a termination event-id
CO-size: takes default value

The above gives the definition of the TCO. The initial integer value of a TCO is 0.

OIW has defined a number of control objects, some specific to a VTE-profile and some shared by the VT profiles. The shared control objects are as follows:

- **Sequenced Application (SA):** This control object is used to convey signals from an application to a terminal sequentially with other updates.
- **Unsequenced Application (UA):** This control object is used to convey urgent signals (hence unsequenced) from an application to a terminal.
- **Sequenced Terminal (ST):** This is a control object used to convey signals from a terminal to an application.
- **Unsequenced Terminal (UT):** This is a control object used to convey urgent signals from a terminal to an application. Values are the same as those for ST.

Example 19.5

CO-structure: 1 (i.e., simple)
CO-priority: "normal"
CO-category: "symbolic"
CO-size: 11

The above SA control object shows that the symbolic values which can be sent from an application to a terminal are audible_alarm, newlines_enabled, newlines_disabled, restore, visual_alarm, keypad_enabled, keypad_disabled, keyboard_locked, keyboard_unlocked, device_disconnected, and break_signal.

Example 19.6

```
CO-structure: 1
CO-priority: "normal"
CO-category: "integer"
CO-size: 65535
```

The above gives the definition of the ST control object. The integer values of the ST control object are composite and are given in hex. The control, shift, and alt keys may appear in any combination with the special or function keys. The hex value "100" means that the special key is depressed. The hex value "200" means that the function key is depressed. The hex value "400" means that the control key is depressed. The hex value "1000" means that the alt key is depressed. Examples of composite values to be used with the special key are break, tab, escape, rightArrow, bell, backTab, pageUp, print, insert, etc.

Example 19.7

There are six control objects defined for the TELNET profile: SY (SYNCHRONIZE), DI (DISPLAY-SIGNAL), KB (KEYBOARD-SIGNAL), NI (NEGOTIATION BY INITIATOR), NA (NEGOTIATION BY ACCEPTOR), and GA (GO-AHEAD). The TELNET SYNCH command is simulated by updating the SY control object with the single symbolic value of "SYNCH" and immediately updating the DI (or KB) control object and selecting the DM (data mark) boolean. The definition of SY is as follows:

```
CO-name: SY
CO-access: "NSAC"
CO-category: "symbolic"
CO-size: 1
CO-priority: "urgent"
```

An update to the GA control object is equivalent to the TELNET Go Ahead command signalling for half-duplex data transfer. The definition of GA is as follows:

```
CO-name: GA
CO-access: "NSAC"
CO-category: "boolean"
CO-size: 1
CO-priority: "normal"
CO-trigger: "selected"
```

The TELNET IP (interrupt process), AO (abort output), AYT (are you there), and BREAK commands may be accompanied by a SYNCH command by updating the SY control object and then updating the DI or the KB control object which selects both the DM and the other desired booleans. The DI and the KB control objects, storing up to 5 booleans, are used to select a TELNET command. The first boolean value, corresponding to the TELNET IP command, requests the current user process to be interrupted. The second boolean value, corresponding to the TELNET AO command, requests the current user process to be allowed to run to completion but no more output be sent to the printer. The third boolean value, corresponding to the TELNET AYT command, requests a visible or an audible signal to indicate that the remote signal is still operating. The NI and NA control objects are boolean control objects used to negotiate options. For example, the first boolean is the remote echo option and the second boolean is to suppress the go ahead option.

19.2.3 Device Object VTE-parameters

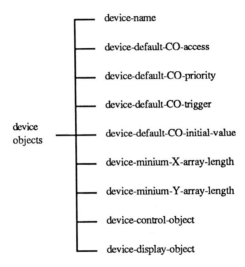

device objects
- device-name
- device-default-CO-access
- device-default-CO-priority
- device-default-CO-trigger
- device-default-CO-initial-value
- device-minium-X-array-length
- device-minium-Y-array-length
- device-control-object
- device-display-object

FIGURE 19.11   VTE-parameters for Device Objects

The following VTE-parameters (Figure 19.11) are used to describe a device object:

- device-name: This parameter, of type PrintableString, is used to identify a device.
- device-default-CO-access: This specifies any valid access rules for the default control object associated with the device object.
- device-default-CO-priority: This specifies a priority for the default control object.
- device-default-CO-trigger: This specifies a trigger value for the default control object.
- device-default-CO-initial-value: This specifies the initial eight Boolean values in the default control object.
- device-minimum-X-array-length: This specifies the shortest X-array length acceptable to both VT-users when a display object is mapped to this device object.
- device-minimum-Y-array-length: This specifies the shortest Y-array length acceptable to both VT-users.
- device-control-object: This parameter, which can have multiple occurrences, specifies a potential control object that can be associated with the device object. For

example, control objects such as FDCO and CCO can be used to control data entry at a terminal.
* device-display-object: This is the DO-name of a display object associated with the device object.

Example 19.8

```
Device-objects = *(double occurrence)*
{
    {
    device-name = DISPLAY-DEVICE,
    device-display-object = D,
    device-default-CO-initial-value = 1,
    device-minimum-X-array-length = 1,
    device-minimum-Y-array-length = 1,
    device-control-object = SY,
    device-control-object = NA,
    device-control-object = DI,
    device-control-object = GA,
    device-default-control-access = "WACA",
    device-control-CO-priority = "normal"
    *(other device object parameters for attributes assume corresponding DO values)*
    }
    {
    device-name = KEYBOARD-DEVICE,
    device-display-object = K,
    device-default-CO-access = "WACI",
    device-default-CO-priority = "normal",
    device-default-CO-initial-value = 1,
    device-minimum-X-array-length = 1,
    device-minimum-Y-array-length = 1,
    device-control-object = SY,
    device-control-object = NI,
    device-control-object = KB,
    device-control-object = GA,
    *(other device object parameters for attributes assume corresponding DO values)*
    }
}
```

Two device objects used in the TELNET profile: the display device object and the keyboard device object. The definition of these two device objects is shown above. Note that each device object is associated with some control objects, the meanings of some have been described in Section 19.2.2.

In addition to the above VTE-parameters, there are also device object VTE-parameters for attributes and termination VTE-parameters.

The VTE-parameters for attributes are used to assign device object dependent semantics to the logical attribute values in the display object. They consist of device-repertoire-assignment, device-font-assignment, device-emphasis, device-foreground-color-assignment, and device-background-color-assignment.

When the device object is associated with an object updating device such as a keyboard, three more VTE-parameters can be associated with the device object: device-termination-event-list, device-termination-length, and device-termination-timeout. These termination parameters allow conditions to be defined under which input is to be regarded as terminated and hence accumulated data can be forwarded.

An entry in the device-termination-event-list is used to notify the peer VT-user that some event has occurred. The event may define one or more characters from a repertoire such that input of any of the defined characters causes forwarding action with respect to any previously accumulated input, together with the character that is concerned. The device-termination-length parameter is of the form <length, event-id>. It defines the maximum number of characters which may be entered before any forwarding action occurs. The device-termination-timeout parameter defines when forwarding should occur after a previous forwarding action. Sometimes it is useful to allow more than one set of termination conditions. For example, we can arrange a set of termination conditions for text input and another set of termination conditions for command input. We associate more than one device object with an object updating device, with each device object defining some termination conditions.

19.3 Block and Field Structuring Capabilities

The BCVT service also provides block and field structuring capabilities. These capabilities can be used when the appropriate functional units are active.

19.3.1 Block Capabilities

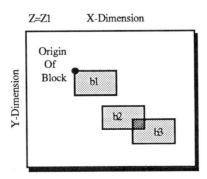

FIGURE 19.12   An Y-array with Three Blocks

Blocks are a display object addressing mechanism which allows frequently used sets of display object updates to be written in an address independent manner. For example, a company's logo may appear at different locations. With the use of the block addressing mechanism, display object updates to generate a logo can be written once. Thereafter whenever it is necessary to generate the logo, a new block of the appropriate size can be created at the desired location and the existing set of logo updates is copied over. In this way, updates for the logo can be performed independently of where the logo will be placed later on.

A block is simply a rectangular subarea of a Y-array. It has a width, a depth, and an origin designated by the upper left hand corner. Blocks can overlap, as illustrated by Figure 19.12.

An array element within a block can be addressed relative to the origin of the block. Suppose a block is addressed by the pair (b, z) where b identifies a block in a Y-array and z is the fixed z-value. An array element within this block can be addressed by a quadruple (p, q, b, z) where p, q are offsets from the origin of the block.

Block operations are needed to create and delete blocks. Addressing operations using the extended display pointer work similar to addressing operations using the primitive display pointer.

19.3.2 Field Capabilities

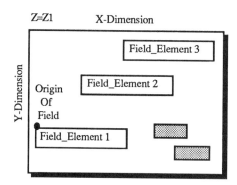

FIGURE 19.13   A Field Consisting of Non-contiguous Field Elements

Fields are primarily used for controlling data entry. To control a terminal VT-user to enter data in a proper manner, an application VT-user defines entry rules to be followed by the local processing function of a terminal VT-user. These rules are specified using a set of control objects.

First, we consider the structure of a field. Field structuring is similar to block structuring, i.e. it subdivides a Y-array. A field, however, may have a shape more complex than that of a simple rectangle. For example, Figure 19.13 shows a single field consisting of a set of non-contiguous rectangular field-elements. The origin of each field-element is given by the upper left corner. These field-elements are "serialized" in such a way that when the logical display pointer reaches the last array element of the last X-array of a field-element, the NEXT operation will move the pointer automatically to the first array element of the first X-array of the next field-element. Thus, only one coordinate, known as the k-coordinate, is needed to specify an arbitrary array element of a field. Suppose that a field in a Y-array is identified by a pair (f,z), where f identifies a particular field and z is the z-value of the Y-array. Then an array element within a field can be identified by the triple (k,f,z) which is sometimes known as the logical address.

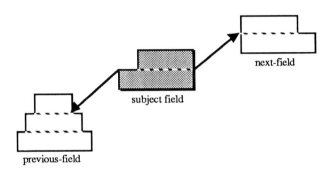

previous-field

subject field

next-field

FIGURE 19.14   A Navigation Path for a Set of Fields in a Y-array

More than one field can be defined on a single Y-array. A set of fields in a Y-array can be serialized to form a **navigation path** (Figure 19.14) although no array element can be in more than one field.

Field operations are quite similar to display object operations. There is a logical pointer that contains the logical address of an array element in the field which will be updated by the LOGICAL-TEXT operation. The effect of the LOGICAL-TEXT operation is to increase the k-coordinate of the logical pointer. Other field operations include the LOGICAL-ATTRIBUTE and LOGICAL-ERASE operations.

The definition of a field is stored in a **Field Definition Record (FDR)**. FDRs form the contents of a non-parametric control object known as the **Field Definition Control Object (FDCO)**. Some of the components of a FDR (Figure 19.15) are described below:

- field status: Its value can be either "active", "inactive", or "non-extant". A field with the "non-extant" value has no elements. Therefore, a field can be deleted by setting its field-status to "non-extant". A field with the "inactive" value means that it is temporarily deleted, and may be restored sometime in the future.
- field-extent: This defines a sequence of field-elements.
- next-field: This specifies the next field if one is present. The NEXT-FIELD operation when applied to a field will give the next field value.
- previous-field: This specifies the previous field if one is present. This field and the next-field allow several fields to be linked together to form a navigation path. Inactive fields are skipped by a navigation path. The PREVIOUS-FIELD operation when applied to a field will give the previous field value.

• T-policy: This specifies the transmission policy. Possible values are "transmit all of this field", "do not transmit any of this field", "transmit those portions of this field, if any, which have been changed", and "transmit all of this field if any portion of it has been changed".

• entry-control-list: Perhaps the most important of all the components, this parameter specifies a sequence of entry-controls. An **entry-control** specifies constraints on data entry into a field, including reactions which should be performed when the constraints are violated. This component will be discussed next in more detail.

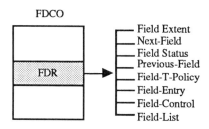

FIGURE 19.15   Field Definition Record (FDR) VTE-parameters

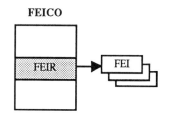

FIGURE 19.16   Field Entry Instruction Control Object

Each entry-control specifies a device-object-list, FEIR-list (i.e., a list of FEIRs), and a FEPR-list (i.e., a list of FEPRs). Basically, it links a set of FEIRs and FEPRs to a field. The FEIRs and the FEPRS are stored in two global objects, known as the **Field Entry Instruction Control Object (FEICO)** and the **Field Entry Pilot Control Object (FEPCO)** respectively (Figures 19.16 and 19.17).

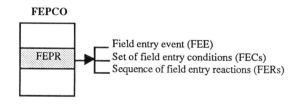

FIGURE 19.17   Field Entry Pilot Control Object

A **Field Entry Instruction Record (FEIR)** is a set of **Field Entry Instructions (FEIs)** with each FEI specifying constraints on the data to be entered into the field. Examples of Field Entry Instructions are:

- certain field entry is mandatory,
- certain field is protected from field entry,
- the maximum number of characters to be entered into the field,
- the list of authorized/forbidden characters to be entered into the field,
- the list of authorized logical attribute operations which may be performed on the field content, and
- the entry waiting time indicating the time after which a lack of action by the terminal VT-user will cause a reaction.

A **Field Entry Pilot Record (FEPR)** is specified by a Field Entry Event, a set of Field Entry Conditions, and a sequence of Field Entry Reactions. A **Field Entry Event (FEE)** identifies some potential violation of an FEI. A **Field Entry Condition (FEC)** is used to test the current position of the cursor at the time the FEE occurs. Finally, a **Field Entry Reaction (FER)** is used to specify a set of actions to be performed if the FEC is evaluated to true at the time the FEE occurs. For example, suppose that a terminal VT-user enters a character in the last array element of a field (FEE). If the current cursor is already in the last field of the navigation path (FEC), then control is returned to the application (FER). In general, an FEPR can be defined by taking one FEC ("if") and two FERs ("then" and "else") as parameters. The "if" parameter takes an FEC as a value while the "then" and "else" parameters each take a sequence of FERs as values. Semantically, this means that if the "if" FEC is satisfied, then the "then" FERs are performed, otherwise the "else" FERs are performed. The next few examples give examples of FEEs, FECs, and FERs.

Example 19.9

Examples of FEEs are:

- field entry complete -- this event is generated by a character entry into the last position in a field,
- end of field entry -- this event is generated by reaching the maximum number of characters allowed in a field,
- erroneous character entered -- this event is generated when a forbidden character is entered, and
- entry waiting time expired.

Example 19.10

Examples of FECs are:

- entry cursor is in the field which is currently at the start of a navigation path,

- entry cursor is in the field which is currently at the end of a navigation path, and
- entry position is in the first position to be entered in the field.

Example 19.11

Examples of FERs are:

- deliver all undelivered updates entered up to this point,
- ignore event,
- stop further entry and relinquish WAVAR access rights if in the S-mode,
- erase data entered into the current field and restart the field,
- present a visual/audible indication in response to an FEI violation,
- change the entry cursor to the first array element of the next field, if any, on the forward navigation path, and
- change the entry cursor to the first array element of the previous field, if any, on the backward navigation path.

The **Context Control Object (CCO)** is another important control object to be used in conjunction with field structuring. It is made up of two parts. The first part identifies an array element where data entry can start, and the second part identifies a reason for termination.

The next example illustrates the definitions of some of the control objects used to support field-oriented data entry.

Example 19.12

```
-- Field Definition Control Object
CO-name: FD
CO-type-identifier: vt-b-sco-fdco
CO-structure: "non-parameteric"
CO-access: "WAVAR + profile-argument-r12
CO-priority: "normal"
CO-trigger: "not-selected"


-- Field Entry Instructions Control Object
CO-name: EI
CO-type-identifier: "mandatory-feico"
CO-structure: "non-parameteric"
CO-access: "WAVAR" + profile-argument-r12
CO-priority: "normal"
CO-trigger: "not-selected"


-- Context Control Object
```

CO-name: CC
CO-type-identifier: vt-b-sco-cco
CO-structure: 6
CO-access: "WAVAR"
CO-priority: "normal"
CO-trigger: "not-selected"

The profile-argument-r12 above says if the VT-association initiator is the terminal VT-user, then it takes the access value of "WACA", otherwise it takes the value of "WACI".

19.4 VT Service

Functional Unit	Facility	Service	Type
Kernel	Establishement	VT-ASSOCIATE	confirm
	Termination	VT-RELEASE VT-U-ABORT VT-P-ABORT	confirm non-confirm
	Delivery Control	VT-DELIVER VT-ACK-RECEIPT	non-confirm non-confirm
	Access-right Management	VT-GIVE-TOKENS VT-REQUEST-TOKENS	non-confirm non-confirm
	Data Transfer	VT-DATA	non-confirm
Switch Profile Negotiation	Switch Profile Negotiation	VT-SWITCH-PROFILE	confirm
Multiple Interaction Negotiation	Multiple Interaction Negotiation	VT-START-NEG VT-END-NEG VT-NEG-INVITE VT-NEG-OFFER VT-NEG-ACCEPT VT-NEG-REJECT	confirm confirm non-confirm non-confirm non-confirm non-confirm
Negotiated Release	Termination	VT-RELEASE	confirm
Urgent Data	Data Transfer	VT-DATA	non-cofirm
Break	Interrupt	VT-BREAK	confirm

TABLE 19.1   VT Functional Unit Facilities and Associated Service Elements

Functional units provide the means for VT-users to negotiate facilities. In addition to the mandatory Kernel functional unit, there are ten optional functional units. Some functional units provide facilities which can be described in terms of service elements (Table 19.1), but some do not. Functional units such as Blocks and Field functional units do not provide added service elements. However, their presence makes some VTE-parameters available for use. First, we give a short description of each functional unit.

- Switch Profile Negotiation functional unit: This is used to switch from one VTE-profile to another.
- Multiple Interaction Negotiation (MIN) functional unit: This allows the negotiation of a set of VTE-parameters to be carried in a series of steps.
- Negotiated Release functional unit: This is used to reject a request to release a VT-association.
- Urgent Data functional unit: This allows urgent information to be conveyed.
- Break functional unit: This allows a VT-user to interrupt an activity and discard all updates which have not been processed.
- Enhanced Access-rule functional unit: This is used to extend the access rules to control objects and provide the WACI and WACA access rights in the S-mode as well as the A-mode.
- Structured Control Object functional unit: This is used to allow a control object to have more than one data element of the same or different category, to separate updating of the individual data elements, and to allow a control object defined non-parametrically to be partially updated.
- Reference Information Object functional unit: This allows a particular CO to be used in a VTE.
- Block functional unit: This provides the block structuring capability .
- Field functional unit: This provides the field structuring capability.

- **establishment facility**

VT-users use **VT-ASSOCIATE** to establish a VT-association and an initial VTE. The two mandatory parameters of VT-ASSOCIATE.request are VT-class and VT-mode. The VT-class parameter specifies the virtual terminal service class to be used. Its value will be "BASIC" for the BCVT service. The VT-mode parameter enables the initiating VT-user to select the initial mode of operation and determines whether mode switching is allowed during the VT-association. The mode value can be "S-mode", "A-mode", "either-S", or "either-A". The first two values do not allow mode switching while the last two do.

The VT-functional-units parameter of VT-ASSOCIATE allows VT-users to negotiate which VT functional units to be used. The VTE-profile-name parameter identifies a VTE-profile which forms the basis for the initial VTE. If this parameter is absent, the VT service provider would select the default VTE-profile based on the value of the VT-mode parameter. For example, if the VT-mode is asynchronous, then the default asynchronous VTE-profile will be used as the initial VTE. If the VT-mode value is either "S-mode" or "either-S", then the VT-WAVAR-owner parameter is used to negotiate the initial ownership of the WAVAR access-right.

- **termination facility**

The termination facility provides service elements for a VT-user to terminate a VT-association either in a non-destructive manner (using **VT-RELEASE**) or in a destructive manner (using **VT-U-ABORT**). It also provides **VT-P-ABORT** by means of which the VT service provider can abort the VT-association.

• **negotiation facilities**

The negotiation facilities enable peer VT-users to select, modify, and replace the current-VTE.

If the Switch Profile Negotiation functional unit is chosen, then the **VT-SWITCH-PROFILE** service element is used to negotiate a switch to a full-VTE from a named VTE-profile. This negotiation takes the form of a proposal made by one VT-user using a named VTE-profile. The named VTE-profile is not negotiable although the offered VTE-profile argument values may be adjusted by both the VT service provider and the accepting VT-user within the range offered by the initiating VT-user.

If the Multiple Interaction Negotiation (MIN) functional unit is chosen, then negotiation of VTE-parameter values can be carried in a series of steps. The following service elements are available: VT-START-NEG, VT-END-NEG, VT-NEG-INVITE, VT-NEG-OFFER, and VT-NEG-ACCEPT. The **VT-START-NEG** service element is used to negotiate a transition to the negotiation phase and optionally name a VTE-profile as the initial draft-VTE. If the VTE-profile-name parameter is not supplied, the current-VTE is used as the initial draft-VTE. **VT-END-NEG** is used to terminate the negotiation. The only mandatory parameter of the VT-END-NEG.request primitive is VT-vte-choice which indicates which of the available VTEs may be chosen as the current-VTE. Its value is either "draft", "current", or "either". The VT-END-NEG.response primitive contains a VT-result parameter. If the result is "success", the data handling phase is entered and the new current-VTE is determined by the value of VT-vte-choice parameter of the VT-END-NEG.response primitive. If the result is "failure", then both VT-users remain in the negotiation phase and the draft-VTE is retained.

During the negotiation phase, a VT-user uses **VT-NEG-INVITE** to invite its peer to propose values for one or more VTE-parameters. It uses **VT-NEG-OFFER** to propose a set of acceptable (to the initiating VT-user) VTE-parameter values and/or value ranges. It uses **VT-NEG-ACCEPT/VT-NEG-REJECT** to select/reject values for one or more VTE-parameters from those proposed in a VT-NEG-OFFER.indication primitive. Counter-offers are possible during the negotiation. An example of a valid MIN sequence is (VT-NEG-OFFER, VT-NEG-OFFER, VT-NEG-ACCEPT), where one VT-user issues a VT-NEG-OFFER.request primitive and the other VT-user counter-offers by issuing another VT-NEG-OFFER.request primitive. Counter-offering is not allowed after an INVITE. Therefore, the MIN sequence (VT-NEG-INVITE, VT-NEG-OFFER, VT-NEG-ACCEPT) is allowed but the MIN sequence (VT-NEG-INVITE, VT-NEG-OFFER, VT-NEG-OFFER, VT-NEG-ACCEPT) is not allowed.

• **data transfer facility**

A VT-user uses **VT-DATA** to update the contents of display and/or control objects.

•   **delivery control facility**

The delivery control facility provides two service elements: VT-DELIVER and VT-ACK-RECEPT. A VT-user uses **VT-DELIVER** to indicate a delivery point in a sequence of VT-DATA service initiations, and, optionally, to request acknowledgement of receipt. This service element is not available if the type-of-delivery-control VTE-parmeter has the value "no-delivery-control". A VT-user uses **VT-ACK-RECEPT** to acknowledge receipt of a delivery point. Hence, the activities of two communicating VT-users can be synchronized.

•   **access-right management facility**

Used only for the S-mode, this facility enables VT-users to request or transfer ownership of the WAVAR access-right. **VT-REQUEST-TOKENS** is used by a VT-user to request transfer of ownership of the WAVAR access-right. **VT-GIVE-TOKENS** is used by a VT-user to pass ownership of the WAVAR access-right to its peer.

•   **destructive break facility**

Used during the data transfer phase, the destructive **VT-BREAK** service element enables a VT-user to interrupt an activity and discard all the previously initiated object updates which have not yet been processed. When used in the S-mode, it is not necessary for a VT-user to own the WAVAR access-right to initiate VT-BREAK. The mandatory VT-information parameter contains information to assist the VT-users to resynchronize their activities following VT-BREAK.

19.5 VT Protocol

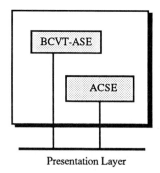

Presentation Layer

FIGURE 19.18   BCVT Application Context

The BCVT standard specifies only one application context. As shown in Figure 19.18, this application context contains two ASEs: BCVT-ASE and ACSE. The BCVT standard specified a number of procedures used by the protocol machine of the BCVT-ASE. These procedures will not be covered. The purpose of this section is to show how the BCVT service elements are mapped to the underlying service elements.

Table 19.2 shows how each VT APDU is generated as a result of some incoming event received from either the VT-user, ACSE, or Presentation Layer. It also gives the fields of each VT APDU.

The ASQ APDU is conveyed as user-data of an A-ASSOCIATE.request/indication primitive, while the ASR APDU is conveyed as user-data of an A-ASSOCIATE.response/confirm primitive. The session requirements parameter of A-ASSOCIATE.request/indication contains the following functional units: Typed Data, Duplex (if A-mode), Half Duplex (if S-mode), Resynchronize (if the VT Break functional unit is selected), Expedited (if the VT Urgent Data functional unit is selected), Negotiated Release (if the VT Negotiated Release functional unit is selected), and Major Synchronize (if either the VT Negotiation or the VT Break functional unit is selected).

The RLQ APDU generated as a result of a non-destructive release is carried by the A-RELEASE service element. The AUQ APDU and the APQ APDU generated as a result of a destructive release are carried by the A-ABORT service element.

From the session requirements parameter above, it is obvious that BCVT uses the following presentation service elements: P-DATA, P-EXPEDITED-DATA, P-RESYNCHRONIZE, P-SYNC-MAJOR, P-TOKEN-GIVE, P-TOKEN-PLEASE, and P-TYPED-DATA. The following describes how each presentation service element is used.

The P-DATA service element carries as user-data the NAQ APDU for data manipulation to either display object(s) or control objects which have "normal" priority, and the NAQ, NIQ, NJQ, NOQ APDUs generated during the VT negotiation phase.

The P-EXPEDITED-DATA service element carries as user-data the UDQ APDU generated as a result of the issuance of the VT-URGENT-DATA.request primitive.

The P-RESYNCHRONIZE service element carries as user-data the BKR and BKQ APDUs generated during the use of the VT-BREAK service element.

The P-SYNC-MAJOR service element carries as user-data the SPQ and SPR APDUs generated during the use of the confirmed VT-SWITCH-PROFILE service element. It also conveys as user-data the SNQ and SNR APDUs generated during the use of the confirmed VT-START-NEG service element, and the ENQ and ENR APDUs generated during the use of the confirmed VT-END-NEG service element.

The GTQ APDU generated as a result of the issuance of a VT-GIVE-TOKEN.request primitive is conveyed by the P-TOKEN-GIVE service element. The RTQ APDU generated as a result of the issuance of a VT-REQUEST-TOKEN.request primitive is conveyed by the P-TOKEN-PLEASE.request service element.

The P-TYPED-DATA service element is used by BCVT in three different ways. When updates to control objects with "high" priority are made via the VT-HIGH-PI-DATA.request primitive, the HDQ APDU generated is conveyed as user-data of P-TYPED-DATA. When updates to control objects with "urgent" priority are made via the VT-URGENT-DATA.request and the P-EXPEDITED-DATA service is not available, the UDQ APDU generated is conveyed as user-data of P-TYPED-DATA. Finally, P-TYPED-DATA is used to carry the DLQ and DAQ APDUs generated as a result of the issuance of the VT-DELIVER.request and VT-ACK-RECEIPT.response primitives.

VT PDU	Generated as a result of an incoming event	Fields
ASQ	VT-ASSOCIATE.req	Called-application-entity-title, Calling-application-entity-title, VT-class, VT-mode, VT-WAVAR-owner, VT-profile-name, VT-functinal-units, protocol-version, implementation-identifier
ASR	VT-ASSOCIATE.res	responding-application-entity-title, VT-WAVAR-owner, VT-profile-arg-value-list, VT-result, failure-reason, protocol-version, VT-functional-units, implementatin-identifier
AUQ	VT-U-ABORT.req	VT-user-failure-reason
APQ	VT-P-ABORT.req	VT-reason
BKQ	VT-BREAK.req	VT-WAVAR-owner, VT-information
BKR	VT-BREAK.res	VT-token, VT-information
DLQ	VT-DELIVER.req	VT-ack-request
DAQ	VT-ACK-RECEIPT.res	
NIQ	VT-NEG-INVITE.req	VT-param-ident-list
NOQ	VT-NEG-OFFER.req	param-offer-list
NAQ	VT-NEG-ACCEPT.req	VT-param-value-list
NJQ	VT-NEG-REJECT.res	VT-param-ident-list
ENQ	VT-END-NEG.req	VT-vte-choice, VT-failure-allowed
ENR	VT-END-NEG.req	VT-vte-choice, VT-result, failure-reason
GTQ	VT-GIVE-TOKEN.req	
RTQ	VT-REQUEST-TOKEN.req	
RLQ	VT-RELEASE.req	
RLR	VT-RELEASE.res	VT-result, failure-reason
NDQ	VT-DATA.req	object-updates, echo-now, start-entry
UDQ	VT-URGENT-DAT.req	object-updates
HDQ	VT-HIGH-PRI-DATA.req	
SPQ	VT-SWITCH-PROFILE.req	VT-profile-name, VT-profile-arg-offer-list
SPR	VT-SWITCH-PROFILE.res	VT-profile-arg-value-list, VT-result, failure-reason
SNQ	VT-START-NEG.req	VT-profile-name, VT-profile-arg-offer-list
SNR	VT-START-NEG.res	VT-profile-arg-value-list, VT-result, failure-reason

TABLE 19.2 VT APDUs

19.6 Summary

The VT standard defines a means for users to access applications in remote computer systems through a terminal regardless of the make of the computer systems and the terminal. It introduces the notion of a virtual terminal which is an abstraction of a class of real terminals. In this chapter, we study the Basic Class Virtual Terminal (BCVT) which is character-oriented and provides limited services for manipulating blocks and fields.

The information model of BCVT is defined in an object-oriented manner. All the objects are organized in the shared conceptual communication area (CCA). This CCA contains display objects, device objects as well as control objects. Each object is described in terms of a set of VTE-parameters. Because there are many choices of VTE parameters, profile organizations define VTE-profiles. A VTE-profile is a predefined set of VTE-parameters. For example, the OIW has defined profiles such as the TELNET profile, the Transparent profile, the Forms profile, the Scroll profile, the X3 profile, and the Paged profile. These profiles form a basis of negotiation by VT-users during the VT-association establishment.

The BCVT service supports two modes of operation, the S-mode and the A-mode. These two modes have their origins from two of the common terminal types, the IBM 3270 (S-mode) and the DEC VT 100 (A-mode). It defines access rules to be used with the S-mode. It provides delivery control mechanisms by which a VT-user can mark the end of a sequence of updates to objects in the CCA. It also provides a break-in service for VT-users to interrupt each other.

The BCVT protocol is quite straightforward. To provide the delivery control and the break-in services, it relies on the presentation resynchronization and expedited data services.

Related Standards

ISO 9040: Information Technology - Open Systems Interconnection - Virtual Terminal Basic Class Service

ISO 9040 DAM 2: Information Technology - Open Systems Interconnection - Virtual Terminal Basic Class Service - Amendment 2: Additional Functional Units

ISO 9041-1: Information Technology - Open Systems Interconnection - Virtual Terminal Basic Class Protocol - Part 1: Specification

ISO 9041-1 DAM 2: Information Technology - Open Systems Interconnection - Virtual Terminal Basic Class Protocol - Part 1: Specification - Amendment 2: Additional Functional Units

DIS 9041-2: Information Technology - Open Systems Interconnection - Virtual Terminal Basic Class Protocol - Part 2: Protocol Implementation Conformance Statement (PICS) Proforma

CD 10184: Information Technology - Open Systems Interconnection - Terminal Management Model

20

Transaction Processing

A **transaction** is a logical set of operations characterized by the ACID properties (see Chapter 12). The **OSI Transaction Processing (TP)** standard, as defined in ISO/IEC 10026, provides an infrastructure to support distributed transaction processing which may span across one or more open systems. It provides mechanisms to ensure the ACID properties of a distributed transaction, and a transaction processing environment involving a number of application associations.

The TP protocol makes use of the facilities of CCR-ASE and ACSE. It acts as a mediator for these protocols and operates in an environment of many communicating pairs over many application associations. On the other hand, CCR-ASE and ACSE operate in a single peer-to-peer environment. As a mediator, TP does not specify any style of data transfer. It does provide an environment for an ASE to transfer data. It is up to a TP application to determine its user-ASE(s) to transfer data. Although there are user-ASEs such as RPC-ASE and RDA-ASE that can operate with TP, one can define a user-ASE that is specific for a TP application.

Section 20.1 gives a high-level description of the TP concepts. Section 20.2 describes the TP model. Section 20.3 describes the TP service. Section 20.4 describes the TP protocol machine which is more complicated than most of the other protocol machines because the TP environment involves many associations.

20.1 TP Concepts

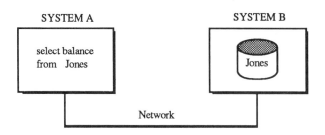

FIGURE 20.1   An Example of a Transaction

Figure 20.1 shows a simple example of a distributed transaction. In this example, user Jones in system A issues a database query to find out his account balance in system B. The query is processed on system B, and the resulting balance is transferred to system A. The transaction is complete when the information is posted on system A. In this example, the transaction spans over two systems.

Within each system involved in the distributed transaction processing, there is an entity called the **Transaction Processing Service User (TPSU)**. A TPSU, typically an application program, is a user of the TP services provided by the TP service provider. Consider a simple example of a banking transaction with an ATM (i.e., Automatic Teller Machine). With the help of the ATM controller, a user can open a session on the ATM and move funds from his savings account to his checking account. We can identify four different systems in this example. First, there is the ATM system for interfacing with a user. There is the controller system which is responsible for managing transactions. There is the checking_system which is responsible for maintaining the database of users' checking accounts. Finally, there is the savings_system which is responsible for maintaining the database of users' saving accounts. Each system has a TPSU. For example, the TPSU on the ATM system can open a new user session for a user, validate the user with the controller system, direct requests from the user to the controller system, and close the user session. At a given instant, the controller system may maintain three associations, one with each of the other systems. That is, in a **TPSU invocation (TPSUI)** of the TPSU at the controller system, one can find up to three SAOs (i.e., single association objects), with one for each association.

As mentioned earlier, the TP protocol provides an environment to manage multiple communicating pairs involved in a distributed transaction. A peer-to-peer relationship between two TPSUIs is modelled as a **dialogue**. Over a dialogue, the two TPSUIs can exchange data and error notifications, perform a transaction, and synchronize their activities based on the application semantics. Two separate control modes for a dialogue are possible: polarized, and shared. In the **polarized control mode**, a TPSUI must own a token to initiate actions other than error notification, rollback, and abrupt termination of the dialogue. In the **shared mode**, a TPSUI is not required to own a token to initiate an action.

A **dialogue tree** is simply a tree with TPSUIs as nodes and dialogues as edges. For example, based on Figure 20.1, we can build a simple dialogue tree with only two nodes. As the initiator of the transaction to retrieve an account balance from system B, system A is the root node of the dialogue tree. System A is also the superior node to system B (because A is the one that initiates a dialogue with B), while system B is a subordinate node to system A.

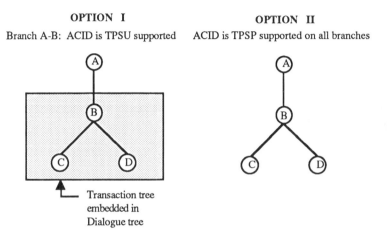

FIGURE 20.2 Examples of Transaction Trees

The dialogue branch from system A to system B in our example can be viewed as a branch without bark, i.e., the branch is unprotected. By setting the coordination level of a dialogue to "COMMITMENT", the dialogue branch is made a **transaction branch**. A transaction branch has bark, i.e., it is protected. This means that the TPSP (i.e., TP service provider) must ensure the ACID properties of a transaction branch. If the coordination level of a dialogue is set to "NONE", then the TPSUIs must ensure the ACID properties of the dialogue branch.

This distinction between a dialogue branch and a transaction branch means that both dialogue trees and transaction trees should be examined. A **transaction tree** is a tree with TPSUIs as nodes and transaction branches as edges. TP allows a dialogue tree to contain several non-overlapping transaction subtrees. Extend the example of system A and system B in Figure 20.1 such that the user's account balance desired on system B is actually a company balance. In this case, system B must request a balance from system C for the retail division, and a balance from system D for the wholesale division. Our dialogue tree would span all four nodes. Each node in the tree, however, only sees his immediate superior and subordinate(s). Therefore, the root node, system A, does not know that the tree has grown to include systems C and D for this transaction. In this example, the transaction tree thus spans all 4 nodes (option II in Figure 20.2), or possibly span only nodes B, C, and D (option I in Figure 20.2). In option I, the entire dialogue tree is a transaction tree. In option II, the dialogue tree contains a transaction subtree which consists of nodes B, C, and D.

Although more than one transaction subtree can exist within a dialogue tree, transaction subtrees cannot overlap, i.e., they are disjoint among themselves. Thus between two transaction subtrees, there is at least one dialogue whose coordination level is equal to "NONE".

For developers building TP products, three levels of conformance are defined:

• **Application-supported transactions**: Applications written to this level of conformance will not depend on CCR to preserve data integrity when finishing a transaction.

• **Chained provider-supported transactions**: A **chained transaction** is a sequence of contiguous provider-supported transaction branches of the same nature. Chained transactions thus cause a new transaction branch to be immediately initiated at the termination of the current transaction. For example, a payroll manager can use the same transaction tree to process the employees' accounts repetitively.

• **Unchained provider-supported transactions**: An **unchained transaction** is a sequence of non-contiguous provider-supported transaction branches aimed at achieving a common goal. "Unchained" means that within the sequence, there is a dialogue whose coordination level is equal to "NONE". For example, a payroll manager, after processing the accounts of 50 employees, may want to unchain the transaction tree to do something else and then rechain the transaction tree later on to resume the processing of employees' accounts.

Choosing a level of conformance is important for both application developers and users. In some cases, a lower level of conformance does not mean that the application provides less functionality. It may only mean that the application makes less use of the TP services to provide the same functionality as other applications do.

Recovery is an integral part of TP. A **TP channel** allows the TPSP on a system to exchange error messages for recovery with the TPSP on another system, without letting the TPSUIs ever realize that the channel exists. The TP channel is just another tool that the TPSP uses to get the job done for its TPSUIs.

20.2 TP Model

In this section, we will elaborate on dialogue trees and transaction trees. We will also discuss the naming issues of TPSUIs, the coordination of resources based on the two phase commit protocol, and the TP recovery mechanisms.

• **dialogue trees**

A dialogue, modelled as a dialogue branch in the dialogue tree (Figure 20.3), represents some binding between two TPSUIs that communicate with each other over an application association. To support a dialogue, an application association must first be established with an application context that provides the communication requirements of the TPSUIs. A dialogue can span over more than one application association. This means that if an association fails, a dialogue recovery mechanism can be used to establish another association to continue the dialogue. On the other hand, the same association may span over more than one dialogue. This means that when two TPSUIs are done with a dialogue, they can retain the association for some future dialogues. As a result, associations may stay for a long period of time, and potentially be used by several TPSUIs. TP applications typically establish an **association pool**, so that an association can be quickly obtained and used for service without making the transaction initiator wait on the network latency required to set up an association.

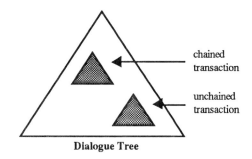

FIGURE 20.3   A Dialogue Tree

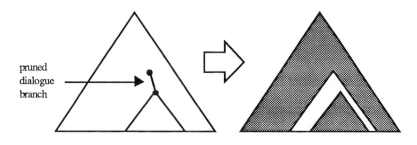

FIGURE 20.4   Pruning of a Dialogue Tree

A dialogue tree is not necessarily static. It grows when a dialogue branch is added. It shrinks when a dialogue branch is removed. Let us consider the growth of a dialogue tree. A TPSUI may want to activate a new TPSUI to execute part of a distributed transaction, which causes a dialogue branch to be added to the existing dialogue tree. During the dialogue establishment, the two TPSUIs negotiate on the control mode which is either polarized or shared, and the use of the commitment service which is either application-supported or provider-supported. A dialogue with an initial coordination level of "NONE" may be added to a dialogue tree at any time. However, a dialogue with a coordination level of "COMMITMENT" may only be added when it is permitted to start a transaction, or to add a transaction branch to the current transaction.

Next, we consider the pruning of a dialogue tree. A dialogue can be terminated if and only if there is no transaction branch in progress on that dialogue. This is possible when the coordination level is "NONE" or the current transaction branch is terminated and the next one has not yet been started. Of course, a dialogue may be terminated when a communication failure or a node crash occurs. Figure 20.4 shows that when a dialogue is terminated, a new dialogue tree is created.

- **transaction trees**

A transaction branch is a dialogue branch whose coordination level is equal to "COMMITMENT". A transaction tree, within a dialogue tree, is a tree with transaction branches as arcs. Since a transaction tree is used to model a transaction, it lasts only for the duration of a single transaction. The TPSUI in the transaction tree that has no superior is called the root TPSUI, a TPSUI that has no subordinate is called a leaf TPSUI, and a TPSUI that has both a superior and at least one subordinate is called an intermediate TPSUI. The root TPSUI together with its **TP protocol Machines (TPPMs)** form the **commit coordinator** of the transaction. Note that the root of the transaction need not be placed at the root of the dialogue tree.

A transaction tree may need to grow to meet the initial requests of the commit coordinator. There are two ways to grow a transaction tree. A new transaction branch can be added to a transaction tree by establishing a new dialogue branch with the coordination level of "COMMITMENT". When the coordination level is allowed to change dynamically, an existing dialogue branch becomes a transaction branch and its coordination level changes from "NONE" to "COMMITMENT".

Chained and unchained transactions are modelled as follows. In a dialogue tree, a dialogue can be used to model a chained sequence of transaction branches (all on the same edge) that operate at the same coordination level of "COMMITMENT". It can be also used to model an unchained sequence of transaction branches such that there is at least one transaction whose dialogue coordination level transition to "NONE" in the sequence.

Completion of a transaction is initiated by the root TPSUI. When concurrence is obtained from all the participants in the tree, the transaction is completed.

- **TP naming**

Naming in TP is complex. Some of the names defined by the TP model are described below.

- **TPSU-Title:** This is used at dialogue establishment to identify the target TPSU, typically located on a remote node.
- **TPSUI-ID:** This is used to identify a TPSUI.

• **Dialogue-ID**: This is used to reference a dialogue within the scope of a TPSUI. Note that all the dialogues of a TPSUI belong to the same dialogue tree.
• **Transaction-ID**: This is used to reference a transaction within the OSIE. For example, the Transaction-ID is qualified by: the AP-invocation identifier, the TPSUI-ID of the root TPSUI, and some identifier unique within the scope of the TPSUI.
• **Transaction-Branch-ID**: This is used to identify a transaction branch. For example, it can be qualified by the Transaction-ID and the Dialogue-ID.

• **two-phase commitment procedure**

The first part of a transaction, called the **active phase**, is typified by two TPSUIs which exchange user data, and get themselves ready for the commitment (Figure 20.5). The second part of the transaction, called the **termination phase**, is entered when the commit coordinator asks its subordinate(s) to commit. This is the phase where the two phase commit procedure is executed. There are also two phases within the termination phase.

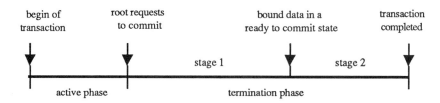

FIGURE 20.5 Lifetime of a Transaction

The first stage of the termination phase is characterized by the propagation of the commit request message originated from the root down the tree to all its subordinates. A subordinate in the transaction tree is informed by its superior to go ahead to commit. From this point onwards, the subordinate will not receive any more data from its superior. If it agrees to proceed, it attempts to make its local bound data ready for commitment. Bound data are said to be **ready for commitment** if they can be released to either the initial state or the final state when the transaction is terminated by commitment or rollback,. The subordinate has to not only attempts to make its local bound data ready for commitment, but also inform its subordinate(s), if there is any, to go ahead to commit. However, if the subordinate is unable to make the bound data ready for commitment, it initiates rollback of the transaction and instead of propagating the commit request down the tree, it propagates the rollback request up the tree.

If all the bound data are ready for commitment, the transaction may be committed. If the transaction is provider-supported, it will be actually committed by the TPSP instead of the root TPSUI. This shows how the TPSP contributes its share of decision making in the transaction processing. The second stage begins when the TPSP at the commit coordinator tells its subordinate(s) to to release their bound data to their final state. This is possible since each subordinate has earlier claimed that its bound data are in a "ready to commit" state. This is done in a recursive way in the sense that when a subordinate receives the go ahead signal to release its bound data to the final state, it will also send a message to each of its subordinates (if there is any) to go ahead to do the same thing. After a subordinate has released its bound data to the final state, it will inform its TPSP that the release on its part is completed. As far as a subordinate is concerned, the transaction is complete as soon as all the bound data of its subtree have been released to the final state. In particular, when all the bound data have been released to the final state, the transaction is complete for the root TPSUI, i.e., the commit coordinator.

After a node has declared itself ready to commit in the first stage, it may decide to release part or all of its bound data to the initial state even though it has not been notified by its superior of the final outcome of the transaction. Such a decision, as we explained in the chapter on CCR, is called a heuristic decision. Whenever a node makes a heuristic decision, it does not need to propagate its decision to other nodes although it is required to record that decision on a **log-heuristic record** in some secure storage. This record may be used later on to compare with the final outcome of the transaction to see if the guess is right or wrong.

- **recovery**

The major reason for using the two-phase commit protocol is to ensure that a failure will not damage the ACID properties of a transaction. Typical causes of failure in TP are application errors, transaction aborts, dialogue aborts, node crashes, and storage media failure. The TP model provides rich support for recovery. Recovery mechanisms for provider-supported transactions assume that the atomic action data (i.e., control information about the transaction) is appropriately logged. An important consideration here is that the system overhead (e.g., of making log writes) is fairly limited. The **Presumed Abort** technique is used. This technique requires the commit coordinator to inform its subordinates of the final outcome if and only if the transaction tree has been committed. When a failure occurs, it requires a subordinate which has indicated its readiness to commit to ask its superior the final outcome of the transaction. If the superior has no knowledge, the subordinate "presumes" that the transaction must rollback. This technique has an advantage that only one log-write is required on both the commit coordinator and the subordinates.

Let us describe the recovery procedure. TP recovery actions can be divided into three phases: fault detection and containment, transaction recovery, and dialogue recovery. Fault detection and containment is entered upon recognition of one or more failures. If possible, transaction recovery is entered after fault detection and containment. It is entered to restart failed components of the transaction. It then determines the type of recovery actions possible depending on the state of bound data and other items in the failed transaction. Recovery of a transaction means that, after occurrence of a failure, all the bound data involved will be reinstated to either the final state or the initial state. Dialogue recovery is entered if and only if transaction recovery completes successfully. Recovery of a dialogue means that the TPSUIs can initiate the next transaction if they choose to. The current TP standard does not specify any dialogue recovery mechanism.

Recovery actions of a node depend on the role and the state of the node. If the node is a commitment coordinator, its state can be either "ACTIVE" or "DECIDED". "ACTIVE" means that the transaction is still in the active phase. "DECIDED" means that the node has made the decision and has written a log-commit record in the recovery log if the decision was to commit. If a node is a subordinate, it has a third possible state, namely, "READY". "READY" means that the node, earlier invited by the commit coordinator to commit, has indicated that it is ready to commit and has written a log-ready record in its recovery log. Should the node make a heuristic decision here, it will also write a log-heuristic record in its recovery log and still remain in the "READY" state.

Let us examine the first two phases of TP recovery in more detail. The fault detection and containment phase is entered when a failure is detected. The action taken here is to try to recover from the log records which indicate the current state. If the state is "ACTIVE", then the node tries to bring its bound data to the initial state and propagate rollback to all other nodes with which it communicates. The recovery terminates as soon as the rollback is complete. Transaction recovery is not even entered in this case. If the state is "DECIDED", the outcome of the transaction is commit. In case that the node has made a heuristic decision before the failure occurred, the log-heuristic record should give the heuristic decision. This phase of the recovery does not re-establish communication with the superior or the subordinate(s) of the node if there is failure in communication. After this phase, transaction recovery is started.

The transaction recovery phase is entered when communication with an adjacent node has been disrupted and the final outcome of the transaction needs to be communicated. There are two possible situations. In the first case, a node in the "READY" state needs to re-establish communication with its superior. In the second case, a node in the "DECIDED" state needs to re-establish communication with its subordinate(s). Re-establishment of communication is done by means of a channel. To illustrate the recovery actions, suppose that a subordinate is in the "READY" state. First it re-establishes communication with its superior. Then it finds out from its superior about the outcome of the transaction. Upon receipt of the superior's response, it enters the "DECIDED" state. If the superior indicates that it has no knowledge of the transaction, then the subordinate presumes that the transaction must rollback. In this case, it releases its bound data to the initial state, and may propagate rollback to its subordinate(s) if there is any. If the superior indicates that the final outcome is to commit, the node releases its bound data in the final state (unless a heuristic decision was taken earlier by the node) and may need to propagate the final outcome of the transaction to its subordinate(s) if there is any.

20.3 TP Service

The TP service specification organizes the functionality of TP into seven functional units (Table 20.1). An overview of these functional units is given below:

Functional Unit	Services
Dialogue	TP-BEGIN-DIALOGUE TP-END-DIALOGUE TP-U-ERROR TP-U-ABORT TP-P-ABORT
Shared Control	no associated services
Polarized Control	TP-GRANT-CONTROL TP-REQUEST-CONTROL
Handshake	TP-HANDSHAKE TP-HANDSHAKE-AND- GRANT-CONTROL
Commit	TP-DEFERRED-END-DIALOGUE TP-DEFERRED-GRANT-CONTROL TP-COMMIT TP-COMMIT-RESULT TP-DONE TP-COMMIT-COMPLETE TP-PREPARE TP-READY TP-ROLLBACK TP-ROLLBACK-COMPLETE TP-HEURISTIC-REPORT
Chained Transactions	no associated services
Unchained Transactions	TP-BEGIN-TRANSACTION

TABLE 20.1 TP Functional Units

• Dialogue functional unit: Formerly called the Kernel functional unit, this unit provides the basic services required to establish a dialogue (via TP-BEGIN-DIALOGUE), allows invocation of U-ASE service primitives, signals user-initiated errors (via TP-U-ERROR), and terminates the dialogue (via TP-END-DIALOGUE). A TPSU or the TPSP may also signal abnormal termination (via TP-U-ABORT and TP-P-ABORT).

• Shared Control functional unit: When this functional unit is active, both TPSUIs can transfer data. There is no service elements associated with this functional unit.

• Polarized Control functional unit: Being mutually exclusive with the Shared Control functional unit, this functional unit ensures that only one TPSUI has control of the dialogue at any time. Many TP service request primitives can only be issued by the TPSUI which has the control. For example, a handshake may only be requested by the TPSUI which has control of the dialogue. The TPSUI which does not have the control can request for the token (via TP-REQUEST-CONTROL), but it is up to its peer to grant the request (via TP-GRANT-CONTROL).

• Handshake functional unit: This functional unit allows a pair of TPSUIs to synchronize their processing (via TP-HANDSHAKE) and possibly transfer control (TP-HANDSHAKE-AND-GRANT-CONTROL).

• Commit functional unit: This functional unit supports commitment and rollback of provider-supported transactions (via TP-PREPARE, TP-READY, TP-COMMIT, TP-ROLLBACK, TP-COMMIT-RESULT, TP-DONE , TP-ROLLBACK-COMPLETE, TP-COMMIT-COMPLETE, and TP-HEURISTIC-REPORT).

• Chained Transactions functional unit: Selected only when the Commit functional unit is also selected, this functional unit supports coordination of the TPSUIs with a chained sequence of provider-supported transaction branches. Thus, repetitive provider-supported transactions are possible. There are no service elements associated with this functional unit.

• Unchained Transactions functional unit: Selected only when the Commit functional unit is also selected, this functional unit allows a superior to exclude a transaction subtree from a sequence of provider-supported transactions, and to include this subtree in later provider-supported transactions (via TP-BEGIN-TRANSACTION). This is analogous to a boss who has a group of workers on a job. If the boss has the unchained functional unit, he could tell some of the workers at the end of the job that he wants to keep them around, but that they would not be working on the next job. However they may work on a later job. This functional unit and the Chained Transactions functional unit are obviously mutually exclusive of each other.

Next we describe each functional unit in more detail, with emphasis on how the service elements are used.

• **Dialogue Control functional unit**

This functional unit contains the following service elements: TP-BEGIN-DIALOGUE, TP-END-DIALOGUE, TP-U-ERROR, TP-U-ABORT, and TP-P-ABORT.

The **TP-BEGIN-DIALOGUE** service element is used by a superior to create a subordinate and to establish a dialogue. It uses a number of parameters. Some of the parameters have to do with the naming of the TPSUI initiator and the TPSUI recipient. The functional-units parameter is used for the negotiation of TP functional units. The confirmation parameter is used by the initiator to specify if a confirmed dialogue establishment is required. Hence, this service element can be either confirmed or non-confirmed. When the Unchained Transactions functional unit is selected, the begin-transaction parameter is used to specify whether a provider-supported transaction branch is initiated on the dialogue.

The **TP-END-DIALOGUE** service element is used to terminate a dialogue. The only parameter here is the confirmation parameter which indicates whether the TP-END-DIALOGUE service request should be confirmed.

The **TP-U-ERROR** service element is used by a TPSUI to notify its peer of a processing error. It also serves as a negative response to the handshake service. It operates as follows: it invokes TP-U-ERROR, then sends a description of the error using TP-DATA. Figure 20.6 shows the use of TP-U-ERROR to respond negatively to a TP-HANDSHAKE service request in shared control.

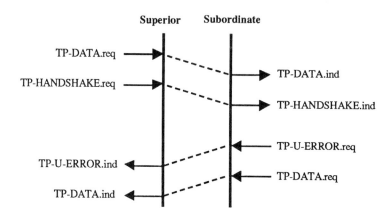

FIGURE 20.6   Use of TP-ERROR to respond negatively to TP-HANDSHAKE.request

The **TP-U-ABORT** service element is used by a user to abort a dialogue. If used for a dialogue with a coordination level of COMMITMENT, the request causes a rollback of the current transaction.

The **TP-P-ABORT** service element is used by the TPSP to notify a TPSUI of any failure which causes the dialogue to be terminated. The indication primitive of this service element carries a rollback parameter to indicate whether the transaction, if provider-supported, is being rolled back or not.

• **Shared Control and Polarized Control functional units**

The Shared Control functional unit contains no service element. Each TPSUI can issue primitives subject only to the normal sequence constraints of the primitives. For example, with Shared Control, data can be transferred by both TPSUIs at the same time. When the Polarized Control functional unit is selected, the control is modelled as a token which is initially owned by the initiator of the dialogue establishment.

The Polarized Control functional unit has two service elements: TP-REQUEST-CONTROL and TP-GRANT-CONTROL. The **TP-REQUEST-CONTROL** service element is used by a TPSUI to request control of the dialogue. The **TP-GRANT-CONTROL** service element is used by a TPSUI to grant control of the dialogue to its peer. Both TP-REQUEST-CONTROL and TP-GRANT-CONTROL cannot be requested during the termination phase of a provider-supported transaction.

Many TP service elements require the requestor to have control of the dialogue when the Polarized Control functional unit is selected. These service elements include TP-

BEGIN-DIALOGUE, TP-END-DIALOGUE, TP-HANDSHAKE, TP-HANDSHAKE-AND-GRANT-CONTROL, TP-PREPARE, TP-COMMIT, TP-BEGIN-TRANSACTION, TP-DEFERRED-END-DIALOGUE, TP-DEFERRED-GRANT-CONTROL, and TP-BEGIN-TRANSACTION. Some service elements in the above list automatically grant control to the acceptor upon completion of the service request.

- **Handshake functional unit**

This functional unit allows the TPSUIs to synchronize their processing with one another and possibly transfer control. It contains two service elements: TP-HANDSHAKE and TP-HANDSHAKE-AND-GRANT-CONTROL. The **TP-HANDSHAKE** service element is used by a TPSUI to request confirmation of processing to a known point by another TPSUI. The semantics of this service are determined by the TPSUIs and not the TPSP. The only parameter of TP-HANDSHAKE is confirmation-urgency which applies only if the Shared Control functional unit has been selected. It has the value "URGENT" if the requestor asks for minimal delay in receiving the confirmation primitive, and the value "NORMAL" if the requestor does not care when to receive the confirmation primitive. Figure 20.7 illustrates the case when the confirmation-urgency has the value "NORMAL".

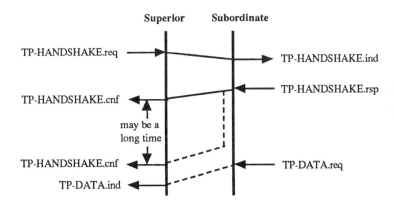

FIGURE 20.7 Use of Confirmation-urgency Parameter

The **TP-HANDSHAKE-AND-GRANT-CONTROL** service element is used by the TPSUIs not only to synchronize their processing with one another but also to transfer control. This service element is only used if the Polarized Control functional unit is selected. The requestor of this service element relinquishes control of the dialogue to the recipient.

- **Commit functional unit**

This functional unit is selected if a TPSUI wants the TPSP to maintain the ACID properties. The service elements associated with this functional unit are based on the two-phase commit procedure that is executed during the termination phase of a transaction. There are two phases within the termination phase. In the first phase, all the related bound data for the transaction are brought to the "ready to commit" state. Rollback is possible during first phase. The first phase uses TP-COMMIT, TP-ROLLBACK, and TP-READY (optional). If all the subordinates are ready to commit, the second phase begins when the TPSP at the commit coordinator sends requests to its subordinate(s) to release their bound data to the final state. Note that in an application-provided transaction, the TPSUI at the commit coordinator can choose to rollback even if its subordinates are ready. Phase II uses TP-COMMIT-RESULT, TP-DONE, TP-ROLLBACK, TP-ROLLBACK-COMPLETE, TP-COMMIT-COMPLETE, and TP-HEURISTIC-REPORT. These service elements are explained below.

First we explain the service primitives which may be used in the first stage of the termination phase. The **TP-PREPARE.request** primitive is (optionally) issued by a superior to request a subordinate to complete processing of the current transaction, place its bound data in the "ready to commit" state, and tell the subordinate that no more data will be sent to it. The subordinate will receive a **TP-COMMIT.indication** primitive. If the Polarized Control functional unit is selected, both the TP-PREPARE.request and the TP-COMMIT.indication primitives carry a boolean data-permitted parameter. If the value of this parameter is "YES", the subordinate is allowed to issue data requests to its superior. The superior remains in the active phase of the transaction although the subordinate subtree can proceed with the first stage of the termination phase.

The use of TP-PREPARE is optional because as we will see shortly, the superior may issue a TP-COMMIT.request primitive which is quite similar in intent to a TP-PREPARE.request primitive. We should point out that TP-PREPARE provides a potential way to optimize a large transaction tree, while waiting for a portion of the transaction to complete elsewhere. Subtrees of the transaction tree may complete in their operations. TP-PREPARE allows the completed subtrees to be prepared for commit.

When the subordinate's subtree is ready (i.e., all the TPSUIs in the subordinate's subtree are ready to commit), the subordinate will issue a TP-COMMIT.request primitive to indicate to the superior that its bound data are in a "ready to commit" state. The superior will receive a **TP-READY.indication** primitive. If the subordinate or any node in the subordinate's subtree is not ready to commit, the subordinate will issue a TP-ROLLBACK.request primitive to terminate the transaction and release its bound data to the initial state. The TPSP will propagate the rollback message up the transaction tree via the **TP-ROLLBACK.indication** primitive. When a TPSUI receives a TP-ROLLBACK.indication primitive, it releases its bound data to the initial state and then issues a **TP-DONE.request** primitive. The TP-DONE.request serves to tell the subordinate TPSP that the bound data held by the TPSUI have been already released to the initial state. After all the TPSUIs involved in a transaction have rolled back, the TPSP at the commit coordinator issues a **TP-ROLLBACK-COMPLETE.indication** primitive to tell all the TPSUIs that the transaction has been rolled back. This indication message is propagated down the tree by the TPSP.

As mentioned earlier, instead of issuing a TP-PREPARE.request primitive, the superior can issue a TP-COMMIT.request primitive to request its subordinate to enter the READY state. By issuing a **TP-COMMIT.request** primitive, the superior enters the first stage of the termination phase. In particular, this implies that it will not receive any more bound data from its subordinate and it cannot send any more data to its subordinate. It also means that all bound data held by the superior are placed in the ready to commit state. In contrast, a superior issuing a TP-PREPARE.request primitive instead may not have its bound data in the "ready to commit" state. The subordinate will receive a TP-COMMIT.indication primitive. However, the TP-COMMIT.indication primitive here does not carry the data-permitted parameter as in an earlier case when the superior issues a TP-PREPARE.request primitive.

Next, we examine the service primitives that may be used during the second stage of the termination phase. The second stage is entered when both the superior and its subordinates have issued a TP-COMMIT.request primitive. At this stage, the transaction can be committed. The TPSP issues a **TP-COMMIT-RESULT.indication** primitive to both the superior and its subordinates to indicate that the outcome of the transaction is commitment and to order them to release their bound data to the final state. On receiving a TP-COMMIT-RESULT.indication primitive, a TPSUI can release its bound data in their final state if it has not done so. It then issues a TP-DONE.request primitive to indicate to its TPSP that the release is complete. This request primitive carries an optional heuristic-report parameter which is only used if the TPSUI, before issuing the TP-DONE.indication primitive, has made a heuristic decision and the guess is wrong. The heuristic-report parameter has two possible values: heuristic-mix and heuristic-hazard. The value is **"heuristic-mix"** if the bound data handled by the TPSUI are inconsistent with the final outcome of the transaction, and the inconsistency cannot be corrected. The value is **"heuristic-hazard"** if some failure in the TPSUI prevents the TPSUI to report the inconsistency.

When a TP-DONE.request primitive signalling the release of the bound data to the final state is received from each TPSUI involved in a transaction, the commitment is complete. In this case, the TPSP at the commit coordinator issues a **TP-COMMIT-COMPLETE.indication** primitive to the TPSUIs involved in the transaction, indicating the completion of commitment. This indication message is propagated down the tree by the TPSP.

In the case of a rollback, a TPSUI, in response to a TP-ROLLBACK.indication primitive, issues a TP-DONE.request primitive to tell its TPSP that its bound data have been released to the initial state. Thus, TP-DONE.request primitive can be used in response to either a TP-COMMIT-RESULT.indication or a TP-ROLLBACK.indication primitive. When a TP-DONE.request primitive is received from each TPSUI involved in a transaction, the rollback is complete. In this case, the TPSP at the commit coordinator issues a TP-ROLLBACK-COMPLETE.indication primitive to the TPSUIs involved in the transaction, indicating the completion of rollback. This indication message is propagated down the tree by the TPSP.

We pause here for some examples.

Example 20.1

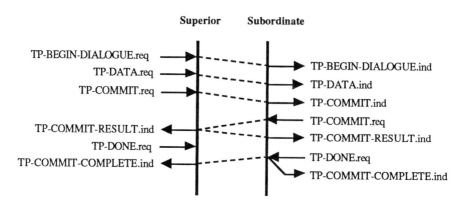

FIGURE 20.8   A Successful Transaction

Figure 20.8 illustrates a successful transaction on a tree with 2 nodes. As soon as the TPSP receives a TP-DONE.request from the subordinate, it issues a TP-COMMIT-COMPLETE.indication primitive, possibly before the TPSP at the superior issues a TP-COMMIT-COMPLETE.indication to the superior.

Example 20.2

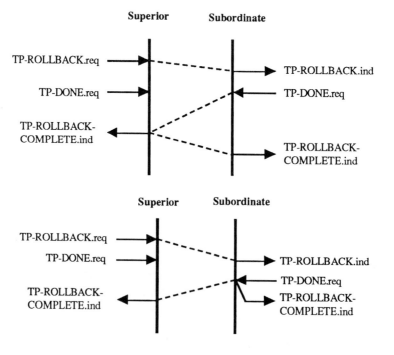

FIGURE 20.9   Rollback

The first part of Figure 20.9 illustrates rollback when the Chained functional unit is selected. The second part illustrates rollback when the Unchained functional unit is selected. Note the timing on receipt of the TP-ROLLBACK-COMPLETE.indication by the subordinate in either case.

Example 20.3

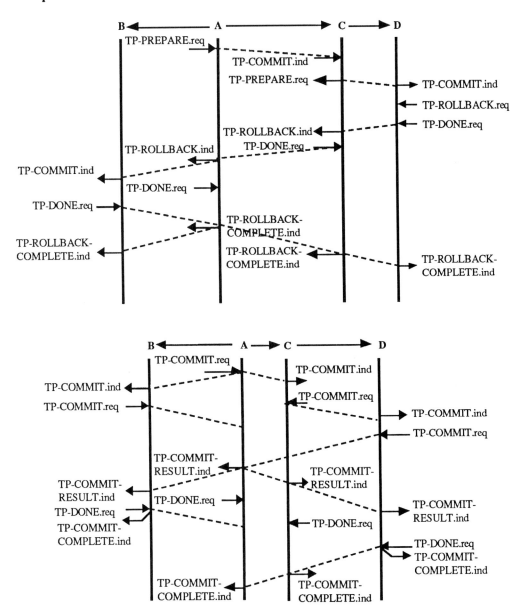

FIGURE 20.10   A Successful Transaction

The transaction here consists of four nodes, where A is the root, B and C are subordinates of A, and D is a subordinate of C. The first part of Figure 20.10 illustrates rollback. A issues a TP-PREPARE request to C which then propagates the request to D. D is not ready to commit, hence it initiates the rollback. The second part of Figure 20.10 illustrates a successful transaction.

When the coordination level of a dialogue is "COMMITMENT" and if the transaction is not in the termination phase, the superior can use **TP-DEFERRED-END-DIALOGUE** to tell its subordinate that the dialogue is ended as soon as the current provider-supported transaction is committed. The following example illustrates.

Example 20.4

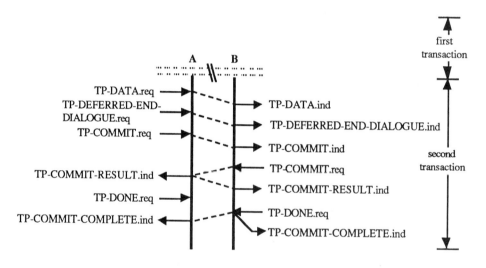

FIGURE 20.11   Use of TP-DEFERRED-END-DIALOGUE

The dialogue in Figure 20.11 is terminated at the end of the second transaction.

TP-DEFERRED-GRANT-CONTROL is quite similar to TP-DEFERRED-END-DIALOGUE but instead of terminating a dialogue, a superior will turn the control of the dialogue over to its subordinate.

Suppose that a subordinate makes a heuristic decision prior to the reception of a TP-COMMIT-RESULT.indication or a TP-ROLLBACK.indication primitive. If the bound data of the subordinate is inconsistent with the outcome of the transaction, it can use **TP-HEURISTIC-REPORT.request** to indicate the heuristic inconsistency to its superior.

• **Unchained Transactions functional unit**

This functional unit allows a user to switch between application- and provider-supported transactions. It allows a dialogue to continue with a subordinate, but not to include the subordinate in a future transaction. The Unchained Transactions functional unit is what allows us to have several transaction subtrees within a dialogue tree. The primary benefit of additional complexity is flexibility, which allows for optimization of the transaction environment.

A TPSUI uses the TP-BEGIN-TRANSACTION service element to reinclude a branch in the next provider-supported transaction. At the time the request is made, the coordination level must be "NONE". As a result of the request, the coordination level of the dialogue is changed to "COMMITMENT".

We have completed our examination of almost all the TP service elements. To address data transfer, the TP service specification provides the TP-DATA service element. This service element, however, is for modelling only. Application developers are free to choose their own methods of data transfer. TP can be viewed as a traffic cop coordinating the transaction. Just as a traffic cop does not care what type of cars it is directing, TP does not care what data transfer methods are used. The Presentation Layer can be used for data transfer. This method provides possibly the greatest level of flexibility. Since many options are available, the end-user must also investigate what data transfer methods TP products use. Two products from different vendors, both written to the TP standard, could not interwork if they each use different data transfer methods.

20.4 Structure of a TPSUI

TP is the first application protocol to require the use of SAOs (i.e., Single Association Objects) and MACFs (i.e., Multiple Association Control Functions). Accordingly, the structure of a TPSUI is quite complex. In fact, a TPSUI can contain a number of protocol machines. In this section, we examine the structure of a TPSUI. What we will not examine here are the elements of procedures associated with the protocol machines.

Because a TPSUI can be involved in channel recovery as well as a number of TP dialogues, it contains a **Channel Protocol Machine (CPM)** and a number of TPPMs (i.e., TP Protocol Machines). Interactions between a TPPM and the CPM are described by the **Channel Auxiliary Facility (CAF)** service. In the following, we examine the structure of each type of machine.

- **TPPM**

A TPPM contains the MACF and a number of SAOs. Internally, an SAO comprises of the following:

- TP-ASE: The TP-ASE is responsible for the exchange of TP APDUs with its peer. The interaction between the TP-ASE and the MACF is described by the **Auxiliary Facility (AF) service**. This AF service provides a definition of events to describe the operation of the protocol machine of TP-ASE.
- ACSE: ACSE is driven directly by the MACF.

• CCR-ASE: The CCR-ASE is needed if the Commit functional unit is selected. The CCR protocol requires that the issuer of a C-BEGIN.request, C-COMMIT.request, or C-RECOVER.request primitive own the minor-synchronize token. This requirement is guaranteed by the TPPM.

• one or more user-ASEs: A user-ASE, which is used to define some style of data transfer, can be the RDA-ASE, the RPC-ASE, or a specific user-ASE.

• SACF (i.e. Single Association Control Function): This function controls the above ASEs to maintain the consistency and integrity of a single application association. The interaction between the SACF and the MACF is represented by the **SACF Auxiliary Facility (SAF) service**. The SAF service, provided by the SACF, models the ability for an SAO to be attached to or detached from the MACF. While a dialogue is in use on the association, the SAO is attached to the MACF. At the completion of the dialogue, the SAO is detached from the MACF although the association used for the detached SAO can be retained for use by the MACF in another TPPM within the TPSUI.

Thus, the TPSUI interacts with the MACF using the TP service interface. The MACF interacts with the SACF of an SAO using the SAF service interface. The SACF can interface directly with either ACSE, TP-ASE, CCR-ASE, or one or more user-ASEs. In particular, it interacts with TP-ASE using the AF service interface. Note that a TPSUI never sees the AF and the SACF services. Since these two services are used for modelling purpose, a TP implementation is not required to implement a module for either service.

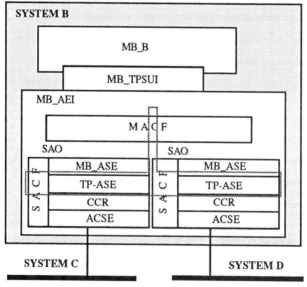

= TPPM boundary for manage_balances function

FIGURE 20.12 Structure of TPPM at System B in Figure 20.2

Referring to Figure 20.2, Figure 20.12 shows the structure of a TPSUI at system B. Here, we assume that the TPSUI has a TPPM which is responsible for the communications with systems C and D. Not shown in the figure are the CPM and the other TPPM which is responsible for the communication with system A. Note that the MB_ASE is a user-ASE defined by the application at system B.

- **CPM**

The CPM interacts with a TPPM using the CAF service. The CAF service, provided by the CPM, models the ability for channels to be dynamically attached to and detached from a TPPM. Whenever the CPM receives a request from a TPPM to perform recovery, the CPM assigns an unused channel to that TPPM. As soon as the TPPM completes recovery, the channel is returned to the CPM.

Like the TPPM, the CPM consists of the MACF and a number of SAOs. Unlike an SAO in a TPPM, an SAO in the CPM does not contain any user-ASE, although it does contain ACSE, TP-ASE, CCR-ASE (optional), and SACF.

20.5 Summary

The purpose of OSI Transaction Processing (TP) is to provide an infrastructure to support distributed transaction processing which may span across one or more systems. Unlike many other protocols, the TP protocol provides an environment which may involve a number of communicating pairs, and it leaves the style of data transfer to its users.

TP models a distributed transaction as a dialogue tree where each tree edge is a dialogue between two TPSUs (i.e., TP service users) consisting of a superior and a subordinate. Within a dialogue tree, there can be a number of non-overlapping transaction subtrees. Transaction processing in a transaction subtree is supported by the TP service provider via the use of CCR.

TP provides two kinds of provider-supported transactions. A chained provider-supported transaction is a sequence of contiguous provider-supported transaction branches of the same nature. An unchained provider-supported transaction is a sequence of non-contiguous provider-supported transaction branches aimed at achieving a common goal. Thus an unchained transaction can have certain branches not participate in a transaction, and then participate later in other transactions.

The structure of an invocation of a TPSU involves the CPM (i.e., Channel Protocol Machines) and a number of TPPMs (i.e., TP Protocol Machines). The primary responsibility of the CPM is to perform TP recovery. Within a TPPM, there is the MACF (i.e., Multiple Association Control Function) and a number of SAOs (i.e., Single Association Objects). Each SAO is involved in a TP dialogue with an application context consisting of ACSE, TP-ASE, CCR-ASE (optional), and one or more user-ASEs. The MACF is primarily responsible for the coordination of the SAOs.

Related Standards

DIS 10026-1.2: Information Technology - Open Systems Interconnection - Distributed Transaction Processing - Part 1: OSI TP Model

DIS 10026-2.2: Information Technology - Open Systems Interconnection - Distributed Transaction Processing - Part 2: OSI TP Service

DIS 10026-3: Information Technology - Open Systems Interconnection - Distributed Transaction Processing - Part 3: Protocol Specification

CD 10026-4: Information Technology - Open Systems Interconnection - Distributed Transaction Processing - Part 4: Protocol Implementation Conformance Statement Proforma

CD 10026-5: Information Technology - Open Systems Interconnection - Distributed Transaction Processing - Part 5: Application Context Proforma

CD 10026-6: Information Technology - Open Systems Interconnection - Distributed Transaction Processing - Part 6: Unstructured Data Transfer

21

Remote Database Access

In a manufacturing environment, it is typical to find heterogeneous database systems on different floors of a building. The **Remote Database Access (RDA)** standard provides the communication mechanisms to integrate these systems. It provides independence such that a RDA user can use the same front-end to access different database systems, and a single database may be shared by different workstations.

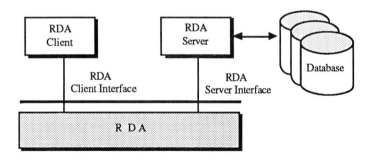

FIGURE 21.1   The Basic RDA Model

RDA is based on a client-server model (Figure 21.1). A RDA client, modelled by an application process running in some workstation, reads or updates a remote database system. The interface between a RDA client and the RDA service provider can operate in either a synchronous or an asynchronous mode. A RDA server, which is attached to a database system, responds to requests from a RDA client. Both the RDA client and the RDA server are RDA service users.

The RDA standard, as documented in ISO/IEC 9579, is currently a DIS (i.e., Draft International Standard). It consists of two parts. Part 1, the **generic RDA standard**, defines the common aspects of RDA applications. The RDA-ASE described here is not directly usable. In an application, it has to be specialized to a specific class of database systems. A **specialization standard** describes how the generic standard can be optimized for a specific class of database systems. Part 2 describes the specialization standard for SQL access.

Section 21.1 examines the Dialogue State Model. Section 21.2 examines the Generic RDA Services. Section 21.3 describes the rules used by a RDA server. Finally, Section 21.4 gives an overview of the RDA Specialization standard for SQL access.

21.1 Generic RDA Services

The generic RDA services can be classified into five groups: Dialogue Management service, Transaction Management service, Control service, Resource Handling service, and DBL service. The first two groups are concerned with database management, and the last three are concerned with database access. The **Dialogue Management service** provides facilities for the management of a RDA dialogue. The **Transaction Management service** supports the management of transactions. The **Control service** is used for the cancellation and status determination of outstanding RDA operations. The **Resource Handling service** is used to manage database resources. The **Database Language (DBL) service** deals with the definition and dropping of DBL operations, the invocation of already defined operations, and the execution of DBL operations.

Each RDA service element is modelled by an abstract operation. Its service parameters can be divided into a request group, a result group, and an error group. Service parameters in the request group correspond to arguments of an abstract operation. Parameters in each group which are subject to assignment by a specialization standard are called **specialization parameters**.

An early draft of the RDA standard included the use of ROSE in the RDA application contexts. The use of ROSE was dropped later, because ROSE can only support data queries in an interactive environment. It is sometimes necessary to transfer large tables of data between two systems. ROSE does not support such kind of communication. In the following, we will examine the service elements in each group.

- **Dialogue Management service**

The Basic Dialogue functional unit provides the Dialogue Management service. There are two service elements: R-BeginDialogue and R-EndDialogue (Table 21.1). A client invokes **R-Initialize** to establish a RDA dialogue with a server. During the dialogue establishment, RDA functional units are negotiated. The RDA functional units are Termination, Transaction, Cancel, Status, Resource, Immediate-DBL, and Stored-DBL. A client can terminate a dialogue in an orderly manner by invoking **R-Terminate**. All the resources which are opened for the dialogue must be closed before the dialogue is terminated. Note that a RDA dialogue cannot be terminated within a RDA transaction.

Functional Unit Name	Service Elements
Basic Dialogue Functional Unit	R-Initialize, R-Terminate

TABLE 21.1　Service Elements in the Basic Dialogue functional Unit

• **Transaction Management service**

The provision of the Transaction Management service depends on the RDA application context. RDA provides two application contexts: the RDA Basic Application Context and the RDA TP Application Context. The **RDA Basic Application Context** is the minimum application context which can provide RDA services. It contains ACSE and the RDA-ASE. Transaction management here is provided by the RDA-ASE. The **RDA TP Application Context** contains ACSE, the RDA-ASE, the CCR-ASE, and the TP-ASE. Transaction management here is provided by the TP-ASE.

Functional Unit Name	Service Elements
Transaction Management Funtional Unit	R-BeginTransaction, R-Commit, R-Rollback

TABLE 21.2　Service Elements in the Transaction Management functional unit

The Transaction Management functional unit is only supported by the RDA Basic Application Context. There are three service elements (Table 21.2). A client invokes **R-BeginTransaction** to begin a new transaction, **R-Commit** to order a commit, and **R-Rollback** to order a rollback. Note that the commitment protocol here is one-phase instead of two-phase, hence it is relatively simple compared with the commitment protocol provided by the CCR-ASE. If the RDA user wants to use the two-phase commit protocol for transaction management, it should use the RDA TP Application Context.

• **Control service**

If the interface between the client and the server is chosen to operate in the asynchronous mode, then a number of RDA operations may be outstanding at any time. The Control service allows a client to query a server for the status of an outstanding operation, or to cancel an outstanding operation. There are two functional units for the Control service: Cancel functional unit and Status functional unit (Table 21.3).

Functional Unit Name	Service Elements
Cancel Functional Unit	R-Cancel
Status Functional Unit	R-Status

TABLE 21.3   Service Elements in the Control and the Status functional unit

A client invokes **R-Cancel** to cancel one or more outstanding operations, and **R-Status** to determine the status of one or more outstanding operations. The value of the operationStatus result parameter of R-Status is either "operationIDUnknown", "awaitingExecution", "executing", "finished", "cancelled", or "aborted". For example, an operation is "finished" if it has completed execution, but has not yet returned the result or error response.

• **Resource Handling Service**

Functional Unit Name	Service Elements
Resource Handling Functional Unit	R-Open, R-Close

TABLE 21.4   Service Elements in the Resource Handling functional unit

The Resource Handling functional unit is used to manage database resources. The resources are defined by the implementors and are subject to constraints specified in a RDA specialization standard. A database resource must be opened before its content or capabilities can be accessed. There are two service elements in the Resource Handling functional unit: R-Open and R-Close (Table 21.4). These service elements are used to control the availability of data resources.

A client invokes **R-Open** to open a data resource which may be accessed in subsequent operations. R-Open has three specialization request parameters: specificAccessControl, specificUsageMode, and specificOpenArgument. For example, the specificAccessControl parameter contains access control data which is used to verify whether the user has authority to open the data resource, and the specificAccessControl parameter gives the access mode of the data resource. A client invokes **R-Close** to close one or more data resources. When a data resource is closed, any DBL (i.e., database language) command handle referencing the resource is made unavailable.

• **DBL service**

Functional Unit Name	Service Elements
Immediate Execution DBL Functional Unit	R-ExecuteDBL
Stored Execution DBL Functional Unit	R-DefineDBL, R-InvokeDBL, R-DropDBL

TABLE 21.5　Service Elements in the Immediate Execution DBL and the Stored Execution DBL functional units

The DBL service is by far the most important RDA service. It provides facilities for defining and dropping DBL operations, the invocation of already defined operations, and the execution of DBL operations. It has two functional units: the Immediate Execution DBL functional unit and the Stored Execution DBL functional unit (Table 21.5).

A client invokes **R-ExecuteDBL** to execute a single DBL statement a number of times. This number is specified by the user. The **DBL statement** together with the associated arguments and results define a database operation. The result parameters of R-ExecuteDBL contain the outcome of the execution which will be returned to the client. All the result parameters and almost all the request parameters of R-ExecuteDBL are defined in a specialization standard, since the RDA generic standard does not want to constrain the function of DBL operations at a database server.

The Stored Execution DBL functional unit is used by a client to define and store a DBL command for a future execution. A **DBL command** has a DBL statement, a command handle, (optional) argument parameters, and (optional) result parameters. The statement and the command handle are supplied by the client. The handle is valid until either the command is dropped, the referenced data resource is closed, or the dialogue is terminated. The Stored Execution DBL functional unit has three service elements: R-DefineDBL, R-InvokeDBL, and R-DropDBL. A client invokes **R-DefineDBL** to define a DBL command, and to allow a database server to validate and store the command. It invokes **R-InvokeDBL** with a command handle request parameter to execute an already stored command a number of times. Finally, it invokes **R-DropDBL** to nullify one or more defined DBL commands. Note that R-ExecuteDBL is equivalent to R-DefineDBL followed by R-Invoke/R-Drop.

21.2   RDA Dialogue State Model

The relationship between a RDA client and a RDA server can be modelled by a **RDA dialogue**. A RDA dialogue is a contract liaison between a client and a server. It can last for more than one application association. When a dialogue is active, a client can invoke operations while waiting for the results of previous RDA operations. A dialogue fails if either the RDA server, the RDA client, or the application association fails. A dialogue failure cancels the results of any transaction which have not yet been successfully committed.

A RDA server makes use of the objects in the **Dialogue State Model** to keep track of its dialogues. The objects in the Dialogue State Model are explained next.

• **dialogue entities**

A **dialogue entity** is created by the server whenever a dialogue is successfully established. It lasts until the dialogue is terminated.

A dialogue entity can be described by a set of attributes. The DialogueID attribute is used to identify the dialogue. The identityOfUser attribute is used to identify a user. The controlServicesAllowed attribute is used to indicate whether the server has agreed to allow control services for the dialogue to be issued on another dialogue. If the value is "FALSE", then RDA services such as R-Cancel and R-Status for this dialogue cannot be issued over another dialogue. The controlAuthenticationData attribute contains authentication information which is used to authenticate a control service request for this dialogue when it is used on another dialogue. The RDATransactionStatus attribute indicates the RDA transaction status of the dialogue. Its value can be either "RDATransactionNotOpen" (i.e., no RDA transaction in progress), "RDATransaction Open", or "RDATransactionTerminating" (i.e., a RDA transaction in progress and it has entered the transaction terminating phase). The RDATransactionRolledBack attribute is used to indicate whether or not the server has decided to roll back the current transaction.

• **opened data resource entities**

A data resource is a named collection of data and/or capabilities known to both the client and the server. A data resource must be opened before its content or capabilities can be accessed by the client. An **opened data resource entity** is created after a data resource is open. It may be nested within another resource, which is called the parent resource. Whenever a parent resource is present, it must be opened before a subordinate resource can be opened.

An opened data resource entity can be described by the dataResourceHandle, the parentDataResourceHandle, and the dataResourceName attributes. The dataResourceHandle attribute is used to qualify the data resource within a set of data resources known to the client within a dialogue. The parentDataResourceHandle attribute identifies the parent of the data resource if the parent exists. The dataResourceName attribute is a descriptive name which can be used to open the resource. The above three attributes are supplied as request parameters when a client invokes R-Open.

- **defined DBL entities**

An opened data resource entity, once created, is available for subsequent use in DBL services. Whenever the client invokes a DBL request on an opened data resource entity, another object, known as the **defined DBL entity**, is created. The need to introduce the defined DBL entity stems from the fact that there may be more than one DBL request on the same data resource entity. A defined DBL entity can be described by the dialogueID, the commonHandle, and the dataResourceHandle attributes. The dialogueID attribute is used to reference the dialogue to which the defined DBL entity belongs. The commonHandle attribute identifies the DBL entity within a dialogue. The dataResourceHandle attribute identifies the opened data resource entity associated with the defined DBL entity. Note that every defined DBL entity is associated with an opened data resource entity.

- **operation entities**

Whenever the server receives a request from the client, an **operation entity** is created. This entity will last until the request has been processed. An operation entity can be described by a number of attributes. The dialogueID attribute identifies the dialogue to which an operation entity belongs. The operationID attribute identifies the operation, i.e., the service request. The status attribute indicates the current status of the operation. Its value can be either "AWAITING EXECUTION", "EXECUTING", "FINISHED", "CANCELLED", or "ABORTED". The cancelRequestReceived attribute indicates if a cancellation request has been received for the operation. The operationArgument attribute gives the arguments of the operation. The operationResult attribute gives the result if the operation has been executed successfully. Finally, the operationError attribute gives the error value if the operation has been executed unsuccessfully.

- **states of a dialogue**

A RDA dialogue can be described using an operational status state and a transaction status state. The transaction status state is described by the RDATransactionStatus attribute which is one of the attributes of a dialogue entity. There are three **operational status states**: "idle", "active", and "interrupted". The "idle" state means that there is no dialogue between the client and the server. The "active" state means that there exists an application association for the dialogue. The "interrupted" state means that the dialogue is not currently supported by an application association because of a failure.

21.3   RDA Server Rules

When the server receives an operation request, it will execute the operation, modify the attributes of the relevant objects in the Dialogue State Model, and returns either a result or an error to the client. The generic RDA standard defines a set of server rules which are to be used by the RDA servers. There are three types of server rules: entity modification rules which specify constraints on the objects defined in the Dialogue State Model, result rules which specify constraints on the result responses from the server, and error rules which specify conditions for specific errors to be returned. Below, we will give simple examples to illustrate some of the server rules.

Example 21.1

Consider the server rules associated with R-Initialize. If there is no error, a dialogue entity is created (entity modification rule). Results such as controlServicesAllowed, and functionalUnitsAllowed (result rule) may be returned. An error is returned if the dialogueID is not unique (error rule).

Example 21.2

Consider the entity modification and the result rules associated with the R-Commit service element. When serving the R-Commit service element, the server sets the RDATransactionStatus attribute of the dialogue entity associated with the current dialogue to "RDATransactionNotOpen" (entity modification rule). The RDATransactionRolledBack attribute value of the dialogue entity is set to "TRUE" if the transaction has been aborted and all changes made to the database have been rolled back. It is set to "FALSE" if all changes to the database have been secured (entity modification rule). TransactionResult, one of the result parameters of R-COMMIT, is set to "ROLLEDBACK" if the RDATransactionRolledBack attribute value is "TRUE"; otherwise, it is set to "COMMITTED" (result rule).

Example 21.3

When serving the R-Close service element, the server will delete all the related opened data resource and the defined DBL entities if an error is not returned (entity modification rule).

Example 21.4

Consider the entity modification and the result rules associated with the R-Cancel service element. All the target operation entities with the "AWAITING EXECUTION" status will be updated as follows: the status attribute value is set to "CANCELLED", the cancelRequestReceived attribute value is set to "TRUE", and the operationError attribute value is set to "operationCancelled" (entity modification rule). A R-Cancel result must be returned before any response is issued for an operation entity whose cancelRequestReceived attribute value is set to "TRUE" as the result of R-Cancel (result rule).

We close this section by examining the server rules associated with the service elements in the DBL service. The entity modification rules for the R-ExecuteDBL service element says that if an error occurs and causes a transaction to be rolled back, then the server should set the RDATransactionRolledBack attribute value of the dialogue entity to "TRUE". If a result is returned, then it should set the listOfResultValues attribute value of the dialogue entity to the repetitionCount parameter value on the R-ExecuteDBL.indication primitive (if the DBL operation has only one argument).

When serving the R-DefineDBL service element, the server generates a defined DBL entity with the following constraints on the initial attribute values. The dialogueID attribute value is set to the current dialogueID value, the commandHandle attribute value is set to the commandHandle parameter value of the R-DefineDBL.indication primitive, and the dataResourceHandle attribute value is set to the dataResourceHandle parameter value of the R-DefineDBL.indication primitive (entity modification rule).

When serving the R-InvokeDBL service element, the server should set the RDATransctionRolledBack attribute value of the current dialogue entity to "TRUE" whenever the transaction needs to be rolled back. Suppose that a result is to be returned. If the DBL operation has a single argument, the number of entries in the listOfResultValues attribute value should be assigned the repetitionCount parameter value of the R-InvokeDBL.indication primitive. If the DBL operation has more than one argument, it should be assigned the number of entries in the listOfSpecificDBLArgument parameter value of the R-InvokeDBL.indication primitive.

When serving the R-DropDBL service element, the server should delete all the defined DBL entities whose dialogueID attribute value is equal to the current dialogue value and whose commandHandle attribute value is equal to the commandHandle parameter value of the R-DropDBL.indication primitive (entity modification rule).

21.4 SQL Specialization Standard

A RDA specialization standard defines the characteristics and capabilities of a set of RDA data resources, and the characteristics and semantics of a set of RDA DBL commands. It may specify which optional facilities provided in the generic standard should be made mandatory. For each service element, it may define constraints on the permissible parameter values. If a parameter is defined by a specialization standard, it must either specify the valid values and their meanings, which include whether the parameter is mandatory, optional, or conditional, or state that the parameter is not used. It may define additional server rules, additional entities, and additional attributes of the existing entities.

Presently, the only specialization standard that has been defined is the SQL specialization standard. The RDA specialization is formally defined as an ASN.1 module that is derived from a specialization module template given in the generic RDA standard. The RDA specialization module provides definitions for those types listed in the template as being undefined by the generic standard. In that module, the generic RDA data types named Specificxxx are renamed to SQLxxx. The current draft of the RDA specialization standard is defined for version 1.0 of SQL. It is anticipated that there will be RDA specialization standards defined for versions 2.0 and 3.0 of SQL in the future.

In this section, we will use examples to illustrate some of the constraints added by the SQL specialization standard to the generic RDA standard.

- **additional attributes in the RDA Dialogue State Model**

Two more attributes are added to a dialogue entity: SQLConformanceLevel and userData. The SQLConformanceLevel attribute indicates the year of the SQL standard for the DBL statements to be used in the RDA DBL operations. The userData attribute is user data specified by the implementor of the SQL server.

As far as data resources are concerned, there are no hierarchical data resources in the SQL specialization. Thus, parentDataResourceHandle should not be supplied as a parameter to R-Open. Two more attributes are added to an opened data resource entity: SQLAccessControl and SQLUsageMode. The SQLAccessControl attribute is supplied by the client to authenticate the right to open SQL DB resources for the required usage. The SQLUsageMode attribute indicates the access mode to an SQL DB resource. If the "retrieval" mode is selected, all the objects within that resource can be accessed for read-only purpose. If the "update" mode is selected, operations such as update, insert, delete, and drop can be applied to all the objects within that resource.

- **additional parameters of RDA service elements**

Almost all the service elements (except those associated with the transaction management and the control services) acquire SQL specific parameters. We will use examples to illustrate some of the additional SQL specific parameters.

Example 21.5

R-Initialize has three additional parameters. The SQLInitializeArgument request parameter is used to negotiate the level of support desired by a RDA client. The SQLInitializeResult result parameter is used by a SQL server to report the support it can provide when it cannot meet the support requested by a RDA client. The SQLInitializeError parameter is used by a SQL server to report errors.

Example 21.6

R-Open has three additional request parameters: SQLOpenArgument, SQLAccessControl, and SQLUsageMode. The SQLOpenArgument parameter contains information specific to SQL. The SQLAccessControl and SQLUsageMode parameters are mentioned earlier as additional attributes added by

SQL to an opened data resource entity. R-Open also has a result parameter, SQLOpenResult, which contains information returned by an SQL server, and an error parameter, SQLOpenError, which is used by an SQL server to report errors.

Example 21.7

R-ExecuteDBL has four additional request parameters. The SQLDBLStatement parameter specifies an SQL DBL statement. The SQLDBLArgumentSpecification parameter is composed of a sequence of SQL data type descriptors, where each SQL data type descriptor describes an input formal parameter in the DBL statement. The SQLDBLResultSpecification parameter is also composed of a sequence of SQL data type descriptors, where each SQL data type descriptor describes an output formal parameter in the DBL statement. Finally, the SQLDBLArgumentValues parameter contains the argument values.

   R-ExecuteDBL contains additional result parameters. The SQLDBLException parameter defines the completion code carried in the result of an SQL DBL operation. The SQLDBLResultValues parameter carries the result parameter values.

* **additional server rules**

The SQL specialization adds additional rules to the server rules defined in the generic RDA standard. The only service group to which no additional rules are added is the Transaction Management service group. Only the server rules added to the DBL service group are discussed here. We will illustrate these rules with an example.

Example 21.8

We consider the server rules for R-ExecuteDBL. There are altogether six error rules. The first rule says that the SQLDBLArgumentSpecification, the SQLDBLResultSpecification, the SQLDBLStatement, and the SQLDBLArgumentValues parameters will be validated and any exceptions will be returned. The second rule says that if the number of SQL data type descriptors in SQLDBLArgumentSpecification is not the same as the number of occurrences of input formal parameter values for the DBL statement, then the server returns the SQLDBLArgumentSpecificationError error. The third rule says that if the number of SQL data type descriptors in SQLDBLResultSpecification is not the same as the number of occurrences of output formal parameter values for the DBL statement, then the server generates the SQLDBLResultSpecificationError error. The fourth rule says that if the "host identifier" of an "embedded variable name" of an SQL statement is not "H", then the server generates the HostIdentifierError error. The fifth rule says that if a data resource was opened in a "retrieval" mode and the specified DBLstatement will modify one or more objects in that data resource, then the usageModeViolation error will be returned. Finally, the sixth rule says that if no execution of the statement is completed, an error will be generated.

   The execution rule says that SQL statements are executed by the database system at the SQL server exactly as if they were embedded in a host program which is local to the database system.

   The result rule says that for each execution of a DBLstatement, a specificDBLException returned by the database system will be included in the result. The specificDBLResult, if returned by the database system, must be also included.

21.5 Summary

The RDA standard is intended to support interworking between an application program in an open system and a database management system in a remote open system. The RDA service provides independence such that a user may use the same front end to access different database systems. The generic RDA standard defines the common aspects of a class of RDA applications, and a specialization standard defines an optimization of the generic standard for a particular type of database systems. At present, only the SQL specialization standard has been defined.

RDA uses a client-server model. Typically, a RDA client is an application program running in an intelligent workstation, and a RDA server is a remote database server. Both the RDA client and the RDA server are users of the RDA service.

A RDA server may have multiple dialogues with its RDA clients. It uses the objects in the Dialogue State Model to keep track of its dialogues. Objects in the dialogue state model consist of dialogue entities, opened data resource entities, defined DBL entities, and operation entities. These entities are manipulated by the RDA server.

The RDA services are divided into five groups. The Dialogue Management service allows a client to establish or terminate a dialogue with a server. The Transaction Management service allows transactions to be handled within a dialogue. The Control service allows a client to query the database server for the status of a particular outstanding operation, and to cancel an outstanding operation. The Resource Handling service is used by a client to make available data resources on a remote server. The DBL service is used by a client to execute DBL statements.

The server rules specify constraints on a RDA server when it is processing a RDA request. There are three types of server rules. They are the entity modification rules, the result rules, and the error rules. For example, the result rules specify constraints on the result responses from a server.

A RDA specialization standard defines those aspects that are specific to a particular type of database systems. For example, it defines the format and meaning of any data item that are unspecified by the generic standard. It may define additional entities in the Dialogue State Model, and additional attributes of the existing entities.

Related Standards

DP 9579-1: Information Technology - Database Languages - Remote Database Access - Part 1: Generic Model, Service and Protocol

DP 9579-2: Information Technology - Database Languages - Remote Database Access - Part 2: SQL Specialization

22

Manufacturing Message Specification

One of the most celebrated requirements for all manufacturing applications is the need for plant floor computers and devices to communicate. Fifty years ago, "Islands of Automation" was not a problem for manufacturing plants. "Islands of Automation" refer to various sections of a plant, each under the control of some supervisory computer system, and none of these supervisory computer systems have the ability to communicate with each other. As a plant continues to automate all phases of its operation with computers, the need to eliminate "Islands of Automation" grows. **MMS (Manufacturing Message Specification)** grew out of the standardization work at General Motors during the early 1980s. The early work at General Motors, as a part of the **MAP (Manufacturing Automation Profile)** task force effort, produced the **Standard Message Format (SMF)** specification. Using SMF as a base, development of the **Manufacturing Message Format Specification (MMFS)** began. MMFS was an extension of SMF, but also had input from a group developing a protocol for computer numerical control machines. MMFS was fairly complete from a service definition standpoint, however, three years of effort were required to add ASN.1 syntax encoding, and to further define and develop the standard to its recognizable form for publication with MAP 3.0 as MMS.

MMS is one of the largest and most complex application protocol standards. The scope and magnitude of MMS is quite extensive. This is partially due to the various traditional technologies that MMS supplements, and also due to the wide variety of factory floor devices available. Companion standards also contribute to the extensive scope and magnitude of MMS. MMS specifies how messages are assembled and sent using a client/server environment. The MMS service definition and protocol specification are given in ISO 9506.

In Section 22.1, we examine some of the key MMS concepts, including the notion of a virtual manufacturing device and the structuring of an MMS object. In Section 22.2, we review each of the eleven functional units, paying more attention to the objects involved and the service elements available in each functional unit. In Section 22.2, we briefly describe the MMS protocol specification. Finally in Section 22.4, we describe three companion standards: robots, numerical controllers, and PLCs.

22.1 MMS Concepts

MMS defines a communication language for manufacturing computers and devices. It is the child of both the OSI standardization groups, and the MAP standardization groups. It overlaps several traditional technologies associated with plant floor computers and devices. These technologies include Man Machine Interface technology, supervisory control technology, device operating system technology, and device communication technology. These traditional technologies are represented as actual product families available for manufacturing, along with de facto industry standards. For example, supervisory and cell control technology is available in the form of programmable logic controllers (PLCs) supervised by personal computers or workstations running specialized software. Figure 22.1 illustrates how these traditional technologies relate to each other, and how MMS overlaps. This overlap gives MMS somewhat of a disjoint feeling, since it specifies communications standards for several distinct areas under manufacturing computing. MMS services are listed in each area of overlap with traditional technology.

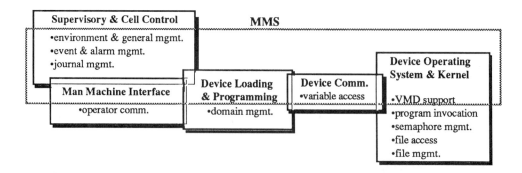

FIGURE 22.1   MMS Overlap with Traditional Technologies

MMS uses object oriented methodology to model the items and entities required for communication among manufacturing devices. MMS services operate on MMS objects. An object model is specified for the various components of an MMS environment: Virtual

Manufacturing Devices (VMDs), domains within VMDs, program invocations within VMDs, variables and data within VMDs, and several others. MMS objects are built from attributes and constraints (Figure 22.2).

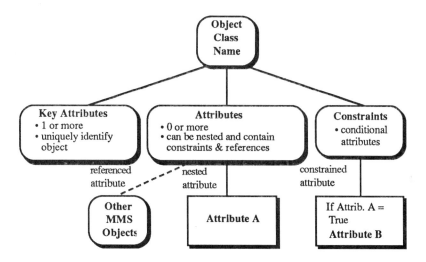

FIGURE 22.2 Structure of Objects

MMS uses the client/server approach to distribute services across devices on the network. Typically, the client is a host computer and the server is some factory floor device.

MMS is unique among the OSI application standards due to companion standards. Companion standards allow MMS to provide additional detail focused on a particular type of factory floor device. The companion standard mechanisms are inherent throughout the base MMS specification. For example, 53 of the 86 MMS services are specifically designed for extension. Additionally, 8 of the 18 MMS objects are specifically designed for extension. For example, the MMS companion standard for robots provides a description of a robot arm object. This description then becomes an extension of the base VMD object. A companion standard can add to the base MMS specification the following items: specification of extra parameters in the service primitives, specification for additional detail attributes in MMS object definitions, and additions to the protocol procedures and the protocol behavior.

A companion standard requires details for both the MMS service and protocol specification. Thus, the core of MMS is considered to be the service and protocol specification, with companion standards encircling this core, adding definition and specific meaning for families of devices (Figure 22.3). It is important to note that companion standards have been written for areas beyond families of devices. The PLC companion standard applies to over a hundred PLC manufacturers worldwide. However, a companion standard for Production Management exists. Production management is not a factory floor device. Robots, PLC's, Numerical Controllers, and Vision Systems are actual factory floor devices. Production Management is concerned with the coordination of these devices. This use blurs the original definition and intention of the companion standard, but conversely shows the flexibility of MMS as an extensible standard.

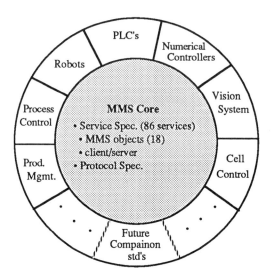

FIGURE 22.3   Core MMS with Companion Standards

22.2   MMS Service

The MMS service definition gives 86 service elements, grouped into eleven functional units. Each functional unit typically operates on a single object type, or on several closely related object types. These functional units are Event Management, Variable Access, Semaphore Management, Domain Management, Virtual Manufacturing Device Support, Program Invocation, Environment and General Management, File Management, Journal Management, Operator Communications, and File Access functional units.

22.2.1   Environment and General Management

The Environmental and General Management service elements allow two MMS users to establish communication with each other, and control some aspects concerning their connection (Table 22.1). The five service elements are explained below:

- **Initiate:** This is used to establish an application association between two MMS users. The association is established within a particular context, indicating supported level of service and conformance, with attributes such as maximum message size, number of outstanding requests that can be handled, and others.
- **Conclude:** This is used to terminate an application association between two MMS users and to free the resources allocated to that association.

- **Abort**: This is used to terminate an application association abruptly. Unlike the Conclude service, this service is destructive.
- **Cancel**: This is used to cancel a previous request of some MMS service. Most MMS services may be cancelled regardless of how fast they are normally acted upon. However, a few may not be cancelled, including the Cancel service itself.
- **Reject**: This is used by the MMS provider to indicate that a protocol error was detected.

Environment and General Management Services		
Services	**Objects**	**States**
Initiate Conclude Abort Cancel Reject		No MMS environment MMS environment (all other states are a subset of this one)

TABLE 22.1   Environment and General Management Service Elements

Establishing service levels for a MMS association is a part of the initial negotiation between the MMS users. Conformance levels are also negotiated with the initiate service. The INITIATE request primitive asks for a conformance level via the init request detail parameter. This parameter specifies a version number of MMS to use, the conformance building block (CBB) parameter, and the supported services. The supported services are simply a listing of which of the 86 MMS services the MMS user can support. CBB is a listing of other abilities that an MMS user may support.

Most of the CBB abilities have to with data types, variable naming, event management, and other abilities associated with variable modeling and transfer. Some examples of items which would be specified in CBB are: support for complex data types such as arrays and structures with or without nesting, use of alternate access for variables, and use of scattered access for variables.

22.2.2 VMD Support

VMD services are used to map the real factory floor device to an MMS addressable entity. Viewed from another standpoint, the **Virtual Manufacturing Device (VMD)** allows for translation between the device and MMS. This situation is analogous to an international soccer team. Each member of the soccer team is a factory floor device. The coach is a supervisory computer controlling and communicating with the various devices. The soccer coach of an international team will speak to the team with terms and language particular to the sport. For example, suppose that the coach talks to the team in English, using the terms and concepts relative to soccer. Each player will carry out his instructions individually on the field, but may think about his actions in his native language. This is unimportant to the coach, as long as the actions are properly communicated initially.

For the soccer coach, the English language coupled with the additional terms that comprise the language of soccer allow for an effective, coordinated, well controlled team. Additionally, the players may communicate with each other on the field in English also. For manufacturing, OSI is analogous to the soccer team using English as the primary language of communication. MMS is analogous to the language of soccer. In particular, each of the players on the soccer team is modelled as a virtual soccer player, just as each plant floor device is modelled with a VMD, to be spoken to using OSI and MMS.

Under a stricter interpretation than the soccer team analogy, the VMD in conjunction with the MMS services model the externally visible behavior of an MMS server. The relationship between VMDs and the application process is flexible. For example, an MMS system which is connected to a non-MMS environment containing multiple attached manufacturing devices could be modeled as a single application process containing one VMD for each attached device, or as several application processes each containing a single VMD for a single, distinct, attached device. In either case, the clients of the VMD will see a particular attached device as a single VMD independent to all other VMDs.

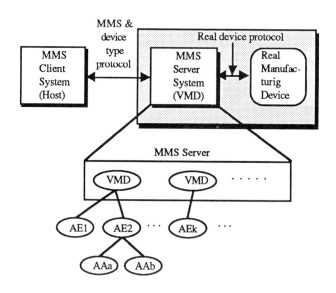

FIGURE 22.4 VMD Mapping

Therefore, an MMS server can have several VMDs. Additionally, a VMD can map to multiple application entities, each of which can map to multiple application associations (Figure 22.4).

From a practical standpoint, most implementations will not use the flexibility outlined above. In most cases, a single VMD will be allocated per server, on a device by device basis. The MMS server and VMD may be located in the same hardware unit as the real device. Or, the MMS server may be located on another computer. For example, several of the MMS products available for PLCs are implemented as a card which resides in the same backplane with the PLC. This implementation imposes a structure of a single VMD per MMS server. Another method is to use a single supervisory computer connected to a "data highway" connecting many PLCs together, and implement the MMS server in the supervisory computer. The PLC's "data highway" is used to communicate to the real devices. The MMS server at the supervisory computer requires multiple VMDs.

VMD Support Services		
Services	**Objects**	**States**
Status UnsolicitedStatus GetNameList Identify Rename GetCapabilityList	VMD Transaction	

TABLE 22.2   VMD Support Service Elements

Six service elements are available for VMD support (Table 22.2). Many of the service elements in other functional units will access the VMD or some portion of it. These service elements are explained below:

• **Status**: This is used to determine the general condition of an MMS server application and its associated VMDs. The information included with a Status response depends on the type of device as specified in companion standards.

• **UnsolicitedStatus:** This is used to indicate the local status of a server application and its associated VMDs. The response information for this service is the same as for a Status response(+). Issuing an unsolicited status message by a server application when appropriate makes it unnecessary for the client application to constantly poll the server via the status service.

• **GetNameList:** This is used to request a server to return a list of MMS object names defined for the VMD. Due to packet size restrictions for large lists, returning the entire list of names may require multiple requests of this service. This is indicated by the "more follows" parameter.

• **Identify**: This is used to obtain identifying information about the VMD, such as vendor name, model, and revision.

• **Rename:** This is used to rename an MMS object at the server. For example, this could be used to change the name of a temperature variable when an existing temperature sensor is reused on another piece of equipment.

• **GetCapabilityList**: This is used to request that a server return a list of capabilities associated with a VMD. Capabilities are any nameable ability inherent to the VMD. For example, in a robotics application, the capability "Arm1" may represent the set of sensors, actuators, and logic needed with a specific arm of a multi-arm robot.

Due to packet size restrictions for large lists, returning the entire list of capabilities may require multiple requests of this service. This is indicated by the "more follows" parameter.

Next, we examine the VMD service class objects. MMS services are said to define the externally visible behavior of an MMS server. This behavior is modelled by describing the VMD. An implementation of an MMS server must provide a mapping of the VMD model to a real device.

The VMD object model specifies an executive function as the key attribute. The executive function can be thought of as the operating system of the real device. The VMD object model then specifies certain identifying information such as vendor name, model name, revision. An attribute is included to specify abstract syntaxes supported, which may be specified in companion standards. Two status attributes are specified: logical status, and physical status. Logical status defines access modes for the VMD. For example, the logical status of NO-STATE-CHANGES-ALLOWED allows for 28 of the 86 MMS services to operate on the VMD. These 28 services do not induce state changes in the VMD.

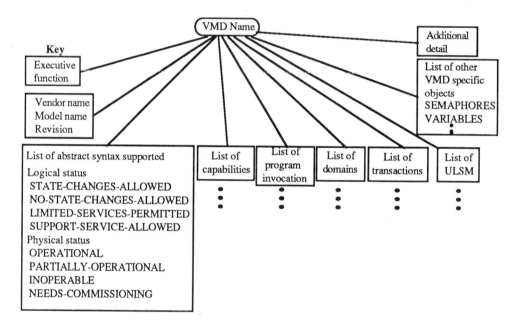

FIGURE 22.5   VMD Object Model

Transaction objects are created when a VMD receives a request for one of the MMS confirmed services. The transaction object is created to govern the operation of the service. Since most of the MMS services are confirmed, the list of transaction objects associated with a VMD shows the currently progressing operations on the VMD. The maximum number of transaction objects is governed by the negotiated number of outstanding requests returned by the Initiate service. The transaction objects are initialized in order of receipt at the VMD, and each is given a unique identifier. The transaction object then processes pre and post execution modifiers for the service it governs, and also holds an attribute which allows the service to be cancellable or not.

The VMD object model includes the attribute "list of other VMD specific objects" so that additional items such as semaphores, variables, events, journals, and others can be associated with the VMD. Therefore, this attribute allows for further extension of a specific VMD model to a real manufacturing device. Figure 22.5 below gives a summary of the VMD object model.

The actual nature of the VMD implemented at a server will reflect the real device. Figure 22.6 gives a representation of a typical VMD implementation.

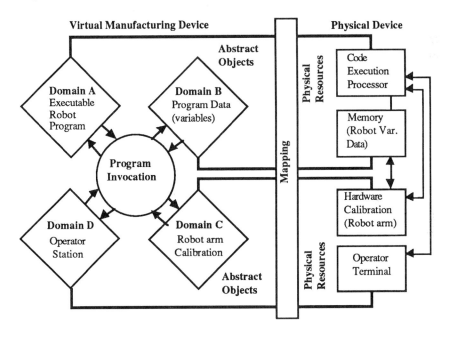

FIGURE 22.6   Example VMD Object

22.2.3 Domain Management

A **domain** is a named group of resources within a VMD. Typically, a domain is intended for a specific use, and in the strictest interpretation, a domain is a specific instance of use of these resources. For the soccer player analogy, a domain could be represented by the soccer player used for the specific purpose of a shot on goal after a penalty. The soccer player (VMD) is going to be used by the coach for one of his specific talents: kicking a shot on goal (domain). For a PLC, a domain may be a ladder logic subroutine which does analog signal processing.

Domain management services are intended for three primary duties:

- uploading/downloading domains to the VMD;
- loading/storing domain contents from/to a local or third party file store; and
- obtaining information about domains, and deleting domains.

Domains provide flexibility to a VMD. A single VMD can contain multiple domains. Domains are also closely related to program invocations. A single domain may contain the load image for multiple program invocations. Conversely, multiple program invocations may access and use a domain if the domain is sharable.

Domain Management Services		
Service	**Objects**	**States**

InitiateDownloadSeq
DownloadSegment
TerminateDownloadSeq
InitiateUploadSeq
UploadSegement
TerminateUploadSeq
RequestDomainDownload
RequestDomainUpload
LoadDomainContent
StoreDomainContent
DeleteDomain
GetDomainAttributes
	Domain
	UploadStateMachine
		For Domain
		    Loading
		    Complete
		    Incomplete
		    Ready
		    InUse
		
		For ULSM
		    Non-existent
		    Uploading
		    Uploaded

TABLE 22.3   Domain Management Service Elements

Twelve service elements are available for domain management (Table 22.3). These service elements specifically concern domains, and represent the primary method of transferring mass data and definitions between the client and the server. They are described below.

- **InitiateDownloadSequence, DownloadSegment, and TerminateDownloadSequence:** This is used as a domain download suite of services to transfer and load domain content information from the MMS client to the MMS server. The resulting domain may be one of several domains that constitute an executable program and its loaded data. A domain may be shared by more than one program if it is specified to be a sharable domain. A domain may have only one download sequence active at any time. An MMS client wishing to initiate a download would typically call the services in the order listed above. Multiple DownloadSegment calls may be required to download the entire domain, depending on domain size. A state diagram in the MMS service specification defines the interdependence of these three services.
- **InitiateUploadSequence, UploadSegment, and TerminateUploadSequence:** This is used as the domain upload suite of services to upload to the MMS client the domain content and loading information corresponding to the specified load

image at the MMS server. The upload information must be in a form that the domain may be downloaded later with the same information using the download suite of services. A MMS client wishing to initiate an upload would typically call the services in the order listed above. Multiple UploadSegment calls may be required to upload the entire domain, depending on domain size.

• **RequestDomainDownload and RequestDomainUpload**: This is used by the MMS server to request the client to perform a download to the server or an upload from the server. These services are contrasted to the previous six services in that they initiate a download or upload from the MMS server as opposed to the MMS client. A domain may have only one download sequence active at any time.

• **LoadDomainContent**: This is used to request the MMS server to load a file from its filestore, or from its file server into a designated domain. Certain implementations may require the CBB parameter of TPY (third party), since the load image may be stored on a third party filestore.

• **StoreDomainContent**: This is used to request that the contents of a specified domain at the MMS server be stored in a file on some filestore. "Storing" requires whatever processing is necessary so that it may be loaded later using the LoadDomainContent service. Certain implementations may require the CBB (i.e., Conformance Building Block) parameter of TPY, since the load image may be stored on a third party filestore.

• **DeleteDomain**: This is used to delete an existing domain and release associated resources at the VMD.

• **GetDomainAttribute**: This is used to get the attributes associated with a particular domain. Attributes returned include: domain name, list of capabilities, state, MMS deletable, sharable, list of program invocations, and upload in progress.

Next, we consider the domain class objects. Two MMS objects are listed in association with the domain management service class: domain object, and the upload state machine object. The **domain object** specifies: domain name, list of capabilities, state, MMS deletable, sharable, domain content (including a list of subordinate objects), list of program invocations, additional detail, and two constrained attributes: assigned application association, and upload in progress. The **upload state machine (ULSM) object** is analogous to the transaction object associated with the VMD object model. Typically, both the transaction object and the upload state machine object would not be visible to the end user. However, an implementor of MMS might be concerned with either of these objects. The ULSM object governs the operation of a particular upload. Each ULSM is given a unique identifier. Multiple ULSMs may be active on the association. All references to an ULSM are through the identifier, and the ULSM object is deleted upon completion of the TerminateUploadSequence service for that ULSM.

Domains are perhaps one of the most abstract concepts in MMS. However, for those familiar with factory floor devices, domains are directly relatable to the technology of programming devices. For example, most PLC programmers use some type of PLC programming software. This software typically gives the ability to upload and download programs into the PLC. Domain management services are providing this functionality via MMS.

22.2.4 Program Invocation Management

Program invocation management MMS services allow MMS users to control programs running in the real device via the MMS server. The program invocation management services and object modelling most closely resemble a multi-tasking operating system. In effect, the MMS standardization defines the external control mechanisms for a rudimentary operating system. The execution of a program invocation need not necessarily occur in the real device, but could be emulated in the MMS server. This concept is valid for devices such as PLCs which often offer co-processor modules, which can extend the functionality of the base device. Co-processors with OSI communications capabilities could implement MMS and also extend the functionality of the base device.

MMS strictly defines the execution of a program invocation as a time series of operations on a device. This limits MMS to providing any meaning to the sequence of operations. The meaning and the effect are local issues. In most implementations, a single program invocation will be active at a factory floor device. The operating systems of most factory floor devices are simple. In many cases, they are not multi-tasking or multi-threaded. It can be a matter of definition, however, since starting a program invocation at the factory floor device could mean starting a subroutine, or starting an entirely new process depending on the complexity of the device operating system. This flexibility is due to the wide range of devices which are available. Program invocations are very closely tied to domains. This allows for many different combinations and uses of program invocations, each of which must be specified for a family of devices in the MMS companion standards.

Program Invocation Management Services		
Services	Objects	States
CreateProgramInvocation DeleteProgramInvocation Start Stop Resume Reset Kill GetPgmInvAttributes	ProgramInvocation	Non-existent Idle Starting Running Stopping Stopped Resuming Resetting UnRunnable

TABLE 22.4   Program Invocation Management Service Elements

Eight service elements are provided for program invocation management (Table 22.4). Collectively, these eight service elements can be thought of as the control mechanisms for process management at the VMD. This process management is analogous to managing processes in a traditional multi-tasking operating system.

- **CreateProgramInvocation** and **DeleteProgramInvocation:** This is used to specify or delete one or more domains at the MMS server that together make up an executable program, called a "program invocation." Only a program invocation can be executed. A domain may not be executed directly, hence the CreateProgramInvocation service must always be invoked before the invocation of the Start service. The MMS execution model allows multiple program invocations to be running simultaneously in a multi-tasking environment. These multiple program invocations could possibly share one or more common domains.
- **Start:** This is used to start a program invocation executing from the "idle" state at the MMS server. Examples of the idle state are after a program invocation has been created but before it has been run, or after it has run to completion.
- **Stop:** This is used to temporarily stop a running program invocation at an MMS server. A stopped program invocation can later be restarted using the Resume service, or it can be placed back in the idle state using the Reset service.
- **Resume:** This is used to restart a program invocation that has been temporarily stopped at a MMS server.
- **Reset:** This is used to put a stopped or running program invocation back into the idle state at an MMS server.
- **Kill:** This is used to put a stopped or running program invocation into the "unrunnable" state at a MMS server. The only means of exiting this state is by deleting the program invocation. A program invocation can get to the unrunnable state because of an execution error, or because of a failure to perform the Stop, Start, Resume, or Reset service.
- **GetProgramInvocationAttributes**: This is used by an MMS client to attain the attributes of a program invocation at the server. The following attributes are returned with the result primitive: state, list of domain names, MMS deletable, reusable, monitor, and execution argument.

Next, we examine the program invocation class objects. A single MMS object is listed in association with the program invocation management service class. The **program invocation object** specifies a single key attribute: program invocation name. Other attributes are: state, list of domain references, MMS deletable, re-usable, monitor, execution argument, and additional detail.

The program invocation object also contains three constrained attributes. When the monitor mode is true, the attributes: event condition reference, event action reference, and event enrollment reference are active. These constrained attributes pertain to the ability of a program invocation to be run in monitored mode. When run in monitored mode, the MMS server will provide asynchronous notification via the event services when the program invocation leaves the running state. This represents a very powerful capability for both diagnostic processing and causing action when a sequence of operations are completed.

For example, many PLC manufacturers provide "watchdog" functions which flag irregular operation. A typical "watchdog" function is to take action if a fault occurs which causes the PLC program to leave the run mode. A monitored program invocation can provide this same functionality via MMS. Figure 22.7 shows the structure of the PI object when it uses the monitored mode feature and when it does not.

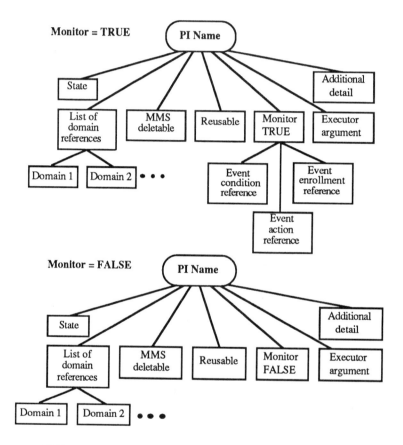

FIGURE 22.7   PI Object for Monitor Mode Settings

22.2.5   Variable Access

Variable access service is the most important class of services for MMS. It allows an MMS user to get at the variables associated with a VMD. Variable access implies exchanging valuable data between plant floor devices.

The complexity of MMS variables originates from the modelling and access options available. MMS specifies five types of variable objects. The variable access services have eight associated parameters. The variable objects combined with the parameters allow for a very wide range of variable modeling options. Variable type definitions can be built up in a tree structure. Also, elements of a tree can be of different types, and can contain substructures.

Many of the options and differences in MMS implementations currently available are concerned with variable access services. MMS variable access services are intended to serve the needs of a wide variety of systems, from the most simple to the most complex. For example, vendor A might offer a software product which supports variable access services, but does not support alternate access. Another vendor might support alternate access, but only support a nesting level of two for recursive structure type variables. Both of these products might have problems interoperating with a PLC vendor which has the need to support deeply nested structured variables, including alternate views of the variables.

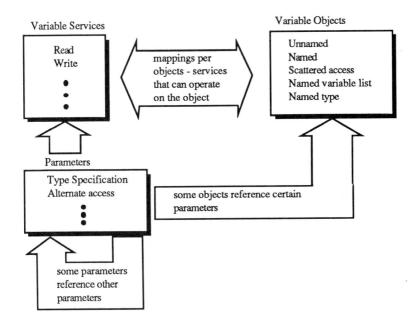

FIGURE 22.8   The World of MMS Variables

MMS variables are complex and diverse enough to comprise their own world (Figure 22.8). The five variable objects could be further subclassified. Two of the objects, unnamed variable, and named variable, define two basic methods of mapping the MMS variable at the VMD to the real variable. The scattered access object and named variable list object act as grouping mechanisms for the two basic options. The named type object acts in support of the other objects concerned with named variables. The term contiguous variables is used to refer to any variables which are not of the scattered access type.

MMS also specifies a V-Get and a V-Put function. These functions represent a element of variable modelling at the MMS server. These functions are the underlying mechanisms used to obtain the value of an MMS variable from the VMD. In effect, a remote MMS user which invokes the Read service eventually causes execution of the V-Get function at the targeted MMS server to retrieve the value from the real device via the VMD model. Sometimes, protection of variables is a capability inherent in the real device, and must be mapped into the VMD such that the MMS server can honor the protection.

Variable Access Services		
Services	**Objects**	**Parameters**
Read Write InformationReport GetVariableAccessAttrib DefineNamedVariable DefineScatteredAccess GetScatteredAccessAttrib DeleteVariableAccess DefineNamedVariableList GetNamedVariableListAttrib DeleteNamedVariableList DefineNamedType GetNamedTypeAttrib DeleteNamedType	UnnamedVariable NamedVariable ScatteredAccess NamedVariableList NamedType	TypeSpecification AlternateAccess AccessResult DataParameter VariableAccessSpec VariableSpecification ScatteredAccessDesc Address

TABLE 22.5   Variable Access Service Elements

Fourteen services are available for management of MMS variables (Table 22.5). A particular subset of these services will apply to each of the five variable access objects. Certain services are applicable to all of the variable object types.

- **Read**: This is used to read the value of a variable (or the values of a list of variables) at a remote MMS user. The variable may have a name that is assigned either locally or remotely, or it may be specified by an address and a data type. The variable type may be simple, or it may be an array or a structure, consisting of possibly many simple types and even other arrays or structures in a recursive fashion.
- **Write**: This is used to write a new value into a variable at a remote MMS user.
- **InformationReport**: This is used to indicate the value of a local variable to a remote MMS user. This service is normally invoked by the server application, and contains the same information that is contained in a Read response(+) primitive. Issuing an InformationReport by a server application when appropriate makes it unnecessary for the client application to constantly poll the server via the Read service.
- **GetVariableAccessAttributes**: This is used to get information about a variable, such as its address and data type. Variable addresses may be public or hidden. In the case that the value of the variable is calculated each time the variable is accessed (as opposed to being retrieved from memory), or if the variable address is hidden, then the address would not be "public" and would not be provided in the

response. This service is valid with either contiguous variables or scattered-access variables.

• **DefineNamedVariable**: This is used for defining a single contiguous variable and specifying its type at a remote MMS user. This variable may be based on another existing variable, but may differ in its data type. This means that a different type is overlaid over the same memory of another variable. When this occurs, the new variable is said to represent an "alternate view" of the primary variable.

• **DefineScatteredAccess and GetScatteredAccessAttributes:** This is used to define a new structured variable, composed of other variables at the MMS server which may be scattered in memory. GetScatteredAccessAttributes is used to get information about such a variable.

• **DeleteVariableAccess**: This is used to delete either contiguous or scattered access variables.

• **DefineNamedVariableList, GetNamedVariableListAttributes, and DeleteNamedVariableList**: This is used as a suite of services to manage named variables. The services are used to define a list of variables (possibly including scattered variables), used to get the definition of a previously defined list, or to delete a specified list. A variable list differs from a scattered-access variable in that accessing a list is equivalent to a number of separate accesses to each element in the list. In particular, when reading a variable list, it is possible to have partial success, where a subset of the variable list was read successfully. When reading a scattered-access variable, partial success is not allowed. Partial success is also not allowed for contiguous variables. These constraints also apply for writing variable lists.

• **DefineNamedType, GetNamedTypeDefinition**, and **DeleteNamedType**: This is used as a suite of services for naming a data type at a remote MMS user, getting a previously defined data type definition, and deleting a specified data type name.

Next, we consider the variable access class objects. Five MMS variable objects are designed for modelling the data for simple and complex real devices. **Unnamed variable** objects are intended for older devices, which typically specify data elements by a physical address. Unnamed variable objects are never created or destroyed. Their existence is inherent in the architecture of the VMD. Unnamed variable objects have attributes of: address (key), MMS deletable (always FALSE), access method (always PUBLIC), and type description. Additionally, unnamed variables can not have their access restricted. An example of an unnamed variable might be a general purpose byte addressable device with a fixed memory bound. MMS might assign the type "octet" to each public address.

The **named variable** object is intended for devices designed for MMS. Access to named variable objects is much like accessing variables in a programming language. Named variable objects have attributes of: variable name (key), MMS deletable (TRUE, FALSE), type description, access method (PUBLIC, . . .), and address (constrained, valid when access method is PUBLIC). The type description is unique in that it refers to the TypeSpecification parameter. Parameters in the variable access services are unique because they support and add additional detail to both the services and the objects.

The scattered access and named variable list objects describe access to multiple variables. These objects are groupings of base objects. The scattered access object has attributes: name (key), MMS deletable (TRUE, FALSE), and list of components. The list of components attribute is sub-divided into: kind of reference (NAMED, UNNAMED, SCATTERED), reference (actual "pointer" to component), component name, and access description. Access description is either UNDEFINED, or specifies an alternate view of the component using the alternate access parameter. UNDEFINED means that a full view of the component named in the reference is used.

A scattered access object is a collection of typically non-contiguous memory elements grouped into a single presentable entity. For example, a factory floor device such as a numerical controller may run several programs, each controlling a portion of a machine. Each program resides in its own memory space. A scattered access object could be defined to reference the process status table for each of the individual programs. All the status tables could then be presented to an inquiring MMS user as a single entity: a scattered access object providing status for all machine operations.

The **named variable list** object has similar goals to the scattered access object. The primary difference is that the named variable list object allows for partial success when performing read and write with the data. Therefore, the named variable list object is treated more as a collection of elements, versus the scattered access object, which is treated as a single, possibly large unit.

A named variable list could be used for the simple task of identifying an array of ten integers. Or it could be used for representing a very complex, structured, recursive, nested data type. Because the complexity can be so formidable, most products support a very shallow level of nesting (one to three). Additionally, support of alternate access for variables is not available in all products, or it is only available for simple data types and structures.

The fifth type of MMS variable objects is the **named type** object. This object specifies a named type which may be applied to a real variable in order to allow its value to be communicated using MMS. The attributes of the named type object are: name (key), MMS deletable (TRUE, FALSE), type description. Type description is supplied using the TypeSpecification parameter.

The use of specified parameters are unique to the variable access class of MMS services. As Figure 22.8 shows, eight parameters support both the object definition and the MMS services. In effect, these parameters are the basic building blocks of the MMS variable access service specification. A large measure of the complexity is due to the flexibility and range of options available with these parameters. Just as MMS objects and services depend on or reference these parameters, these parameters reference each other. For example, the scattered access description parameter references the variable specification and, optionally, alternate access parameter. Some of the parameters are explained below.

- TypeSpecification: This parameter provides the abstract syntax, range of valid values, and basis for alternate access (if used) for a variable.

• AlternateAccess: This parameter provides an alternate view of a variable. For example, this allows the read service to write to the value of a single element in an array of integers, given that the array of integers is a named variable list. Alternate access is very important in this situation because without alternate access, a MMS user needing to write a value to the list would have to either write the entire list, or keep separate definitions for each element in the list requiring writes. The AlternateAccess parameter, however, can be used to overlay simpler views of complex variable types. The parameter defines a list of alternate access selections. Each of these selections can be a direct access, or another alternate access.

• AccessResult and DataParameter: This parameter is used by the Read, Write, and InformationReport services. The AccessResult parameter holds or represents the result of the V-Get function. The DataParameter holds or represents the input for the V-Put function. Scattered access objects would require multiple V-Get or V-Put functions, with a successful response reported only if all V-Get or V-Put function executions were successful. These parameters are simpler than those previously mentioned. The AccessResult parameter provides for data access errors to be reported. The DataParameter can be specified for either an array, structure, or simple data type.

• VariableAccessSpecification, VariableSpecification, Scattered-AccessDescription, and Address: All these parameters are used to specify base access to a variable. In effect, these parameters provide structure datatyping. The VariableAccessSpecification parameter indicates whether the variable is referenced as a single named variable list, or as an enumerated list of VariableSpecifications with possible alternate access. The VariableSpecification parameter specifies access to a single MMS variable, or constructed variable represented by a scattered access object. The ScatteredAccessDescription parameter gives a list of components via the VariableSpecification parameter and optionally AlternateAccess parameter. The Address parameter specifies an unnamed variable object.

22.2.6 Semaphore Management

Semaphore management service provides a resource management mechanism for the MMS environment. Semaphores allow access control to a resource by more than one remote application. The semaphore model is rich enough to be used for the traditional purposes of mutual exclusion, but can also be used to specify a multiple priority queuing service mechanism.

Two types of semaphores exist: **token** or **pool**. Each type has its own specific state machine and queuing mechanism. The primary difference is that pool semaphores are mapped to the physical device, while token semaphores typically exist only in the MMS server via the VMD model. Pool semaphores can only be predefined, since they are dependent on the real device. A token semaphore provides one or more identical tokens for the control of a resource. A pool semaphore provides one or more individual, specifically named tokens; each pool token controlling a resource (or state of a resource) at the real device. Therefore, the pool semaphore is a grouping mechanism for named entities.

Each type of semaphore has a different mission. Pool semaphores control access to resources of the real device. Token semaphores are intended to coordinate activities among MMS users. In effect, token semaphores represent an "inter-process" communication mechanism for MMS users. Each semaphore is modelled as a queue, and has a list of owners for the resource, and a queue of requestors.

Semaphore Management Services		
Services	**Objects**	**States**
TakeControl RelinquishControl DefineSemaphore DeleteSemaphore ReportSemaphoreStat ReportPoolSemaphoreStat ReportSemaphoreEntryStat	Semaphore SemaphoreEntry	For Semaphore Entry Non-Existent Queued Owner Hung

TABLE 22.6   Semaphore Management Service Elements

Seven service elements provide for semaphore management (Table 22.6). They are described below.

• **TakeControl and RelinquishControl**: This is used to take control or relinquish control of a semaphore at an MMS server. The semaphore is used to coordinate activities with other MMS clients and may control access to a single resource, or to a set (pool) of resources.

• **DefineSemaphore and DeleteSemaphore**: This is used to create or delete a semaphore at a MMS server.

• **ReportSemaphoreStatus, ReportPoolSemaphoreStatus, and Report-SemaphoreEntryStatus**: This is used to obtain various amounts of information about a semaphore or semaphore entry at an MMS server. Since each semaphore is modelled as a queue, ReportSemaphoreStatus returns the state of the queue, including the number of tokens in queue, the number of owned tokens, the number of hung tokens, and other information. ReportPoolSemaphoreStatus is similar, returning the name and status of named tokens (resources) controlled by the pool semaphore. ReportSemaphoreEntryStatus provides the detailed status of specific entries in a semaphore queue, including the application process names of the clients using a semaphore or queued up to use it, and other information.

Next, we consider the semaphore class objects. The **semaphore object** has the following attributes: name (key), MMS deletable (TRUE, FALSE), class (TOKEN, POOL), list of owners, list of requestors, and event condition reference. Two sets of constrained attributes are also a part of the semaphore object. When class equals TOKEN, the constrained attributes are number of tokens, and number of owned tokens. When class equals POOL, the constrained attributes are list of named tokens, and list of named token states. The list of owners and list of requestors both reference the semaphore entry object. The event condition reference allows a network triggered event condition of normal priority and severity to be tied to the semaphore.

The **semaphore entry object** has the following attributes: entry id (key), entry class (SIMPLE, MODIFIER), semaphore reference, requestor application reference, application association local tag, invoke id, named token, priority, remaining acquisition delay, remaining control time out, abort on time out (TRUE, FALSE), relinquish if connection lost (TRUE, FALSE), and entry state (QUEUED, OWNER, HUNG).

The attach-to-semaphore modifier is included in the semaphore management specification. This modifier is used to delay the processing of a service until the control of a semaphore is granted.

22.2.7 Event Management

An event at a factory floor device can be defined as either a change in some value in the device, a change in time, or an operator initiated action. MMS event management service provides for sophisticated notification and detection facilities at the MMS server. These abilities are then used by the MMS client to monitor and control the operation.

The event management service specifies nineteen services, and three objects: event conditions, event actions, and event enrollments. Alarms are a special type of event enrollment. MMS specifies a very detailed event detection and notification model. Event conditions define what the event is, event actions define what to do when the event occurs, and event enrollments tie the two together. An event action must be tied to the event condition to specify the action to be taken.

As a monitoring and detection engine, the event management specification details very specific procedures. The top level procedure specified is a procedure for event condition monitoring. This procedure is implemented as a part of the VMD (MMS server). The event monitoring procedure invokes the procedure for event transition processing when it detects a change of state in the monitored event condition, or when a network triggered event condition is fired. The procedure for event transition processing will then determine the necessary actions and call one or more of the following procedures:

- event condition object update,
- event condition object attribute value capture,
- event enrollment object attribute value capture,
- event enrollment object update,
- event action execution,
- establishment of an application association for notification,
- invoking an event notification, and
- acknowledgement of event notifications.

Each of these procedures defines how to treat transitions between the event objects. For example, the "procedure for event condition object attribute value capture" is executed when required to issue the EventNotification service. The procedure captures the event condition name, value of the state attribute, and value of the severity attribute. Most of the other procedures are significantly more complicated than this example. The sum of the these procedures comprises the event monitoring and detection engine.

Figure 22.9 shows the relationship between the different types of event objects. Event enrollments tie event conditions and event actions together. However, event enrollments do not have to be tied to actions to be useful.

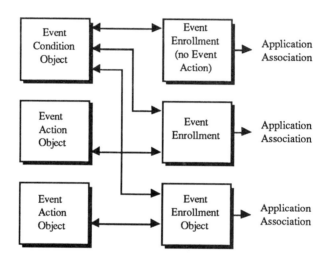

FIGURE 22.9   Event Objects

MMS events are of two types: monitored, and event triggered. **Monitored events** are more traditional. These are events which are watched locally at the MMS server in conjunction with the real device. Thus a robot might define a monitored event with a event condition of: the robot arm has cycled through its movement 1000 times. The MMS specification requires monitored event conditions to be supplied to the VMD from the real device via a boolean type variable. In this example, the robot would have to count the number of cycles, and when it reached 1000, set a variable value to true. This variable, if mapped to the VMD via the V-Get function, could be used as the source variable for a monitored event condition.

Network triggered events provide another layer of flexibility to MMS event services. Network triggered events are not watched locally, but are defined at the MMS server, and then "fired" from the MMS client. This allows for actions to be predefined or scheduled at the MMS server, and then started at will by the MMS client. This feature could possibly be accomplished without network triggered events, but with different implications. For example, a supervisory computer might wish to predefine five actions at the MMS server, so that later it just has to start the actions. Perhaps it is an automatic control application which cannot afford the latency of sending direct MMS service requests when it needs to start the actions. Network triggered events can be thought of as an indirect way of executing MMS service requests, since event action objects specify MMS confirmed services. A primary use of network triggered events is for acknowledgement of MMS alarms (notification event enrollment objects).

Event Management Services		
Services	**Objects**	**States**
DefineEventCond	EventCondition	For Event Cond:
DeleteEventCond	EventAction	Non-existent
GetEventCondAttrib	EventEnrollment	Disabled
ReportEventCondStat		Idle
AlterEventCondMonitoring		Active
TriggerEvent		Only first two apply
DefineEventAction		for network triggered
DeleteEventAction		type
GetEventActionAttrib		
ReportEventActionStat		For EventAction:
DefineEventEnroll		Non-existent
DeleteEventEnroll		Defined
GetEventEnrollAttrib		
ReportEventEnrollStat		For Event Enrollments
AlterEventEnroll		Rule = None
EventNotification		Rule = Simple
AckEventNotification		Rule = AckActive
GetAlarmSum		Rule = AckAll
GetAlarmEnrollmentSum		States composed of
		major states and
		minor impled states

TABLE 22.7   Event Management Service Elements

Not all of the nineteen event management service elements apply to all the event objects (Table 22.7). In this regard, event management service is similar to variable access services, in that the service could be partitioned into sets according to the objects they operate on. MMS alarms provide an emulation of traditional alarm functionality. Alarms are notification event enrollment objects. Alarms provide the ability for detected conditions to be summarized and sent to the MMS client. Typically, an alarm will be detected and displayed for an operator in a centralized control room. Handshaking then occurs between the operator and the control computer concerning the alarm. The control computer may wish to know if the operator has seen the alarm. This handshaking is accomplished via the alarm acknowledgement. The alarm acknowledgement is a message from the operator to the control computer that he has seen the alarm. MMS event enrollment objects provide several methods to handle alarm acknowledgements. Event management service elements are explained below:

• **DefineEventCondition, DeleteEventCondition, and GetEvent-ConditionAttributes**: This is used as the suite of services to create or delete an event condition, or obtain the attributes of an existing event condition at the MMS server. An event condition can either be enabled or disabled, and if enabled, can have a state of "active" or "idle."

• **ReportEventConditionStatus**: This is used to report the status of a defined event condition at the MMS server.

• **AlterEventConditionMonitoring**: This is used to alter certain attributes of a locally monitored event condition. For example, this service would be used to enable or disable the event condition. This service applies to the monitored events, and is not applicable to network triggered events.

• **TriggerEvent**: This is used to trigger a network triggered event condition. Network triggered event conditions are not monitored locally by the MMS server. When triggered, the event actions associated with the event are performed at the MMS server.

• **DefineEventAction, DeleteEventAction, and GetEventAction-Attributes**: This is used as the suite of services to create or delete an event action, or to obtain the attributes of an existing event action at the MMS server. An event action is an MMS service request that is not acted upon until a specified event condition triggers it. For example, the event could trigger the read of a variable, or start of a program invocation. When the event action is triggered, the specified MMS service request is executed. The response is sent to one or more "enrolled" clients via EventNotification service requests.

• **ReportEventActionStatus**: This is used to report the status of a defined event action at the MMS server. This service returns a count of the number of event enrollment objects which are specified for an event action object.

• **DefineEventEnrollment, DeleteEventEnrollment, and GetEvent-EnrollmentAttributes**: This is used as the suite of services to create or delete an event enrollment, or obtain the attributes of existing event enrollments at the MMS server. Event enrollments are references to client applications which are to receive either: event notification each time an event occurs, or a single response to a service request containing the AttachToEventCondition modifier when the event occurs.

• **ReportEventEnrollmentStatus**: This is used to report the status of a defined event enrollment at the MMS server. This service returns the current state of the event enrollment and other information.

• **AlterEventEnrollment**: This is used to modify an event enrollment object. Only specific parameters concerning the event enrollment can be modified: transitions attribute, and the alarm acknowledgement rule attribute. The service cannot be used to alter a modifier event enrollment object (an event enrollment which results from a service request which contains the AttachToEventCondition modifier).

• **EventNotification**: This is used to notify enrolled clients of the occurrence of a particular event and to include the response information of a specified event action (typically execution of a service request) that was performed when the event occurred.

- **AcknowledgeEventNotification**: This is used by a MMS client receiving an EventNotification request to acknowledge receipt of the information.
- **GetAlarmSummary**: This is used to get a summary of the alarms that have occurred at an MMS server regarding a specified set of event conditions.
- **GetAlarmEnrollmentSummary**: This is used to obtain a report of the status of all event enrollments that specify an alarm type of event. This service also provides the ability to filter alarms that are reported to the MMS client. This means that only the alarms of a particular severity might be reported.

Next we consider the event management class objects. The **event condition object** provides for event detection and prioritization. For monitored events, the event condition object contains information which assists in determining active alarms. The event condition object defines an entry for the MMS server event detection and monitoring engine to watch. This entry can be fired by either: a transition of the monitored variable (if monitored type), or by "triggering" from a MMS client.

The attributes of the event condition object are: name (key), MMS deletable (TRUE, FALSE), event condition class (NETWORK-TRIGGERED, MONITORED), state (DISABLED, IDLE, ACTIVE), priority, severity, additional detail and list of event enrollment references. For a monitored event condition object, the following constrained attributes are also active: enabled (TRUE, FALSE), alarm summary reports (TRUE, FALSE), monitored variable reference, evaluation interval, time of last transition to active, and time of last transition to idle.

Priority and severity are both represented as integers in the range of 0 to 127. Priority and severity allow for filtering of alarms when using the GetAlarmSummary and GetAlarmEnrollmentSummary service. The constrained attribute "enabled" determines if the procedures for event processing should be executed when the event condition object changes state. State is always disabled for network triggered objects. The constrained attribute: alarm summary reports, is an override which says: all attached event enrollment objects will be included in alarm reports regardless of the state of the event condition and regardless of the alarm acknowledge rule setting for each individual event enrollment object.

The primary drawback, or lack of capability in the event condition object concerns the type of variable which can be monitored. The monitored variable reference must be of type boolean. This does not address a wide range of other alarm and event detection requirements: for example, the ability to detect that an analog value is greater than 120. What is required is an expression mechanism, where the event condition object references an expression, the result of the expression evaluation either TRUE or FALSE. This additional capability would greatly expand the usefulness of the MMS event management services.

The **event action object** is concerned with the execution of MMS confirmed services upon the occurrence of an event. The event action object has attributes: name (key), MMS deletable (TRUE, FALSE), confirmed service request, list of modifier, list of event enrollment reference, and additional detail. The confirmed service request attribute contains the service request and associated arguments. The list of modifiers applies to the execution of the service request (for example, the AttachToSemaphore modifier might be included here). When the confirmed service request is executed at the MMS server, the request and the results are sent back to the MMS client using the EventNotification service.

It is interesting to note that an event action can be tied to multiple event enrollments. This means several different conditions in the system could be made to perform the same action. An example of when this is necessary is an emergency stop situation. An entire group of event conditions may all be critical enough to require a shutdown. Each could be tied to separate event enrollments that all point back to an event action object which causes an emergency stop of the manufacturing process. This is possible, because the event action object specifies a list of event enrollments which can trigger the action. This flexibility is important. It allows the emergency stop to occur because of either a tank overflow, a power interruption, or an auxiliary system shutdown. An event condition can fire multiple event enrollments, and an event action can be triggered by multiple event enrollments. This allows multiple actions to occur from one event condition, and allows multiple event conditions to fire multiple actions, or a single action.

The **event enrollment object** serves several functions: tie the event condition to an event action, tie event notifications to a MMS client (and therefore to an Application Association), manage state information concerned with tracking and coordinating client responses for alarm event notification, and managing services which were executed with the AttachToEventCondition modifier. An event enrollment represents a request from an MMS client to be notified of an occurrence of one or more specified state transitions of an event condition object.

The event condition transitions attribute provides a list of the event condition state transitions which should trigger notification (from a list of seven possible transitions). For example, notification could be triggered on the transitions: IDLE-TO-ACTIVE, and ANY-TO-DELETED.

The constrained attributes for notification event enrollment objects contain the attributes which are concerned with alarm processing, specifically, acknowledging alarms. Once an event condition has triggered the event enrollment object, the values of these attributes are used to determine if this event enrollment should be included on alarm reports, unless the override attribute in the event condition object is TRUE.

It is important to emphasize that alarms are for operators. The event enrollment object provides several methods for dealing with alarms because of the variety of ways different companies use alarms. The purpose of requiring operators to acknowledge alarms is that the control system is assured that the operator has seen them. Additionally, this comprises a part of the audit trail of operator actions.

How does a MMS client acknowledge alarms (event enrollment objects)? What is the mechanism to do this? The acknowledgement is performed via the acknowledgement event condition reference. This reference is to a network triggered event condition object. This means that the mechanism to acknowledge an alarm generated by a monitored type event condition object is another event condition object: a network triggered event condition object. At first glance, this seems exceedingly complex, however, this method provides an extreme amount of flexibility. It allows a single network triggered event condition object to acknowledge a group of alarms, or the implementation could allow for individual acknowledgments.

The client application attribute allows for notification to a MMS client. The time active and idle acknowledged attributes log times for acknowledgements when appropriate (alarm acknowledgement rule equals NONE). The state attribute is related to the alarm acknowledgement rule attribute. The alarm acknowledgement rule primarily specifies if alarm acknowledgement is required or allowed for a transition into a particular state. For example, SIMPLE designates that alarm acknowledgements are allowed for transitions of the event condition to active. When the acknowledgements are received, they will affect the state diagram (and therefore value of the state attribute) of the event enrollment object. When the alarm acknowledgment rule equals ACK-ACTIVE, this designates that acknowledgements are required for a transition to active, and will affect the state. Additionally, acknowledgements are accepted for transitions to the idle state, but will not affect the state.

The use of these different choices for the alarm acknowledgement can be related to operator needs. An alarm that the control system requires the operator to see would typically be implemented with the acknowledgement rule equal to ACK-ACTIVE. When the various choices for alarm acknowledgements are coupled with priority and severity designations for the event condition, a very flexible range of specifications are possible for alarm reporting using the GetAlarmSummary and GetAlarmEnrollmentSummary services. For example, it is possible to have the GetAlarmEnrollmentSummary service return all the active alarms within a certain severity range. Both of these services provide additional flexibility in that they can return summaries on named lists of event conditions or event enrollments, and also can return summaries for all of the objects associated with a particular application association or client application.

22.2.8 Other MMS Service Classes

In this section, we consider briefly the remaining MMS service classes.

• **Operator Communication**

Operator Communication Services		
Services	Objects	States
Input Output	OperatorStation	Idle Waiting for Input Str Display list of Prompts InputBufferFilled OutputBufferFilled

Table 22.8 Operator Communication Service Elements

Operator communication service provides MMS users with a rudimentary operator interface capability for control and monitoring of plant operations (Table 22.8). MMS operator communications are intended to be restrictive and simple. The VMD model at the MMS server will include an operator station object if this service class is to be used.

Operator communication service at the device typically does not require elaborate graphics displays. Typically, many devices have a one or two line display for showing messages or taking operator input. Operator communications are intended to be available primarily at the MMS server.

A single object is specified for operator communication service. The concept of virtual functions are applied to map values from the operator station to the real device. The D-Put (display put) function writes values to the physical display of the operator station device. The E-Get (entry get) function obtains an input string from an operator station.

• **Journal Management**

Journal Mangement Service		
Services	Objects	States
ReadJournal WriteJournal InitializeJournal ReportJournalStatus CreateJournal DeleteJournal	Journal JournalEntry	

TABLE 22.9   Journal Management Service Elements

Journal management service provides MMS users with a facility to record and retrieve information concerning events, variables associated with events, and operator comments (Table 22.9). Based on the flexibility of the event management objects, the definition of journal management services is flexible enough to provide for several traditional needs, such as historical alarms summaries, logging of operator actions, system event archiving and logging, taking operator input in association with journal entries, and capturing data snapshots related to important system occurrences.

• **File Access**

File Access Services		
Services	Objects	States
ObtainFile		

TABLE 22.10   File Access Service Elements

The file access service is used to direct the MMS server to an auxiliary or third party filestore (Table 22.10). This service class is very simple, and includes only a single service. Once a file is obtained with the file access service, it can be used via the file management services. This service is also unique in that it does not operate on an explicitly defined MMS object.

- **File Management**

File Management Services		
Services	**Objects**	**Parameters**
FileOpen FileRead FileClose FileRename FileDelete FileDirectory		FileAttributes

TABLE 22.11　File Management Service Elements

File management service provides the ability to read files and data from file systems in control devices (Table 22.11). These file systems in the real devices can themselves be virtual filestores, depending on the MMS server implementation. The MMS virtual filestore is mapped to a real object. This provides the ability of a control device filestore to be located on another computer. This object is termed the MMS virtual filestore.

MMS file management services are intended to provide only the simplest capability of file access. The only format supported is a sequential, unstructured binary file. If more robust file access services are required by the application, it is expected that the MMS server implementation will use FTAM to meet that need.

22.3　MMS Protocol Specification

The MMS protocol specification is organized around the same functional units defined in the service specification. Each functional unit is related from an applications standpoint (they are all useful for communications with factory floor devices), however, the functional units are not highly coupled: the state of the services in one functional unit does not usually affect the state of the services in the other functional units. For example, a program invocation service to start a process does not care if at the same time some variables are being read by a variable access service. The application may care, but the protocol doesn't.

Fourteen PDU types are specified for the MMS protocol. Four of these PDU types are generic, and are used as the carrier for the majority of the MMS services. The other ten are used specifically for the services in the Environment and General Management services functional unit.

The generic PDU types and their mapping to the lower OSI layers are given in Table 22.12. PDU types specific to the Environment and General Management services and their mapping to the lower OSI layers are also given in Table 22.12.

MMS Protocol Specification PDU	OSI Lower Layer PDUs
Generic MMS PDUs which carry most of the services	
confirmed-RequestPDU	P-DATA.req, ind
confirmed-ResponsePDU	P-DATA.req, ind
confirmed-ErrorPDU	P-DATA.req, ind
unconfirmed-PDU	P-DATA.req, ind
MMS PDUs which carry Environment and General Management Services	
rejectPDU	P-DATA.req, ind
cancel-ResquestPDU	P-DATA.req, ind
cancel-ResponsePDU	P-DATA.req, ind
cancel-ErrorPDU	P-DATA.req, ind
initiate-RequestPDU	A-ASSOCIATE.req, ind
initiate-ResponsePDU	A-ASSOCIATE.req, ind (with Result para. accepted)
initiate-ErrorPDU	A-ASSOCIATE.req, ind (with Result para. rejected)
conclude-RequestPDU	P-DATA.req, ind
conclude-ResponsePDU	P-DATA.req, ind
conclude-ErrorPDU	P-DATA.req, ind

TABLE 22.12   Generic PDU types and Their Mapping to the Lower Layers

The companion standard idea serves to keep the level of detail in the MMS protocol specification relatively low compared to the number of services available. Since each class of devices can have unique protocol needs, a particular limitation on the sequencing of primitives could be fully defined in a companion standard. Another method used by the protocol specification to keep the level of detail low is by "supporting productions" and importing data type definitions. Both of these techniques are used to keep the ASN.1 definitions more concise and readable. Supporting productions are a defined type which is referenced in many places, like a structure definition in the C programming language. Imported data types allow the type definitions of other OSI standards to be used without explicit declaration.

22.4 Companion Standards

Companion standards allow MMS to provide additional detail focused on a particular type of factory floor device. The purpose of this section is to provide an overview of each of them, focusing on building understanding of the device, and what its unique communication requirements are. Examples of how MMS has been extended for each device will be given.

22.4.1 Robots

The robot companion standard defines the use of MMS specific to a "Manipulating Industrial Robot." This distinction is made to focus on MMS use for robots used in the manufacturing environment, since robots are available in other environments such as medicine. Manipulating industrial robots are typically used in discrete manufacturing operations such as the automotive industry. Welding is one of the primary applications for industrial robots in the automotive industry. Other robot applications include assembly and packaging.

The model for communications among robots allows for: a robot server and a single client, a robot server and multiple clients, a robot client, and peer to peer configurations where a robot acts as both client and server at the same time. Non-intelligent devices associated with the robot such as teach pendants and operator interfaces are considered part of the robot server. Typically, the communication between such devices and the robot is non-OSI.

The robot model specifies a robot arm with several associated sub-systems, and several types of geometric coordinate systems. A "robot controller" entity is described, which can be a computer within the robot itself, or a separate supervisory computer.

The robot model extends the VMD object definition, and also defines two new objects: the robot arm object, and the auxiliary device object. A single robot system may contain one or more arms. Multiple arms may be either coordinated or independent, depending on the application.

The extended robot VMD object is listed below as an example of how a companion standard would need to extend the VMD model.

Object: Robot VMD
All MMS defined Attributes
Attribute: Safety Interlocks Violated (TRUE, FALSE)
Attribute: Robot VMD State (ROBOT-IDLE, ROBOT-LOADED, ROBOT-READY, ROBOT-EXECUTING, ROBOT-PAUSED, MANUAL-INTERVENTION-REQUIRED)
Attribute: Any Physical Resource Power On (TRUE, FALSE)
Attribute: All Physical Resources Calibrated (TRUE, FALSE)
Attribute: Local Control (TRUE, FALSE)
Attribute: Metric Measure (TRUE, FALSE)
Attribute: Reference to Selected Controlling Program Invocation

The program invocation object is also extended. Robot programs are typically not very complex from a logic standpoint. Typically, a particular robot will run a single program from a library of programs. For example, different programs may run for different models of an automobile that is being produced. Most robots run a single controlling program, which may call other programs. This situation is modeled with an additional attribute shown in the robot VMD object model: control (CONTROLLING, CONTROLLED, NORMAL). A set of constrained attributes are active when the control attribute equals CONTROLLING.

The robot companion standard also extends several of the MMS services. For example, the CreateProgramInvocation service is extended to allow the service to specify that the created program invocation is the controlling program invocation. The robot companion standard also defines four additional services: VMDStop, VMDReset, Select, and AlterProgramInvocationAttributes.

22.4.2 Numerical Controllers

Numerical controllers are application specific devices which control plant floor machinery. The numerical control companion standard defines MMS communications for these devices. Numerical controllers typically are used in discrete manufacturing applications. An automatic metal press is a classic example of a numerical controller application. This specialized machine may be able to punch pieces out of a sheet of metal. The device which controls this machine is a numerical controller. Another example is an automatic lathe or drill press. These are often controlled by a numerical controller.

Numerical controllers differ from robot controllers in that they are more application specific. The devices that a numerical controller supervises are not as general purpose as robots or PLCs. The model for numerical controller communication distinguishes between the numerical controller (which is modelled as a VMD), and one or more supervisory computers. Two fundamental modes of operation are available in this model: local control (via an operator panel located at the device), and remote (via a supervisory computer).

The model of the numerical controller is based on multiple controlling processes, each with its individual program and date, mapped to the image of a device to be controlled (Figure 22.10). Thus, a single numerical controller can control a single device, or multiple devices.

The numerical controller companion standard describes a switching model for the remote and local control modes, and describes a model for alarm processing. The basic functions of the numerical controller are: request data transfer (machine programs, tooling data, etc.), alarm processing (state transitions, fault occurrences, etc.), provide status information, interact with the operator, switching functions, identify available functions, and process management (create state transitions, activate machine programs).

The basic status information is contained in extensions to the VMD model. However, named variables are used to identify modes of operation. The numerical control model uses semaphores to manage a control token when multiple supervisors are mapped to a single numerical controller.

An interesting feature of the numerical controller companion standard is the use of named variables and named variable lists to represent information that would intuitively be considered as part of the VMD object. This includes status information concerning the numerical controller, as well as application specific objects. For example, an alarm object is defined which is mapped to a named variable. This provides another ability to transfer alarms to the operator and supervisory computer, in addition to the event management services which the numerical controller standard also can use.

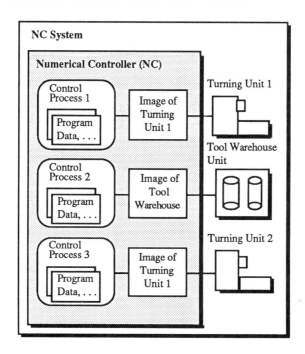

FIGURE 22.10   An Numerical Controller Example

22.4.3 Programmable Logic Controllers

Programmable logic controllers can be thought of as generalized numerical controllers, with additional capabilities. A PLC is more generic than a numerical controller, and therefore is useful to a wide range of applications. A PLC can also be described as an industrial computer with a very specific I/O system. PLCs typically do not have a disk storage. PLCs are used to control devices by switching or modulating electrical signals to the devices. The generation of the electrical signals is accomplished via the very specialized I/O subsystem of the PLC. In contrast, the output capabilities of a desktop personal computer are limited to displaying items on the screen or to a printer, and maybe producing sound. A PLC can turn on a 120 volt signal to a device to start its operation.

PLC's are programmed via a pictorial form of assembler termed as "ladder logic." Ladder logic is designed to resemble electrical schematics used to specify plant control systems before the advent of PLCs. The PLC companion standard allows a MMS client to invoke PLC functions to be delivered by a server. The server may conform to the IEC standard for a PLC or not; or may be represented by some sub-system that performs PLC functions, but exists in a device that is not a PLC.

The PLC companion standard defines ten areas of specific functionality that PLCs are expected to perform. Table 22.13 outlines these ten areas, and gives a brief indication of the major considerations for each area of functionality.

Area of Functionality	Major Considerations
Device Verification	state information fault detection fault isolation
Data Acquisition	polled unsolicited programmed configured
Control	parametric interlocked
Synchronization between user applications	
Alarming	programmed alarm report configured alarm detection alarm summary
Operator Interface	programmed operator interface direct operator interface
Program Management and Control	application program state start and stop control application program transfer
Recipe Manipulation	recipe data recipe procedure
Programming, Debugging, and Process Verification	not required by PLC companion standard
Protection and Connection Management	access right database in MMS server

TABLE 22.13 Specific Functionality Areas that PLCs are expected to perform

The PLC companion standard makes use of an "intermediate object model" technique. This technique is in fact the same technique as applied in previous companion standards: extending the base MMS objects for the specific needs of the family of devices. The PLC companion standard chooses to term the extended objects as Programmable Controller Message Specification (PCMS) objects. The extended objects include: VMD (adding a PLC status and access rights database), domain (defining several types), and program invocation (defining superiors, subordinates, and I/O states).

A new object, called the gate object, is defined for the purposes of interlocked control. This also requires the definition of two new services: ReportGateState, and DataExchange. DataExchange is used to request and perform interlocked control at a PLC server with the gate object.

The PLC companion standard also makes use of named variable objects to create application specific objects. For example, the "programmed data acquisition" object and the "programmed alarm detection" objects are both mapped to named variables.

Another unique aspect of the PLC companion standard concerns meta-services. Meta-services are used to describe functions a PLC can perform when acting as an MMS client. The meta-services can be thought of as short subroutines or sequences of one or more base MMS services, controlled by an individual state diagram. The concept of meta-services is used to focus the actions a PLC as a client can take within the ten categories described in the table above.

- **Other MMS Companion Standards**

The robot, numerical controller, and PLC companion standards are the most prominent factory floor devices defined for MMS. Other devices and "areas" can also be attacked with MMS. These include: process control, production management, vision systems, and cell control. Of these, vision systems most closely resemble robots, numerical controllers, and PLC in that vision system classifies a family of devices.

The process control companion standard is designed to define MMS for a **Distributed Control Systems (DCS)**. A DCS is a family of factory floor devices provided from a single vendor which are linked together to control an operation. DCS have traditionally been applied in process applications which have a high requirement for analog control. The strength of DCS systems is the ability to handle large applications with high point counts, and configuration flexibility. However, DCS can benefit from sharing data with supervisory computers. Traditionally, enhanced supervisory capabilities in DCS have been limited, and sharing data with DCS has been difficult.

The process control companion standard is modelled to access the DCS via a gateway to a vendor specific network which connects the components of the DCS. The future use of MMS as an internal communications vehicle from component to component radically changes the potential for DCS. This would allow an end user to potentially build a DCS with components from several vendors, perhaps choosing vendor A for strengths in operator interface consoles, and combining this equipment with vendor B's automatic control and PID control modules.

The production management companion standard seeks to define the operation of a discrete factory operation in MMS terms. MMS objects and services are defined to act as the building blocks to accomplish the following: inventory control, inventory monitoring, general operation monitoring, quality control, maintenance, and error notification.

In another characterization, the production management standard seeks to provide a diversified standard for distributing interfacing of man and machine at a higher level. This leads to the eventual benefit of more intelligent and centralized input from production schedulers and planners, or artificial intelligence applications which provide this guidance to the manufacturing operation.

Vision systems represent a large class of devices available from many vendors. Vision systems can be classified from a low end to a high end. It is difficult to distinguish between some low end vision systems and intelligent sensors.

The companion standard for vision systems seeks to model MMS communications for automated vision inspection systems. These systems are typically standalone controllers receiving input from one or more cameras, processing the picture, and making control decisions. Often vision system are implemented as a part of system that also talks to PLCs or robots. In other applications, like inspection or quality control, the application may be standalone. Additionally, some PLC vendors offer vision systems as part of their I/O sub-system.

The cell control companion standard is very similar to the production management companion standard, but reduced in scope to the activities within a particular manufacturing "cell" as opposed to plantwide activity.

22.5 Summary

One of the most celebrated requirements for all manufacturing applications is the need for plant floor computers and devices to communicate. MMS is designed to provide a solution to meet this requirement.

MMS is one of the largest and most complex application protocol standards. This is partially due to the various traditional technologies that MMS supplements, and also due to the wide variety of factory floor devices available. MMS specifies how messages are assembled and sent. An object model is specified for the various components of an MMS environment: These models are the virtual manufacturing devices (VMDs), domains within VMDs, program invocations within VMDs, variables and data within VMDs, and several others. The client-server model is used to distribute services across the devices on the network. Typically, the client is a host computer and the server is some factory floor device.

The MMS service definition gives 86 service elements, grouped into eleven functional units. Each functional unit typically operates on a single object type, or on several closely related object types. These functional units are:

- Event Management,
- Variable Access,
- Semaphore Management,
- Domain Management,
- Virtual Manufacturing Device Support,
- Program Invocation,
- Environment and General Management,
- File Management,
- Journal Management,

- Operator Communications, and
- File Access.

The Variable Access functional unit provides the most important class for services for MMS. The variable access services allow an MMS user to get at the variables associated with a factory floor device.

MMS is unique among the OSI application standards due to its companion standards. Companion standards allow MMS to provide additional detail focused on a particular type of factory floor device. The robot, numerical controller, and PLC companion standards are the most prominent factory floor devices defined for MMS. Others include process control, production management, vision systems, and cell control.

Related Standards

ISO 9506-1: Industrial Automation Systems - Manufacturing Message Specification - Part 1: Service Definition

ISO 9506-2 : Industrial Automation Systems - Manufacturing Message Specification - Part 2: Protocol Specification

23

Electronic Data Interchange over MHS

As the business world grows, industries require more and more paper work associated with the postal exchange of trade documents. In order to prosper in this complicated arena and be able to trade competitively with external partners, they need to standardize the structure of trade documents and utilize a global communication network. The interchange format of a trade document is called an **Electronic Data Interchange (EDI)**. The notion of an EDI has been used for quite some time by the transportation industry, the automobile industry, the grocery industry, and the aerospace industry. Today, there are many EDI user communities such as SWIFT (Society for Worldwide Funds Transfer), IATA (International Air Transport Association), AIAG (Automobile Industry Action Group), and CCC (Customs Coordinating Committee).

The problem with the early work on EDI is the lack of an international EDI standard. Indeed, there are a number of proprietary or national EDI standards, with each defining its own EDI structure. As early as 1968, the US transportation industry developed the US EDI message standard through the Transportation Data Coordination Council (TDCC). This standard includes a common dictionary of data elements. In 1983, the ANSI X12 Committee created a more generic standard which could be applied to industries outside the transportation industry. On the international side, the major driving force for the development of EDI standards came from the United Nations Economic

Commission of Europe (UN ECE). In 1988, UN ECE published the **EDIFACT** **(Electronic Data Interchange for Administration, Commerce and Transport)** standard. TC 154 of ISO which deals with Trade and Commerce ratified the EDIFACT syntax and trade dictionary, and produced two ISO documents: ISO 9735 and ISO 7372. Since then, EDIFACT has been widely accepted as a worldwide de facto standard.

It is important to note that although the EDIFACT standard focuses on the structure of an EDI document, it leaves the communication community to develop a solution for the transfer of the document. Here we can apply OSI, which is a set of international communication standards, to the exchange of an international interchange format. The benefits of applying OSI to EDI include reduced clerical overhead and faster transmission, which imply lower cost and better service to the customers.

Either the MHS standard or the FTAM standard can be used to transfer an EDI document. In particular, the security features of the 1988 version of the MHS standard are of great importance to the business world. Therefore in 1990, CCITT brought together MHS and EDI, and produced two CCITT Recommendations, namely, F.435 and X.435. F.435 describes the MHS-EDI messaging service, while X.435 describes the MHS-EDI Messaging System in more depth. The framework of the 435 documents is general in the sense that it applies MHS to carry not only EDIs conforming to EDIFACT, but also EDIs conforming to TDCC, ANSI X.12, and others. It is robust because it can be used to carry EDI documents of different formats in the future.

The purpose of this chapter is to examine how MHS is used to carry an EDI document. Section 23.1 examines the structure of an EDIFACT interchange. Section 23.2 describes the functional model of an EDI Messaging System, and the structure of EDI messages and EDI notifications. Section 23.3 explains how to apply the OSI DS standard to an EDI Messaging System.

23.1 Structure of an EDIFACT Interchange

As mentioned earlier, every EDI standard defines its own EDI structure. In particular, an EDI structure conforming to the EDIFACT standard is called an **EDIFACT interchange**. The purpose of this section is to give an overview of the structure of an EDIFACT interchange.

An EDIFACT interchange is built using data elements, segments, and messages. A **data element** is the smallest named item that can convey data. For example, a product number or an address is a data element. A **segment** is a defined group of data elements. For example, a line on an invoice or a purchase order is a segment. A **message** is equivalent to a single purchase order or invoice. An **interchange** is a group of messages sent by a sender to a receiver. A **functional group** is a special case of an interchange where all the messages are of the same type (e.g., all invoices or all purchase orders).

Figure 23.1 shows the structure of an EDIFACT interchange. On the top of the structure is a **UNA (United Nations, service string advice)** which is used to provide the **data element separators** and the **data element terminator** to the receiving party's software so that the translation software can decode an EDIFACT document properly. The common data element separators are ":" (component data element separator) and "+" (segment tag and element separator). The only data element terminator is "," (segment terminator). If the separators adhere to the EDIFACT standard defaults, the use of the UNA is not necessary.

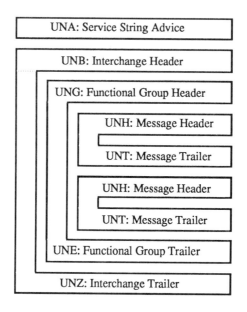

FIGURE 23.1   Structure of EDIFACT Interchange

An interchange has a **UNB (United Nations, interchange header)** and a **UNZ (United Nations, interchange trailer)**. The UNB specifies the sender, the receiver, the transmission date/time, and the password. The UNZ indicates an interchange control number and the number of functional groups included in the interchange.

An interchange may contain a number of functional groups. As mentioned earlier, a functional group contains only one message type. The purpose of functional groups is to facilitate different departments in a large organization to create their own application level envelopes. For example, we can have a department for processing invoices and a different department for processing purchase orders. Each functional group has its own envelope which contains a **UNG (United Nations, functional group header)** and a **UNE (United Nations, functional group trailer)**. The UNG specifies the message type, the application sender identity, the application receiver identification, the group date/time, and the password. The UNE specifies a functional group control number and indicates the number of messages included within the functional group.

A functional group can contain a number of messages which must be of the same message type. Each message in a functional group has its own message envelope. A message envelope contains a **UNH (United Nations, head of a message)** and a **UNT (United Nations, termination of a message)**. The UNH specifies a message control number and a message type. The UNT specifies a message control number (same as that of the UNH) and indicates the number of segments included within the message. Some of the more common message types are INVOIC (international invoice), CUSDEC (customs declaration), CUSREC (customs response), ORDERS (purchase order), DEBADV (debit advice), and PAYORD (payment order).

A message can contain a number of segments. Each segment corresponds to a line. An EDIFACT segment begins with a **segment tag** followed by one or more data elements. It ends with a **segment terminator**. A segment tag implicitly specifies the data elements and the order in which they appear within the segment. The EDIFACT trade dictionary (i.e., ISO 7372) contains descriptions of all the segment tags. The common segment tags used for an invoice are BGM (beginning of message), NAD (name and address), CTA (contacts), RFF (references), PAT (payment terms basis), LIN (line item), TDT (details of transport), TMA (total message amount), and CNT (control totals).

A data element corresponds to an item within a line. It can be either simple or composite. A simple data element contains a single data item while a composite data element contains multiple data items. Data elements within a composite data element are separated by the "+" data element separator. For example, 500811 + 1720 is a composite data element showing the date (August 11, 1950) and the time (5:20 pm). Each data element has a data type associated with it.

Example 23.1

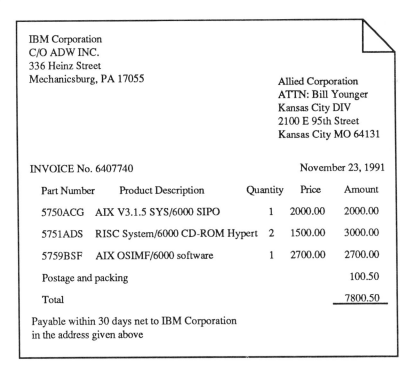

FIGURE 23.2   An Invoice Example

```
UNA:+.?'
UNB+UNOA:1+134571+134638+911123:1405+REF771'
UNH+INV001+INVOIC:1++1'
BGM+380+6407740+911123'
REF+87756-T001: PO+006+910915'
NAD+BY+134638:91++BILL YOUNGER+2100 E
95TH ST+KANSAS CITY+MO+64131'
NAD+SE+134571:92++IBM CORPORATION+336
HEINZ ST+MECHANICSBURG+PA+17055'
UNS+D'
LIN++5750ACG+1:21:PC+2000:CA:1+1+2000'
LIN++5751ADS+2:21:PC+1500:CA:1+2+3000'
LIN++5759BSF+1:21:PC+2700:CA:1+1+2700'
LIN++999-9901++++100.50'
UNS+S'
TMA+7800.50'
UNT+12+INV001'
UNZ+1+REF771
```

FIGURE 23.3   EDIFACT format of Invoice Example

Figure 23.2 shows an invoice, and Figure 23.3 shows the resulting EDIFACT format.

23.2 EDI Messaging System

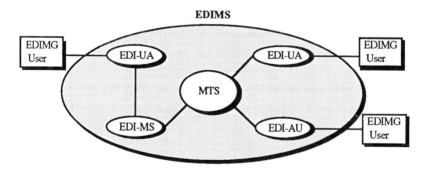

FIGURE 23.4   EDI Messaging System

An **EDI messaging system (EDIMS)** consists of an MTS (i.e., message transfer system) and a number of peripheral objects (Figure 23.4). Peripheral objects are of three kinds: **EDI User Agents (EDI-UAs)**, **EDI Message Stores (EDI-MSs)**, and **EDI Access Units (EDI-AUs)**. An **EDIMS user**, as a user of an EDIMS, originates/receives **EDI messages (EDIMs)**. An EDIM is similar to an interpersonal message in MHS. It has to be placed inside an MHS envelope before it is ready for submission to an EDIMS. An EDI-UA assists an EDIMS user in originating and receiving EDIMs. An EDI-MS assists an EDI-UA to submit, take delivery of, store, and retrieve EDIMs. An EDI-AU provides access to an EDIMS for those EDIMS users who are not directly attached to an EDIMS. It can be a physical delivery access unit, a facsimile access unit, etc. Figure 23.5 expands the concept illustrated in Figure 23.4 and shows the principal information flow.

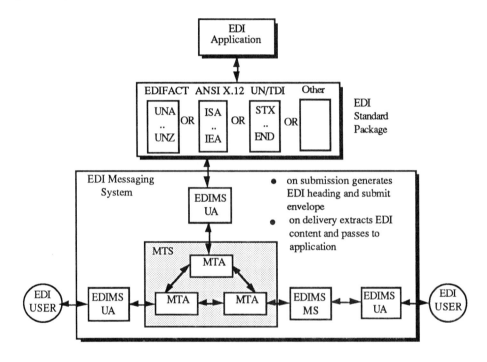

FIGURE 23.5   Expanded View of an EDIMS

The MHS standard defines the notion of a content type. The content type relevant to an EDI document is called the **EDIM content type**. It is studied in Section 23.2.1. In Section 23.2.2, we study EDINs which are related to forwarding of responsibility.

23.2.1 Structure of the EDIM Content Type

In this section, we examine the structure of the EDIM content type which is also known as the Pedi content type. An EDIM content consists of two parts: a heading and a body (Figure 23.6). The heading contains various fields of information, some of which are MHS-specific and some of which are EDI interchange-specific. The body contains a number of body parts, one of which is the **primary body part**. The EDI is carried within the primary body part. It can be EDIFACT, ANSI X.12, UN/TDI, or any format which can be mapped entirely within the primary body part. The other body parts of the body are related to the primary body part. They contain drawings, explanatory text, etc.

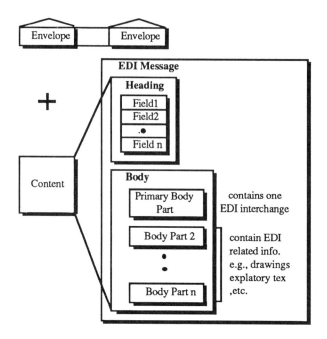

FIGURE 23.6 Structure of EDIM content type

X.400 Fields	EDI Interchange Fields
this-EDIM	cross-referencing-informtion
originator	edi-message-type
recipients	service-string-advice
edin-receiver	syntax-identifier
edi-bodypart-type	interchange-sender
incomplete-copy	date-and-tim Ä-preparation
expiry-time	application-reference
related-messages	heading-extensions
obsoleted-EDIMs	responsibility-forwarded
edi-application-security-elements	

TABLE 23.1 EDIM Heading Fields

The heading contains both MHS-specific and EDI interchange-specific data. Some of the fields of the heading are given in Table 23.1. Below is an explanation of some fields:

- this-EDIM: This field identifies the EDIM.
- originator: This field, which is defined as an O/R name, identifies the EDIM's originator.
- recipients: This field identifies the recipient(s) of the EDIM.

- EDIN receiver: This field identifies the recipient to whom EDINs should be sent.
- responsibility-forwarded: This field is used to indicate whether responsibility was forwarded. The default value is FALSE.
- edi-bodypart-type: This field indicates the EDI standard that is used in the primary body part. The default value is EDIFACT.
- expiry-time: This field indicates the time when the originator considers this-EDIM to be invalid.
- related-messages: This field identifies the EDIMs to which this EDIM are related.
- obsoleted-EDIMs: This field identifies the EDIMs which will be made obsolete by this EDIM.
- edi-application-security-elements: This field allows an EDI application to exchange security elements having an end-to-end significance.
- cross-referencing-information: This field allows an EDI application to reference individual body parts within the same EDIM or different EDIMs.
- edi-message-type: This field indicates the message type(s) present in the EDI. Examples of message types are purchase orders and invoices.
- interchange-sender: This field indicates the sender of the EDI. Note that the sender may not be the same as the originator.
- date-and-time-of-preparation: This field indicates the date/time of the preparation of the EDIM.

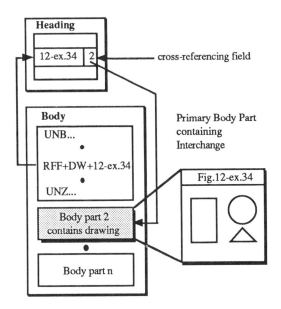

FIGURE 23.7   Example of Cross Referencing Usage

An interesting field above is the **cross-referencing** field. Upon receiving an EDIM, an EDI-UA can use this field to forward to different recipients the body part containing the EDI (i.e., the primary body) and the referred-to-body parts. It looks up the cross-referencing field in the heading to correlate a body part which may or may not be a body part in the received EDIM. The cross-referencing field is available to all recipients, even if they may not receive all the body parts. Figure 23.7 shows an example of how to use the cross-referencing field. In this example, the EDI in the primary body part contains an application-cross-referencing field field whose value is 12-ex.34. This application-cross-referencing field is correlated to the body-part-reference field which identifies a body part in some EDIM. In our case, the correlated body-part-reference has the value 2. Body part 2 happens to be in the same EDIM.

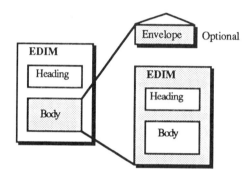

FIGURE 23.8   EDIM Forwarded without Changes

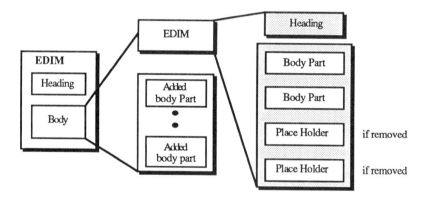

FIGURE 23.9   EDIM Forwarded with Changes

Another interesting heading field is the responsibility-forwarded field. It is related to the notion of an EDIN which will be explained in the following section. For the time being, let us explain forwarding and how it would affect the body parts of an EDIM. **EDI forwarding** is the onward transfer of a received EDIM to one or more recipients determined by a **forwarding EDI-UA/EDI-MS**. The **forwarded EDIM** is different from the received EDIM. When the EDIM is forwarded with no change to the body, the received EDIM together with its envelope are packed into the primary body part which becomes the only body part of the forwarded EDIM. Figure 23.8 illustrates the case when the EDIM is forwarded with no change, where the EDIM on the right is the received EDIM and the EDIM on the left is the forwarded EDIM. In some cases, body parts may be added to or removed from a received EDIM. If body parts are added, they appear as additional body parts after the body parts of the received EDIM. If body parts are removed, they are replaced by place holders to indicate what type of body parts have been removed. This case is illustrated in Figure 23.9. The forwarded EDIM is shown on the left.

23.2.2 Structure of an EDIN

An EDIN is used to convey to the originator EDI-UA/EDI-MS the disposition of the EDIM responsibility of an EDIM. An **EDIM responsibility** indicates whether the subject EDIM has been made available to an EDIMS user by its EDI-UA/EDI-MS. An EDI-UA/EDI-MS can request the recipient EDI-UA/EDI-MS or a "gateway" EDI-UA/EDI-MS (which is different from the recipient EDI-UA/EDI-MS) to indicate its disposition of responsibility. An EDIM cannot leave the EDIMS unless its EDIM responsibility has been accepted somewhere. An EDI-UA/EDI-MS accepts the responsibility of an EDIM if it adds or removes a body part from the received EDIM.

There are three kinds of EDINs. An EDIN can be a **Positive Notification (PN)**, a **Negative Notification (NN)**, or a **Forwarded Notification (FN)**. The following scenario will illustrate the different kinds of EDINs.

Suppose that in a large corporation, there is a "gateway" EDI-UA which happens to be the only EDI-UA which can interface with the outside world. Any originator EDI-UA, who wants to send an EDIM to a recipient EDI-UA within the corporation, must first send the EDIM to the gateway EDI-UA. Eventually, the gateway EDI-UA will forward the EDIM to the recipient EDI-UA. The gateway EDI-UA may have various levels of power. In some cases, it accepts responsibility by adding or deleting a few body parts of the received EDIM before forwarding it to the recipient EDI-UA. In other cases, it simply forwards the responsibility and the EDIM to the recipient EDI-UA. Whatever the case, the originating EDI-UA may need to know whether the gateway EDI-UA has forwarded the responsibility, and whether the recipient EDI-UA has received the EDIM. It achieves this by requesting an EDIN from the gateway EDI-UA, the recipient EDI-UA, or even both. If the gateway EDI-UA accepts the responsibility, it returns a PN. In this case, the gateway EDI-UA may add or delete body parts from the received EDIM. If the gateway EDI-UA refuses responsibility, it returns an NN. This happens if the gateway EDI-UA has tried in vain to forward the EDIM to the recipient EDI-UA. If the gateway EDI-UA does not accept responsibility, it can forward both the responsibility and the EDIM to the intended recipient EDI-UA, then return an FN to the originator EDI-UA. In this case, if the recipient EDI-UA has received the forwarded EDIM and accepted the responsibility, it sends a PN to the originator EDI-UA. If the recipient EDI-UA receives the forwarded EDIM and notes that the EDIMS user no longer subscribes to the EDIMS, it can refuse the responsibility and sends an NN to the originator EDI-UA.

Heading Fields	Responsibility Forwarded	Responsibility not Forwarded
edim-identifier	new value	new value
notification-request	unchanged for one recipient	any value
edin-receiver	unchanged	not same value as in original EDIM
responsibility-forwarded	TRUE	not present

TABLE 23.2   EDIM Heading Fields used for Forwarding

Forwarding of responsibility is achieved by setting the appropriate heading fields in the EDIM. Table 23.2 shows the heading fields and the values which are set in both the responsibility forwarded and the responsibility not forwarded cases.

For a better understanding, we will illustrate the forwarding and the disposition of EDIM responsibility in various scenarios. We assume that EDI-UA1 is the originator EDI-UA, EDI-UA3 is the recipient EDI-UA, and EDI-UA2 is the "gateway" EDI-UA. We also assume that EDI-UA1 wants to know which EDI-UA has eventually accepted the responsibility.

*   **scenario 1:   no forwarding**

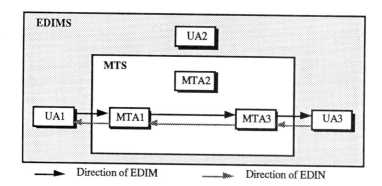

FIGURE 23.10   No Forwarding

No forwarding is performed in this scenario. The EDIM prepared by EDI-UA1 is submitted to MTA1, transferred to MTA3, and delivered to EDI-UA3. Upon receiving the EDIM, EDI-UA3 responds with an appropriate EDIN. If it accepts the EDIM responsibility, it responds with a PN. If it refuses the EDIM responsibility, it responds with an NN. Figure 23.10 illustrates this scenario.

- **scenario 2:   EDIM responsibility forwarded and not accepted by EDI-UA2**

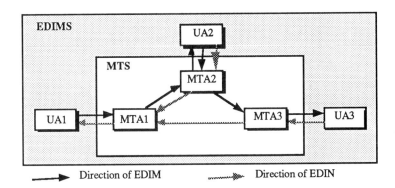

FIGURE 23.11   EDIM Forwarding with responsibility forwarded

In this scenario, EDI-UA2 does not accept the responsibility and forwards the received EDIM to EDI-UA3. The EDIM prepared by EDI-UA1 is submitted to MTA1, transferred to MTA2, delivered to EDI-UA2, and forwarded to UA3. In this case, EDI-UA2 cannot modify the EDIM. If EDI-UA1 does request an EDIN from EDI-UA2, then EDI-UA2 must request it from EDI-UA3 by placing the ORName of EDI-UA1 in the EDIN Receiver Field of the forwarded EDIM (Table 23.1). Figure 23.11 illustrates this scenario.

- **scenario 3:   EDIM responsibility accepted by EDI-UA2**

In this scenario, EDI-UA2 accepts the responsibility. Hence, it can add or remove body parts of the EDIM before it forwards the EDIM to EDI-UA3.

In the first part of Figure 23.12, the EDIM prepared by EDI-UA1 is submitted to MTA1, transferred to MTA2, and delivered to EDI-UA2. EDI-UA2 accepts the responsibility. It returns a PN to the EDI-UA1. It then creates the forwarded EDIM, so EDI-UA1 will receive no further EDINs from EDI-UA2.

The second part of Figure 23.12 is a continuation of the first part. EDI-UA2 submits the forwarded EDIM to MTA2, which transfers it to MTA3, which then delivers it to EDI-UA3. Since the initial EDIM responsibility has been accepted, EDI-UA2 is free to request the EDIM responsibility from EDI-UA3. If EDI-UA2 requests the responsibility, the resulting EDIM responsibility relationship applies between EDI-UA2 and EDI-UA3 only. That is, EDI-UA2 must not place the ORName of EDI-UA1 in the EDIN Receiver Field of the forwarded EDIM. In this scenario, we assume that the responsibility has been requested, hence EDI-UA3 has to respond to EDI-UA2 with an appropriate EDIN.

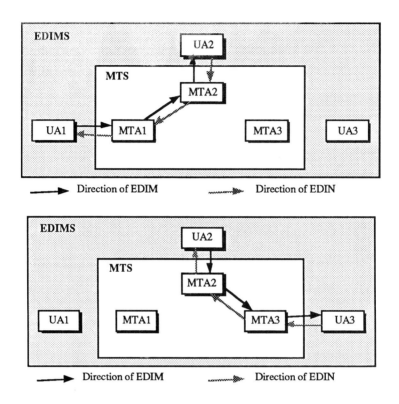

FIGURE 23.12   EDIM Forwarding with Responsibility not Forwarded

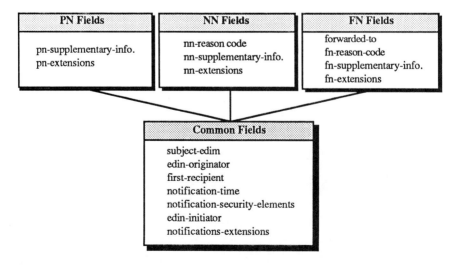

FIGURE 23.13   Structure of an EDIN

Let us examine the structure of an EDIN which can be described by a set of fields (Figure 23.13). Some of the fields are common to a PN, an NN and an FN. A brief description of some of the common fields is given below.

- subject-edim: This contains the EDIM identifier.
- edin-originator: This contains the ORName of the EDI-UA which sends the EDIN.
- first-recipient: This contains the ORName of the originator EDI-UA.
- notification-time: This contains the date and time at which the notification for the subject EDIM is generated.
- notification-security-elements: This is used to provide a proof/non-repudiation of content received and other EDI security services.

23.3   EDI Use of the Directory Services

For an EDIMS user, there are two main purposes of using the Directory services. One is to obtain the ORAddress of an EDIMS user, and the other is to obtain EDI-specific attributes of an EDI-UA.

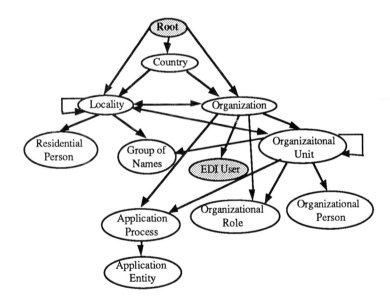

FIGURE 23.14   Directory Containment Hierarchy for EDI Requirements

An EDI name is essentially an alphanumeric string. Although it is normally unique within a particular EDI community, it needs not be globally unique. It is carried in the EDIFACT UNB segment. Before an EDIM can be transmitted, the originator EDI-UA must obtain the ORAddress of the recipient EDI-UA. The mapping of EDI names to ORNames is considered a local issue and is not covered in the X.435 standard. However, the Directory services can be used for this purpose. This method will be briefly described below.

A new generic object class, EDI user, is created in the Directory containment hierarchy (Figure 23.14). One of the attributes of this object class is the name of an EDIMS user (e.g., DUNS 64110). A qualifier (e.g., DUN in the name DUNS 64110) is used in the name to identify the naming authority that assigns or endorses the name. Given an EDI name in the form of some DN (i.e., distinguished name), a Directory query is issued to a DUA. If successful, the DUA returns the DN of the EDI-UA with the given EDI name. Given the DN of the EDI-UA, a second Directory query is issued. This time, the DUA returns the ORAddress of the EDI-UA with the given DN, and perhaps some EDI-specific attributes of the EDI-UA.

Example 23.2

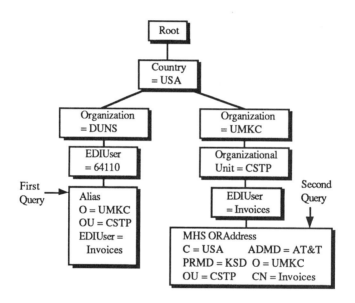

FIGURE 23.15   Use of Directory Services

Referring to Figure 23.15, suppose the EDI-UA calls the DUA with a DN which is {C = USA, O = DUNS, EDIUser = 64110}. Note that this DN contains an EDI name (i.e., Invoices). The DUA returns an alias DN which is {C = USA, O = UMKC, OU = CSTP, EDIUser = Invoices}. The EDI-UA then calls the DUA with the returned alias DN. The DUA returns the ORAddress of the recipient EDI-UA which is {C = USA, ADMD = AT&T, PRMD = KSD, O = UMKC, OU = CSTP, CN = Invoices}.

As mentioned earlier, the Directory can be also used to obtain EDI-specific attributes of a recipient EDI-UA. Some of these attributes are:

- EDIBodypartType: This can be either EDIFACT, ANSI X.12, UN/TDI, or others.

- StandardVersion: This gives the version of the EDI syntax supported by the recipient EDIM user.
- DocumentType: This gives the edi-message-type such as purchase order, invoice, etc.

Therefore by using the Directory services, an originator EDI-UA can find out the recipient ORAddress and can also discover whether or not the recipient can accept and process an EDIM that the originator intends to send.

23.4 Summary

Published in 1988 by the United Nations, the EDIFACT standard is the de facto worldwide standard for the electronic exchange of business documents. It defines the format of an EDI document which can be described using data elements, data segments, and messages. While the EDIFACT standard focuses on the structure of an EDI document, the transfer of the document is left to the communication industry. F.435/X.435 described how MHS is used to convey an EDI document.

The EDIM content type, which is also known as the Pedi content type, is an MHS content type used to carry an EDI document. It consists of a heading and a body. The body contains a number of body parts, one of which is the primary body part. The primary body part is used to hold an EDI document. The other body parts contain drawings or explanatory texts which are related to the EDI document.

An important EDI concept is the forwarding of responsibility. In short, an EDI message cannot leave the EDI Messaging System unless its responsibility has been accepted by some EDI-UA. By accepting the responsibility, an EDI-UA makes available the body parts of the EDI message to its user. In order to know whether an EDI-UA has accepted responsibility, the originator EDI-UA can request for an EDI notification.

Related Standards

ISO 9735: Electronic Data Interchange for Administration, Commerce and Transport (EDIFACT) - Application level Syntax Rules

CCITT Draft Recommendation F.435: Message Handling - EDI Messaging Service

CCITT Draft Recommendation X.435: Message Handling Systems - EDI Messaging System

24

Office Document Architecture

The modern electronic office incorporates a rapidly growing variety of complex systems. Although exchanging documents among these systems is useful, the different representations of a document in different systems make it difficult to do so. Conversion is a way to make the exchange possible, but the number of conversions required is O(n*n), where n is the number of systems in the office. Using a standard interchange representation can substantially reduce the number of conversions needed.

ISO 8613 describes the **Office Document Architecture (ODA)** which provides an abstract view of an office document. It describes a couple of **Office Document Interchange Formats (ODIFs)**. And it also describes a number of content architectures to embrace a variety of content types of a document. The ODA standard does not prescribe any particular editing, layout, or imaging processes which are considered to be local issues. It also does not prescribe any particular communication protocol used for the exchange of documents. An ODA document may be conveyed by MHS or FTAM. Thus, ISO 8613 does not describe a communication protocol.

In Section 24.1, we introduce the general ODA concepts. In Section 24.2, we show how each component of an ODA document is described in terms of attributes. Section 24.3 describes ODIF, the data stream format used to represent a document in the interchange.

24.1 ODA Concepts

Like any object in the object-oriented world, a document contains information relating to its structure and content. A **document architecture** is a set of rules for defining the structure and representation of a document. It consists of a structural model and a descriptive representation. The **structural model** describes the **structural elements** of a document and the relationships among these elements. The **descriptive representation** describes how the structural elements are represented by attributes. The structural model is explained in this section, and the descriptive representation is explained in the next. A content architecture is different from a document architecture. Imagine that the document content is partitioned into content portions. A **content architecture** defines rules for positioning content portions within a document. For example, it specifies the nature of the content, the presentation attributes, the coding methods, the control functions that can be applied to the content elements within a content portion, and the content positioning rules. Since a document may contain mixed contents (e.g., text and graphics), different content portions with different content architectures can coexist within a document. So far, three different content architectures have been defined by the ODA standard. They are:

- **Character Content Architecture:** This architecture supports the character repertoire defined in ISO 6937 (Coded Character Sets for Text Communication) and other character sets as long as they are defined according to the rules of ISO 2022 (ISO 7-bit and 8-bit Coded Character Sets - Code Extension Techniques).
- **Raster Graphics Content Architecture:** This architecture supports raster graphics which represent images as pixels or, in ODA terms, **pels (picture elements)**.
- **Geometric Graphics Content Architecture:** This architecture supports a content type consisting of a series of geometric constructs such as points, lines, arcs, polygons, etc. The geometric graphics in ODA are based on ISO 8632 CGM (Computer Graphics Metafile for the Storage and Transfer of Picture Description Information).

Future versions of the ODA standard may include content architectures for sound, speech, and 3-D images.

Before we introduce the structural model, let us first examine the various cycles involved in document processing (Figure 24.1). The ODA standard does not prescribe any editing, layout, or imaging processes. Instead, it provides the notion of a document form which represents a document between the various processes. A document progresses through the following sequence of steps:

- **creation/editing process**: The creation/editing process is concerned with creating a new document or modifying an existing one. The output of the process

produces a document in the **processable form**. A processable document can be edited again or presented to the layout process.
•   **layout process**: The layout process is concerned with where the content will appear on an output media (such as paper, CRT screen, etc.). It makes no changes to the content. It takes the output of the creation/editing process and generates a **formatted form** which can only be imaged but not altered by a receiver, or a **formatted processable form** which can be processed further. A formatted processable form document is suitable for input to any one of the imaging, layout, or editing processes. The information contained in a formatted processable document is basically a "union" of the information in a processable form and the information in a formatted form. It allows the document to be either imaged or processed and re-formatted as intended by the originator.
•   **imaging process**: The imaging process is concerned with presenting an image of a document for human perception. The input of the imaging process is either a formatted document or a formatted processable form document. Although the ODA standard does not prescribe the imaging process, it does allow a document to contain attributes relating to the imaging process. Such attributes would allow the creator of a document to specify how the document should be imaged.

The above steps are not rigid. Ideally, a document does not have to follow the above steps. It can be composed and edited until both parties have a common understanding of its appearance.

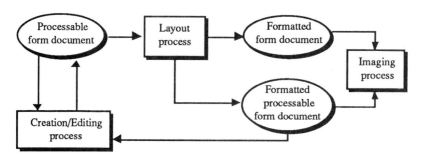

FIGURE 24.1   Document Processing Cycle

Next we describe the structural model. An ODA document is described in terms of components such as document profile, generic structures, specific structures, styles, and content portions. The ODA standard provides two different but complementary views of a document: a logical view and a layout view. A **logical structure** represents a logical view of a document. It describes how a document is broken into parts and how these parts are organized logically. The key to these notions is that this breakdown follows patterns that are easily understood by people. For example, a memo is composed of a header, a message, and a signature, where the header is made up of a logo, a title, a date, and a subject.

A **layout structure** represents a layout view of a document. It describes the physical positioning and presentation of the content on an output medium. Layout information can cover things such as stating what font should be used to image text, its style and type size, how many columns are there on a page, and what appears in which column. For example, a memo can be laid out in a single page which has two frames. The first frame contains four blocks, one for the logo, one for the title, one for the date, and one for the subject, The second frame contains two blocks, one for the message, and the other for the signature. The logical structure of the same memo can be laid out in two pages, with each page containing a frame.

Layout directives are used to map a logical structure to a layout structure. These directives tell how a logical structure is realized in a layout structure. For example, they indicate how a block is positioned within a frame (e.g., aligned to the right, left, or center), whether a logical object should be placed in a new layout object (e.g., a chapter always starts on a new page), the spacing between two adjacent layout blocks (e.g., the spacing between two paragraphs), etc.

We have seen that a document can be described by a logical structure and a layout structure. Each structure is described by a set of structural elements. Thus there are logical structural elements as well as layout structural elements. Examples of logical structural elements are titles, dates, messages, and signatures in the memo document. Examples of layout structural elements are pages, blocks, and frames. Since there are many logical structural elements and layout structural elements, it is useful to group the related ones into logical object classes and layout object classes respectively. Most documents have well known or generic logical and layout structures. For example, everyone has a clear notion of what a memo looks like. A **document class** is a class of documents with similar characteristics. We can define a document class for memos, a document class for letters, a document class for reports, etc. Each document class has a **generic logical structure** and a **generic layout structure**. From the generic structures of a document class, we can build the specific structures of a document. The specific structures are the **specific logical structure** and the **specific layout structure**. Two documents from the same document class have identical generic logical and generic layout structures, although they differ from each other in their specific logical and specific layout structures. For example, they may differ from each other in the size of a block within a frame.

Next, we examine how a generic structure is represented. The generic logical structure of a document class can be arranged as a tree, where the nodes of the tree are called **logical object classes** because of their generic nature. Similarly, the generic layout structure of a document class can be arranged as a tree, where the nodes of the tree are called **layout object classes**. For an example on the representation of a generic structure, we consider the letter document class. Every letter has a header and a body. A header has a logo, a date, an addressee, a subject, and a summary. A body has paragraph(s), figure(s), an ending, a signature, and a name. Thus, the logical object classes here are letter-header, letter-body, logo, date, addressee, subject, summary, paragraph, figure, ending, signature, and name. They are the non-leaf nodes of the tree in Figure 24.2. Note that the edges of the tree are labelled, where "SEQ" means a sequence construction, "AGG" means an aggregate construction, "CHO" means a choice construction, "REP" means that the construction can be repeated one or more times, "OPT" means that the construction is optional, and "OPT REP" means that the construction can be repeated any number of times. Next we consider the generic layout structure of the letter document class. A letter can be laid out in a header page and one or more body pages. A page can be laid out into frames, and a frame can be laid out in blocks. And a body page can be laid out in body frames. Thus the layout object classes here are header, body-page, logo frame, date frame, addressee frame, subject frame, summary frame, body-frame, and a logo block page. They are the non-leaf nodes of the tree in Figure 24.3.

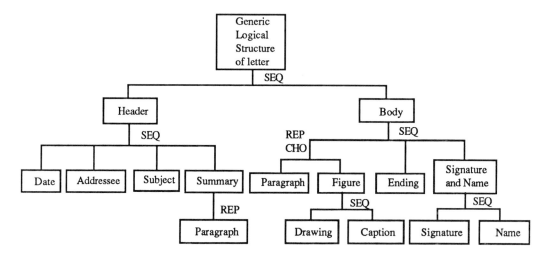

FIGURE 24.2   Generic Logical Structure of the Letter Document Class

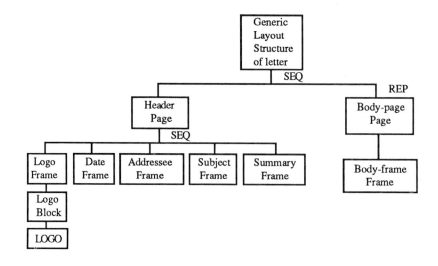

FIGURE 24.3   Generic Layout Structure of the Letter Document Class

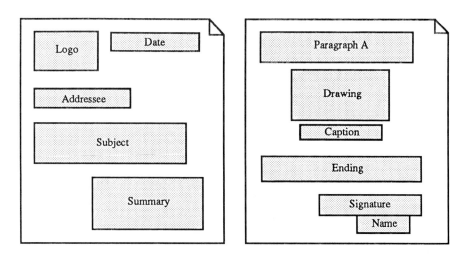

FIGURE 24.4   Header and Body Page of a Letter

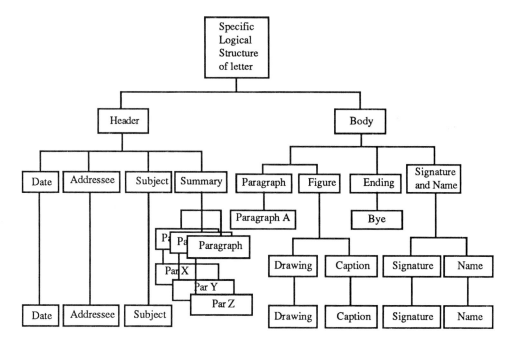

FIGURE 24.5   Specific Logical Structure of a Letter

Like the generic structures, both specific structures can be arranged as tree structures, where the nodes are called **logical objects** and **layout objects** respectively. For example, we consider a letter. Figure 24.4 shows the layout of a letter which consists of a header page and a body page. In the specific logical structure of this letter, there is one paragraph (i.e., paragraph A), one drawing, and one signature. In the specific layout structure, there are five frames on the header page, one for logo, one for date, one for addressee, one for body, etc. In the body frame, there are six blocks, one for paragraph A, one for drawing, one for caption, etc. Figures 24.5 and 24.6 illustrate the specific logical and specific layout structures of the letter respectively. Note that in the specific structures, we do not find such terms as "REP", "CHO", or "AGG" which appear as labels of trees for the generic structures. The point is that when a specific structure is derived from a generic structure, specific decisions have to be made on the above terms. Thus, although a generic layout structure of the letter document class says that a body page can be repeated, a specific logical structure must specify the exact number of body pages.

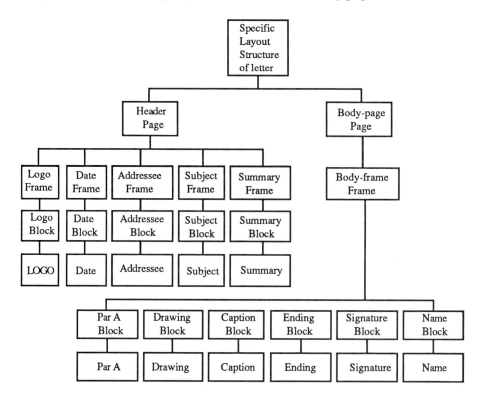

FIGURE 24.6　Specific Layout Structure of a Letter

Suppose that we modify our letter example by allowing two body pages instead of one. We assume that there are three paragraphs in the body, namely, paragraph A, paragraph B, and paragraph C. Paragraph A appears in body page one, paragraph B appears in both body page one and body page two, and paragraph C appears in body page two. In the specific layout structure of this letter, there will be two layout objects for paragraph B. However in the specific logical structure of this letter, there is only one logical object for paragraph B.

Although the specific logical structure and the specific layout structure provide two complementary views of a document, they refer to the same content. The content of a document is made up of content portions. These content portions appear as leaf nodes of the specific structures. Some leaf nodes of the specific structures may not have any content portions associated with them. This is the case if the relevant content is generic to a document (such as a logo) or is generated by a set of content generator rules (such as automatic page numbering).

There is a minor difference between the leaf nodes of a specific logical structure and the leaf nodes of a layout structure. Suppose that a paragraph in a letter is split between two pages. As a result, the paragraph logical object is laid out on two different layout objects, and there is a content portion associated with each layout object in the specific layout structure. On the other hand, there is only one content portion associated with the paragraph logical object in the specific logical structure.

A document also contains a document profile, a layout style, and a set of presentation styles in addition to the logical and the specific structures. Document styles and document profiles are discussed next.

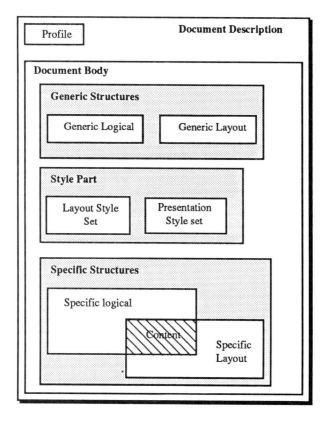

FIGURE 24.7 Components of an ODA Document

The **document profile** of a document contains information that relates to the document as a whole, but is not part of the user perceived view of the document. It identifies the form of the document, the content architecture(s) associated with the content portions, the ODIF class (whether it is class A or class B), and management information such as document description, dates and time, filing/retrieval, information for change control (e.g., release date and expiration date), and security information. Quite often, it duplicates information (e.g., document name, author, etc.) found within the body of the document. It can be interchanged by itself without the rest of the document. The receiver can review it to decide if its system can handle the document.

A **document style** contains rules for positioning the content of a document during the layout process (**layout styles**), or the appearance of the content resulting from the imaging process (**presentation styles**). For example, having a caption for a picture appear directly beneath it on the same page is a layout style, and using a 9 point font is a presentation style. A layout style is specified in the form of layout directives which, as we mentioned earlier, define the mapping between a logical structure and a layout structure. One obvious difference between a layout style and a presentation style is that a layout style is not concerned with any characteristics of the content whereas a presentation style can specify characteristics specific to a content architecture. For the convenience of reference, related presentation styles can be grouped into a **presentation style set**. To save time, a user can simply choose a presentation style set and does not have to explicitly enumerate the styles in the set.

Figure 24.7 illustrates the various components of an ODA document. Although the document styles are set aside, they are actually referenced from the logical structures and the layout structure.

Given the four different structures (i.e., generic logical and layout structures, and specific logical and layout structures) of a document, it is time to point out the effects of editing and formatting on these structures. Editing can change the specific logical structure. For example, by adding a new paragraph in the body page, we obtain a new specific logical structure. However, editing does not change the generic logical/layout structure because all the letters in the letter document class share the same generic logical/layout structure. Either editing or formatting can change the specific layout structure. Finally altering the generic or specific layout structure will change the document's appearance, but it will not change its generic or specific logical structure. The above observations on the effects of editing and formatting are important because they tell us which structures should be used as inputs to editing, layout, and imaging. As we mentioned earlier, a document can have three different forms (i.e., processable, formatted, and processable formatted). Depending on the form of the document, some of the structures contained in a document are mandatory, some are optional, and some are not permitted. Consider the interchange of a letter. The letter can be interchanged in a processable form with a specific logical structure only. It can be interchanged in a processable form with a generic logical structure and a generic layout structure to accompany the specific logical structure; the generic structures are used here to facilitate the subsequent editing of the document by a recipient. It can be interchanged in a formatted processable form with a specific layout structure to accompany the specific logical structure and perhaps the generic structures. Finally it can be interchanged in a formatted form, in which case only the specific layout structure is present. Table 24.1

summarizes the permitted components of the various forms of a document. For example, it says that a formatted document must have a specific layout structure, may have a generic layout structure, but cannot contain any generic structure.

	Generic Logical Structure	Specific Logical Structure	Generic Layout Structure	Specific Layout Structure	Layout Style	Presentation Style
Processable	Optional	Mandatory	Optional	Not Permitted	Optional	Optional
Formatted	Not Permitted	Not Permitted	Optional	Mandatory	Not Permitted	Optional
Formatted Processable	Optional	Mandatory	Optional	Mandatory	Optional	Optional

TABLE 24.1   Permitted Components in different Document Forms

24.2   Descriptive Representations

A document architecture consists of a structural model and a descriptive representation. The structural model was explained in the previous section. In this section, we examine the descriptive representation and show how each structural element in the structural model is described using attributes. The ODA standard provides a descriptor in the form of an ASN.1 module for the definition of each structural element. The use of such descriptors promotes consistency in the definition of structural elements by the profile groups. Examples to illustrate how these modules are used will be given in our discussion.

- **attributes for a document profile**

The attributes used to describe a document profile include:

- presence-of-document-attributes: This attribute indicates which components (e.g., specific layout structure, specific logical structure, layout styles, presentation styles, etc.) are present in a document. A "1" bit is assigned to a component which is present.
- document-application-profile: This attribute is used to reference a **Document Application Profile (DAP)** to which a document is conformed. A DAP, as defined by an implementation workshop, contains specific definitions of structural elements and specific choices of values. It also specifies a set of default values which may apply to a document architecture (such as page dimension and content type) or a content architecture (such as line spacing, character spacing, and indentation). When the document-application-profile attribute is absent in a document profile, the default settings from the ODA standard are used.
- document-architecture-class: This attribute specifies the form of a document.

- content-architecture-classes: This attribute specifies a list of content architecture classes associated with content portions of a document.
- interchange-format-class: This attribute defines which class of interchange (either Class A or Class B) is used.
- oda-version: This attribute gives the version number and the date of the ODA standard to which a document conforms.
- document profile management attributes: These attributes include document description (such as title and subject), dates and time, filing and retrieval (such as keyword, reference number, and other information used to facilitate filing/retrieval), status, copyright, distribution list, and a set of security attributes.

In the following examples, we will illustrate how to define document profiles.

Example 24.1

```
document-profile {
    specific layout structure "1",
    document-characteristics {
        document-architecture-class formatted,
        content-architecture-classes {
            {....},
            .
            {....}}
        interchange-format-class if-b,
        oda-version {
            standard-or-recommendation "ISO 8613",
            publication-date "1988"}}}
```

The document is in a formatted form containing only the specific layout structure. Note that the interchange format class is if-b (i.e., B), and that the application profile and the document profile management attributes are absent. Since the document is in a formatted form, it should not contain any document styles.

Example 24.2

```
document-profile {
    generic-layout-structure "1",
    generic-logical-structure "1",
    presentation-styles "1",
    layout-styles "1",
    specific-logical-structure "1",
    document-characteristics {
        document-architecture-class processable,
```

```
content-architecture-classes {
     {...},
     .
     {...}}
interchange-format-class if-a,
oda-version {
     standard-or-recommendation "ISO 8613"
     publication-date "1988"}}}
```

The document is in a processable form containing the generic layout, the generic logical, and the specific logical structures. It also contains layout styles and presentation styles.

- **attributes for logical objects and logical object classes**

Recall that logical objects and logical object classes, which represent the specific logical structures and the generic logical structures respectively, appear as nodes of trees. A logical object is one of three types: a document logical root (i.e., the root), a composite logical object (i.e., a non-leaf node), or a basic logical object (i.e., a leaf). Referring to the specific logical structure of a letter in Figure 24.6, the header logical object is composite since there are five other logical objects (date, addressee, subject, logo, and summary) subordinate to it.

Examples of attributes to describe logical objects and logical object classes are:

- type: This is one of the three types mentioned above.
- object identifier: This is an object identifier assigned to a logical object or a logical object class. According to the ODA standard, identifiers of logical object classes have the leading digit of "2", and identifiers of logical object have the leading digit of "3".
- user visible name: This is a user friendly name assigned to a logical object or a logical object class.
- generator for subordinates: This attribute type is used to define the existence and order of object classes subordinate to a logical object class. The order can be described by SEQ, AGG, or CHO. It can be further qualified by REP, OPT, or OPT REP.
- layout styles and presentation styles: A basic logical object, which can be associated with some content portion, can reference layout styles and presentation styles. Recall that a layout style is specified by a set of layout directives such as block assignment, offset, and separation.
- content portion: This is used to specify the content portion attached to a basic logical object. Note that the same content portion may be attached to a layout object.
- content architecture class: This is used to specify the content architecture class of the content portion.

In the following examples, we will show how to define some of the logical objects and the object classes in the letter document class.

Example 24.3

```
logical-object {
    object-type composite-logical,
    descriptor-body {
        object-identifier "30",
        user-visible-name "Header",
        subordinates {"0", "1", "2", "3"}}}
```

The above gives the definition of a composite logical object, "Header", in the specific logical structure of a letter. Note that this object has four subordinates.

Example 24.4

```
logical-object {
    object-type basic-logical,
    descriptor-body {
        object-identifier "3111",
        user-visible-name "Drawing",
        presentation-attributes { content-architecture-class {28280}},
        content-portions {"0"}}}
```

The above gives the definition of a logical object, "Drawing", in the specific logical structure of a letter. Note that presentation styles are referenced in "Drawing".

Example 24.5

```
logical-object-class {
    object-type composite-logical,
    descriptor-body {
        object-class-identifier "20",
        user-visible-name "Header",
        generator-for-subordinates {
            sequence-construction
                required-construction-factor
                    object-class-identifier "200",
                required-construction-factor
                    object-class-identifier "201"}}}
```

The above gives the definition of a logical object class, "Header", in the letter document class. It specifies how the subordinates of "Header" can be generated. It is useful to contrast this definition with the definition of the specific header logical object in Example 24.3.

Example 24.6

```
logical-object-class {
    descriptor-body {
        object-class-identifier "200".
        user-visible-name "Date",
        layout-style "40",
        presentation-attributes {
            content-architecture-class {28261}}}}
```

This example shows that presentation attributes can be specified within the definition of a logical object class which appears as a leaf of a tree for a generic logical structure (Figure 24.2).

•   **attributes for layout objects and layout object classes**

Recall that layout objects and layout object classes, which represent the specific layout structures and the generic layout structures respectively, appear as nodes of the trees. A layout object is one five types: a document layout root (i.e., the root of a layout structure tree), a page set (i.e., a group of pages), a page (i.e., a rectangular area of the imaged output), a frame (i.e., a rectangular area in a page/frame), or a block (i.e., a leaf node holding some content). Examples of attributes of layout objects a/object classes are:

   •   type: This is one of the five types mentioned above.
   •   object identifier: This is an object identifier assigned to a layout object/object class. According to the ODA standard, object identifiers of layout object class have the leading digit of "0", and object identifiers of layout objects have the leading digit of "1".
   •   user visible name: This is a user friendly name assigned to a layout object or a layout object class.
   •   generation of subordinate objects: This is used to define the subordinates of a layout object class and the order in which they appear.
   •   presentation style: These are presentation and layout attributes used to control the appearance of the content associated with a "basic" layout object such as block ("basic" means that the layout object appears as a leaf of a tree). For example, we can stipulate the dimension of a block and its position relative to the immediately superior object. We can control the color (either colorless or white) and transparency. We can stipulate the direction in which immediate subordinate layout objects are to be laid out (e.g., from top to bottom, left to right, etc.).
   •   content portion and content architecture class: These attributes are used to describe the content within a block.

Note that all the above attributes are also used to describe logical objects and logical object classes. The layout style attribute, which is used to define a mapping from a logical structure to a layout structure, is used strictly for logical objects and logical object classes.

In the following examples, we will show how to define some of the layout objects and layout object classes in the letter document class.

Example 24.7

```
layout-object {
    object-type page,
    descriptor-body {
        object-identifier "10",
        user-visible-name "Header Page",
        dimensions {
            horizontal 9920,
            vertical fixed 14030}},
        subordinates {
        "0", "1", "2", "3", "4"}}}
```

The above defines a layout object, "Header Page". It gives the dimension of the page and the number of its subordinates. The dimensions are measured in basic measurement units (BMUs) where each BMU is equal to 1/1200 of an inch.

Example 24.8

```
layout-object {
    object-type block,
    descriptor-body {
        object-identifier "110",
        user-visible-name "Paragraph A",
        position {
            horizontal 1000
            vertical 1000},
        dimensions {
            horizontal 7800
            vertical fixed 1600},
        presentation-attributes {
            character-attributes {
                line-spacing 300
                alignment justified }}
        content-portions {"0"}}}
```

The above defines a layout object, "Paragraph A", which appears in Figure 24.4. "Paragraph A" is a block. The definition gives the dimension of the block and where it appears on a page. It also gives the presentation attributes which are specific to the Character Content Architecture.

Example 24.9

```
layout-object-class {
    object-type page,
    descriptor-body {
        object-class-identifier "01",
        user-visible-name "Body",
        dimensions {
            horizontal 9920,
            vertical fixed 14030}
        generator-for-subordinates {
            single-term-construction
            required-construction-factor
            object-class-identifier "010"}}}
```

Th above defines a layout object class, "Body". It specifies the dimension and the way its subordinates should be generated.

- **attributes for a layout style**

A layout style is a mechanism that allows a logical structure to impose particular requirements on a layout structure. It can be referenced from a logical object or a logical object class. It is made up of a set of layout directives. The effect of a reference to a layout style is to apply its layout directives to a logical description. Thus, layout styles affect the layout of objects but they do not affect the content.
    A few examples of layout directives are given below:

- offset: This attribute type specifies the minimum offset between the boundary of a block and the boundary of an immediately superior layout object such as a frame.
- separation: This attribute type is used to specify the distance between two blocks (e.g. paragraphs).
- new layout object: We can use this attribute type to specify that the content associated with a logical object should be laid out starting within the next layout object which does not contain any content associated with the preceding logical object (e.g., a chapter should start on a new page).

According to the ODA standard, the object identifier of a layout style must have the leading digit of "4".

Example 24.10

```
layout-style {
    style identifier "47"
```

```
layout-directives {
     offset {
          right-hand 2665,
          left-hand 525},
     separation {
          trailing 745}}}
```

This example specifies the offset and the separation.

- **attributes for presentation styles**

A presentation style is used to specify information for the layout process and the imaging process. It may be referenced from a logical or a layout description. Thus, a presentation style may affect the layout and the imaging of the content, hence it is content architecture specific.

There are many presentation attributes used to describe a presentation style. In fact, we have seen some of them in the previous examples. There are presentation styles relating to the color, the transparency, and the border (e.g., which edges of a frame/block include a border line, and if so, the width of the line and its distance from the edge of the frame/block). Some presentation attributes are specific to a content architecture such as the spacing and font size attributes for the Character Content Architecture, the number of pels per line attribute for the Raster Graphics Content Architecture, and the picture dimensions attribute for the Geometric Graphics Architecture. According to the ODA standard, an object identifier for a presentation style must have the leading digit of "5".

Examples 24.11

```
presentation-style {
     style-identifier "50",
     presentation-attributes {
          character-attributes {
               line-spacing 300}}}

presentation-style {
     style-identifier "51",
     presentation-attributes {
          character-attributes {
               first-line-offset 1417,
               alignment justified}}}
```

This example illustrates a presentation style set containing two presentation styles, both of which are specific to the Character Content Architecture.

•   **attributes for content portions and content elements**

A content portion is made up of content elements. Examples of attributes used to describe content portions are the type of encoding and content information. The type of encoding attribute provides information that is used to encode/decode a content portion. The content information attribute specifies the content architecture governing the structure of a content portion.

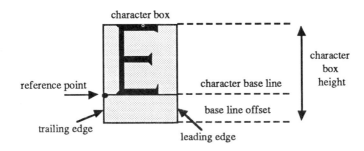

FIGURE 24.8   A Character Content Element

Attributes to describe a content element are specific to a content architecture. Let us consider attributes used to describe a content element for the Character Content Architecture (Figure 24.8). A character box is the rectangular area in which a character is drawn. The lines of characters on a CRT screen are composed of rows of character boxes. The size of a box, the number of boxes in a line, the character path (which specifies the direction in which a line of boxes is drawn), line progression (which specifies the direction in which successive lines are drawn) are examples of attributes. Attributes may be needed to specify the margin surrounding a character. Enough room is needed so that "tails" used by letters such as "y", "j" and "p" can be clearly drawn, and so that one row of letters will not rest directly on top of another. The other attributes of a character content element include:

•   font: This specifies a font set.
•   active position: This specifies the character following which the next character will be imaged.
•   size: This may affect both height and width, but sometimes only height or width are altered. An example is compressed text.
•   tabulation: The characters in a line can be left or right aligned, centered around the mid-point of a line of boxes, or centered around a "." in the line. The last one is used to make a column of money values line up vertically around their decimal points.

The above attributes do not exhaust all the qualities one can have with regard to characters. The situation is further complicated by the need to designate "fall back positions". If it is impossible to image a character as its creator desires, then it would be useful to have a set of default values to substitute for the desired values so that an approximate image could be produced. It is possible that the fall back values might be also unavailable. If we suppose a fall back for fall backs, then we can readily see that a hierarchy of less desired approximations could be composed.

The ODA standard defines a text unit to contain the content portion attributes and the content information. An example is given below.

Example 24.12

```
text-unit {
    content-portion-attributes {
        content-identifier-layout "1030"},
    content-information ("SUBJECT: ON THE PROGRESS OF THE GEOMETRIC DAPS")
        }
```

This example shows the use of a text unit.

24.3   Office Document Interchange Format

Description of interchange data stream

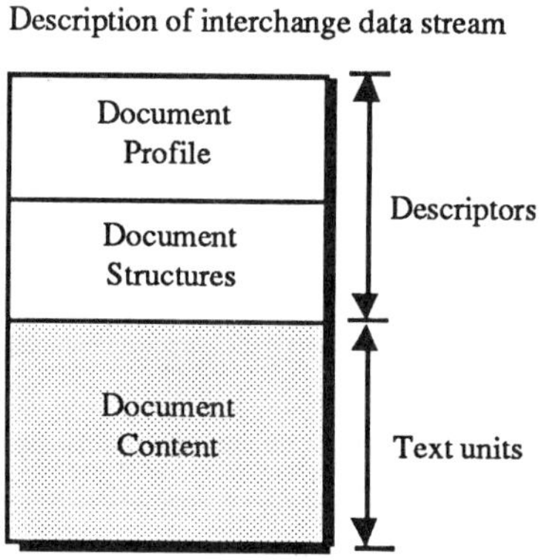

FIGURE 24.9   ODIF Data Stream

Office Document Interchange Format (ODIF) defines the format of a document based on the ODA Document Architecture. ODIF is not the only document interchange format. Another interchange format is SGML/SDIF. **Standard Generalized Markup Language (SGML)**, as specified in ISO 8879, is a language-based approach to represent a document. It is very popular in the publishing arena. Unlike ODA, SGML is used primarily to represent the logical structure of a document. **Standard Document Interchange Format (SDIF)**, as defined in ISO 8824, is the interchange format of SGML-based documents.

ODIF defines two permissible interchange format classes: Class A and Class B. They differ from each other in the data stream used to represent an interchange format. A **data stream** is a sequence of **data elements** such as the document profile, the generic and the specific structures, the document styles, and the document content (Figure 24.9). As we mentioned in the last section, the ODA standard provided a descriptor in the form of an ASN.1 module to assist the definition of each component of a document. A data element is an instance of the use of one of these descriptors. We have seen quite a number of examples of data elements in the previous section.

An interchange format class identifies the data elements in a data stream and the order in which they appear. The two interchange format classes are described below.

• **ODIF Class A**

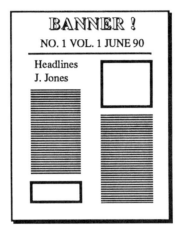

FIGURE 24.10   A Newsletter

Class A is intended for interchanging processable, formatted, and formatted processable documents. The first data element that a Class A data stream contains is a data element for the document profile. The rest of the data stream contains the following optional data elements in the order shown: data elements for the layout object classes, data elements for the logical object classes, data elements for the text units representing generic content portions, data elements for the presentation styles, data elements for the layout style, data elements for the layout objects, data elements for the logical objects, and data elements for the text units representing specific content portions.

Within each group of related data elements for the layout/logical objects or logical classes, the order of appearance of the data elements is given by the pre-order traversal algorithm on the associated tree for the layout/logical structure. A data element for a text unit must appear immediately after a layout object with which it is associated. No order is required on the data elements for layout styles/presentation styles, although they must appear as a group.

To illustrate the order in which the data elements in a data stream appear, we consider the newsletter in Figure 24.10.

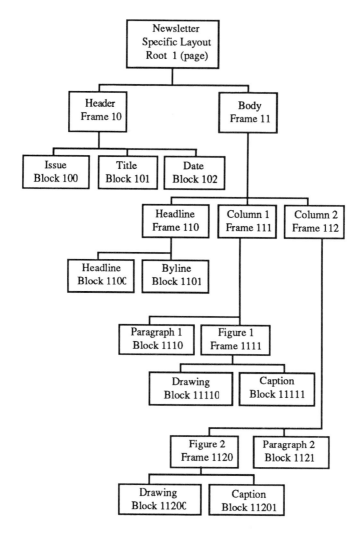

FIGURE 24.11   Specific Layout Structure of a Newsletter

This newsletter in Figure 24.10 has one page and one article with two illustrations. The page has a banner, which incorporates a title, an issue, and a date. Here the title is "BANNER!". The illustrations are arranged in two columns. Figure 24.11 gives the specific layout structure of the newsletter. Each node in the specific layout structure is mapped to a data element. Note that an object identifier is assigned to each node of the tree. According to the ODA standard, an object identifier of a layout object begins with the digit of "1". The pre-order traversal sequence of the data elements for the layout objects is:

{1, 10, 100, 101, 102, 11, 110, 1100, 1101, 111, 1110, 1111, 11110, 11111, 112, 1120, 11200, 11201, and 1121}

- **ODIF Class B**

Class B is only suitable for interchanging formatted documents. These documents do not have any specific or generic logical structure. A Class B data stream contains the following data elements in the given order: data element for the document profile, data elements for layout object classes and associated text units, data elements for presentation styles, and data elements for layout objects and associated text units.

24.4 Summary

The ODA standard defines the ODA Document Architecture and a number of content architectures. The ODA Document Architecture defines the structure of an office document. There are logical structures and layout structures. A logical structure represents the logical view of a document. It describes how a document is broken into parts and how these parts are organized logically. A layout structure shows the physical positioning and the presentation of the content of a document on an output medium. Layout information can cover everything from stating what fonts to use, the style and type size, how many columns are there on a page, and what appears in each column. A document class specifies the generic logical structure and the generic layout structure that are common to a set of documents. A document is an instance of a document class. Every document has a specific logical structure and a specific layout structure. In addition, it contains a document profile, presentation styles, and content portions. The document profile provides information that relates to the document as a whole, but is not part of the user perceived view of the document. A presentation style guides the format and the appearance of the content of a document on an output medium.

The content of a document, given by a set of content portions, is defined using a content architecture. A content architecture is a set of rules used to define the representation of each content portion. Three content architectures have been defined by ISO/IEC. They are the Character Content Architecture, the Raster Graphics Content Architecture, and the Geometric Graphics Content Architecture.

Office Document Interchange Format (ODIF) defines the format of the data stream used to interchange a document. There are two format classes. ODIF A is suitable for interchanging processable, formatted, and formatted processable documents. ODIF B is suitable for interchanging formatted documents.

Related Standards

ISO 8613 DAD 1: Information Processing - Text and Office Systems - Office Document Architecture (ODA) and Interchange Format - Addendum 1: Tiles Raster Graphics

ISO 8613 DAM 2.2: Information Processing - Text and Office Systems - Office Document Architecture (ODA) and Interchange Format - Amendment 2: Colour

ISO 8613 DAD 3: Information Processing - Text & Office Systems - Office Document Architecture (ODA) and Interchange Format - Addendum 3: Alternate Representation

ISO 8613 DAD 4: Information Processing - Text & Office Systems - Office Document Architecture (ODA) and Interchange Format - Addendum 4: Security

ISO 8613 DAD 5.2: Information Processing - Text & Office Systems - Office Document Architecture (ODA) and Interchange Format - Addendum 5: Streams

ISO 8613 DAD 6: Information Processing - Text & Office Systems - Office Document Architecture (ODA) and Interchange Format - Addendum 6: Styles Extension

ISO 8613-1: Information Processing - Text and Office Systems - Office Document Architecture (ODA) and Interchange Format - Part 1: Introduction and General Principles

ISO 8613-1 DAD 1: Information Processing - Text and Office Systems - Office Document Architecture (ODA) and Interchange Format - Part 1: Introduction and General Principles - Addendum 1: Document Application Profile Proforma and Notation

ISO 8613-1 DAM 1: Information Processing - Text and Office Systems - Office Document Architecture (ODA) and Interchange Format - Part 1: Introduction and General Principles - Amendment 1

ISO 8613-1 DAM 2: Information Processing - Text and Office Systems - Office Document Architecture (ODA) and Interchange Format - Part 1: Introduction and General Principles - Amendment 2: Conformance Testing Methodology

ISO 8613-2: Information Processing - Text and Office Systems - Office Document Architecture (ODA) and Interchange Format - Part 2: Document Structures

ISO 8613-4: Information Processing - Text and Office Systems - Office Document Architecture (ODA) and Interchange Format - Part 4: Document Profile

ISO 8613-5: Information Processing - Text and Office Systems - Office Document Architecture (ODA) and Interchange Format - Part 5: Office Document Interchange Format (ODIF)

ISO 8613-6: Information Processing - Text and Office Systems - Office Document Architecture (ODA) and Interchange Format - Part 6: Character Content Architectures

ISO 8613-7: Information Processing - Text and Office Systems - Office Document Architecture (ODA) and Interchange Format - Part 7: Raster Graphics Content Architectures

ISO 8613-8: Information Processing - Text and Office Systems - Office Document Architecture (ODA) and Interchange Format - Part 8: Geometric Graphics Content Architectures

ISO 8613-10: Information Processing - Text and Office Systems - Office Document Architecture (ODA) and Interchange Format - Part 10: Formal Specifications

ISO 8613-10 DAM 1: Information Processing - Text and Office Systems - Office Document Architecture (ODA) and Interchange Format - Part 10: Formal Specifications - Amendment 1: Formal Specification of the Document Profile

ISO 8613-10 DAM 2: Information Processing - Text and Office Systems - Office Document Architecture (ODA) and Interchange Format - Part 10: Formal Specifications - Amendment 2: Formal Specification of the Raster Graphics Content Architectures

ISO 8613-10 DAM 4: Information Processing - Text and Office Systems - Office Document Architecture (ODA) and Interchange Format - Part 10: Formal Specifications - Amendment 4: Formal Specification of ODA Geometric Graphics Content Architectures

ISO 8613-10 DAM 5: Information Processing - Text and Office Systems - Office Document Architecture (ODA) and Interchange Format - Part 10: Formal Specifications - Amendment 5: Formal Specification of the the Defaulting Mechanism for Defaultable Attributes

ISO 8613-10 ANNEX C: Information Processing - Text and Office Systems - Office Document Architecture (ODA) and Interchange Format - Part 10: Formal Specifications - Annex C: Formal Specification of ODA Character Content Architectures

DTR 10183-1: Information Processing - Text and Office Systems - Office Document Architecture (ODA) and Interchange Format - Testing Methodology and Abstract Cases - Implementation Testing Methodology - Part 1: Framework

PDTR 10183-2: Information Processing - Text and Office Systems - Office Document Architecture (ODA) and Interchange Format - Testing Methodology and Abstract Cases - Implementation Testing Methodology - Part 2: Abstract Test Suites

25

Design of an OSI Module

Since OSI software comprises of multiple layers of complex protocols, it is a challenging task to implement an OSI software. Given the OSI service definitions and protocol specifications, implementors face numerous problems. Some are related to the specific protocols, such as how to clear ambiguities, how to choose among options, and how to choose an attribute value. Others are related to software engineering aspects, such as portability, interfaces to other products, compatibility with older versions, efficiency, testing, and documentation. In this chapter, we address two of the software engineering aspects: portability and efficiency.

Portability, one of the desirable requirements in an OSE, means that an implementation must be robust enough to run in diverse environments. A portable implementation is often designed as a "black box", with the external interfaces clearly defined and the internal operations made invisible to the user. In Section 25.1, we examine the interfaces of a portable OSI module.

Efficiency means that the software should provide low delay and high throughput despite overheads caused from interprocess communication. One common technique to improve efficiency is to group multiple OSI layers into a single module. Each layer in the module is realized as a thread. Section 25.2 examines the design of a multi-layer module.

In Section 25.3, we examine an implementation of ACSE. Finally in Section 25.4, we examine an implementation of ROSE.

25.1   Interfaces of a Portable OSI Module

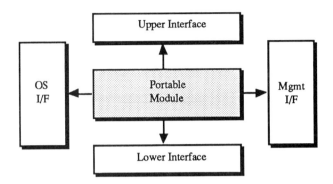

FIGURE 25.1   **Four Interfaces of a Portable OSI Module**

The most effective technique in the design of portable software is the use of modularity. Modularity means that the software has well defined external interfaces so that the internal operations are invisible to the module users. With well-defined interfaces, it is possible to mix and match modules from different vendors. Modules can be replaced when needed with little impact on the modules in its environment. In this section, we examine four interfaces of a portable OSI module. They are the upper interface, the lower interface, the operating system interface, and the management interface (Figure 25.1).

The **upper interface** of an OSI module defines the interface between the module and a module user. It must "mesh" with the **lower interface** of the module user. In some cases, the module and the module user may come from different vendors. To provide portability, a standardized lower interface should be used whenever it is possible. For example, the lower interface of many existing OSI software is XTI, the transport interface specification by X/Open.

The **operating system interface** defines the interface between the module and the operating system. It can be described in terms of operating system facilities such as buffer management, timer management, and file management. In almost all the existing OSI software, the POSIX operating system interface is used.

The **management interface** defines the interface between the module and a management module. It is described in terms of systems management functions or layer-specific management functions. Systems management systems can be given by the CMISE functions. Layer-specific management functions have not yet been standardized.

The upper interface of a module can be either asynchronous or synchronous. An **asynchronous interface** allows a module user to continue its own processing after sending a request to the module. When the module has finished processing of the request, it alerts the module user of the completion. The asynchronous interface is often used when the module can support more than one module user. A **synchronous interface** is used if the module and the module user are closely coupled with each other in an application. It is based on the use of procedure calls. When the module user sends a request to the module, it makes a procedure call (sometimes called a **downcall** procedure) and waits for the completion of the request. When the module completes the request or detects some processing error, it calls a registered procedure (sometimes called an **upcall** procedure) to notify the module user. The module user registers the notification procedure at the time it binds to the module. Of the two interfaces, the asynchronous interface is more fundamental because a synchronous interface can be always implemented on top of an asynchronous interface.

The management of the upper interface can be functionally divided into three parts: SAP management, action management, and event management. SAP management provides facilities for a module user to register or deregister with the module. Registration binds a module user to the module. Action management provides facilities for a module user to send requests or responses to the module. Event management provides facilities for a module user to review or process notifications posted by the module. After a module user is notified of an outstanding event, it retrieves and processes the event, and may send a response to the module using the facilities of action management.

We consider here a small sample of functions which can be used in the management of the upper interface. A module user first invokes function sp (i.e., service provider) to bind itself to the module. During the invocation of sp, the module user passes names/addresses information, access control/authentication information, default values, mode of operation (i.e., synchronous or asynchronous), and addresses of upcall procedures to the module. A module user invokes the send function whenever it wants to send a request/response to the module. Parameters of send may include an invocation identifier, a specification of the type of request/response, and a specification of the user-data. A module user invokes the receive function to retrieve events from the module. The receive function carries the description of the event as an argument.

Example 25.1

We illustrate here the functions associated with the upper interface of a session module. The session module supports three functions at its upper interface: s_activate, session, and *ssu, corresponding to sp, send, and receive respectively. There s_activate function has two arguments: a session selector, and the address of an SS-user function, ssu, which is used by the session module to pass events to an SS-user. The session function is used by an SS-user to send a request/response to the session module. This function has two arguments: a session control block and a structure describing the request/response. The session control block maintains state information of a session connection, assuming that more than one session connection can be maintained by the session module. It is created when a session connection is established. The function *ssu is supplied by an SS-user at the time it registers with the session module using s_activate. When the session module needs to notify an SS-user of an event, it calls *ssu. This function has two arguments: a session control block, and a structure describing the event.

Next, we examine the objects exchanged between the module and a module user. Such objects are called **IDUs (i.e., interface data units)**. An IDU can be an object exchanged between two adjacent OSI layers, between two ASEs/ASOs, or between an

ASE/ASO and an application. It can be used to carry local processing information such as local errors or information exchanged during registration/de-registration. Local processing information is not propagated to the remote system. An IDU can be also used to carry an OSI event. For example, Figure 25.2 shows that four distinct IDUs are used to carry the four primitives of a confirmed OSI service element.

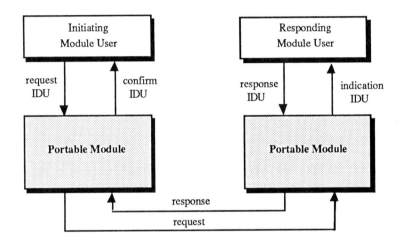

FIGURE 25.2   A Realization of Service Primitives using IDUs

The structure of an IDU is examined next. This structure is implementation dependent. It depends on the needs of the module and the operating environment. Consideration should be given to the IDU fields so as to avoid excessive buffer copying.

```
struct generic-IDU {
        struct generic-IDU      *next;
        struct generic-IDU      *previous;
        unsigned int            event-type;
        unsigned int            event-struct-type;
        genericptr              user-entity-reference;
        genericptr              provider-entity-reference;
        genericptr              user-con-reference;
        unsigned int            local-error;
        genericptr              event-struct;
        }
```

The above gives an example of a generic IDU structure used at the upper interface of the Presentation Layer. It is generic in the sense that a specific IDU can be built using this generic IDU. Hence, it can be used by any ASE/ASO which wants to exchange information with the Presentation Layer, an ASE/ASO, or an application. The event-type field indicates the event carried by the IDU. The user-entity-reference field identifies the module user which will receive an upward bound IDU. The provider-entity-reference field identifies a protocol control block which will receive a downward bound IDU from the module user, where a protocol control block here maintains state information about an invocation of the module. The user-con-ref field is similar to an application association identifier. The local-error field identifies a local error. Finally, the event-struct field contains information specific about an IDU.

IDUs used at the upper interface of the Session Layer/Transport Layer contain more specific information about the layer. Since they are quite different in structure from the IDUs used above the Presentation Layer, we will give an example below to illustrate the structure of a session IDU.

Example 25.2

```
struct s_idu {
        unsigned int        event;
        ssap_selector       *loc_ssap;
        struct rem_addr     *rem_addr;
        unsigned int        fu;
        unsigned char       token;
        unsigned char       type;
        unsigned int        reason;
        unsigned long       sync;
        struct buffer       *buffer;
        unsigned char       credit;
        unsigned char       version;
        struct act_id       cur_act_id;
        struct act_id       old_act_id;
        struct sc_id        sc_id;
        qos_type            qos;
        unsigned char       *perm;
        };
```

The above gives the structure of a session IDU. The event field carries the code for the session service primitive event. The ssap_selector field points to a session selector structure. The rem_addr field points to the remainder of the session address, i.e., the transport address. The fu field specifies the functional units negotiated at session connection establishment. The type field indicates the type of resynchronization which is either restart, abandon, or set. The sync field contains the synchronization point serial number. The buffer field points to a user data buffer. The cur_act_id field identifies the current activity. The sc_id field identifies a session connection.

Not all the fields here are used during a session function call. For example, when an SS-user establishes a session connection, only the following fields are used: event, loc_ssap, rem_addr, fu, credit, sc_id, token, sync, buffer, version, and qos (if implemented).

Next, we examine the operating system interface. In particular, we examine the buffer management and timer management aspects. The functions used for buffer management depend on the buffer structure. Not all the layers of the OSI model use the same buffer structure. For example, the lower layer buffers are typically smaller in size than the upper layer buffers. A buffer pool is shared by a group of adjacent OSI layers. The purpose of using a common buffer pool is to avoid excessive copying. When two adjacent layers share the same buffer pool, a layer only needs to pass a pointer to the adjacent layer whenever it passes data, thereby eliminating copying. However, sharing a common buffer pool creates management problems, such as which layer is responsible for deallocating a buffer and how much buffer space should a layer occupy.

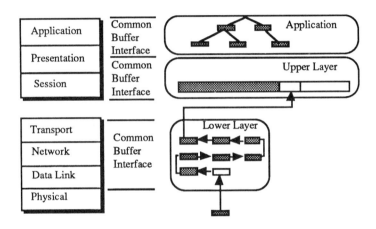

FIGURE 25.3   Different Buffer Structures

There can be more than one common buffer pool used for the entire OSI architecture. The obvious question is which layers should be grouped to share a common buffer pool. Figure 25.3 shows that three common buffer pools can be used for the OSI architecture. The Application Layer and the Presentation Layer use a tree-like buffer structure. The reason for choosing a tree-like buffer structure is that BER is used in practically all the existing OSI software. Recall that encoding by BER is accomplished by first parsing an abstract value into a parse tree and then applying encoding to the nodes of the tree bottom up from the leaves. To facilitate the use of BER, the Application Layer performs the parsing, allocates a tree-like buffer structure for the resulting parse tree, then passes the tree to the Presentation Layer which performs the encoding.

The second common buffer pool is used for the Presentation Layer and the Session Layer. Note that the Presentation Layer shares a buffer pool with the Application Layer and another buffer pool with the Session Layer. This, in a way, demonstrates that the upper layer software is very tightly coupled. Each buffer structure in the second buffer pool is a contiguous block of memory which is large enough to hold a session PDU. Whenever the Presentation Layer passes a presentation PDU to the Session Layer, it first allocates a buffer from the pool, inserts a presentation PDU into the proper location, then passes to the Session Layer a location in the buffer where a session entity can insert a session protocol header. Creation of this common buffer pool is normally performed by a presentation entity. The number of buffers required by the presentation entity depends on the number of simultaneous outstanding events that a presentation entity expects the Session Layer to maintain. In general, at least two buffers should be reserved for each session connection.

The third common buffer pool is used by the lower layers. While the buffer structures in the first two pools are user-defined, the buffer structure in this pool is system-supplied. A point worth mentioned is that system-defined buffers, by their nature, are smaller than the upper layer buffers. As a result, several operations may be needed to transfer a single session PDU to the Transport Layer.

Timer management functions are used extensively by the lower layer software. Typical timer management routines are init_timer to initialize a timer, newtimer to create a new active timer, cancel-timer to cancel an active timer, and do_timer_queue to process the timer queue. A timer queue is used to maintain the active timers. Whenever the newtimer routine is called, a new active timer is added to the timer queue. On a regular basis, do_timer_queue checks for timer expiration.

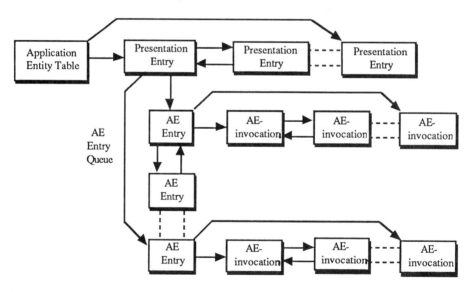

FIGURE 25.4   AE-table

We close this section by examining the Application Entity Table (AE-table), a useful internal data structure used by most OSI implementations. Conceptually, an AE-table maintains information about the module users as well as the data structures used to serve the module users. The users here are the AE-invocations. The AE-table is two-dimensional, made up of Presentation Entries as columns, and AE Entries as rows (Figure 25.4). A Presentation Entry is a list of AEs which are of the same AE-type. Since all the AEs in a Presentation Entry have the same capabilities, they share the same presentation address. An AE Entry is a list of AE-invocations associated with an AE. Each AE-invocation is characterized by a set of SAOs (i.e., single association objects) and MACFs (i.e., multiple association control functions). An SAO is implemented as a **protocol control block (PCB)** which maintains the state and application context of the association, addresses of functions that may be called during the association, and a pointer to a state table. One can imagine that every ASE in the application context is implemented by a library of functions. The PCB contains an address of every ASE that is used in the application context. The state table, which is used to specify the operation of the machine, is provided in a protocol specification standard. Essentially, the machine is driven by a simple table look-up. In an implementation, the state table from the standard is normally expanded to include local events which are chosen by the implementors.

25.2   Designing a Multi-layer OSI Module

The previous section described the interfaces of an OSI module, but did not specify how layer are implemented within the module. To improve performance, two or more layers are normally grouped together in a single module. In this section, we describe how to use threads to design of a multi-layer module.

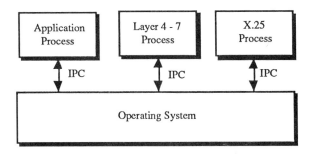

FIGURE 25.5   Transport Software not in Kernel of Operating System

Numerous ways to group OSI layers exist in OSI implementations. Some layers are implemented in the kernel code and some in the user code. The basic objective in all the implementations is the same: performance. For example, if layers 1 through 6 are implemented in the kernel, throughput will be improved because context switching in the kernel is more efficient than context switching in the user code. Three common groupings are examined next.

Figure 25.5 shows an OSI architecture comprising three processes: an application process, an OSI process containing layers 4 and above, and an X.25 process. It is assumed in this architecture that the operating system does not provide any OSI functionalities other than some network interfacing facilities at the lower two layers. The OSI process may be an FTAM process within which the session and presentation functionalities are implemented as function calls. The three processes communicate with each other using interprocess communication facilities in the operating system.

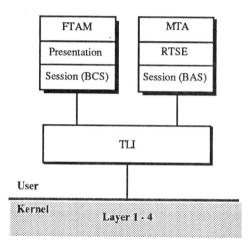

FIGURE 25.6   Transport Software within Kernel of Operating System

Figure 25.6 shows an OSI implementation where the kernel of the operating system provides the OSI transport facilities. The system also provides a TLI (i.e., Transport Level Interface) above which OSI application programs can be written.

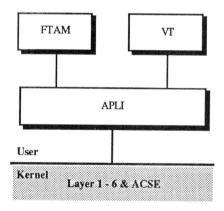

FIGURE 25.7   First 6 Layers plus APLI

Figure 25.7 shows an OSI implementation where the kernel of the operating system implements the lower six OSI layers and ACSE. APLI (i.e., ACSE/Presentation Library Interface) is present to provide an interface above which OSI application programs can be written. The figure shows two application programs, one for VT and one for FTAM.

Since ACSE is already included in the kernel, neither of the application programs has to support the ACSE functionality.

A multi-layer OSI module can be implemented using threads. **Threads** are a modern concurrency mechanism designed to support efficiency. A thread is a single sequential flow of control within a process. Within a single thread, there is a single point of execution. With threads, an application can be designed to be multi-threaded. Each thread can independently carry out sequential processing of different parts of an application. For example, while one thread executes an OSI layer, another thread executes a different OSI layer. All the executing threads in a process share the same address space. Thus, threads are "lighter-weight" than processes. However, care must be taken to ensure that shared data is accessed correctly. Semaphore objects can be introduced to resolve the access control problem. Almost all the modern operating systems today provide support for threads.

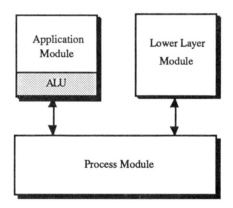

FIGURE 25.8   A Process Module

Using threads, we can implement a multi-layer module as a **process module**. Figure 25.8 shows that the process module interacts with an application module at its upper interface, and a lower layer module at its lower interface. Not shown in the figure are the operating system and the management interfaces, although we assume that the operating system interface is always present.

The part of the application module interfacing with the process module is sometimes called the **application layer user (ALU)**. An ALU is used to send work orders to the process module. After the process module completes its part of the work order, it responds to the ALU. Examples of these commands are "get me connected to site A" and "send the following message to John Doe".

The process module also needs to interact with a lower layer module for communication support. For example, the lower layer module may be asked to establish an X.25 connection with a remote site. Depending on the functionalities of the process module, the lower layer module may contain some upper layer functionalities. For example, if the process module contains only the Application Layer functionalities, then this lower layer module has to provide the presentation, the session, the transport, and the lower layer functionalities.

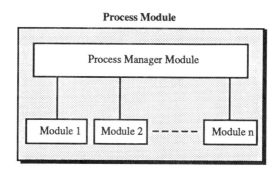

FIGURE 25.9   Internal Configuration of a Process Module

Figure 25.9 shows the internal configuration of the process module. There are n layer modules and a process manager module. Each internal module is implemented as a thread. A layer module provides the functionality of an OSI layer or an ASE/ASO. All the layer modules are monitored and coordinated by the process manager module. Given an incoming event which may be either external (from the application module or the lower layer module) or internal (from one of the layer modules), the process manager decides which layer module to activate. Whenever a layer module receives a work order from the process manager, it will complete its part of the job first before returning to the process manager. Thus the layer modules run serially, i.e., when a layer module is executing, no other layer module can run.

Each layer module within the process module is designed more or less the same as a single layer module. It may not have all four interfaces. In some cases, it may have just one interface with the process manager module. In other cases, it may have an interface with another layer module in the process module. When the layer module happens to be the lowest layer module within the process module, it can also have its lower interface directly linked to a lower layer module.

If any of the layer modules requires operating system support, it requests the service from the process manager module since we assume that the process module has an interface with the operating system. Thus, the process manager module acts as an operating system module to the internal modules.

The following example explains the operation of the process module in detail. In particular, it shows that each internal module runs as a thread.

Example 25.3

Figure 25.10 shows a process module containing the GEN-ASE, the ACSE, the presentation, the session, and the transport modules as layer modules. We assume that the GEN-ASE and the ACSE modules can directly communicate with each other. To illustrate the operation of this module, we assume the process module receives a work order to connect to a remote site A from the ALU of an application module. The process manager sends the GEN-ASE module a work order which requests a connection establishment with site A. The GEN-ASE module calls the ACSE module to establish an application association. The ACSE module returns the call to the ASE module with an AARQ APDU. The ASE module then returns to the process manager with the indication that the AARQ APDU needs to be passed to the presentation module.

The process manager sends the presentation module the AARQ APDU and a work order which requests a presentation connection establishment. The presentation module, after preparing a CP PPDU, returns to the process manager with the indication the CP PPDU needs to be passed to the session module.

The process manager sends the session module the CP PPDU and a work order which requests a session connection establishment. The session module, after preparing a CN SPDU, returns to the process manager with the indication the CN SPDU needs to be passed to the transport module.

The process manager sends the transport module the CN SPDU and a work order which requests a transport connection establishment. Assume there is no available network connection to site A. Therefore, when the transport module receives the work order from the process manager, it calls the X.25 module to establish an X.25 connection with site A. It then posts an event with the process manager indicating that the X.25 module has been sent a message to establish a network connection with site A.

Upon receipt of the event from the transport module, the process manager checks if there are other activities which it can initiate. If, for example, it has another work order from the ALU to establish a connection with site B, then it will send a work order to the ASE module as before. In this way, the process module will not sit idle while it is waiting for a confirmation message from the X.25 module regarding the connection to site A.

Eventually, the X.25 module establishes a network connection with site A and sends a notification event to the process module.

Upon receipt of the notification, the process manager communicates the notification message to the layer modules in the following order: the transport module, the session module, the presentation module, and the ASE module. This step is necessary because the layer modules have to maintain a protocol control block for each established connection. Finally, the process module sends the following message to the ALU: "you are connected to site A".

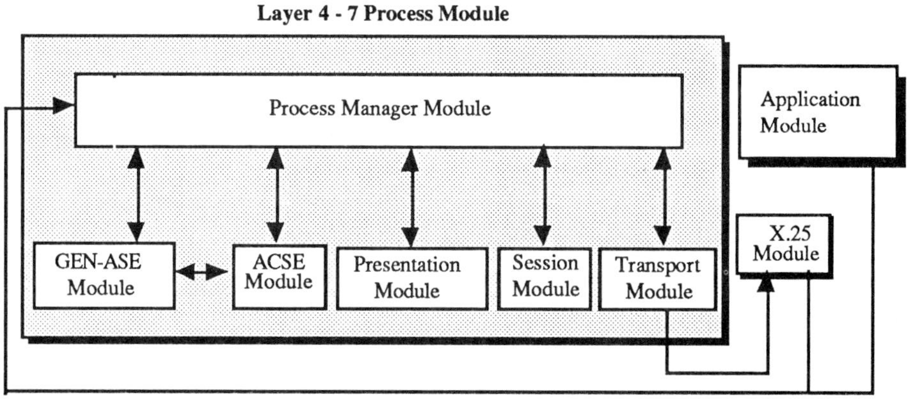

Layer 4 - 7 Process Module

FIGURE 25.10   An Example of a Multi-layer Process Module

The next example illustrates the operation of a process module when it contains a set of ROS-based ASEs as layer modules.

Example 25.4

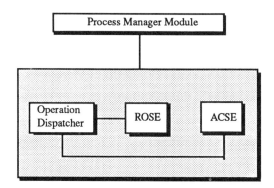

FIGURE 25.11   A Process Module containing ROSE

Figure 25.11 shows a process module containing the operation dispatcher, the ROSE module, and the ACSE module.

Recall that a ROS-based ASE does not have its own protocol engine to generate or process APDUs. All it does is to supply parameters to the ROSE interface. Thus, there is no point in having a layer module for each ROS-based ASE. Instead, all these ROS-based ASEs are grouped into one layer module which is the operation dispatcher.

The operation dispatcher maintains two data modules. The first data module is a table of application contexts defining the rules for the ROS-based ASEs. The second data module is a set of ASE tables, where each table contains the definition of the operations used by a ROS-based ASE. This operation dispatcher together with the two data modules can model a set of ROS-based ASEs.

Suppose that the operation dispatcher receives a bind/unbind work order from the process manager, it calls the ACSE module directly. If it receives an operation invocation as a work order, it checks if the operation has been registered and the argument types are used correctly. If both checks are correct, it calls the ROSE module. The ROSE module, after preparing an appropriate ROSE APDU, returns directly to the operation dispatcher which then returns to the process manager.

Figure 25.12 shows the internal data structures of the process manager module. It maintains an event queue. The event queue receives inputs from the event mapper and any layer module within the process module. An event destined for the event queue should specify the target layer module, the type, the parameters, and the user data pointer pointing to a data buffer pool which will be shared by the events. The event mapper, upon receipt of an event from an external module or the operating system, needs to adjust the event to an appropriate one for the event queue. For example, if the process module receives an external event through some IPC facilities, it strips off the IPC header. Contained within the process manager module is an event driver module. The event driver removes an event (if there is any) from the head of the event queue, determines the target module for the event, and then sends a work order to the target module. It then waits for a reply from the target module before it continues processing.

Process Manager Module

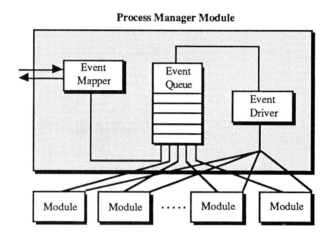

FIGURE 25.12   Internal Configuration of a Process Manager Module

Figure 25.12 shows only one event queue. In practice, more than one event queue can be maintained with each queue assigned a priority value. For example, there can be a queue for messages from the lower layer module, a queue for messages from the application module, and a queue for messages from the layer modules. In an effort not to lose packets from the network, the lower layer module should have a high priority. The event driver first examines the queue with the highest priority to see if it is empty before examining the queue with the next lower priority. If all the layer modules are implemented as procedures, then at any time there should be at most one message from the layer modules. In this case, only two queues need to be maintained, one queue for messages from the application module and the other for messages from the lower layer module.

One advantage of using the process module design is that future expansions/deletions can be accommodated with little effort. If there is a need to add another layer module to the process module in the future, all we have to do is to add another target module name to the event structure. Another advantage is that pass-through services can be managed very efficiently. For example, assume that the process module contains a presentation module and a session module. If the process manager receives a presentation pass through service request from the ALU, it can pass the work order directly to the session module instead of the presentation module.

25.3 Implementation of ACSE

In this section, we examine an implementation of ACSE. Because ACSE is present in the application contexts of all the existing OSI application protocols, the most common approach to implement ACSE is to build ACSE as a library of functions which can be linked to any OSI application program. In the function library approach, every ACSE service primitive is mapped to a function.

> int Association-request(calling-paddr, called-paddr, calling-title, called-title, mode, ap-context, p-context-list, def-context-list, p-requirements, s-requirements, setting, initial-ser-num, settings, user-data, qos, ac-connect, ac-indication, async)
> struct PSAPaddress calling-paddr, called-paddr;
>
> .....
> .....
>
> int async;

Let us examine one of the functions in the function library approach. Consider the A-ASSOCIATE.request primitive which is mapped to the association-request() function. The C declaration of the association-request() function is shown above. The ac-connect parameter contains the association information after the association is successfully established. The ac-indication parameter is used to contain error information if there is any error. The async parameter is used by the calling program to indicate an operation mode which can be either synchronous or asynchronous.

```
{
        /* Variable declaration and initialization*/
    int acs-result;
    struct PSAP *pc;
    struct AARQ-PDU *pdu;

        /* Check all the parameters */
    check-title(calling-title);
    check-title(called-title);
    check-context(context);

        /* Block the I-O. Useful in case of asynchronous operation */
    smask = sigioblock();

        /* Create a new association control block */
    if (( acblk = create-new-acblk()) == NULL){
            error-routine(aci, ACS-MEMORY, "out of memory");
            return(NOTOK);
    }

        /* Allocate memory for AARQ-PDU */
    if (( pdu = (struct AARQ-PDU *) calloc(1, sizeof *pdu)) == NULL){
            error-routine(aci, ACS-MEMORY, "out of memory");
```

```
        return(NOTOK);
        }

        /* Build AARQ-PDU */
    pdu->ap-context = ap-context;
    pdu->called-ap-tittle = called-ap-title;
        .
        .
        .
        /* Release all unwanted memory space */
    release(data);

        /* Make call to p-connect-request() */
    acs-result = p-connect-request(calling-paddr, called-paddr...async);

    (void) sigiomask(smask);
    return(acs-result);
    }
```

The above gives the coding structure of association-request(). First, all the variables are initialized and all the parameters are checked for syntax correctness. For example, the PSAP structure which is used to hold information (such as address of responding peer, list of negotiated presentation contexts, default context name, presentation requirements, initial serial number, and session connection identifier) about the presentation connection is initialized with the appropriate parameters of the function call. If any of the mandatory field is missing, the appropriate error function is called. If the asynchronous mode has been chosen, the sigioblock() function is called to block I/O signals. This is to prevent the internal data structures from improper access. When the control is returned, the sigiomask() function is called to restore the signal state to its previous values.

The next step is to create an ACSE control block which contains all the significant information (such as state, and addresses of libraries of functions) about the requested association. Once the ACSE control block is created, the next step is to create the AARQ APDU. This can be carried out in two steps. First, the calloc() function is called to allocate memory for the AARQ APDU. Then the AARQ APDU is filled with the values of relevant parameters. Once the APDU is built, all the unwanted memory space is released.

Finally, the P-CONNECT.request primitive is issued by calling the p-connect-request() function, assuming that the Presentation Layer is also implemented as a library of functions.

25.4 Implementation of ROSE

Recall that ROSE must be used along with one or more user-ASEs in an application context. In many situations, only one user-ASE is used. Hence, it is useful to combine ROSE and the user-ASE into a single module. This suggests that ROSE, like ACSE, is implemented as a function library in practice. In this section, we will examine an implementation of ROSE as a function library. At the end of the section, we will briefly examine an implementation of ROSE based on the exchange of IDUs.

First, we consider the function library approach. The interaction with the ROSE system is usually specified in a remote operations module. An application uses the remote operations module to register the definition of a set of operations with the ROSE system. At compile time, the remote operation module is passed to a rose-stub-generator function. The rose-stub-generator function produces a stub procedure and two data structures for each operation.

The stub procedure is used to perform front-end processing of an operation invocation during run-time. In the initiator side, it first checks if the call to the operation is valid. If it is valid, then the arguments are encoded by the respective functions, and an operation-control-block is generated to maintain the state of the operation invocation. In the performer side, the stub procedure is used to check if the requested operation can be performed.

One data structure generated by the rose-stub-generator function, one data structure contains information about the operation name, the operation code, addresses of routines to encode/decode the arguments, and addresses of routines to encode/decode the results. The other data structure contains information about error names, error codes, and addresses of routines to encode/decode errors encountered during the execution of the operation. Once the stubs and data structures are generated, the application is ready to run.

At run-time, an application association has to be established first. Depending on the application context, the user calls a function which corresponds to either a RT-OPEN.request or an A-ASSOCIATE.request primitive. When the function corresponds to the RT-OPEN.request primitive, it means that the user wants to include RTSE in its application context. In this case, RTSE is the sole user of ACSE and the presentation services. On a successful application association establishment, an ACSE PCB (i.e., protocol control block is created and an association descriptor is returned to the user. The ACSE PCB maintains state information about the application association. Furthermore, it contains addresses of the important functions which are needed for this particular application context. The association descriptor is used to reference the ACSE PCB.

After an application association has been established, the ROSE service primitives can be issued. Each service primitive is mapped to a function. For example, the RO-INVOKE.request primitive is mapped to a stub procedure and the ro-invoke-request() function. The stub procedure is generated by the rose-stub-generator at compile-time. Let us examine the code of the ro-invoke-request() function.

```
int ro-invoke-request(assoc-desc, op-value, class, op-args, invoke-id, linked-id, priority, rose-indicator)
int assoc-desc,
    op-value,
    class,
    invoke-id,
    linked-id,
```

```
        priority;
char * op-args;
struct rose-indicator rose-indicator;

{
        /* Parameter declarations */
 int result;
 int smask;
 struct assoc-control-block * assoc-block;
 struct ro-invoke-pdu * pdu;

        /* Check for the validity of the class parameter */
 if (check-class(class) == NULL){
        error-routine(rose-indicator, RO-CLASS, "Invalid class specified");
        return(NOTOK);
 }

        /* Block the I-O */
 smask = sigioblock();

        /* Get the association control block for the given association descriptor */
 if (get-assoc-block(sd, assoc-block) == NULL){
        error-routine(rose-indicator, RO-SD, "Invalid association descriptor specified");
        return(NOTOK);
        }

        /* Check to see if the user can initiate and also if it is users turn */
 if (check-assoc-block(assoc-block) == NULL){
        error-routine(rose-indicator, RO-EVENT, "Event not allowed");
        return(NOTOK);
        }

        /* Check to see if all the arguments are present */
 if (check-args(op-value,op-args) == NULL){
        error-routine(rose-indicator, RO-ARGS, "Argument is missing");
        return(NOTOK);
        }

        /* Steps to build the invoke APDU. Allocate memory */
 if (( pdu = (struct RO-IV *) calloc(1, sizeof *pdu)) == NULL){
        error-routine(rose-indicator, RO-MEMORY, "out of memory");
        return(NOTOK);
        }
```

```
                /* call the function to build the pdu */
        build-invoke-pdu(pdu, invoke-id,.., op-args);


                /* Call the appropriate function depending on the underlying service to convey the PDU. The
        function to be used is stored in the structure assoc-block */
        if ((* assoc-block->write-fn(assoc-block, pdu,..) == NULL)
                error-routine(rose-indicator, RO-PERROR, "error by provider");
                return(NOTOK);
                }


                /* Get the result. In case of synchronous mode result is in the rose-indicator structure and in
        case of asynchronous mode appropriate wait function is called */
        result = (class == SYNC
                ? (* assoc-block->rose-wait)(assoc-block, invoke-id, rose-indicator)
                : OK);
        (void) sigiomask(smask);
        return(result);
        }
```

The above gives the code of the ro-invoke-request() function. Let us examine the code in detail. The assoc-desc parameter is used to store the association descriptor which is returned by ACSE at the end of a successful association establishment. The rose-indicator parameter is used to contain information about any error occurred during the association.

First, the class parameter is checked to find out if the valid operation class is passed. Note that the association class, which specifies whether the initiator or the responder can invoke an operation, is an integral part of an application context. If there is an error, the function calls the error-routine function which updates the rose-indicator parameter. It returns the constant "NOTOK". After blocking the I/O signals to maintain consistency of the internal data structures, the ACSE control block identified by the assoc-desc parameter is retrieved. Checking is done to see if the current event is allowed and if it is the turn of the initiator. If the event is allowed, ROSE proceeds to build the ROIV APDU. Memory is allocated and the function which is used to build ROIV is called. The address of this function can be found in the ACSE PCB. ROIV is ready to be passed to the peer ROSE. If the operation mode is synchronous, ROSE is blocked and the rose-wait() function is called. The address of the rose-wait() function can be found in the ACSE PCB. If the operation mode is asynchronous, the ro-invok-request() function returns "OK". The result is later conveyed to the user using the event-handler()function which is used to indicate an incoming event.

Next, we sketch a ROSE implementation using IDUs. In the IDU implementation, the upper and the lower interfaces of the ROSE module are described by the exchange of event related structures. At the upper interface, two functions are used to pass these structures. They are the rose-app-provider and the rose-app-user functions. Both functions take only one argument, generic-IDU, whose definition was given in Section 25.1. The rose-app-provider function is used to send an IDU to the ROSE module, while the rose-app-user function is used to convey indications to a ROSE user.

The user of the ROSE module first sets up the ROSE environment by calling the rose-init function after a successful initialization of the presentation module. Next, it calls the rose-register-apx function to register a set of operations and errors. Then it calls the rose-activate function to activate the PSAP, register the abstract syntaxes along with their transfer syntaxes, and register an event-handling function. After all these steps, the user can request services from the ROSE module.

To request a service, the user must build an IDU. It first allocates a generic-IDU. Then it proceeds to build an event structure which is used to describe the specific request. This structure is mapped to the event-struct field of the generic-IDU. The event-struct-type field of the generic-IDU is set to indicate the type of the event structure.

The IDU is passed to the ROSE module using the rose-app-provider function. Once the IDU is received, the ROSE module checks if the syntax is correct. The appropriate ACSE control block is retrieved. Using the ACSE control block and the event-type field of the IDU, the ROSE module can check if the requested operation is valid for the association.

Next, the ROSE module prepares an IDU to be sent to the presentation module. An appropriate event structure is first built. Then, a generic-IDU is allocated and the event structure is mapped to the event-struct field of the generic-IDU. Similar to its upper interface, the ROSE module has two functions at its lower interface. The pres-provider function is used to pass an IDU to the presentation module. When the presentation module wants to pass an indication to ROSE, it calls the pres-user function. The pres-user function is registered with the presentation module during the activation of the presentation module.

25.5 Summary

In this chapter, we examined two of the software engineering issues in the design of an OSI module: portability and efficiency. We first considered a single layer module and then a multiple-layers module.

Modularity is the most effective technique to provide portability. Modularity means that the software has well-defined external interfaces. Four interfaces of an OSI module were identified in this chapter: the upper interface, the lower interface, the operating system interface, and the management interface. For example, the upper interface has functions to send IDUs up/down, as well as functions to allow a module user to bind or unbind with the module. The operating system interface is characterized by the possible use of more than one buffer pool. Use of a common buffer pool eliminates copying.

Most OSI implementations merge two or more layers into a single module for efficiency reasons. In this chapter, we introduced the multi-layer process module design. Within the process module, there is a process manager module, a set of layer modules, and a set of ASE/ASO modules. Each layer or ASE/ASO module can be implemented as a thread. Using an event queue, the process manager monitors and controls the execution of the layer and the ASE/ASO modules in a serial manner. One advantage of using the process module design is that future expansions/deletions can be accommodated with little effort. Another advantage is that pass-through services can be managed very efficiently.

References

RETIX Upper Layers Common Facilities Manual, Document Number (1080149-01)

ISODE Reference Manual, Marshall Rose

26

Conformance Testing

Conformance testing is an examination of the static capabilities and the dynamic behavior of an OSI implementation. It serves to verify the claims made by the supplier of an implementation. These claims may make reference to OSI protocol standards or functional profiles.

There are two aspects of conformance testing that need to be standardized. The first aspect, conformance testing methodology, identifies the various test methods. Conformance testing methodology is specified in ISO/IEC 9646. The second aspect is the identification of test suites used for conformance testing. In this chapter, we are mainly concerned with the conformance testing methodology although we will also examine the structure of a generic test suite.

In Section 26.1, an overview of conformance testing is provided. Section 26.2 describes abstract test methods and shows how they are applied to conformance testing. Section 26.3 describes the structure of an abstract test suite.

26.1 Overview of Conformance Testing

This section gives an overview of conformance testing. First, we describe the objects involved in conformance testing. Second, conformance requirements are described.

Third, the various kinds of tests that can be applied during conformance testing are discussed. Finally, an overview of the conformance assessment process is provided.

- **objects involved in conformance testing**

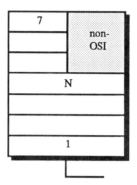

FIGURE 26.1   SUT Containing Non-OSI Protocols.

The implementation to be tested is called the **Implementation Under Test (IUT)**. An IUT may be an entire system or part of a real system known as the **System Under Test (SUT)**. The configuration of a SUT may affect the test methods that can be applied to the IUT. For example, the SUT shown in Figure 26.1 contains non-OSI protocols, in which case the **points of control and observation (PCOs)** used during the conformance testing must be confined only to the OSI part of the SUT.

Conformance testing involves a testing laboratory and a client. The **client** is an organization which submits an IUT for conformance testing while the **test laboratory** is an organization which carries out conformance testing using a tester. Conformance assessment is based on the external behavior of the IUT which is monitored and controlled at one or more points external to the IUT.

- **conformance requirements**

Conformance requirements are defined in terms of static conformance requirements and dynamic conformance requirements. They are defined by either protocol standards or functional profiles. **Static conformance requirements** define the minimum allowed capabilities of an implementation i.e., what a protocol implementation must contain. Examples of static conformance requirements are the service elements and functional units that an implementation must support. **Dynamic conformance requirements** define the allowed behavior in instances of communication. They are defined in terms of the elements of protocol procedures specified in the protocol standards.

Before testing begins, the client must provide a **Protocol Implementation Conformance Statement (PICS)** per protocol implemented as stated in the **Systems Conformance Statement (SCS)**. The SCS is a document summarizing which OSI protocols are implemented and to which conformance is claimed. The PICS describes the capabilities of each protocol mentioned in the SCS.

Status	Predicates	References	Support	Type/Length/Values	
				Allowed	Supported
m/o/c/-	XXXX	XXXX		XXXX	
m/o/c/-	XXXX	XXXX		XXXX	
.	.	.		.	
.	.	.		.	
.	.	.		.	

TABLE 26.1   Generic PICS Proforma Table

ACSE APDUs	Sending		Receiving	
	Base	F/S	Base	F/S
A-associate-request APDU (AARQ)	c1	c1	c2	c2
A-associate-response APDU (AARE)	c2	c2	c1	c1
A-release-request APDU (RLRQ)	o	*	m	m
A-release-response APDU (RLRE)	m	m	c3	c3
A-abort APDU (ABRT)	c4	c4	c4	c4

c1 - m if initiator capability else -   m - mandatory for base and
c2 - m if responder capability else -   supported for F/S
c3 - m if 3 sender is m, else -   o - optional
c4 - m if session V2 is supported else -   * - upto the referencing implementation

TABLE 26.2   Requirements on ACSE APDUs

The format in which the PICS is written is called the **PICS proforma**. A PICS proforma should be part of a protocol or functional profile specification. It is basically a set of tables with one table for each static conformance requirement. An example is given in Table 26.1. The status column indicates the status of an item as defined in the standard or profile (this is always preprinted). Examples of items are parameters of a service element and fields of a PDU. The predicate column specifies a predicate upon which a conditional status is based. The references column (also preprinted) gives references to static conformance requirements in the relevant standard(s) or profile(s). The support column is the place where the client must fill in the capabilities supported by the implementation. The type/length/values column gives the allowed values (preprinted) and the supported values.

Table 26.2 is a table taken from the PICS proforma on ACSE. This table is used to specify the ACSE APDUs supported by a referencing implementation. Considering the

RLRQ APDU, a receiver can claim conformance by supporting the syntax of the received RLRQ but not necessarily the procedure associated with the processing of the RLRQ APDU.

Another form that a client should supply to the testing laboratory is the **Protocol Implementation eXtra Information for Testing (PIXIT).** This form provides the test laboratory with necessary information about the SUT. Information about the SUT may include network addresses, power requirements, and protocol values required by the tester. The **PIXIT proforma** is the form in which the PIXIT is written. It is issued by the test laboratory and completed by the client. The test laboratory uses the PIXIT information to determine the means of testing.

• **types of conformance tests**

No conformance testing can be exhaustive because infinite events can occur at a PCO in general. Thus there is a trade-off between the coverage of a test and the cost of its execution. A non-conforming implementation may pass a conformance test in a given environment but fail a conformance test in a different environment.

Three types of conformance testing have been identified according to the extent to which they provide an indication of conformance. They are basic interconnection tests, capability tests, and behavior tests. **Basic interconnection tests** provide limited testing of the major features to establish sufficient conformance for interconnection without trying to perform thorough testing. These tests cannot be used as a basis for claims of conformance by the supplier of an implementation. **Capability tests** provide testing for each of the static conformance requirements. They check the consistency of the PICS with the IUT thoroughly. **Behavior tests** endeavor to provide as comprehensive a testing as possible over the full range of dynamic conformance requirements. They include tests for the behavior by the IUT in response to valid, invalid, and inopportune PDUs sent by the tester. Capability tests and behavior tests together provide a basis of claims of conformance.

• **conformance assessment process**

There are three major steps in the conformance assessment process: test preparation, test operation, and production of test reports (Figure 26.2).

The test preparation step involves production of the SCS, the PICs, the PIXIT, and choice of abstract test methods and abstract test suites. Before the client contracts with a test laboratory for the performance of any conformance test, it must first ensure that the SUT is testable using at least one of the **abstract test methods (ATMs).** An ATM identifies the points closest to the IUT at which control and observation can take place. It also determines the set of test cases, collectively known as an **abstract test suite (ATS),** that can be applied to the IUT during conformance testing. The client should ensure that the SUT provides the necessary means of control and observation as stipulated by any proposed ATMs. After this preliminary effort by the client, the client must complete a PICS for each protocol standard or functional profile which is implemented in the IUT and for which conformance is to be tested. The client must also complete a PIXIT for each ATM that may be used during the conformance assessment process.

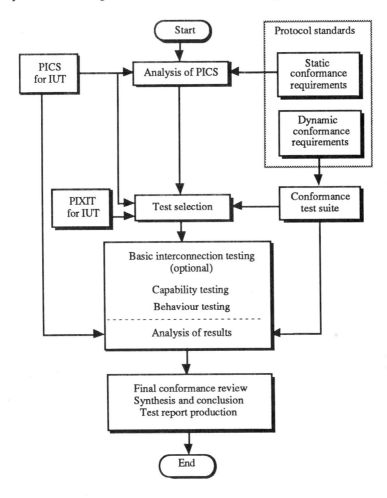

FIGURE 26.2   Flowchart of the Overall Conformance Assessment Process

The completed lists are reviewed by the testing laboratory which accommodates the client's choice of ATMs. For each relevant ATS, the testing laboratory identifies a means of testing. A **means of testing (MOT)** specifies a test system, an executable test suite, and necessary test supporting tools, where an **executable test suite** is a realization of an ATS written in some executable programming language.

The final step in this preparation phase is to prepare the MOT and the SUT for the test operations phase. The test operations phase involves a static conformance review, a test selection and parameterization based on the PICS and the PIXIT, and one or more test campaigns. During the static conformance review, the testing laboratory analyzes the

PICSs to check if they are self-consistent. Based on the information in the PICS, the test laboratory selects the abstract test cases that are appropriate for the IUT. These test cases include both capability and behavior test cases. The selected set of abstract test cases is known as the **Selected Abstract Test Suite (SATS)**.

Next, the information provided in the PIXIT is used to determine the appropriate parameter values in the SATS. Examples of parameter values include values of network addresses, timers, and counters. The resulting **Parameterized Executable Test Suite (PETS)** is then ready to be executed. Should any test coordination procedure be needed for an ATM, it must also be checked whether the MOT and the SUT are able to use the required test coordination procedures.

A **test campaign** is the process of executing the PETS and producing log information if requested by the client. Therefore, this is the stage where dynamic conformance testing takes place. During the test campaign, the following verdicts may be assigned to a test: pass verdict, fail verdict, inconclusive verdict, test case error, and abnormal test case termination. Prior to entering the test report production step, the test laboratory will inform the client of any test cases for which it might indicate a fail verdict. Negotiated exits can be made during the test campaign. For example, if an error is found, the client may take a negotiated exit and end the conformance testing process.

After the test operations are complete, an assessment of the conformance of the IUT is made, resulting in the production of two test reports: the SCTR and the PCTR. The **System Conformance Test Report (SCTR)** gives an overall summary of the conformance of the system. The **Protocol Conformance Test Report (PCTR)** gives the details of the testing carried out for each protocol involved.

26.2 Abstract Test Methods and Applicability

An ATM identifies the PCOs at which control and observation are to be exercised. PCOs can be at the same site of the IUT or at a remote site, all depending on the architecture of the IUT and the agreements made between the test laboratory and the client. ATMs form a basis for the design of ATSs. In this section, various ATMs are discussed.

26.2.1 Abstract Test Methods

From the testing point of view, an IUT is a black box. The behavior of an IUT is defined in terms of events observed and controlled above and below the IUT. These events are known as **Abstract Service Primitives (ASPs)**. Examples of ASPs are reception of service primitives above the IUT, and reception of PDUs below the IUT. If the ASPs below the IUT cannot be controlled and observed locally, then they must be controlled remotely (or externally) provided that some reliable communication service is available. Similarly, the ASPs above the IUT may not be controllable nor observable at all.

Figure 26.3 shows the various PCOs where ASPs can be observed and controlled. Note that they are dispersed around the tester and the IUT. When the IUT contains more than one protocol to be tested, PCOs may also appear within the IUT, depending upon whether the layer boundaries within the IUT are exposed. An IUT does not have to provide access to layer boundaries at all. For example, many 1984 MHS implementations implement the Session Layer as a library of function calls. Hence they do not provide an exposed interface to the Session Layer.

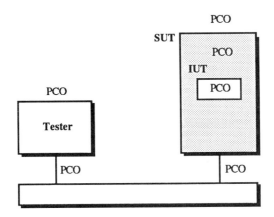

FIGURE 26.3   PCOs with Observable and Controllable ASPs

A **conformance tester** performs control and observation. It must have an operator interface to allow test execution. It must be able to execute test cases, record test events, and perform results analysis to match test events and assign test case verdicts. Results analysis may be performed off-line. A **lower tester**, also called a **test driver** or **encoder/decoder**, is the means for providing control and observation of ASPs beneath the IUT. It acts as a peer entity of the IUT and exchanges PDUs with the IUT. The **upper tester**, also called a **test responder**, is the means for providing control and observation of ASPs above the IUT. In general, a lower tester is more complex than an upper tester. **Test coordination procedures** are used to define rules for cooperation between the upper tester and the lower tester during testing.

SUTs can be end systems or relay systems. In this section, only test methods applicable to IUTs within end system SUTs are considered. ISO/IEC 9646 identifies four conformance test methods for single layer testing when the IUT contains only one layer. They are the local, distributed, coordinated, and remote methods. For the last three methods, the test system and the IUT reside in two different locations, hence they are also called external methods.

The fault detection capacity of one test method versus another is the subject of open debate. Fault detection is not only related to the test method, but also related to the test suite coverage and synchronization issues. If all other issues are equal, assumptions often made are: the fault detection capacity from most powerful to least is local, coordinated, distributed, and remote methods for single layer testing. The reason is, for the coordinated, distributed, and remote methods, the lower tester and the upper tester are at different sites and therefore, synchronization is more difficult.

- **local method**

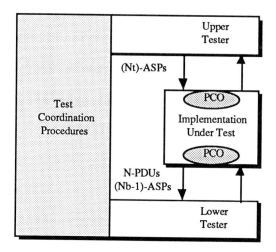

FIGURE 26.4   Local Method

The local method assumes that PCOs can be placed above and below the IUT. This model comprises a test harness around the IUT which coordinates the actions of the upper and lower testers (Figure 26.4). Even though the lower tester is below the IUT, it functionally behaves as a peer protocol entity.

- **remote method**

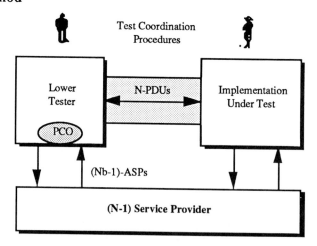

FIGURE 26.5   Remote Method

The remote method, which is used for X.25 testing, assumes that there is no upper tester, that the lower tester and the IUT reside in different systems, and that direct access to the lower interface of the IUT by a test laboratory is not possible (Figure 26.5). Human operators may be provided on top of the IUT and the lower tester to provide coordination.

- **distributed method**

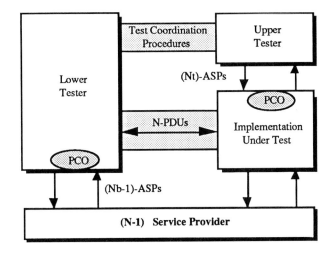

FIGURE 26.6   Distributed Method

The method assumes that the lower tester and the IUT reside in two different systems, and an upper tester can be placed above the IUT (Figure 26.6). Test coordination procedures are used to synchronize between the lower tester and the upper tester.

- **coordinated method**

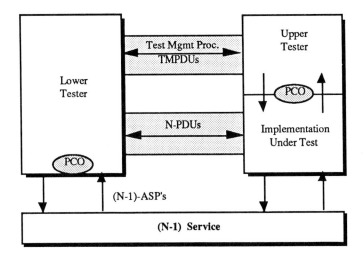

FIGURE 26.7   Coordinated Method

The two features which distinguish the coordinated method (Figure 26.7) from the distributed method are: (1) no exposed upper interface is assumed above the IUT, and (2) a standardized **Test Management Protocol (TMP)** is used to automate the test coordination procedures. Architecturally, the coordinated method is the most sophisticated model because the TMP allows a very high degree of coordination and synchronization of the upper and lower testers.

We have examined four single layer test methods. For a multi-layer IUT where either all the layers are tested or only a single layer is tested, an embedded variant of the above test methods was defined by the ISO/IEC 9646. Whenever control and observation can be applied to the upper boundary of the entities under test within the IUT, then the test methods are normal, otherwise they are **embedded**. Embedded methods limit observability and control, and are generally considered to be weaker than the single layer method.

By convention, the characters "L", "R", "C", and "D" are used to denote local, remote, coordinated, and distributed test methods respectively. Test methods are further classified based on the composition of the IUT. The letter "S" denotes a single layer IUT while the letter "M" denotes a multi-layer IUT. Whenever the method is embedded, the letter "E" is added to the suffix. For example, RSE stands for remote single layer embedded test method, DS stands for distributed single layer, and RS stands for remote single layer.

26.2.2 Choice of Abstract Test Methods

The applicability of an ATM to test an IUT depends on the availability of PCOs above and below the protocol. This in turn depends on whether the real open system is used for several applications or only one application, and whether the protocol is symmetrical or asymmetrical.

Some general observations of the test methods studied in Section 26.2.1 are made below:

- Local test methods are useful for systems under development.
- External test methods are useful for testing complete or partial end systems which can be attached to telecommunications networks.
- Coordinated test methods apply when there is a standardized TMP for use between the upper tester and the lower tester.
- Remote test methods apply when it is possible to make use of some functions of the SUT to control the IUT, instead of using a specific upper tester.
- Distributed test methods apply when it is possible to allow complete freedom for the implementation of the test coordination procedures between the SUT and the lower tester.
- Embedded test methods permit the application of single layer testing to all layers of a multi-layer IUT.

- For a complete seven layer open system, the preferred method is the incremental use of external single layer embedded methods, with PCOs provided by the upper interface of the Application Layer and PCOs starting from the lowest protocol of the IUT and working upwards.

Two examples are given below to illustrate the application of the test methods to the transport protocol, FTAM, and MHS.

Example 26.1

Consider the single layer testing of a transport entity in a real open system. When the system is used for several applications, normally the transport service is accessible either directly or indirectly via the session services. When the transport service can be accessed directly, then either the CS or the DS method can be used. If the transport service can be accessed indirectly, then either the CSE or the DSE method can be chosen.

Example 26.2

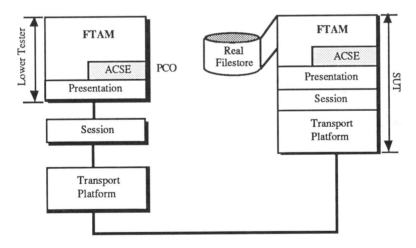

FIGURE 26.8   Application of the DS method to an FTAM Responder

FTAM is an asymmetrical protocol in the sense that an initiator only communicates with a responder. In practice, observation and control of ASPs is different for FTAM initiators and responders. Observation and control are possible with initiators but not with responders. This is because the user of the FTAM responder service in a responder is the virtual filestore, whose behavior can only be observed via the behavior of the real filestore which is highly system dependent. Observation of the behavior of the real filestore is only possible if the test laboratory is furnished with a detailed description of the mapping of the abstract file service primitives onto system-specific file operations through the PIXIT. Therefore, the DS test method which requires an upper interface on the IUT is not applicable to the testing of an FTAM responder. An FTAM responder can be tested with either the RS or the CS method. Figures 26.8 and 26.9

illustrate the applications of the DS method and the CS method to an FTAM responder implementation respectively. The RS method can also be used to test an FTAM initiator.

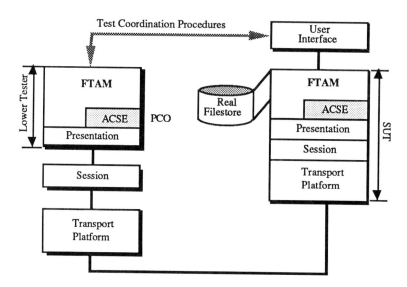

FIGURE 26.9   Application of the CS Method to an FTAM Responder

Example 26.3

There are two basic system configurations for testing MHS. One is the end system test configuration which is used to test P1, P2, and RTSE. The other is the relaying MTA configuration which is used to test P1. Consider the end system test configuration to test P1 and P2. The P1 protocol test suite assumes a PCO at the boundary between the MTA and the RTSE and a PCO at the upper boundary of the IUT. Therefore, the DS method is used for end system testing of P1. The P2 protocol test suite assumes a PCO at the boundary between the UA and the MTA and a PCO at the upper boundary of the IUT. Again, the DS method can be used for end system testing of P2.

26.3 Abstract Test Suite Specification

An ATS consists of a number of test cases where each test case has an identified purpose. It is abstract because it does not take into account the environment surrounding the tester and the SUT. Therefore, before the test operations begin, it has to be converted to an executable test suite which takes into account the programming environment.

The design of an ATS depends on the location of the PCOs and the ATM chosen. In general, there is one or more ATSs for each applicable ATM. The rest of this section examines the structure of an ATS.

Every test case has a test purpose. Test cases of an ATS can be grouped into **test groups**. If necessary, test groups can be nested within test groups. The following hints can be used to group test cases:

• capability tests can be subgrouped based on mandatory features and optional features,

• behavior tests can be further subgrouped into tests of valid behavior, tests of invalid behavior, and tests of inopportune behavior,

• each of the above behavior test subgroups can be further subgrouped into test subgroups for the connection establishment phase, the data transfer phase, and the connection release phase, and

• the data transfer phase can be further subgrouped into tests that focus on PDUs sent to the IUT and PDUs received from the IUT.

Because of the abstract nature of an ATS, the test body should be specified in some formal notations. ISO/IEC 9646-3 defined a notation called **Tree and Tabular Combined Notation (TTCN)** for this purpose. TTCN is a specification language for describing trees of behavior and actions associated with exchanging PDUs. The next two examples illustrate the use of TTCN.

Example 26.4

```
U! Initialize
     Start (A, time-duration)
          L? FINIRQin [is-valid-fus AND is-valid-ctl]
               Cancel (A)
               + abort-postamble
```

In the notation above, "!" means send and "?" means receive. The test body here is used to test an FTAM initiator's ability to generate a valid F-INITIALIZE.request FPDU. First, the upper tester (denoted by "U") prompts the IUT to set up an FTAM regime with the lower tester. In the meantime, the lower tester starts a timer to wait for an arrival of the F-INITIALIZE.request (denoted by "FINIRQ") FPDU. When the FPDU does arrive in time, the lower tester checks if the functional units and contents type are valid. If valid, it assigns a "PASS" to the test, cancels the timer, and aborts the connection.

Example 26.5

```
L! Clodes
     Start (A, time-duration)
          L? Clodes
               Cancel (A)
                    + Terminate, Postamble
          ? Timeout (A)
```

The above test body is used to test an FTAM responder's ability to accept requests for file closing and deselection. First the lower tester sends grouped F-CLOSE.request and F-DESELECT.request FPDUs to the initiator. It then starts a timer, expecting the arrival of a response to both request FPDUs. If the lower tester does receive the expected FPDU in time, then it assigns the "PASS" verdict, cancels the timer, and terminates the FTAM regime. If it does not receive a response when the timer expires, an "INCONCLUSIVE" verdict will be assigned.

Structurally, a test case consists of a preamble, a test body, and a postamble. Let us assume that the test case is used to test a certain edge in the FSM specification of a protocol. Associated with the edge is an initial state, an ending state, and an (input, output) pair. The idea is that if the FSM receives an input event in the starting state, it should perform the output event and move to the ending state. The **preamble** of a test case serves to lead the IUT to the starting state of the edge. The **test body** is used to simulate the input event and observe the output event. The **postamble** is used to determine if the IUT ends up with the state corresponding to the ending state. In practice, an edge subsequence is assigned individually to the preamble, the test body, and the postamble. An edge sequence is the concatenation of the three edge subsequences. A **test sequence** is a sequence of edge sequences, with an edge sequence for each edge in the FSM specification. **Test sequence generation** is the generation of a test sequence based on cost and fault coverage. There are many test generation methods around. The major differences among the various test generation methods is how the edge sequences are connected and what techniques are used to verify the ending state.

Presently, most of the ATSs are written by implementors. None of them has an international status. The fact that there may be more than one ATS for a protocol standard or functional profile poses the problem as to which test suite to choose. Another problem with ATSs is the absence of criteria to judge the fault coverage.

26.4   Summary

Conformance testing is used to verify the claims made by the supplier of an implementation. It examines the static capabilities and the dynamic behavior of an implementation known as the IUT.

Several abstract test methods are used to perform conformance testing. They differ from each other in the location of the points of control and observation. There is at least one abstract test suite for each abstract test method. An abstract test suite consists of a set of test cases, where each test case has a test purpose.

Before testing begins, the supplier of the implementation and the test laboratory exchange information about the Protocol Implementation Conformance Statement (PICS) and the Protocol Implementation eXtra Information for Testing (PIXIT). Based on the information, the test laboratory determines the means of testing. The means of testing is a realization of each abstract test method and each abstract test suite involved.

A test campaign is basically the process of executing the test suite. During the test campaign, verdicts are given to the test cases. After the execution of the test cases is complete, two test reports are produced, the Systems Conformance Test Report (SCTR) and the Protocol Conformance Test Report (PCTR). The former report gives the overall summary of the conformance of the system, while the latter report gives the details of the testing carried out for each protocol involved.

Given the complexity of the OSI protocols, exhaustive testing is impossible. There is a trade-off between the coverage of a test suite and the cost of its execution. Thus, it is possible for a non-conforming implementation to pass a conformance test in a given environment but fail in a different environment.

This chapter only covered the basic issues. We did not mention multi-party testing. Applications such as MHS and Directory Services require the testing over several related associations when the IUT needs to communicate with several partners concurrently. A methodology is being developed to handle this kind of multi-party testing.

Related Standards

DIS 8882-1.2: Information Technology - X.25-DTE Conformance Testing - Part 1: General Principles

DIS 8882-2: Information Technology - Telecommunications and Information Exchange Between Systems - X.25-DTE Conformance Testing - Part 2: Data Link Layer Test Suite

ISO 8882-3: Information Technology - Telecommunications and Information Exchange Between Systems - X.25-DTE Conformance Testing - Part 3: Packet Level Conformance Suite

ISO 8882-3 PDAM 1: Information Technology - Telecommunications and Information Exchange Between Systems - X.25-DTE Conformance Testing - Part 3: Packet Level Conformance Suite - Amendment 1: Use of Data Link Service Primitives in ISO/IEC 8882-3

ISO 9646-1: Information Technology - Open Systems Interconnection - Conformance Testing Methodology and Framework - Part 1: General Concepts

ISO 9646-1 PDAM 1: Information Technology - Open Systems Interconnection - Conformance Testing Methodology and Framework - Part 1: General Concepts - Proposed Draft Amendment 1: Protocol Profile Testing Methodology and Multi-Protocol Testing

ISO 9646-1 PDAM 2: Information Technology - Open Systems Interconnection - Conformance Testing Methodology and Framework - Part 1: General Concepts - Proposed Draft Amendment 2: Multi-Party Testing Methodology

ISO 9646-2: Information Technology - OSI Conformance Testing Methodology and Framework - Part 2: Abstract test suite Specification

ISO 9646-2 PDAM 1: Information Technology - OSI Conformance Testing Methodology and Framework - Part 2: Abstract Test Suite Specification - Proposed Draft Amendment 1: Protocol Profile Testing Methodology

ISO 9646-2 PDAM 2: Information Technology - OSI Conformance Testing Methodology and Framework - Part 2: Abstract Test Suite Specification - Proposed Draft Amendment 2: Multi-Party Conformance Testing Methodology

DIS 9646-3: Information Technology - OSI Conformance Testing Methodology and Framework - Part 3: The tree and Tabular Combined Notation (TTCN)

ISO 9646-4: Information Technology - OSI Conformance Testing Methodology and Framework - Part 4: Test Realization

ISO 9646-4 PDAM 1: Information Technology - OSI Conformance Testing Methodology and Framework - Part 4: Test Realization - Proposed Draft Amendment 1: Protocol Profile Testing Methodology

ISO 9646-4 PDAM 2: Information Technology - OSI Conformance Testing Methodology and Framework - Part 4: Test Realization - Proposed Draft Amendment 2: Multi-Party Conformance Testing Methodology

ISO 9646-5: Information Technology - Open Systems Interconnection - Conformance Testing Methodology and Framework - Part 5: Requirements on Test Laboratories and Clients for the Conformance Assessment Process

ISO 9646-5 PDAM 1: Information Technology - Open Systems Interconnection - Conformance Testing Methodology and Framework - Part 5: Requirements on Test Laboratories and Clients for the Conformance Assessment Process - Proposed Draft Amendment 1: Protocol Profile Testing and Multi-Protocol Testing

ISO 9646-5 PDAM 2: Information Technology - Open Systems Interconnection - Conformance Testing Methodology and Framework - Part 5: Requirements on Test Laboratories and Clients for the Conformance Assessment Process - Proposed Draft Amendment 2: Multi-Party Testing Methodology

DP 10025: Information Processing Systems - Transport Conformance Testing for Connection Oriented Transport Protocol Operating Over the Connection Oriented Network Service - Part 1: General Principles

CD 10025-3: Information Technology - Telecommunications and Information Exchange between Systems - Transport Conformance Testing for Connection Oriented Transport

Protocol Operating over the Connection Oriented Network Service - Part 3: Transport Test Mgmt Protocol

DIS 10168-1: Information Technology - Open Systems Interconnection - Conformance Test Suite for the Session Protocol - Part 1: Test Suite Structure and Test Purposes

DP 10168-4: Information Technology - Open Systems Interconnection - Conformance Test Suite for the Session Protocol - Part 4: Test Management Protocol Specification

ISO 10169-1: Information Technology - Open Systems Interconnection - Conformance Test Suite for the ACSE Protocol - Part 1: Test Suite Structure and Test Purposes

ISO 10170-1: Information Technology - Open Systems Interconnection - Conformance Test Suite for the File Transfer, Access and Management (FTAM) Protocol - Part 1: Test Suite Structure and Test Purposes

DIS 10729-1: Information Technology - Open Systems Interconnection - Conformance Test Suite for the Presentation Layer - Part 1: Test Suite Structure and Test Purposes for the Presentation Protocol

CD 10739-1: Information Technology - Open Systems Interconnection - Conformance Test Suite for 9041 - Virtual Terminal Basic Class Protocol - Part 1: Test Suite Structure and Test Purposes

27

US GOSIP

Governments are by far the largest buyers of Information Technology. The functional standards used by governments are known as **GOSIPs,** standing for government OSI profiles. Examples include US GOSIP, UK GOSIP, SOSIP (S for Swedish), etc. In this chapter, we examine the specification of US GOSIP.

US GOSIP is the US Government program for the adoption and standardization of OSI across all government agencies. Managed by NIST, it aims at achieving network connectivity and interoperability across the heterogeneous environments within the government agencies, while increasing competition in the procurement of networking products. Network connectivity is achieved through the adoption of OSI. Interoperability is achieved through the adoption of functional standards defined at OIW. Competition is enhanced through standardization on a small number of subnetwork technologies and application functions.

The first version of US GOSIP, published as **FIPS (Federal Information Processing Standards Publication Series) 146,** was released in February 1989. As of August 15 1990, GOSIP has been mandatory in the government procurements of network products. It is planned that any future version of GOSIP will be mandated eighteen months after its release. FIPS 146 contains two sections: the announcement and the specifications. The announcement section contains information about the GOSIP objectives, the applicability criteria, the waiver process, and the procurement procedures.

The specifications section contains technical description such as the specifications of the required OSI application protocols and network services. GOSIP Users' Guide, another publication from NIST, serves as a companion document to FIPS 146. It is designed to assist government users in understanding GOSIP technical information.

In Section 27.1, we summarize the announcement section. In Section 27.2, we examine the GOSIP technical requirements. Interoperability in a profile requires some of the OSI objects to be registered and assigned unique names. In Section 27.4, we identify the US GOSIP objects. While FIPS 146 laid out the ground rules for the sake of procurement, procedures are needed to check whether a product conforms to the GOSIP specification. NISTR 4595, known as GOSIP Conformance and Interoperation Testing and Registration, contains guidelines for agencies wishing to specify testing requirements for GOSIP acquisitions. Some of these guidelines are described in Section 27.4.

27.1   FIPS 146:   Announcement Section

The following summarizes the key issues in the announcement section.

* **applicability**

After August 15, 1990, GOSIP 1.0 must be used by all government agencies in the procurements of network communication functionalities that can be supported by GOSIP. This applies not only to new networking systems, but also to expansion of existing non-GOSIP networks. The communication must be host to host rather than terminal to host. Consider the following four implications of the GOSIP mandate. First, since only FTAM and MHS are included in version 1.0, government agencies have to use GOSIP FTAM and GOSIP MHS whenever they consider file transfer and electronic mail applications. Second, if government agencies want to implement a new subnetwork before version 2.0 is mandated, they have to use either X.25, Ethernet, Token Bus, or Token Ring. Third, government agencies are permitted to buy network products whose functionalities are not supported by GOSIP for the indefinite future. So for example, they can procure proprietary products on EDI or RDA in the year of 1992 since EDI and RDA are not expected to be included in version 3.0 of GOSIP. Fourth, it is not necessary for the terminal-to-host configurations to be GOSIP compliant.

* **waivers**

In situations where compliance may adversely affect accomplishment, performance, or budget of the mission, the heads of the government agencies may apply for a waiver. A waiver is an exception from the mandatory requirement to purchase GOSIP compliant products. A waiver request submitted to NIST must specify the reasons as well as the length of time during which the waiver is to be in effect. It is granted only for a designated period of time and is reviewed regularly to determine continued validity. A notice for each waiver granted is sent to the Committee on Government Operations of House and the

Committee on Government Affairs of Senate, and published in the Federal Register. A copy of the waiver finding and all of its supporting documents is considered to be part of the procurement documentation and must be retained by the government agency.

*   **procurement steps**

Procurement regulations are developed by each government agency following the general regulations mandated by Congress and the Office of Management and Budget. One of the most important regulations, the Federal Acquisition Regulation, covers acquisition, leasing, rental property, and services. It also prescribes the policies and procedures for the selection process of a source or sources in competitive negotiations.

The GOSIP procurement procedure is outlined as follows. First, the "Mission Element Needs Statement" is outlined and accompanied by functional requirements which can be either network requirements, application requirements, or both. After determining that GOSIP does meet the functional requirements, the requirements are submitted to an **Acquisition Authority (AA)** which determines a procurement package. The AA structures procurements as open competition with negotiated acquisitions. The procurements also specify the tests involved. **NCSL (National Computer Systems Laboratory)** at NIST has established policy and procedures aimed at ensuring that procured data communication products adhere to the technical products referenced by GOSIP. These policy and procedures can be found in NISTR 4595. The Request for Proposal (RFP) sent out to bidders can reference NISTR 4595. Bidders or offerers must demonstrate compliance to the GOSIP requirements by test certification. Conformance testing shall be conducted by accredited test laboratories using accredited test methods. After the bids arrive, they are evaluated. The AA has the responsibility to determine if the required tests have been passed. The best and final offers are evaluated in accordance with the solicitation's evaluation criteria. An award is made to the offerer which offers the greatest value in terms of cost, performance, and possibly other factors.

To aid government agencies in their evaluation of bids, NIST developed guidelines on the evaluation of MHS and FTAM implementations. For example, FIPS 182, known as "Guidelines for the Evaluation of MHS Implementations", gives a rating to each MHS functionality. An agency can use FIPS 182 to assign an overall rating to an MHS implementation based on the vendor's claimed MHS functionalities.

GOSIP does not provide performance criteria. However, an AA must specify some performance related features and benchmarking criteria. Specifying performance requirements may not be easy. At the least, an AA may specify performance requirements for the principal operating environment of the end system.

27.2   FIPS 146:   Specifications Section

Figure 27.1 shows the architecture of version 2.0 of US GOSIP. Each layer may contain a range of protocol choices reflecting the different subnetwork technologies and the application protocols that ought to be supported within the government agencies. Most of these choices are based on the functional standards defined at OIW. At a few places, GOSIP imposed extra constraints to reflect the needs of the US Government. The architecture and constraints are examined below.

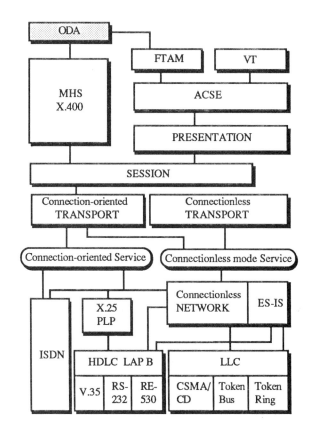

FIGURE 27.1   Version 2.0 Architecture of US GOSIP

*   **subnetwork technologies**

The subnetwork technology can be either a WAN or a LAN technology. The WAN technologies can be either X.25, point-to-point, or ISDN. The LAN technologies can be either Ethernet, Token Bus, or Token Ring. Version 3.0 of GOSIP may include FDDI as a LAN technology.

*   **Physical Layer**

GOSIP did not mandate any specific physical interface standard. However, an AA must specify Physical Layer requirements. The following interfaces are recommended:

- for X.25 technology: use RS-232-C for low rates up to 19.3 kbps, V.35 for rates between 19.2 kbps and 20 kbps, and RS-530 for higher rates.
- for LAN technologies: use the ISO 8802 OIW agreements.
- for ISDN technology: use either the Basic Rate Interface (two B channels at 64 kbps and one D channel at 16 kbps) or the Primary Rate Interface (twenty three B channels and one D channel).

- **Data Link Layer**

The following data link protocols along with the OIW agreements are mandatory:

- for point-to-point subnetworks and X.25: use HDLC LAP B.
- for ISO 8802 LAN: Use LLC Type 1.
- for ISDN: Use HDLC LAP D on the D channel and HDLC LAP B on the B channels.

- **connectionless network service**

CLNP per OIW agreement is mandatory. GOSIP requires the value of the lifetime parameter to be adjustable (recall that the lifetime parameter appears in the fixed part of the header of an IP datagram). It also specified the values and procedures for the use of the security parameter in an IP datagram. Furthermore, it required implementation for the calculation and verification of the checksum value in the IP header.

- **connection oriented network service**

CONS is an option for ESs directly connected to X.25 or ISDN. X.25 must be provided by X.25 PLP per ISO/IEC 8878 OIW agreement. For ISDN, control of B and D channels must be provided per ISO/IEC DIS 9574 plus OIW agreement.

A parameter has been identified to be used as needed for security reasons. This parameter, called the Reason for Discard parameter, appears in the Error Report PDU of CLNP. It consists of three parts: code, length, and values. The parameter code is assigned by ISO/IEC 8473. The parameter value is further divided into three subfields: security format code, basic portion, and extended portion. Only two bits of the security format code octet are described in ISO/IEC 8473. The remaining six bits are reserved and must be zero. The basic portion identifies the US classification level to which a PDU is to be protected. If the extended portion is required by an authority for a specific system, it must be specified explicitly in any RFP (i.e., Request For Proposal) for that system.

- **ISs**

An IS must operate in the connectionless mode unless it is connected to two X.25 subnetworks, in which case it operates in the connection oriented mode. For routing using

LAN or point-to-point technologies, an IS must support IS-ES routing per ISO/IEC 9542 and OIW agreement. For routing using WANs, the use of IS-ES is optional.

- **network addresses**

IDP		DSP							
AFI	IDI	DSP							
47	0005	DFI	Admin. Author.	Reserved	Routing Domain	Area	End System	NSel	
1	2	1	3	2	2	2	6	1	

FIGURE 27.2   GOSIP NSAP Address Structure

ISO 8348 AD2 subdivided an NSAP address into an IDP and a DSP. An IDP is further divided into an AFI and an IDI. The format of the DSP, as shown in Figure 27.2, is established by GSA. The DFI (i.e., DSP Format Identifier) which specifies the version of the DSP format has its current value equal to '80'H. The DSP format was examined earlier in Chapter 4 on Naming and Addressing. It suffices to note that AFI value of 47 (decimal) means that the IDI format is an ICD (ISO 6523) and the abstract syntax of the DSP is binary. The IDI value of '0005'H is used for US GOSIP. The AAI identifies the entity which is responsible for the organization of ISs and ESs into Routing Domains and Areas. GSA, which is responsible for assigning the AAI values, may assign a block of 256 values one at a time. The Reserved field which is used for expansion in the future has its current value equal to '00 00'H.

- **Transport Layer**

TP 4 per OIW agreement is a must while TP 0 is an option for use with MHS. CLTP is used if CLTS is to be provided. GOSIP mandated no direct access to the transport service.

- **Session Layer and Presentation Layer**

The session protocol (ISO/IEC 8327), the presentation protocol (ISO/IEC 8823), and ASN.1/BER (ISO/IEC 8824 and 8835) per OIW agreement are mandatory.

- **ACSE**

ACSE per OIW agreement is mandatory for use with all applications except the 1984 version of MHS which does not use ACSE. GOSIP required ACSE implementations to support the entry of AETs (i.e., application entity titles).

•   **MHS**

MHS is provided per X.400 (1984) and OIW agreement. In particular, this means that a conforming implementation will provide MTS and IPMS. All ESs on PRMDs must use TP4, must use TP0 over X.25 while communicating with ADMDs. An O/R address must support the country name, the ADMD name, the PRMD name, the organization name, the organization unit, and the personal name attributes. GSA is the Address Registration Authority for organization names. It delegates the authority to an organization to assign its own organization units. As a matter of fact, the organization name of an agency is registered automatically when an agency requests an AAI for its NSAP address. Country names and ADMD names are assigned by CCITT.

•   **FTAM**

ISO/IEC 8571 per OIW agreement is mandatory to fulfill the FTAM requirements. GOSIP used six document types. They are FTAM-1, FTAM-2, FTAM-3, NBS-6, NBS-7, and NBS-9. The use of these document types depends on whether an FTAM implementation is limited-purpose or full-purpose. A **limited-purpose FTAM system** must support at least the T1 (Simple File Transfer) and M1 (Management) implementation profiles defined at OIW. A **full-purpose FTAM system** must support at least the T2 (Positional File Transfer), A1 (Simple File Access), and M1 (Management) implementation profiles that are also defined at OIW. A short description of these profiles follows:

•   **T1 (Simple File Transfer)**: The purpose of this profile is to support the transfer of entire files with the unstructured constraint set. Document types FTAM-1 (i.e., unstructured text files) and FTAM-3 (i.e., unstructured binary files) must be supported. Support of NBS-9 (i.e., directory files) is optional.
•   **T2 (Positional File Transfer)**: T2 is basically an enhancement of T1 to include the transfer of files with the flat constraint set. T1 document types plus FTAM-2 (i.e., sequential flat text files), NBS-6 (i.e., sequential flat files), and NBS-7 (i.e., sequential ordered flat files) must be supported.
•   **A1 (Simple File Access)**: This allows locating or deleting FADUs to T2 document types.
•   **M1 (Management)**: This allows an initiator to manage remote files.

The AA must determine the requirements for each FTAM implementation in terms of initiator-sender, initiator-receiver, responder-sender, or responder-receiver. GOSIP recommended the use of AETs to identify FTAM users.

•   **VT**

Basic Class VT is provided per ISO/IEC 9041 and OIW agreement. Both simple and forms-capable VT systems are defined for procurement purposes. A **simple VT system** supports the OIW registered TELNET profile while a **forms-capable VT system** supports the OIW registered Forms profile.   All systems must support the "No Negotiation" option, i.e., the VTE-profile proposed by the initiating VT-user cannot be negotiated. Both simple and forms-capable systems must support the ASCII character set specified in ISO/IEC 646.

*   **ODA**

ODA is provided according to the specification in ISO/IEC 8613 plus OIW DAP (i.e., Document Application Profile). Each implementation should provide a mapping between the word processing/desktop publishing products and the ODA interchange. The transfer of ODA data streams can be achieved by either MHS or FTAM. With MHS, the IPM body part, encoded per OIW plus GOSIP, is used. And with FTAM, the FTAM-3 document type is used.

The major constraints of US GOSIP version 2.0 have been examined. Below is a list of the planned future GOSIP enhancements through version 4.0.

*   **Directory Services**

The DS standard is currently not included in version 2.0 of GOSIP since the OIW DS implementation agreements are not very stable. However, it is scheduled for version 3.0. The following capabilities are identified to be contained in version 3.0: name to data record mapping, host name to NSAP mapping, service name to T-selector, S-selector and P-selector mapping, inclusion of a host's capabilities, and security information about Directory service users.

*   **FTAM extensions**

The following FTAM extensions are considered to be in version 3.0: more document types, error recovery and restart capabilities, overlapped access and full concurrency control, full file transfer and full file access, and file directory service capability.

*   **MHS extension**

MHS extensions for version 3.0 will be based on the 1988 MHS standard.

*   **VT extension**

VT extensions for version 3.0 are expected to include the X3, Scroll, and Page profiles.

Other possible candidates for inclusion in version 3.0 are FDDI, IS-IS routing, CGM and SGML for ODA, Network Management, and security enhancements. Version

4.0 of GOSIP may include TP, RDA, EDI, and perhaps additional security enhancements and network management functions.

27.3   GOSIP Registration Issues

Registration of certain OSI objects is important to provide unique identification in a GOSIP environment. There are two basic issues in registration. What are the OSI objects to register and how are they registered?

GOSIP identified two categories of objects to be registered. Objects in the first category consist of NSAP AAIs (i.e., administration authority identifiers) and MHS PRMD names. Objects in the second category are technical objects that are normally defined and registered by standards groups or implementation workshops. They include FTAM document type names, message body parts, VT profiles, and control objects. Besides objects in these two categories, there are other objects such as application contexts, application entity titles, abstract syntaxes, managed objects, and relative distinguished names. These objects should be registered by government agencies when there are agency specific requirements for defining these objects.

Let us consider registration of objects in the first category. The objects here are AAIs and PRMD names. Registration of NSAP addresses boils down to registration of AAIs. GSA has been delegated by NIST to be the registration authority for AAIs under {iso(1) identified-organization(3) ICD(5)}.

NIST has also delegated GSA the authority to assign values for PRMD names. The organization name of an agency is registered automatically when the agency requests an AAI from GSA. It is recommended that a PRMD name have the syntax GOV + Name, where Name is the name of the government agency to be registered. For example, GOV + DOE is a valid PRMD name.

In some cases, the ADMD attribute may not appear in an O/R name. This is the case when a PRMD is connected to another PRMD under a bilateral agreement. In this case, the PRMD name becomes the top level name under the country name US. Registration of such a PRMD name with GSA may not make this PRMD name unique in the US. To make it unique, a government agency should register the name with ANSI.

Finally there is the situation where a PRMD is attached to multiple ADMDs. Making such a PRMD unique under a broader context in this situation would require some joint agreements among the ADMDs. As of now, there is no final resolution on this issue.

Objects in the second category are technical objects which are application specific and are normally registered by standard groups or implementation workshops. NIST has delegated GSA the authority to assign values to these technical objects under {iso(1) member-body(2) US(840) GOV(101) technical objects(0)}. Note that the numeric code of "101" for the US Government was assigned by ANSI, and the numeric code of 840 for the US was assigned according to ISO 3166 (Codes for the Representation of Names of Countries).

Technical objects include FTAM document type names, private message body parts, VT profiles, etc. Both the standards group or the implementation workshops have defined and registered a number of common and useful technical objects. Thus, registration of the technical objects other than the common ones is rare, although possible. Under special circumstances, a government agency can register a technical object with GSA. It is, however, encouraged that the government agencies should try to use the existing technical objects.

The GSA GOSIP Registration Services Document provides information on the registration procedures.

27.4 GOSIP Conformance and Interoperability Testing

This section describes how NIST helps government agencies and vendors in the testing of GOSIP compliant products. As far as government agencies are concerned, the most natural question to ask is: how can vendors' claims of GOSIP compliance be substantiated? To help answer this question, NIST established a GOSIP Testing Program in 1989. As far as vendors are concerned, the question to ask is: what is the GOSIP testing policy? NIST addressed this question by publishing NISTR 4594 which identified the policy, procedures, and testing mechanisms employed for GOSIP products. First we outline the GOSIP Testing Program, and then the GOSIP testing policy.

The objective **GOSIP Testing Program** is to identify the relevant ATSs (i.e., Abstract Test Suites) and MOTs (i.e., Means of Testing), establish a program to accredit laboratories, define the role of interoperability testing, and create a set of publicly accessible registers. Each aspect of the testing program is described next.

Since an ATS is the basis for evaluating MOTs and vendor products, the first priority is to identify the ATSs covering GOSIP functionality. This is not an easy task, considering the fact that an ATS may not cover all the functions in appropriate breadth and depth.

A MOT is a combination of hardware and software used to execute and evaluate test cases. In 1990, NIST announced an informal call for potential MOT suppliers. Each responding MOT supplier received the MOT Assessment Book which described the MOT assessment procedures. Three levels of merits within the GOSIP test program are defined.

GOSIP testing laboratories can be accredited through the **National Voluntary Accreditation Program (NVLAP)**. The accreditation procedures are described in a GOSIP Test Laboratory Accreditation Handbook. An accredited test laboratory must provide at least one or more MOTs qualified by NIST. Test Laboratories can be either first party (i.e., supplier of the product) or third party (i.e., an organization independent of the supplier of the product).

As far as interoperability testing is concerned, NIST identified two types of interoperability testing. The first type is based on the testing of a supplier product with a GOSIP Reference Implementation. The idea is that if the product can interoperate with the GOSIP Reference Implementation, then it is highly probable that the product can interoperate with other OSI products of similar nature. The second type of testing is bilateral testing of pairs of supplier products. NIST published interoperability test suites for FTAM and MHS (1984) covering the application functionalities of version 1.0 of GOSIP.

The public registers at NIST provide the key to the GOSIP Testing Program. Currently, the NIST Register maintains the following:

- abstract test suites,
- accredited test laboratories,
- assessed means of testings,
- interoperability test suites,
- GOSIP reference implementations,
- conformance tested GOSIP products, and
- successful interoperability testing with either reference implementations (if approved) provided by NIST or other supplier's products.

If a supplier claims GOSIP conformance for a product, then the product must be tested in accordance to the criteria described in NISTR 4594. If the test passes, it will be registered at NIST. Whenever a government agency requires validation of supplier claims of GOSIP conformance, it can consult the register of conformance tested GOSIP products.

Under NVLAP, NCSL published procedures to conduct GOSIP product testing. Any product claiming conformance to GOSIP must be tested in accordance with these procedures. Conformance testing should be conducted by accredited test laboratories using accredited MOTs. This leads to a certificate of conformance testing to be added to the register of conformance tested GOSIP products. Interoperability testing is done after conformance testing. Successful interoperability testing against a registered GOSIP reference entity also leads to an addition to the register of interworking GOSIP products.

NISTR 4594 described a framework for conformance testing and interoperability testing, and defined constraints for supporting profile testing and application profile testing. The remainder of this section examines NISTR 4594.

First we examine the testing framework. Whether it is conformance testing or interoperability testing, the following issues must be addressed: how should it be tested and what should be tested? The GOSIP conformance testing procedure is consistent with ISO/IEC 9646 which was described in Chapter 26. Therefore, only the GOSIP objects to be tested are addressed here. The GOSIP objects to be tested are basically profiles. A profile here is a consistent selection of protocols from the GOSIP architecture. Examples of GOSIP profiles from version 1.0 of GOSIP are given below:

- end system profiles:
  FTAM/ACSE/Presentation/Session/TP4/CLNP/LLC1/8802.3
  FTAM/ACSE/Presentation/Session/TP4/CLNP/X.25/HDLC/RS232C
  X.400/Session/TP4/LLC1/8802.3
  X.400/Session/TP0/X.25/HDLC/V.35
- application relay profiles:
  X.400/Session/TP4/8802.4

X.400/Session/TP0/X.25/HDLC/RS232C
- network layer profiles:
  CLNP/LLC1/8802.3
  CLNP/X.25/HDLC/RS232C

An IUT (i.e., implementation under test) supplied by a vendor is tested on one of the above profile objects. GOSIP conformance testing may be applied to the following types of IUTs:

- application stacks,
- application relay stacks,
- transport stacks,
- network stacks, and
- intermediate system stacks.

An important need in the GOSIP testing policy is to reduce the cost of testing. To achieve this, previously tested end systems substacks may be carried forward into larger substacks. To illustrate how this is done, we consider how conformance testing of the FTAM/ACSE/Presentation/Session/TP4/CLNP/LLC1/8802.4 profile is conducted. First, the LLC1/8802.4 is tested and an SCTR (i.e., system conformance test report) is produced. Then TP4/CLNP is tested over 8802.4. CLNP as well as TP4 may be tested separately by the coordinated single layer embedded means. If conformance to both protocols is passed, a second SCTR is produced. Finally, FTAM is offered for testing over TP4 with the second SCTR providing conformance to TP4, CLNP and 8802.4. Let us assume that the FTAM IUT contains embedded session, presentation, and ACSE functionalities. In this case, the Session Layer, the Presentation Layer, and ACSE are tested by the remote single layer embedded means for the FTAM responders, and by the distributed single layer embedded means for the FTAM initiators. If all the conformance tests are passed, a third SCTR is produced for the FTAM stack.

GOSIP interoperability testing may be applied to either an application stack or an intermediate system stack. In the case of application stacks, the two systems involved must be compatible. For example, an FTAM initiator should be tested with an FTAM responder. Therefore, before interoperability testing can take place, a static analysis must be executed to see if the two systems are compatible.

Next we examine the constraints for supporting profile testing and application profile testing. When conformance testing is performed on an application profile, it is done on an incremental basis starting from a supporting profile such as a transport profile. For each permissible supporting profile, NISTR 4594 identified configurations, characteristics of the MOT, and the associated test suite constraints. The test methods are those identified in ISO/IEC 9646. The common characteristics of a MOT include the capability to analyze PICS and PIXIT to select tests, the capability to monitor and initiate PDU exchanges, the capability to construct valid as well as invalid PDUs, the capability to produce conformance test reports, and the capability to record the PDUs exchanged in a conformance log.

The only application profiles supported by GOSIP version 1.0 are FTAM and MHS. If the application is an FTAM responder, the remote single-layer test method is used. If the application is an FTAM initiator, the distributed single-layer test method is used. For an MHS implementation with an embedded RTSE, either the distributed single-layer embedded RTSE test method, the distributed single-layer embedded P1 test method, or the distributed single-layer P2 test method can be used. Furthermore, P1 relay testing must be performed.

27.5 Summary

Different countries have different OSI profiles for their governments. US GOSIP, however, is the one of the few that is mandated for the government agencies. The first version of US GOSIP took effect on August 15, 1990. It contains two sections: the announcement section and the specifications section. The announcement section contains information about GOSIP objectives, applicability, waiver process, and procurement steps. The specifications section contains the technical description. It is characterized by the use of the CLNP in the Network Layer, and MHS (1984) and FTAM in the Application Layer. In this chapter, we examined the architecture of version 2.0 GOSIP and possible extensions through version 4.0.

While the standards bodies and the OSI implementation groups define OSI objects, the users in a community must register the objects they need for meaningful communication within the community. For version 1.0 of GOSIP, the most important objects for government agencies to register are NSAP addresses and MHS organization names. Both are registered with GSA. FTAM document type names may be registered whenever needed.

Also described in this chapter is the GOSIP Testing Program, a program in NIST to help government agencies and vendors in the testing of GOSIP compliant products. This program provides public registers to maintain abstract test suites, names of accredited test laboratories, interoperability test suites, conformance tested GOSIP products, and successful interoperability test results.

Related Standards & References

ISO 3166: Codes for the Representation of Names of Countries

ISO 6523: Structure for the Identification of Organizations

ISO 8348 AD2: Information Processing Systems - Data Communications - Network Service Definition - Addendum 2: Network Layer Addressing

FIPS 146, Government Open Systems Interconnection Profile (GOSIP), Version 1.0, National Institute of Standards and Technology, 1989

GOSIP User Guide, National Institute of Standards and Technology, 1989

The US GOSIP Testing Program, National Institute for Standards and Technology

GOSIP Conformance and Interoperation Testing and Registration, NISTR 4594, National Institute of Standards and Technology

Means of Testing Assessment Handbook, GOSIP Testing Program, National Institute of Standards and Technology

Operational Requirements of the Laboratory Accreditation Program for GOSIP Conformance Testing, National Institute of Standards and Technology

Message Handling Systems Evaluation Guidelines, National Institute of Standards and Technology

Stable Implementation Agreements for Open Systems Interconnection Protocols, Version 3 Edition 1, National Institute for Standards and Technology

US GOSIP Registration Services, Instructions to Applicants, GSA, Office of Telecommunications Services

28

Open Distributed Processing

In distributed processing, discrete components of the overall processing activities may be distributed in more than one system. **Open Distributed Processing (ODP)** serves to extend the OSI concept of "openness" from communication to distributed processing. It characterizes systems whose components, if designed to conform to ODP standards, can interoperate with other systems. There will be multi-vendor interoperability of distributed applications, extending multi-vendor interoperability of OSI communication software.

The work item on ODP, announced in 1987, was assigned to ISO/IEC SC21 WG7. The goals of this work group is to create an **ODP Reference Model** which serves to:

- model distributed processing in terms of functional components,
- identify levels of abstractions at which services can be described,
- classify the boundaries between components,
- identify the generic functions performed by distributed systems, and
- show how the elements of the model can be combined to achieve ODP.

Shortly after the ISO started the work on ODP, CCITT initiated the study question on a **Framework for Distributed Applications (DAF)**. Work on the DAF has been carried in cooperation with ISO's ODP from the start.

The structure of the ODP Reference Model is divided into five parts:

- Part 1: This part gives an overview of ODP, which provides both the scoping and the explanation of key definitions.
- Part 2: Known as the **Descriptive Model**, this part introduces concepts and notations for the description of distributed processing systems.
- Part 3: Known as the **Prescriptive Model**, this part contains the specification of required constraints that qualify distributed processing to be open.
- Part 4: This part contains a description of the ODP environment from the users' point of view.
- Part 5: This part attempts to use formal FDTs (i.e., formal description techniques) to formalize the concepts in Part 2.

Most of the preparatory work on Parts 2 and 3 has been done.

In Section 28.1, we introduce a few ODP architectural concepts. In Section 28.2, we explain aspects and views. Aspects correspond to components of a distributed system, while views correspond to ways of approaching an aspect. Aspects together with views provide a framework for ODP. Once the framework is in place, ODP standards can be specified for the various components. In Section 28.3, we examine two components: remote procedure call and trading. Almost all the existing distributed applications are built on top of these two services. In Section 28.4, we examine DCE, a distributed processing model by OSF.

28.1   ODP Architectural Concepts

ODP architectural concepts are used to build a distributed system, hence they are more specialized than the general modelling concepts presented in Section 3.2. Transparency, behavior, and organizational concepts are described below. The ODP standard also introduced naming, management, and security concepts.

- **transparency concepts**

Perhaps the most important requirement of a distributed system software is the hiding of the distributive nature of the system from its users. A user in a distributed system needs not know where an object is located (**location transparency**), when an object changes its location (**migration transparency**), and the address structure of an object being accessed (**address transparency**). Other kinds of transparency include:

- **configuration transparency**: This is used to hide from a user the way an object being accessed is configured.
- **replication transparency**: This is used to hide from a user the existence of replicas of an object.
- **fault transparency**: This is used to hide from a user any fault occurrences in the system.

- **concurrency transparency**: This is used to hide from a user the existence of concurrency in the system.
- **access transparency**: This is used to hide from a user the way access actually takes place.

Mechanisms to provide the above transparencies may introduce transparency related objects in between the users and the distributed system.

- **behavior concepts**

There are two interesting behavior concepts: liaison and casuality. A **liason** is a binding that specifies some common context among a set of cooperating objects. An OSI application association is an example of a liaison between two application entities. A dialogue between two TPSUs (i.e., transaction processing service users) is another example of a liaison. The ODP standard differentiates between contractual liaisons and engagement liaisons. A **contractual liaison** delimits the period of a contract. For example, a dialogue used in Transaction Processing is a contractual liaison between two TPSUs. An **engagement liaison**, which is defined relative to a contractual liaison, delimits the period of an active communication. An application association is an example of an engagement liaison. Since a contract may span more than one period of active communication because of communication failures, a contractual liaison can contain multiple engagement liaisons.

     Casuality is a constraint to which the behavior of each of the cooperating objects in the distributed system must conform during the interaction. It can be specified by a cause and effect relationship. In particular, it specifies the role of a cooperating object. Here are some examples of roles. An **initiating object** is an object which causes communication to take place. A **responding object** is an object which participates in a communication. A **producer object** is an object which is the source of information conveyed during communication. A **consumer object** is an object which is the sink of the information during communication. A **client object** is an object which requests some function to be performed by another object. Finally, a **server object** is an object which performs some functions as a result of requests from a client object.

- **organizational concepts**

A useful concept here is the notion of a domain. A domain refers to a set of objects managed by the same organization. We have seen the use of domains in MHS (e.g., PRMDs), Directory Services (e.g., DMDs), and routing standards (e.g., routing domains) in this text. Domains can be generalized to include non-OSI objects. An **X-domain** is a set of controlled ODP objects which is related to some controlling object via some relationship X. For example, X can be "OSI management". The idea is that the controlled objects in an X-domain are administered by a controlling object under a common administration policy. A controlling object needs not be a member of the X-domain.

28.2　Views and Aspects

An **aspect** is a logical grouping of the functional requirements of a distributed system. Each aspect can be viewed as a modular component of a distributed system. The current ODP work has identified seven different aspects. Thus an ODP system can be refined into seven objects, one for each aspect. If any such object needs to be distributed, it can be refined further into seven subobjects. These seven aspects are :

- **storage**: This aspect is concerned with the structures and functions for the retention of information in an ODP system .
- **process**: This aspect is concerned with the information processing operations of an ODP system.
- **user access**: This aspect is concerned with the presentation of information from/to an ODP system.
- **separation**: This aspect enables the separation of objects in an ODP system.
- **identification**: This aspect is concerned with the naming and addressing of objects in an ODP system.
- **management**: This aspect is concerned with the management of ODP resources.
- **security**: This aspect is concerned with the provision of security services to an ODP system.

Of the seven aspects above, the first three may require distribution while the last four support distribution.

Each aspect of an ODP system can be viewed in different ways, depending on who is viewing it. The ODP standard introduced five different viewpoints. Each **viewpoint** leads to a representation or an abstraction of an aspect of the system with emphasis on a particular set of concerns. In this way, we do not need to build a huge model incorporating every possible viewpoint. Instead, we only need to build a model for each viewpoint of an aspect. The five viewpoints are:

- **Enterprise viewpoint** (why?): This viewpoint focuses on the functional requirements which an enterprise places on its information systems. It is concerned with rules and policies for business and management, and human user roles with respect to the ODP system and their environment. It provides members of an enterprise with a description showing how and where the system is placed within the enterprise.
- **Information viewpoint** (what?): This viewpoint is concerned with the information requirements of the enterprise in terms of conceptual groupings of information elements, the relationship rules between the groupings, the information flows between sources and sinks, and the logical partitions of the information.
- **computational viewpoint** (how to do?): This viewpoint is concerned with the data structures that represent information and the algorithms that automate the information processing functions. Application developers use this viewpoint to specify an abstract service model to detail the information exchanges. The abstract service

model can be described using abstract operations. Invocations and replies of these operations essentially mark the significant events of an activity in a distributed system.

• **engineering viewpoint** (how to support?): This viewpoint is concerned with a realization of the computation model. Here we find mechanisms used to support the abstract service model in the computation viewpoint. It also includes mechanisms to provide the various forms of transparency that are assumed in the computation view.

• **technology viewpoint** (build or select?): This viewpoint is concerned with the details of the components and the links from which the distributed system is constructed. A designer uses this viewpoint to select or build ODP products.

The above viewpoints can be seen as a top-down approach, starting from the enterprise viewpoint which is mainly concerned with functional requirements to the technology viewpoint which is used to support the abstract viewpoints at a concrete level.

These viewpoints can be used to describe not only an ODP system but also any system or application. Applying the above viewpoints to describe an OSI application, we can see that the enterprise viewpoint corresponds to the OSI users' requirements (e.g., the OSI management functional areas), the information viewpoint corresponds to the OSI information models (e.g., the FTAM virtual filestore, the Directory Information Model, and the Management Information Model), the computation viewpoint corresponds to the abstract service specifications, the engineering viewpoint corresponds to the OSI application protocols, and the technology viewpoint corresponds to the OSI vendors' products.

Since each aspect of an ODP system can be described using any one of the viewpoints, there are as many as thirty-five steps in the design of an ODP system. Because of the interdependencies of some of the aspects (e.g., the process and storage aspects are very tightly coupled with each other), some of the steps can be designed simultaneously. The following suggests a possible logical sequence in the design of an ODP system. First, all the aspects should be examined from the enterprise viewpoint to get an overall idea of the users' requirements. The process and storage aspects can be examined together because of their tight coupling. Each one of them can be examined first from the information viewpoint, then the computation viewpoint, and finally the engineering viewpoint. The user access aspect is examined next to find out the presentation constraint. The remaining four aspects to examine are the aspects that enable distribution. They can be examined in the following order: identification, distribution, management, and security. After the above steps are completed, we then examine the aspects from the technology viewpoint to determine what products are available in the market to meet the requirements of the engineering viewpoint.

To illustrate the above steps, we will give the computational and the engineering viewpoints of each aspect.

Assuming an information model is in place, application developers use the computational viewpoint to specify abstract operations that can manipulate the information in the information model. Operations used in the computation viewpoint of each aspect are examined next:

- storage: Treating a storage as an information container, the computational view would provide operations to create/destroy objects in the storage and read/write attributes of objects in the storage.
- process: Processes can interact asynchronously or synchronously with each other. Assuming an information model such as a process precedence graph, the computational view would provide operations for process synchronization and transactions.
- user access: Given an information structure of a dialogue, the computational view would provide operations to control the style of the dialogues (such as character-based styles, graphic-based styles, or query-based styles) between users and applications.
- separation: The computational view would provide operations to control the mode of interaction (such as connection oriented and connectionless) among a set of interacting objects.
- identification: Assuming the use of some dictionary in the information model, the computational model would provide a directory interface to allow the registration for ODP objects.
- management: The computational model would provide operations for management monitoring, control, and reporting.
- security: The computational model would provide access control and authentication operations to control the use of resources in an ODP system.

Once the computational models are formulated, engineering models to provide mechanisms for the abstract services can be pursued as follows:

- storage: From the engineering viewpoint, the physical storage containers are visible. The engineering viewpoint would provide mechanisms to supply reliable containers, to cache frequently used data, to replicate data at more than one container, and to map data between the logical form and the physical form.
- process: The engineering viewpoint would provide process synchronization mechanisms, concurrency control mechanisms, recovery mechanisms, as well as mechanisms to schedule processes to run on different processors.
- user access: The engineering viewpoint would provide mechanisms such as X-Windows and Virtual Terminal.
- separation: The engineering viewpoint would provide transparency mechanisms such as the use of RPC.
- identification: The engineering viewpoint would provide mechanisms for name resolution, name registration, and maintenance of naming database systems.
- management: The engineering viewpoint would provide mechanisms to generate and exchange management information.
- security: The engineering viewpoint would provide security mechanisms to provide security services.

As the enterprise viewpoint is defined according to the needs of an enterprise, it is outside the scope of ODP standardization. The information viewpoint has not received too much attention because some of the information flows do not have to be automated. Thus the ODP Reference Model does not specify any constraint on the enterprise and the information viewpoints. Choosing a common computational model would give a consistent computational view of the different aspects of an ODP system. Standardizing the mechanisms used in the engineering models is useful so that different vendors can interoperate with each other using a common mechanism. Thus the computational and the engineering viewpoints would probably receive the most attention in the ongoing work of ODP.

28.3   Evolving ODP Supporting Standards

The last section described the ODP framework. Once the architecture is in place, the next step is to define standards for the components called for by the computational and the engineering viewpoints. For example, standards are needed to provide transparencies and security mechanisms. This section explains two ongoing ODP standards: remote procedure call and trader. Both standards are primarily used to provide transparency.

28.3.1   Remote Procedure Call

RPC extends the local procedure call to a distributed environment. In a RPC, a process can invoke a remote procedure as if it were invoking a local procedure. By hiding the communication details from the invoking process, RPC promotes applications portability.

RPC is extremely useful for distributed applications. For example, a client application involving a computationally complex procedure can use RPC to have that procedure run on a remote high speed computer. This will improve the throughput of the application dramatically.

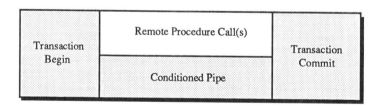

FIGURE 28.1   RPC used with TP

Since RPC only defines a style of interaction, it can be combined with any OSI application standard which leaves the data transfer facilities open to the users. For example, it can be used with the OSI Transaction Processing standard. Since TP does not provide a method for transferring data, it is up to a TP application to determine its own style of data transfer. Figure 28.1 shows how RPCs can run within a transaction envelope. Figure 28.2 shows how RPC primitives can be mixed with TP primitives in a TP application.

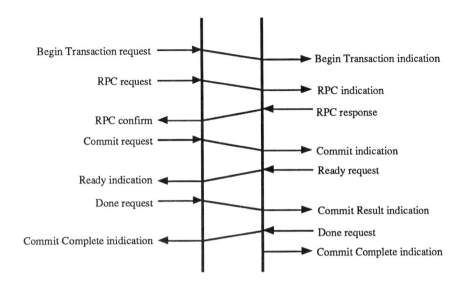

FIGURE 28.2 RPC Primitives mixed with TP Primitives

The RPC standard specified a RPC computational model and a RPC engineering model. The RPC computational model describes the style of program interaction, while the RPC engineering model describes the protocol used to support the RPC computational model. First we describe the RPC computational model. RPC is based on a client-server model. Figure 28.3 shows how RPC works. The steps are described below:

• step 1: The client invokes a local procedure called a **client stub** on the local machine. The purpose of the stub is to "marshall" (i.e., package up) the arguments to the remote procedure and then build one or more network messages.
• step 2: The client stub transmits the network message(s) to the underlying communication platform (e..g., an OSI platform) and waits for a reply from the server.
• step 3: The local communication platform transfers the messages to the communications platform of a remote server system.
• step 4: Upon arriving at the remote communication platform, the network messages are passed to a server stub.
• step 5: The **server stub** "unmarshalls" the arguments from the network messages and calls the server.
• step 6: After the server executes the procedure, it returns the result to the server stub.
• step 7: The server stub marshalls the result and sends it to the underlying communication platform.
• step 8: The server system sends the result messages to the client system.
• step 9: Upon receiving the result messages, the communication platform on the client machine passes the messages to the client stub.
• step 10: The client gets the result.

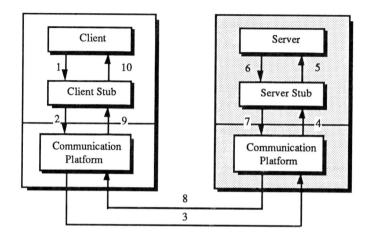

FIGURE 28.3   RPC Flow Control

With the use of RPC, there is a question as to the number of times a remote procedure was executed. If the server crashed before being called by the server stub, then nothing is executed. If it crashed after control is returned to the server stub, then the remote procedure is executed exactly once. In some cases, the client system might have timed out and retransmitted the request to the server system. It is conceivable then that the remote procedure might have been executed more than once as a result. If the result of executing a remote operation once is the same as the result of executing the remote operation more than once, we say that the operation is **idempotent**. For example, setting a variable to a constant is an idempotent operation, and adding a constant to a variable is a non-idempotent operation. As a result of the confusion over the number of times a remote operation is executed, three different kinds of RPC semantics are defined. They are:

- **at most once semantics**: This means that the RPC software has to guarantee that the remote procedure is either never executed or executed once. An implementation would require the server to keep track of the invocation identifiers of all the procedures it has previously executed in order to avoid duplicate execution. This semantics is adopted by the first release of the RPC standard.
- **exactly once semantics**: This means that the RPC software guarantees that the remote procedure is executed exactly once. Because of network and server failures, this semantics is hard to achieve.
- **at least once semantics**: Also called the idempotent semantics, this semantics means that the RPC software guarantees that the remote procedure is executed at least once. This semantics is fine if the remote operation is idempotent. At least once semantics is the easiest to implement. The client simply keeps on calling until a result or error is received.

The design of the client or the server stub only depends on the interface between the client and the server. It certainly does not depend on how the remote procedure is implemented or the context in which the client makes the call. The interface between the client and the server declares all the procedures used together with the numbers and the types of their arguments. They are specified in an **Interface Definition Notation (IDN)**. An IDN, which is a data declaration language, provides most of the basic data types and data structuring facilities. As part of a RPC run-time library, an IDN compiler takes an interface definition as input. From the interface definition, the compiler generates a client stub and a server stub. The client stub is linked to the client program which calls the remote procedure, and the server stub is linked to the server program which implements the remote procedure.

A RPC run-time library also provides routines to create and manage RPC handles. When a client makes a RPC, the RPC run-time library needs the following information: the object on which the operation is to be performed and the location of the server that exports the interface containing the operation. The information about the object and the server's location is represented in a **RPC handle**. Routines are provided by a RPC run-time library to create and manage RPC handles. Once created, a handle always represents the same object although it may be bound to different servers at different times, or it may not be bound to any server at all. If the handle is bound to a server, the RPC run-time library can send the message directly to the server. If the handle is not bound to a server, the RPC run-time library may try to send the request to all the hosts in the network, hoping that some server that exports the requested interface and supports the requested object will respond. A handle can be bound to a host but does not identify a particular server that exports the requested interface. In this case, the request goes to that host and will rely on some local directory service to identify a particular server exporting the requested interface.

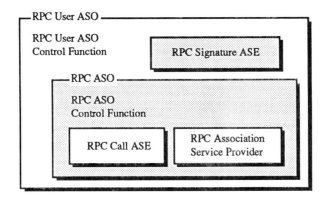

FIGURE 28.4   Seven RPC Components

Next, we describe the RPC computational model. The material here is taken from a working draft of the RPC standard. This RPC standard may be the first standard which uses the extended ALS concepts. It defined seven components to perform remote procedure calls. They are the RPC Call ASE, the RPC Association Service Provider, the

RPC ASO and its control function, the RPC Signature ASE, and the RPC User ASO and its control function (Figure 28.4). These seven components are explained next.

The RPC Call ASE provides the generic RPC service, allowing peer entities to make remote procedure calls and to cancel outstanding remote procedure calls.

The RPC Association Service is used to maintain the association between the client and the server. For example, this service can be provided by ACSE.

The RPC ASO contains those Application Layer components which are involved in the manipulation and use of the underlying communications channels to provide the generic RPC service. At the minimum, it contains the RPC Call ASE, a RPC Association Service Provider, and a control function to coordinate the information flow between these components and the user of the ASO, i.e., the RPC User ASO. Figure 28.5 shows a situation where the RPC ASO also includes a Security Exchange ASE and a Directory ASE.

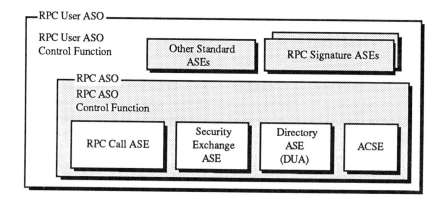

FIGURE 28.5   An Example of a RPC user ASO

The RPC Signature ASE is responsible for generating the interface definition specific portions of the RPC protocol.

The RPC User ASO provides a set of composite services required by a particular application. Besides containing the RPC ASO, it may contain some other ASEs (such as the VT ASE) and a control function to perform the mapping of the composite services to the individual services of components within.

We close our discussion in this section by briefly describing the service elements of the RPC Call ASE (Table 28.1). A client uses **RPC-INVOKE** to call a remote procedure. The permitted parameters include an operation-value, an argument, a cancel-flag, and an invocation-id. The operation-value parameter identifies a remote procedure. The cancel-flag parameter specifies if a cancel is pending. A server uses **RPC-RESULT** to return the input/output parameters at the end of the normal execution of the invoked procedure or to indicate that an error has occurred. **RPC-CANCEL** is used to cancel an outstanding RPC. Finally, **RPC-REJECT** is used by the RPC service provider to indicate to the users that an error has been detected.

It is conceivable that the above service elements can be mapped to ROSE service elements. For example, the RPC-INVOKE.request primitive is mapped onto the RO-INVOKE.request primitive. The cancel-flag and the argument parameters of the RPC-INVOKE.request primitive are concatenated and mapped to the argument parameter of the RO-INVOKE.request primitive.

Service	Type
RPC-BIND	Confirmed
RPC-UNBIND	Confirmed
RPC-INVOKE	Non-confirmed
RPC-RESULT	Non-confirmed
RPC-ERROR	Non-confirmed
RPC-CANCEL	Non-confirmed
RPC-REJECT	Provider-initiated

TABLE 28.1   RPC Services

28.3.2 Trading

Before a client can request a service from a server, it must first obtain a service reference that includes the location of a server in particular. With the service reference, the client can establish a binding with the server and start invoking services. The trading service provides the means for clients to obtain service references. In general, **trading** refers to the process of importing, exporting, and matching of proposals. In the following, we will explain some of the trading concepts and describe the computational model.

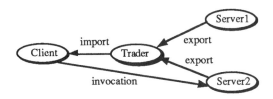

FIGURE 28.6   Trader

Consider Figure 28.6 where we have three objects interacting with each other: a client, a **trader** (also called **location broker**), and one or more servers. The client plays the role of an **importer** which makes a proposal to use some particular service, the server plays the role of an **exporter** which makes a proposal to provide some particular service, and the trader performs activities pertaining to imports and exports such as matching imports with exports. Both the client and the server are users of the trading service.

A server which wants to export some service must register a service type with a trader. A service type specification must include the interaction signature that specifies the set of operations and their parameters, and the interaction structure that specifies any synchronization and concurrency constraints on the interaction. Along with the service type specification, the server may also include some access control information and a trading context name. Since a service type is the subject of importing and exporting, it is important that a formal service type specification exists for every service type and that both the client and the server have a common understanding of the ingredients of the service type specification. The service type specification may be expressed in an IDN. Hence IDNs are important to the standard groups on RPC as well as the standard groups on trading.

In order to use the trading service, a client must establish a binding with a trader first. After a binding is established, the client can send a request containing a service type to the trader. Some trading attributes such as quality of service may accompany the request. In general, there may be more than one server exporting the requested service type. The trader tries to match the request with the best available service in the environment based on the trading attribute information. If there is a match, the trader will return a service reference to the client. A service reference corresponds to a RPC context handle. With the returned service reference, the client can establish a binding directly with a specific server.

We can imagine that the trader maintains a conceptual trading information base which stores the exported service types. Each entry in this conceptual information base contains information about a service type object and locations of servers that export the particular service type. It is conceivable that the trader can make use of the OSI Directory Services to maintain such an information base. It would be useful to co-locate a trading object with a DSA object. Unlike the DIB which is designed to hold data that is to be accessed by different applications, the information base maintained by a trader may contain information that is not necessarily shared with any application. Thus independent naming trees, i.e., trees that do not all have a common root, are used by a trader.

28.3.3 An Example of a Distributed Application

A simple application is explained here as an example of a distributed application based on Network Computing Systems. The application generates grade reports for students who are taking a particular course. The application is divided into 3 modules: a client, a server, and an interface definition. The server runs on the Professor's machine which maintains a grade file. The client module can be invoked from any host on the network. The client program gets the student's id number from the student and calls the show_grade() procedure which runs on the server's host. The show_grade() procedure then looks up the grade file and gets the grade corresponding to the student's id_number. The grade is returned to the client and the client displays it on the screen.

```
%c
[ uuid(4880fe5a1000.0d.00.02.18.e9.00.00.00), version(1) ]
interface gr   {
    const    int      GR_MAX_STRLEN = 128;
    typedef  [handle]  string0 [GR_MAX_STRLEN]        gr_string_t;
    void show_grade {
```

```
gr_string_t        [in]     id_num,
gr_string_t        [out]    grade_ptr
    };
}
```

The interface definition between the client and the server (grade.idl) is shown above. The %c indicates that the definition follows C syntax. The next line assigns a particular UUID (i.e., Universal Unique IDentifier) and the version number for the above interface. The procedure show_grade and its arguments and argument types are defined in the above interface definition. The compiler generates the client and server stub files and the header file "grade.h".

```
#include        <stdio.h>
#include        "grade.h"
main(argc,argv)
int  argc;
char            *argv[];
{
    int         status,ret_code;
    char        grade;
    if ( argc != 2 ) {
            fprintf(stderr,"usage: %s id#\n", argv[0]);
            return(1);
    }
    show_grade( argv[1], &grade );
    if ( grade != 0 ) {
            printf("Your grade is a %c\n",grade);
            ret_code = 0;
    } else {
            fprintf(stderr,"Could not find grade in grade file\n");
            ret_code = 1;
    }
}
```

The program shown above, client.c, is the client program which gets the student's id number from the command line and passes it as an argument to the procedure show_grade(). It displays either the student's grade or the error message on the screen.

```
#include        <stdio.h>
#include        "grade.h"
#define         GRADE_FILE    "grades.dat"
#define         NO                      0
#define         YES                     1
```

```
#define       ID_NUM_SIZE  3
void show_grade(id_num, grade_ptr)
char          *id_num;
char          *grade_ptr;
{
    FILE    *fp;
    char    tmp_id_num[ID_NUM_SIZE+1];
    int     done;
    done = NO;
    if ( fp = fopen(GRADE_FILE,"r")) != NULL ) {
    while (done == NO && fscanf(fp,"%s %c",tmp_id_num,grade_ptr) != EOF) {
            if ( strncmp(id_num,tmp_id_num,ID_NUM_SIZE) == 0 ) {
                    done = YES;
            }
    }
    fclose(fp);
    } else {
            fprintf(stderr,"Error : Cannot open file: %s\n",GRADE_FILE);
    }
    if ( done == NO )
            *grade_ptr = 0;
}
```

The above program, manager.c, implements the show_grade() procedure which runs on the server's host. It searches the GRADE_FILE for the grade of the id_number passed as its argument.

```
#include      <stdio.h>
#include      <lb.h>
#include      "grade.h"
#include      "socket.h"
extern uuid_$t uuid_$nil;
handle_t      gr_string_t_bind()
{
    status_$t           status;
    socket_$addr_t      address;
    unsigned long       address_length;
    lb_$entry_t         entry;
    unsigned long       no_entries_returned;
    lb_$lookup_interface (
            &gr_v1$if_spec.id,
            lb_$default_lookup_handle.
            (unsigned long) 1,
```

```
                &no_entries_returned,&entry,&status
    );
    address = entry.saddr;
    address_length = entry.saddr_len;
    return rpc_$bind(&uuid_$nil, &address, address_length, &status);
}
void gr_string_t_unbind( rpc_handle )
handle_t      rpc_handle;
{
    status_$t            status;
    rpc_$free_handle( rpc_handle, &status);
}
```

The above file bind.c is linked with the client module. It looks up the location broker to find out the socket address of the server and binds to the server and returns an rpc_handle. This handle is used by the client stub in communicating with the server. The routine gr_string_t_unbind() takes care of releasing the rpc_handle when the client's job is done.

```
#include      "grade.h"
#include      <pfm.h>
#include      "lb.h"
#include      "socket.h"
extern        uuid_$t uuid_$nil;
gr_v1$epv_t            gr_v1_manager_epv = {show_grade};
int main()
{
    status_$t                 status;
    pfm_$cleanup_rec          cleanup_record;
    socket_$addr_t    address;
    lb_$entry_t               lb_entry;
    unsigned long     address_length;
    rpc_$use_family (
            (unsigned long) socket_$internet,
            &address, &address_length, &status
    );
    rpc_$register_mgr (
            &uuid_$nil, &gr_v1$if_spec, gr_v1$server_epv,
            (rpc_$mgr_epv_t) &gr_v1_manager_epv, &status
    );
    lb_$register (
            &uuid_$nil,  &uuid_$nil, &gr_v1$if_spec.id,
            (lb_$server_flag_t) 0,
```

```
                    (unsigned char *) "Saravan's grade reporting program",
                    &address, address_length, &lb_entry, &status
          );
          pfm_$init( (unsigned long) pfm_$init_signal_handlers);
          status = pfm_$cleanup(cleanup_record);
          if ( status.all != pfm_$cleanup_set ) {
                    status_$t           u_status;
                    lb_$unregister(&lb_entry, &u_status);
                    rpc_$unregister(&gr_v1$if_spec, &u_status);
                    pfm_$signal(status);
          }
          rpc_$listen(1L, &status);
  }
```

The file server.c is linked with the server module which registers the interface with the location broker and listens to the socket assigned to this interface.

After compiling the interface definition grade.idl, the following files are produced: grade_cstub.c, grade_sstub.c, grade_cswtch.c, grade.h. To compile the client module, we do:

```
%cc -c -I/usr/include/idl/c client.c bind.c grade_cstub.c grade_cswtch.c
%cc -o client client.o bind.o grade_cstub.o grade_cswtch.o -lnck
```

And to compile the server module, we do:

```
%cc -c -I/usr/include/idl/c server.c manager.c grade_sstub.c
%cc -o server server.o manager.o grade_sstub.o -lnck
```

The server is run in background in any host which has the grades.dat file. When the server module is run in background in the host where the grades.dat file is kept, the server registers the interface show_grade with the Global location broker and listens to the socket assigned to it for any incoming rpc calls.

The client can be run from any other host on the network. For example:

```
% client
usage : client id#
% client 123
Your grade is a A.
```

The client calls the show_grade() procedure with 123 as argument. The client stub then calls the gr_string_t_bind() function to get an RPC handle for this call. The gr_string_t_bind in turn looks up the global location broker for the interface show_grade() and gets the socket address for the show_grade() interface. It then allocates and binds an RPC handle and returns that handle to the calling function. The client stub then passes the

handle returned by gr_string_t_bind() along with the marshalled parameters in its call to
NCK. Since the socket address of the server is found, it makes a RPC call to the server.
The server stub unmarshalls the parameters of the call and calls the show_grade() function
which in turn returns the grade corresponding to the student id_number. In the above case,
the grade "A" corresponding to the id_number 123 is returned.

28.4 Distributed Computing Environment

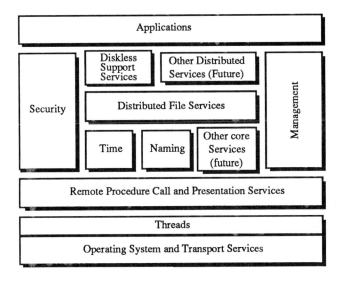

FIGURE 28.7   OSF/DCE Architecture

Although the ODP standard groups are still in the process of drafting the ODP architectural
standard, a few distributed processing models have been established by open systems
groups. In this section, we will review the **Distributed Computing Environment**
(DCE) by OSF (Figure 28.7). The objective of OSF/DCE is to provide a comprehensive
offering of fundamental services that support the development, the use, and the
maintenance of distributed applications. To satisfy this objective, OSF integrates a set of
mature technologies into an architecturally coherent system that provides a layer of logical
simplicity to hide the physical complexity of a distributed environment.

The notion of a **cell** is used in the DCE architecture. A cell is basically an
organizational unit of a distributed environment. It is a natural domain for naming,
security, and management. Different cells may have different levels of trust and different
administration policies. Multiple cells are integrated into a global context. Although both
intracell communication and intercell communication are possible, users do not see the
difference between the two.

Below we will describe each DCE component in more detail.

• **threads**

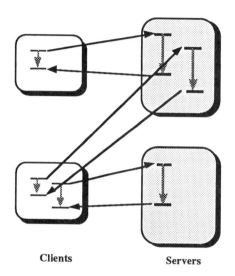

Clients   Servers

FIGURE 28.8   Multiple Threads

Threads, which were briefly mentioned in Chapter 25, support the development of distributed applications that can utilize the inherent computational parallelism. With threads, an application can be designed to be multi-threaded, where each thread is a single sequential flow of control within the application. Although it is possible to do the same thing with processes, threads impose less system overhead because all the threads within a process share the same address space. It is expected that threads will be included in the next generation operating systems. For the time being, DCE includes threads in its architecture in case the underlying operating system does not support threads. One peculiar property of DCE's threads is that even when a blocking system call is made by an application, the thread, but not the process, will block.

As Figure 28.7 shows, the support of threads is used by a number of DCE components: RPC, Security, Directory, Time, and Distributed File System. In RPC, for example, a client can use multiple threads to make RPCs to multiple servers, and a server can use multiple threads to service multiple clients (Figure 28.8).

• **remote procedure call**

DCE's RPC originated from Network Computing System. It allows application developers to choose one of the three semantics: at most once, at least once, and broadcast. The broadcast semantics, a special case of at least once semantics, specifies that an operation is to be broadcast to all hosts in a LAN.

DCE's RPC is made up of two components. The first component is the DCE **Interface Definition Language (IDL)** and its associated compiler. IDL is a high-level declarative language which is very similar to C. It imposes no limits on the number or the size of parameters to RPCs. The IDL compiler accepts an IDL interface definition as input and generates the client and the server stubs. The second component is a run-time facility that provides glues to the underlying communication service, the security service, and the naming service (Figure 28.9). DCE's RPC allows multiple transport protocols to be supported simultaneously on a system. The security service of the RPC run-time library works in conjunction with the Authentication run-time which implements the DCE security. Finally RPC can access the naming service to find out the address of a server and the network communication protocols required to access a server.

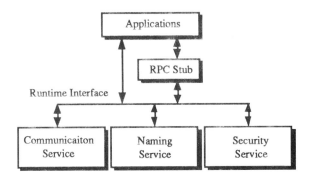

FIGURE 28.9   RPC Runtime Facility

DCE's RPC is also integrated with the DCE thread service. When a client makes a RPC, it initiates a calling thread in its local address space. RPC essentially extends this calling thread from the client's address space to the server's address space. The extension is a logical thread. After the remote procedure finishes executing, the logical thread returns any call results and releases control to the client's calling thread.

DCE's RPC resolves the data representation problem using the "receiver makes it right" scheme. All RPCs are tagged with a description of the calling machine's representation. A receiver would convert the data from the sender's representation to the receiver's representation only when the tag shows that the sending and receiving machines use different representations. Negotiations of transfer syntaxes is also supported.

• **naming service**

DCE uses two naming services: a Cell Directory Service (CDS) for intracell naming service and a Global Directory Service (GDS) for global naming service (Figure 28.10). An application program interfaces to both services using XDS.

GDS uses an integrated name space. Figure 28.11 shows that this integrated name space incorporates each individual cell name space. GDS is quite similar to the OSI Directory Services. It has caching, replication, and security capabilities. It is designed to cope with very large configurations. Transactions are used to update the naming database. This preserves integrity and minimizes startup time.

CDS offers support for caching and replication. Figure 28.12 shows a typical cell name space. As we can see, a cell name space provides naming for security principles, RPC handles, and file objects.

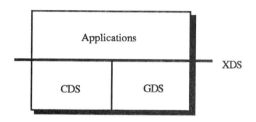

FIGURE 28.10   A Single Interface to CDS and GDS

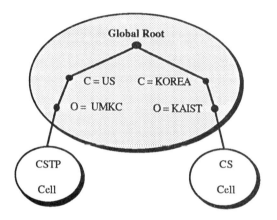

FIGURE 28.11   An Integrated Global Name Space

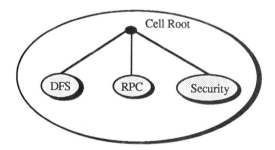

FIGURE 28.12   A Typical Cell Name Space

• **security**

The security component of DCE provides authentication service, integrity service, confidentiality service, and authorization service. This component is well integrated with the DCE's RPC component in the sense that the user only needs to specify the level of security service and the RPC software does all the dirty work of encryption and decryption.

Authentication is used to verify identity of principals within a cell. The authentication mechanism is based on the **Kerberos** approach taken from the Athena Project at MIT. Kerberos uses a secret (instead of public) cryptography. It works as follows. Suppose a client wants to make a RPC to a server. In the first place, both the client and the server need to obtain a secret key from a trusted third party called the ticket granting server. There is a secret key shared between the client and the ticket granting server, and another secret key shared between the server and the ticket granting server. We assume that these two keys are obtained in some out-of-band fashion. Next, the client makes a RPC to the ticket granting server, specifying the server from which it would want to request the service. The ticket granting service will return a session key and a session ticket to the client. Within the session ticket is a copy of the session key, but since the session ticket is encrypted with the server's shared key, the client has no idea of it. When the client makes a RPC to the server, it also sends the opaque session ticket together with an encryption of its own identity using the session key provided by the ticket granting server. After receiving the ticket, the server decrypts the session ticket and unveils the session key. It then uses the session key to unveil the identity of the client. This in a way proves the identity of the client because the session key can only be obtained from the ticket granting server which is assumed to be trusted by both the client and the server.

Data integrity is provided through DCE's RPC. RPC ensures data integrity using cryptographic data checksums. A sophisticated checksum algorithm prevents unauthorized individuals from altering the data and then updating the checksum.

Data confidentiality is also provided using RPC. Like authentication, it makes use of a trusted third party which is called the key distribution center. Somehow the client and the server obtain the same secret key from the key distribution server. No one else besides the client, the server, and the key distribution center would have any knowledge about the secret key. In this way, confidentiality is provided.

Once users are authenticated, they can request to have certain operation performed on a resource. DCE uses ACLs (i.e., access control lists) to control user access to a remote resource. ACLs are maintained with the resource. They are a superset of the ACLs specified by the POSIX 1003.6 ACL working group because the POSIX ACLs were designed to control user access to a single computer.

• **distributed time service**

Distributed applications need a single time reference to schedule events, to determine the ordering of events, to measure the duration of an event, and to time-stamp an event report. The goal of DCE's **Distributed Time Service (DTS)** is to synchronize the clocks of the computers in a distributed environment so that all systems have a time close to the Coordinated Universal Time (UTC), the "true" time. Distributed time in DTS is expressed as an interval rather a single value. The interval indicates an inaccuracy consideration. The midpoint of the interval represents the time value.

DTS is designed as a client-server system. The DTS clients are also called **clerks**. A clerk periodically issues a request for the required synchronization. During synchronization, it requests a few servers to send their time intervals. The received intervals are intersected to derive the clerk's new time and inaccuracy. If the clerk receives a time interval that does not intersect with the majority, the time interval is declared to be faulty. For example, the time interval received from C in Figure 28.13 is faulty. The clerk adjusts its time clock by changing the clock tick increment. For example, if it adjusts one time unit of an error in 60 time units, then a minute is required to correct a one second error.

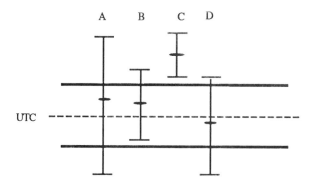

FIGURE 28.13   Time Intervals from Different Time Servers

A DTS server provides time to clerks and other servers. There are four types of servers. They are local servers, global servers, couriers, and time provider servers. A local server synchronizes with other local servers on a LAN, while a global server is available across a WAN. A courier is a local server synchronizing with global servers. A time provider server synchronizes with a UTC time provider. Clearly, a local server will try to synchronize with a time provider server if available.

- **distributed file system**

Some of the goals of DCE's **Distributed File System (DFS)** are uniform name space, good performance, and high availability.

As we saw earlier, DFS is integrated with the naming service. Every file has a name that is part of the global name space. A typical file name is of the form ./.../{cell name}/{intracell name}/fs/{DFS pathname}. Note that the name does not tell which host the file can be found although it does tell which cell the file can be located.

Good performance is provided by a cache manager running on the client's machine. Caching consistency is needed to ensure that each client can see changes that others are making to their cached copies. This can be achieved by means of **tokens**. A token is assigned to the client by the server when the client wants to cache data. Tokens are typed. For example, if a client wants to modify a cache entry, it must first obtain a "write" token from the server. The server must keep track of all the tokens that it has handed out. In this way, if part of a file changes, the server can notify the clients which hold copies of the data that their copies are no longer up to date by revoking their tokens. To minimize the number of server requests, the cache manager may try to pull large amounts of data when a file is opened.

Availability means that when the file server is in operation and available to users, the system administrators are still able to perform routine maintenance such as moving of disk data across file servers, backuping files, and checking file system consistency after a server crashes. DCE achieves high availability by many means. One means is replication when a fileset, which is a basic unit of replication in DFS, is moved from a primary server to a secondary server. The second means is the ability to backup a system without taking the system off line. The idea here is to create a replicated copy first and then back up the copy. Thus even if a user is changing the original file, the replicated file remains stable. The third means is to use a log to record all disk operations that occur between updates of housekeeping information (such as the size of unallocated disk areas). In this way, if the server crashes, only changes made to the disk since the last update are checked and reconstructed. This allows quick file server restarts.

- **distributed management environment**

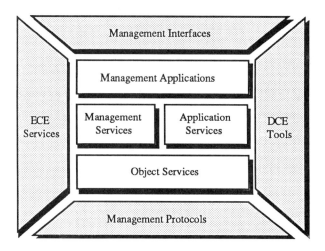

FIGURE 28.14   DME Framework

DCE's **Distributed Management Environment (DME)** is an attempt to unify the management of stand-alone and distributed systems. It wants to provide a consistent graphical user interface, and the ability to manage system resources and application services.

Figure 28.14 illustrates the DME architecture. At the very top is the manager user interface which provides a consistent interface to both system administrators and management application developers.

The application services component provides services such as license management, software management, printing, and host services.

Treating managed resources and management applications as objects, the object services component provides **management request brokers** to register and locate objects which are maintained in object servers. Furthermore, it provides event services which handle the forwarding of event notifications between systems, the filtering of events, and the subscription to specific events by management applications.

The management services component provides fundamental services for management applications such as defining management policy, structuring a large system into manageable domains, and assigning administrative roles to administrators. By isolating this component, the DME architecture does not prescribe any specific management model, but offers defaults, which may be customized locally.

Finally, the management protocols component is used to provide communication support for management applications. DME supports CMIP, SNMP (the management protocol used in the Internet), and a specific OSF management protocol based on DCE's RPC. DME also provides the Consolidated Management API which provides direct access to the above protocols.

28.5 Summary

ODP serves to extend the OSI concept of "openness" to distributed processing. It characterizes systems whose components, if designed to conform to ODP standards, can interoperate transparently with other systems.

The ODP standard identifies seven different aspects of an ODP system. Each aspect is a logical grouping of the functional requirements of a distributed system. These seven aspects are storage, process, user access, separation, identification, management, and security.

Each aspect can be viewed in five different ways. These five viewpoints are enterprise viewpoint, information viewpoint, computational viewpoint, engineering viewpoint, and technology viewpoint. Each viewpoint leads to a representation or an abstraction of an aspect of the system with emphasis on a particular set of concerns. The above viewpoints can be seen as a top-down approach, starting from the enterprise viewpoint which is mainly concerned with functional requirements to the technology viewpoint which is used to support the abstract viewpoints at a concrete level. The computational and engineering viewpoints would probably receive the most attention in the ongoing work of ODP.

Aspects and viewpoints together define the ODP framework. Once the architecture is in place, the next step is to define supporting standards giving the specifications of components called for by the computational and engineering viewpoints. In this chapter, we examine two evolving ODP standards, RPC and trading, both primarily used to provide transparency. The RPC services allow a process to call a remote procedure as if it were calling a local procedure. The trading services provide the function of maintaining knowledge of the services currently available and matching client requirements with suitable service offers.

Related Standards

CD 10746-2:　Information Technology - Basic Reference Model of Open Distributed Processing - Part 2: Descriptive Model

DIS 10148:　Information Technology - Basic Remote Procedure Call (RPC) using OSI Remote Operations

APPENDIX A: OSI Acronyms

AAA	Autonomous Administrative Area
AAI	Administration Authority Identifier
ACDF	Access Control Decision Function
ACIA	Access Control Inner Areas
ACID	Atomicity, Consistency, Isolation, and Durability
ACL	Access Control List
ACS	Access Control Store
ACSA	Access Control Specific Area
ACSE	Association Control Service Element
ACSP	Access Control Specific Point
AD	Addendum Document to an OSI standard
ADMD	Administrative Management Domain
AE	Application Entity
AEI	Application Entity Invocation
AF	Auxiliary Facility
AET	Application Entity Title
AFI	Authority and Format Identifier (NSAP)
ALS	Application Layer Structure
ALU	Application Layer User
ANSI	American National Standards Institute
AOW	Asian and Oceanic Workshop
AP	Application Process
APDU	Application Protocol Data Unit
API	Application Program Interface

APLI	ACSE/Presentation Library Interface
APP	Applications Portability Profile
APT	Application Process Title
ASC	Accredited Standard Committee
ASCII	American Standard Code for Information Interchange
ASDC	Abstract Service Definition Convention
ASE	Application Service Element
ASN.1	Abstract Syntax Notation One
ASO	Application Service Object
ASP	Abstract Service Primitive
ATM	Abstract Test Method
ATS	Abstract Test Suite
AU	Access Unit
AVA	Attribute Value Assertion
BACM	Basic Access Control Model
BAS	Basic Activity Subset
BCS	Basic Combined Subset
BCVT	Basic Class Virtual Terminal
BMU	Basic Measurement Unit
BSS	Basic Synchronization Subset
CA	Certification Authority
CAE	Common Applications Environment (X/Open)
CAF	Channel Auxiliary Facility
CASE	Common Application Service Elements
CCA	Conceptual Communication Area
CCITT	Comite Consultatif Internationale de Telegraphique et Telephonique
CCO	Context Control Object
CCR	Commitment, Concurrency & Recovery protocol
CD	Committee Draft
CDS	Conceptual Data Storage
CEI	Connection Endpoint Identifier
CEN/ELEC	Committee European de Normalization Electrotechnique
CF	Control Function
CGM	Computer Graphics Metafile
CHILL	CCITT High-Level Language
CIGOS	Canadian Interest Group on Open Systems
CIM	Computer Integrated Manufacturing
CLI	Connectionless Internetworking
CLNP	Connectionless Network Protocol
CLNS	Connectionless Network Service
CLTP	Connectionless Transport Protocol

CLTS	Connectionless Transport Service
CMIP	Common Management Information Protocol
CMISE	Common Management Information Service Element
CNMA	Communication Network for Manufacturing Applications
COI	Connection-oriented Internetworking
CONS	Connection-oriented Network Service
COS	Corporation for Open Systems
COTP	Connection-oriented Transport Protocol
COTS	Connection-oriented Transport Service
CSS	Control, Signalling, and Status Store
DACD	Directory Access Control Domain
DAD	Draft Addendum
DAF	Framework for Distributed Applications
DAP	Directory Access Protocol
DCC	Data Country Code
DCE	Distributed Computing Environment
DCS	Defined Context Set
DES	Data Encryption Standard
DFI	DSP Format Identifier
DIB	Directory Information Base
DIS	Draft International Standard
DISP	Draft International Standardized Profile
	Directory Information Shadowing Protocol
DIT	Directory Information Tree
DMD	Directory Management Domain
DMI	Definition of Management Information
DMO	Domain Management Organization
DN	Distinguished Name
DOP	Directory Operational Binding Management Protocol
DP	Draft Proposal
DS	Directory Services
DSA	Directory Service Agent
DSE	DSA specific Entries
DSP	Directory Service Protocol
DTE	Data Terminal Equipment
DU	Data Unit
DUA	Directory User Agent
EBCDIC	Extended BCD Interchange Code
ECMA	European Computer Manufacturers Association
ECO	Echo Control Object
EDI	Electronic Data Interchange

EDIFACT	EDI For Administration, Commerce and Transport
EDIM	EDI Message
EDIME	EDI Messaging Environment
EDIMS	EDI Messaging System
EDI-MS	EDI Message Store
EDIN	EDI Notification
EDI-UA	EDI - User Agent
EEI	External Environment Interface
EIT	Encoded Information Type
ES	End System
ESH	End System Hello
ES-IS	End System-Intermediate System
ESTELLE	Extended State Transition Language
EWOS	European Workshop on Open Systems (CEN)
FADU	File Access Data Unit
FDCO	Field Definition Control Object
FDR	Field Definition Record
FDT	Formal Description Technique
FEC	Field Entry Condition
FEE	Field Entry Event
FEI	Field Entry Instruction
FEICO	Field Entry Instruction Control Object
FEIR	Field Entry Instruction Record
FEPCO	Field Entry Pilot Control Object
FEPR	Field Entry Pilot Record
FER	Field Entry Reaction
FIPS	Federal Information Processing Standard
FOD	Office Document Format
FSG	SGML Interchange Format
FSM	Finite State Machine
FTAM	File Transfer Access and Management
GDMO	Guidelines for the Definition of Managed Objects
GFI	General Format Indicator
GOSIP	Government OSI Profile
GSA	General Services Administration
HDLC	High level Data Link Control
IA5	International Alphabet number 5
IAP	Inner Administrative Point
ICD	International Code Designator

ICI	Interface Control Information
ICV	Integrity Check Value
IDI	Initial Domain Identifier
IDN	Interface Definition Notation
IDP	Initial Domain Part
IDU	Interface Data Unit
IEC	International Electrotechnical Commission
IEEE	Institute of Electrical and Electronics Engineers
IMIL	International Managed Information Library
INTAP	Interoperability Technology Association for Information Processing
IONL	Internal Organization of Network Layer
IPC	Interprocess Communication
IPI	Initial Protocol Identifier
IPICS	ISP Implementation Conformance Statement
IPM	Interpersonal Message
IPM-UA	Interpersonal Messaging User Agent
IPMS	Interpersonal Messaging System
IPN	Interpersonal Notification
IS	International Standard
	Intermediate System
ISAM	Index-Sequential Access Method
ISH	Intermediate System Hello
IS-IS	Intermediate System-to-Intermediate System
ISO	International Organization for Standardization
ISODE	ISO Development Environment
ISP	International Standard Profile
ISPSN	Initial Synchronization Point serial Number
IT	Information Technology
ITU	International Telecommunications Union
IUT	Implementation Under Test
IWU	Interworking Unit
LAN	Local Area Network
LAP	Link Access Procedure
LCF	Log Control Function
LCN	Logical Channel Number
LLC	Logical Link Control
LOTOS	Language of Temporal Ordering Specifications
LSE	Local System Environment
MAC	Media Access Control
MACF	Multiple Association Control Function
MAP	Manufacturing Automation Profile

MFA	Management Functional Areas
MH	Message Handling Package
MHS	Message Handling System
MIB	Management Information Base
MIM	Management Information Model
MIN	Multiple Interaction Negotiation
MIT	Managed Information Tree
MMI	Man Machine Interface
MMS	Manufacturing Message Specification
MOTIS	Message Oriented Text Interchange System
MOT	Means of Testing
MS	Message Store
MTA	Message Transfer Agent
MTS	Message Transfer System
MTSE	Message Transfer Service Element
NC	Numerical Controller
NIST	National Institute of Standards and Technology
NM	Network Management
NRN	Non-receipt Notification
NSAP	Network Service Access Point
NVLAP	National Voluntary Accreditation Program
OAM&P	Operations Administration, Maintenance and Provisioning
ODA	Office Document Architecture
ODIF	Office Document Interchange Format
ODP	Open Distributed Processing
OIT	Object Identifier Tree
OIW	OSI Implementation Workshop
OM	Object Management
O/R	Originator/Recipient
OSE	Open Systems Environment
OSF	Open Software Foundation
OSI	Open System Interconnection
OSIE	Open System Interconnection Environment
PAD	Packet Assembler/Disassembler
PAI	Protocol Address Information
PCI	Presentation Context Identifier
	Protocol Control Information
PCO	Points of Control and Observation
PCTR	Protocol Conformance Test Report
PKCS	Public Key Cryptosystems

PDAD	Proposed Draft Addendum
PDAU	Physical Delivery Access Unit
pDISP	Proposed Draft International Standard Profile
PDN	Public Data Network
PDU	Protocol Data Unit
PDV	Presentation Data Value
PETS	Parameterized Executable Test Suite
PICS	Protocol Information Conformance Statement
PIXIT	Protocol Implementation eXtra Information for Testing
PLC	Programmable Logic Controller
PLP	Packet Level Protocol
POSIX	Portable Operating System Interface
PPDU	Presentation Protocol Data Unit
PRMD	Private Management Domain
PTLXAU	Public Telex Access Unit
PTT	Post, Telegraph and Telephone
P1	Protocol 1 (message transfer protocol/MHS/X.400)
P2	Protocol 2 (interpersonal messaging MHS/X.400)
P3	Protocol 3 (submission and delivery protocol/MHS/X.400)
P5	Protocol 5 (teletext access protocol)
P7	Protocol 7 (message store access protocol in X.400/1988 standard)
QOS	Quality Of Service
QUIPU	X.500 conformant directory services in ISODE
RD	Routing Domain
	Route re-direction
RDA	Remote Database Access
RDN	Relative Distinguished Name
RFP	Request for Proposals
RIB	Routing Information Base
RM	Reference Model
RN	Receipt Notification
RO-Notation	Remote Operation Notation
ROSE	Remote Operation Service Element
RPC	Remote Procedure Call
RPOA	Recognized Private Operating Agency
RS	Relay System
RTSE	Reliable Transfer Service Element
SA	Sequenced Application
SAA	Specific Administrative Areas
SACF	Single Association Control Function

SAF	SACF Auxiliary Facility
SALI	Source Address Length Indicator
SAO	Single Association Object
SAP	Service Access Point
	Specific Administrative Point
SATS	Selected Abstract Test Suite
SC	Subcommittee
SCS	System Conformance Statement
SCTR	System Conformance Test Report
SDIF	Standard Document Interchange Format
SDL	System Description Language
SDSE	Shadowed DSA Entries
SE	Session Entity
SG	Study Group (CCITT)
SGFS	Special Group on Functional Standardization
SGML	Standard Generalized Markup Language
SHL	SNARE Hello
SIA	Stable Implementation Agreements
SMAE	System Management Application Entity
SMASE	Systems Management Application Service Element
SMFA	Systems Management Functional Area
SMI	Structure of the OSI Management Information Service
SMIB	Stored Message Information Base
SNAcF	Subnetwork Access Function
SNAcP	Subnetwork Access Protocol
SNARE	Subnetwork Address Routing Entity
SNDCP	Subnetwork Dependent Convergence Protocol
SNICP	Subnetwork Independent Convergence Protocol
SNPA	Subnetwork Point of Attachment
SPAG	Standards Promotion and Application Group
SPDU	Session Protocol Data Unit
SPI	Subsequent Protocol Identifier
SPSN	Synchronization Point Serial Number
SQL	Structured Query Language
SRH	SNARE Request Hello
SSA	Subschema Specific Area
SSAP	Session Service Access Point
ST	Sequenced Terminal
SUT	System Under Test
TC	Technical Committee
TCO	Termination Control Object
TCP	Transmission Control Protocol

TEP	Transport End Point
TI RPC	Transport Independent RPC
TLI	Transport Layer Interface
TLMAU	Telematic Access Unit
TLV	Type, Length, and Value
TLXAU	Telex Access Unit
TMP	Test Management Protocol
TOP	Technical Office Profile
TP	Transaction Processing
TPSP	Transaction Processing Service Provider
TPSU	Transaction Processing Service User
TPSUI	TPSU Invocation
TP0	TP class 0 - simple
TP1	TP class 1 - basic error recovery
TP2	TP class 2 - multiplexing
TP3	TP class 3 - error recovery and multiplexing
TP4	TP class 4 - error detection and recovery
TR	Technical Report
TTCN	Tree and Tabular Combined Notation
TTP	Transport Test Platform
UA	Unsequenced Application
	User Agent
User-ASE	User Application Service Element
UT	Unsequenced Terminal
UTC	Coordinated Universal Time
VMD	Virtual Manufacturing Device
VT	Virtual Terminal
VTE	Virtual Terminal Environment
WACA	Write Access Connection Acceptor
WACI	Write Access Connection Initiator
WAN	Wide Area Network
WAVAR	Write Access Variable
WD	Working Document
WG	Working Group
WP	Working Party
XAPIA	X.400 API Association
XDS	X/Open Directory Services API
XTI	X/Open Transport Interface

Appendix B: Glossary of OSI Terms

abstract model: a macroscopic description of a distributed application/system in ASDC.

Abstract Syntax Notation One: the OSI language for describing an abstract syntax in a machine independent manner.

abstract service: a microscopic description of a distributed application/system in ASDC.

abstract syntax: a set of machine independent types and values, defined using an ASN.1 module

abstract test case: a specification of the actions required to achieve a specific test purpose.

abstract test method: an abstract description of how an implementation under test is to be tested.

abstract test suite: a test suite composed of abstract test cases.

activity attributes: attributes used to describe the activity of an FTAM dialogue.

Administration Management Domain (ADMD): a management domain managed by an administration such as a central PTT authority or a recognized private agency, used in MHS.

alias entry: a leaf entry in the Directory Information Tree, pointing to another entry.

allomorphism: the capability of an object to imitate or emulate the behavior of another object class.

application association: a cooperative relationship between two application-entity-invocations, characterized by an application context.

application context: an attribute of an application association specifying the shared knowledge between the communicating objects. Shared knowledge includes rules, bind/unbind type, application service elements/appliction service objects involved, abstract syntaxes, etc.

application entity: a communication component of an application process.

Application Entity Invocation (AEI): an invocation of an application entity. It maintains states of an application association.

AEI Identifier: identifies an application entity invocation.

Application Entity Title (AET): name of an application entity in an application process.

application entity type: a description of a class of application entities in terms of a set of capabilities.

Application Layer: layer seven of the OSI Reference Model. It is concerned with providing communication support for system-independent application services.

applications portability: the ability of application software to be used in multiple platforms/environment with minor modification.

application process: a human being or an application program.

application process invocation: an invocation of an application process.

Application Process Title: a title of an application process.

application process type: a description of a class of application processes in terms of a set of interworking capabilities.

Application Program Interface: an interface that allows the specific characteristics of the platform to be transparent to application programs.

Application Service Element: an atomic subobject of an application entity. It defines a set of capabilities of an application entity.

Application Service Object: a composite subobject of an application entity. It may contain application service elements or appliction service objects as subobjects.

application wide tag: a class of tag intended for types expected to be of common utility to an application protocol.

ASN.1 macros: a facility in ASN.1 that allows an application protocol designer to use non-standard notations to define types and values.

association classes: rules in an application context to determine which application entity may invoke operations.

Association Control Service Element: an application service element which is used to establish and terminate application associations.

at least once semantics: an RPC semantics to guarantee that the remote procedure is executed exactly once.

at most once semantics: an RPC semantics to guarantee that the remote procedure is never executed or executed once.

atomic action data: control information about an atomic action.

atomic action tree: a tree constructed as a result of performing an atomic action using CCR.

atomic synchronization: used in CMISE to mean that a management operation is successfully applied to all the specified objects, otherwise no operation is performed.

atomicity: a property of a unit of work such that the operations of the unit of work are either all performed, or none of them are performed.

Autonomous Administrative Area (AAA): a convex substructure of the Directory Information Tree managed by a single organization.

attribute-based name: a descriptive name that is composed of attributes.

Basic Activity Subset: a subset of the session functionalities to provide MHS support.

Basic Combined Subset: a subset of the session functionalities needed for a simple application, where the only consideration is whether communication is half duplex or full duplex.

Basic Encoding Rules: a set of encoding/decoding rules for ASN.1.

basic interconnection tests: limited tests of an implementation under test to determine whether or not there is sufficient conformance to the relevant protocol(s) for interconnection to be possible, without trying to perform thorough testing.

basic layout object: an object in the specific layout structure that has no subordinate. It is a leaf in the tree representing the specific layout structure.

basic logical object: an object in the specific logical structure that has no subordinate. It is a leaf in the tree representing the specific logical structure.

Basic Synchronized Subset: a subset of the session functionalities to support checkpointing. It is used by FTAM.

behavior tests: tests to determine the extent to which the dynamic conformance requirements are met by the IUT.

best effort synchronization: attempts to perform the required management operation on all the managed objects selected, whether or not the operation can be performed.

block: a rectangular substructure of a display object in Virtual Terminals.

body part: a structured set of fields containing the information that users wish to transmit via MHS.

capability test: a test for a static conformance requirement.

casuality: a constraint to which the behavior of each of the cooperating objects in a distributed system must conform to during the interaction.

certification authority: an authority trusted by one or more users to create certificates.

certification path: an ordered sequence of certificates of objects in the Directory Information Tree which, together with the public key of the initial object in the path, can be processed to obtain that of the final object in the path.

chained sequence: a sequence of related provider-supported transactions which are aimed at achieving a common goal.

chaining: a mode of interaction used by a Directory Service Agent to relay a Directory request to another Directory Service Agent.

character-box graphic element: an atomic element of a character-repertoire where use of the repertoire has been agreed through negotiation by the VT-users.

character-repertoire: a set of objects which can be represented by primary attribute values. An object represented by its primary attribute value can occupy an array element in a display object when the character-repertoire is in use for that array element.

CCR-ASE: an ASE which ensures that open systems communications are restarted in an orderly way if the link is broken for any reason.

Common Management Information Protocol: the OSI protocol for systems management.

Common Management Information Service Element: the ASE responsible for carrying systems management information.

composite layout object: an object in a document layout structure that has one or more subordinate objects.

composite logical object: an object in a document logical structure that has one or more subordinate objects.

conditional package: a collection of attributes, notifications and operations which are either all present or all absent in an instance of a managed object class.

configuration interval: the interval between the transmission of Hello packets in IS-ES routing.

conformance assessment process: the complete process of accomplishing all conformance testing activities necessary to enable the conformance of an implementation or a system to one or more OSI standards to be assessed.

conformance test: a set of tests to decide whether a product conforms to the OSI standard specification.

connection oriented internetworking: a strategy to interconnect a set of subnetworks to provide connection-oriented network service.

connection-oriented service: a service that has three distinct phases: connection establishment, data transfer and, connection release.

connectionless internetworking: a strategy to interconnect a set of subnetworks to provide connectionless network service.

connectionless service: a service without a connection setup.

consistency: a property of a unit of work, such that the operations of the unit of work, if performed at all, are performed accurately, correctly, and with validity, with respect to application semantics.

constraint set: a set of refinements of the hierarchical file model to specify a less general model tailored to the needs of a particular class of file applications.

content architecture: rules for defining the internal structure and representation of the content of an office document .

content portion: the result of partitioning the content of a document according to its logical and/or layout structure.

content type: specification of the content of an MHS structure (e.g., IPM, EDIM).

Context Control Object: a type of control object which provides the local context of the VT-user at certain stages of the data entry dialogue.

context management: ability to modify the presentation defined context set dynamically.

context prefix: the distinguished name of the root of a naming context.

context restoration: the ability to resynchronize the presentation defined context set during resynchronization.

context-specific tag: a class of tags used to achieve local distinctness for components of sets and sequences and choices.

control object: an abstract object for modelling the exchange of unstructured information of a single type.

coordinated test method: an external test method for which a standardized test management protocol is defined as the test coordination procedures, enabling the control and observation to be specified solely in terms of the lower tester activity.

coordination level: an agreement between two TPSU invocations on what mechanism will be used to guarantee the ACID of a transaction in transaction processing.

cross reference: a knowledge reference containing information about the Directory Service Agent that holds an entry.

Data Link Layer: layer two of the OSI Reference Model. It synchronizes transmission and handles error correction for a data link.

data unit: the smallest unit of a file content meaningful to an FTAM file action.

defined context set: a set of presentation contexts negotiated between peer presentation entities.

destructive service: a service that may cause the loss of information in transit.

device object: an abstract object used to model certain logical characteristics of a real device used in virtual terminal applications.

Directory Access Protocol: the protocol used between a Directory User Agent and a Directory System Agent.

Directory entry: an object in the Directory Information Base to model information. It can be an object entry or an alias entry.

Directory Information Base: a set of Directory entries. It contains objects to which the Directory provides access and which includes all of the pieces of information which can be read or manipulated using the Directory operations.

Directory Information Shadowing Protocol: a protocol used for shadowing between two Directory Service Agents in the Directory Services standard.

Directory Information Tree: a tree structure of the Directory Information Base.

Directory name: names for Directory entries in the Directory Information Base.

Directory Operational Binding Management Protocol: a protocol used by the Directory Service Agents to activate a shadowing agreement. This allows Directory Service Agents to establish, modify, and terminate operational bindings.

Directory schema: rules used to specify the structure of the Directory Information Base.

Directory Service Agent: an application entity that offers the Directory services.

Directory Service Protocol: the protocol used between two Directory System Agents.

Directory User Agent: an application entity that provides the Directory services.

display object: an object to model the information exchanged between a virtual terminal user and an application.

display pointer: used to refer to either the primitive display pointer or the extended display pointer.

distinguished attribute: a selected attribute of a Directory entry.

Distinguished Name: name of a Directory entry .

distinguished value: a selected attribute value of a distinguished attribute.

Distributed Processing: a set of information processing activities in which discrete components of the overall processing activities may be distributed in more than one system.

Distributed Test Method: an external test method in which there is a point of control and observation at the layer boundary at the top of the implementation under test.

Distribution List: a group of recipients under one name.

document: a structured amount of information intended for human perception, that can be interchanged as a unit between users and/or systems.

document architecture: (1) rules for defining the structure of documents, in terms of a set of components and content portions, and the representation of documents in terms of constituents and attributes; and (2) the structural information of a document consisting of a specific logical structure, a specific layout structure, a generic logical structure and/or generic layout structure.

document body: the part of a document that may include a generic logical and layout structure, specific logical and layout structure, layout and presentation styles but excludes the document profile.

document profile: a set of attributes which specifies the characteristics of a document as a whole.

document style: a set of rules for positioning the content of a document during the layout process, or the appearance of the content resulting from the imaging process. It is made up of presentation and layout styles.

document type: a specification of a class of documents.

domain defined attribute: attributes used to provide domain specific information in an O/R name.

domain specific part: part of an NSAP address.

durability: a property of unit of work such that all the effects of the completed unit of work are not altered by any sort of failure.

dynamic conformance requirements: all those requirements (and options) which determine what observable behavior is permitted by the relevant OSI standard(s) in instances of communication.

EDIFACT: a de facto standard for Electronic Data Interchange for Administration, Commerce and Transport.

EDIFACT interchange: an EDI structure conforming to the EDIFACT standard.

EDI forwarding: EDI forwarding is the onward transfer of a received EDIM to one or more recipients determined by the forwarding EDI user agent/message store.

EDI Message Responsibility: indicates whether the subject EDI message has been made available to a specific user by its EDI user agent/message store.

EDI message: information in electronic form that is transferred between EDI messaging users.

EDI Messaging System: consists of a Meesage Transfer System and a set of peripheral objects such as EDI User Agents, EDI Message Stores, and EDI Access Units.

EDI Notification: used to indicate to the originator of an EDI message the disposition of EDIM responsibility for an EDI message.

Electronic Data Interchange: a set of standard data formats for information exchange which could eliminate much of the inter-company paperwork.

embedded testing: testing the behavior of a single layer within a multi-layer implementation under test without accessing the layer boundaries for that layer.

embedding: a simultaneous connection establishment method to optimize the cost incurred during connection establishment.

encoded information type: the type of a body part of an MHS message, can be IA5 text, fascimile, voice, telex, etc.

end system: a system performing functions for all layers of the OSI model, commonly thought of as hosting applications.

End System Hello: a configuration packet periodically generated by an ES and transmitted to every IS on the subnetwork in ES-IS routing.

envelope: structured set of fields that comprises the beginning of an MHS message, and that contains the information required by the Message Transfer System. The envelope is followed by a content.

ES-IS routing: a routing exchange protocol that provides an automated means for ISs and ESs on a subnetwork to dynamically determine the existence of each other, and allows an IS to inform an ES of a potentially better route towards a destination

exactly once semantics: an RPC semantics to guarantee that the remote procedure is executed exactly once.

executable test case: a realization of an abstract test case.

executable test suite: a test suite composed of executable test cases.

explicit normal release: a transport release procedure that involves an exchange of transport protocol data units.

extended display pointer: a set of coordinate values which identify a particular array element in a block defined on a display object.

external test methods: abstract test methods in which the lower tester is separate from the system under test and communicates with it via an appropriate lower layer service-provider.

field: provides one-dimensional logical addressing over a designated subset of the array elements of a Y-array of a display object.

field-element: a rectangular area of a Y-array of a display object forming part of a field.

Field Definition Control Object: a type of control object which holds the definition of fields for a display object as Field Definition Records.

Field Definition Record: holds the status and definition of one field.

field entry condition: a condition of the data entry which when taken with an entry event predicates an entry reaction.

Field Entry Event: an event which may occur during controlled data entry and cause an entry reaction.

Field Entry Instruction: applies a rule for controlled data entry into a field.

Field Entry Instruction Control Object: A type of control object which holds data entry instructions as Field Entry Instruction Records.

Field Entry Instruction Record: holds a set of data entry rules as Field Entry Instructions.

Field Entry Pilot Control Object: a type of control object which holds data entry pilots as Field Entry Pilot Records.

Field Entry Pilot Record: holds a data entry pilot consisting of field entry event, field entry conditions and a sequence of field entry reactions.

Field Entry Reaction: a reaction to an entry event and entry condition defined in terms of operations on other objects in the virtual terminal service.

File Transfer, Access and Management: the OSI application protocol standard which allows remote files to be transferred, accessed and managed.

file access context: a file access data unit according to the view of an initiator.

file access data unit: a subtree of the hierarchical access structure. It is used to specify a location in a file structure.

file attributes: properties of a file that do not depend on an FTAM dialogue.

file-directory: OSI equivalence of a directory in a file system.

file management: the creation and deletion of files/filestores, and the inspection or manipulation of the file/filestore attributes.

file transfer: a function which moves a file's content between open systems.

Formal Description Techniques (FDT): a formal specification language used to specify a distributed application/system.

formatted form: a form of representation of a document that allow the presentation of the document as intended by the originator and that does not support editing and (re)formatting.

formatted processable form: a form of representation of the document that allows presentation of the document as intended by the originator and also supports editing and (re)formatting.

forward responsibility: action performed by the EDI-UA to inform a recipient EDI-UA that it must generate any notifications requested by the original originator.

frame: a type of composite layout component that corresponds to a rectangular area within a page or another frame.

frozen references: a transport connection reference that is frozen from use.

functional unit: a grouping of related service elements or capabilities into a single unit.

functional group: a set of EDI messages that are grouped together. An interchange may contain several functional groups.

functional profile: selections from the options within OSI standards and brought together under the name of a profile.

geometric graphics content architecture: a content architecture that supports an ODA content type consisting of a series of geometric constructs such as lines, arcs etc.

Government OSI Profiles: functional standards used by the government agencies in their procurement of open system equipments and software.

heading (MHS): a structured set of fields that comprises the beginning of the content of an MHS message, and that contains the information required by the UA. The heading is followed by a body.

heuristic decision: a decision of a subordinate to commit/rollback its part of a transaction after the node has declared to be ready to commit, but before it has received the decision of the commit coordinator by means of the commit protocol.

hierarchical file model: a model of the structure of a file which takes the form of a tree of file access data units.

implementation under test: an implementation to be tested.

implicit normal release: a transport release procedure without an exchange of transport PDUs

Initial Domain Part: the initial part of an NSAP address.

Initial Protocol Identifier: used to identify a network protocol type.

initiator: a file service user which requests an FTAM regime establishment.

interconnection: linking systems together so that data can be passed between them.

Intermediate System: a system performing functions of the lower three layers of the OSI Reference Model, commonly thought of as routing data for end-systems.

Intermediate System Hello: a packet generated by an IS and transmitted to every ES on the subnetwork to convey both the SNPA and NSAP addresses of a system.

interoperability: the ability of OSI products from different vendors to communicate with each other.

interoperability testing: tests used to demonstrate interoperability between a pair of OSI products.

interpersonal messaging system: an MHS system supporting the communication of interpersonal messages.

interpersonal message: a message type used for human-to-human communication in MHS.

interworking: the ability for application processes to communicate meaningfully with each other.

IS-IS routing: routing between ISs within a routing domain.

isolation: a property of a unit of work such that the partial results of the unit of work are not accessible, except by operations of the unit of work.

knowledge information: name resolution information which a Directory Service Agent maintains about other Directory Service Agents.

layers: in the OSI scheme, the communication task is broken up into layers. Each layer provides services to the layer above it, uses services from the layer below it, and communicates with an equivalent layer on another system.

layout directives: rules used in ODA to map a logical structure to a layout structure.

layout object: an element of the specific layout structure of a document, for example, page, block.

layout structure: (1) the result of dividing and subdividing the content of a document on the basis of the presentation, e.g., into pages, blocks; and (2) all layout objects and associated content portions forming the layout structure of a document.

layout style: a set of layout directives.

link state algorithm: a routing algorithm which requires each IS to maintain link information and a complete topology map.

Local System Environment: an abstract representation of that part of the real system that is not pertinent to OSI.

logical pointer: a set of two or three coordinate values which identify a particular array element in a field defined on a display object.

logical structure: (1) the result of dividing and subdividing the content of a document on the basis of the human-perceptible meaning of a document content; and (2) all logical objects and associated content portions representing the logical structure of a document.

lower tester: a component of the tester system which acts as a peer to the implementation under test.

macro: an extension to the ASN.1 notation, allowing the users to define non-standard types and values.

major synchronization point: a means to begin or end a dialogue unit within a session dialogue.

managed object: a management view of a real resource for managing the resource.

management functional area: a specific set of users' requirements in management. It provides a framework for defining management functions.

Management Information Base: a collection of managed objects.

Management Information Tree: a tree structure of the Management Information Base.

management support object: a system managed object defined specifically to support a systems management function (e.g., log, discriminator).

Media Access Control: a sublayer in the Data Link Layer which controls access to the physical medium of a network.

message (EDI): a set of segments that, taken together, comprise a single business transaction (e.g., purchase order, invoice order).

message (MHS): a structured set of data that is sent from a user agent to one or more recipient user agents.

message store: an entity acting as an intermediary between an user agent and its local message transfer agent.

Message Transfer System: a collection of message transfer agents cooperating to provide the message transfer service.

Message Transfer Agent: an object in the Message Transfer System. Message transfer agents use a store and forward method to relay message from originator to recipient. They interact with user agents when a message is submitted, and upon delivery.

minor synchronization point: a means to insert a checkpoint within a session dialogue unit.

multicasting: a mode used by the Directory Service Agent to chain a request to many other Directory Service Agents simultaneously.

multi-layer testing: testing the behavior of a multi-layer implementation under test as a whole, rather than testing it layer by layer.

multiple association control function: a component of the application-entity-invocation that co-ordinates a set of single association objects.

multiple interaction negotiation: a process which enables a draft VTE to be modified or extended in stages to create a new full VTE acceptable to the service provider and both VT-users.

(N)-address: a name unambiguous within the OSIE which is used to identify a set of (N)-service-access-point which are all located at a boundary between an (N)-subsystem and an (N+1)-subsystem in the same open system.

(N)-concatenation: a function performed by an (N)-entity to map multiple (N)-protocol-data-units into one (N-1)-service-data-unit.

(N)-connection: an association established by the (N)-layer between two or more (N+1)-entities for the transfer of data, which provides explicit identification of a set of (N)-data-transmissions and agreement concerning the (N)-data-transmission services to be provided for the set.

(N)-connection-endpoint-identifier: an identifier of an (N)-connection-endpoint which can be used to identify the corresponding (N)-connection at an (N)-service-access-point.

(N)-connection-endpoint: a terminator at one end of an (N)-connection within an (N)-service-access-point.

(N)-connection-mode transmission: (N)-data-transmission in the context of an (N)-connection.

(N)-connectionless-mode transmission: (N)-data-transmission not in the context of an (N)-connection. It does not require to maintain any logical relationship between (N)-service-data-units.

(N)-entity-invocation: a utilization of part or all of the capabilities of a given (N)-entity.

(N)-entity-type: a description of a class of (N)-entities in terms of a set of capabilities.

(N)-entity: an object within an (N)-subsystem embodying a set of capabilities defined for the (N)-layer that corresponds to a specific (N)-entity-type.

(N)-function: a function of (N)-entities.

(N)-interface-control-information: information transferred between an (N+1)-entity and an (N)-entity to coordinate their joint operation.

(N)-interface-data-unit: the unit of information transferred across the (N)-service-access-point between an (N+1)-entity and an (N)-entity in a single interaction. Each (N)-interface-data-unit contains (N)-interface-control-information and may also contain the whole or part of an (N)-service-data-unit.

(N)-layer managed object: a managed object specific to the (N)-layer.

(N)-layer: a subdivision of the OSI architecture, constituted by subsystems of the same rank (N).

(N)-multiplexing: a function within the (N)-layer by which an (N-1)-connection is used to support more than one (N)-connection.

(N)-protocol-control information: control information exchanged between communicating (N)-entities, using an (N-1) connection, to coordinate their joint operation. It is also known as a header.

(N)-protocol-data-unit: the objects exchanged between two communicating (N)-entities using an (N)-protocol.

(N)-protocol-identifier: an identifier used between communicating (N)-entities to select a specific (N)-protocol to be used on a particular (N-1)-connection.

(N)-protocol: a set of rules and formats (semantic and syntactic) which determine the communication behavior of communicating (N)-entities.

(N)-reassembling: a function performed by an (N)-entity to map multiple (N)-protocol-data-units into one (N)-service-data-unit. It is the reverse function of segmenting.

(N)-reset: a function which sets the corresponding (N)-entities to a predefined state with a possible loss or duplication of data.

(N)-segmenting: a function performed by an (N)-entity to map a (N)-service-data-unit into multiple (N)-protocol-data-units.

(N)-selector: part of an (N)-address to address an (N+1)-entity.

(N)-separation: a function performed by an (N)-entity to identify multiple (N)-protocol-data-units which are contained in one (N-1)-service-data-unit.

(N)-sequencing: a function performed by the (N)-layer to preserve the order of (N)-service-data-units that were submitted to the (N)-layer.

(N)-service-access-point: the point at which (N)-services are provided by an (N)-entity to an (N+1)-entity.

(N)-service-access-point-address: an (N)-address used to identify an (N)-SAP.

(N)-service-data-unit: an amount of (N)-interface-data-unit whose identity is preserved from one end of an (N)-connection to the other.

(N)-services: a capability of the (N)-layer and the layers beneath it, which is provided to (N+1)-entities at the boundary between the (N)-layer and the (N+1)-layer.

(N)-splitting: a function within the (N)-layer by which more than one (N-1)-connection is used to support one (N)-connection.

(N)-subsystem: an element in a hierarchical division of an open system which interacts directly only with elements in the next higher/lower division of that open system. It is viewed as a component of the (N)-layer residing in an open system.

(N)-user-data: the data transferred between (N)-entities on behalf of the (N+1)-entities for whom the (N)-entities are providing services.

name resolution: the process of locating an entry by sequentially matching each relative distinguished name in a purported name to a vertex of the Directory Information Tree.

naming context: a convex substructure of the Directory Information Tree which starts at a vertex and extends downwards to leaf and/or non-leaf vertices. Subordinates of non-leaf vertices belonging to the border denote the start of further naming contexts.

naming context tree: a tree structure where each node represents a naming context.

net-effecting: the conversion of a sequence of items, representing the content of one or more update operations into a different, usually shorter sequence, which results in the same final states of the objects being updated.

network: a collection of subnetworks connected by intermediate systems and populated by end systems.

Network Layer: layer three of the OSI Reference Model. It is responsible for data transfer across the network, independent of both the media coomprising the underlying subnetworks and the topology of these subnetworks.

non-destructive service: a service that does not cause the loss of information in transit.

notification (management): information given by a managed object relating to an event that has occurred within the managed object.

notification (MHS): MHS messages that are used to carry information related to the disposition of other MHS messages.

O/R name: the address of a user agent in MHS.

object entry: a Directory entry which is the primary collection of information in the Directory Information Base about an object in the real world, not an alias entry.

object identifier-based name: names based on the OBJECT IDENTIFIER type.

object identifier tree: a tree where tree edges are labelled with integers.

object identifier type: an ASN.1 type whose values are the path names of the nodes of the object identifier tree.

octet aligned: property of an encoding method where an encoded value is an integral number of octets.

Office Document Architecture: define the OSI view of an office document.

Office Document Interchange Format: describes an interchange format of an office document, consisting of a sequence of data elements where each data element represents a component of the document.

Open Distributed Processing: the distribution of inter-related processing tasks across a number of open systems.

Open System Environment: an environment in which computer systems and software of different vendors are interchangeable.

Open System Interconnection: a strategy defined in the OSI Reference Model which will allow open systems to be interconnected to and interwork with each other.

Open Systems Interconnection Environment: a "subset" of an open systems environment where open systems use OSI in their communiction.

open systems: systems particpating in an open systems environment.

operation class: used to describe a remote operation such as whether results or errors should be returned to the invoker.

operational attributes: attributes required by the Directory Service Agents for the regulation of Directory user information.

OSI Reference Model: the generic model by which OSI communication services are structured.

package: a group of logically related object classes.

page: a layout component that corresponds to a rectangular area on an output medium.

peer-entities: entities within the same layer.

Physical Layer: layer one of the OSI Reference Model. It is responsible for the electromechanical interface to the communication media.

PICS proforma: a document, in the form of a questionnaire, which when completed for an OSI implementation, becomes the PICS.

picture element: the smallest graphic element that can be individually addressed within a picture, used in ODA.

PIXIT proforma: a document, in the form of a questionnaire, provided by the test laboratory, which when completed during the preparation for testing, becomes a PIXIT.

point of control and observation: a point, defined for an abstract test method, at which test events are controlled and observed.

polarized control: a mode of communication over a dialogue where only one TPSU invocation involved in the dialogue is allowed to have control at a time.

presentation context: a pair of abstract syntax and transfer syntax.

presentation context identifier: an integer identifying a presentation context active on a presentation connection.

presentation data value: a logically indivisible part of a presentation service data unit

Presentation Layer: layer six of the OSI Reference Model. It is concerned with the representation of information structures exchanged between the communicating application entities.

presentation style: a constituent of the document, referred to from a basic logical or layout component, which guides the formal and appearance of the document content.

presumed rollback recovery mechanism: a mechanism used in CCR to determine when a superior or a subordinate acquires recovery responsibility in case of a failure.

primary attribute: the attribute of an array element of a display object which is a coded representation of the character-box graphic element assigned to that array element.

primitive display pointer: a set of one to three coordinate values which identify a particular element in a display object.

print value: a representation of an ASN.1 value in printable form for presentation to human beings.

Private Management Domain: a Management Domain managed by an organization that may be a company or a non-commercial organization.

processable form: a form of representation of a document that allows editing and formatting.

profile: a set of one or more base standards, and, where applicable, the identification of chosen classes, subsets, options and parameters of those base standards, necessary for accomplishing a particular function.

protocol: rules which govern the way communicating applications/systems interact.

protocol address information: a field in a protocol data unit where the addressing information is put, and carried between two open systems.

protocol conformance test report: a document written at the end of the conformance assessment process, giving the details of the testing carried out for a particular protocol. It includes the identification of the abstract test cases for which corresponding executable test cases were run. It also includes the test purposes and verdict for each test case.

protocol control information: that part of a protocol data unit which conveys specific, layer-dependent, instructions between peer layer entities.

protocol data unit: a message exchanged between peer layer entities in their communication. It is made up of protocol control information and, optionally, user data.

protocol implementation conformance statement: a statement made by the supplier of an OSI implementation or system, stating which capabilities and options have been implemented, for a given OSI protocol.

protocol implementation eXtra information: a statement made by a supplier or implementor of an implementation under test which contains or references all of the information (in addition to that given in the Protocol Information Conformance Statement) related to the implementation under test and its testing environment, which will enable the test laboratory to run an appropriate test suite against the implementation under test.

Quality of Service: the desired or actual characteristics of a service.

referral: an outcome which can be returned by a Directory Service Agent which cannot perform an operation itself, and which identifies one or more other Directory Service Agents able to perform the operation.

relative distinguished name: a component of a Directory entry's Distinguished Name, consisting of a set of distinguished attributes.

relay: an intermediate system which passes messages between two OSI end systems. A relay need only handle communications up to the third or fourth layer of the OSI model.

release: an activity that closes a connection or association between cooperating peers.

Reliable Transfer Service Element: an ASE responsible for reliable transfer of application protocol data units.

Remote Database Access: an OSI standard to integrate heterogeneous database systems.

Remote Operations Service Element: an ASE concerned with providing a basis for remote requests for operations to be submitted to an end-system, and for that end system to be able to issue a reply to the initiating end-system.

remote operation: an action invoked by an application entity and performed by another.

Remote Procedure Call: a request by an application program on a system for a procedure to be executed on another system.

remote test method: an external test method in which there is neither a point of control and observation above the implementation under test nor a standardized test management protocol.

rendition attributes: secondary attributes of an array element which qualify the character-box graphic element and provide information specifying how it is intended to be presented.

requestor: a user that initiates a service by invoking the request primitive associated with that service.

responder: that file service user which accepts an FTAM regime establishment requested by the initiator.

resynchronization: a service provided by the Session Layer to support controlled restarting of an information exchange between peer application processes, usually after some failure in the lower layers.

RO-notation: a set of tools defined using the ASN.1 macro facility, that convey the semantics of remote operations.

routing: a function within a layer which translates the title of an entity or the service-access-point-address to which the entity is attached into a path by which the entity can be reached.

routing information base: a repository for outputs from route calculations, and routing updates from other nodes.

self delimiting: an encoding property by which the end of an encoded value can be deduced.

service definition: an ISO document defining a set of services.

service element: an OSI abstraction of a service.

service primitive: a part of a service element. There are four types: request, indication, response, and confirm.

service provider: the whole of the subordinate OSI communications environment as seen by cooperating peer service users.

service user: a user of services provided by the cooperation of peer layer entities. Access to these services is provided by service primitives.

session dialogue: a structuring of one or more transport connections by the Session Layer to model the interaction between two session service users.

Session Layer: the fifth layer in the OSI Reference Model. It coordinates the dialogue between two communicating application processes.

shadowing: a form of replication specified by the Directory Services standard.

single association control function: the component of a single association object which coordinates the interactions among the application-service-elements within the single association object.

single association object: The collection of things in an application entity invocation related to a single application association.

static conformance requirements: constraints which are specified in OSI standards to facilitate interworking by defining the requirements for the capabilities of an implementation.

subnetwork access protocol: a protocol used to access a particular subnetwork technology.

subnetwork dependent convergence protocol: a protocol used to augment the service offered by a particular subnetwork technology to the OSI network service.

subnetwork independent convergence protocol: a protocol used to provide the network service between two end-systems.

Subnetwork Point of Attachment: the point in a subnetwork to which an open system is attached.

system conformance statement: a document summarizing which OSI standards are implemented and to which conformance is claimed.

system conformance test report: a document written at the end of the conformance assessment process, gives the overall summary of the conformance of the system to the set of protocols for which conformance testing was carried out.

system under test: the real open system in which the IUT resides.

Termination Conditions Control Object: a type of control object which holds termination conditions effective on the operation of one or more device objects linked to it.

termination-event: a locally defined atomic event relative to input from an object updating device (for example, entering a character, pressing a function key, setting a flag) which the VT-user agree (through negotiation) to designate as causing input data to be delivered to the peer VT-user.

test body: the set of test steps that are essential in order to achieve the test purpose and assign verdicts to the possible test outcomes.

test campaign: the process of executing the parameterized executable test suite for a particular IUT and producing the conformance log.

test case: a generic, abstract or executable test case.

test coordination procedures: the rules for cooperation between the lower and upper testers during testing.

test group: a named set of related test cases.

test management protocol: a protocol which is used as the test coordination procedures for a particular test suite.

test purpose: a prose description of a narrowly defined objective of testing.

test suite: a set of signals and responses which tests a product as an implementation of a standard.

test verdict: a statement of 'pass', 'fail' or 'inconclusive', specified in the abstract test suite, concerning conformance of an IUT with respect to a test case that has been executed.

threads: an efficient mechanism to support concurrency within a process, is is single sequential flow of control within the process.

token: a object whose ownership conveys permission to request the service associated with the token.

transaction: a unit of work characterized by four properties: atomicity, consistency, isolation, and durability.

transaction branch: the portion of a distributed transaction performed by a pair of TPSU invocations sharing a dialogue.

transfer syntax: a specification for the encoding of information of a given abstract syntax that will be applied to the abstract syntax while in transit between peer application processes, also means a description of an instance of a data structure that is expressed as a string of bits.

Transmission Policy Control Object: a type of control object which holds variable values which determine how field contents are transmitted after a controlled data entry.

Transport Layer: the fourth layer in the OSI Reference Model. It provides a reliable end-to-end service to its users.

Tree and Tabular Combined Notation: a formal notation to specify test cases.

universal tag: a class of tags allocated to the built-in and useful types of ASN.1.

update-window: a mechanism associated with display object addressing which defines a range of coordinate values for an array below which an update operation cannot be performed. The absolute coordinate values in the range may increase in value during operation, but cannot decrease.

upper tester: the representation of the means of providing during test execution, control and observation of the upper service boundary of the implementation under test.

user agent: an application entity that makes the message transfer service available to the user.

vector state algorithm: a routing algorithm in which an intermediate system periodically sends its routing table to the adjacent neighbors.

virtual file: OSI abstraction of a file.
virtual filestore: OSI abstraction of a collection of files, directories, and references.

Virtual Manufacturing Device (VMD): an abstraction of a real device on a manufacturing floor.

Virtual Terminal: an ISO standard which aims to allow access to an application in an open system from different kinds of terminals.

VT-association: an application association between two peer VT-users.

VT-environment: a set of parameters that together define the data structure and operational characteristics for a particular VT-association. The VTE exists only during the life time of that VT-association. The parameters of the set are mutually related by a directed graph structure. The VTE may be modified during the existence of the VT-association by negotiation.

VT-user: a user of the virtual Terminal Service.

VTE-parameter: an individual parameter of a VTE. Each VTE-parameter is given a unique name in the service which is used as the identifier for the VTE-parameter.

VTE-profile: a pre-defined set of VTE-parameter values making up a VTE.

wavar access-right: an access-right which can be held by at most one VT-user at any time. It is used to ensure that control and display objects cannot be updated by both VT-users simultaneously.

INDEX

T